PREFACE

Aim of the Book

In writing this book, we have had three main aims: firstly, to provide a guide to UML that condenses the material in the UML Specification (Object Management Group, 1999*a*) and in the books by the main authors of UML; secondly, to do this by means of practical case studies that are developed throughout the book; and, thirdly, to provide plenty of practical examples and exercises for the reader. None of these is an easy task. The UML Specification is 800 pages long, and the books by Rumbaugh, Booch and Jacobson (see Bibliography) together run to 1,500 pages. Experienced practitioners know that a fully elaborated set of models for a system would be at least as much paper as in a copy of this book when printed out. A single case study does not always provide opportunities to develop all the rich notation of UML.

We have nonetheless tried to achieve all three. We have described the key features of the notation of each kind of diagram in UML, and have pulled out the notational conventions that they share. We have also provided a 'How To' section in each chapter in which we develop examples from one of our two case studies. We have used these case studies to provide worked examples, within and at the end of each chapter, and exercises, and believe that there is plenty of material in them that could be developed by a reader who wants more practical experience. We have tried, by using two case studies, to provide examples that cover business modelling, information system development and real-time system development. We hope that we have succeeded.

Structure

The first two chapters of the book introduce the case studies that we are using and provide background to UML. The next eleven chapters explain the notation of UML diagrams and how to produce them. For each type of diagram, there are sections on the notation, on how to produce the diagrams or of modelling guidance, on how each diagram is related to other diagrams, on how each diagram can be used in business modelling, and on how each diagram fits into the Unified Software Development Process. Within each chapter we introduce examples from the case studies. We also provide a set of review questions, with answers at the back of the book, solved problems and supplementary problems for the reader. Chapter 14 covers features of UML that are common to many kinds of diagram. The final two chapters provide information on related topics: Computer-Aided Software Engineering (CASE) Tools and Design Patterns. The book concludes with a summary of UML notation, answer pointers for the review questions, a glossary and a bibliography.

Conventions

All three authors are British and we have used British English spelling conventions (those of the Oxford English Dictionary) and punctuation throughout. We have tried to avoid terms that do not carry the same meaning in the varieties of English spoken around the world as they do in British English.

In the text, we have used an italic style to highlight new terms that have a special meaning in UML at the point where they are introduced, for example *classifier*, we have used a sans serif font for terms that are part of a UML model, for example CarSharer, and we have used a fixed width font for sample pieces of code and syntax, for example `sequence-term`. Examples within chapters and the solutions to solved problems at the end of each chapter are printed in a slightly smaller font than the main text.

In diagrams, we have used a sans serif font for labels that are part of the diagram and an italicised serif font for notes that describe elements of a diagram.

Acknowledgments

Our thanks go to David Howe, who provided invaluable help by reading every chapter and making suggestions for improvements, and to David Hatter, our publisher at McGraw-Hill, who made sure that we delivered the book on schedule. All errors are nonetheless the responsibility of the authors.

Simon Bennett, John Skelton, Ken Lunn
January 2001

CONTENTS

DEDICATION

To Helen, Joe and Laurie for putting up with another book.

Simon

To Angela, Kate and Matthew. Thanks.

John

To Simon, Charlotte and Nicole, who gained an author as a dad and lost their taxi driver for a while. Thanks for the forbearance.

Ken

Introduction to the Case Studies

1.1 INTRODUCTION

These two case studies are used throughout the book. The first one, CarMatch, is used for illustration of points and worked examples in each chapter. The second case study, VolBank, is used for worked examples and for problems for the reader. You should read the material in this chapter in order to understand the examples and complete the problems.

1.2 CASE STUDY 1—CARMATCH

1.2.1 CarMatch Background

CarMatch is a franchising company that is being set up to promote car sharing. In many cities, traffic congestion poses a threat to the quality of life as well as causing considerable pollution. This includes the release of carbon dioxide into the atmosphere. Many countries are trying to meet their obligations under international agreements to reduce carbon emissions in an attempt to prevent the worst effects of global warming. CarMatch is a response to this situation. In many areas, public transport has declined as car ownership has increased, and the public transport infrastructure is not available to take up the demand from people not using their cars to travel to work. Car sharing schemes offer one short-term way of reducing traffic without the immediate investment in public transport infrastructure that is required in the medium to long term.

CarMatch seeks to promote car sharing and to provide a service to potential car sharers by matching up people who both live and work near one another. While many people who work together share transport informally, it is more difficult for people who work near one another to find a suitable person to share transport with, and in some very large organizations, even people who work on the same site may not know one another.

CarMatch consists of three layers of structure: the global operation, which is a not-for-profit trust, the central operating company in each country and local franchise operations. Depending on the country in which it is operating, CarMatch's central operation will offer its services to local government and large corporations, which have legal obligations to reduce traffic in some countries or states. It will also publicize its services to the general public. People who join up will pay a small membership fee, which will be refunded if the local CarMatch franchise is unable to match them up with one or more other people who require or are offering transport. The CarMatch franchise will draw up model agreements between the participants, to prevent the money that changes hands to cover fuel costs being treated as taxable income, and advise on the insurance implications of car sharing. It will act as an agent for companies that sell insurance policies that specifically cover car sharing. Research has shown that car sharers are a good insurance risk.

Staff in the local franchises will undergo a comprehensive training course, which covers the consultancy that they must be able to offer to companies and local government, the legal situation in their own country or state, insurance requirements, safety considerations and how to operate CarMatch's systems. In some countries, regulation of the insurance industry means that franchise staff must also meet the requirements of regulatory bodies.

CarMatch expects to make its money from a combination of membership fees, consultancy income and the commission on insurance sales. A percentage of all income will be taken by the central operation, and the rest kept by the franchise. As road-pricing schemes based on radio communication between vehicles and road-side transponders become more widespread, CarMatch franchises will sell and install the necessary equipment and work with toll authorities and road-pricing schemes to negotiate discounts for members on the basis that they are reducing traffic demand.

1.2.2 CarMatch Computer Support

CarMatch has a requirement for a computer system that can be used by its franchisees. The aim is to launch the new service with computer support right from the start. In each country there will also be at least one web-server. These web-servers will provide up to date information and insurance brokerage services to franchisees as well as allowing members to register with CarMatch on-line. Information about members will then be downloaded to the franchisee's system in the relevant area. Where there is not a franchisee in an area, the central service will try to match members.

1.2.3 CarMatch Requirements

The requirements listed here are those of the systems that franchisees will use. The central system is the subject of a separate development process.

1 To develop a system that will hold information about members of the CarMatch scheme.

- 1.1 To record the details of potential car sharers, whether they are offering transport, seeking transport or both and the geographical location of their home and their work addresses.
- 1.2 To transfer details of potential car sharers from the central web-server if they have registered on-line.
- 1.3 To provide an interface to credit card transaction systems and the Automated Bank Transfer System (ABTS) in order to process membership fee payments and refunds.

2 To match members up with other members as car sharers.

   2.1 On the basis of geographical locations and travel times to match up members who may be able to share transport.

   2.2 To record details of sharing arrangements that result.

3 To record insurance sales.

   3.1 To record details of the policies sold to members and to process renewals.

   3.2 To record the commission income from these policies.

4 To record details of potential and actual consultancy customers in the area of operation.

   4.1 To maintain a mailing list of potential customers.

   4.2 To record details of actual customers, contacts within the companies, addresses etc.

   4.3 To record visits made by the franchisee's staff and other contacts with consultancy customers.

5 The system must be capable of future expansion to incorporate information about toll and road-pricing schemes and equipment sold to and installed for members.

1.3 CASE STUDY 2—VOLBANK

1.3.1 VolBank Background

VolBank is a not-for-profit organization that matches volunteers with people and groups in need of help. Its overall aims are to promote citizenship and a sense of community by involving people in voluntary activities in their local area. It does this by maintaining a list of voluntary opportunities and a list of volunteers and seeking to match volunteers to the right opportunities. Part of VolBank's philosophy is that everyone has skills to offer and needs to be met. Because of this, it encourages volunteers to register their own needs and the recipients of help to offer their own skills. For example, Pete Duffield volunteered to help with painting and decorating. He was matched up with a local after school centre for the under-tens whose centre needed repainting. The children offered their time to put on a show for a local old people's home. One of the elderly residents of the old people's home, Mrs Hernandez, offered her time to give someone a chance to practise Spanish conversation. Pete Duffield took her up on the offer so that he could brush up his Spanish before his holiday in Mexico.

The name VolBank comes from the idea that people can deposit the time that they are prepared to give, as well as a list of the skills that they are willing to offer. Information about VolBank is available through a number of sources including local radio, television advertising and the Internet. VolBank has been set up in partnership with local voluntary organizations that put forward voluntary work that needs doing. They also act as local contact points for volunteers to put themselves forward.

Volunteers can register the skills they are offering with VolBank, by telephone to a volunteer organizer, in person through a local voluntary organization or by filling out their details on a web page. Once they are registered they can deposit time with VolBank by the same means. If the volunteer registers through a local voluntary organization, then the information is passed on in writing to VolBank, where it will be recorded by a volunteer organizer in the same way as if the volunteer had contacted VolBank directly by telephone.

Voluntary organizations and individuals (including volunteers) can register their needs for help by contacting a volunteer organizer. This volunteer organizer then tries to match up the people offering their time with the opportunities. This can happen in two different ways: a new volunteer can be matched against opportunities, or a new opportunity can be matched against a pool of volunteers. Matching is done on a geographical basis, using zip or postal codes, and by matching skills to needs.

Once volunteers have been matched to an opportunity, they are notified of the details, and, if they are interested, their details are passed on by the volunteer organizer to the voluntary organization or individual that requested the help. It is made clear to volunteers that this does not mean that they will automatically be accepted. For some kinds of work, such as work with children, there may be further vetting procedures or even police and social services checks. These are the responsibility of the organization requesting the help.

VolBank is in the process of setting up a computer system to handle all the business of registering and matching volunteers and opportunities, and notifying the participants.

1.3.2 VolBank Computer Support

VolBank needs a computer system to handle the matching of volunteers with opportunities and opportunities with volunteers. This computer system will need a link to the VolBank web-server. Member organizations will be notified whenever a match is made between an opportunity that they have registered and a volunteer. This will be done by fax or email. Volunteers will be notified when a match has been made by letter.

1.3.3 VolBank Requirements

The requirements listed here are for the system to handle registration, carry out the matching and notify participants. The web-server is a separate system.

1 To develop a system that will handle the registration of volunteers and the depositing of their time.
   - 1.1 To record the details of volunteers, including the skills and the address of each one.
   - 1.2 To record the time that each volunteer deposits in the system.
   - 1.3 To transfer from the web-server details of volunteers and the time they are depositing.

2 To handle the recording of opportunities for voluntary activity.
   - 2.1 To record details of member voluntary organizations.
   - 2.2 To record the needs of voluntary organizations for help.
   - 2.3 To record the needs of individuals (including volunteers) for help.

3 To match up donors and recipients of voluntary activity and record the results.
   - 3.1 To match a volunteer with suitable voluntary activities in his or her area.
   - 3.2 To match a voluntary activity with suitable volunteers in the same area.
   - 3.3 To record every match between volunteer and activity.
   - 3.4 To notify volunteers of matches.
   - 3.5 To notify voluntary organizations of matches.
   - 3.6 To record the success of each match and to produce a volunteering agreement for each successful match.

4 To produce statistical analyses of the number of volunteers and opportunities and the amount of time deposited.

Background to UML

2.1 INTRODUCTION

The Unified Modeling Language (UML) is a visual language that provides a way for people who analyze and design object-oriented systems to visualize, construct and document the artefacts of software systems and to model the business organizations that use such systems. Rational Software Corporation and the Object Management Group (OMG) have brought together elements of three significant object-oriented diagramming notations and aspects of many other notations to produce a standard modelling language that represents best practice in the software development industry. UML is still evolving as a standard, and is likely to become an international standard accepted by the International Organization for Standardization (ISO) in the near future.

This chapter explains the history of UML, describes its current state and outlines its likely future development. It also explains the structure of UML and how it is documented.

2.2 ORIGINS OF UML

Object-oriented software development techniques have gone through three stages of evolution.

1. Object-oriented programming languages were developed and began to be used.

2. Object-oriented analysis and design techniques were produced to help in the modelling of businesses, the analysis of requirements and the design of software systems. The number of these techniques grew rapidly.

3. UML was designed to bring together the best features of a number of analysis and design techniques and notations to produce an industry standard.

2.2.1 Programming Languages

Simula-67 is usually credited as the first object-oriented language. Simula 1 was developed in the early 1960s as a language for writing discrete-event simulations. A simulation system is used to analyze and predict the behaviour of a physical system, such as a traffic intersection, a chemical reaction or an assembly line. A discrete-event simulation simulates the real system in terms of a set of discrete states that change over time in response to events that occur at specific instances in time. This distinguishes a discrete-event simulation from a continuous simulation in which the state is continuously evolving. Modelling a traffic intersection is a discrete-event simulation: vehicles arrive and the lights change at specific instants in time. A chemical reaction is normally modelled as a continuous simulation: the chemicals react together continuously and the rate of reaction is dependent on variables such as temperature and pressure.

Simula-67 was developed in 1967 by Kristen Nygaard and Ole-Johan Dahl from the University of Oslo and the Norwegian Computing Centre. It built on Simula 1 and is a general-purpose programming language. In 1986 the language became known just as Simula and it is still in use today. Simula introduced many of the features of object-oriented languages such as classes and inheritance (discussed in more detail in Chapters 4 and 5).

The first explicitly object-oriented language was Smalltalk which was developed by Alan Kay at the University of Utah and later with Adele Goldberg and Daniel Ingalls at Xerox PARC (Palo Alto Research Centre) in the 1970s. It became more widely used in the 1980s with the release of Smalltalk-80. Smalltalk introduced the ideas of objects communicating by passing messages and of encapsulated attributes inside objects that are accessible to other objects only in response to a message.

Smalltalk was followed by the release of other object-oriented languages: Objective C, C++, Eiffel and CLOS (Common Lisp Object System). Since its release in 1996, Sun's Java has thrust object-oriented development into the limelight. More recently, Microsoft has released the details of its new language C♯ (C-sharp), which is meant to combine the best of Java and C++. Between Simula and C♯, many other object-oriented languages have been developed and continue to be developed, but it is Java with its relationship to the rapid growth of the Internet that has made object-oriented development more widespread.

2.2.2 Analysis and Design

A few years after the emergence of Smalltalk, books on object-oriented analysis and design began to appear. Some of these were closely tied to specific languages, such as Objective C and C++, while others were more general purpose. First among these were the work of Shlaer & Mellor (1988) and of Coad & Yourdon (1990 & 1991). They were closely followed by Booch (1991), the team of Rumbaugh, Blaha, Premerlani, Eddy & Lorensen (1991) and, slightly later, Jacobson, Christerson, Jonsson & Övergaard (1992). These are just the most widely known and used; there were many others.

Different authors adopted different diagramming notations to represent classes and objects and the associations among them. Often different authors used the same notational element to represent different things. For example Coad and Yourdon used a triangle to represent a whole-part association (aggregation in UML terms), while Rumbaugh and his co-workers used a triangle to represent inheritance. As well as providing a notation, all these authors also presented a method for using their notation, consisting of more or less clearly defined stages and activities and specifications of the analysis and design products.

The early 1990s were characterized by a confusing diversity of different object-oriented notations and methods, referred to by some authors as 'Method Wars'. Between 1989 and 1994, the number of modelling languages went from fewer than 10 to more than 50. In the mid 1990s this situation began to change. The methods of three key authors had become prominent: Rumbaugh, Booch and Jacobson. Rumbaugh had revised his *Object Modeling Technique* (OMT) as OMT-2; Booch had produced a second edition of his book outlining what is known as *Booch'93*; Jacobson's method was known either as *Object-Oriented Software Engineering* (OOSE) or as *Objectory,* the name of his company.

2.2.3 Emergence of UML

These three methods were also beginning to grow more similar as the authors incorporated the best features of other methods. In 1994 Rumbaugh and Booch began to work together at Rational Software Corporation to unify their two methods. In October 1995 they released the draft Version 0.8 of the *Unified Method.* In autumn 1995 Jacobson and his company, Objectory, joined Rational, and the three authors started developing both UML and the Unified Software Development Process, which was based largely on the Objectory method.

In June and October 1996 Versions 0.9 and 0.91 were released, incorporating feedback from people and organizations interested in the development of a standard object-oriented modelling language. At this time, the *Object Management Group* (OMG), an industry standards body, issued a Request for Proposal (RFP) for a standard object modelling language. Rational Software Corporation recognized that there was a need for wider involvement in the process and formed the UML Partners consortium with other organizations such as IBM, HP, Microsoft and Oracle, which were willing to commit resources to the further development of UML as a response to the OMG.

In January 1997 the UML Partners and a number of other companies and groups submitted proposals to the OMG. Subsequently, the others joined up with the UML Partners to produce Version 1.1 of UML. In November 1997, UML 1.1 was added to the OMG's list of Adopted Technologies, and the OMG took on the responsibility for the further development of UML.

The OMG set up a *Revision Task Force* (RTF) led by Cris Kobryn of MCI Systemhouse to take on the task of refining the UML specification—handling bugs, rectifying omissions, and resolving inconsistencies and ambiguities. The RTF produced an editorial revision of the UML specification (Version 1.2) in June 1998 and the current full version (Version 1.3) in June 1999.

2.3 UML TODAY

The current release of UML is Version 1.3. The responsibility for further development lies with the Revision Task Force set up by the OMG. The planned future development of UML is explained in Section 2.5.

UML Version 1.3 is documented in the UML Specification (Object Management Group, 1999*a*). The contents of the specification are listed in Table 2-1.

The UML Specification is not written as a document for ordinary users of UML, but for members of the OMG, standards organizations, companies that produce CASE tools, authors of books and trainers who need to have a detailed understanding of UML. In particular, Chapters 5 and 6 are written for CASE tool builders. The CORBAfacility Interface Definition specifies the contents of a data repository suitable for creating, storing and manipulating UML models using the Interface Definition Language (IDL) for the Common Object Request Broker Architecture (CORBA). The XMI (XML Metadata Interchange) DTD (Document Type Declaration) Specification uses XML (eXtensible Markup Language) to provide

Table 2-1: Contents of the UML Specification

Chapter 1	UML Summary
Chapter 2	UML Semantics
Chapter 3	UML Notation Guide
Chapter 4	UML Standard Profiles
Chapter 5	UML CORBAfacility Interface Definition
Chapter 6	UML XMI DTD Specification
Chapter 7	Object Constraint Language Specification
Appendix A	UML Standard Elements
Appendix B	UML Modeling Glossary

a specification for how data about UML models can be exchanged among applications. The only other part of the Specification whose title is not self-explanatory is Chapter 4. This documents two standard UML profiles (ways of applying UML to different kinds of development projects): one for software development processes and the other for business modelling.

2.4 WHAT IS UML?

UML is a visual language that can be used in developing software systems. It is a formal specification language. The term 'language' confuses some people. It is not a language like a human language, nor is it a programming language. However, like both of these other kinds of language, it has a set of rules that determine how it can be used.

Programming languages consist of a set of elements and a set of rules that define how you are allowed to combine those elements to make valid programs. Formal specification languages like UML also consist of a set of elements and a set of rules that determine how you can combine the elements. Most of the elements of UML are graphical: they consist of lines, rectangles, ovals and other shapes, and many of these graphical elements are labelled with words that provide additional information. However, the graphical elements of UML are only a graphical representation of whatever is being modelled. It is possible to produce a UML model purely in terms of the data that describes the model (and this is what the CORBAfacility and the XMI DTD do). Nonethless, the graphical representation helps people to understand the model or parts of the model, and it is the graphical representation that makes UML a visual specification language rather than a textual one.

The rules about how the elements of UML can be combined are set out and explained in the UML Specification (Object Management Group, 1999*a*). There are three kinds of rules: *abstract syntax*, *well-formedness rules* and *semantics*. The abstract syntax is expressed as diagrams and natural language (English), the well-formedness rules in Object Constraint Language (OCL)(see Chapter 12) and English, and the semantics in English with some supporting diagrams. The rules that are expressed as diagrams use a subset of the notation of UML itself to specify how the elements of UML can be combined. This is an important feature of UML, but not one that you really need to understand in detail. It is called the *Four-Layer Metamodel Architecture* of UML and is summarized here.

2.4.1 Four-Layer Metamodel Architecture

UML can be viewed as four layers. Each layer is an abstraction of the one below it, and each layer is defined in terms of the one above it. The lowest layer consists of *user objects*. These are the instances of objects that are in the system: <Insurance_Policy_2123434>, 21.34, set_premium and <Insurance_Quote_Server_213>. The next layer up consists of the *model*. These are the modelling concepts that define the user objects in the particular modelling domain: InsurancePolicy, monthlyPremium, setPremium and InsuranceQuoteServer. (Much of the work of systems analysis and design lies in determining what the elements of the model are.) The layer above the model is the *metamodel*. The metamodel defines the elements of the model. (A meta-something is a higher order something. So metadata is data that describes data, a metamodel is a model that describes another model.) The elements of the metamodel are the elements of UML, for example, Class, Attribute, Operation, Component. The top layer is the OMG Meta Object Facility's (MOF) *meta-metamodel*. This defines the language for defining metamodels. Its elements are MetaClass, MetaAttribute and MetaOperation. In the same way as the UML metamodel can be applied to produce models of different domains—air-traffic control, banking, volunteering, libraries, car sharing, robotics, telecommunications and many others—the meta-metamodel can be used to specify many different metamodels—if you wanted to define other visual specification languages. For the purpose of understanding the abstract syntax of UML, it is the metamodel layer that is important.

2.4.2 Abstract Syntax

The abstract syntax of UML is specified using the notation of the metamodel. This is a subset of UML notation, using the UML class diagram to specify the elements of UML models and the relationships among them. Figure 2-1 shows a part of the diagram that expresses the abstract syntax of the UML core package.

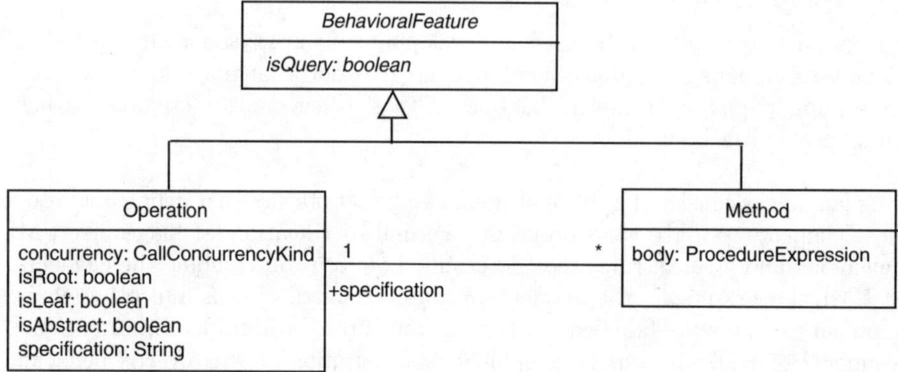

Fig. 2-1: Part of the abstract syntax of the UML core package

This diagram shows that Operation and Method are metaclasses and are both subclasses of the abstract metaclass BehavioralFeature, and that an Operation is a specification of a Method. While an Operation has a specification as one of its attributes, a Method has a body as its only attribute: the specification in the Operation metaclass is a string that specifies the signature of the operation (its return-value, name and parameters); the body in the Method metaclass is a procedure, probably in a programming language, which defines how the method implements the operation. A particular instance of an operation in a class is an instance of the metaclass Operation.

The specification of a Method and its attributes and associations is also provided in natural language in the UML Specification (Object Management Group, 1999*a*), as follows.

Method

A method is the implementation of an operation. It specifies the algorithm or procedure that effects the results of an operation. In the metamodel, a Method is a declaration of a named piece of behavior in a Classifier and realizes one (directly) or a set (indirectly) of Operations of the Classifier.

Attributes

body	The implementation of the Method as a ProcedureExpression.

Associations

specification	Designates an Operation that the Method implements. The Operation must be owned by the Classifier that owns the Method or be inherited by it. The signatures of the Operation and Method must match.

There is a similar specification for Operation and for every other metaclass in the metamodel.

2.4.3 Well-formedness Rules

The well-formedness rules apply to instances of metaclasses (that is to operations, methods, classes and so on in the model layer). They provide the rules that instances of the metaclasses must conform to as a set of *invariants.* Invariants are constraints which cannot be broken: they must always be true for the model to be meaningful. They are specified in Object Constraint Language (OCL), which is explained in detail in Chapter 12. For example, the specification for the metaclass Class states that if the class is concrete (not abstract), then every operation should have a method that realizes it. This constraint is written in OCL.

```
not self.isAbstract implies self.allOperations->forAll (op | self.allMethods->exists (m |
m.specification->includes(op)))
```

These constraints on the metamodel can be applied to check that the model conforms to the rules of UML and is well-formed.

Note that OCL is used **within** UML in order to document constraints within a model. For example, if one of the rules in the CarMatch system is that every journey that is linked to a sharing agreement must belong to a different car sharer, this could be documented in OCL as follows.

```
context SharingAgreement inv:
self.isSharedIn->forAll (i, j | (i.makes = j.makes)
    implies i = j)
```

What this says in English is that in the context of the SharingAgreement class there is an invariant rule as follows. If you take every possible pair of links between an instance of SharingAgreement and instances of Journey based on the association isSharedIn, and for each member of the pair you follow the link based on the association makes to an instance of the class CarSharer, then if the two CarSharers are the same, then the two journeys must be the same. Because they must be the same, it follows that two different journeys belonging to the same car sharer cannot be shared in the same sharing agreement.

2.4.4 Semantics

The semantics of UML are documented in English. For example the following is the description of the metaclass Operation.

> Operation is a conceptual construct, while Method is the implementation construct. Their common features, such as having a signature, are expressed in the BehavioralFeature metaclass, and the specific semantics of the Operation. The Method constructs are defined in the corresponding subclasses of BehavioralFeature.

However, much of the information about operations is to be found in the definition of Class, and you would need to read the entire section to understand the semantics fully.

2.4.5 Notation Guide

The 'Notation Guide' section of the UML Specification is the largest part of the specification and the most useful to anyone intending to apply UML. While the abstract syntax is specified in the notation of the metamodel and the well-formedness rules are specified in OCL, the notation of UML is described in English with supporting diagrams. However, because English is used, the notation is ambiguous in places, and it is sometimes necessary to refer to the other sections of the specification.

The Notation Guide includes a section on common elements of the UML notation, which we have covered in Chapter 14. For each kind of diagram this section explains the diagram and includes the semantics of the diagram and its elements, the notation, the mapping between elements of the notation and the metamodel, and optionally examples of its use, style guidelines and presentation options. Presentation options are possible alternative ways of representing aspects of the notation that are not inherently part of the notation, for example the use of colour to distinguish different types of message.

EXAMPLE 2.1 A UML Use Case Diagram is made up of ovals representing use cases and stick figures representing users. These are joined together by lines to show which users use which use cases. Which of the following is a valid use case diagram?

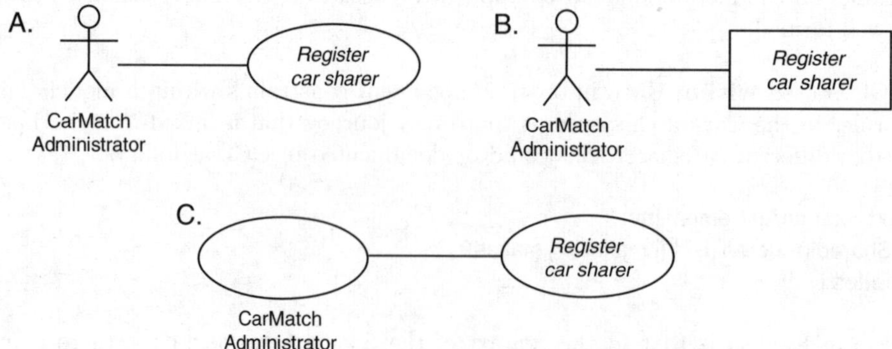

Solution

Only A is a valid use case diagram. B uses a rectangle instead of an oval for the use case, and C uses an oval instead of the stick person for the actor.

EXAMPLE 2.2 Here are two rules from the metalanguage used to define UML. Names of stereotypes are delimited by guillemets and begin with lowercase (e.g., «type»). Initial embedded capital is used for names that consist of appended nouns/adjectives (e.g., ownedElement, allContents).

Which of the following stereotypes follows these syntax rules?

«Type» «new type» «newType» «longGreenDottedLine»

Solution

«Type» does not, as it begins with a capital letter. «new type» does not, as it has a space in it. The other two do follow the rules.

2.4.6 Model Management

2.4.6.1 Packages

UML itself is organized into *packages.* Each package contains some of the diagrams that make up UML. Metaclasses are grouped together into packages depending on the degree of cohesion that they have with one another. Figure 2-2 shows the top-level packages and the dependencies among them.

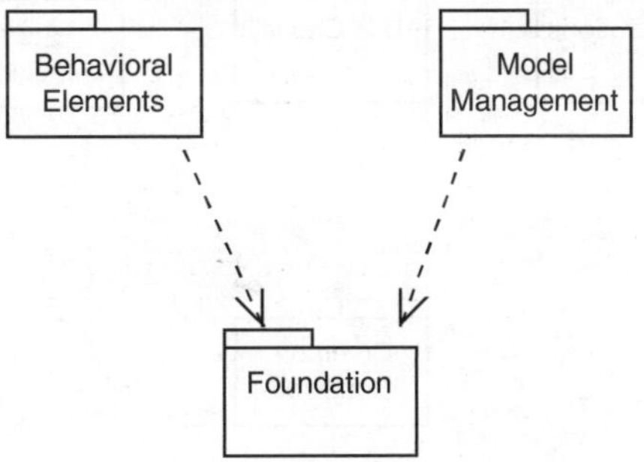

Fig. 2-2: Top-level packages of UML

The *Model Management* package contains the metaclasses for the organization of models into packages like these. Packages can be used within a project to organize the different diagrams that are produced into coherent groupings. These packages are purely an organizational convenience and do not necessarily map to subsystems in the finished system.

The other two packages in the top-level package diagram are broken down into their component sub-packages in Figures 2-3 and 2-4.

The containment of one or more packages within another package can be shown using the notation of Figure 2-5, as a tree structure with a plus sign in a circle drawn at the end of the line that is attached to the container.

Alternatively, this can be shown by including packages within another, in which case the name of the package is displayed in the tab rather than the body of the package, as in Figure 2-6.

The relationships among packages can be stereotyped as «import» or «access».

As we stated above, packages provide the mechanism for organizing model elements. The different views of a project, *Use Case View*, *Logical View* or *Component View*, can be represented as packages.

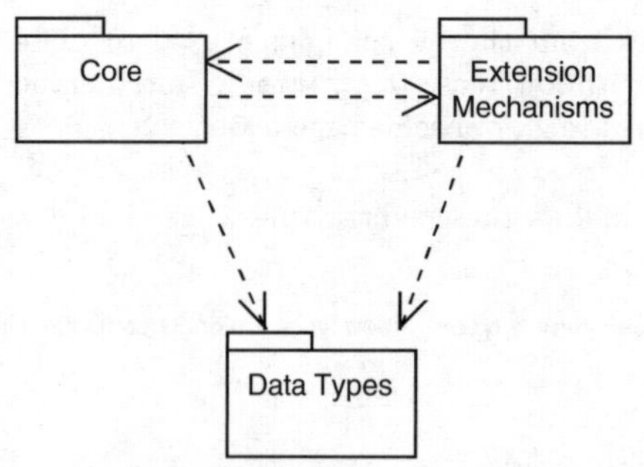

Fig. 2-3: Foundation packages of UML

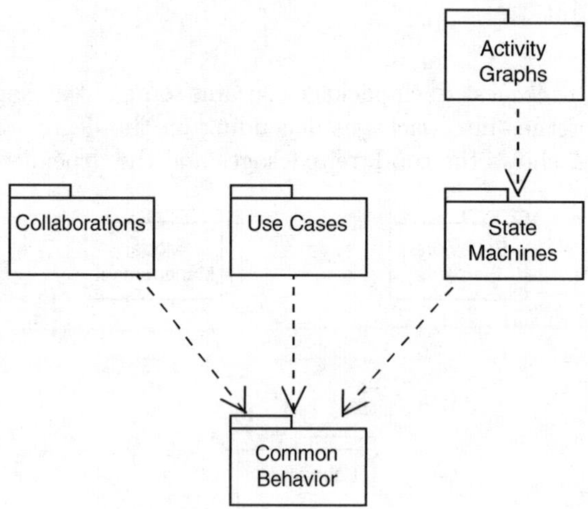

Fig. 2-4: Behavioral elements packages of UML

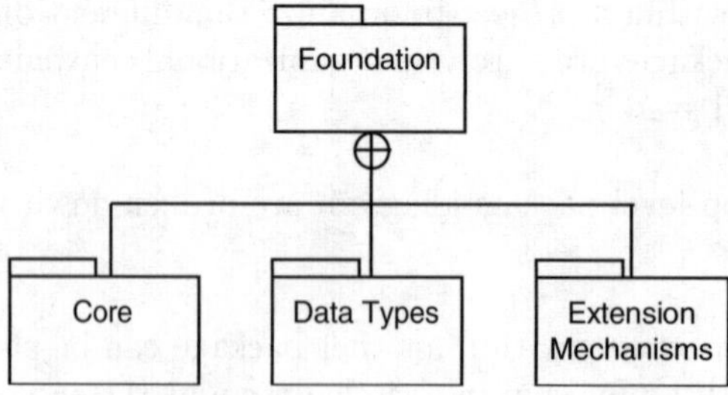

Fig. 2-5: Tree structured containment notation for packages of UML

2.4.6.2 Subsystems

Subsystems represent units of the physical system that can be organized in stereotyped packages as in Figure 2-7. They are stereotyped either with the fork symbol shown or with the stereotype «subsystem».

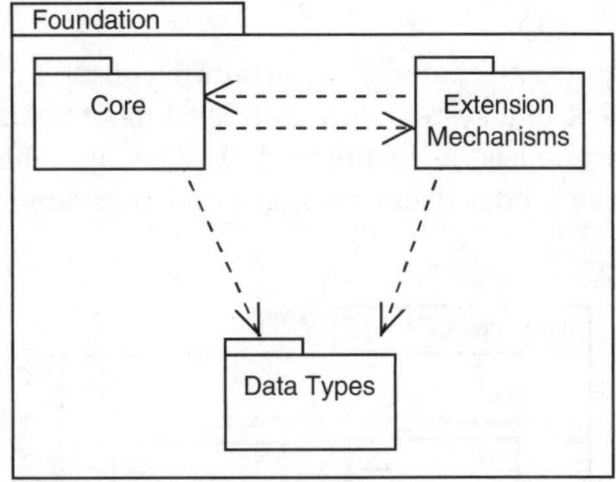

Fig. 2-6: Alternative containment notation for packages of UML

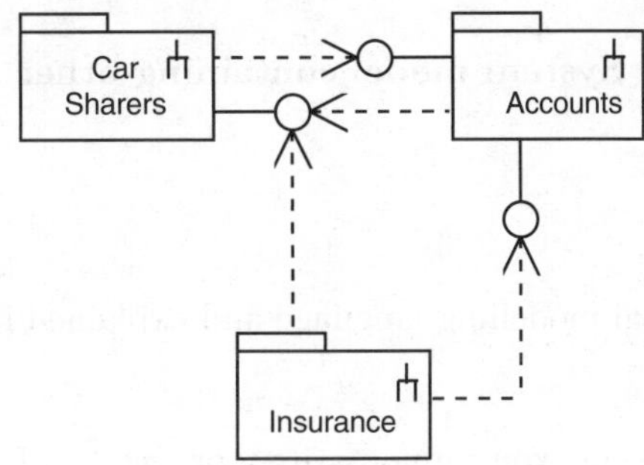

Fig. 2-7: Example subsystems for the CarMatch case study

The subsystems in Figure 2-7 offer interfaces on which the other subsystems have dependencies. These elements of notation are explained in more detail later in the book.

Subsystems can also be shown as large icons divided into three compartments, one for *Operations*, one for *Specification Elements* and one for *Realization Elements*. (The notation is flexible and allows compartments to be omitted or collapsed into a single compartment.) Figure 2-8 shows this notation.

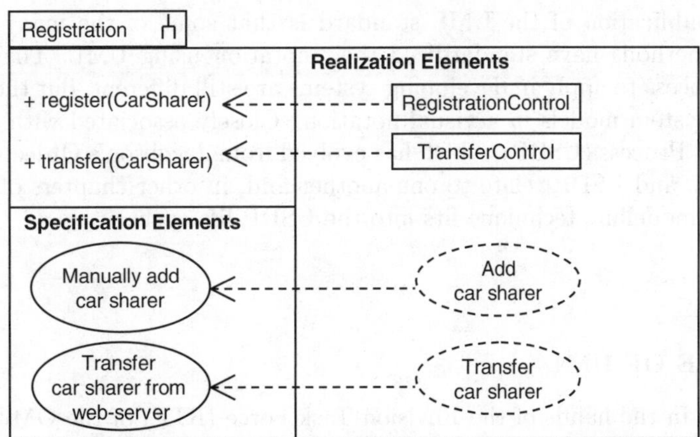

Fig. 2-8: Subsystem with compartments

2.4.6.3 Models

Models are abstractions of a physical system with a certain purpose. Typically models are used for the different stages in the development of a system. The top-level model of a system can be stereotyped as «systemModel» and contains other models, as in Figure 2-9. This also shows the use of a small triangle as a stereotype icon to distinguish models from packages and subsystems. The stereotype «model» can also be used.

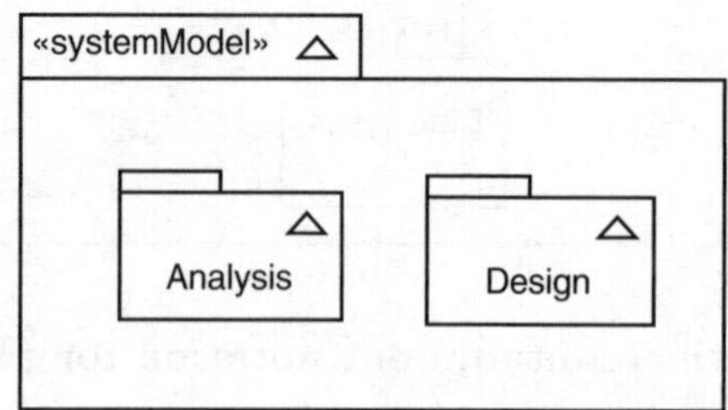

Fig. 2-9: System model containing other models

2.4.7 What UML is Not

We have said that UML is a visual modelling language and explained its structure. It is worth stating briefly what UML is not.

UML is not a programming language. You cannot write a program in UML. Some CASE tools can take a UML model and generate program code in different languages from it, but this will be little more than a framework. The developer will still have to write code to implement the methods.

UML is not a CASE tool. There are a number of CASE tools that implement the UML standard to a greater or lesser extent, and the UML specification has been written in part for CASE tool developers to enable them to implement the standard and to exchange models between applications using the XMI DTD.

UML is not a method, methodology or software development process. The UML notation can be applied in projects that use different approaches to the process of software development and that break the system development life-cycle into different activities, tasks, stages and steps. One thing that has happened since the publication of the UML standard is that some of the many competing systems analysis and design methods have standardized their notation using UML. Their authors' views of what is the correct process to apply in developing systems are still different, but they can at least agree on how to represent system models in a visual notation. Closely associated with UML is the Unified Software Development Process (USDP), which has evolved from Jacobson's Objectory process. Section 2.8 explains how UML and USDP relate to one another and, in other chapters of this book, we have explained where each modelling technique fits into the USDP life-cycle.

2.5 THE FUTURE OF UML

The future of UML is in the hands of the Revision Task Force (RTF) of the OMG. The plans for the development of UML are described in an article in the *Communications of the ACM* by Cris Kobryn, Chair of the RTF, (Kobryn, 1999). There is also information about the development of UML in the future on the RTF's web site.

The current release of UML is Version 1.3. The RTF is working on Version 1.4, at the time of writing. Version 1.4 is a minor revision and will be an editorial correction of Version 1.3, correcting errors and resolving ambiguous points in the specification. Much of this is based on feedback from users. Users of UML submit issues to the RTF's web site for consideration, and the RTF examines each issue and decides what action to take. The release of Version 1.4 was planned for late 2000, but the deadline for recommended changes was extended to 22nd December 2000 in September 2000, and it is likely to be 2001 when it is finally available.

Version 2.0 is also being developed at the time of writing. Requests for Proposals for Version 2.0 were issued in September 2000, and it is planned for release in 2001. This is a major revision and will include more significant changes to the specification. The areas that are being addressed in Version 2.0 are the following.

- **Architecture**—More rigorous specification of the metamodel, including a clearer separation between what is in the core of UML and what is defined in standard profiles.
- **Extensibility**—Improve the mechanisms for extending UML with notation for specific domains (see Chapter 14).
- **Components**—Better support for component-based development through the notation and semantics of component diagrams (see Chapter 13).
- **Relationships**—Better definition of the semantics of associations, including refinement and trace dependencies.
- **Statecharts and activity graphs**—Separate the semantics of the two types of diagrams, so that activity graphs can be defined independently of statecharts (see Chapters 10 and 11).
- **Model management**—Better notation and semantics for model management.
- **General mechanisms**—Support for model version control and diagram interchange.

As well as these points, users have also requested a change to the way that the UML specification is produced. At over 800 pages, it is an unwieldy document, and it is planned to take out the physical model specifications (CORBAfacility and XMI) into a separate document.

The other major event in the future development of UML is that the OMG is planning to submit it to the International Organization for Standardization (ISO) as an international standard for information technology.

2.6 UML PROFILES AND EXTENSIBILITY

Versions 1.4 and 2.0 of UML continue the mainstream evolution of UML for general systems development. One of the features of UML is that it is intended to be capable of being customized for different kinds of projects. The mechanisms for doing this are *constraints*, *stereotypes* and *tagged values*, and these are described in more detail in Chapter 14. These extension mechanisms can be packaged together into *profiles* for different domains. (Note that the term *process extension* is sometimes used instead of profile, but profile is the term used in the UML Specification.) There are two profiles in the Specification: Software Development Profile and the Business Modelling Profile. The OMG has issued RFPs for profiles that can be applied in other domains. Work is also under way on the development of a profile for CORBA and another for enterprise distributed computing.

The most significant profile under development is the profile for scheduling, performance and time. The work on this is being carried out by the OMG's Real-time Analysis and Design Working Group. This has a submission deadline in June 2001. Currently extensions to UML for developing real-time applications have been included in the product range from Rational Software Corporation in the form of Rational Rose RealTime. This CASE tool uses stereotypes to represent the notation from the ROOM (Real-Time Object-Oriented Modeling) method (Selic, Gullekson & Ward, 1994). However, other CASE Tool products use other notations for real-time systems design, and there is an urgent need for standardization.

2.7 WHY USE UML?

In this section we discuss why you should use UML. For those who are new to systems analysis and design, we first discuss the reasons for using a visual approach to designing systems. We then look at some of the benefits that are claimed for UML before finally giving some examples of projects on which UML has been used.

2.7.1 Why Use Analysis and Design Diagrams?

People who design all kinds of artefacts use pictures or diagrams to assist in the design process. Fashion designers, engineers, architects and system analysts and designers all use diagrams to visualize their designs. System analysts and designers use diagrams to help them visualize the software systems that they are designing, despite the fact that the products of the design process—computer programs—are not themselves inherently visual. What advantages does using diagrams bring to the design process?

There are two main uses of diagrams in producing a design:

- to abstract features of the design;
- to show relationships between elements of the design.

When an architect designs a building, he or she will produce a number of drawings with different purposes. These include diagrams that show an overall view of the building with very little detail, diagrams that show particular features of the design, such as the location of the pipework for the plumbing, and diagrams that show details of the design, such as the shape of wooden mouldings or the colour and texture of an external surface. No one diagram can embody every aspect of something as complex as a building, and no human can handle all the information about a building design in one go. It is the same with software systems: they are very complex, and the designer will represent different aspects of the design with different diagrams. Each of these diagrams picks out one or more specific aspects from the overall design. Even then, each diagram cannot represent every detail of those aspects of the design. A diagram of the plumbing in a building might simply use lines to represent each pipe rather than attempting to show the width of the pipe in scale. Similarly, a diagram showing communication between different elements in a software system might use lines to show the communication without attempting to represent the way that the communication is intended to take place.

This use of diagrams to simplify systems and to represent certain key features is known as *abstraction*. Abstraction is a mechanism that we use to represent a complex reality in simplified terms using some kind of model. The term abstraction can also be used to apply to the product of this process. More often, if the abstraction is represented in some physical way, such as a diagram on paper or a physical object, we use the term *model.*

In systems analysis and design, models are produced that abstract the important features of real-world systems. A UML class that describes a customer includes only those features of the customer that are of interest to a business information system. A UML class that models the behaviour of an aircraft in an air traffic control system models only those features of the aircraft that are of interest to a real-time control system. In both cases, part of the role of the system analyst or designer is to decide which features are of interest and which are not.

EXAMPLE 2.3 In most business systems, the features of a customer that might be of interest include name, address, telephone number, fax number and email address. Hair colour, weight and height are unlikely to be relevant features. However, if the business system belongs to a slimming club then weight will be a relevant feature of clients that should be modelled. Abstracting the right features and building the correct model is part of the skill of systems analysis.

System analysts and designers use diagrams for all of these reasons and purposes. Computer systems are complex artefacts made up of hardware and software; diagrams provide a way of modelling these systems, how they are structured and how they are intended to work.

The relationships among elements of a design can also be shown graphically or in the supporting text that accompanies a model. In architecture, the relationships between elements can include the need to model the structural relationship between floors and the parts of the building (walls and joists) that support them. In modelling any subject, these relationships are as important as the things that they relate together. Relationships in models can include the following types.

- Structural relationships between elements of a model that have some dependency on one another.
- Organizational relationships between elements of a system that must be packaged together in the final system for it to work.
- Temporal relationships between parts of the model in order to illustrate a sequence of events over time.
- Cause and effect relationships between elements of a model, for example to show preconditions that must exist before something else will work.
- Evolutionary relationships between models over time, showing how one element has been derived from another during the life-cycle of a project.

UML includes all these kinds of relationships between its elements. The following list gives an example of each.

- Structural relationships—associations between classes.
- Organizational relationships—packages as a way of organizing model elements.
- Temporal relationships—the time sequence of messages in an interaction sequence diagram.
- Cause and effect relationships—states in statechart diagrams.
- Evolutionary relationships—trace dependencies between diagrams in the design model and the analysis model.

EXAMPLE 2.4 In a slimming club, each customer's weight will be recorded on a number of occasions, so a set of weight measurements will gradually be accumulated. There is a structural relationship between each customer and the set of weight measurements that belongs to that customer. This relationship can be abstracted into a relationship between the class Customer and the class WeightMeasurement. We may also want to model cause and effect relationships, for example, if a customer loses more than a certain amount of weight then the customer is awarded a certificate.

2.7.2 Why Use UML Specifically?

In an object-oriented systems development project, UML is a candidate modelling language for the analysis and design of the product. (Note that not all development projects use object-oriented languages, despite the hype. For projects using procedural languages or functional languages and for projects that are to be implemented using a relational database, models in UML may be difficult to convert to an implementation.)

The strongest reason for using UML is that it has become the *de facto* standard for object-oriented modelling. If it is necessary to involve a team of developers or to convey the information in models to other people, then UML is the obvious choice as it will facilitate communication among participants.

A second reason lies in the fact that it is a *unified* modelling language. It brings together the ideas of three leading players in object-oriented modelling and combines them into a single notation. Since the early versions, the organizations involved in the development of UML have also tried to incorporate the best features of other modelling languages, so it could be regarded as a combination of best practice in the field. However, there is a danger in this, and that is that in trying to incorporate many views on object-oriented modelling, UML will become bloated with superfluous notation. The OMG's RTF has tried to avoid this by keeping the core of UML simple and using profiles and other extensibility mechanisms to extend it to new domains.

This is a third reason for using UML. Special profiles already exist to help the user to apply it to specific kinds of problem, and more are being developed. If a profile does not exist for a specific problem domain, then it is possible to extend the notation to apply to that domain. Jim Conallen's work on applying UML to modelling web-based systems is a good example of this, and one which we discuss in more detail in Chapter 14 (Conallen, 2000).

Finally, although UML itself does not include a specification of how it should be applied—a process—the Unified Software Development Process does provide guidance on how to develop a system using UML and is designed specifically to work with UML.

2.8 THE UNIFIED SOFTWARE DEVELOPMENT PROCESS

UML is a language for specifying systems in a formal way; it does not define a process for the analysis, design and implementation of systems. The developers of UML have also produced a specification of a software development process that explains how they think developers should go about developing systems using UML (Jacobson, Booch & Rumbaugh, 1999). This software development process is known as the Unified Software Development Process, the Rational Unified Process or simply the Unified Process. Throughout the rest of this book we shall refer to it as the Unified Process.

The Unified Process involves *people*, *projects*, *products*, *process* and *tools*. *People* are the participants and developers in one or more system development *projects* which produce a software *product* or *products* following a *process* and using automated *tools* to assist in the development. The Unified Process is a use-case-driven process. This means that the users' requirements are captured in use cases, as sequences of actions performed by the system that provide some value for users. These use cases are used as the basis of subsequent work by developers to produce design and implementation models that implement the use cases. (The technique of producing use cases is explained in Chapter 3.) The Unified Process is also architecture-centric, iterative, and incremental. Architecture-centric means that the system architecture is developed to meet the requirements of key use cases in terms of the platform the system will run on and the structure of the system and subsystems. It is iterative in that the project is broken down into mini-projects. In each mini-project or iteration some part of the system is analyzed, designed, implemented and tested. Each such part is an increment and the system is built up in increments. Iterations are not all the same; the kinds of activities involved in each iteration will change as progress is made through the overall cycle. In the Unified Process, the life-cycle is broken down into four phases: *Inception*, *Elaboration*, *Construction* and *Transition.* An overall project may consist of a number of cycles, each of which consists of these four phases, and each phase consists of several iterations.

The Unified Process produces more than just the finished system. A number of intermediate artefacts are produced; these are known as models. Each model specifies the modelled system from a particular viewpoint. As such, they are abstractions of the system, each one abstracting certain features of the system. The main models in the Unified Process are the *Use-Case Model*, the *Analysis Model*, the *Design Model*, the *Deployment Model*, the *Implementation Model* and the *Test Model.* It should be possible to trace parts of each model back to its predecessor; for example, it should be possible to trace classes in the design model back to classes in the analysis model, and to trace these back to requirements in the use case model. This is known as a *trace dependency* between models.

The process aspect of the Unified Process is defined in terms of the *activities* that are needed to transform users' requirements into a working system. These activities are grouped together into *workflows*, and each workflow is represented graphically using an activity diagram. Figure 2-10 shows the analysis workflow.

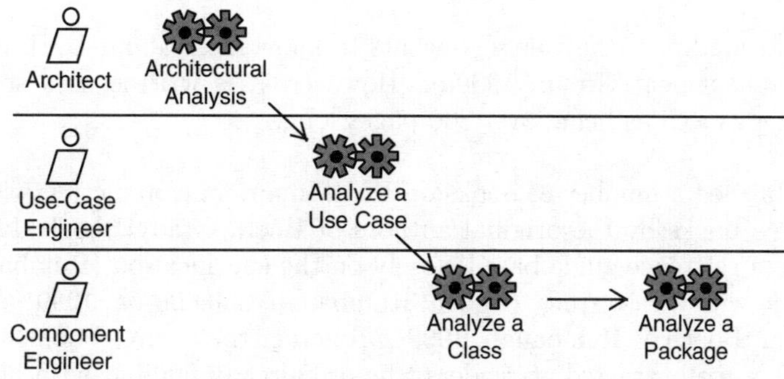

Fig. 2-10: Analysis workflow as an activity diagram

Note that the authors of the Unified Process have used a stereotyped form of the UML activity diagram to represent workflows. Stereotypes are explained in Chapter 14 and activity diagrams in Chapter 10.

Workflows also specify the workers who will carry out the activities. Workers are not specific people but abstract roles. More than one person may fill a particular worker role, or more than one worker role can be filled by the same person. The workers involved in the analysis workflow are shown in the activity diagram. Each activity is broken down into more detailed *steps.* Each activity is also specified in terms of the models and other project artefacts that are used as inputs in that activity and in terms of the artefacts that are produced as results of the activity. Figure 2-11 shows this for the activity *Analyze a Use Case.*

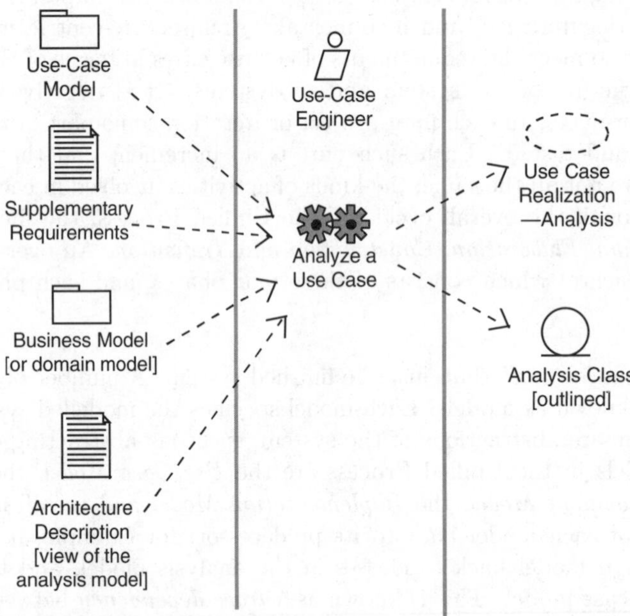

Fig. 2-11: The input and result of analyzing a use case

2.9 WHERE TO FIND MORE INFORMATION

The obvious source of information for anyone who wants to know more about UML is the UML Specification itself (Object Management Group, 1999*a*). However, it is written as a specialist reference manual and is heavy going as well as being over 800 pages long.

Addison-Wesley have published a number of books on UML, many in conjunction with Rational Software. These include three books by the original authors of UML, Grady Booch, Ivar Jacobson and Jim Rumbaugh. There is a reference guide based closely on the specification (Rumbaugh, Jacobson & Booch, 1999), a user guide with a case study (Booch, Rumbaugh & Jacobson, 1999) and a guide to the Unified Process (Jacobson, Booch & Rumbaugh, 1999). Together these three books amount to around 1,500 pages. These books are all targeted at readers who are already familiar with how to carry out a systems analysis and design project.

McGraw-Hill have published a more general systems analysis and design textbook using UML notation co-authored by one of the authors of this book (Bennett, McRobb & Farmer, 1999).

Information on the current version of the specification and on the development of UML is available on the Rational Software web-site (www.rational.com), and on the OMG web-site (www.omg.org). The OMG site has links to the UML Forum and pages maintained by the Revision Task Force members as well as other UML resources. The Rational Software Corporation web-site has links to case studies of organizations that have used UML and Rational Rose in development projects.

The article by Cris Kobryn (Kobryn, 1999) in the *Communications of the ACM* gives an overview of the roadmap for development of UML, although the timescales are now out of date.

Review Questions

2.1 Who were the three lead authors of earlier notations who joined Rational Software Corporation to develop UML?

2.2 Which organization is now responsible for the UML standard?

2.3 What is the purpose of the UML XMI DTD?

2.4 What are the three kinds of rules used to define UML?

2.5 What are the four layers of the UML metamodel architecture?

2.6 How are well-formedness rules specified?

2.7 What are packages used for in UML?

2.8 What body within the OMG is responsible for the future of UML?

2.9 What are UML profiles used for?

2.10 Which of the following is an abstraction?

- a A map that you draw using just a few lines on a scrap of paper for a friend to show the way to your home
- b A road atlas of London, England
- c London, England
- d A UML class diagram

2.11 Which of the following is a model?

- a A UML class diagram
- b A set of UML class diagrams describing the classes in a software system
- c A 1:100 scale clay replica of a new sports car that will be used to test its aerodynamics in a wind tunnel
- d A full scale, working prototype of a new sports car

2.12 Give three reasons for using UML.

2.13 What are the four phases of the Unified Process life-cycle?

2.14 Explain the relationships among workflows, activities and steps in the Unified Process.

Supplementary Problems

2.1 Investigate one of the notations that were the forerunners of UML (Rumbaugh's, Booch's or Jacobson's). Choose a UML diagram and its equivalent in the other notation and list what they have in common and what is different.

2.2 Investigate the three notations that were the forerunners of UML (Rumbaugh's, Booch's and Jacobson's). Choose one type of diagram and compare the notation in each.

2.3 One of the principles of human–computer interaction design is 'affordance'. This means that the form of an object should suggest its purpose. Based on your research for the previous two questions, do you think that the diagramming symbols used in UML have obvious affordances, or are they just an arbitrary set of symbols? Are there examples of both categories?

2.4 Find some case studies of the use of UML. (There are several on Rational Software Corporation's web-site, though they are really promoting the CASE tool Rational Rose.) Identify any benefits that are claimed for using UML.

Use Cases

3.1 INTRODUCTION

Many projects begin with use cases, as they provide a good way of getting an overall picture of what is happening in the existing system or is planned to happen in the new system. The *use case diagram* is very simple with very little in the way of notation to remember. It is an effective means of communicating with users and other stakeholders about the system and what it is intended to do. Use cases can also be used as the basis of the test specifications that will be drawn up later in a project.

Use case diagrams show *use cases* and *actors* and the associations among them. Figure 3-1 shows what a simple use case diagram looks like. Use cases represent sequences of actions carried out by the system, and actors represent the people or other systems that interact with the system being modelled. Use case diagrams are supported by *behaviour specifications*, which define the interactions within a particular use case.

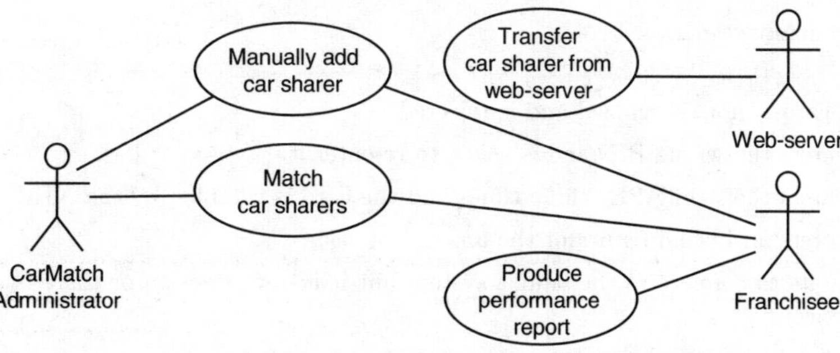

Fig. 3-1: Example use case diagram

Use cases have come into UML from the work of Jacobson et al. (1992), originally carried out within Ericsson in Sweden. In Jacobson's approach, use cases are the starting point for the development of a new system.

In UML terms, the *Use Cases package* is a *subpackage* of the *Behavioural Elements package.* This means that it is used to specify the behaviour of some entity such as a system or subsystem. Use cases do not specify the detail of how that behaviour is carried out. However, the detail will be elaborated using other models as the process of designing the system develops. Typically, how a use case will be realized in the eventual system is defined in one or more collaboration diagrams that show the interaction between co-operating objects.

EXAMPLE 3.1 In a banking system, use cases define the interaction that takes place between customers and automated teller machines (ATMs). Figure 3-2 shows an example of a simple use case diagram for an ATM subsystem. The Customer actor represents the *class* of all customers who will use the ATM subsystem. When you use your local ATM to withdraw cash, you are an *instance* of Customer using a particular instance of the use case Withdraw cash. The person standing in line behind you is another instance of Customer, who will use a different instance of the use case Withdraw cash. Someone else may use an instance of the use case Check balance or Print mini-statement. You may successfully withdraw cash from the machine, but the person behind you may find that he or she does not have enough money deposited, and the use case instance will proceed along a different course from yours, rejecting the request.

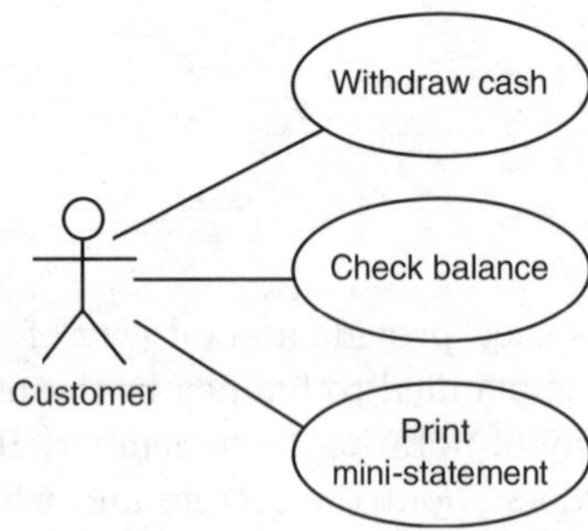

Fig. 3-2: Example use case diagram for ATM subsystem

The term *scenarios* is often used to refer to the different possible courses that different instances of the same use case might take. The use case diagram names only the use cases, but additional documents or diagrams may show the alternative scenarios that could occur.

EXAMPLE 3.2 What different scenarios might exist for the use case Withdraw cash?

Clearly, there could be many scenarios.

- The customer's card is not recognized and is rejected.
- The customer enters the wrong PIN and is asked to re-enter it.
- The customer enters the wrong PIN three times and the card is retained by the ATM.
- The customer enters an invalid figure for the amount of cash.
- The ATM attempts to connect to the bank's system but it is out of action or there is a network failure, so it cannot connect.
- The ATM does not have enough cash to meet the customer's request.
- The customer's account does not have enough funds to meet the request.
- The customer cancels the transaction part way through.

You may have thought of others. All these different scenarios are represented by the use case Withdraw cash. Eventually, the use case will have to be specified in enough detail for all these possible courses of events to be handled correctly by the objects that make up the subsystem. Initially, it is usual to specify the normal course of events (in which the customer successfully withdraws the amount of cash requested) and the most likely alternatives. As you will see later in Section 3.3, use case descriptions are often used to define the different scenarios.

3.2 PURPOSE OF THE TECHNIQUE

Use cases are created during the early stages of a project. Producing use case diagrams and the associated documents is an analysis technique rather than a design technique. Use cases can also be used later in the development process, for example to specify test cases. Use cases can be used to model what happens in the existing system (if there is one), or they can be used to model the new system that is going to be developed. The main purposes of producing use cases are as follows.

- They are used to model sequences of actions that are carried out by the system and that provide an observable result to someone or something outside the system, known as an actor.
- They provide a high level view of what the system does and who uses it.
- They provide the basis for determining the human–computer interfaces to the system.
- They can be used to model alternative scenarios for specific use cases that may result in different sequences of actions.
- They use a simple diagrammatic notation that is comprehensible to end users and can be used to communicate with them about the high level view of the system.
- They can be used as the basis for drawing up test specifications.

3.3 NOTATION

Use cases describe a sequence of actions that a system performs to achieve an observable result of value to an actor. They may be described informally in text, in a more structured form, for example using pseudocode, or through a behaviour specification represented by a link to another diagram, for example a collaboration diagram. The high-level view of the use cases in a system or subsystem is represented by use case diagrams.

3.3.1 Basic Notation—Use Cases, Actors and Relationships

Use cases are represented graphically in a use case diagram to allow the analyst to visualize each use case in the context of the other use cases in the system or subsystem and to show its relationships with actors and other use cases.

In a use case diagram use cases are drawn as an ellipse, as in Figure 3-3. The name of the use case is usually written inside the ellipse, but can be placed beneath it. Do not mix these two styles in the same model.

Use case names are text strings that contains letters, numbers and most punctuation marks—except for the colon, which is used to separate use case names from the names of packages (see Section 2.4.6 for an

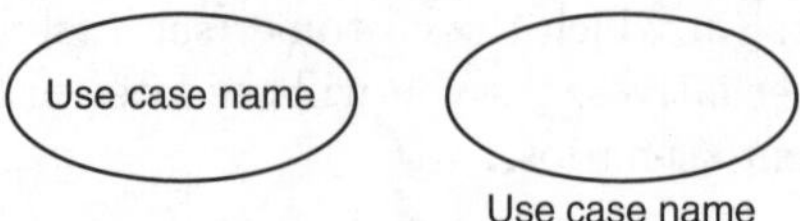

Fig. 3-3: Use case notation

explanation of packages)—and it is a good idea to keep them short. Use case names are normally made up of an active verb and a noun or noun phrase that concisely describe the behaviour of the system that you are modelling, for example Register car sharer, Match car sharers or Record sharing agreement. Figure 3-4 shows examples.

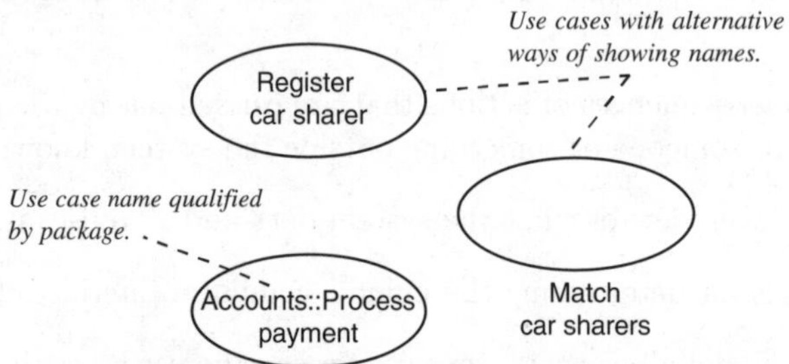

Fig. 3-4: Use cases with suitable names

Actors are the people or systems that interact with use cases. For the most part, you will find that they are users of the system that you are modelling. In a use case diagram each actor is drawn as a stick pereson with the role name written beneath (see Figure 3-5).

Fig. 3-5: Actor notation

When dealing with human actors, it is important to remember that the name of an actor is the name of the role that the actor performs in relation to the system and not just the job title. In a CarMatch office there may be people with different job titles (clerk, receptionist and supervisor) who can all register new car sharers in the system. Rather than drawing three different actors, we identify what is common to their jobs and create an actor for that role, in this case CarMatch Administrator (see Figure 3-6).

Actors are connected to the use cases with which they interact by a line which represents a relationship between the actors and the use cases (see Figure 3-7).

An example of this is shown in Figure 3-6. (There are other kinds of relationships between actors and other actors and between use cases and other use cases, which are described in Section 3.3.3.) The relationship indicates that there is an association between an actor and a use case. This means that particular people or systems in that actor role will communicate with particular instances of the use case; they will participate in the sequence of events that is represented by the use case. In practical

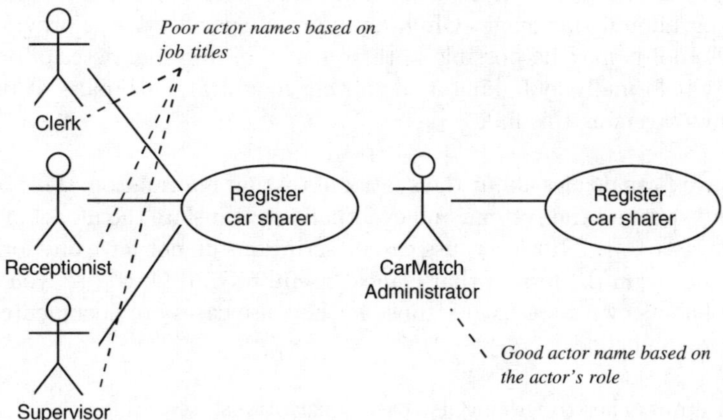

Fig. 3-6: Actors with unsuitable and suitable names

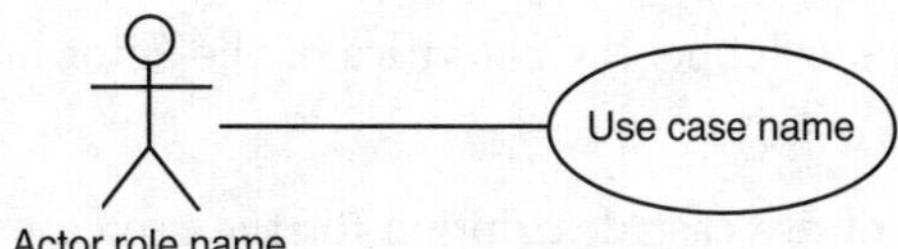

Fig. 3-7: Relationship between an actor and a use case

terms, the use case will eventually be implemented as some kind of computer program and the actors will use the program by entering information, receiving information or both.

A single actor may be associated with more than one use case, and a single use case may be associated with more than one actor. Figure 3-8 shows this for part of the CarMatch system.

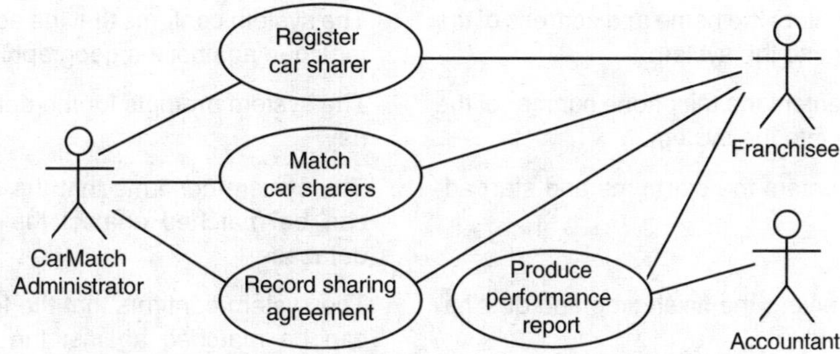

Fig. 3-8: Actors and use cases

3.3.2 Behaviour Specifications

Each use case represents a sequence of activities that results in some observable outcome for the actor or actors who interact with it. This sequence of activities is documented in a *behaviour specification.* The link to a behaviour specification may be represented in a CASE tool by a link to a diagram that provides the specification. This could be a sequence diagram or a collaboration diagram, a statechart diagram or text in a programming language. Often an informal specification is provided as a *use case description*. In a CASE tool it may be possible both to enter an informal description of a use case's behaviour and to specify it formally by linking it to another diagram. This makes it possible to 'zoom into' the specification by traversing this link.

Some UML diagrams have formal rules about the syntax of textual information. This makes it possible to execute the model and simulate the system, and eventually to translate the model into program code in a language such as Java or C++. However, use case descriptions do not have any formal syntax, and you can write the descriptions in the format that is most useful to you. Of course, you may be working in an organization that has its own rules or guidelines for how use cases are documented, in which case you should abide by those guidelines.

There are two common approaches to writing use case descriptions.

- The first is simply to write one or a few statements or paragraphs that describe the typical sequence of activities that the use case involves.
- The second is to list in two columns the activities of the actor and the responses of the system.

Figure 3-9 shows the first type of use case description for the use case Register car sharer, while Figure 3-10 shows the second type for the same use case. It may be that initially you produce the first type, and later when you have a better understanding of the requirements you produce the second type.

The user will enter the name, address and telephone number of the potential car sharer. For each journey that this person wants to share, the start address, the destination address, the start time and the finish time of the journey are entered.

Fig. 3-9: Simple use case description for Register car sharer

	Actor	*System*
1	The user enters the name and address of the car sharer into the system.	The system confirms that the address can be matched against the geographical database.
2	The user enters the telephone number of the car sharer into the system.	The system prompts for the details of a journey.
3	The user enters the start time and start address.	The system confirms that the start address can be matched against the geographical database.
4	The user enters the finish time and destination address.	The system confirms that the finish address can be matched against the geographical database. The system prompts the user to indicate if another journey is to be entered.
5	The user either enters another journey (Loop back to 3) or saves and exits.	The system either prompts for another journey (loop back to 3) or saves the car sharer and journey details and exits the use case.

Fig. 3-10: Use case description for Register car sharer using columns

Constantine (1997) classifies use case descriptions in a different way, according to whether they represent a logical view of the use case or a physical view. He distinguishes between 'essential' use cases and 'real' use cases. The word 'essential' here does not mean that these are somehow necessary use cases, but use cases that capture the essence of what is to be done. An essential use case describes the interaction in a way that is not dependent on the design of the eventual system. For example, Figure 3-10 is an essential use case description and contains no information about the physical implementation of the use case. Figure 3-11 is a real use case, as it includes information that defines the way that the physical interface will work.

	Actor	*System*
1	The user enters the name and address of the car sharer in the Car Sharer entry window.	The system confirms that the address can be matched against the geographical database.
2	The user enters the telephone number of the car sharer into the Car Sharer entry window.	The system prompts for the details of a journey by displaying the Journey entry dialogue box.
3	The user enters the start time and start address.	The system confirms that the start address can be matched against the geographical database.
4	The user enters the finish time and destination address.	The system confirms that the destination address can be matched against the geographical database. The system prompts the user to indicate if he or she wants to enter another journey by enabling two buttons labelled Another and Done.
5	The user clicks on Another to enter another journey (Loop back to 3) or clicks on Done to save and exit.	The system either clears the Journey entry dialogue box (Loop back to 3) or closes the dialogue box, saves the car sharer and journey details and exits the use case instance.

Fig. 3-11: Real use case description for Register car sharer

The use cases within a use case diagram can be shown enclosed by a rectangle. The rectangle either maps onto the complete use case model, which contains all the use cases and actors, or onto the system or subsystem to which the use cases belong. Figure 3-12 shows an early draft of the Registration subsystem of the CarMatch system.

3.3.3 Other Types of Association and Relationships

There are four other types of association or relationship that can be shown in a use case diagram. These are:

- Generalization between use cases
- Generalization between actors
- Include relationship between use cases
- Extend relationship between use cases

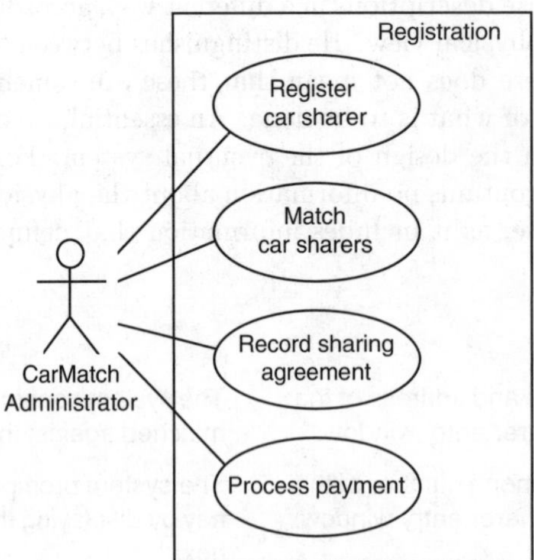

Fig. 3-12: Use cases in a subsystem

Note that in UML Version 1.1, *include* and *extend* were called *uses* and *extends.*

3.3.4 Generalization between Use Cases

Sometimes it becomes apparent that there is more than one version of a use case, and that the different versions have some actions in common and some that are unique to each one. Consider the use cases to add new car sharers to the system: there is one use case for adding new car sharers manually, and another for transferring them in from the web-server. These two use cases both serve the same overall function, but they are different in some aspects of how they operate. We can consider the two use cases as specializations of the use case Register car sharer, and Register car sharer as the general case. This can be represented in a use case diagram through the use of *generalization.* The generalization association is drawn with a triangular icon on the line, which points towards the use case that is the general case, as in Figure 3-13.

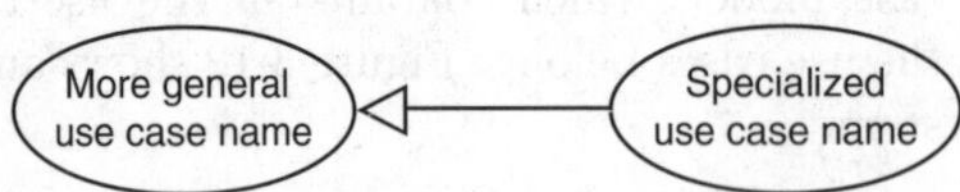

Fig. 3-13: Use case generalization notation

An example of the notation for this is shown in Figure 3-14.

This diagram indicates that the two use cases Manually add car sharer and Transfer car sharer from web-server inherit some of the functionality from the use case Register car sharer, but that they differ from it in some way. In this case, it is because one will be linked to a user interface to allow the CarMatch Administrator actor to enter the details, while the other will have an interface to the data on the web-server. Note that actors are not necessarily people, and can be other systems.

Sometimes the more general use case is one that will never exist in a real system, it is there only to define what is common to the specialized use cases. In this case, it is called an *abstract* use case, and

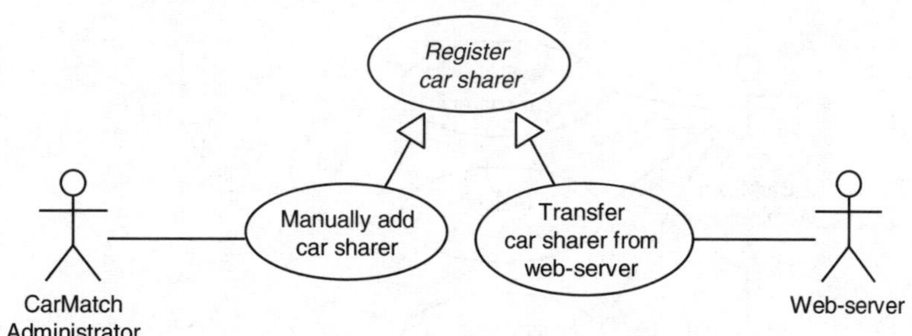

Fig. 3-14: Use cases in a generalization association

its name is printed in italics. The specialized use cases are sometimes referred to as *concrete* use cases. In their book on the Unified Process Jacobson et al. (1999) call these 'real' use cases, but this is not part of the UML terminology and is likely to lead to confusion with Constantine's use of the word 'real' as described in Section 3.3.2.

Generalization is often implemented by the mechanism of *inheritance* and is covered in more detail in the case of classes in Chapter 5.

3.3.5 Generalization between Actors

It is also possible for a generalization association to exist between actors (Figure 3-15).

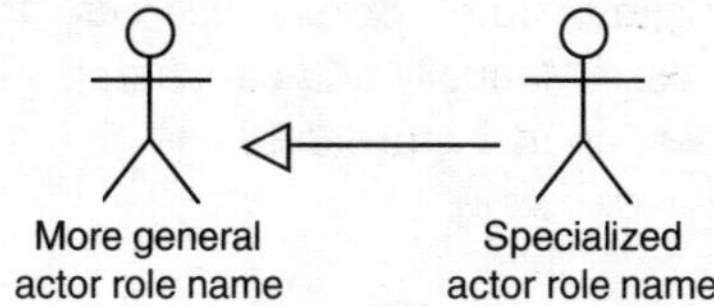

Fig. 3-15: Actor generalization association notation

At CarMatch, the Franchisee can handle the registration of new car sharers, but can also be the recipient of management reports. Rather than show both the Franchisee and the CarMatch Administrator in association with every use case that they share as in Figure 3-8, it is possible to show the Franchisee as a specialization of the CarMatch Administrator. This means that the Franchisee can do everything that the CarMatch Administrator can do, and more. This is shown in Figure 3-16.

3.3.6 Include Relationship between Use Cases

Sometimes one use case includes the functionality of another use case. The *include* relationship is drawn as an open arrow with a dashed line that points towards the use case that is being included. The word «include» is written in *guillemets* («...») alongside the relationship arrow, as in Figure 3-17.

This happens at CarMatch, where there is a use case to process payments from car sharers. This

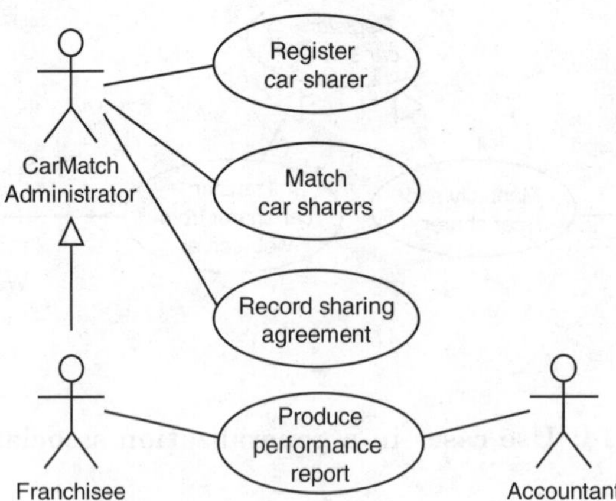

Fig. 3-16: Actors in a generalization association

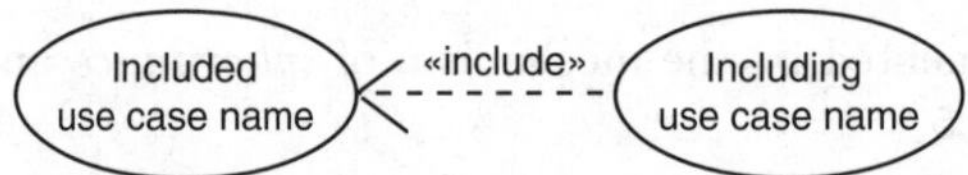

Fig. 3-17: Include relationship notation

can exist as a free-standing use case to deal with payments that come from members whose details were transferred from the web-server, but when a new car sharer is added manually, the membership payment is always processed at the same time. So the use case Process payments is both a use case on its own and included in the use case Manually add car sharer. This can be shown with an include relationship between the two use cases, as in Figure 3-18.

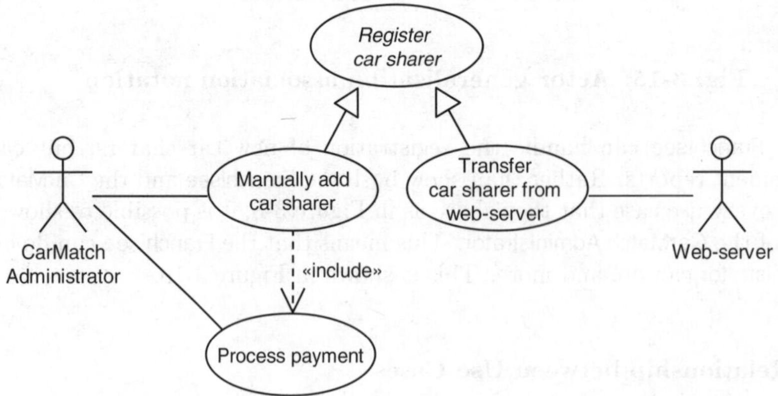

Fig. 3-18: Use cases in an include relationship

An include relationship can also be used when a particular use case is included in other use cases because it encapsulates some functionality that is used at several points in the system. This avoids having to define the same sequence of actions in multiple use cases. The including use case will continue up to the point where it includes the included use case, the full sequence of activities in the included use case will be carried out, and then the including use case will carry on at the point where it left off.

3.3.7 Extend Relationship between Use Cases

While an include relationship means that one use case always includes another, there are occasions where one use case may optionally be extended by the functionality in another use case. The relationship is drawn as an open arrow with a dashed line that points towards the use case that is being extended. The word «extend» is written in guillemets alongside the relationship arrow, as in Figure 3-19.

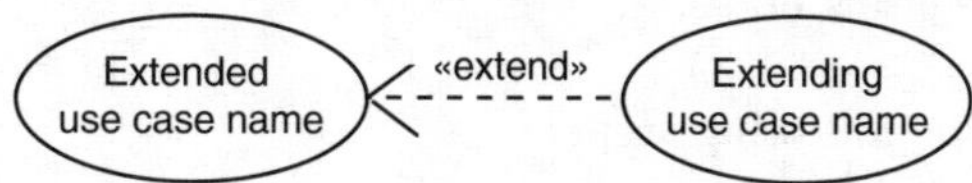

Fig. 3-19: Extend relationship notation

For example, if a car sharer is paying by cash or cheque, then the Process payment use case contains all the functionality that is required. However, if payment is by bank direct debit, or by credit or debit card, then the Process payment use case can be extended by either the use case Process card payment or the use case Process direct debit. An example of this is shown in Figure 3-20.

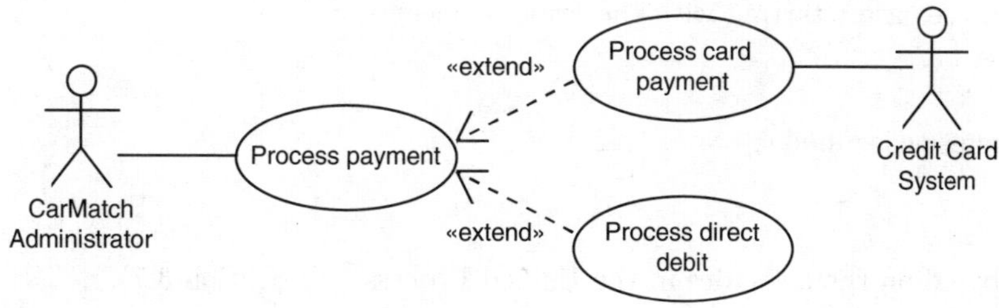

Fig. 3-20: Use cases in an extend relationship

Details of the point or points in the use case at which the extension takes place can be shown in a compartment in the use case ellipse in the diagram. This compartment is headed *Extension points* (even if there is only one) and is shown in Figure 3-21.

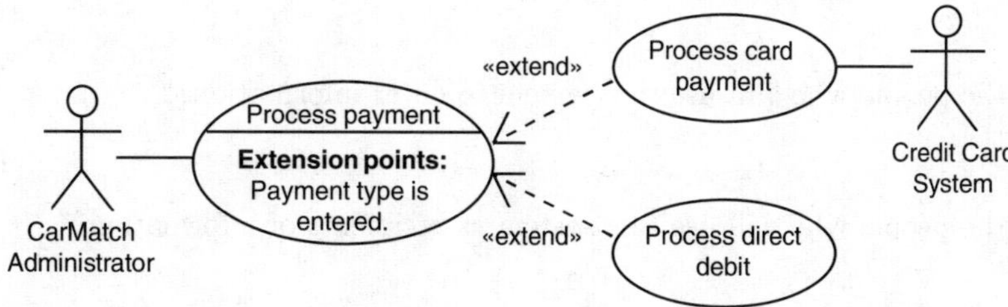

Fig. 3-21: Use case showing extension points

For the link to be followed into an extending use case and the sequence of activities in that use case to be carried out, some condition must evaluate to be true. In the example in Figure 3-21, there are three conditions, paymentType = credit or debit card, paymentType = cash or cheque and paymentType = direct debit. In this case, only one of these can be true, so at most one of the extending use cases will be used. If the member is paying cash then neither of the extending use cases will be used.

3.4 HOW TO PRODUCE USE CASES

A systems analyst who is producing use case diagrams and descriptions will normally be working from source documents such as notes and transcripts of interviews. (A transcript is produced when an interview has been recorded on tape and the contents of the tape are then transcribed word for word into a word processed document.) The analyst may have carried out the fact-finding him or herself or may be working from someone else's notes.

Producing use cases involves the following steps.

- Find actors and use cases.
- Prioritize use cases.
- Develop each use case (starting with the priority ones).
- Structure the use case model.

This approach is based on the activities in the Unified Process (see Section 3.7).

3.4.1 Find Actors and Use Cases

The actors represent the roles that people perform in using the system and that other systems fulfil in interacting with the system. It is easier to find people and systems than actors to start with. Ask yourself these questions:

- "Who are the people who will use this system to enter information?"
- "Who are the people who will use this system as recipients of information?"
- "What are the other systems that this system will interact with?"

EXAMPLE 3.3 Here is a short excerpt from an interview transcript with one of the directors who is setting up CarMatch. Mick Perez is the systems analyst and Janet Hoffner is the director.

Mick Perez: So you're saying that car sharers will be able to register by telephoning the office and speaking to someone there who will enter their details into the system.
Janet Hoffner: Yes. Either the franchisee, or more likely one of the office staff will take the call and enter the details into the computer.
MP: Who are the office staff?
JH: Well, there's one or two clerks, a receptionist and a supervisor. They all have a role in the administration of the system.
MP: What will they be entering?
JH: Oh, the person's name and address, details of the journeys they want to share, any preferences they have, such as being a non-smoker.
MP: Is that the only way that this information will get into the system?
JH: No, it could also be transferred in from the national web-server.
MP: How will this information be used?
JH: Two ways. Firstly it will be used to match up potential car sharers, and secondly, it will be used to produce a management report for the franchisee showing the number of registrations per week, whether they come from the web-server or by telephone and breaking them down by area.

If we ask these three questions about this description of the system being used, we can identify the franchisee, the clerks, the receptionist and the supervisor as people who enter information into the system. The franchisee is also a recipient of information from the system, and the web-server is another system that interacts with this one. Note that for this example, the car sharers do not interact directly with the system, and so they are not actors. There is nothing to distinguish the roles that the clerks, receptionist and supervisor play in this part of the system; they all administer the registration process, so we can use the actor role CarMatch Administrator to include all of them. Franchisee is also an actor, as the franchisee has a separate role as recipient of the management report. The final actor role is the Web-server, as this is another system that the CarMatch system interacts with.

Use cases represent sequences of actions carried out by the system, so to find use cases we need to look for the actions of the system. In this example there are four distinct use cases.

- Manually add car sharer.
- Transfer car sharer from web-server.
- Match car sharers.
- Produce management report.

These are shown in Figure 3-22. Note that we have not broken down the use cases into the level of detail that is described in the transcript. We are trying to group sequences of actions together into units that are meaningful in the context of the business. We do not create use cases with names like Take call or Enter details. The detail will be in the behaviour specifications.

3.4.2 Prioritize Use Cases

The next step is to prioritize the use cases. The purpose of this is to ensure that the important use cases are developed in early iterations of the next activity.

EXAMPLE 3.4 Of the use cases listed in the previous example, getting the details of car sharers into the system in the first place and matching them up are probably more important than producing management reports, and they would be the priorities for further elaboration.

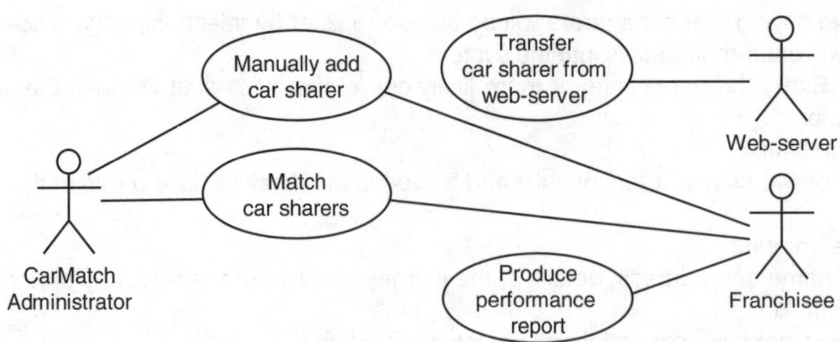

Fig. 3-22: First cut use cases and actors

3.4.3 Develop each Use Case (Starting with the Priority Ones)

The purpose of this activity is to produce the detailed specification of each use case along the lines of the use case descriptions in Section 3.3.2. This activity may also result in new use cases coming to light. In the Unified Process there is a staff role for *Use Case Specifiers*, people who produce the detailed step by step specification of use cases. In most projects, it is likely to be a systems analyst who is carrying out this role.

EXAMPLE 3.5 Here is another brief excerpt from an interview with Janet Hoffner describing what happens when a new car sharer is entered into the system in more detail.

Janet Hoffner: Whether we are entering a new car sharer manually or by transferring the data from the web-server, the processing is the same apart from how we deal with membership payments. If we are entering a new car sharer into the system manually, then we need to process their membership payment at the same time. If their data is being transferred from the web-server, then we process it separately later. When we process the payment, the person can either pay by a regular direct debit or using a credit or debit card. If it's a direct debit payment, then the data about the payment is stored, and we transfer a batch of payment details to the ABTS system at the end of the month.
Mick Perez: What's ABTS?
JH: The Automated Bank Transfer System. It handles electronic payments, okay. If it's a card payment, it's processed there and then.
MP: What about the matching process?
JH: That'll be based on several factors, mostly it's geographical...

At this point, the analyst will begin to produce use case descriptions to define the use cases informally. The transcript on page 37 can be used to draw up a use case description like the one in Figure 3-9. The information in the transcript above also tells the analyst a number of things.

- Manually entering car sharers and transferring them from the web-server are two versions of the same thing.
- When a car sharer is entered manually, payment details are always processed, but this needs to be a separate use case because it can also happen on its own.
- The Process payment use case can be extended in two different ways: to handle payment by credit or debit card, or to handle payment by bank debit.

These aspects of the use cases can be used to add further structure to the use case model.

3.4.4 Structure the Use Case Model

In this activity structure will be added to the use case diagram through the use of generalization, include and extend relationships and through the grouping of use cases in packages.

EXAMPLE 3.6 There are two different ways of registering car sharers. Both perform the same core function, but one responds to the CarMatch Administrator entering data through a user interface, while the other happens in response to the data about a new Car Sharer being transferred from the web server. Generalization can be used to represent this part of the model.

The use case Process payment is a use case in its own right but is also included in the use case Manually add car sharer. This can be represented by an «include» relationship.

The use case Process payment can optionally be extended in one of two ways, depending on the payment type. This can be represented by an «extend» relationship.

We have also already noted that the Franchisee is a specialization of the CarMatch Administrator, so we can use generalization to represent this.

Figure 3-23 shows the combination of all these structural aspects of the use case diagram for this Registration subsystem.

3.5 BUSINESS MODELLING WITH USE CASES

The UML includes special *profiles* that can be used to apply the notation of UML to particular aspects of system development. One of the profiles that is described in the UML 1.3 Specification is the UML Profile for Business Modelling. In this profile, use case diagrams can be applied to the activity of business modelling.

The use cases that have been given as examples in this chapter have all been use cases within a system that communicate with actors who are direct users of the system.

It is possible to draw use case diagrams to represent business processes and their interaction with people and systems that are external to the business.

EXAMPLE 3.7 CarMatch as a business interacts with a number of external actors. These can be identified from the material in Chapter 1. They include CarMatch Member, Credit Card Company and ABTS.

The use cases in a business model are the functions that these people and organizations interact with. For example, a CarMatch Member interacts with the business use cases Register with CarMatch, Agree to car sharing arrangement and Pay membership. These business use cases are shown in Figure 3-24.

3.6 RELATIONSHIP WITH OTHER DIAGRAMS

As was stated in Section 3.3.2, the behaviour of a use case may be specified using another UML diagram: a collaboration diagram, a sequence diagram or a statechart diagram. In a CASE tool, this would be handled by a hyperlink from the use case to the related diagram that specifies its behaviour.

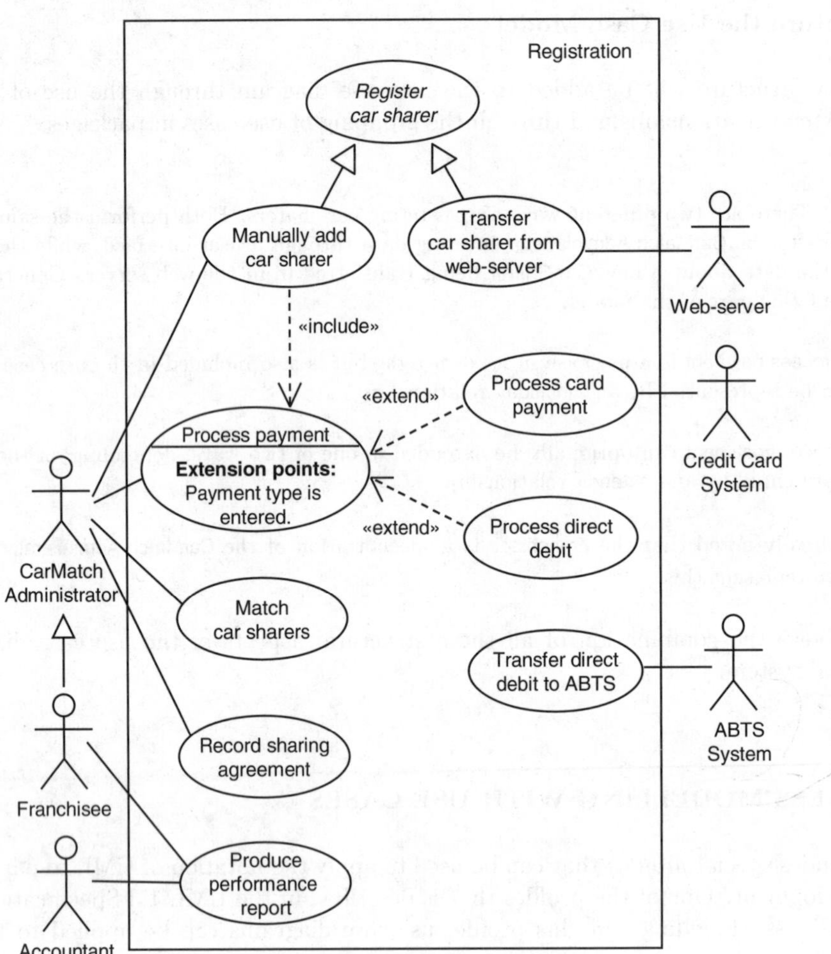

Fig. 3-23: Structured version of use case diagram

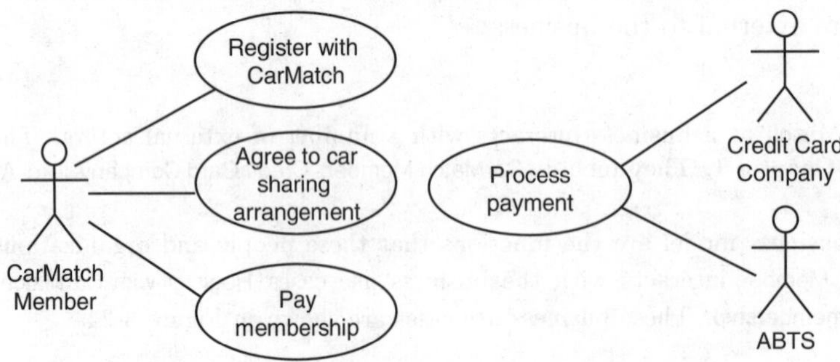

Fig. 3-24: Business profile use case diagram

Like all other UML models, the use case model is organized in packages as part of the *Model Management View.*

3.7 USE CASES IN THE UNIFIED PROCESS

Jacobson et al. (1999) describe the Unified Process as use-case-driven, and use cases are central to the way that users' requirements are identified and documented in the Unified Process.

In Chapter 2 we explained how the Unified Process comprises five workflows. Each workflow consists of a number of related activities that are carried out by different workers. By carrying out the activities in each workflow, the workers produce models, which are elaborated as the development proceeds. In the Unified Process, the first of these workflows is the Requirements Workflow, and the *Use Case Model* is one of its outputs. Figure 3-25 shows the workflow as an activity diagram (see Chapter 10) using stereotyped icons (see Chapter 14) to represent the workers and activities. The one activity that we have not discussed in the current chapter is *Prototype User-Interface.* This activity involves producing a prototype of the user interface for selected use cases. It does not use UML notation, but is part of the Unified Process workflow.

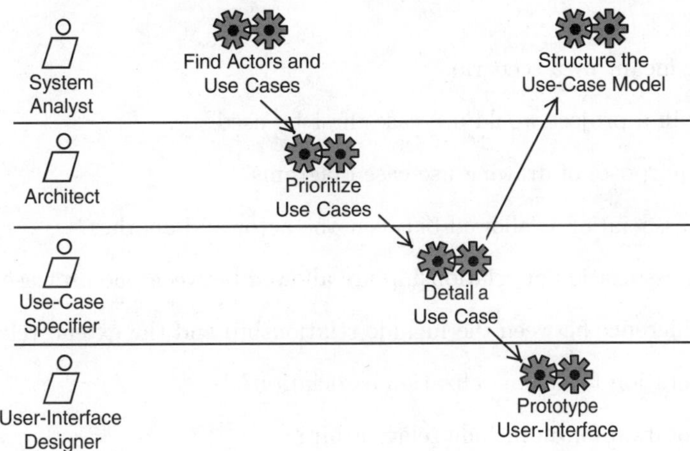

Fig. 3-25: Requirements workflow as an activity diagram

In the Unified Process, use cases are *realized* by a collaboration with a *trace* dependency between the use case and its realization. A trace dependency is a special kind of dependency between elements of different models that make it possible to trace the requirements through to their final implementation. It is shown in a diagram as a «trace» stereotype in guillemets. The trace represents a relationship between elements of two models that is either historical or based on some process that has resulted in one being derived from the other. Figure 3-26 shows the trace dependency between the use case Manually add car sharer and its realization. (In the Figure, UI is an abbreviation for user interface.) The notation of the dependency will be explained in Chapter 7.

Review Questions

3.1 Define what is meant by a use case.

3.2 What is the notation for a use case?

3.3 Define what is meant by an actor.

3.4 What is the notation for an actor?

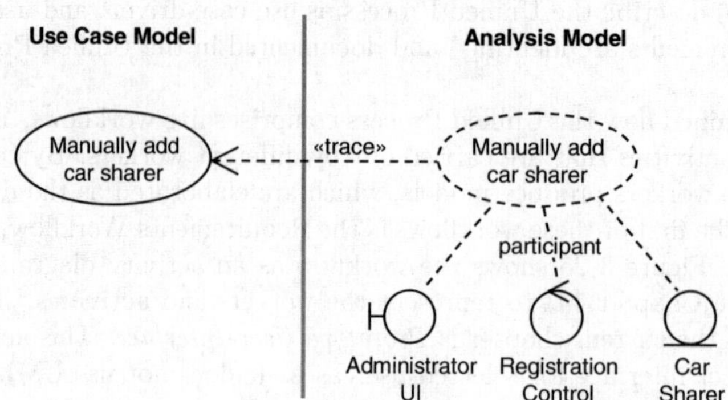

Fig. 3-26: Trace dependency between use case and realization

3.5 Define what is meant by a scenario.

3.6 At what stage in a project would use cases first be used?

3.7 What are the purposes of drawing use case diagrams?

3.8 What kind of association is allowed between one actor and another?

3.9 What kinds of association or relationship are allowed between one use case and another?

3.10 What is the difference between the include relationship and the extend relationship?

3.11 What is the notation for a generalization association?

3.12 What is the notation for an include relationship?

3.13 What is the notation for an extend relationship?

3.14 What is meant by an extension point?

3.15 In which workflow are use cases developed in the Unified Process?

3.16 What are the Unified Process activities to produce use cases?

Solved Problems

3.1 In the insurance subsystem for CarMatch, staff will search for suitable policies for a member based on the member's age and occupation and where he or she lives. They will then recommend one or more policies to the member. If the member wants to buy a policy, then they will sell it to him or her. What use cases are involved here? What should they be called?

There are three activities carried out by the staff using the system: searching for the policies, recommending the policies to the member and selling a policy. The names should be kept simple: Search for Policy, Recommend Policy and Sell Policy.

3.2 In the CarMatch system, there will be an Insurance Supervisor and an Insurance Assistant in each franchise office. Their role will be to deal with insurance sales to CarMatch members. They will both use the same use cases in the system. How many actors are involved and what should their name or names be?

Because both the assistant and the supervisor use the same use cases, there is no need to differentiate between them as actors, so one actor is all that is required. The exact name is not important, but Insurance Administrator would be suitable.

3.3 Here is a transcript of an interview with Janet Hoffner.

Janet Hoffner: When we are selling insurance, the first thing is to get the details of the member: their age and occupation, where they live and their insurance history, that is whether they've had any recent accidents.
Mick Perez: Where does that come from?
JH: Some of it comes from their membership details in the system, some of it we'll get from them over the 'phone.
MP: What happens next?
JH: We'll try to find a suitable policy. We'll be searching for the best policy for them, based on the information we have. The system could come up with more than one policy. We'll recommend the ones that best meet the member's needs.
MP: Do you always get a sale?
JH: No, obviously sometimes the person will decide to buy a policy, but sometimes they won't.
MP: So you set out to recommend a suitable policy. You always do a search for a suitable policy, and sometimes you sell a policy.
JH: Yep! That's about it.

Using extend and include, represent the relationships among the three use cases here.

The key factors here are that the overall task is to recommend a policy to a member. This always includes the functionality of searching for suitable policies. We have made Search for policy into a separate use case already, so it is linked to the use case Recommend policy by an include relationship: Recommend policy always includes Search for policy. However, the use case Sell policy only happens sometimes, so the link between it and Recommend policy is an extend relationship: sometimes it is extended by the additional functionality. This is shown in Figure 3-27. Note the direction of the arrows for extend and include relationships.

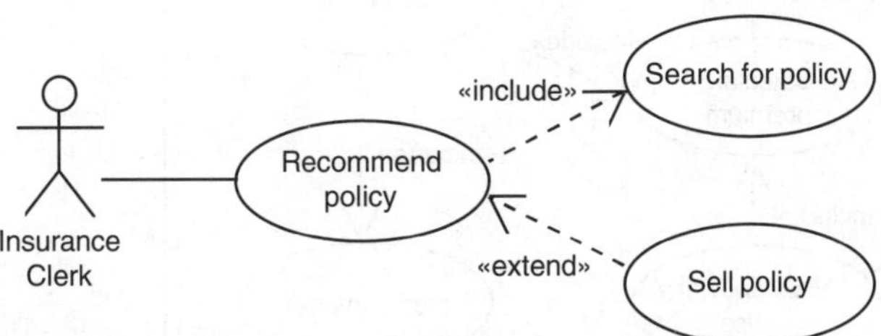

Fig. 3-27: Use cases for selling insurance

3.4 What do you think is the condition on the extension point for the use case Sell policy to be invoked from Recommend policy?

The condition will be Member agrees to purchase policy. At this stage we do not know how this will be implemented. Later it could be specified in terms of a specific piece of data being entered in a field on screen.

3.5 Here are some other requirements for the Insurance subsystem. Draw a use case diagram to include them as well as the use cases from the examples above.

- To notify the insurance company system of all sales.

- To receive notification of new policies and the criteria that enable them to be matched to members' needs from the insurance company system.
- To receive notification of premium changes from the insurance company system.
- To generate on a weekly basis renewal notices for all policies one month before they are due for renewal. (These will be mailed out to the policy holders.)
- To renew a policy.
- To notify the insurance company system of all renewals.
- To calculate the insurance premium for recommendations, sales and renewal notices.

Note that all the transfers of information between the insurance company system and CarMatch are intended to be automatic transfers between the two computer systems.

A possible solution is shown in Figure 3-28. Note that this solution assumes that notifying the insurance company system happens as part of the use cases to sell and renew policies. If the use case Notify insurer happens at a later time, say once a week on a Friday, then the include relationships from Sell policy and Renew policy to Notify insurer would not be required.

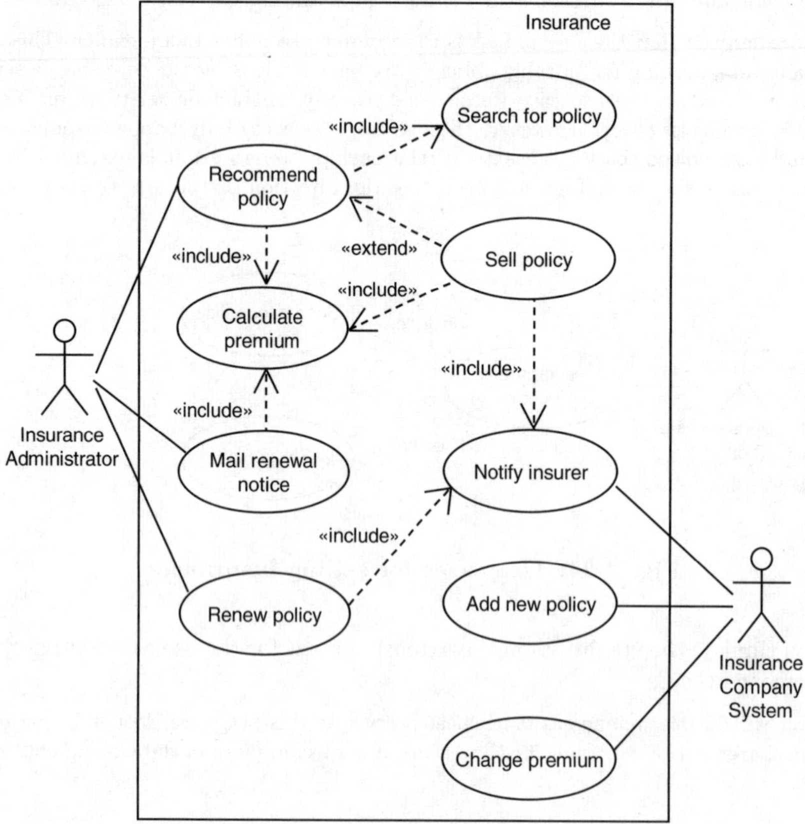

Fig. 3-28: Use case subsystem for insurance

Supplementary Problems

3.6 The first three problems apply to the CarMatch consultancy subsystem. Draw a use case diagram showing the actor Consultant with an association with each of the use cases Record consultancy visit and Record consultancy expenses.

3.7 Add the actor Senior Consultant and a generalization association between the actors Consultant and Senior Consultant to the diagram from the previous problem. A Senior Consultant can do all that a Consultant can do, and also the use cases Initiate consultancy project, Conclude consultancy project and Invoice customer. Add these two use cases to your diagram.

3.8 The use case Record consultancy visit is sometimes extended by the use case Record consultancy expenses. The use case Conclude consultancy project always includes the use case Invoice customer. Add the necessary relationships to the diagram from the previous problem. (Take care which way the arrows point.)

3.9 Read the case study material for VolBank in Chapter 1. (All the following problems use this case study material. Each problem builds on the previous ones.) List the actors that you think are involved in this system.

3.10 List the use cases that you think are involved in the VolBank system.

3.11 Which actors have an association with which use cases? (Note that every actor should be associated with at least one use case, and every use case should be associated with at least one actor.)

3.12 Which are the priority use cases for elaboration?

3.13 Here is a short transcript of an interview between Said Hussain, a systems analyst, and Martin Page, Recruitment Director of VolBank.

Said Hussain: So, how will you get information about volunteers into your system?
Martin Page: Well, most volunteers will call into a local voluntary organization, and their information will be passed on by 'phone to one of our volunteer organizers, some will ring us directly, and some will use our web-server, and then we'll transfer the data from the web-server.
SH: What about the voluntary time they're banking in the system?
MP: They can either do that at the same time as they register, or they can do it separately.
SH: So, that data needs to be transferred from the web-server or entered manually by a volunteer organizer as well?
MP: Yes.

Develop and structure your use case diagram based on the information in the transcript.

3.14 Here is some additional information about VolBank. Use this to complete your use case diagram.

- Some local voluntary organizations will have their own computer systems, and will transfer details of opportunities into VolBank's computer system. Others will telephone or send in a paper form with the details.
- There are two processes for matching volunteers and opportunities. The first process takes place when someone volunteers, and matches the volunteer against all the unfilled opportunities on file. The second takes place when a new opportunity is registered, and matches the opportunity against all the volunteers with available time. In both cases the matching is done on the basis of the geographical location of both the volunteer and the opportunity, and by matching the skills and interests of the volunteer against the needs of the organization.

- Once a volunteer is matched with an opportunity, the volunteer will be notified and, if he or she is interested, the voluntary organization that requested help will then be notified. If they accept the volunteer, then an entry will be made in the system recording a successful match.
- The recruitment director requires a statistical report of numbers of volunteers, how they registered, how much time they have deposited and how much time has been used.

3.15 Write a use case description for each of the use cases that you have found for the VolBank system in the previous problems.

Class Diagram Classes and Associations

4.1 INTRODUCTION

The class diagram shows the building blocks of any object-oriented system: the classes that make up a system. The potential for collaboration among those classes, through message passing, is shown in the relationships between these classes.

The range of concepts that can be represented through the UML class diagram notation is extensive. Non-technical participants in the development process are less likely to understand the more detailed concepts and notation of a class diagram than the other, more intuitive, 'problem domain' diagrams such as use case diagrams (Chapter 3) and activity diagrams (Chapter 10). In this chapter the basic elements of the class diagram notation will be covered, with subsequent chapters introducing further notational elements.

In terms of the framework of UML the concepts shown in a class diagram are part of the *core subpackage* of the *foundation package* of UML. That is to say, the class diagram forms an essential and fundamental part of any object-oriented model produced using UML.

A class diagram shows a static view of the classes in a model, or part of a model. The attributes and operations of classes are shown along with the various different kinds of relationship that bind the classes together. The analogy of a class diagram as a road map or atlas could be used. The classes are the towns or cities with the relationships being the routes between those places.

The interactions and collaborations that actually take place to support any one particular functional requirement represent one specific route across the map. That route will navigate from class to class, traversing the relationships between those classes. It is only possible to navigate between two points by following valid relationships from the start point, via intermediate points to the intended destination.

The class diagram itself does not show the specific route through the class model to be taken to satisfy any one use case. Instead the class diagram shows all points available and the possible routes between them. The actual route taken for any one specific 'journey' through the class model is shown on interaction diagrams such as sequence diagrams (Chapter 9) or collaboration diagrams (Chapter 8).

For example, the class diagram in Figure 4-1 for a banking system shows the static structure of the core model components from the problem domain. In this instance, the class diagram shows only the name of each class and the relationships between the classes. In the diagram, the Customer class represents a general *type* or *class*, of which there will many *objects* or *instances*. The association between the Customer and Account classes indicates that there is some kind of collaboration between these two classes. From the label on the association, it can be seen that the nature of the association is that a customer holds an account.

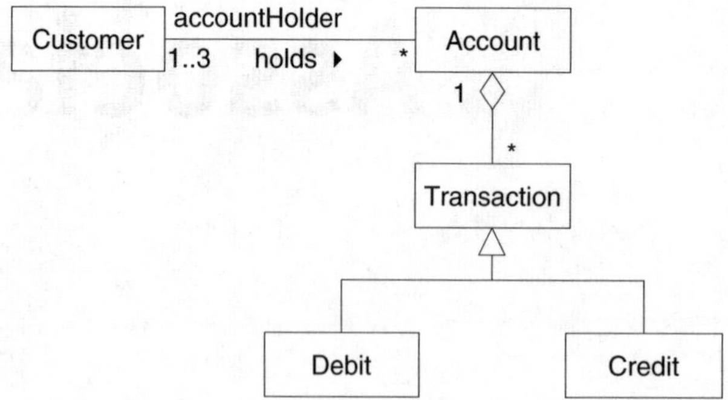

Fig. 4-1: Example class diagram for banking system

By inspection of the class diagram in Figure 4-1, it may be possible to infer other aspects of the class diagram notation. However, as already mentioned, the complete notation set for class diagrams is extensive. In order to approach the complete notation in a structured and coherent manner, the notation will be covered in Chapters 4 to 7.

In this chapter we will introduce the basic class diagram notation for showing classes, their features and the basic associations among them. In subsequent chapters the more detailed and advanced aspects of the notation will be introduced to build up a complete understanding.

4.2 THE CLASS DIAGRAM THROUGH THE DEVELOPMENT PROCESS

The classes that are shown on a class diagram will depend on the phase of the development process and the level of detail being considered.

In the analysis phase, the classes apparent in the problem domain are of primary interest. The end-user stakeholder would recognize many of these problem domain classes. At this stage, the classes that may be used in the implementation of a solution are of little interest or may not have even been considered yet.

As the development moves into the design phase, classes and relationship structures that reflect the solution model will be introduced. These classes may not be part of the understanding of the end-user community but are necessary in order to produce a coherent and well-structured model.

Classes that allow us move towards an implementable solution will be added. Such classes may relate to the interface of an application or to the persistent data management for an application. The relationship structure between classes may be amended to reflect implementation considerations. Additional attributes and operations may be added to classes in order to enhance the quality or performance of the implemented solution.

The contents of a class diagram will reflect this change in emphasis during the development process. As the class diagrams for a solution model will include many implementation classes they can quickly become very large. As with other UML notations, model management can be used to help deal with these issues of complexity and size (Chapter 14).

4.3 PURPOSE OF THE TECHNIQUE

As mentioned above, class diagrams are used throughout the development process. Class diagrams show the static structure of the classes that make up a system or subsystem. The static structure of classes includes the classes of interest themselves and the features of those classes—that is, their attributes and operations, and the relationships among them. The classes of interest in a system or subsystem will provide the capabilities for fulfilling some part of the functional requirements for the system.

Class diagrams do not show how different components of a class model interact with each other. That is the purpose of techniques such as interaction sequence diagrams (Chapter 9) or collaboration diagrams (Chapter 8).

Class diagrams show the behavioural and data management responsibilities of each class, and thus how this responsibility is delegated across the class model. They do not show the functional requirements of a system (or subsystem) from the perspective of the end-users of a system. That is the purpose of use case diagrams (Chapter 3).

Strictly speaking the UML notation specification (Object Management Group, 1999*b*) describes Static Structure Diagrams. However, as the notation specification itself points out, the term class diagram is 'shorter and well established'. The main purposes of producing class diagrams are as follows.

- They are used to document the classes that constitute a system or subsystem.
- They are used to describe the associations, generalization and aggregation relationships among those classes.
- They are used to show the features of classes, principally the attributes and operations of each class.
- They can be used throughout the development lifecycle, ranging from the specification of the classes in the problem domain to the implementation model for a proposed system, to show the class structure of that system.
- They can document how the classes of a particular system interact with existing class libraries.
- They can be used to show individual object instances within the class structure.
- They can show the interfaces supported by a given class.

4.4 CLASS DIAGRAM—BASIC NOTATION

The class model for a system may consist of a large number of classes and relationships between those classes. The complexity of such a large model can be managed by showing fragments of the class model on different class diagrams. A class diagram may correspond to a specific (sub)system, package or model. Alternatively, a class diagram may show the relationships that exist among classes from different (sub)systems, packages or models. Any contextual relationship between a particular class diagram and a specific (sub)system, package or model must be clearly asserted by the developer producing the class diagram in the documentation associated with a class diagram.

4.4.1 Classes

The basic building block for class diagrams is the class. Classes are shown as a rectangle, with the name of the class centred in the rectangle. The class name should start with a capital letter. By convention a class's name should have no spaces between multiple words in the name, but should start each subsequent word with a capital letter. For example, BankAccount, not Bank account, CustomerInvoice not Customerinvoice. This minimal form of a class is shown in Figure 4-1.

Each class symbol may also include list compartments for attributes, operations and either none, one or more predefined compartments for other features. A list compartment is an area containing a list of whichever class feature is contained by that compartment. (Attributes and operations are referred to collectively as the *features* of a class.) The list compartments for attributes and operations can be independently omitted. In other words it would be acceptable to show a class as:

- a class name only;
- a class name and a list of attributes;
- a class name and a list of operations;
- a class name, a list of attributes and a list of operations.

These four cases are shown in Figure 4-2.

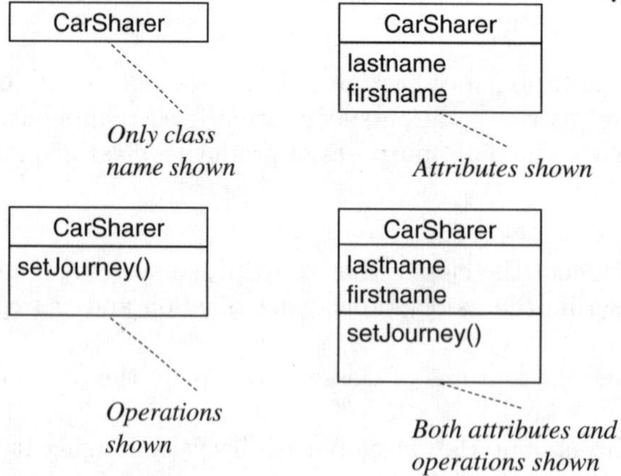

Fig. 4-2: Classes with basic compartments

Each list compartment may be named, though the names for the attribute and operation compartments are usually assumed (that is, they are not normally named). It is, however, good practice to name the list compartments that are used in addition to the attribute and operation compartments. Additional

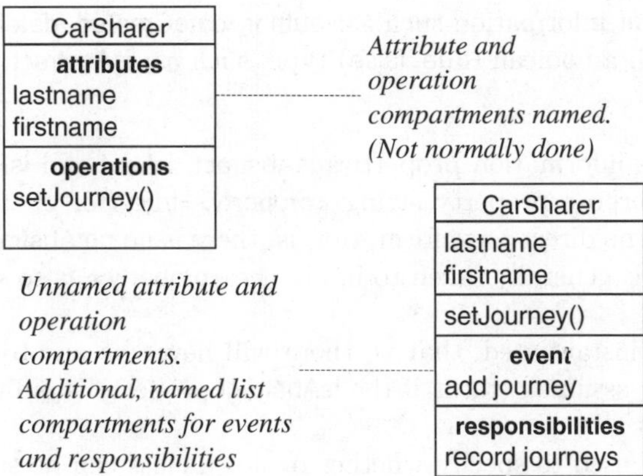

Fig. 4-3: Named class list compartments

list compartments are commonly used for the events which a class may be subject to, or the functional responsibilities of a class (Figure 4-3).

As shown in Figure 4-4, the class name compartment can also be used to show the *stereotype* or generic type to which the class conforms and any properties of the class as a list of tagged values enclosed in curly braces ({...}, see Chapter 14).

In the context of the class diagram, stereotypes would typically be used to show where a model component conforms to a well understood behaviour. Figure 4-4 class indicates that the RegisterCarSharerController conforms to the pattern of behaviour understood by the «controller» stereotype.

> ***Aside***
> A controller class can be used to coordinate the interaction between classes in the core class model of an application and the interface of that application. Structuring the implementation in this way shields the interface implementation from many types of change to the underlying class model. Similarly, different interfaces can be commissioned without requiring reworking of the underlying class model.

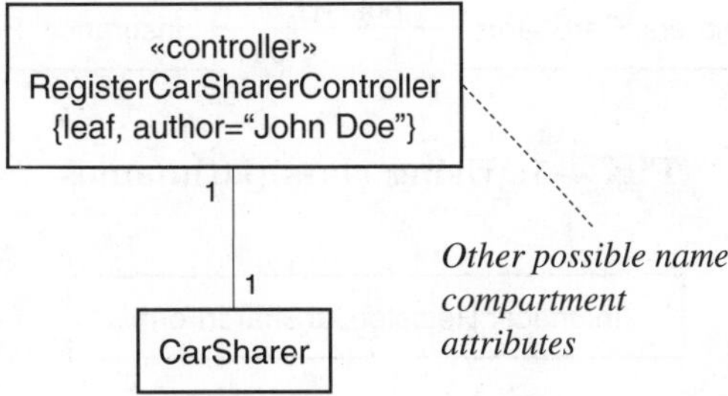

Fig. 4-4: Information shown in the class name compartment

Class properties provide descriptive information about the class to other people involved in the modelling process. The class properties are listed in curly brackets, that is `{<property-list>}`. Class properties could include:

- modelling management information such as: author, dateCreated, dateLastModified, and status;
- class information with a boolean (true/false) type, such as: isAbstract, isLeaf, and isRoot.

The terse form of the class information properties isAbstract, isLeaf and isRoot (for example, abstract) is identical to the more verbose property string <property>=true (for example, isAbstract=true). The <property>=false setting has no direct terse form, that is, there is no notAbstract form. However, omission of a property specification is generally taken to imply the <property>=false setting.

Abstract classes are never instantiated, that is, there will never be an object instance of an abstract class. isAbstract=false is the assumed status if the isAbstract property is omitted.

The isLeaf property can be used to specify whether or not a class can be subtyped through a generalization structure. See Chapter 5 for a discussion of generalization. Setting isLeaf to true (isLeaf=true or isLeaf) means that a class may not be specialized (or subtyped). Setting isLeaf to false (isLeaf=false) means that a class may be specialized. The property isLeaf=false is the default if the isLeaf property is omitted.

The isRoot property can be used to specify whether or not a class may be a specialization of another class. Again, see Chapter 5 for a discussion of generalization. Setting isRoot to true (isRoot=true or isRoot) means that a class may not be a specialization (or subtype) of another class. Setting isRoot to false (isRoot=false) means that a class may be a specialization of another class. The property isRoot=false is the default if the isRoot property is omitted.

One last notation of the class name compartment is the ability to include the path name, or package structure, for a class. This can be useful when it is necessary to make clear the lineage of a class. The *class pathname* takes the form `<path or package name(s)>::className.` Where a list of package names is used (package—subpackage, etc.), each package name in the package hierarchy is separated by double colons, "::", for example java::sql::Connection. The pathname context of a class is known as the *namespace* of a class. Class names must be unique within a namespace.

This notation is useful where model management principles have been used to organize a large class model into a series of packages (subsystems, etc.). Some class diagrams will need to show the associations between classes from different packages. Figure 4-5 shows the class pathname being used to show two classes from different packages.

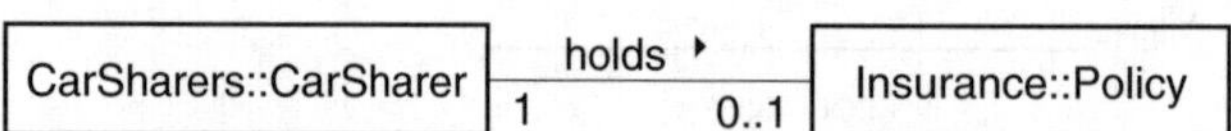

Fig. 4-5: Using class pathnames

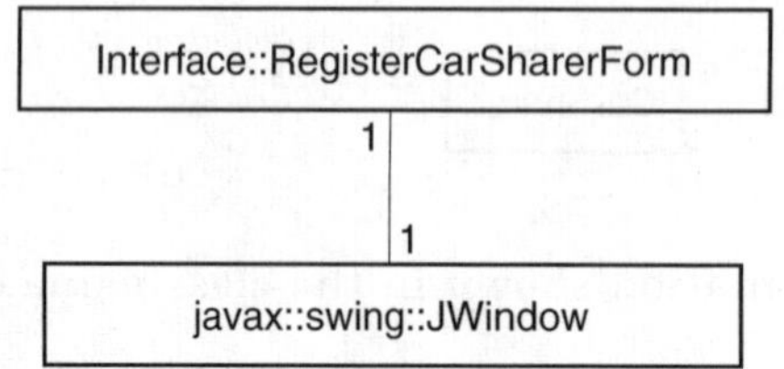

Fig. 4-6: Using class pathnames to access an external class library

Figure 4-6 shows the class pathname being used to show access to a class from an external class library (in this case, the Java Swing interface library).

4.4.2 Object Instances

The UML class diagram notation allows for class instances, that is, objects to be shown on a class diagram. In this Chapter, only the most basic object notation will be introduced. A more thorough treatment of object notation is provided in Chapter 7.

The basic object notation is very similar to the basic class notation. The name compartment of the object shows the name of the object instance and its class type. The name of an object is of the form `instanceName: className`, all underlined. For example, aDocument: Document, salesReport: Document. As with classes, the class name can be preceded by the class pathname, for example newPolicy: Insurance::Policy (Figure 4-7).

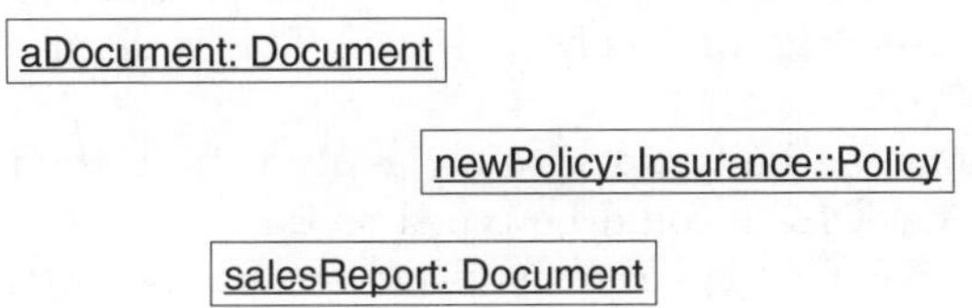

Fig. 4-7: Object instances

4.4.3 Attributes and Operations

The other two common components of a class symbol are the attribute and operation lists. Each list has a well defined format in the UML Specification (Object Management Group, 1999*b*). Both attributes and operations are listed, one per line, in the appropriate compartment. Each attribute and operation listed in its respective list compartments may be suffixed with a property list in the form of a list of tagged values enclosed in curly braces ({...}).

Each attribute and operation name should start with a lower case letter. The exception to this is for the set of constructor operations of a class, which will have the same name as the class itself in exactly the same upper and lower case format. Constructors are not always shown in class diagrams, as their existence may be assumed. By convention, attribute and operation names should have no spaces between multiple words in the name, but should start each subsequent word with a capital letter. For example, setSharingAgreement, not SetSharingAgreement and addRequirement not add requirement.

The level of detail known or displayed for attributes and operations will vary depending upon the phase of the development life cycle that the class diagram is being used in. In the analysis phase, only general information may be known or shown. For example, the parameters of an operation may not yet have been clearly established. In the design phase, levels of detail necessary to allow successful implementation will have been established. For example, not only will the parameters required for an operation be known, but also the data types of each of those parameters.

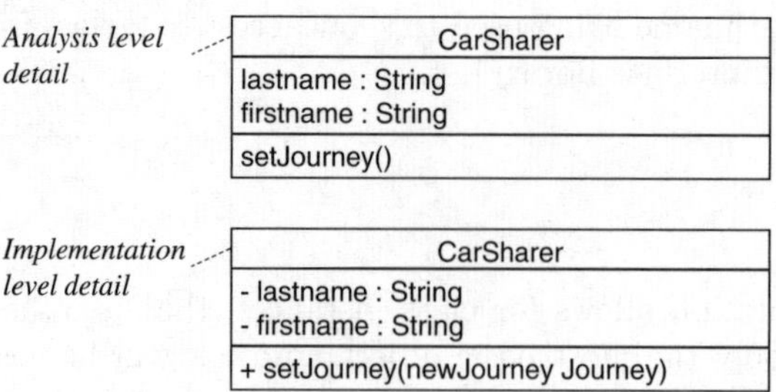

Fig. 4-8: Attribute and operation lists

4.4.3.1 Attribute and Operation Types

Examples of analysis and implementation level representations for attributes and operations are shown in Figure 4-8. Both attributes and operations take the basic form `<featureName>:<type>`, where type is the data type of the attribute or the data type returned by the operation.

Omitting the return type of an operation, as in Figure 4-8, has different connotations depending on the perspective from which the class diagram has been drawn. This is discussed further in Section 4.5.

Both attributes and operations can be typed with a class type from the implementation environment class libraries. For example dateOfBirth could be typed as Date (a class commonly found in the class library of object-oriented development environments and languages). Attributes and operations could also be typed as a class from the class model currently being specified. For example, a getHomeAddress() operation on CarSharer could be typed as Address (Figure 4-9).

CarSharer
- homeAddress : Address - dateOfBirth : Date
+ getHomeAddress(): Address

Fig. 4-9: Features typed with a class

The implication of using this typing is that the attribute or value returned by a feature will provide all the operations available on the class it was typed as. So, an attribute typed as Date could provide formatting and internationalization operations that could be used by the class containing the Date typed attribute.

It is not uncommon to use both primitive types and class types in class models. Primitive types such as int can be used to represent an integer value where only simple arithmetic operations are carried out on that value. Languages such as Java often provide class representations of these primitive values. For example, the Java class Integer acts as a wrapper around an int value, providing additional operations such as comparisons (for example, equals) and conversion to other types (for example, floatValue). Thus type names such as String, int and Date reflect the use of both primitive and class types.

4.4.3.2 Attribute and Operation Visibility

Attributes and operations can be assigned a level of visibility shown on the class diagram with a *visibility* indicator. The visibility of a feature can be defined by either a keyword or a symbol. There are three specific types of visibility, private (with the symbol –), public (+), or protected (#).

The visibility of an attribute or an operation relates to its availability to other classes. *Private* visibility means that a feature is available only within the class that owns that feature. *Public* visibility means that the feature is available to any class associated with the class that owns that feature. *Protected* visibility means that the feature is available within the class that owns that feature and any subtype of that class. Protected visibility relates to the concepts of generalization covered in Chapter 5.

EXAMPLE 4.1 What is the visibility of each of the attributes and operations shown in Figure 4-9?

SOLUTION homeAddress and dateOfBirth are private. getHomeAddress is public.

By convention, attributes are normally private and operations are mostly public. Private operations can be used however, for internally delegated responsibilities. There is no default value for visibility. The omission of a visibility indicator simply means that the visibility is not shown or has not yet been defined.

The general extension mechanism of UML permits a implementation language specific visibility. This allows specification of visibility in terms of the intended implementation language. For example, if a C++ implementation is intended then it may be desirable to use a friend visibility, with an appropriate symbol.

The set of publicly visible operations for a class is commonly referred as the interface of that class. UML notations relating to class interface are covered in Chapter 7.

4.4.3.3 Attributes in Detail

There are three other properties of attributes that will be discussed here, namely; *initial values*, *derived attributes* and *multiplicity* . The notation for all three properties is shown in Figure 4-10.

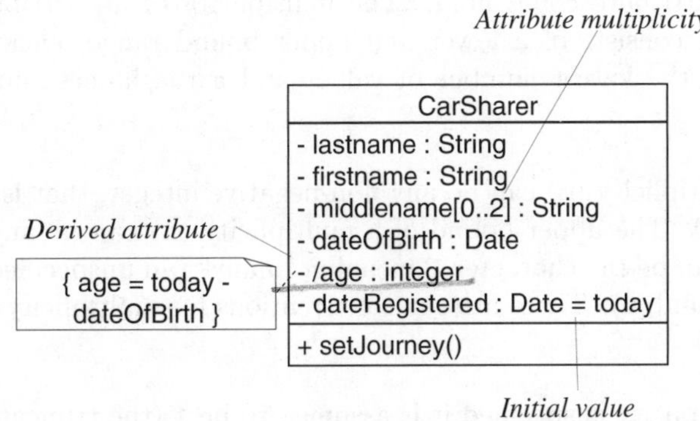

Fig. 4-10: Attribute features: initial value, default value and multiplicity

Initial Values

The initial value for an attribute can be specified as part of a class diagram by including the clause `=<initialValue>` after the attribute type. The specification in the example given in Figure 4-10 is that the value for the dateRegistered for a CarSharer should be set to today (the current system date). This specification comes into effect when an instance of the object is created. The methods that implement the creation operations should take account of this specification and make sure that the dateRegistered is set to the current system date. Subsequent processing in a constructor operation may overwrite this initial value, but the initial value must be set to start with.

Derived Attributes

The value for a derived attribute can be determined from the values of other attributes (or features of other classes). Given that the value for a derived attribute can be determined from other feature values, there is no inherent need to implement an attribute for a specified derived attribute. The presence of a derived attribute in a conceptual or specification model conveys a requirement and is provided to improve the clarity of the model. In reality, a derived attribute could be implemented as part of an operation, as an explicit operation or by implementing a real attribute to hold the derived value. In UML a derived attribute is annotated by the inclusion of a forward slash (/) immediately before the attribute name. The specification for the derivation of a derived attribute can be shown as a constraint in a note attached to the derived attribute.

In Figure 4-10, the attribute age is indicated as being derived. The derivation is shown as a constraint based on the current system date and the value of the dateOfBirth attribute.

Fowler & Scott (1997) point out that the interpretation of a derived attribute may depend upon the context in which the derivation is viewed. The derivation simply expresses a constraint between the derived attribute and other values. For example, it may become desirable for performance reasons to store the age of a CarSharer as an attribute in the implementation of the system. It is then the responsibility of the class to maintain the value of the age attribute in line with the specified constraint.

Multiplicity

A multiplicity clause can be used immediately after the attribute name to indicate the number of separate values that an attribute could hold. The multiplicity of an attribute takes the form of a multiplicity clause, which consists of a lower and upper bound range, enclosed in square brackets, `[m..n]`. Here `m` specifies the lowest number of values and `n` the highest number of values that an attribute can hold.

The lower bound of a multiplicity (`m`) can be any non-negative integer, that is a whole number that is greater than or equal to 0. The upper bound of a multiplicity (`n`) can be any integer that is greater than or equal to `m`, or it can be the character *, meaning "many" (an unspecified and unlimited number greater than the lower bound, `m`). There are some conventions for multiplicity clauses.

- 1..1 is truncated to 1.
- 0..* is truncated to *.
- If no attribute multiplicity is specified it is assumed to be 1 (the truncated version of 1..1).

A single integer value (for example, 7) can be used to indicate a fixed number of attribute values, for example in an array (dayName[7]). Some valid occurrences of an attribute's multiplicity would be:

1. 'telephoneNumber[1..3]'—this definition says 'at least one value will be held for telephone number, and possibly up to three values';
2. 'telephoneNumber[0..1]'—this definition says 'a telephone number can either be null or alternatively a single telephone number can be held'. A null value means no value at all. Null is different from either 0 for an integer or "␣" (space) for a string, for example;

3. 'telephoneNumber[1..*]'— this definition says 'at least one value will be held for telephone number, and possibly up to an unlimited number of values'.

A case may arise where it is clear that an attribute will have a range of values. The specific multiplicity may not yet be known, beyond the fact that it will not be [1]. In such a case using a multiplicity of [*] would provide for the general case of multiple values for an attribute.

The UML Specification (Object Management Group, 1999*b*, Section 3.43) allows a multiplicity clause to be made up of a comma-separated list of sub-clauses. For example the multiplicity attributeName[1,6..12] indicates that one, or between six and twelve attribute values may be held. One illustration of multiple multiplicity clauses such as this might be a system to track teams that register for a volleyball league. In this example system there may be a Team class with an attribute playerName[1,6..12] : String. The multiplicity indicates that either a single name will be held, for example a contact name for a team when the team first registers, or that the names of between 6 and 12 players will be held for that team. (Assuming that the league rules state that a team can have no fewer than 6 and no more than 12 registered players.)

It should be noted that the order of different multiplicity clauses does not imply a temporal sequence. In the example given, nothing in the attribute multiplicity clause says that one value must be held before the six to twelve values. In terms of the specification of the attribute is would be equally permissible for six to twelve values for players names to be held, then one player name, then six to twelve values again, and so on.

4.4.3.4 Operations in Detail

The basic specification of operations has already been outlined. Each operation shown in a class node on a class diagram can include a comma-separated list of the parameters accepted by that operation. The main extensions to the specification of an operation on a class diagram relate to the level of detail shown for these parameters.

Parameters

Each parameter in the list has the basic form `<parameterName>:<type>`. For example, setNextOfKin(name : String), setFirstMatched(firstDate : Date) or equals(testAddress : Address).

Omitting the `<parameterName>:` part of the clause, leaving `<type>` for a parameter is a valid shorthand. For example, setNextOfKin(String), setFirstMatched(Date) or equals(Address).

Using a notation similar to the specification of initial values for attributes, the default value for a parameter can be specified by suffixing a parameter with the clause `=<defaultValue>`. For example, an operation approveApplication that takes a date as a parameter may wish to use the current system date as the default value for a parameter and thus be specified as approveApplication(dateApproved:Date = today).

Parameters may be prefixed with a *parameter kind* clause. The parameter kind can be in, out, or inout. If an explicit parameter kind is omitted, then the default kind is assumed to be in. The parameter kind is of specific use in implementation environments where parameters may be passed by reference instead of by value.

Where a parameter is passed by value, the value of a parameter (a variable) is held as a separate value (that is, it has a separate memory allocation). This means that any modifications made to the value of that parameter by the called operation do not affect the original variable unless those modifications are passed back to the method of the calling operation (using a return value) and explicitly written back to the original variable. This mode of behaviour is illustrated in the pseudocode shown in Figure 4-11.

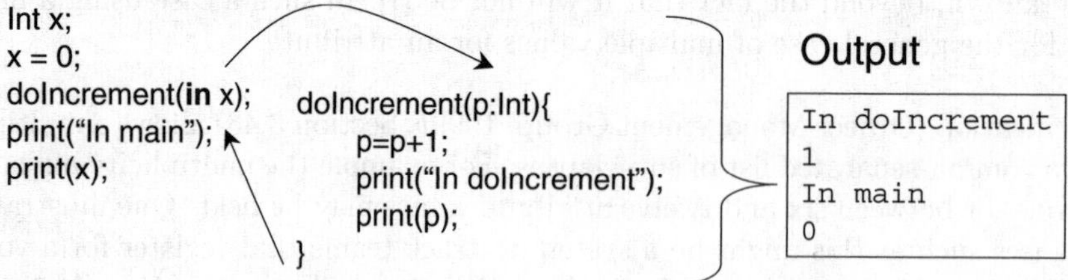

Fig. 4-11: Parameters passed by value

In this example, an integer variable is created and then instantiated to the value 0 (zero). The variable is then passed by value (in) as a parameter to the doIncrement operation. The doIncrement operation then increases the value of the variable passed as a parameter by 1 and prints the context, In doIncrement, and the value of the variable within the operation (1). The doIncrement operation then ends and the processing flow returns to the main routine. The doIncrement operation does not return any value (that is, it has the default return type of void). The main routine then prints the context, In main, and the value of the variable in the main routine. This value (0) was unaffected by the processing within the doIncrement operation. The value of the variable x and the parameter p had different memory allocations and the change made to p did not affect x.

In contrast, where a parameter is passed by reference, the memory location of a variable is passed to the called operation. The original variable and the parameter therefore share the same memory allocation. Any modifications to the variable within the called operation will alter the value of the variable held at the memory location passed to the operation. The effect of this is that the value of the original variable is changed by the processing of the operation. This mode of behaviour is illustrated in the pseudocode shown in Figure 4-12.

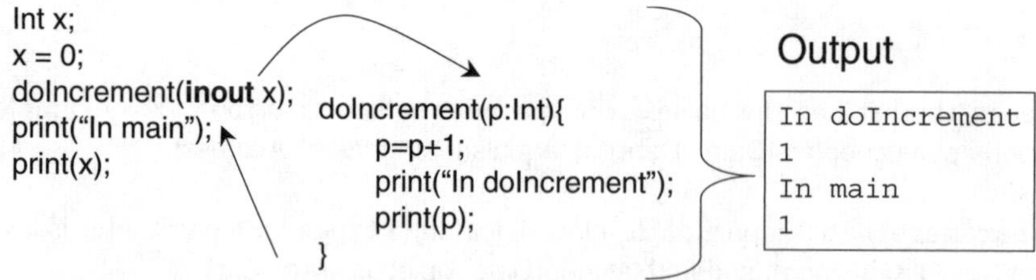

Fig. 4-12: Parameters passed by reference

In this second example, an integer variable is again created and instantiated to the value 0 (zero). The variable is then passed by reference (inout) as a parameter to the doIncrement operation. The doIncrement operation then increases the value of the variable passed as a parameter by 1 and prints the context and the value of the variable within the operation (1, one). The doIncrement operation then ends and the processing flow returns to the main routine. This main routine then prints the context and the value of the variable within the main routine. This value (1, one) was amended by the processing within the doIncrement operation. The value of the variable x and the parameter p had the same memory allocation and the change made to p was, in effect, a direct change to the value of x.

So, in parameters are passed by value, out and inout parameters are passed by reference. An out parameter does not actually provide information to an operation but is passed simply as a means of retrieving data from the operation once it has completed.

Method Note

The specification of a method body for an operation may be included as a note attached to an operation on the class diagram (Figure 4-13). This would normally be done only where the specification for a method is relatively small, and the specification for that method will make a useful contribution to the information documented on the class diagram.

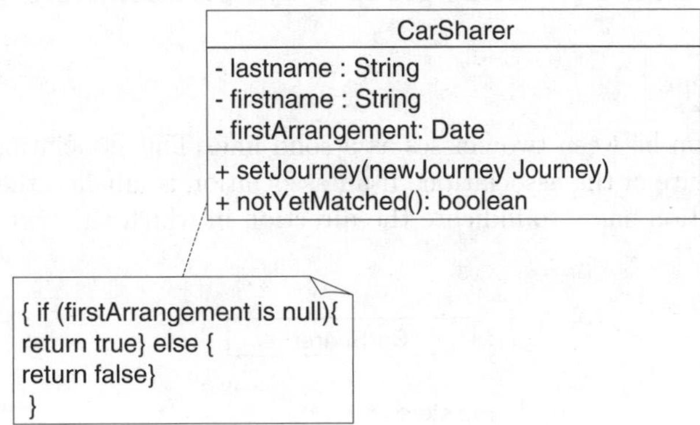

Fig. 4-13: Note showing method specification

It is important to note that the method note does not specify how the method should be implemented. Instead, the method note provides a specification of what the method should do. This specification will normally take the form of a constraint which can be written using the Object Constraint Language (Chapter 12).

Grouping by Stereotype

One final aspect of the UML notation for operations in classes is the ability to group operations by the type of operation. Operation grouping will probably be encountered only in the use of certain CASE tools (Chapter 15) that support this UML notation.

The types used for this grouping are named stereotypes such as «constructor», «query», and «update». Constructor operations bring new instances of the class into being. Query operations will not alter the attribute values of an instance of the class. Update operations may change the attribute values of an instance of a class. Figure 4-14 shows an example of operation grouping.

4.4.4 Associations

An object-oriented system is built from class types that collaborate with each other by passing messages and receiving responses. When running, an object-oriented system is populated with instances which confirm to their class type. Where instances of one class pass messages to instances of another class, an *association* is implied between those two classes.

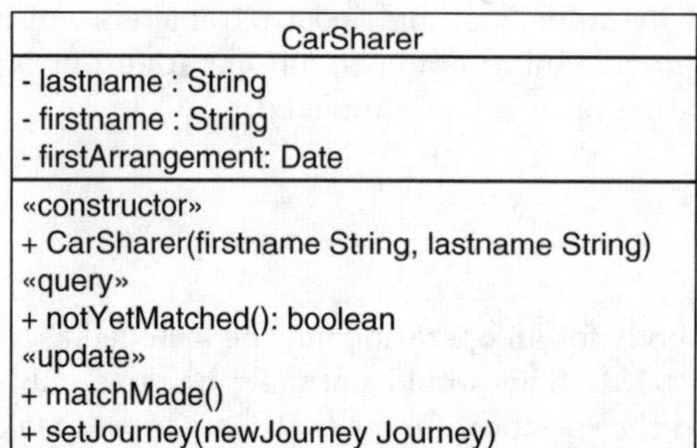

Fig. 4-14: Operations grouped by operation stereotype

4.4.4.1 Association Names

UML shows an association between two classes as a solid line. The association can be labelled with a name to indicate the nature of the association. If an association is labelled then an arrow-head should be used with the association name to indicate the direction in which the text of the association name should be interpreted.

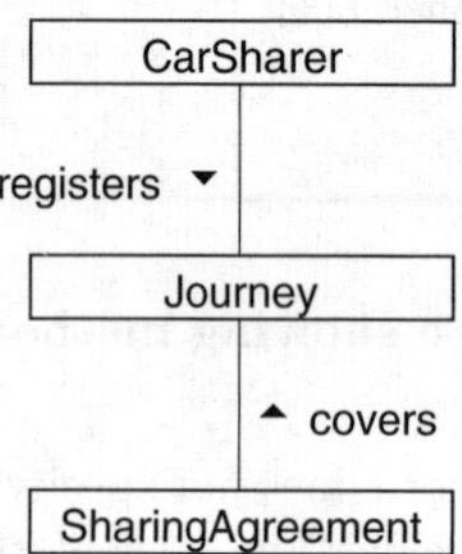

Fig. 4-15: Named associations

Figure 4-15 illustrates two simple associations. One between Journey and SharingAgreement and a second between CarSharer and Journey. These associations indicate that a CarSharer **registers** a Journey and that a SharingAgreement **covers** a Journey.

An association between two classes is also called a 'binary' association. However, as this is the most common form of association, the more concise term (association) is used.

4.4.4.2 Multiplicity

The next thing that can be added to an association is information about the multiplicity of the association. Multiplicity as applied to attributes has already been discussed in this chapter. In terms of an association, multiplicity indicates the number of object instances of the class at the far end of an association for one instance of the class at the near end of an association. This concept of association multiplicity is illustrated in Figure 4-16. (It should be noted that the notation used to show instances of the classes and the association in Figure 4-16 are not part of the UML notation set.)

It might be said that there must be at least two Journeys covered by a SharingAgreement, otherwise they are not shared. CarMatch might set five Journeys as the working maximum for the number of

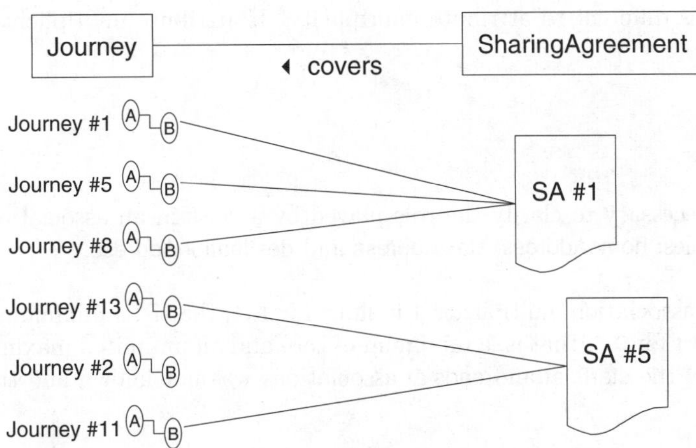

Fig. 4-16: Occurrences of an association between instances of classes

Journeys covered by a SharingAgreement as that is the maximum capacity of most cars. This gives the multiplicity of between two and five Journeys per SharingAgreement.

Looking the other way along this association from Journey to SharingAgreement, it might be established that a Journey can be involved in a minimum of zero SharingAgreements. That is to say that there will be Journeys that have not yet been matched and covered by a SharingAgreement or whose participation in a SharingAgreement has ended. To avoid potential complications or conflicts of interest, CarMatch might wish to limit a Journey to be part of only one SharingAgreement at a time. This gives a multiplicity of between zero and one SharingAgreement per Journey.

> ***Aside***
> Words like 'might' are being used here to indicate that arbitrary choices are being made about the specific lower and upper bounds for the multiplicity. In practice, these bounds will be established from information gathered from the problem domain. At this point the bounds being used are illustrative.

In summary then, the association between Journey and SharingAgreement has the following multiplicity: a SharingAgreement covers 2..5 Journeys and a Journey is covered by 0..1 SharingAgreement.

This information can now be shown on an association on a class diagram. As the phrases above indicate, the multiplicity clause is shown at the end of the association for the direction it is being read in. When reading from Journey to SharingAgreement the 0..1 is shown at the SharingAgreement end.

In class diagrams, the notation for multiplicity on associations is the same as the notation introduced for attributes on page 56. The full notation of the multiplicity for the covers association is shown in Figure 4-17.

Fig. 4-17: Multiplicity of an association

If the multiplicity of an association end it not shown it is assumed to be currently not known or not specified. This is different to attribute multiplicity. If attribute multiplicity is omitted then it is assumed to be '1'.

4.4.4.3 Role Names

On occasions it is necessary to clarify the role played by a class in an association. Figure 4-18 shows three examples of roles; homeAddress, startAddress and destinationAddress.

Remember that the association multiplicity 1 is short for 1..1, that is, a minimum of 1 and a maximum of 1 and that * is short for 0..*, that is, a minimum of zero and an unlimited maximum. The multiplicity of the Journey end of the starts at and ends at associations was not known and therefore omitted from this class diagram.

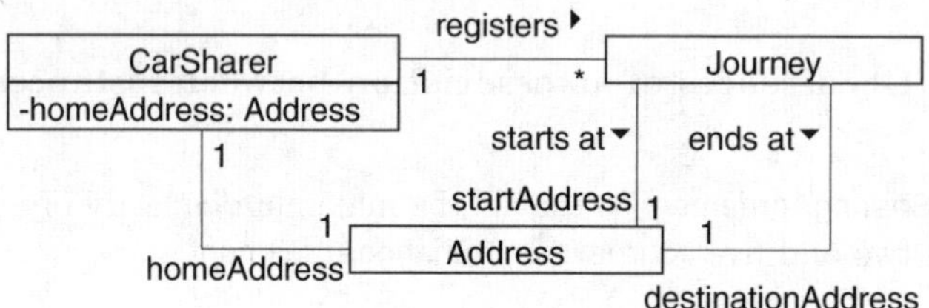

Fig. 4-18: Role names on associations

In the unnamed association between CarSharer and Address, Address plays the role of the homeAddress of a CarSharer. From the multiplicity of the association between the CarSharer and Address classes, it can be seen that a CarSharer will always have a homeAddress and will never have more than one homeAddress. The implementation of this association as a private attribute of type Address in CarSharer is also shown.

The one-to-one association between the CarSharer and Address classes implies that, even if two car sharers have exactly the same home address, those home addresses will be held as two separate and distinct instances of Address. Those instances will have the same attribute values, but will be different instances of Address.

EXAMPLE 4.2 Discuss the role played by Address in the context of the two associations starts at and ends at between the Journey and Address classes shown in Figure 4-18.

SOLUTION From the multiplicity of the two associations, it can be seen that a Journey starts at one Address, and ends at one Address. Instances of Address can then play the roles of the startAddress of a Journey and the destinationAddress of a Journey. This could be shown as the implementation attributes - startAddress : Address and - destinationAddress : Address respectively.

Role names can be useful when specifying method notes as the body of the method note can use the role name to refer to an instance of an associated class (Figure 4-19).

4.5 MODELLING GUIDANCE

Fowler & Scott (1997) discuss the notion of perspective in the development of class models, and hence

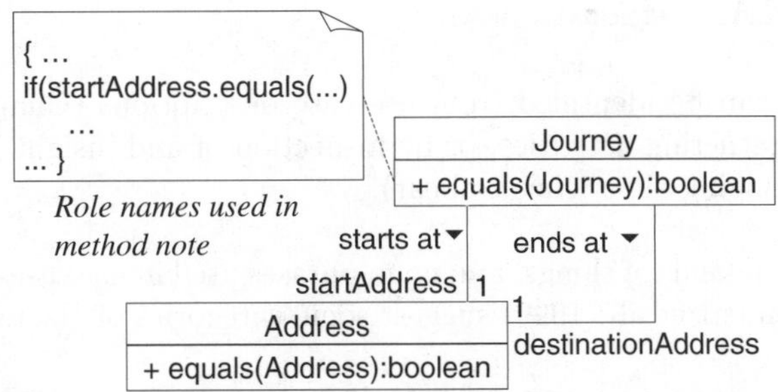

Fig. 4-19: Use of role names in operation specifications

class diagrams. The perspective of a class diagram can be conceptual, specification or implementation.

A model (and diagram) produced from a conceptual perspective, and thus reflecting the requirements of the problem domain being modelled, will consist both of classes apparent to the problem domain and of classes that represent insights into that problem domain. Such a model can be constructed from the products of the initial information-gathering activity undertaken at the outset of a project. These products may include, among other sources, interview transcripts, sample documents, pro-forma, and manuals. The model and diagram can then be refined through an iterative process of critical review and further information gathering.

Models and diagrams produced from a specification or implementation perspective will reflect the intended design or implementation, respectively, of a software system. These models may well draw on the classes in a conceptual model (see above). However, specification and implementation oriented models also suit modelling approaches based on the principles of functional delegation (see Section 4.5.2).

Section 4.4.3 introduced the notation for the return type of an operation. At this point it should be noted that the perspective from which a class diagram is drawn will affect the interpretation of an omitted return type. In a conceptual diagram, the omission of a return type may be interpreted as being no more significant than saying that the return type of the operation is not yet known or has not yet been finalized. In a specification or implementation class diagram the omission of the operation return type implies that the operation does not return a value (equivalent to a return type of :void).

4.5.1 Conceptual Modelling

Producing class diagrams from a conceptual perspective involves the following iterative activities.

- Find classes and associations.
- Identify attributes and operations and allocate to classes.
- Identify generalization structures (see Chapter 5).

It is not necessary to work through the steps in rigorous sequence. Instead, early iterations in conceptual modelling may involve iterations around the identification of classes, attributes and associations. In later iterations, class operations and generalization structures may begin to emerge.

4.5.1.1 Find Classes and Associations

Classes and associations can be identified from use case descriptions (Chapter 3), directly from the products of information gathering activities, or by inspection of and insight into the class model itself (thinking about it and bringing experience to bear).

Nouns, that is, the names of kinds of things, and noun phrases used in use cases and interview transcripts often indicate classes. Bennett et al. (1999) suggest some categories of classes that may be identified.

Specific occurrences of a general type, such as people ('John Doe'), organizations ('Bald Eagle Insurance'), and organizational units ('The sales team').
Structures inherent in the problem domain, such as 'car sharers', 'volunteer team'.
Abstractions of things such as:

- **People and roles** 'Car sharer', 'Volunteer', 'Account holder', 'Insurance sales advisor'.
- **Physical artefacts** 'car', 'cover note', 'insurance policy'.
- **Concepts** 'sale', 'skill', 'requirement'.

Enduring relationships between other identified classes, such as 'agreement', 'registration'.

Verb phrases can indicate associations between classes. In other cases, inherent logical associations between classes might become apparent as the class model is refined. Examples to indicate the type of phrase to be considered as an association might include 'Customer holds account', 'Car sharer registers journey', or 'Volunteer holds particular skills'.

EXAMPLE 4.3 Here is a another excerpt from an interview transcript with one of the directors who are setting up CarMatch. Remember, Mick Perez is the systems analyst and Janet Hoffner is the director. Identify any classes and associations mentioned in the transcript.

Mick Perez: Can we look at the way car sharing is actually organized now. I'd like to find out a bit more about the ideas you work with.
Janet Hoffner: Sure. I guess at the heart of everything there is the car sharer. That's a person who has registered with us so that they can share journeys with other registered car sharers.
MP: Tell me more about how you keep details of the journey that someone wants to share.
JH: Well a car sharer can actually register several journeys with us. They do not have to limit themselves to just one journey to share.
MP: I guess they would have to want to share at least one journey to be classed as a car sharer though?
JH: That's right. Remember that they can register as many journeys as they want. When we find other car sharers that want to share a similar journey we match up the sharers and formalize things with a sharing agreement.
MP: ...

SOLUTION Mick Perez has gone through the transcript, using his experience to pick out possible classes and associations for a conceptual class diagram. Mick has underlined probable class nouns or noun phrases, and drawn a box around probable association verbs or verb phrases.

Mick Perez: Can we look at the way car sharing is actually organized now. I'd like to find out a bit more about the ideas you work with.
Janet Hoffner: Sure. I guess at the heart of everything there is the car sharer. That's a person who has registered with us so that they can share journeys with other registered car sharers.
MP: Tell me more about how you keep details of the journey that someone wants to share.
JH: Well a car sharer can actually register several journeys with us. They do not have to limit themselves to just one journey to share.
MP: I guess they would have to want to share at least one journey to be classed as a car sharer though?
JH: That's right. Remember that they can register as many journeys as they want. When we find other car sharers that want to share a similar journey we match up the sharers and formalize things with a sharing agreement.
MP: ...

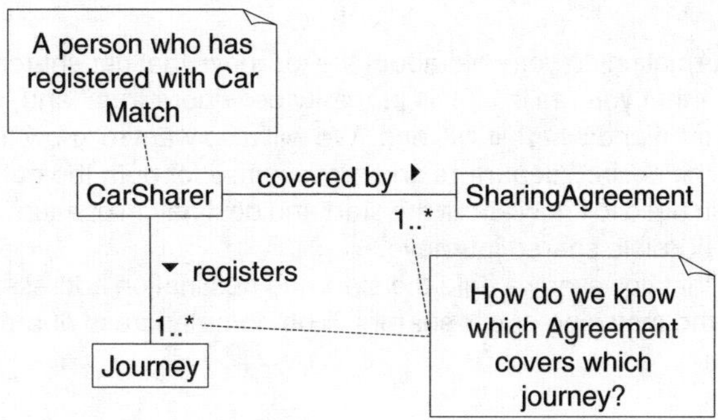

Fig. 4-20: A first draft conceptual class diagram

Mick's first draft class diagram for the interview fragment above is shown in Figure 4-20. The classes CarSharer, Journey and SharingAgreement that were identified in the transcript are included in the class diagram, moreover, the fact that it has been possible to identify associations that relate the classes together encourages Mick that the classes themselves are reasonable.

Mick is not so sure about the associations though. As the note in Figure 4-20 indicates. Mick has identified that the structure of the associations does not seem to make sense. Queries such as this could be resolved, either by further consideration of the concepts being modelled or by taking the diagram (and notes) back to the interviewee and clarifying the conceptual relationships. In this particular case, the notion of a sharing agreement actually relates shared journeys, rather than the car sharers themselves (Figure 4-21).

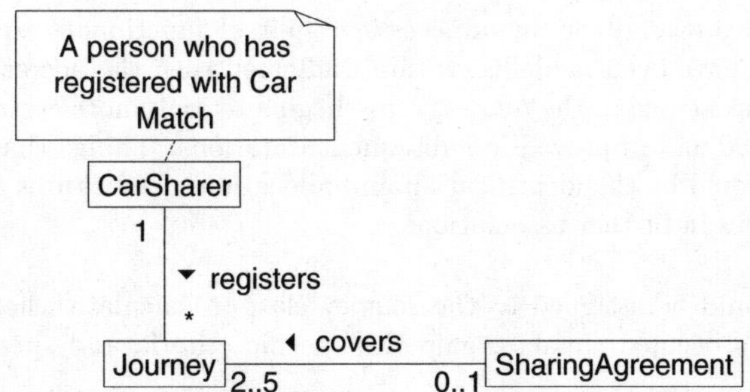

Fig. 4-21: The second draft conceptual class diagram

4.5.1.2 Identify and Allocate Attributes and Operations

The items of data held for each instance of a class are the attributes of that class. As with classes, in conceptual modelling attributes should be reasonably straightforward to identify from the available information sources.

Operations describe the processing capabilities of a class. In conceptual modelling it may not be easy to identify the detailed operations for each class until more detailed work on the interaction diagrams has been completed (see Chapters 8 and 9). However, some operations may be apparent from the available information sources and these should be noted.

EXAMPLE 4.4 Consider another extract from the transcript of the interview between Mick Perez and Janet Hoffner. From this extract, identify and attributes and operations that can be added to the class model.

Mick Perez: What kind of information do you hold about the journeys that car sharers will register with you?
Janet Hoffner: Well, I'm sure that you realize it will primarily be 'where from' and 'where to'. We need to know where each journey will start from and where it will end. We will also want to know travel times for each direction of the journey. That is to say, the desired departure and arrival times for both the outward and return journeys.
MP: What kind of things do you need to know about the start and destination of each journey? Will that information need to be used to match up possible shared journeys?
JH: Good point. Yes, I guess that however we hold the start and destination address, we'll need to be able to use that information to automate the matching of car sharers. The home address of a person might also be used in some journey matching.
MP: . . .

SOLUTION From this transcript it can be seen that some time based attributes are required for departure and arrival times. There are three mentions of address information as well. There are the start and destination addresses. There is also the home address of a car sharer. These addresses could be held as text strings, but this will probably not allow anything more than crude matching for sharing purposes.

One way of modelling addresses in this early iteration might be to create an Address class. The Address class has responsibility for maintaining information relating to an address and also for matching two addresses with each other.

To support this last notion, an equals operation could be defined. This operation returns a boolean true or false value depending on whether or not one address is deemed geographically close enough to another to be considered equal. The actual specification of what constitutes 'close enough' would need to be investigated in subsequent iterations.

If this separate Address class proves to be an unnecessary split of functional responsibility, because address handling and matching could have been modelled within CarSharer, then the Address class could be replaced in subsequent iterations. If the existence of the Address class begins to look more certain then the specification of the Address class can be refined and improved in subsequent iterations. Things that would make the existence of a class look more certain would be the identification and allocation of attributes and operations to that class or the participation of the class in further associations.

A similar equals operation could be assigned to the Journey class to calculate whether two journeys are close enough in requirements to be deemed equal. Again the specific criteria and specification for 'close enough' would need to be established.

Attributes are allocated to the class which is most likely to be responsible for the particular item of data represented by an attribute. By and large, operations will go in the same class as the attributes upon which, or with which, they operate in order to provide their functional responsibility. Attributes and operations may need to be moved to other classes as the class diagram is refined.

The attributes and operations identified from the transcript and discussed above are shown in Figure 4-22.

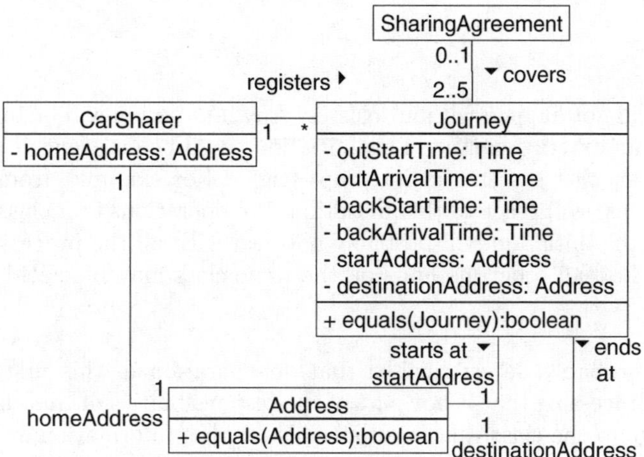

Fig. 4-22: Identification and allocation of attributes and operations

In the next iteration, the Address class may well be assigned suitable attributes to represent address information (for example, street, town, state or county, zipcode or postcode). In Figure 4-22 the implementation of the starts at and ends at associations has been shown as attributes of type Address in the Journey class. The unnamed association between CarSharer and Address has also been implemented as the homeAddress: Address attribute on CarSharer. These implementations are shown to illustrate a possible interpretation of the class model. Associations would not normally be implemented at this early stage.

Modelling in this way can continue until the analyst is satisfied that a comprehensive model exists. The model should incorporate the major classes that exist in the problem domain, their attributes and some of the operations that will be apparent in the solution.

4.5.2 Modelling using Functional Delegation

When generating models and diagrams produced from a specification or implementation perspective, it can be more fruitful to use principles of functional delegation. Specification and implementation class diagrams will reflect the intended design or implementation of a software system respectively.

The principle of functional delegation is that responsibility for data ownership and processing of that data should be delegated to the most appropriate class. We have already seen a simple illustration of this in the section on identification and allocation of operations. The Journey class had responsibility for establishing whether its requirements were the same as (or very similar to) another instance of Journey (the equals(Journey) : boolean operation). As part of determining this, the equals operation on the Journey class will probably need to establish whether start and destination addresses are the same between two journeys. The responsibility for checking that one address is geographically the same as (or very similar to) another address does not lie with Journey though. That responsibility is delegated to the equals(Address) : boolean operation on the Address class.

Modelling by functional delegation is based on the examination of the interactions that will take place between classes in order to fulfil some required, usually externally visible, function in the required system. Given that interactions between classes are being modelled, this implies that three primary components of class models can be investigated using this modelling approach.

- Classes
- Operations
- Associations

Clearly interactions could not happen without classes. Any interaction will be initiated by some kind of probe or message from an external source. This initiation could be an event in an interface, a message passed from a class in another system, an interrupt trigger (for example, from a sensor), and so on. By establishing how a class will react to this initiation, the operations of a class begin to emerge. The operation that handles the initiation will probably not deal with all the processing within the method of that one operation. Instead other methods on the same class may be called to assist in processing the initiating message.

At some point it will probably be established that an operation in this first class needs to obtain information or trigger processing that is not part of the responsibilities of this class. The operation will therefore pass a message to the class that is responsible for that information or the operation required in order to delegate that functional responsibility. This passing of messages from one class to another indicates the presence of an association between those two classes. Thus a picture emerges of a set of classes collaborating through each other's operations to achieve some larger functional goal.

Arguably the most popular technique for simulating this collaboration between classes is the Class-Responsibility-Collaborator (CRC) card technique (Beck & Cunningham, 1989; Wirfs-Brock, Wilkerson & Wiener, 1990). A CRC card is a small piece of card or paper (say 15cm by 8cm). The name of a class is written at the top of the card. Down the left hand side of the card, the responsibilities of the class are listed. Down the right hand side the other classes with which this class collaborates are listed (Figure 4-23).

Journey	
Responsibilities	**Collaborations**
Check if another Journey is the same as this one	Address supports checking for equality between one address and another.
Maintain details of a journey	

Fig. 4-23: CRC card for Journey class

The analysts involved in the development of a system take one or more CRC cards. The collaborations necessary to fulfil a requirement under analysis are enacted by the team of analysts with each analyst playing the part of the classes they hold. As this enaction continues, the need for a new functional responsibility or collaboration may be identified. A negotiation then takes place to agree the most appropriate existing or new class to be responsible for the identified responsibility.

Modelling with the functional delegation approach begins to blur the starting point in terms of UML notations. The interactions between classes that are captured through enacting techniques such as CRC cards should be modelled in notations such as the UML interaction collaboration diagram or interaction sequence diagram (Chapters 8 and 9 respectively).

A class diagram could be produced first, using a conceptual modelling approach, to act as a foundation for interaction-based techniques. Alternatively, using functional delegation based modelling, the class diagram could be drawn as an abstraction of the static structure of the classes identified through the modelling of the interactions necessary to support a particular functional requirement. In some cases (Bellin & Simone, 1997), it is suggested that producing a conceptual class diagram with which to set up a functional modelling enaction is a productive strategy.

4.5.3 Summary of Modelling Approaches

The modelling approach taken will depend upon whether the analyst intends to produce a conceptual class model or a specification or implementation model. For specification and implementation models, a modelling approach based on the dynamic interaction of classes and the functional delegation that takes place as part of that interaction may be appropriate. Producing a conceptual model clearly suggests a conceptual modelling approach. In the former case, a class diagram may be produced as an abstraction of the classes identified during the modelling of the dynamic behaviour required in the system.

In practice, the two approaches may be used alternately or side by side. The conceptual modelling identifies the key classes for the area of the system to be modelled in the CRC exercise, thus creating a set of class (CRC) cards with which to begin the functional delegation modelling.

In practice, the experienced analyst will use whichever modelling approach most suits the particular problem or sub-problem in hand. It would not be unusual or unreasonable for the analyst to switch between approaches demanded by the task in hand. It is important however, that the end product of the modelling phase, the class diagram, is a clear and consistent representation of the concepts modelled. There should be a clear distinction between a version of a class diagram that represents a conceptual model of the problem domain, and a class diagram that represents the specification or implementation of the required software to fulfil the requirements of the problem domain.

4.5.4 Object-Oriented Concepts

At this point it will be useful to identify and discuss some of the fundamental object-oriented concepts that are exemplified by the notational elements covered in the preceding sections.

4.5.4.1 Operation Signature

Collectively the name, parameter list and return type of an operation are referred to as its signature. It is quite possible (and not uncommon) to have several operations with the same name and return type in one class provided that those operations each has a different parameter list to the other same-name operations. The different parameter lists can reflect the different contexts in which the operation can be called.

The ability to specify the signature of an operation without having to specify its method is a useful feature in object-oriented modelling. Knowing the name of the operation to pass a message to, the type to expect in return and the arguments that must be passed as parameters, provides a clear specification for the collaboration between operations.

4.5.4.2 Encapsulation

The notion of an operation's signature and visibility leads to another key object-oriented concept, that of encapsulation. By specifying attributes as private and operations as public and by requiring correct use of operation signatures a class hides the method (the implementation) of an operation from the calling operation.

This encapsulation has the significant benefit of limiting the scope of effect of changes to the implementation of an operation. So long as an operation continues to provide its specified functional capability and continues to conform to its signature then the implementation of the operation can be changed without having to change any of the other operations that call this operation. For example, the algorithm for performing a calculation or the data types used for the data items in that calculation could be changed without effect on the signature of the operation.

4.5.4.3 Object State

Objects are instances of classes. As classes have attributes and participate in associations it follows that, at any instant in time, an object will hold specific values for those attributes and will participate in specific occurrences of the associations with other objects.

Collectively, the set of attribute values and instances of associations with other objects is referred to as the state of an object. If the value of an attribute of the object changes or an association with another object is made or broken, then the state of the object may change. Not all changes to attribute values or associations result in a change of state. As part of the analysis process, the attributes whose values are significant to the state of an object will be identified. Modelling of the effect of state changes can be done in UML using the State Transition Diagram notation (see Chapter 11).

4.6 RELATIONSHIP WITH OTHER DIAGRAMS

The class diagram shows the static structure of the classes in a system. The class diagram can be used to describe the class model from three primary perspectives; conceptual, specification, and implementation. The modelling approach taken may depend on the particular perspective being modelled.

In an object-oriented system, the operations defined in the class diagram will interact with each other to fulfil the functional requirements of the system. The class diagram therefore relates to the functional requirements by virtue of the dynamic use of the static class and operation structure described by the class diagram (Figure 4-24).

The dynamic use of operations and hence classes is documented in interaction collaboration diagrams or interaction sequence diagrams (Chapters 8 and 9 respectively). The functional requirements of the system are described by the use case diagram described in Chapter 3.

Like other UML models, the class model can be organized in packages as part of the *Model Management View* (Chapter 14).

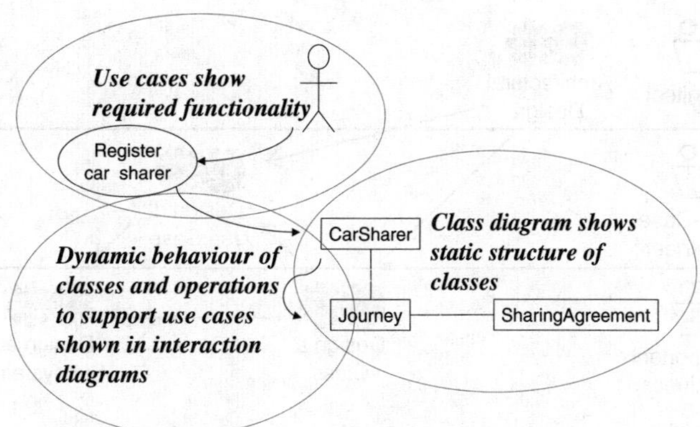

Fig. 4-24: Class diagram relationships with other diagrams

4.7 CLASS DIAGRAMS IN THE UNIFIED PROCESS

Chapter 3 discussed how the Unified Process is use case driven. Given this fundamental approach, the use of the class diagram in the Unified Process is heavily influenced by functional delegation concepts.

In the analysis model, a conceptual class diagram is produced from the use case analysis (Figure 4-25). The class model produced in this activity can be structured using model management concepts such as packages.

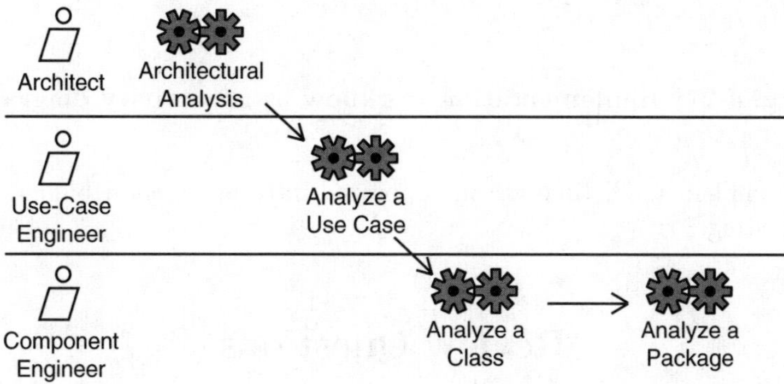

Fig. 4-25: Analysis workflow as an activity diagram

The collaborations required between classes to provide the functional capability necessary to support requirements (in the form of use cases) will be examined in more detail as the design progresses. The consideration of these collaborations will clarify the specification of the classes in the class model (and hence class diagrams, Figure 4-26). As the specification becomes more and more firm, classes can be organized into subsystems of coherent and cohesive functional capability.

As the transition is made from specification to implementation, the subsystems act as a framework for identifying discrete functional components. These components can be built together to provide an identifiable and testable increment to the functional capability of the implemented system (Figure 4-27).

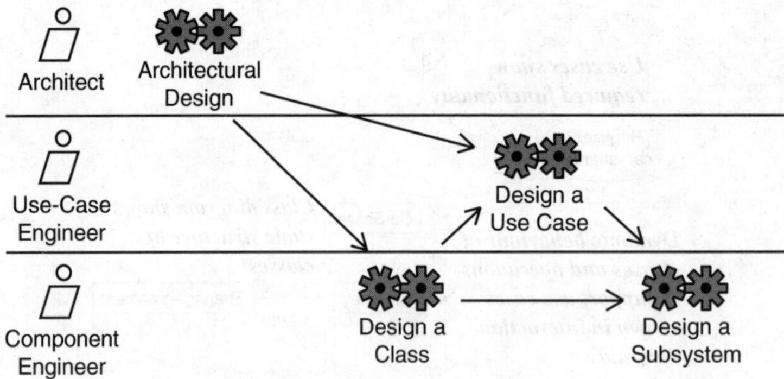

Fig. 4-26: Design workflow as an activity diagram

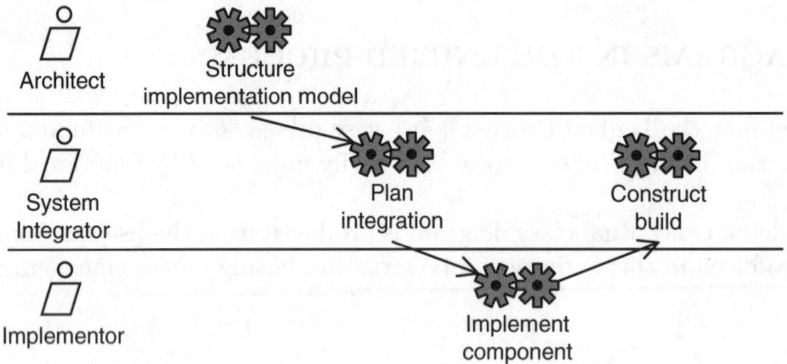

Fig. 4-27: Implementation workflow as an activity diagram

As components are implemented, they are incorporated into incremental builds of the implemented system for system testing.

Review Questions

4.1 What are the basic notational elements of class diagrams?

4.2 What are the purposes of drawing class diagrams?

4.3 Define what is meant by a class.

4.4 What is the most basic notation for a class?

4.5 Define what is meant by a class pathname.

4.6 What is the notation for showing a class pathname?

4.7 Define what is meant by an attribute.

4.8 What is the basic notation for an attribute?

4.9 What other properties can an attribute definition include?

4.10 What is the notation for these other properties of attributes?

4.11 Define what is meant by an operation.

4.12 Define what is meant by a parameter.

4.13 Define what is meant by 'passing parameters by reference' and 'passing parameters by value' and the difference between them.

4.14 What is the basic notation for an operation?

4.15 What is the notation for parameters of operations?

4.16 Define and illustrate how the phase of a project influences the level of detail shown for classes.

4.17 How can initial values for attributes be specified on a class diagram?

4.18 How can default values for parameters be specified on a class diagram?

4.19 Define the meaning of an association between two classes.

4.20 What is the basic notation for a labelled association?

4.21 What is the notation for indicating the role played by a class in an association?

4.22 What is meant by multiplicity?

4.23 What is the notation for multiplicity?

4.24 Which two elements of a class diagram can have multiplicity?

4.25 Define the perspectives from which class diagrams can be drawn.

4.26 What are the two main ways of drawing class diagrams?

Solved Problems

4.1 In the Insurance subsystem for CarMatch, car sharers can take out an insurance policy. Each insurance policy will be part of a particular insurance company's scheme. What classes might there be here?

With the outline, conceptual information presented here, producing a conceptual approach seems to be the most sensible course of action. No class is needed for CarMatch. CarMatch is the context of this conceptual class model, rather than a component in it. The concepts mentioned in this example that could be modelled as classes seem to be: insurance policy, insurance company, insurance scheme and car sharer.

The insurance scheme was a slightly tricky concept to spot. The phrase '*... insurance policy will be part of a particular insurance company's scheme*' implied that a policy is part of a scheme run by a company. The mention of 'company's' was possessive, that is the company 'owns' the scheme.

4.2 The previous example identified classes as part of the Insurance subsystem. What should the proper UML names of the classes be? Use class pathnames to qualify where each class comes from.

As a first attempt, the class names might be InsurancePolicy, InsuranceCompany, InsuranceScheme and CarSharer. However, CarSharer has already been modelled as part of (what might be labelled) the CarSharers package. Thus a suitably qualified class name should be CarSharers::CarSharer.

Given that the other classes are part of the Insurance subsystem, then writing the names of the classes with their pathnames would give, for example, Insurance::InsurancePolicy. This replicates the subsystem context and it might be better to use the names Policy, Scheme and Company (Insurance::Policy, Insurance::Scheme and Insurance::Company when the class pathname is included).

4.3 The premium due for a policy will, in part, be based on the home address of the car sharer taking out the policy. The payment schedule for a policy will generate a number of transactions. The transactions are really part of the Accounts subsystem. Draw a class diagram that incorporates the classes from the Insurance subsystem, along with those just described. Include suitably labelled associations in your class diagram.

See Figure 4-28.

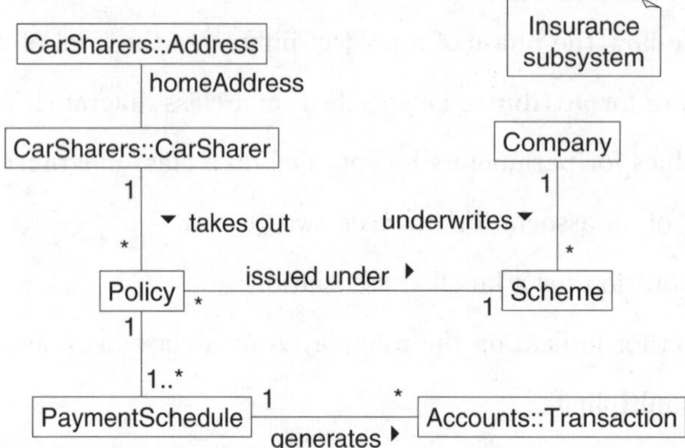

Fig. 4-28: Class diagram showing classes and associations

4.4 The following questions test your understanding of multiplicity notations and have 'Yes' or 'No' answers. Answer the questions based on the multiplicities shown in Figure 4-28.

1. Can a policy be issued under three schemes?
2. Could we hold the details for a scheme without holding details for a policy issued under that scheme?
3. Does a car sharer have to take out an insurance policy?
4. Could a car sharer take out more than one policy?
5. Could we hold details of a policy that has not been taken out by a car sharer?

1. No, a policy can be issued under one and only one scheme.
2. Yes, a scheme does not have to have any policies issued under it (*=0..*).
3. No, again *.
4. Yes, *.
5. No, a policy must be issued for a (1=1..1) car sharer.

4.5 For each insurance policy, it will be necessary to know the policy number, the start date of the policy, when it is due for renewal and the commission rate due on the premium for that policy. The start date is when the policy was first taken out. The renewal date is when the policy next expires. We also need to know how much money has been paid in total as payments against the policy (in the current year of the policy). The current year of the policy is defined as the renewal date minus one year.

Identify any attributes and operations here. Allocate them to appropriate classes. Suggest suitable types for the attributes, operations and any parameters for the operations. Add all these to your class diagram using visibility flags for both attributes and operations.

Clearly there are some attributes for Policy here. policyNumber, startDate, renewalDate, premium and commissionRate are all reasonably easy to identify and allocate to Policy. A derived attribute, startOfCurrentYear has also been included for the start of the current payments year. The specification for this derived attribute can be given in a note. All these attributes could be private. Figure 4-29 shows all these attributes along with their visibility and the derived attribute specification.

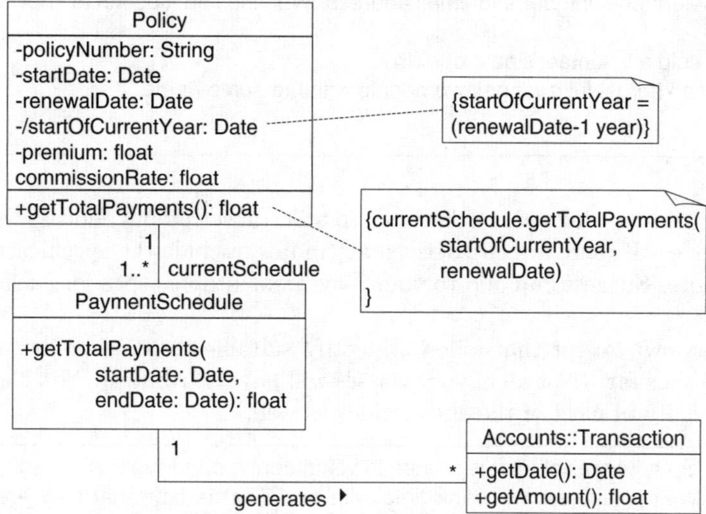

Fig. 4-29: Class diagram showing attributes and operations

In terms of the operations, policy now has a getTotalPayments operation. The note which is included on the diagram indicates that the method for this operation should call the getTotalPayments operation on the instance of PaymentSchedule that is fulfilling the role of the currentSchedule. This call will use the values of startOfCurrentYear and renewalDate as the two Date values passed to currentSchedule.getTotalPayments when it is called.

The class diagram has been specified on the premise that each Transaction made against the currentSchedule PaymentSchedule will be polled to see if it falls into the specified year (using the getDate operation and comparing the value to startOfCurrentYear and renewalDate). If the Transaction does fall in the current year, then the value of the Transaction will be retrieved using the getAmount operation and will be added to a running total.

This dynamic behaviour would be specified in an interaction diagram (Chapter 8 or 9).

It is worth noting that the perspective of this class diagram has now become a little blurred. In terms of the getTotalPayments operation on Policy, the class diagram shows a specification of class functionality required to support that operation. The attributes and other possible operations needed to support this function are not shown. For example, Transaction will probably need to include attributes to represent the date and value of a transaction. These are not shown, yet. By adding in these missing attributes and operations, we would move towards resolving the tension between the conceptual and specification perspectives as well as providing a more complete definition of the classes involved in the system.

Supplementary Problems

4.6 Read the case study material for VolBank in Chapter 1. List any classes that may exist in the description. Sketch out a first draft class diagram.

4.7 Here is part of a transcript of an interview between Said Hussain, a systems analyst, and Martin Page, Recruitment Director of VolBank. (Other excerpts from the same interview are used in subsequent exercises).

Said Hussain: Can you tell me a little more about the information you need to hold about Volunteers please?
Martin Page: Well, we need to know stuff like their name, and contact details...
SH: Contact details?
MP: Yes, their telephone number and email address. We also find it useful to know how old our volunteers are.
SH: So do you hold a volunteer's date of birth?
MP: Yes. That can be useful if we get two people with the same name.
SH: ...

Identify any attributes (derived or otherwise) in this transcript and allocate them appropriately to your list of classes. If there are any derived attributes, include the specification of the derivation as a method note. Suggest and add to your diagram, suitable types for each attribute.

4.8 From the interview excerpt that follows, identify suitable associations between the classes you have identified thus far. (Not all of your classes will have attributes). You should be able to work out the multiplicity of most of the associations as well.

Said Hussain: So how are volunteers related to volunteering opportunities?
Martin Page: Well volunteers will bank time with us. That is time that they are available to work on volunteering projects. Based on their availability we can match them to suitable opportunities.
SH: OK. I can see how you have banked time for volunteers, what about the 'projects' end?
MP: Well, there's a similar set up there with organizations banking time on the various different projects that they need help with.
SH: I see. Do you ever get projects that are set up by more than one organization?
MP: No, but an organization may have several projects on our books at any one time. Volunteers with banked time can work on several different projects. Each time they do some volunteer work it will only be for one project at a time though.
SH: ...

Hint: Part of the last comment by Martin Page actually covers a couple of associations in one phrase. See if you can unpick the multiplicity of all the associations from it.

4.9 Based on the excerpt below identify and allocate operations to support the functional requirements suggested in the transcript.

Said Hussain: How do you intend to match volunteers and volunteering opportunities?
Martin Page: Well, we'd like to be able to start with a volunteer and find the volunteering opportunities that they match against. We'd also like to be able to start with a volunteering opportunity and find any matching volunteers.
SH: Is the matching done on a time basis?
MP: At this stage yes. I'd like to explore other possibilities later, but let's stick to just time matching for now.
SH: So you need to check whether the banked time for a volunteer is the same as the time required for a project?
MP: That would do it.
SH: ...

4.10 Extending the operations you identified in the Problem 4.9, see if you can add a method note to specify how the operation to find volunteers for a project might work. You may need to use role names to clarify the roles played by classes in associations.

4.11 To match the banked time of a volunteer with the required time of a project, some kind of 'equals' operation will be needed. If you do not have such an operation already, add it to the most suitable class. What parameters might the operation take? What might its return type be?

4.12 If you have not done it already, add visibility indicators to all your attributes and operations.

Class Diagram Aggregation, Composition and Generalization

5.1 INTRODUCTION

Chapter 4 introduced the basic UML class diagram notation. Two elements of class diagrams, classes and associations, were covered. The creation of an association between two classes implies collaboration between those classes, achieved through message passing. In this chapter, the UML notation for some extensions to these basic modelling concepts is introduced.

As this chapter extends the consideration of class diagrams covered in Chapter 4, the 'Class Diagram in the Unified Process' and 'Relationship with Other Diagrams' sections are not repeated.

5.2 PURPOSE OF THE TECHNIQUES

When drawing associations between classes on a class diagram, associations are sometimes created where the name of the association is something like consists of or is made up of. Whilst there is clearly an association between the classes, it is desirable to be able to express the more subtle 'objects of this class consist of objects of that class' semantic. This is the purpose of *aggregation* and *composition*. Another notation for showing composition is also discussed in this chapter, namely the *composite object*.

The concept of *generalization* allows the inheritance of properties between classes. Properties inherited can be attributes, operations and participation in associations. Generalization within object-oriented systems is a very powerful construct that can promote the reuse of pre-written, pre-tested code with the resultant benefit of reduced code duplication.

5.3 AGGREGATION AND COMPOSITION NOTATION

In some cases, the associations between classes indicate that objects of one class are made up of or consist of objects of another class. UML has two special kinds of association that are part of the class diagram notation to show this: the aggregation association and the composition association. Both forms of relationship add a notational element to the existing notation for associations covered in Chapter 4. The general concept of aggregation is often referred to as being a *whole-part* or *part of* relationship. One class is a part of another class.

In effect, the aggregation and composition notations convey a property of the association they are used on. An aggregation (or composition) association is not a different type of class-to-class relationship. Rather, it is that the nature of the association being aggregation or composition is something that might be known and expressed about an association.

5.3.1 Aggregation

An aggregation association is used to indicate that, as well as having attributes of its own, an instance of one class may consist of, or include, instances of another class. The actual number of 'part' instances will depend on the multiplicity at the part end of the association. The use of aggregation does not override multiplicity specifications.

A typical example of aggregation would be in a manufacturing system where an assembly is made up of components. This association can be shown in the class diagram as an aggregation association rather than just as a plain association. (See Figure 5-1).

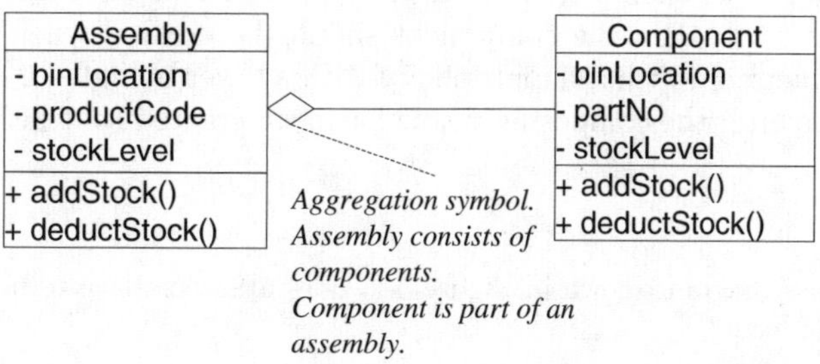

Fig. 5-1: Example of aggregation notation

UML uses a unfilled diamond shape at the end of the association to show that this is an aggregation association. The diamond is always connected to the class that is the aggregate; the class that is made up of something else. The term *whole-part* is sometimes used to refer to aggregation associations. Instances of the class at one end of the association are the *wholes* and they are made up of *parts*, the instances of the class at the other end of the association. The aggregation diamond is always at the whole end of the association. In Figure 5-1, the Assembly is the *whole*, or aggregate and the Component is the *part*.

5.3.2 Composition

Aggregation then, implies a whole-part structure between two classes. This is also the job of the composition notation. However, a composition association also implies *coincident lifetime* (Object Management Group, 1999*b*, p.3-74). A coincident lifetime means that when the whole end of the association is created, then the part components are also created. When the whole end is deleted, the part components are also deleted. In other words, in composition a part cannot exist without being part of a whole.

In aggregation this is not so. In aggregation a part is capable of existence outside of whole-part association. In Figure 5-1, a component can exist without being part of an assembly. Similarly, an assembly could be created from components that exist prior to the creation of the assembly. Composition is, then, a stricter form of aggregation.

In UML, there are two notations for composition. The first notation is very similar to aggregation, except that the diamond is filled to show composition. This notation is arguably the more commonly used notation. Figure 5-2 shows an example of this notation, using classes from a publishing system. As the class diagram shows, a Document is composed of one FrontMatter component, one or more Sections and one Index. As the composition form of aggregation implies, the FrontMatter, Section and Index components do not exist without being part of a Document. Moreover, if a Document is deleted then all the constituent parts of that document will also be deleted.

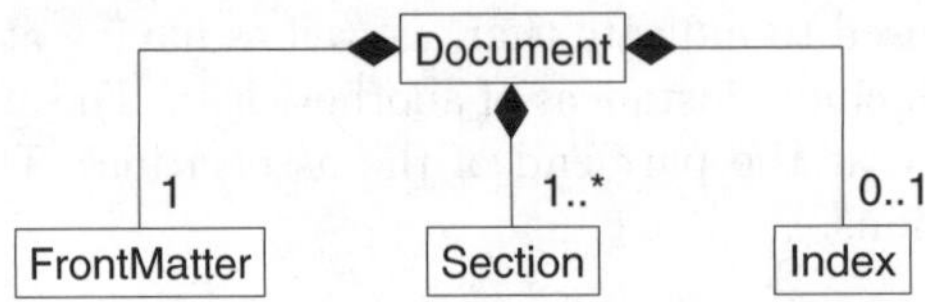

Fig. 5-2: Composition in a publishing system

Where a component object (for example, FrontMatter, Section or Index in Figure 5-2) has a multiplicity with a lower bound of 1 (1..) then the component should be created when the composing whole is created. Where a component object has a multiplicity with a lower bound of 0 (0..) then the component may be created sometime after the composing whole has been created (but before the composing whole is deleted).

EXAMPLE 5.1 In the class diagram shown in Figure 5-2, does a Section have to be created when a Document is created? What about an Index?

SOLUTION With a multiplicity of 1..* at least one Section must be created when a Document is created.

With a multiplicity of 0..1 it is not necessary to create an Index automatically when a Document is created.

The second notation for showing composition is by graphical containment; drawing one node inside another. This graphical containment can be used with either classes or instances of classes (objects).

More commonly, one would expect to use graphical containment to illustrate composition with objects, rather than with classes.

Figure 5-3 shows the portrayal of composition using graphical containment. The basic nature of the composition is exactly the same as that shown in Figure 5-2. The multiplicity of the component objects in the composition is shown in the top right corner of the name compartment of the component objects.

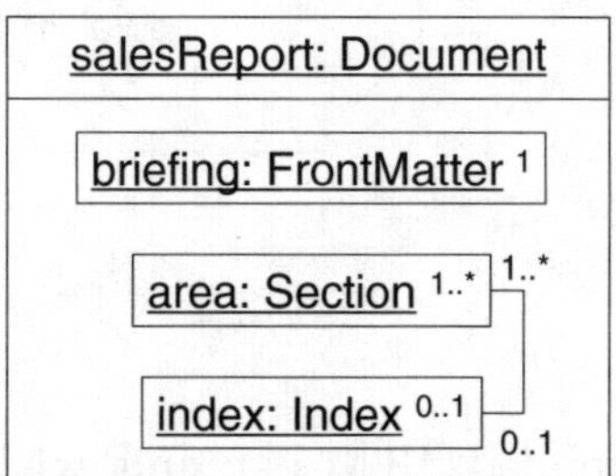

Fig. 5-3: Composition using graphical containment

Classes or objects used in this form of composition can have association either within the composition or to other nodes outside the composition. If that association links two objects inside the composition then it is implied that the association is also part of the component(s). The association between area: Section and index: Index illustrates this. (This association was not shown in Figure 5-2).

5.3.3 Shared Paths

Where more than one association from a class share the same aggregation or composition, those associations can be drawn using converging paths with a shared aggregation or composition symbol. Figure 5-4 illustrates an alternative way of drawing Figure 5-2 using converging paths.

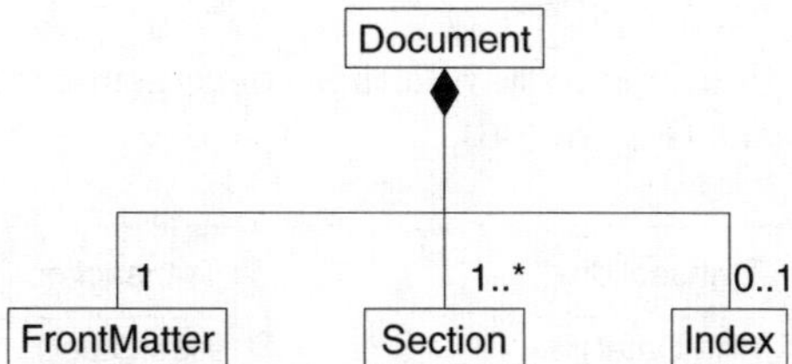

Fig. 5-4: Aggregation with converging paths

5.4 GENERALIZATION NOTATION

Generalization is a different type of relationship between two classes. Generalization relationships therefore do not use the association notation considered in Chapter 4 (nor the aggregation and composition notations covered in this chapter).

The generalization relationship is sometimes described as being a *kind of* relationship. One class is a kind of another class. This is perhaps best illustrated with an example. Figure 5-5 shows an extended version of the ATM class diagram first used at the start of Chapter 4.

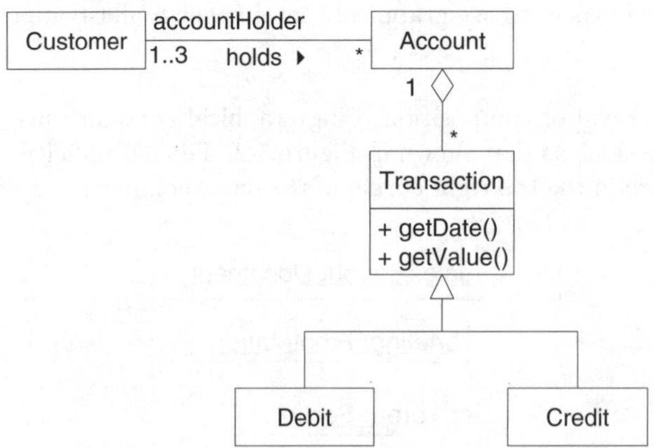

Fig. 5-5: Extended ATM example with inheritance

Generalization is shown in UML as a line ending with a triangular arrowhead at the class which is the more general type. For example, in Figure 5-5 there is a generalization relationship between Debit and Transaction and Credit and Transaction. These two generalizations have converging paths. These generalizations indicate that both Debit and Credit are kinds of Transaction. Every Debit is a kind of Transaction, every Credit is a kind of Transaction. Transaction is a generalization of Debit and Credit. Conversely, Debit and Credit are *specializations* of Transaction.

In a generalization relationship, the specializations are known as *subclasses* (or *subtypes*). In Figure 5-5, Debit and Credit are subclasses. The generalized class is known as the *superclass* (or *supertype*). In Figure 5-5, Transaction is a superclass.

Generalization allows the inheritance of the attributes and operations of a superclass by its subclasses. In the example shown in Figure 5-5, the getDate message could be passed to an instance of the Debit class as this operation is inherited from the Transaction class.

UML allows generalization relationships to have either convergent paths with a shared arrowhead or independent paths and arrowheads (Figure 5-6).

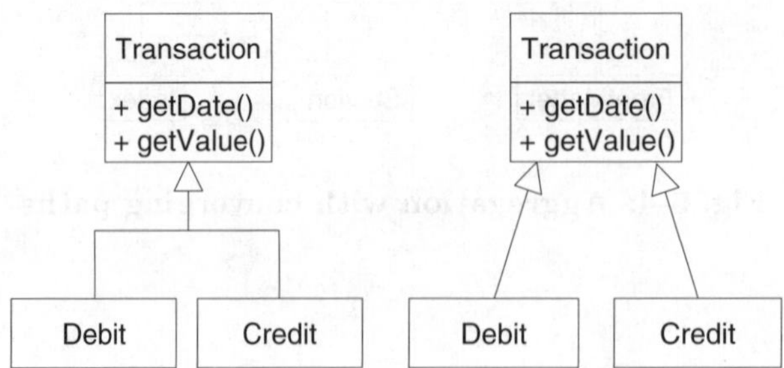

Fig. 5-6: Different ways of drawing paths for generalization relationships

Generalization relationship structures are sometimes referred to as hierarchies, reflecting their tree-like structure. There is no reason why a generalization hierarchy cannot have several layers. In such a case a subclass could also be a superclass. Figure 5-7 illustrates a generalization hierarchy with an example taken from the Java graphics class library (Sun Microsystems, 1999). In UML, the ellipsis (…) can be used to show the existence of additional subclasses that are not shown on a particular class diagram.

This notation has been used in Figure 5-7, which does not show the full class structure at any level of the generalization hierarchy.

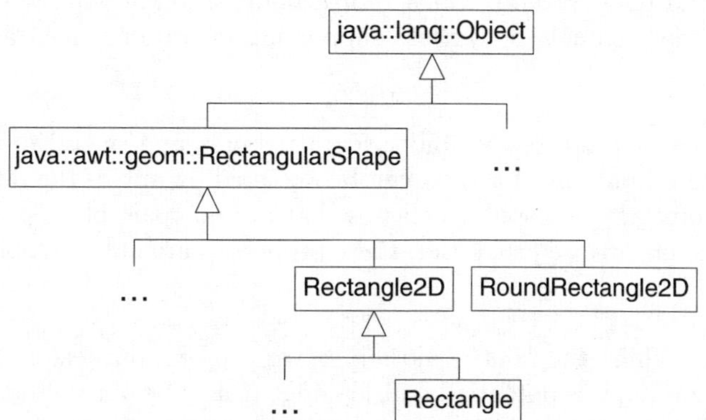

Fig. 5-7: Generalization hierarchy in Java

As Figure 5-7 demonstrates, the subclass to superclass relationship could extend over several generalization relationships.

Any class that is a generalization of a class, regardless of the number of generalization relationships between the two classes, is known as an *ancestor* of that class. For example, in the generalization hierarchy shown in Figure 5-7, java::lang::Object, java::awt::geom::RectangularShape, and Rectangle2D are all ancestors of Rectangle. The immediate ancestor of a class may also be referred to as the *parent class* of that class.

Any class that is a specialization of a class, regardless of the number of generalization relationships between the two classes is known as a *descendant* of that class. For example, in the generalization hierarchy shown in Figure 5-7, Rectangle, Rectangle2D and RectangularShape are all descendants of java::lang::Object.

Where one class is a direct subclass or superclass of another class, then it is more appropriate to use the more specific term subclass or superclass (or parent class) than the more general term descendant or ancestor.

Figure 5-7 also illustrates that a class in one package can be a specialization of a class in a different package. For example, the Object class exists in the java::lang package whereas the RectangularShape class and its descendants exist in the java::awt::geom package.

The interpretation of generalization depends on the perspective of the class diagram. In a conceptual diagram, generalization shows that an instance of one class is also (and at the same time) an instance of another class. In a class diagram drawn from either a specification or implementation perspective, generalization implies a specification of the operations that must be supported by the subtype. For example, in Figure 5-5, the Transaction, Debit, Credit generalization structure implies that Debit and Credit must support the getValue and getDate operations. How they will implement these operations is not specified. The inheritance simply specifies that they must provide those operations. This means that the implementation of an operation and indeed the attributes used in that implementation may vary from subclass to subclass or between subclass and superclass.

As well as the inherited properties and participation in associations of the superclass, subclasses may extend the superclass with subclass-specific responsibilities. For example, for the Java classes shown in Figure 5-7, the RoundRectangle2D class from the Java environment provides a rectangle with rounded corners. The rounding arc to be used at the corners of the rectangle is supported by specific operations such as getArcHeight() and getArcWidth(), which return information about the size of the rounding arc used at the corners of the rectangle, as well as supporting operations, such as getBounds(), inherited from RectangularShape.

In Section 4.4.3 the idea of protected visibility for attributes and operations was introduced. The protected attributes and operations of a class can be accessed by any of the descendants of that class. Protected properties cannot be accessed by classes that are not part of this descendent 'family tree'. Where an ancestor class has private properties, these properties are not available to descendant classes, or any other class.

It should be noted that, whilst the *kind of* notion serves a useful purpose as an introductory way of thinking about generalization, it is potentially misleading. It may be a little too vague when considering the more precise specifications of the behaviour of operations on a class. A more correct and formal notion is one of substitutability. As this book is primarily about the UML notation, rather than object-oriented modelling *per se*, substitutability is not considered any further here. More detailed discussions of substitutability can be found in, for example, Priestley (2000, pp.127-128) and Bennett et al. (1999, p.289).

5.5 MODELLING GUIDANCE

5.5.1 Aggregation and Composition

It is important not to use aggregation and composition too freely. For example, Fowler & Scott (1997) discuss the example of an association between an organization and the employees of that organization. Is this relationship an aggregation? Should a class diagram suggest that an organization is an aggregation of employees?

The answer to the question of whether or not to use aggregation probably lies, in part, with the context of the whole and part ends of the association. What other associations do they participate in? What is the overall intention of the use of the classes in the intended system? Are they to be processed together (as an aggregation) or separately?

For example, the case of an assembly and components used earlier, where both assembly and components are processed together, suggests a closer, aggregation association rather than a 'normal' non-aggregated association. When modelling concepts such as the employees in a department or organization, where employees or departments may be processed independently of each other, a non-aggregated association might be more appropriate.

It should be remembered that aggregation is a conceptual notion. The way in which an association is implemented may be guided by the information represented on a class diagram for an association, but the implementation does not necessarily have to be ruled by that information. For example, Figure 5-8 shows two different ways of modelling an association, one with aggregation, one without. A possible implementation of the association as an attribute of Assembly is also shown. The implementation of the Component end as an attribute of type Component with multiplicity of * is valid for both associations.

Remember that the composition association implies coincident life cycles with the part object instances being deleted when the whole object is deleted. Given this coincident life cycle and the discussion of aggregation above, it should be clear that composition should be used with even more caution than

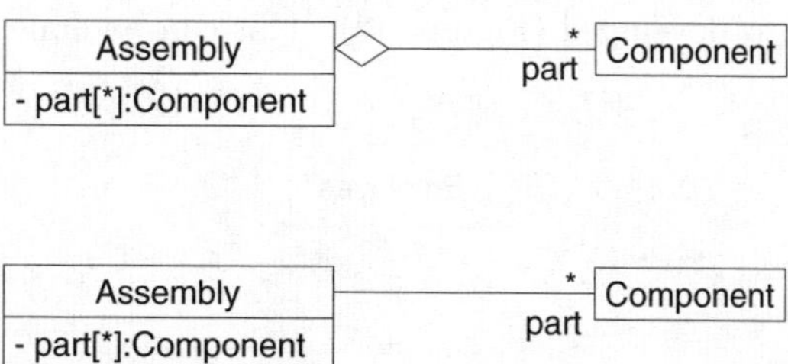

Fig. 5-8: Implementation of associations with and without aggregation

aggregation. If composition is used on an association, then it will carry very specific and more tightly constrained connotations for the implementor of the class model.

5.5.2 Generalization

When developing a class diagram, any generalization structures within the class model will need to be identified and modelled. This is desirable because, as stated above, generalization promotes reuse and improves specification and implementation consistency.

From the discussion in Section 5.4, it should be clear that the perspective of a class diagram will affect interpretation of the generalization used. When working on a conceptual model, an instance of a subclass will at the same time be an instance of the generalized superclass. On a specification or implementation level diagram, use of generalization represents a specification or description of the operations to be implemented in a subclass.

The modelling of generalization structures implies certain features in the code implemented for the specified model. Before modelling approaches are considered, it is worth reviewing these implications so that they can be borne in mind in the subsequent modelling discussion.

Extending class properties Subclasses will inherit the properties of their superclass(es). This means that an instance of a subclass will inherit all the attributes and operations of its superclass. This inheritance iterates up through to the top of the generalization tree. In addition to the inherited properties, a subclass can also possess attributes and operations specific to the subclass. In this way, the subclass can extend the specification of the superclass. Section 5.4 gave an example of this extension of inherited properties for the Java RoundRectangle2D class.

Redefining operations Operations can be inherited 'as is'. In other words, both the operation signature and the method of the operation are inherited from the superclass. It is also possible, and often desirable, for a subclass to redefine the method of an inherited operation in terms of the semantics of the subclass. The signature of the inherited operation remains the same, but the method of the operation is redefined by the subclass.

'Placeholder' operations In some cases, operations on a superclass may be included simply to ensure that subclasses provide that operation. The superclass itself has no method for the operation, but expects subclasses to provide a suitable method for the operation themselves. On the superclass, the operation in effect has the property abstract, though it is not normal to show this property explicitly in the class diagram. In this context, it would be normal to specify the whole superclass as being abstract. This would mean that there would be no instances of the class.

In certain circumstances generalization may be used where only one subclass is apparent in the class model at the time the model is developed (Figure 5-9). This can be done to promote future flexibility in the class model.

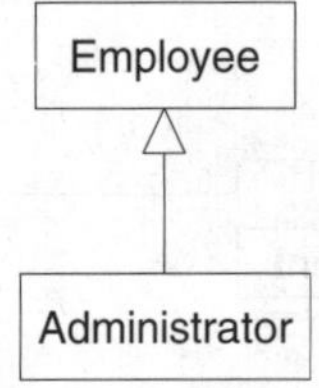

Fig. 5-9: Generalization with a single subclass

For example, for Figure 5-9 the analyst may be reasonably sure that, in the future, it will be necessary to introduce other subclasses of Employee. Each of these subsequent subclasses will specialize the general behaviour of Employee in a suitable way. However the analyst does not invent other subclasses that are not present or required in the current problem domain.

When producing a class model, generalization structures may be identified in either a 'bottom-up' or 'top-down' manner. These terms refer to the means of identifying generalization structures rather than the actual drawing of a generalization structure on a diagram.

5.5.2.1 Bottom-up Generalization

As class models are produced, classes that share properties, responsibilities and collaborations may become apparent. The common properties of those classes can be generalized into a suitable superclass and generalization relationships created between the new superclass and the original classes, which are now subclasses.

EXAMPLE 5.2 In the class model shown in Figure 5-10, both Car and Truck have shared responsibilities (the getRoadLicenceDue(): Date and renewRoadLicence() operations) and collaborations ('Fleet consists of cars' and 'Fleet consists of trucks'). How could the shared features be suitably generalized?

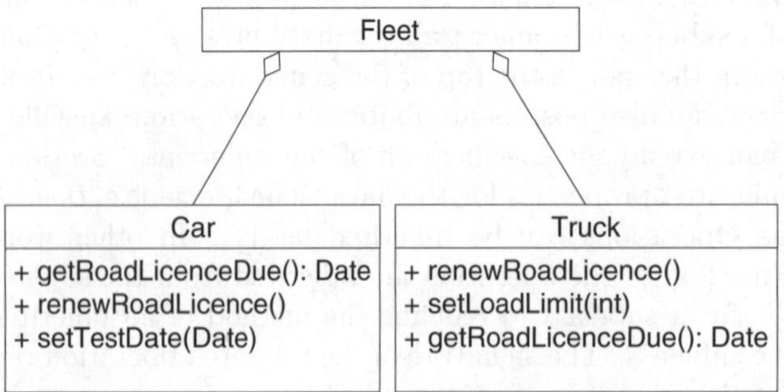

Fig. 5-10: Classes sharing common responsibilities and collaborations

SOLUTION The analyst infers that there is a high degree of commonality between Car and Truck and experiments with a superclass of Vehicle as a generalization of both of those classes. The result of this experimentation is shown in Figure 5-11.

In this example, the generalization seems to be reasonable. Common responsibilities and collaborations can be generalized to the Vehicle class without compromising the semantics of the model. Care should

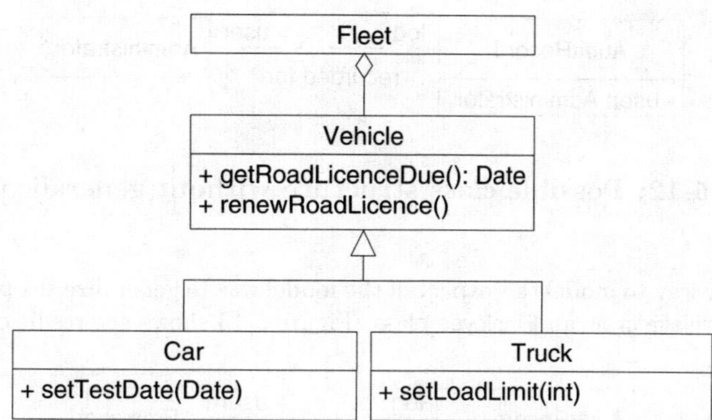

Fig. 5-11: Common responsibilities and collaborations generalized into superclass

be taken with this approach that generalization is not introduced simply as a means of graphical tidying of a complex diagram.

Generalization can be driven by the identification and appropriate abstraction of shared behaviour. Shared behaviour can be defined as the properties of classes (their attributes and operations) or participation in associations.

5.5.2.2 Top-down Generalization

As a class model develops, the analyst may become aware of the need to model classes that have common properties and share common participation in associations. Rather than modelling these classes with the associations seen in Chapter 4, the analyst can use generalization to show the inherent substitutability of one class for another.

EXAMPLE 5.3 Based on the following short transcript extract, identify any necessary classes and construct a suitable generalization relationship.

Janet Hoffner: We would like the system to be able to log which administrator changed records in a system. Is that possible?
Mick Perez: Sure. We are talking about administrators making changes to records here, aren't we?
JH: That's right...
MP: Oh, but there will be other users of the system who could change records in the future won't there?
JH: I guess so, yes. Our initial plan is to have administrators do all the keyboard work, but I guess that won't always be the case.

SOLUTION Mick's first thoughts on modelling the above requirements are shown in Figure 5-12. In this model fragment, the AuditRecord class is associated directly with the Administrator class. Mick has also shown an implementation of this association as an attribute on AuditRecord.

Mick then realized that this structure would not be as resilient against future extension as it might be. If, in future, audit records need to be kept for other types of user, then both the AuditRecord and Administrator classes might need changing.

Fig. 5-12: Possible class structure without generalization

Mick decided that a better way to model this aspect of the model was to generalize the properties, responsibilities and collaborations of Administrator as an Employee class. Figure 5-13 shows the result of this enhancement.

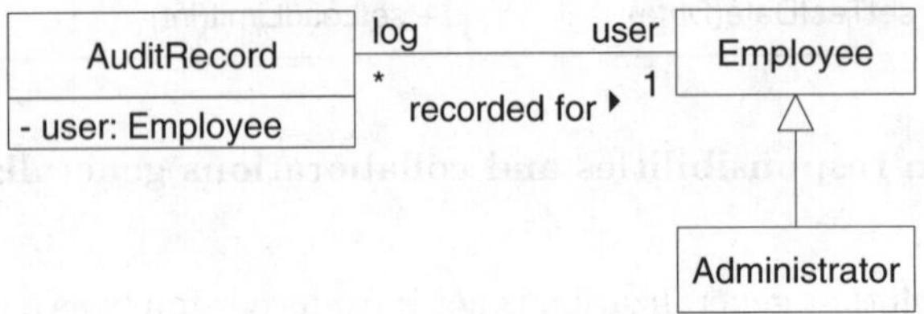

Fig. 5-13: Class structure with generalization

Future changes to the class model, to add other Employee subclasses (for example, Manager, Agent) should not necessarily require amendments to the AuditRecord class.

Where generalization is introduced in a top-down fashion, the analyst should be satisfied that the properties, responsibilities and collaborations of the superclass apply completely to all the subclasses. This compatibility can be tested in a more formal manner with techniques such as the Liskov Substitution Principle (Priestley, 2000; Bennett et al., 1999).

5.5.3 Object-Oriented Concepts

As with the previous chapter, it will be useful to draw out some of the fundamental object-oriented concepts that are exemplified by the notational elements covered in the preceding sections.

5.5.3.1 Object State Revisited

In Chapter 4 the concept of object state was introduced. To recap, object state depends on the values of certain key attributes and the instances of associations with other objects. Changes to these attributes or associations may result in a change in the state of the object.

Generalization hierarchies are sometimes used to manage state-specific object behaviour. Consider the class diagram shown in Figure 5-14. The Booking class delegates responsibility for handling how it behaves in any particular state to the BookingStatus class. The BookingStatus has two subclasses, Provisional and Confirmed.

All the BookingStatus subclasses support the getStatus and cancel operations. The Provisional subclass also provides a confirm operation that allows a provisional booking to be confirmed (for example, with the payment of a deposit). The method of the confirm operation would replace the instance of BookingStatus (BookingStatus.Provisional) with another instance (BookingStatus.Confirmed). The Confirmed class does not provide this operation so a Booking in the Confirmed state cannot confirm itself again. The old instance would copy across all its attribute values to the new instance (barring any values affected by the

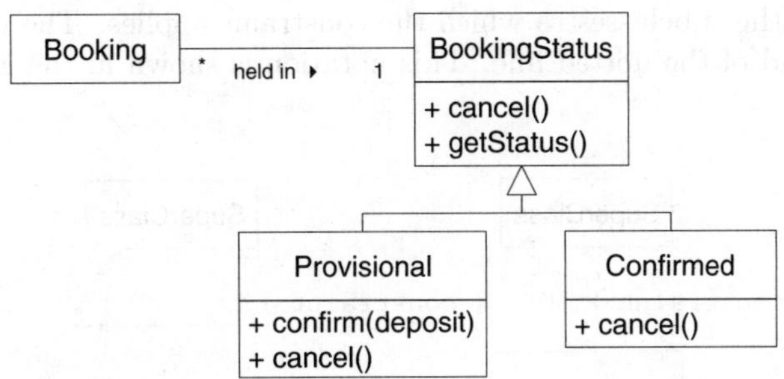

Fig. 5-14: Illustration of state tracking using generalization

state change) and then link the Booking object to the new state object (the new BookingStatus.Confirmed object).

5.5.3.2 Polymorphism

The class diagram shown in Figure 5-14 also illustrates the object-oriented notion of polymorhpism. Polymorphism is the ability of two operations with identical signatures to fulfil the same abstract functional requirement in different ways. For example, the cancel operation in Provisional might simply place the resource allocated to the booking back on an available list (for example, tables in a restaurant or seats in a cinema). However, the cancel operation on Confirmed must also handle the deposit that has been paid. For example, the cancel operation on Confirmed might free up the resource but be specified so as to require another customer to book (and pay a deposit upon) the resource before the deposit can be returned.

5.6 ADVANCED GENERALIZATION NOTATION

UML provides additional generalization notations that can be used to extend the commonly encountered generalization notation covered in Section 5.4.

5.6.1 Generalization Annotations

Generalization structures can be annotated with both constraints and discriminators. Constraints can be used in generalization structures where subclasses of the generalization are subject to certain semantic conditions. Discriminators can be thought of as role names for generalizations, either clarifying the semantics of the generalization or allowing multiple generalizations from one superclass.

5.6.1.1 Constraints

Generalization constraints can be either predefined or user-defined. The abstract UML notation for constraints is shown in Figure 5-15. The constraint itself is shown in curly braces ({...}). Where a shared path generalization is used, the constraint can be placed next to the superclass end of the generalization, near the triangular arrowhead. This notation is shown in the left hand illustration in Figure 5-15. Where separate generalization paths are shown, a dotted line is drawn across the generalization paths for the subclasses to which the constraint applies. The name of the constraint is then written near the end of the dotted line. This notation is shown in the right hand part of Figure 5-15.

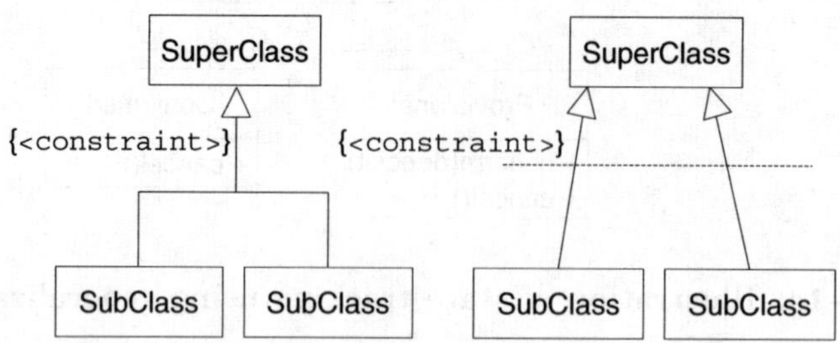

Fig. 5-15: Generalization constraint notation

UML has predefined the following four common constraints.

incomplete The *{incomplete}* constraint indicates that whilst some of the subclasses may have been specified, it is known that not all subclasses that exist in the problem domain have been specified.

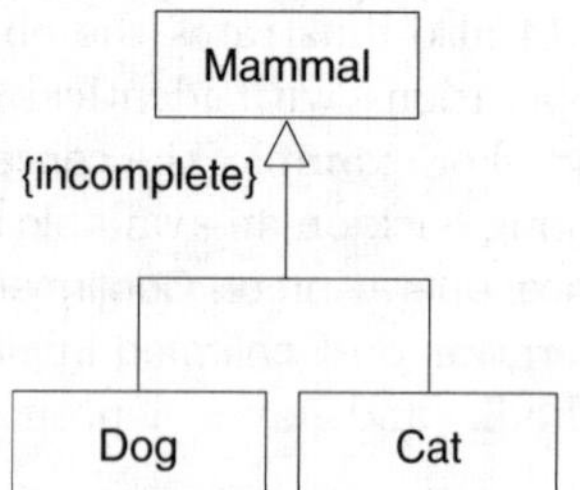

Fig. 5-16: Illustrative example of incomplete constraint

For example, Figure 5-16 shows how the specialization of Mammal into Dog and Cat does not specify all the specializations of Mammal that exist.

complete The *{complete}* constraint specifies that all the subclasses in that generalization have been defined within the class model. Remember though that not all those subclasses may be shown on one class diagram.

disjoint In a disjoint generalization, an instance can only be an instance of one of the subclasses. If any of the subclasses acts as a superclass in a further generalization then the subclasses of that further generalization (the subsubclasses) cannot inherit from more than one of the disjoint subclasses.

The subclasses in a disjoint generalization have no commonality. An instance of one of the subclasses cannot be an instance of one of the other subclasses in the same disjoint constrained generalization.

Figure 5-17 illustrates this using Mammal, Dog and Cat again. The {disjoint} constraint specifies that one instance cannot be an instance of both Dog and Cat. The subclasses constrained to be disjoint are mutually exclusive. Given this disjoint nature, the constraint also specifies that no further class should inherit from both Dog and Cat (nor any other classes covered by the {disjoint} constraint).

The Doat class, which specializes Dog and Cat as shown in Figure 5-17, is incorrect as it specializes two classes governed by the same disjoint constraint.

overlapping An overlapping generalization is an approximate opposite of a disjoint generalization. An instance may be an instance of more than one subclass in the generalization. If any of

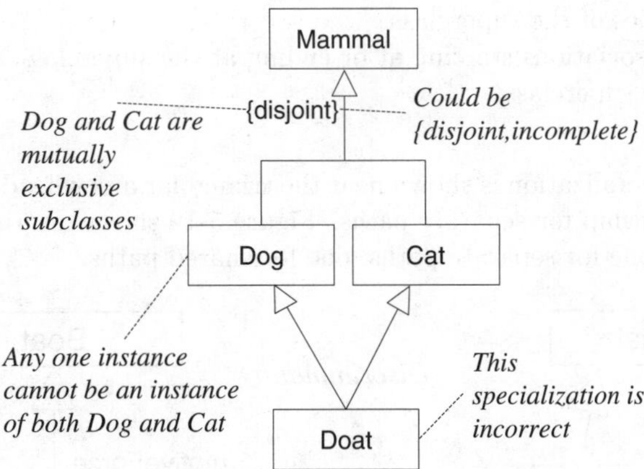

Fig. 5-17: Illustrative example of disjoint constraint

the subclasses acts as a superclass in a further generalization then the subclasses of that further generalization (the subsubclasses) can inherit from more than one of the disjoint subclasses (Figure 5-18).

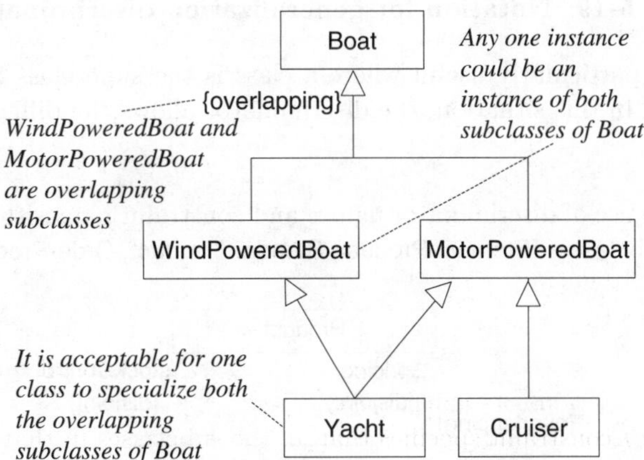

Fig. 5-18: Illustrative example of overlapping constraint

The {overlapping} constraint specifies that one instance can be an instance of both WindPoweredBoat and MotorPoweredBoat. The subclasses constrained to be overlapping are not mutually exclusive. Given this overlapping nature, the constraint also specifies that it is acceptable for further subclasses to inherit from both WindPoweredBoat and MotorPoweredBoat (and any other classes covered by the {overlapping} constraint).

The Yacht class, which specializes both WindPoweredBoat and MotorPoweredBoat as shown in Figure 5-18, is perfectly acceptable as it specializes two classes governed by the same overlapping constraint.

5.6.1.2 Discriminators

Discriminators on generalization relationships are similar to the notion of role names of associations. The discriminator provides a name for the generalization. The name of a discriminator must be different from the following properties of the superclass.

1. The names of any associations starting at or ending at the superclass.
2. The attributes of the superclass.

The discriminator for a generalization is shown near the triangular arrowhead for a shared path, or near each generalization relationship for separate paths. Figure 5-19 shows discriminators for two different generalization structures, one for separate paths, one for shared paths.

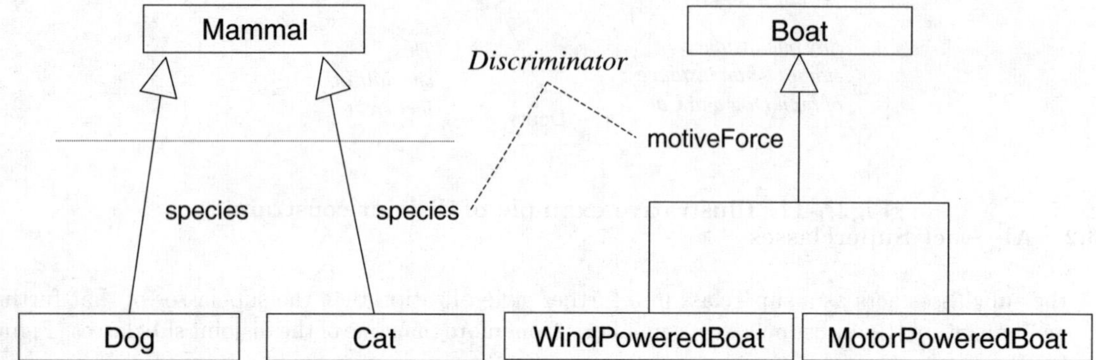

Fig. 5-19: Notation for generalization discriminators

Discriminator names are particularly useful where a class is the superclass for two or more different generalization structures. In this situation, the discriminator allows the different generalizations to be identified.

Figure 5-20 illustrates the use of discriminator names and constraint names together. The Product class is a superclass for four subclasses, PremiumProduct, StandardProduct, OrderProduct and StockProduct.

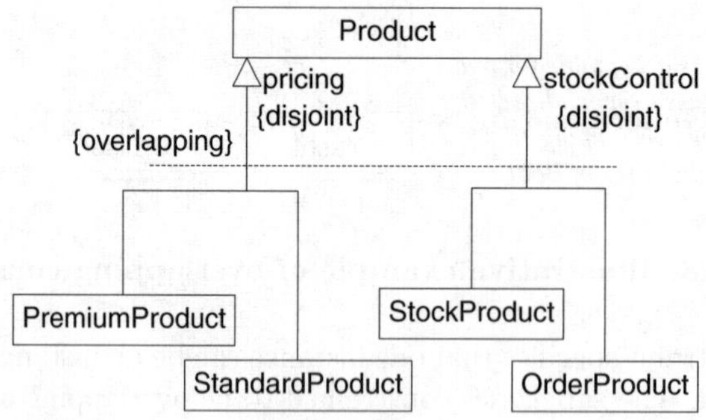

Fig. 5-20: Use of discriminators with multiple generalizations

The implication might be that the pricing subclasses will introduce properties related to processing price based functionality (for example, discount, markup, calculateProfit). Similarly, the stockControl subclasses might introduce properties related to processing stock based functionality (for example, stockLevel, reorderLevel, leadTime, reorderStock).

Both the pricing and stockControl generalizations are constrained as disjoint. This means that a Product can be either a PremiumProduct or a StandardProduct, but not both. Similarly, a Product can be either a StockProduct or an OrderProduct, but not both.

The two generalizations however, have an overlapping constraint specified across them. This constraint indicates that a Product can be one of the pricing products and one of the stockControl products at the same time. Thus an instance could be:

1. An instance of Product, but not specialized as either a pricing product or a stockControl product.
2. A PremiumProduct, but not specialized as a stockControl product.
3. A StandardProduct, but not specialized as a stockControl product.
4. A StockProduct, but not specialized as a pricing product.
5. An OrderProduct, but not specialized as a pricing product.
6. A PremiumProduct, and a StockProduct.
7. A PremiumProduct, and an OrderProduct.
8. A StandardProduct, and a StockProduct.
9. A StandardProduct, and an OrderProduct.

5.6.2 Abstract Superclasses

In a generalization structure it may be possible for an object to be an instance of one or more of the subclasses of the generalization, or an instance of the superclass of the generalization. For example, an organization may employ a person without assigning that person a particular role or job function. Thus, for the generalization structure shown in Figure 5-21, it would be possible to have instances of both subclasses (Administrator and Manager) and instances of the superclass Employee. The latter would represent employees with no specific role as either Administrator or Manager.

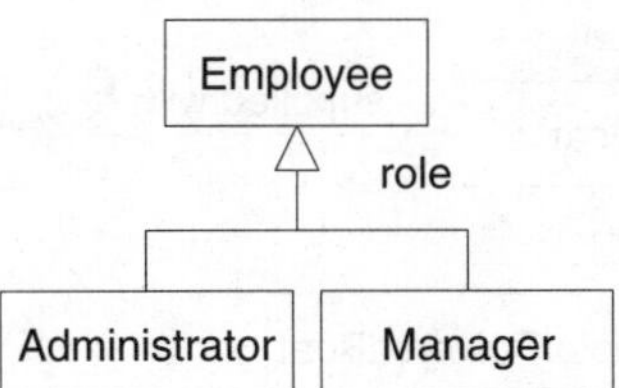

Fig. 5-21: Generalization with instances of superclass permitted

If the opposite were true, and the organization insisted that all staff were allocated a role, then there would be no direct instances of the Employee superclass.

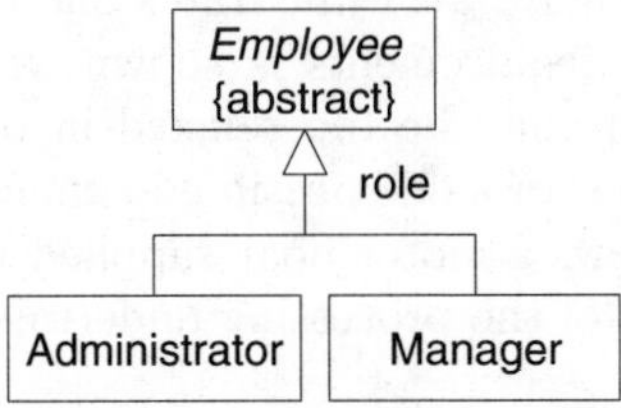

Fig. 5-22: Generalization with abstract superclass

To reflect this requirement in the class diagram, the {abstract} property in the class name compartment can be used to indicate that the Employee class will never have any direct instances (Figure 5-22). The name of an abstract class is shown in italics.

5.6.3 Association Generalization

Thus far, the discussion of generalization has been concerned with the generalization of classes. However, the UML generalization notation can also be applied to associations. The notation for association generalizations is much the same as for class generalizations, with the start and end of the generalization being an association instead of a class. Figure 5-23 illustrates this notation.

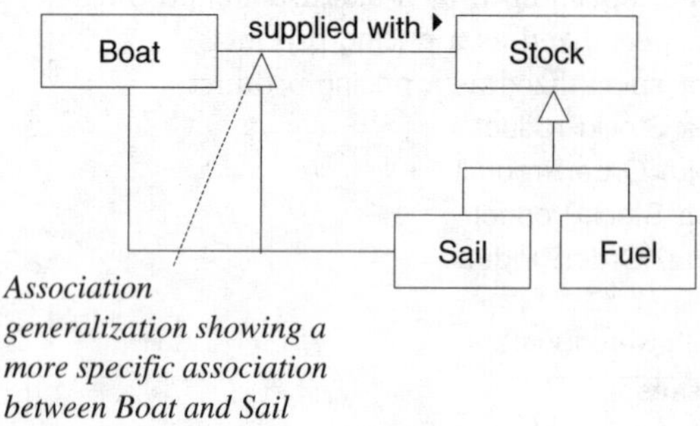

Fig. 5-23: Example of association generalization notation

Figure 5-23 shows a specialized association. The specialization suggests that, whilst the general supplied with association describes the association between boats and stock in general, any specific associations between boats and sail stock should be considered in the light of the more specialized association (which is unnamed in Figure 5-23). This more specific association might include a more rigid multiplicity, a role or constraint.

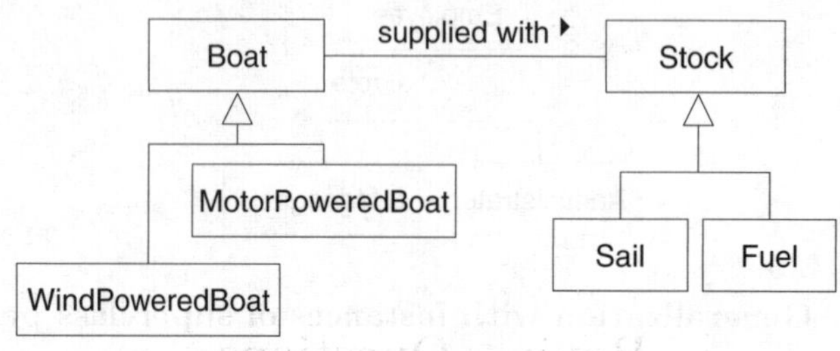

Fig. 5-24: Ambiguity in association between superclasses

Association generalization can be used where an association between superclasses might lead to certain ambiguities or inconsistencies. Figure 5-24 illustrates one possible problem. In Figure 5-24, the association between boats and stock requirements is shown with an association between those two superclasses. This general association may be too relaxed in terms of the possible instances of the association. For example, Figure 5-25 shows one possible instance of the supplied with association. The instance illustrated in Figure 5-25 shows a motor boat supplied with a sail stock item. Clearly, this is not desirable in terms of the integrity of the processing undertaken by the system being modelled.

In this case, the generalized association supplied with needs to be specialized with the addition of more specific associations relating wind powered boats with sail stock and motor powered boats with fuel stock.

Figure 5-26 shows the general association clarified by two specialized associations. Now wind powered boats are (more specifically) associated with sail stock and motor powered boats are (more specifically) associated with fuel stock.

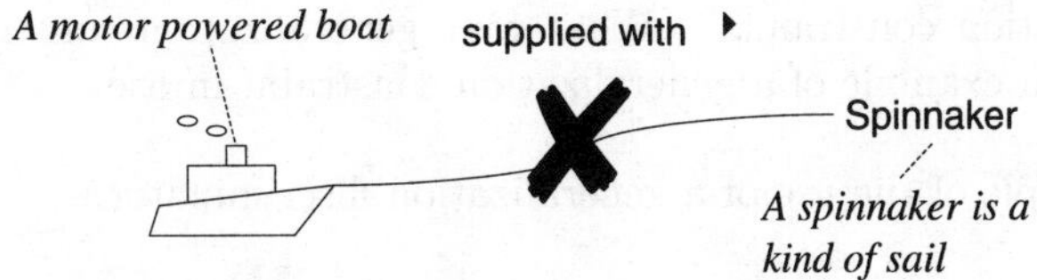

Fig. 5-25: Instance of generalized association (Figure 5-24)

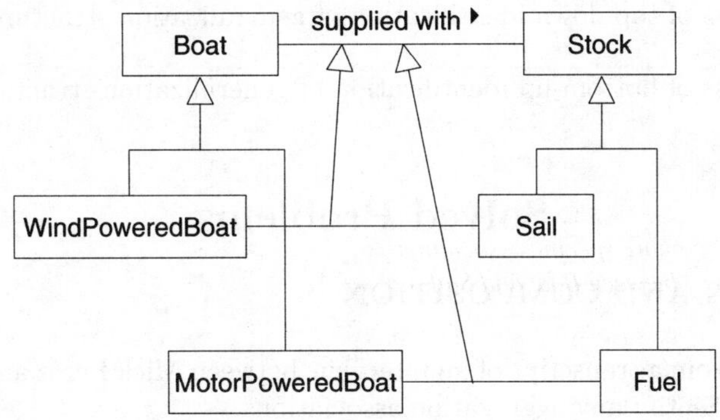

Fig. 5-26: Specialized association linking subclass to subclass

Association generalization will most probably be needed in cases such as the one illustrated here, where associations between subclasses of two generalization hierarchies need to be defined more specifically than is possible with just the general association between superclasses. Association generalization can become visually cluttered though, given the number of lines involved. These lines will inevitably cross over each other, reducing the clarity of the diagram for the reader. A more concise and arguably more precise mechanism for describing these subclass association constraints would be to use Object Constraint Language (OCL) constraints in notes attached to the relevant association (see Chapter 12).

Review Questions

5.1 Define what is meant by aggregation.

5.2 How do aggregation associations differ from 'normal' associations?

5.3 Define what is meant by composition.

5.4 How does composition differ from aggregation?

5.5 What is the UML notation for aggregation?

5.6 What are the two UML notations for showing composition?

5.7 Why might aggregation (or composition) be referred to as a *whole-part* relationship?

5.8 Why might generalization be referred to as a *kind of* relationship?

5.9 What is the UML notation for generalization?

5.10 What are the two UML path notations that can be used for generalization?

5.11 What are generalization constraints? What four generalization constraints are predefined by UML? Give your own example of a generalization constraint in use.

5.12 Give your own example of the use of a generalization discriminator.

5.13 What, arguably, is a more concise way of showing a constraint on a generalized association?

5.14 Why might aggregation and composition associations be misleading on a class diagram?

5.15 Describe the process of top-down identification of generalization structures.

5.16 Describe the process of bottom-up identification of generalization structures.

Solved Problems

AGGREGATION AND COMPOSITION

5.1 Here is an excerpt from a transcript of an interview between Mick Perez and Janet Hoffner. Based on the transcript, identify any aggregation associations.

Mick Perez: Just remind me, what kind of things do you need to know about the start and destination of each journey?

Janet Hoffner: We'd want to know the building name and number, the apartment number, the street, locality, town or city, county and postal code or zip code. We'd also want to hold similar information for the home address of a car sharer as well.

MP: OK. Didn't you say that the journey start and destination address will be used to match up possible shared journeys?

JH: Yes—interesting point that. I'm not quite sure how you'll do this. We want to be able to establish whether two addresses are close enough to each other to be able to consider them a match for a shared journey. For example, two people may want to get from a start destination on adjacent corners of two different blocks to destination addresses in different floors of the same building. A person looking at the addresses would know that the addresses are similar enough to be a match, but in terms of just text of the addresses, they look completely different.

MP: ...

Mick could see that address information was needed for car sharers. An address would need to be held as a car sharer's home address and for the start and destinations of each journey. Given that address information would be kept for these three requirements, Mick modelled an Address class with associations to CarSharer and Journey. Mick assigned all the address attribute information required by CarMatch and an equals operation, to establish whether one Address could be considered the same as another, to the Address class. Figure 5-27 shows Mick's class diagram for this part of the class model.

In terms of processing, the home address (Address) of a CarSharer would always be processed with the CarSharer for which the Address was created. Similarly, the startAddress and destinationAddress of a Journey would always be processed as part of the processing carried out on a Journey. Given this, Mick decided that Address was a part of CarSharer (whole) in the form of the homeAddress of a CarSharer. Similarly, Address was a part of Journey (whole) in the form of the startAddress and destinationAddress of a Journey. For this reason, Mick modelled the associations from Address as aggregations in Figure 5-27.

To indicate the implementation of these associations, Mick put startAddress and destinationAddress attributes in Journey and a homeAddress attribute in CarSharer. All these address attributes were of type Address. (This is actually mixing perspectives a little but helps to show the interpretation of the associations). His class diagram for this part of the system is shown in Figure 5-27. Figure 5-27 includes both the aggregation associations and the implemented attributes (homeAddress, startAddress, destinationAddress).

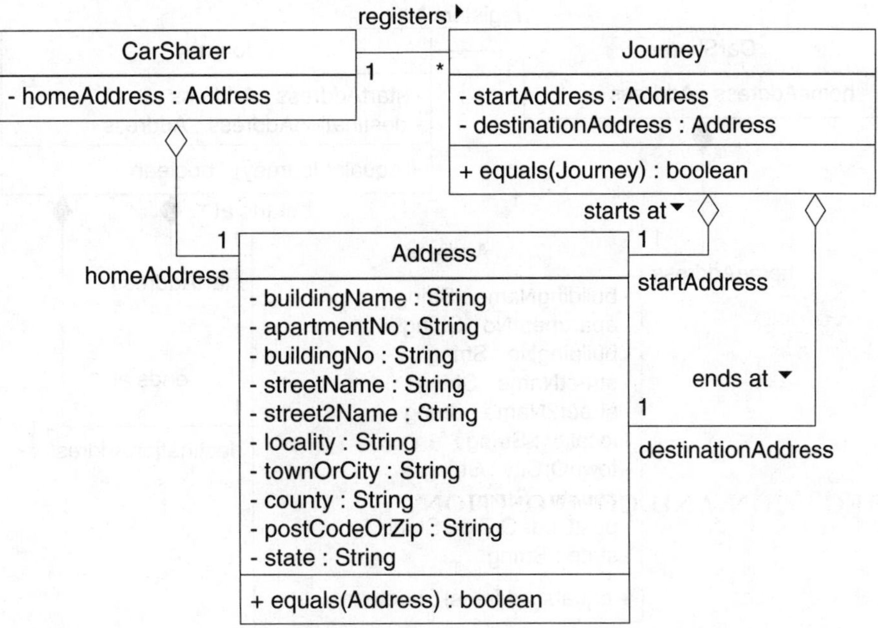

Fig. 5-27: Class diagram with Address aggregation

5.2 Mike then considered the nature of the Address class more carefully. Was the intention to create a new address for every car sharer or journey? If a car sharer registered one or more journeys from his or her home address, would that count as the same occurrence of an address or different occurrences of addresses that happen to have the same state (attribute values)?

(As Mick knew he had not considered this in enough detail yet, he had left the multiplicity of the Journey—Address associations blank at the Journey end in the class diagram shown in Figure 5-27).

Mick decided that each address would probably be a different occurrence. The address matching would work in much the same way regardless of whether addresses were shared or not.

If addresses were shared, that is, if one address occurrence could be used by more than one car sharer or journey, then look-up facilities would be needed in the Address class. This would be necessary to allow new instances of CarSharer and Journey to find out if there was an existing address that was their address. Thus Mick deduced that the most straightforward approach would be to use different occurrences of Address for every car sharer's home address and the start and destination of each Journey.

Given this decision, Mick then knew that the life cycle of an Address instance would be coincident with the CarSharer or Journey for which the Address instance was created. An instance of Address would only come into being when created by the CarSharer or Journey that used that Address and would cease to exist when the CarSharer or Journey that used it was deleted.

Thus, the aggregations could actually be shown as compositions. Furthermore, the multiplicity of the associations between Journey and Address was now clear. These clarifications are shown in Figure 5-28.

GENERALIZATION

Mick then turned his attention to modelling some of the specification for how one Journey might be matched against another. Reviewing his class model thus far, Mick noted that the Journey class delegated responsibility for working out whether one address was the same as another to the Address class. This delegation gave rise to the equals operation on Address.

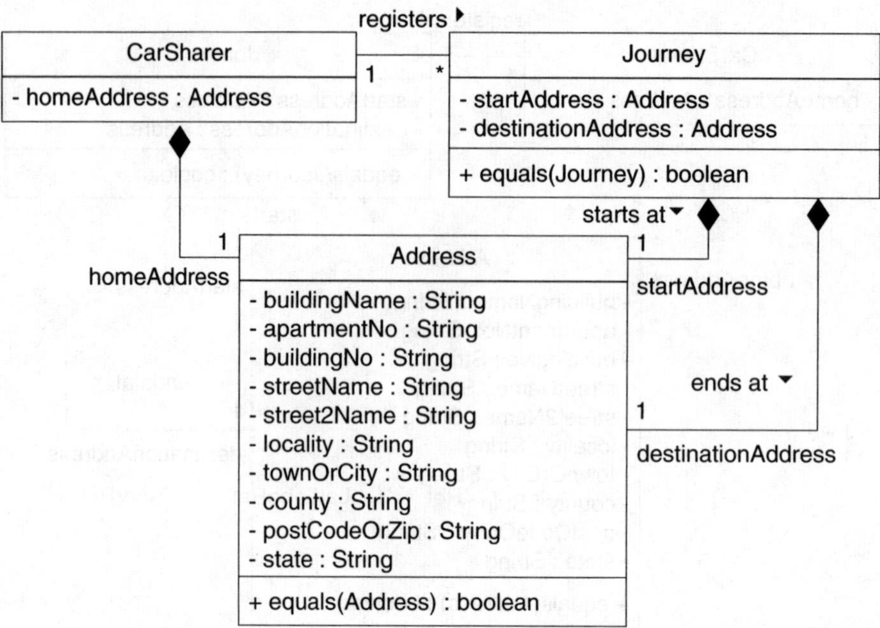

Fig. 5-28: Class diagram with address composition

Mick now had to establish how an address would work out whether it is the same as another. It has already been mentioned that a simple String match is neither accurate enough, nor powerful enough to match similar addresses with each other. Mick therefore decided to look at bringing in some Geographical Information System (GIS) capability. A GIS would give Mick the ability to work out when one address is geographically close to another.

5.3 Mick discussed processing addresses with Jan Cusack, a member of his team who knew about Geographical Information Systems (GIS).

Jan Cusack: I've been looking at the address matching you were talking about.
Mick Perez: Great - do you have any pointers for me?
JC: Well there are three 'standard' geo-locating standard class libraries that you might need to work with. One is the United Kingdom Ordnance Survey (OS) map reference based system, another is based on latitude and longitude, and the third is the 'Tiger' referencing system.
MP: Do they all do the same kind of thing?
JC: Broadly speaking yes. What you'd need to do is wrap up access to each of those class libraries with your own subclasses.
MP: I guess that when it comes to matching locations with each other, I've got to look at converting between a format I can use in the CarMatch system and the format used in one of the standards you mentioned.
JC: I guess so, you'll probably want to provide an 'equals' to do the checking between one location and another.
MP: Great, I'll have a go at modelling that. Can I bounce my model back off you later on?
JC: No... Only joking—of course you can.

Mick knew that he could create his own classes that inherited functions from classes available in the three different GIS class libraries. His own classes could then extend that functionality to provide the operations he needed to match one address with another. However, Mick also realized that he would probably need to manage the conversion between the internal representation formats used by each of the different GIS systems and an external format, and vice versa. Mick sketched out some thoughts based on this discussion (Figure 5-29).

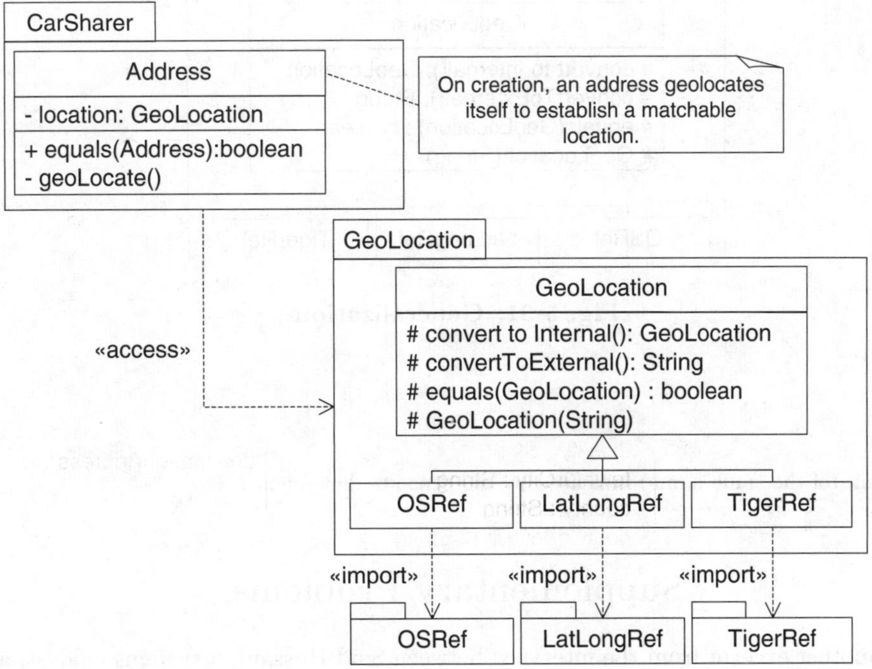

Fig. 5-29: Address modelling with generalization

This diagram is quite complex. Looking at the different aspects of it, a number of features are of interest. Mick has used a model management notation to show use of other packages by his own classes (Figure 5-30). Three different class libraries (packages) are imported. Mick's three classes GeoLocation::OSRef, GeoLocation::LatLongRef and GeoLocation::TigerRef will eventually be specializations of suitable classes in each of the three imported packages. These classes have not been identified yet. Mick is assuming that they are available based on what Jan told him.

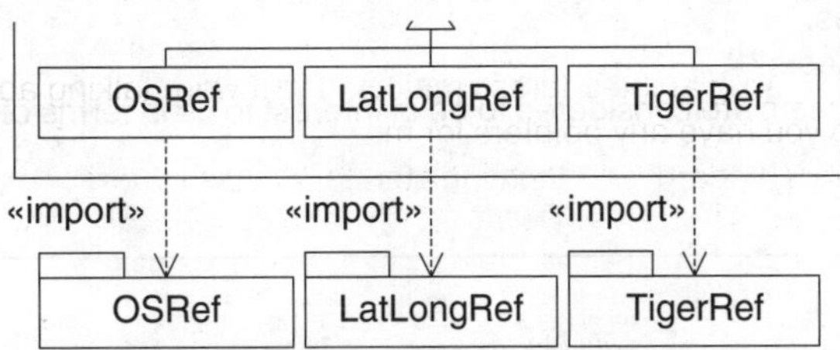

Fig. 5-30: Package imports

Mick's GeoLocation package is accessed by the CarSharer package (the «access» dependency). This indicates Mick's intention to create an association between the Address class and the GeoLocation class. The access dependency indicates that classes in the CarSharer package will be able to access the publicly available classes within the GeoLocation package.

Within the GeoLocation package, OSRef, LatLongRef and TigerRef are specializations of GeoLocation. GeoLocation specifies three operations with protected visibility. The three subclasses will inherit these operations.

Mick's intention is that the equals operation will use the convertToInternal and convertToExternal operations inherited by the OSRef, LatLongRef and TigerRef subclasses to hide the system specific details of each of the three different GIS systems. Each subclass, OSRef, LatLongRef and TigerRef, will implement convertToInternal and convertToExternal so as to encapsulate the attributes and other operations inherited from the specific

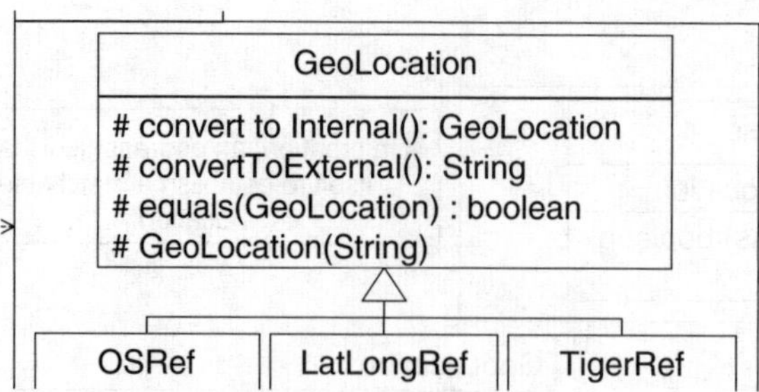

Fig. 5-31: Generalization

GIS system (of the same name) indicated by the «import» dependency.

Supplementary Problems

5.4 Here is another excerpt from the interview between Said Hussain, a systems analyst, and Martin Page, Recruitment Director of VolBank.

Said Hussain: Can we go back to this idea of banked time you mentioned earlier? You seem to be saying that banked time is recorded for both volunteers and organizations with volunteering opportunities.
Martin Page: That's right. We want to be able to match up the banked time for a volunteer with the required time that has been banked for a volunteering opportunity.
SH: So does banked time exist for anything else?
MP: No, only for volunteers and opportunities. We really consider a volunteering opportunity in terms of the time requirements it has.
SH: What about volunteers?
MP: Yes, I guess volunteers are considered to be of interest to us in terms of the volunteering time that they have banked.
SH: . . .

Reconsider the associations you developed in Exercise 4.8. What potential is there for adding the aggregation concept and notation to those associations? What about composition? Justify any decision you make between aggregation, composition and no aggregation at all. Amend your class diagram to include aggregation or composition where you have decided to include it.

5.5 The transcript below moves on to address some of the issues of generalization in the VolBank case study.

Said Hussain: Can we move on from the recording of details for volunteers, banked time and volunteering opportunities? I'd like to look at what you do in terms of assigning volunteers to opportunities.
Martin Page: OK. Well, once we've got a match, we allocate volunteers to projects, I mentioned that already.
SH: Project?
MP: A volunteering opportunity.
SH: OK, could there be a team of people working on a project?
MP: A team, yes. Though we do also have individuals working on other projects. Oh, and on some projects, we have a team large enough to warrant having one or more team leaders.
SH: Go on.
MP: Well, we need to know what role a volunteer is playing in a project.
SH: So you're saying that there are different kinds of assignment?
MP: Just so. There is no reason why one volunteer could not work on one project as an individual or team leader, and on another as a team member though. It varies from project to project.

From the transcript above, identify a possible generalization. Amend your class diagram appropriately.

5.6 VolBank are considering introducing a profile points scheme. In the scheme, volunteers build up a points profile. The more volunteer work they do, the more points they get. The points can be redeemed as a discount on prices at certain retail outlets that are supporting the scheme. All assignments to volunteering opportunities will need to support profile points calculation. The way in which profile points are calculated will vary depending on the type of assignment. Team members on a project will have profile points calculated based on hours worked and the 'team member rate', which is the same for all team members. For team leaders, profile points will be calculated based on hours worked, team size and the 'team leader rate'; again, this will be the same for all team leaders. Finally, for volunteers working as individuals on a project, profile points are to be calculated on hours worked, the 'individual bonus adjustment' and the 'individual rate'.

Amend your generalization superclass and subclasses to include the responsibilities indicated in the passage above.

5.7 Consider the generalization you have created in Exercise 5.5. Could you apply any of the predefined UML constraints to the generalization? Explain your reasoning.

5.8 Again for the generalization you have created in Exercise 5.5, suggest some suitable discriminator names for the generalization structure.

5.9 In the generalization you have created in Exercise 5.5, is the superclass abstract? If so, why? If not, why not? What circumstances affect your conclusion?

Class Diagram More On Associations

The basic notation and semantics of UML associations were introduced in Chapter 4. Two types of textual labelling can be used with associations. The association name, which indicates the basic nature of the association, and role names, which can be used explicitly to describe the nature of the participation of a class in an association.

Examples of association names used in this book included the holds association between Customer and Account (Figures 4-1 and 5-5), and the registers association between CarSharer and Journey (Figure 4-18). Example role names used in this book include the accountHolder role played by Customer in the Customer—Account association (Figures 4-1 and 5-5).

Association multiplicity was introduced as a means of indicating the range of participation of a class in an association as viewed from the other end of the association. Common multiplicity clauses on associations are 1 and *, short for 1..1 and 0..* respectively.

Chapter 5 extended the basic association notation with aggregation and composition. Both these extensions to the association are used to indicate that the nature of the association between two classes is one of *whole-part.* The composition association is a more strict form of association, implying coincident life cycles. In a composition association, when the whole class in the association is destroyed, then any association part classes are also destroyed.

6.1 INTRODUCTION

This Chapter covers the remaining UML notations for associations. These notations represent more specialized semantics which may be used to a greater or lesser extent in the modelling process. All the notations in this chapter are, arguably, less common than the notations covered thus far. This lower rate of use is the primary reason for considering these notations in this separate chapter.

In order to illustrate these notations, the examples used in this chapter may present elements of the common case studies in a slightly differently way to other chapters. Where this has been done, every effort has been made to point out those differences.

6.2 ASSOCIATION END NOTATIONS

The notations covered in this section are all used to add specific meanings to the end of an association where it joins a class. Role names are one such association end notation that has already been covered in Chapter 4. A role name specifies the role played in an association by the class at the end of the association where the role name appears. Figure 6-1 shows an example that was used earlier in this book.

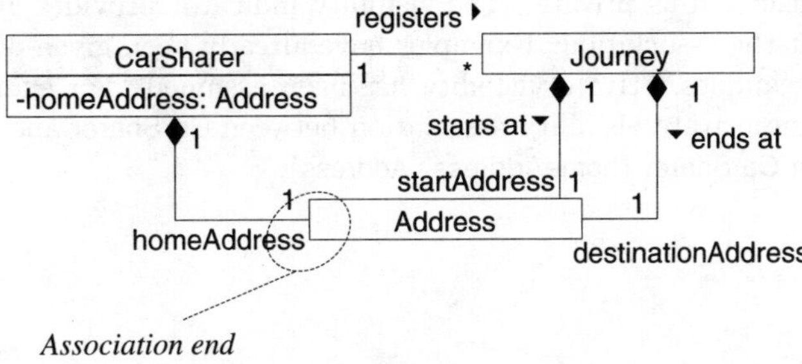

Fig. 6-1: Role name notation

Figure 6-1 shows how the Address class plays the role of homeAddress in the unnamed association with CarSharer. Address also plays the roles of startAddress and destinationAddress in the starts at and ends at associations, respectively, between the Journey and Address classes.

6.2.1 Visibility

A role name can be prefixed with a visibility indicator. Visibility was introduced in Section 4.4.3. Remember that visibility can be shown with the keyword private (or the symbol –), public (+), or protected (#).

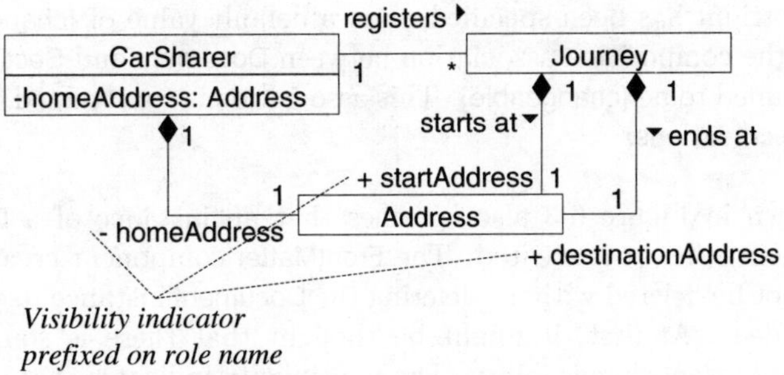

Fig. 6-2: Association visibility shown with role names

The visibility annotation on an association end can be used only as a prefix to a role name. That is to say, association visibility can be used only where a role name has been added to the association end. Figure 6-2 shows an example of the association visibility notation.

EXAMPLE 6.1 What visibility indicators are used in Figure 6-2?

SOLUTION The Address class has private visibility as viewed from CarSharer in the CarSharer—Address association (– homeAddress). The Address class has public visibility as viewed from Journey in both the starts at and the ends at associations between Journey and Address (+ startAddress and + destinationAddress).

The indicator specifies the visibility of the class as perceived when traversing the association towards the role name and visibility indicator. For example, in Figure 6-2, the homeAddress (Address) for a CarSharer should be considered as private. The visibility indicator provides guidance to the designer about how to implement the association. Examples have already been given of the implementation of associations. In those examples, private visibility has been assumed. For example, Figure 6-2 shows the implementation of the private visibility association between CarSharer and homeAddress (Address) as a private attribute on CarSharer (homeAddress : Address).

6.2.2 Changeability

The changeability of an association specifies whether an instance of a class can add or delete instances of the class at the changeability constrained end of the association after it has been created or initialized. The changeability can be changeable, frozen or addOnly and is shown as a constraint. Figure 6-3 illustrates the changeability notation, using the document publishing example seen in Section 5.3.2 .

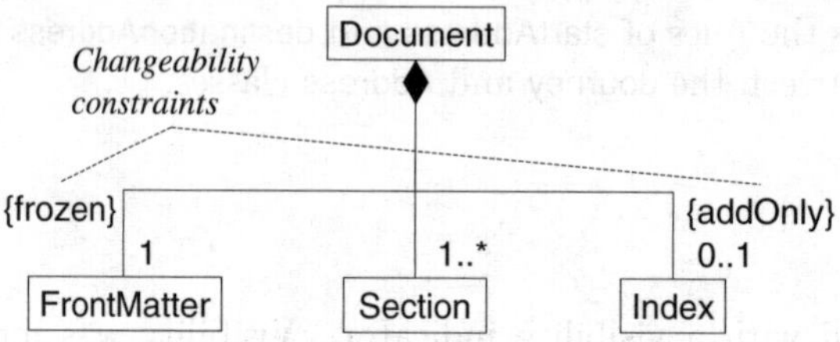

Fig. 6-3: Association changeability constraints

If no changeability constraint has been specified, then a default value of {changeable} is assumed. For example, in Figure 6-3 the composition association between Document and Section has no changeability constraint and so is assumed to be {changeable}. This association is constrained only by the composition and the multiplicity specifications.

The class diagram shown in Figure 6-3 also specifies that an instance of a Document should create one FrontMatter component when it is created. The FrontMatter component created when the Document instance is created cannot be deleted without deleting the Document instance itself. No other FrontMatter components can be added. At first, it might be thought that there is some overlap between the multiplicity of 1 and the {frozen} changeability. The multiplicity indicates that a Document must have a FrontMatter component, and that there can never be more than one FrontMatter component per Document. However, without the frozen changeability constraint, it would be permissible to replace one FrontMatter instance with another. This would not violate the multiplicity. However, the frozen changeability constraint specifies that the FrontMatter instance created with the Document instance cannot be replaced. The association between the two original instances is {frozen}.

Finally, the association between Document and Index has an {addOnly} changeability constraint. Taken in conjunction with the multiplicity and composition, this specifies that a Document instance can be created without an instance of Index being created at the same time. The 0.. part of the multiplicity allows this. When the Document instance is destroyed, then the Index instance must also be destroyed. The coincident life cycle of the composition association specifies this. The {addOnly} changeability constraint specifies that an Index component can only be added to a Document. Once that component has been added it cannot be removed. Taken together with the upper bound of the multiplicity (..1), this means that once an Index component has been added for a Document, it cannot be replaced with another Index component.

6.2.3 Ordering

Where the target of an association has a multiplicity with an upper bound greater than one, it may be necessary to specify whether or not those associated instances have an explicit order.

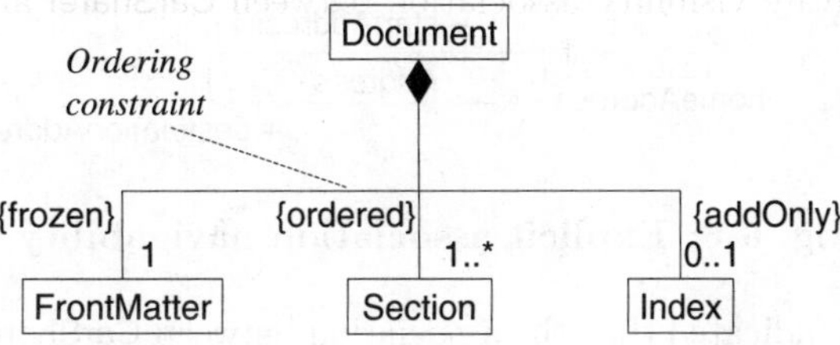

Fig. 6-4: Association ordering constraint

Figure 6-4 shows that the Sections within a Document should be ordered. If an ordering constraint is omitted then the association end is assumed to be {unordered}.

As with other constraints that have already been covered, the ordered constraint should be considered as a specification. The specific mechanism used to implement the ordering is left to the designer of the implementation classes.

Another constraint, {sorted} may be used in a class diagram drawn from an implementation perspective. The sorted constraint refines the ordered constraint. The sorted constraint implies that the ordering is based on the state of the ordered instances. Again, the actual sorting mechanism is not specified by the {sorted} constraint.

6.2.4 Navigability

It is usually assumed that associations can be followed in either direction (indeed this is the UML guideline). This implies that messages can be passed in either direction between two classes connected by an association. For example, in Figure 6-5, the association between CarSharer and Address specifies a path for CarSharer to send a message to Address and also a path for Address to send a message to CarSharer.

This open and general interpretation is fine at the conceptual level, and provides for a general understanding of the class model. However, the design and implementation of a bi-directional association carries an overhead compared to the implementation of an association that is only ever navigated in one direction. This overhead is discussed in more detail in the modelling guidance section for navigability (Section 6.7.4).

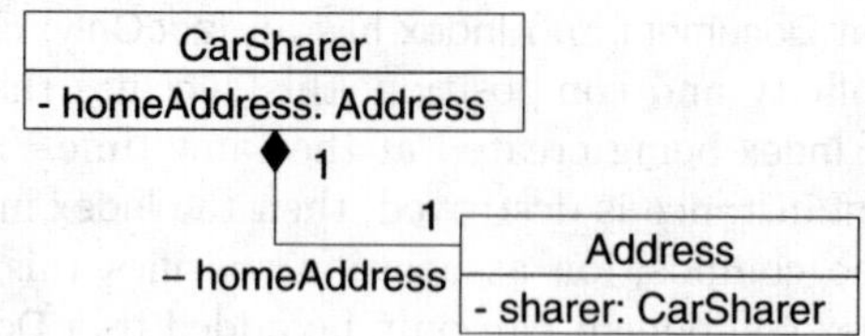

Fig. 6-5: Unspecified association navigability

In UML, an association can be annotated as being navigated in a particular direction by adding an arrow-head to an association to indicate the direction of navigation. Figure 6-6 illustrates this notation.

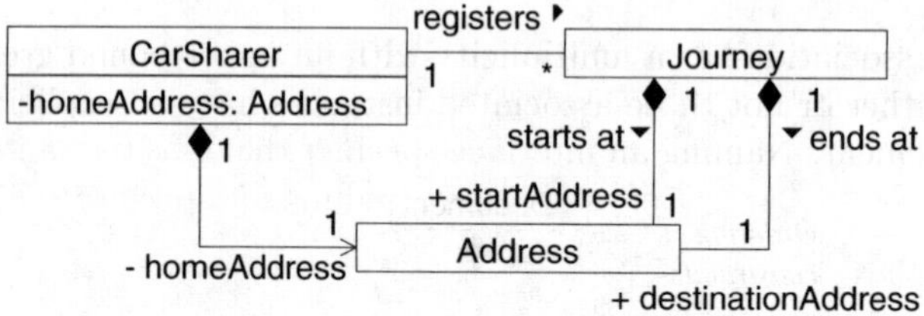

Fig. 6-6: Explicit association navigability

In Figure 6-6 the analyst has indicated that the association between CarSharer and Address is navigated only from CarSharer to Address. More significantly, the annotation shows that it is not necessary to implement navigability from Address to CarSharer.

Navigability arrows can be shown on neither, one or both ends of an association. By convention, omission of navigability implies bi-directional navigability. However, in some software development teams it may be standard practice to implement associations with multiplicity of 1—* (for example, the registers association between CarSharer and Journey) as navigable only from the 1 end (CarSharer) to the * end (Journey). If such a practice is the standard interpretation, then showing navigability arrows for both directions of an association can be used to require explicit bi-directional navigability.

6.2.5 Interface Specifier

Normally, the existence of an association between one class and another would imply that all the public attributes and operations of each class are available to the other class (navigability notwithstanding).

This may not always be the case. The analyst may wish to specify that one class needs only a subset of the publicly visible operations provided by a class in order to fulfil its collaboration requirements with that class. In UML, this can be achieved using an interface specifier. The notation for an interface specifier is shown in Figure 6-7.

The interface specifier is of the form `:<interfaceClassName>`. Adding the interface specifier indicates that the source class (for example, AdminLog) requires only the subset of publicly visible operations of the class named in the interface specifier (for example, Vehicle), rather than the full set of publicly visible operations defined by the target class (for example, Car).

There is a semantic implication that the class upon which the interface specifier is defined (for example, Car) is a specialization of another class, an implementation of an interface class (see Chapter 7), or

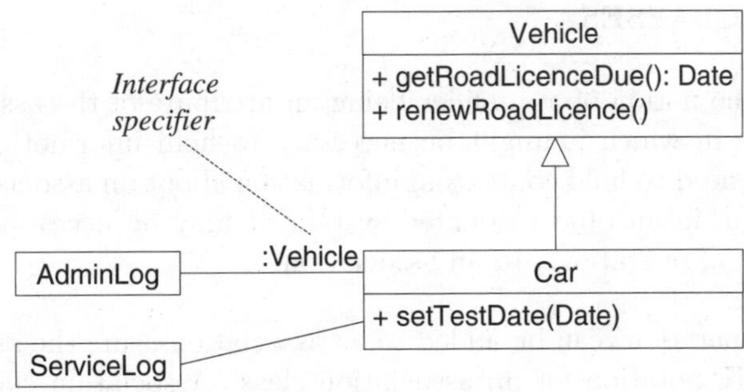

Fig. 6-7: Interface specifier on an association

some other type of refinement. Naming an interface specifier that was the same as the class at the same association end (for example, :Car at Car) would be a redundant specification.

6.3 QUALIFIERS

An association qualifier at the source end of an association specifies a means of identifying zero, one or more of the class instances at the target end of an association.

The UML notation for a qualifier is shown in Figure 6-8. An association qualifier is an attribute list consisting of one or more attributes. Each attribute can be listed as the attribute name on its own, or in the form `name : type`. The qualifier appears in a box that should be slightly smaller than the class symbol and placed adjacent to the class symbol.

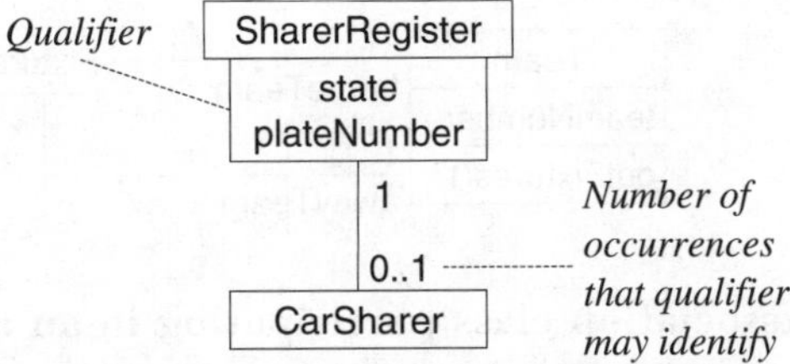

Fig. 6-8: Illustration of notation for qualifiers

The multiplicity at the target end of the qualified association indicates the number of instances that the qualifier may identify. In Figure 6-8, the multiplicity at the target (CarSharer) end of the association is 0..1. The qualifier consists of two attributes, state and plateNumber. If values are known for both of these attributes then, according to the multiplicity given, the qualifier will identify either none or one CarSharer.

The interpretation of the none (0..) depends on the context of the model. In this case it might suggest that state and plate number may not be constrained to be the state and plate number of a car owned by a registered car sharer.

6.4 ASSOCIATION CLASSES

In the previous section, the notion of a qualifier being an attribute of the association was introduced. This is not the only case in which it might be necessary to hold information about the association between two classes. The need to hold contextual information about an association between two classes is not uncommon. Indeed, in an object-oriented system, it may be necessary to delegate functional responsibility, in the form of operations, to an association.

In UML, attributes and operations can be added to an association using the association class notation. Figure 6-9 shows the UML notation for an association class. Association classes are shown with the same notation as other classes on a Class Diagram (See Chapter 4).

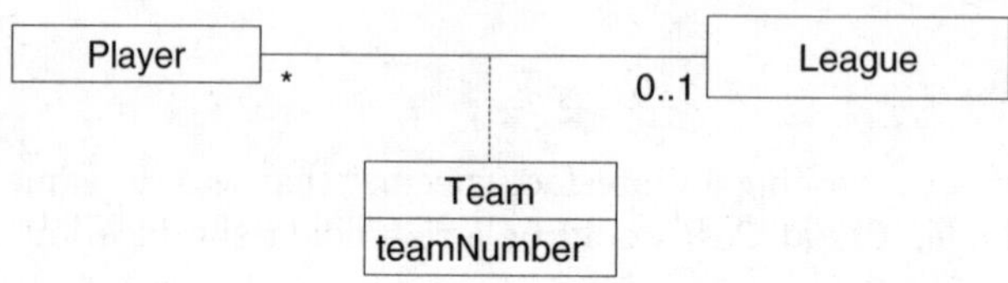

Fig. 6-9: Association class notation

An association class and the association it represents are semantically the same thing. The association class, and the association itself are, however, shown separately in the UML notation. The association class is attached to the association that it represents by a dashed line.

As the association class is the same model artefact as the association, the name of the association class and the association itself are the same. The name of the association can be shown on the association or on the class (as a valid class name).

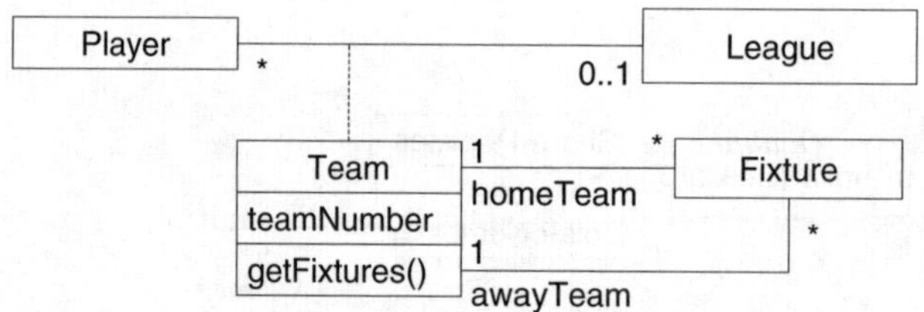

Fig. 6-10: Association class participating in an association

In terms of the underlying semantics of UML, an association class is a specialization of a class and an association. As a specialization of class, association classes may participate in the same types of relationships as other classes (for example, as a superclass in a generalization or in an association). Figure 6-10 illustrates this with the Team association class playing the roles of homeTeam and awayTeam in two associations with Fixture.

6.5 DERIVED ASSOCIATION

The notation for derived attributes was discussed in Chapter 4. The UML notation also allows the specification of derived associations. The notation for derived associations is illustrated in Figure 6-11.

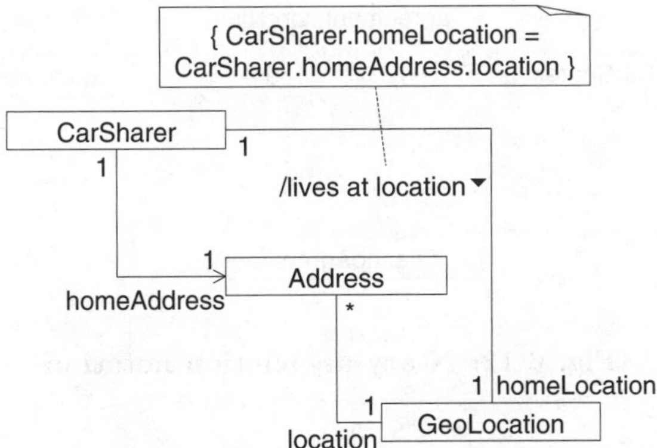

Fig. 6-11: Derived association notation

As with derived attributes, the name of a derived association is prefixed with a / character. The derivation of the association can be shown as a constraint on the class diagram. Figure 6-11 shows a derived association labelled /lives at location between CarSharer and GeoLocation. The specification of the derivation is shown in a method note, which is attached to the association label.

The specification in Figure 6-11 shows that the homeLocation role in the lives at location association can be derived from the associations between CarSharer and Address, and Address and GeoLocation. As with derived attributes, the appropriate use of role names can be helpful in formulating a derivation specification.

EXAMPLE 6.2 How does the multiplicity of the associations traversed in the specification of a derived association affect the multiplicity of the derived association itself?

SOLUTION Looking from the class at the start of the derived association, and traversing to the class at the end of it, the upper and lower bounds of the multiplicity should reflect the highest and lowest multiplicity bounds encountered across all steps of the derivation. For example, in the example shown in Figure 6-11, the lowest multiplicity found in both the CarSharer—Address and Address—GeoLocation associations is 1... Similarly, the highest multiplicity bound encountered is ..1. Therefore, the multiplicity at the homeLocation end of the lives at location association is 1..1 (or 1). The same multiplicity is derived by traversing the associations from GeoLocation to CarSharer.

If the specification had traversed an association with an upper bound of ..* and an association with a lower bound of 0.. then the multiplicity would have been 0..* (or *).

6.6 N-ARY ASSOCIATIONS

The associations that we have considered thus far are binary associations. Binary associations link two classes together. UML also provides a notation for *n-ary associations*, which link three or more classes together.

The UML notation for an n-ary association is a diamond symbol connected to the classes that participate in the association. The notation is illustrated in Figure 6-12.

Figure 6-12 shows an n-ary association. The association is labelled agreement condition. In the present

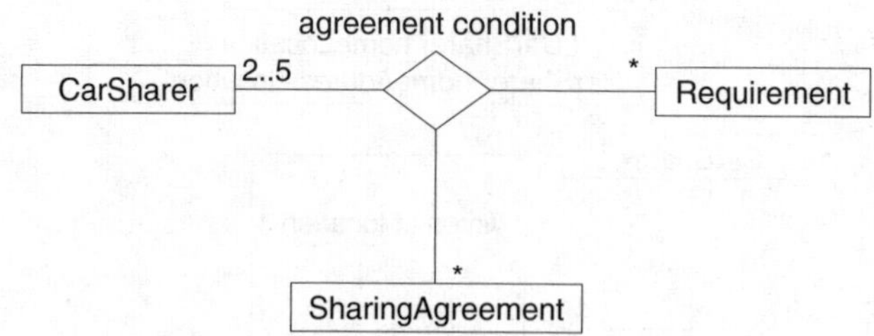

Fig. 6-12: N-ary association notation

example, requirements have been taken to exist independently of CarSharers and are therefore represented by a class. One instance of the agreement condition association would relate instances of CarSharer, Requirement and SharingAgreement with each other.

Multiplicity is more difficult to establish and interpret for n-ary associations than for binary associations. To interpret n-ary association multiplicity, assume that an instance of the n-ary association involves one instance of all bar one of the classes in the association, then read the multiplicity for the remaining class and interpret accordingly.

For example, in Figure 6-12, if one instance of the agreement condition association involves one CarSharer and one SharingAgreement, then between zero and many instances of Requirement will be involved in the association (the * multiplicity of the Requirement class). In other words, an association between CarSharers, SharingAgreements and Requirement may be subject to several (between zero and many) requirements for a car sharer and sharing agreement.

EXAMPLE 6.3 What is the interpretation of the multiplicity of CarSharer and SharingAgreement in Figure 6-12?

SOLUTION Taking one SharingAgreement and one Requirement, an instance of the association will involve between two and five CarSharers. In other words, a SharingAgreement covered by a Requirement could be for between two and five CarSharers.

Taking one CarSharer and one Requirement, an instance of the association will involve between zero and many SharingAgreements.

Role names can be useful in n-ary associations to clarify the nature of the participation of each class in the associations. However, the UML Specification does not permit n-ary associations to use qualifiers, aggregation or composition (Object Management Group, 1999*b*, p.3-74). The use of annotations such as navigability, ordering, changeability and visibility is not prohibited; however, the use of these annotations may be subject to misinterpretation. Given this possibility, caution should be exercised in the use of association end annotations on n-ary associations.

6.7 MODELLING GUIDANCE

This chapter covers relatively specialist annotations that can be used on class diagrams. Given this context, some of the modelling guidance given in this section focusses on the implications of using or not using the annotations. This is particularly true of the following section on association ends.

6.7.1 Association Ends

Visibility

The visibility of an association end can be considered in a way similar to that regarding the visibility of attributes in a class. In object-oriented systems, it is arguably better practice to restrict access to the internal structure of a class. Consider the implications of making an association end public. Figure 6-13 shows an example class diagram used earlier in this chapter.

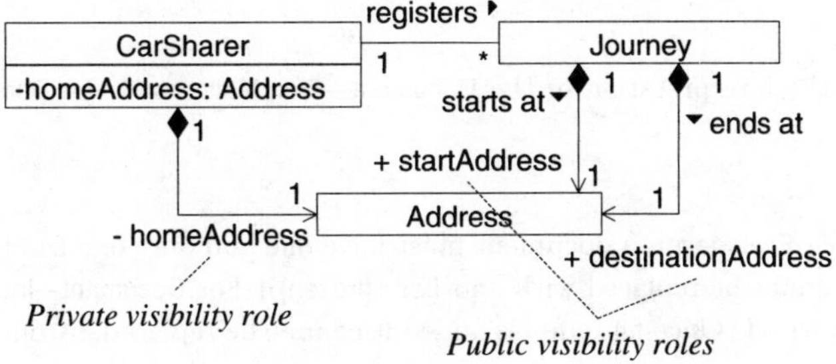

Fig. 6-13: Association end visibility

The startAddress and destinationAddress roles are publicly available. Consider the case where there is a requirement to add a printStartAddresses operation to the CarSharer class. The operation should return the set of addresses that are the start addresses for all the journeys registered by a car sharer.

As startAddress is publicly available, CarSharer could access the instance of Address that is the start-Address of a Journey directly. A specification of this operation might include some code like:

```
forAll(Journey){
    Journey.startAddress.print();
}
```

In other words, for all journeys registered by a car sharer, the printStartAddresses operation will call the print() operation on the instance of Address playing the role of startAddress for that Journey.

At first sight, this approach might seem attractive. The alternative would be to pass a printStartAddress message to each Journey which in turn sends a print() message to its startAddress. This latter approach involves two messages whereas the former approach calls Address.print() directly from CarSharer.

However, this direct calling has a drawback. What would happen if the interface (the set of publicly available operations) on Address were to change, or the method of the print() operation were to change? In this situation, having direct calls to Address operations in classes not directly associated with Address becomes a liability. Tracking down these classes and ensuring that all possible interactions have been re-coded and tested becomes a significant overhead. Instead, it is arguably better practice to keep association end visibility private.

6.7.2 Changeability and Ordering

Changeability constraints can be useful when a class structure has a predefined form that must be adhered to. An illustration of this notion, as applied to document structure was used when the notation was introduced in Section 6.2.2. A slightly amended version of this example is shown in Figure 6-14.

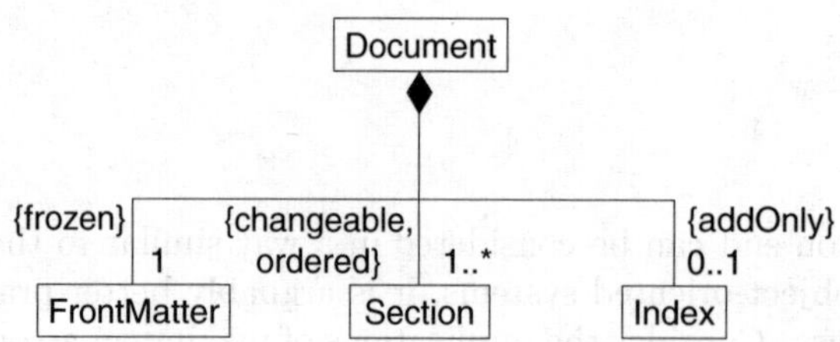

Fig. 6-14: Controlled Document structure

EXAMPLE 6.4 What is the interpretation of the Document—FrontMatter and the Document—Index associations and constraints?

SOLUTION For Document—FrontMatter, a document must have one and only one front matter component. One front matter component cannot be replaced with another ({frozen}). For Document—Index, a document need not have an index when it is created. Once an index is added it cannot be replaced. A document cannot have more than one index.

The {changeable} constraint on Document—Section, taken together with the 1..* multiplicity implies that:

- A document must have one section when it is created (from the multiplicity).
- Sections can be added, removed or replaced (from the changeability constraint) so long as the document always has at least one section (from the multiplicity).

The {ordered} constraint can be useful where the existence of an inherent or explicit order exists across the instances of a class. In Figure 6-14, the ordered constraint on the Document—Section association specifies that the sections that make up a document have an inherent order. The nature of this ordering is not specified. It could, for example, relate to the internal structure of the document within an editor environment, or perhaps to a section number allocated to each section.

6.7.3 Derived Elements

The principles of derivation constraints have already been discussed in the context of derived attributes (Section 4.4.3.3). Taken together with the example discussed in Section 6.5, there is no more to add by way of modelling guidance here.

6.7.4 Navigability

Figure 6-15 shows one possible implementation of a bi-directional association between CarSharer and Address. In this case the association has been implemented as two attributes on the two classes. The homeAddress attribute on CarSharer allows identification of the associated Address instance. The sharer attribute on Address allows the associated CarSharer instance to be identified. Thus two attributes were needed to implement one association. In effect, one attribute is needed for each navigation direction. (It should be noted that different designs could be used to implement the same association.)

As well as this design overhead, there will be a run-time overhead in supporting bi-directional associations. When an Address instance is created as the homeAddress of a CarSharer instance, the Address instance will need to be instructed to point back to the CarSharer instance that created it. If the home address of a CarSharer changes (one instance of Address is replaced by another), then the new Address

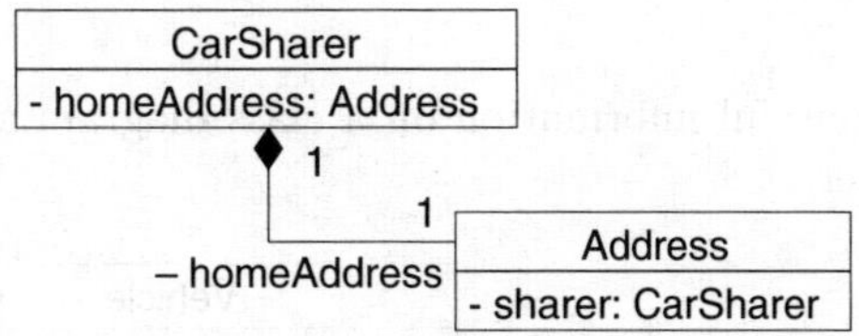

Fig. 6-15: Unspecified association navigability

will need to be associated with CarSharer and the new Address instance will again have to be instructed to point back to the CarSharer. This association maintenance becomes more complicated where the multiplicity is not 1..1.

Specifying navigability for an association can simplify the design and implementation of an association. For example, if the association between CarSharer and Address is specified as navigable only from CarSharer to Address, then it is no longer necessary to implement the sharer : CarSharer attribute on Address (Figure 6-16). Putting a crude metric to this, compared to the example discussed above for Figure 6-15, the specification of uni-directional navigability will halve the design and run-time overhead.

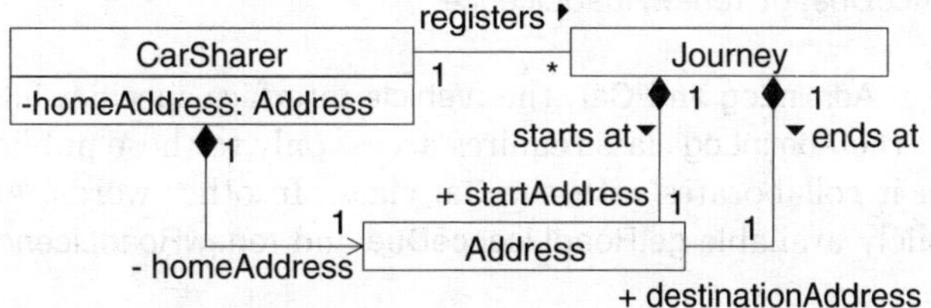

Fig. 6-16: Explicit association navigability

EXAMPLE 6.5 Identify any other associations in the class diagram shown in Figure 6-16 that you think could be uni-directional?

SOLUTION Figure 6-17 shows a probable solution.

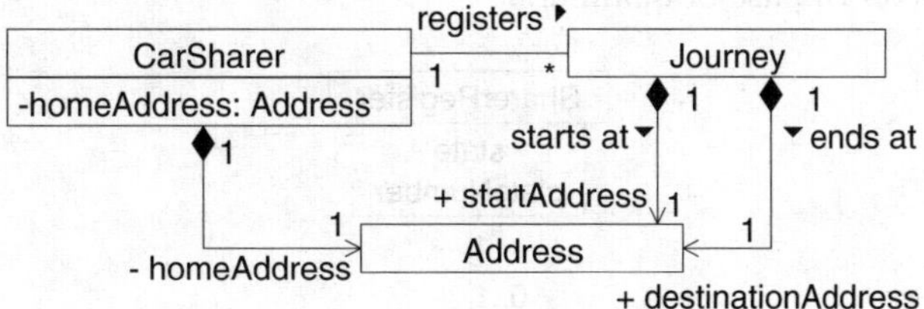

Fig. 6-17: Other uni-directional associations

It might be reasonable to assume that the starts at and ends at associations between Journey and Address will only ever be navigated in the direction from Journey to Address.

6.7.5 Interface Specifier

Interface specifiers can provide useful information on a class diagram as they help to specify the way in which one class treats another.

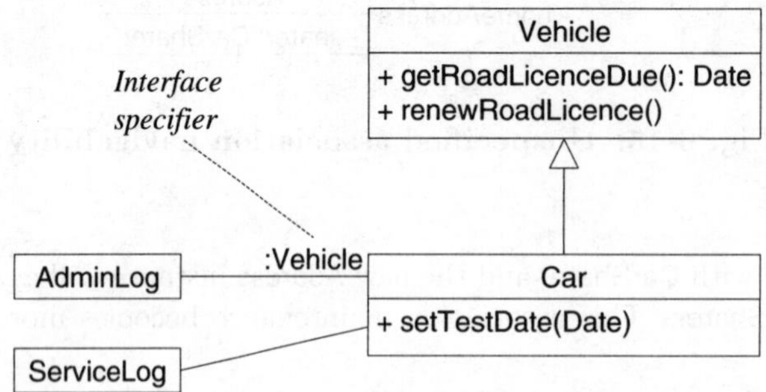

Fig. 6-18: Interface specifier on an association

For example, consider the association between ServiceLog and Car in the class diagram reproduced in Figure 6-18 (from Section 6.2.5). The class model indicates that the ServiceLog class would expect to be able to access any of the operations of the Car class. Specifically, the ServiceLog class could access setTestDate, getRoadLicenceDue, or renewRoadLicence.

In the association between AdminLog and Car, the :Vehicle interface specifier has been used. The use of this specifier implies that the AdminLog class requires access only to those publicly accessible operations of the Vehicle class when it collaborates with the Car class. In other words, AdminLog will expect the Car class to provide publicly available getRoadLicenceDue and renewRoadLicence operations.

There are two specific points to note here. First, AdminLog does not expect to make use of all the publicly available operations of Car. It expects to use only the public operations specified in the Vehicle class. Second, the use of the interface specifier carried the implication that Car must provide the same publicly available operations as Vehicle. It would be unacceptable for Car not to provide getRoadLicenceDue, for example, by overriding the visibility of that operation as private.

6.7.6 Qualifiers

Qualifiers can be useful as a means of specifying how a class may search a set of associated objects using attribute values from the problem domain rather than using specific object identifiers. There are three common variations on the use of qualifiers.

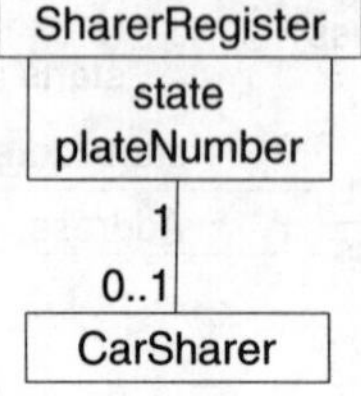

Fig. 6-19: A qualifier with two attributes

Figure 6-19 shows an association between a SharerRegister and a CarSharer. The SharerRegister is CarMatch's list of registered CarSharers. The qualifier consists of two attributes, state and plateNumber.

Taken together, this qualifier and the multiplicity of 0..1 at the CarSharer end of the association indicate that, given values for the two qualifier attributes, it would be possible to identify either none or one CarSharer. The lower bound of the multiplicity (0..) indicates that a state and plateNumber might not identify a CarSharer. The upper bound of the multiplicity (..1) indicates that at most one CarSharer will be identified.

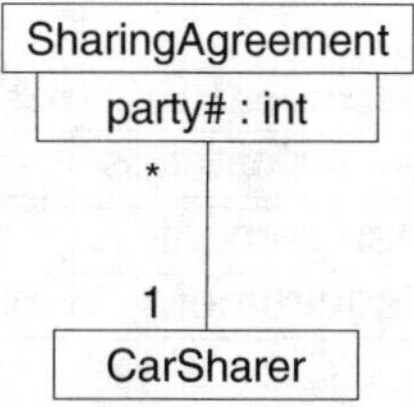

Fig. 6-20: Unique qualifier

The class diagram in Figure 6-20 shows how the parties that are covered by a SharingAgreement can be identified by their party number (party#). In this example, party# is defined as being of type int.

As the lower bound of the multiplicity at the CarSharer end of the association is 1 then the association specifies that a given party# will always identify (at least) one CarSharer. Similarly, as the upper bound of the multiplicity is also 1, then no more than one CarSharer will be identified by a given party#. Putting the upper and lower bounds of multiplicity together, the association specifies that a given party# will always identify one and only one CarSharer in a SharingAgreement.

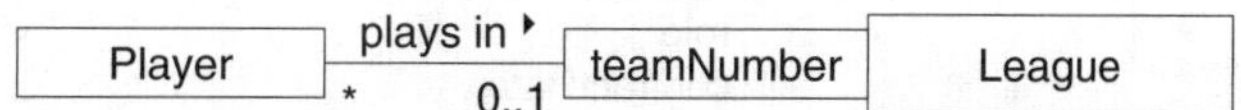

Fig. 6-21: Partitioning qualifier

Finally, Figure 6-21 shows an example of how a qualifier can be used to identify a group of instances. In this case, a teamNumber can be used to identify zero, one or more players in a league. The teamNumber qualifier may not identify any players or it may identify a group of players.

The attribute(s) that make up the qualifier of an association are not attributes of the classes at either end of the association. For example, in Figure 6-21, teamNumber is not an attribute of League or Player. Instead, teamNumber is an attribute of the plays in association between League and Player.

It is intuitively clear that the qualifier attribute is not an attribute of the class at the association end at which the qualifier is placed. For example, if teamNumber were an attribute of League, it would hold multiple values for all the teams in a league. Some kind of link to the actual teams, or the players in those teams would need to be created to instantiate links between leagues and players.

It is perhaps less intuitive that teamNumber is not an attribute of Player. However, the multiplicity of the plays in association allows for players that do not play in a league. In this situation, a teamNumber attribute on Player would not be applicable and would have a null value.

Instead, the teamNumber value is data that is known about the context of a player playing in a league. In other words, it is an attribute of the association itself. If a player is not playing in a league then there is no instance of an association between Player and League and hence no teamNumber value to be held. If a player changes leagues then the context of the association changes, so it is reasonable that the attribute whose value changes is an attribute of the association.

6.7.7 Association Classes

In essence, association classes are used when the association itself has attributes or operations that need to be represented in the class model. One common situation in which association classes are used is to capture the historical or time-based nature of a relationship. Table 6-1 illustrates some examples of possible association classes.

Table 6-1: Examples of historical or time-based association classes

Association	Association class	Possible attributes
Contractor—Project	Assignment	startDate, role, contractRate
CarSharer—RequirementType	Requirement	priority, comment, fromDate, untilDate

One potential indicator that an association class may be required is where it proves difficult to assign attributes to the classes at either end of an association with a *—* multiplicity.

As the association and the association class are one and the same concept, there can only be one occurrence of an association class per occurrence of an association. For example, consider the Contractor—Project association and Assignment association class suggested in Table 6-1. This association is shown in Figure 6-22.

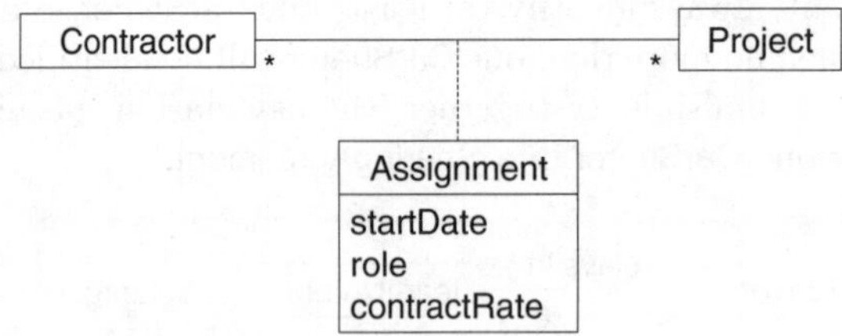

Fig. 6-22: Assignment association class between Contractor and Project

Each assignment of a contractor to a project will result in one occurrence of the association and hence one set of values for startDate, role and contractRate. Where a contractor works on different projects, these three attributes on the association class will hold different values for the different associations. Where a contractor is assigned to the same project a second (or subsequent) time then there can still be only one occurrence of the association between Contractor and Project and hence association class. Thus, the values for startDate, role and contractRate would hold only the latest values for the assignment of a contractor to a project and not a set of historical values.

Modelling this association class as an equivalent set of normal classes and associations would require this 'one association class per association' constraint to be enforced by the multiplicities used. The class diagram shown in Figure 6-23 is not equivalent to Figure 6-22 as it would be possible to create different occurrences of the Assignment class for the same occurrences of Contractor and Project.

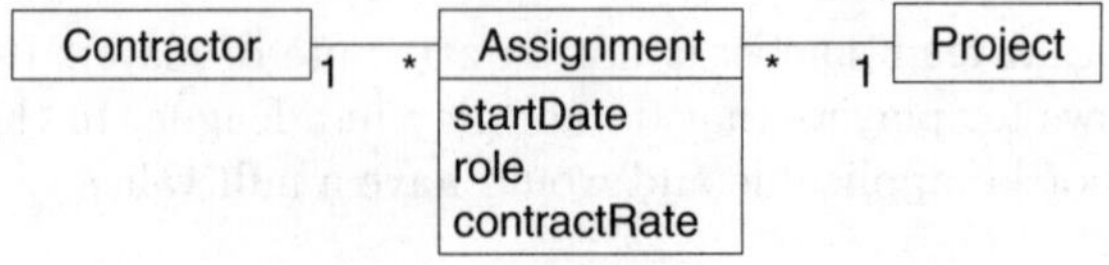

Fig. 6-23: Assignment modelled as class

Thus an association class can be used where the 'one association occurrence, one association class instance' constraint should be enforced. If this is not the case, for example, if a history of assignments of one contractor to one project is required, then the association class should be modelled as a normal class with appropriate associations to the other classes.

6.7.8 N-ary Associations

Section 6.6 introduced the notation for n-ary associations using the example of requirements covered by sharing agreements between car sharers. An investigation of the modelling process that resulted in the use of this notation will illustrate where this notation is useful.

Consider the situation when the analyst begins to model the associations between CarSharer, Requirement and SharingAgreement. Figure 6-24 illustrates some possible occurrences of the associations that need to be modelled.

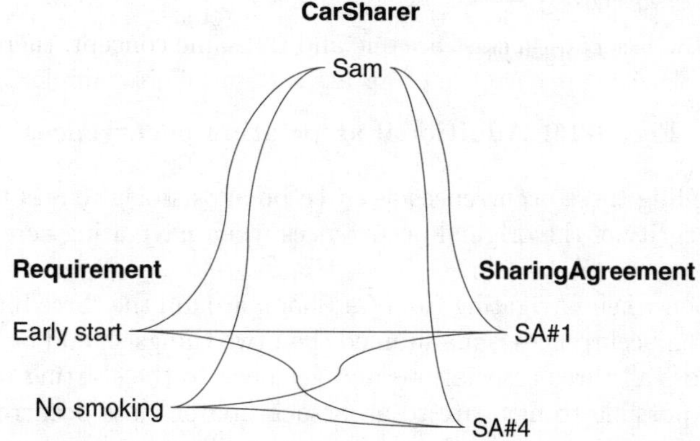

Fig. 6-24: Occurrences of three way association

Figure 6-24 shows that Sam: CarSharer, has two requirements, Early start: Requirement and No smoking: Requirement. Sam participates in SA#1: SharingAgreement and SA#4: SharingAgreement. Both sharing agreements cover the two requirements that Sam has.

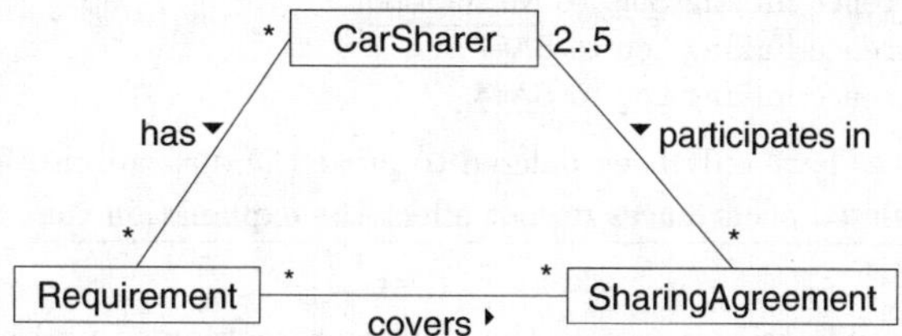

Fig. 6-25: Modelling association occurrences from Figure 6-24

Figure 6-25 shows an initial attempt at modelling these association occurrences. The analyst has modelled three binary associations between the three classes. These binary associations are adequate for the occurrences shown in Figure 6-24. However, if more illustrative occurrences are added, the problem with this binary association structure will begin to become apparent.

Figure 6-26 shows additional occurrences of the associations between the three classes. Lou: CarSharer with requirements of No smoking: Requirement and Allergen filter: Requirement. Lou participates in SA#4:

SharingAgreement with Sam and also in SA#7: SharingAgreement. Both of these sharing agreements cover the requirements of Lou.

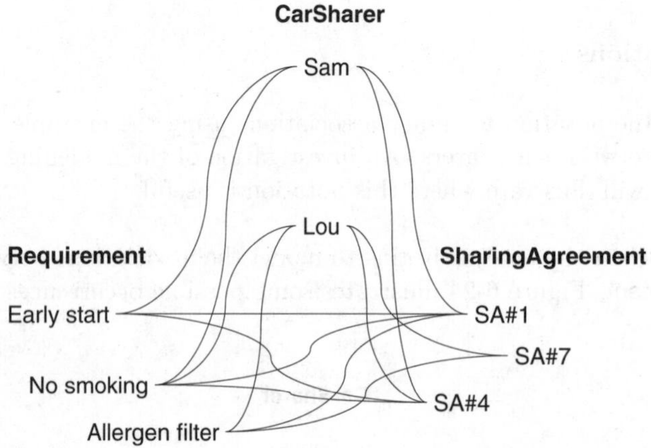

Fig. 6-26: Additional association occurrences

The problem with modelling these occurrences as three binary associations is that it is not possible to preserve the original integrity of the original occurrences when navigating across the associations.

Consider what can happen when navigating from CarSharer around the three binary associations. If the integrity of the association occurrences is maintained then two things should be true. First, it should be possible to navigate across all three associations and get back to the starting point of that navigation. Second, it must not be possible to navigate to an association or class occurrence not covered by the original association occurrences. An example will be used to illustrate these points. Figure 6-27 shows most of the occurrences shown in Figure 6-26.

> ***Aside***
> To make the diagram less cluttered with lines, the following association occurrences have been deleted from Figure 6-27:
>
> - the occurrence linking Sam to Early start
> - the occurrence linking Sam to No smoking
> - the occurrence linking Lou to SA#7
> - the occurrence linking Lou to SA#4
>
> These occurrences have only been deleted to make the diagram in Figure 6-27 easy to read. The deleted occurrences do not affect the explanation that follows.

Starting with Sam, it is possible to traverse to the SharingAgreements in which Sam participates (SA#1 and SA#7). From these occurrences of SharingAgreement, it is possible to navigate to the Requirements satisfied by those SharingAgreements. Here the first problem is encountered. At this point it is possible to navigate from Sam's SharingAgreement SA#1 to the Requirement Allergen filter. This Requirement was met by SA#1, but it was not one of Sam's requirements. Thus it is not possible to navigate from Allergen filter on to Sam, the starting point of this navigation. Continuing with the navigation from SA#1 to No smoking it is then possible to navigate to CarSharer Lou.

The context of this navigation was Sam: CarSharer. Following the occurrences it was possible to get to a Requirement that was not one of Sam's. It was also possible to follow the occurrences through to Lou: CarSharer, a different context to the one the navigation started under. The same loss of integrity will occur regardless of where the navigation starts around the three association structure.

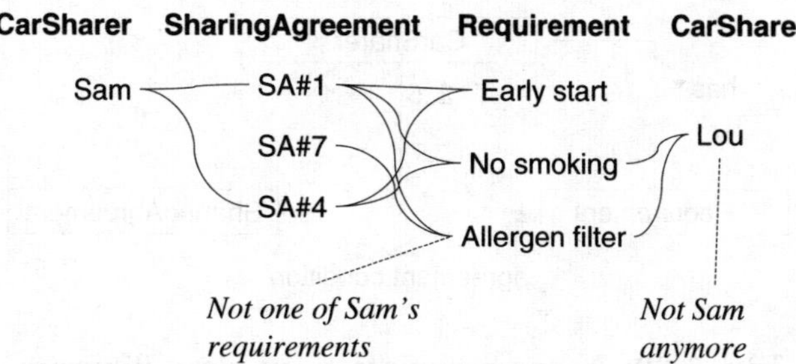

Fig. 6-27: Navigating association occurrences from Figure 6-26

EXAMPLE 6.6 Navigate around the binary associations in Figure 6-26, starting at SA#4: SharingAgreement and the Allergen filter: Requirement in turn. What integrity problems do you encounter?

SOLUTION In brief, it is possible to navigate as follows:

- SA#4—Lou—Allergen Filter (not covered by SA#4)—then to SA#1 or SA#7 (not starting context).
- Allergen filter—SA#1—Sam (does not have Allergen filter as requirement)—then to Early start or No smoking (not starting context).

The conceptual problem here is one of interpretation. Each of the binary associations is valid in its own context. For example, the covers association between the Requirement and SharingAgreement classes is valid as an association between those two classes. It is only when those three separate associations are interpreted as something that links occurrences of all three classes involved that the integrity problems arise.

If there is a conceptual requirement to be able to associate instances of all three classes with each other in one association instance, then an association structure that allows just that is needed. Figure 6-28 illustrates the occurrences of such a three way association, along with the occurrences of the requirements for each car sharer.

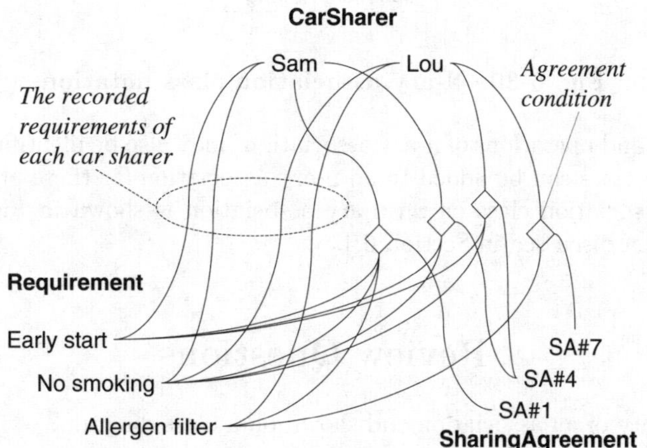

Fig. 6-28: N-ary association occurrences

What Figure 6-28 shows is that there is a hidden type representing occurrences of the association. Each of those occurrences will be associated with occurrences of CarSharer, Requirement and a SharingAgreement. Figure 6-29 models these association and class occurrences as a class diagram.

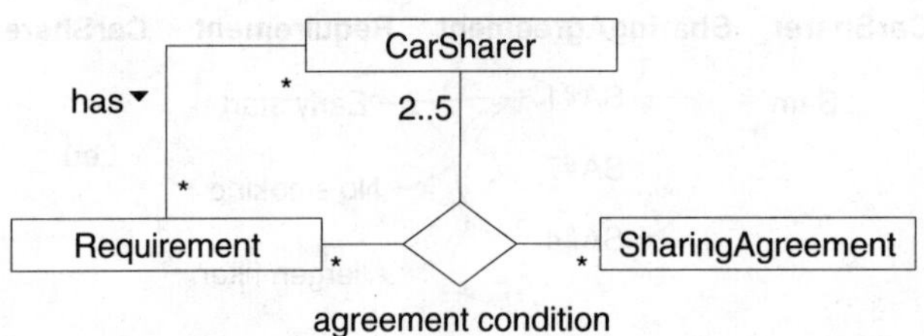

Fig. 6-29: N-ary association on class diagram

The has association between CarSharer and Requirement in Figure 6-29 allows the capture of the requirements for each CarSharer. Those requirements may not yet be satisfied, but they will guide the establishment of sharing agreements to make sure that only those car sharers with the same requirements are put together.

For the sake of clarity it was necessary to limit the number of occurrences shown in these figures. Although it might be inferred from the class and association occurrences used here that all the requirements of a car sharer are met by every agreement they participate in, this is not the intention. The intention is that each occurrence of the n-ary association will meet some, but not necessarily all of the requirements of the car sharers involved in the association. Thus the requirements that are covered will need to be included in the association. The agreement condition association relates car sharers and their requirements to sharing agreements.

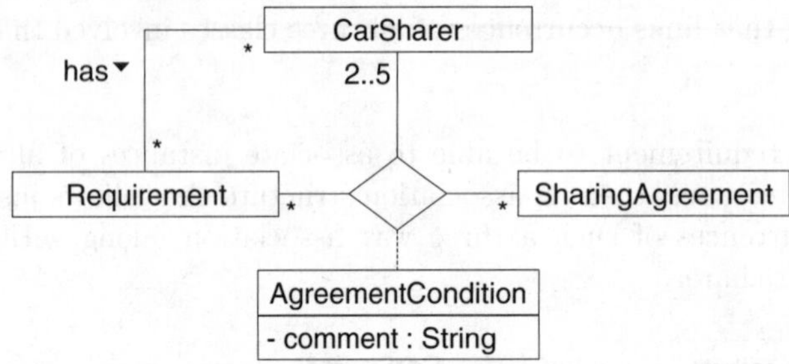

Fig. 6-30: N-ary association class notation

The need for attributes and operations of n-ary associations may also be identified during the modelling process. An association class can be added to an n-ary association for these attribute and operations. The notation for an association class on an n-ary association is shown in Figure 6-30. Association classes have already been discussed in Section 6.4.

Review Questions

6.1 How is the visibility of an association end shown on a class diagram?

6.2 What are the three changeability constraints defined in UML? What is the meaning of each of the three constraints?

6.3 What is the notation for specifying that the objects involved in an association should be ordered?

6.4 How is association navigability shown in UML? Under what circumstances might it be necessary explicitly to specify an association as having bi-directional navigability?

6.5 What is implied by the addition of an interface specifier to an association end? What is the notation for an interface specifier?

6.6 Discuss the meaning of qualifiers as used on a class diagram.

6.7 What features do derived attributes and derived associations share?

6.8 How can a single association that involves more than two classes be modelled in UML?

6.9 If an association is found to have attributes or operations, how can these be modelled in UML?

Solved Problems

6.1 Figure 6-31 shows a class diagram first used for Problem 4.4.

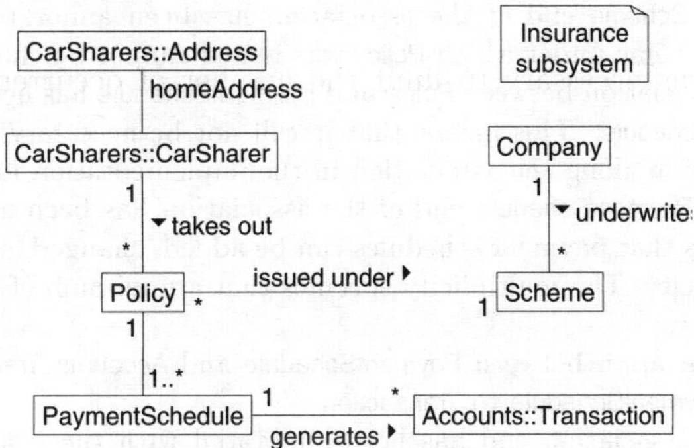

Fig. 6-31: Core Insurance package class model

Annotate the class diagram shown in Figure 6-31 with the changeability and ordering constraints and the navigability suggested in the following transcript. (For the purposes of this question, assume that bi-directional navigation needs to be explicitly specified).

Mick Perez: Can you tell me a little bit more about these insurance classes. [Mick shows Janet the class diagram in Figure 6-31]. I'd like to clarify how some of the information represented here is used. What kind of cross-referencing will you want to do?
Janet Hoffner: Well, when we're analyzing our sales figures we'll need to know which policies were sold under each scheme.
MP: What about needing to know the scheme that a policy was issued under?
JH: Oh yes, we'll need to know that whenever we look at the details of the policy. We'll also need to know the payment schedules for a policy.
MP: Whilst we're in that area—I assume that the scheme that a policy is issued under doesn't change?
JH: That's right. Payment schedules can change though. Sometimes people need to change or amend the way they're paying.
MP: Do you ever need to be able to look-up the policy for a payment schedule?... or the payment schedule that a transaction was paid under?
JH: No and no. Of course we do need to be able to list the payment schedules for a policy as I just said. We'll also need to list the payment transactions made under a payment schedule.
MP: OK—just to finish this bit off, can we look at the transactions? We're into financial regulation territory here. Is it a case of 'normal rules apply'?
JH: Depends what you mean by 'normal rules'. We aren't allowed to delete or amend paid transactions. We can archive them after five years, but not delete them. That means they build up over time. When we list transactions we do it in date order.
MP: OK, that's great. Thanks very much.

Figure 6-32 shows the portion of the model which has been annotated.

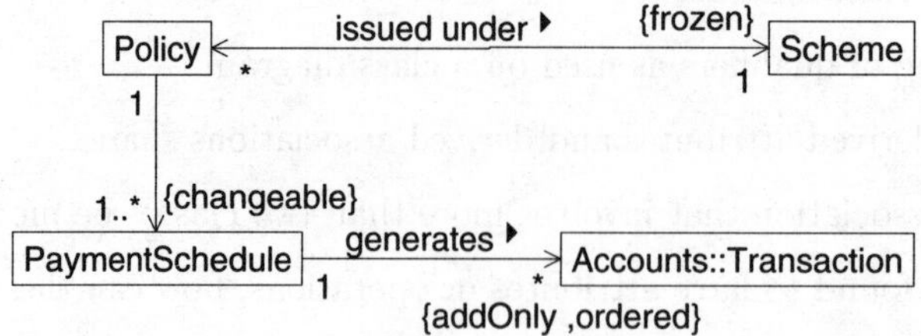

Fig. 6-32: Association end annotations for core Insurance package class model

In Figure 6-32 the following annotations have been made:

- The issued under association between Policy and Scheme has been annotated as bi-directional. This means that navigation support will be implemented in both directions for the association. Furthermore, the Scheme end of the association has been annotated as {frozen}. This constraint implies that the scheme under which Policy was issued cannot be changed.
- The unlabelled association between Policy and PaymentSchedule has been annotated as navigable from Policy to PaymentSchedule. This means that it will not be necessary to directly support navigation in the other direction along the association in the implementation model.
  Furthermore, the PaymentSchedule end of the association has been annotated as {changeable}. This constraint specifies that payment schedules can be added, changed and removed within the confines of the 1..* multiplicity. The multiplicity specifies that a minimum of one payment schedule must be in force for a policy.
- The generates association between PaymentSchedule and Accounts::Transaction has been annotated as navigable from PaymentSchedule to Transaction.
  Furthermore, the association end has been annotated with the {addOnly ,ordered} constraint. The addOnly component specifies that new transactions can be added, but old transactions cannot be deleted or changed. This might seem reasonable in order to comply with financial record keeping regulations. The ordered component of the constraint suggests that the transactions for a PaymentSchedule will be ordered. The fact that the ordering is date based has not been shown, but could be mentioned in a note attached to the ordered constraint.

6.2 Figure 6-33 shows a specification class diagram that includes classes to collate the instances of the CarSharer and Journey classes that will be held in the CarMatch system.

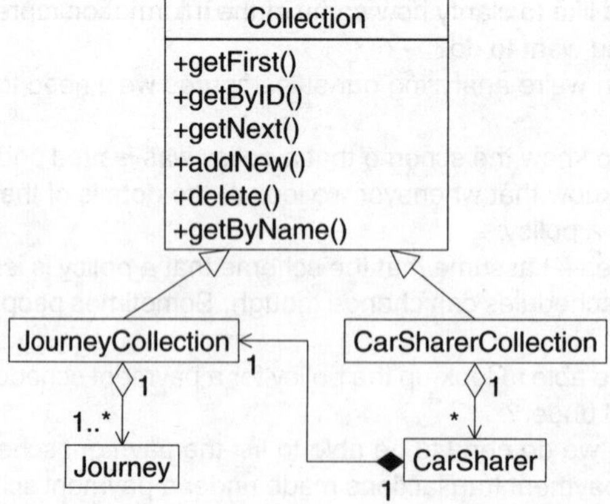

Fig. 6-33: Collection classes for Journey and CarSharer

This class diagram treats the relationship between CarSharer and Journey slightly differently from previous examples. In this example, the relationship is realized by the JourneyCollection collection class. This JourneyCollection class is a component of CarSharer.

It has been determined that CarSharer will require only the generic Collection public operations in its interactions with JourneyCollection. How could this be shown on the class diagram? Annotate the diagram to include an appropriate representation of this requirement.

An interface specifier :Collection could be added to the JourneyCollection end of the CarSharer to JourneyCollection association.

6.3 One interpretation of the +getByName() operation on Collection in Figure 6-33 is that name is a qualifier of the association between CarSharerCollection and CarSharer. Redraw this association to include name as a qualifier. Assume that a value for name might not identify any car sharers, or that it might identify several.

Figure 6-34 shows both the interface specifier from Problem 6.2 and the qualifier for this question.

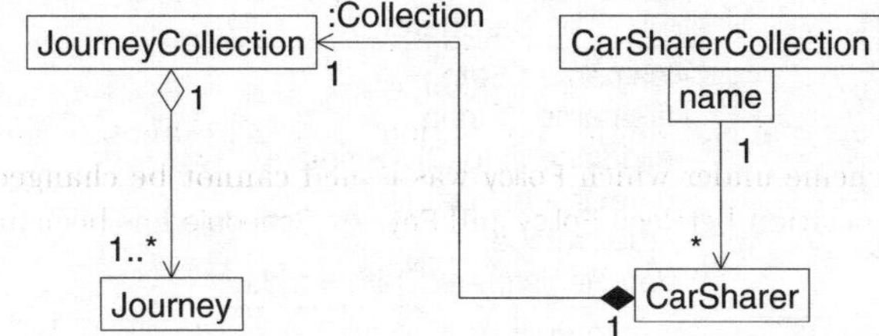

Fig. 6-34: Qualifier and interface specifier annotations added

6.4 (This problem extends the CarMatch case study by introducing elements that are not used elsewhere. Do not worry about integrating this class model with others already produced).

One member service that CarMatch are considering offering is evening talks. The talks would be led by an invited speaker. Occasionally two speakers are used for one talk. The talk will require booking a set of venues. For example, a talk on defensive driving might involve one of CarMatch's seminar rooms for a talk and the parking lot for a hands-on session. Other talks, such as driving to maximize fuel economy would be purely classroom based. Registered car sharers can book a place on a talk. When a talk is first scheduled, a speaker and venue will be known but no car sharers will be booked onto it yet. CarMatch want to be able to extend the proposed system to support a diary of these talks.

Model these requirements as an n-ary association with an association class, adding suitable attributes and operations to any new classes.

Figure 6-35 shows a basic class model showing the multiplicity of the n-ary association.

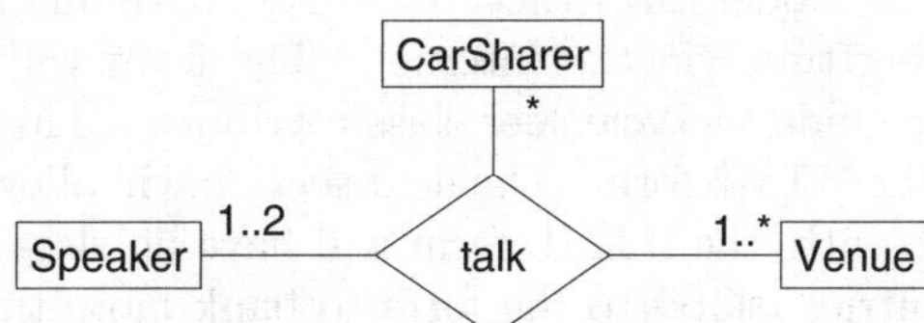

Fig. 6-35: N-ary association for CarMatch evening talks

One occurrence of talk could involve—

1. Between zero and many CarSharers. A talk can be set up with no CarSharers booked on it. CarMatch did not indicate that there was a maximum number of people that could be booked on a talk but there probably is. Even if a specific upper bound to the multiplicity is established of, say, 24, the association will probably be implemented in the same way as for *. If the upper bound were relatively low, that is, only two or three, then the implementation might be different.

2. One or two 1..2 Speakers. The scenario indicated that a talk has a speaker when it is arranged. It was also suggested that two speakers is the normal limit. Care should be exercised in specifying an upper bound of 2 here though. A legitimate implementation of an upper bound multiplicity of 2 would be to have two attributes of type Speaker. In such an implementation a third speaker could not be added under any circumstances. It is wise to check carefully with the stakeholders in such cases.
3. One or more Venues. In line with the discussion about upper bounds in the previous paragraph, the upper multiplicity bound has been modelled as * to allow for a talk with more than the normally envisaged number of venues (for example, a roaming talk on map reading). The lower bound is one, as a talk has at least one venue arranged when it is set up.

Figure 6-36 shows a second draft of the class model.

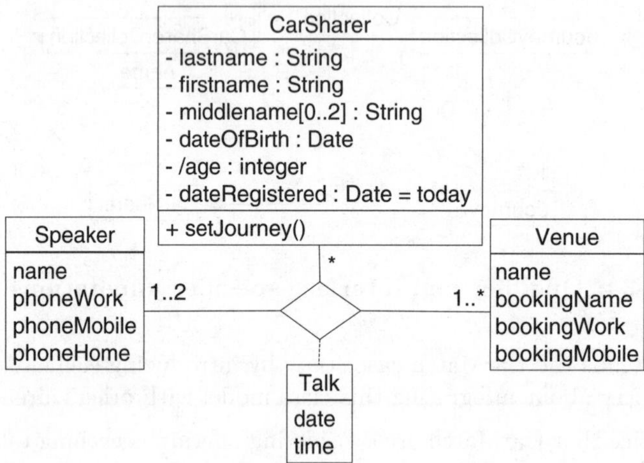

Fig. 6-36: N-ary Association class for CarMatch evening talks

Possible attributes have been added for Speaker, Venue and Talk. The attributes and operations of the CarSharer class used in an earlier chapter have been included here. The Talk association is now represented by an association class.

Supplementary Problems

6.5 VolBank have asked you to model the structure of their (dynamic) HTML form-based interface for registering and banking time via the Internet. The form will have one section relating to the volunteer. This will include the Volunteer class attributes. This section must be present and cannot be removed from the HTML form. The next section will allow the entry of time availability as banked time. To begin with, the HTML form will have no slots for banking time. It must be possible to add further entries (slots) to the form to bank more time. It will not be possible to remove time entries (slots) from the HTML form. In terms of the underlying classes to process the HTML form, it will be necessary to only navigate from the form object down to the volunteer section and each of the banked time entries.

Model the above requirements as a class diagram showing changeability and ordering constraints and navigability.

6.6 Problem 5.5 introduced the notion of an Assignment of a Volunteer to a Project (Volunteering Opportunity). Figure 6-37 shows one possible structure for this part of the class model (attributes and operations have been suppressed).

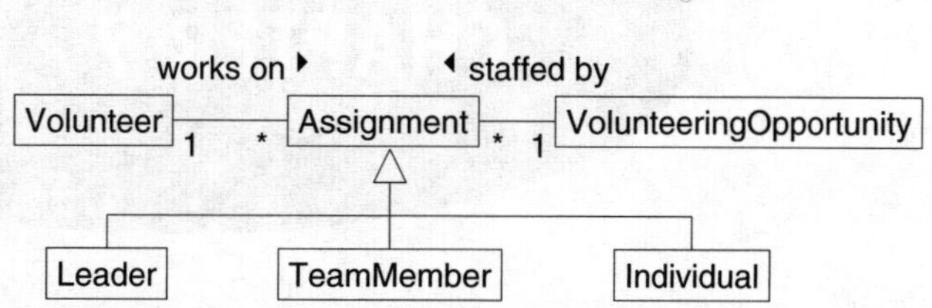

Fig. 6-37: Assignment of Volunteer to VolunteeringOpportunity modelled as class

Redraw Figure 6-37 using an n-ary association and association class. Add the attributes and operations you identified in Problem 5.6.

CHAPTER 7

Class Diagram Other Notations

7.1 INTRODUCTION

The previous three chapters have introduced the major notational elements of class diagrams and certainly those most commonly encountered. This chapter covers the remaining notational elements provided by UML to model class structures. These notations represent specialized semantics that, with the exception of the object notation, may well be encountered only rarely.

As with the previous chapter, the examples used in this chapter may present elements of the common case studies slightly differently to other chapters in order to illustrate the notations covered here. Where this has been done, every effort has been made to point out those differences.

7.2 OBJECT RELATED NOTATIONS

7.2.1 Object Instances

The basic notation for showing object instances on a class diagram has already been introduced in Chapter 4. The name compartment of the object shows the name of the object instance and its class type. The name of an object is of the form `objectName:className`, all underlined.

Figure 7-1 shows some examples of the basic object notation. For example, aDocument: Document, or salesReport: Document. As with classes, the class name can be preceded by the class pathname, for example newPolicy: Insurance::Policy. The name of the object instance can be omitted, resulting in an anonymous object such as :CarSharer.

From a conceptual perspective and in implementation environments that support multiple inheritance, it is quite possible for an object to be an instance of more than one class at the same time. In

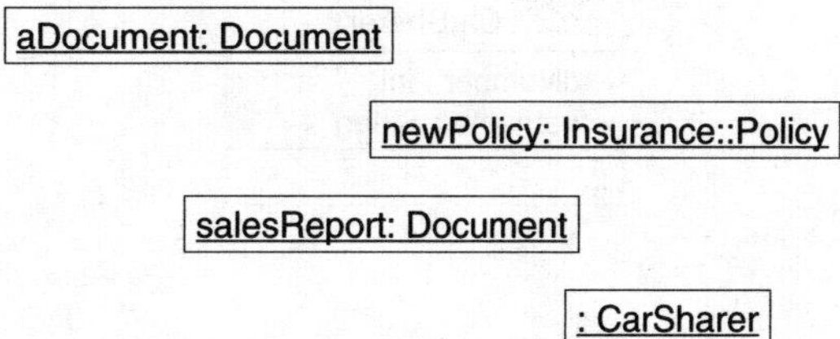

Fig. 7-1: Notation for object instances

UML, multiple class names can be specified for an object in a comma-separated list. Thus the object name compartment can contain a value of the form `objectName : ClassNameA, ClassNameB,...`. For example, aYacht : WindPoweredBoat, MotorPoweredBoat.

One final notational option supported in the object name compartment is to specify that an object is an instance of a class in a particular state. (See Chapter 11 for a discussion of state). The abstract notation for specifying the class state of an object is `objectName : className[stateName]`. For example, an object specified as : SharingAgreement[Provisional] is an anonymous instance of the class SharingAgreement in the Provisional state.

As objects represent occurrences of a classes, some or all of the attributes will hold values reflecting the properties of the object instance. Figure 7-2 shows the notation for specifying the attribute values of objects. The basic notation is of the form `attributeName:type=value`. Figure 7-2 shows two attributes in this form, lastname and age. Age is also a derived attribute. The type of an attribute value must be compatible with the type of the attribute on the class. As such the attribute type in an object can be omitted as it is not needed. The other attributes in Figure 7-2 use the more concise `name=value` notation.

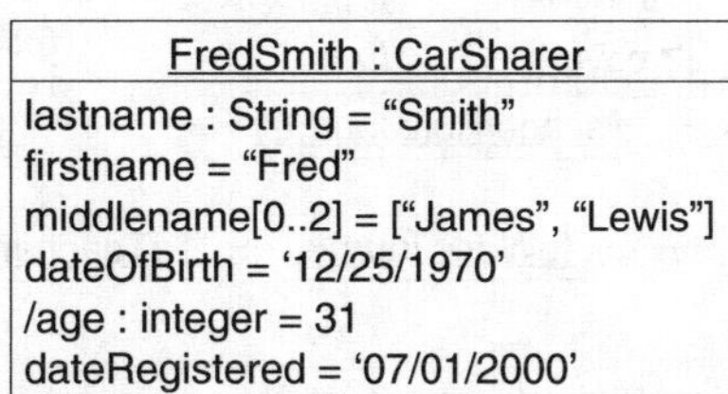

Fig. 7-2: Notation for object attributes

7.2.2 InstanceOf Relationship

Objects are instances of classes. UML provides a notation to link an object to its class. This notation is shown in Figure 7-3.

The object is linked to the class that it is an instance of by a dashed, arrow-headed line with the «instanceOf» stereotype keyword placed near the relationship.

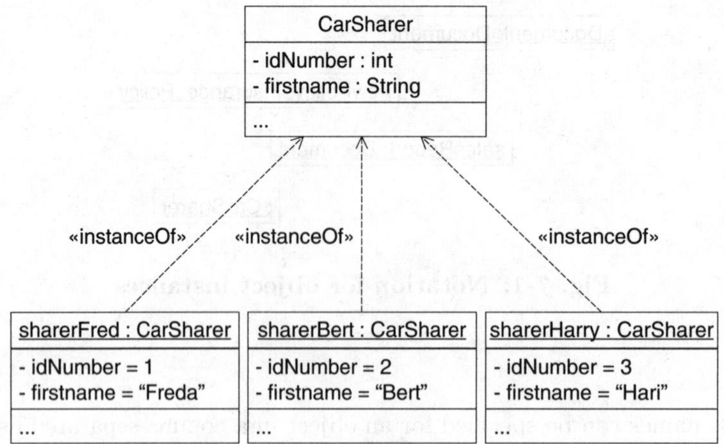

Fig. 7-3: Notation for *object is «instanceOf» class* semantic

7.2.3 Links

As well as showing instances of classes, in the form of objects, instances of associations can be shown between objects. This concept has already been introduced informally in the discussion of multiplicity and n-ary associations in preceding chapters.

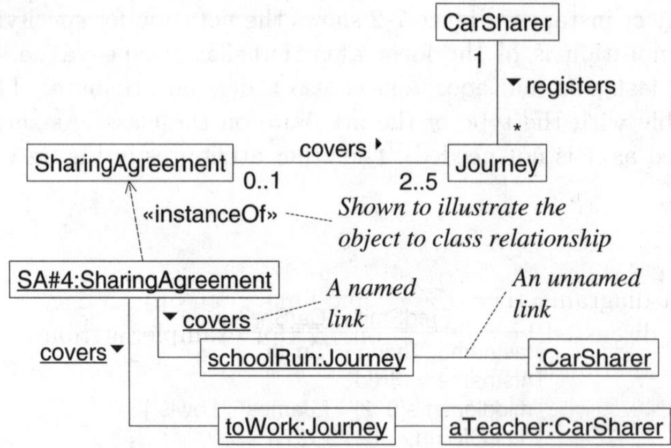

Fig. 7-4: Links between objects

Figure 7-4 illustrates the UML notation for links between objects. A link is shown as a solid line between the objects that it connects. For n-ary associations, links are shown as a small diamond connected by a solid line to each object participating in the link (Figure 7-5).

The name of the association can be added to a link, as shown in Figure 7-4. In the same way that object names are underlined to distinguish them as instances of a class, the association name label is underlined to indicated that the link is an instance of an association.

Role names can be used on links in the same way as they are shown on associations. Multiplicity is not shown for links as each link connects single instances of objects (the multiplicity would always be 1—1). Aggregation, composition and navigation annotations may be shown so long as they are consistent with the association that the link is an instance of. Qualifier instances can also be used at an instance level.

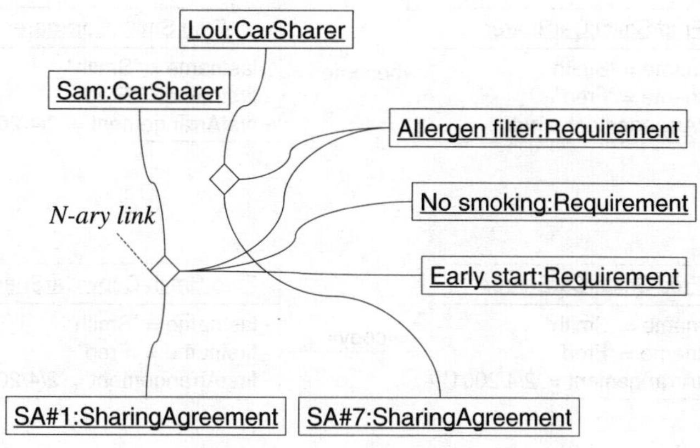

Fig. 7-5: N-ary links

Figure 7-6 illustrates the use of qualifier instances with objects.

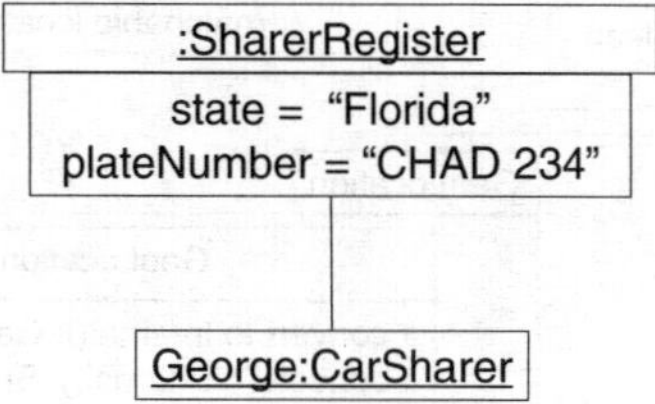

Fig. 7-6: Instance of association qualifiers

7.2.4 Object Diagram

An object diagram can be constructed from objects and links. Figures 7-4, 7-5 and 7-6 are all illustrations of simple object diagrams. The objects and links in an object diagram can incorporate any of the notational elements discussed here in Section 7.2 (for example, attribute values, link role names, class state). Such a diagram might be useful during the elaboration phase of the development process to examine the state of classes and associations between them.

An object diagram consisting of objects and links shows a snapshot of a system at an instant in time. Objects will therefore have a fixed state on an object diagram. UML also provides a notation to indicate the effect of changes to an object's state using «become» and «copy» relationships as shown in Figure 7-7.

Although the object instances Fred Smith and Fred Smith Copy have the same state, they are different instances and will have different object identifiers in the underlying implementation system.

7.3 DEPENDENCY

Dependencies can be used to specify relationships between different model elements. The UML notation for a dependency is a dashed, arrow-headed line. The line goes from the dependent model element to the model element upon which the dependency exists. Figure 7-8 illustrates this notation.

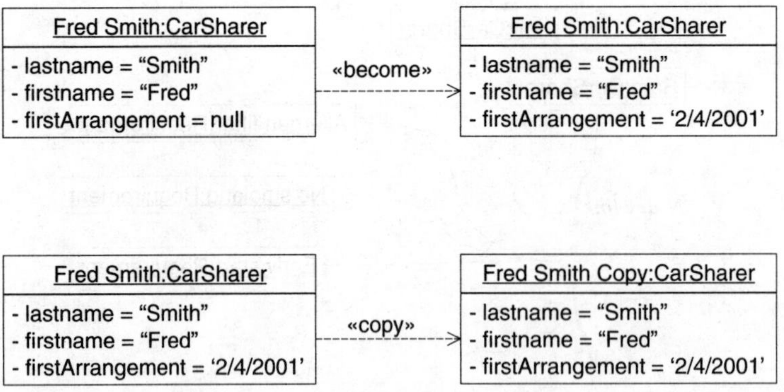

Fig. 7-7: Indicating state change in an object diagram.

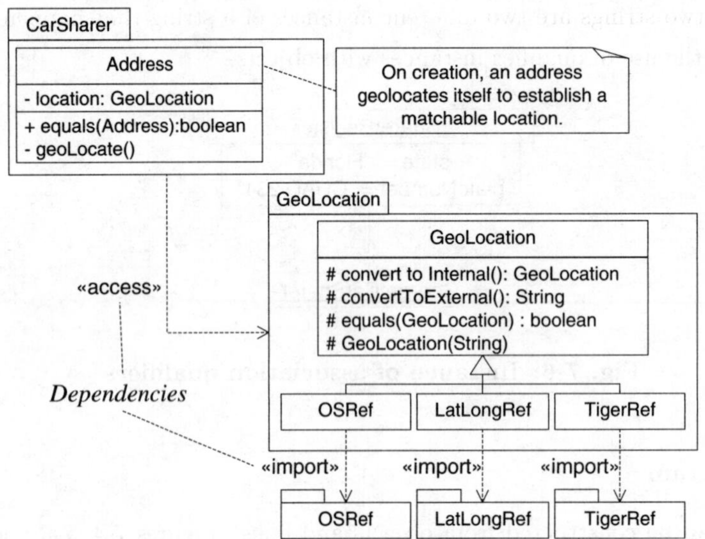

Fig. 7-8: Dependency relationships

In Figure 7-8, the access dependency between the CarSharer and GeoLocation packages indicates that the public classes in the GeoLocation package will be available to classes in the CarSharer package. Not all the classes in the GeoLocation package may be publicly available. Associations cannot be created between CarSharer classes and non-public classes within the GeoLocation package.

Dependencies can be drawn with diverging or converging paths. Figure 7-9 shows an example of diverging dependency paths. Where dependency paths diverge, as with the «refine» dependency of Yacht on WindPoweredBoat and MotorPoweredBoat, a note is attached to the point of divergence to clarify the dependency. With a converging dependency path, the note is attached to the point of convergence.

7.4 CLASS-SCOPE FEATURES

Attributes and operations are normally assumed to be the features that will be manifested by object instances of a class, in other words, they have instance-scope. Different objects will hold different

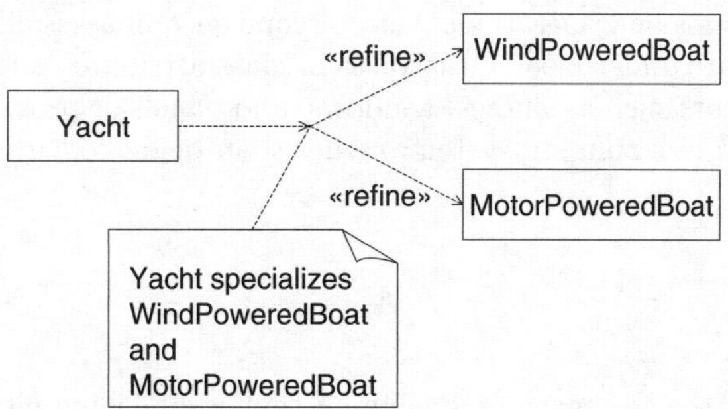

Fig. 7-9: Diverging dependency paths

attribute values for the same class attribute. Two different objects could both have a name attribute set to Fred but those two strings are two different instances of a string that happen to have the same string value.

Sometimes it is desirable to have a class attribute that has the same value across all object instances of a class. Figure 7-10 shows an example of this. In Figure 7-10, three instances of the CarSharer class sharerFred, sharerBert and sharerFred2 are shown. These instances were created one after another.

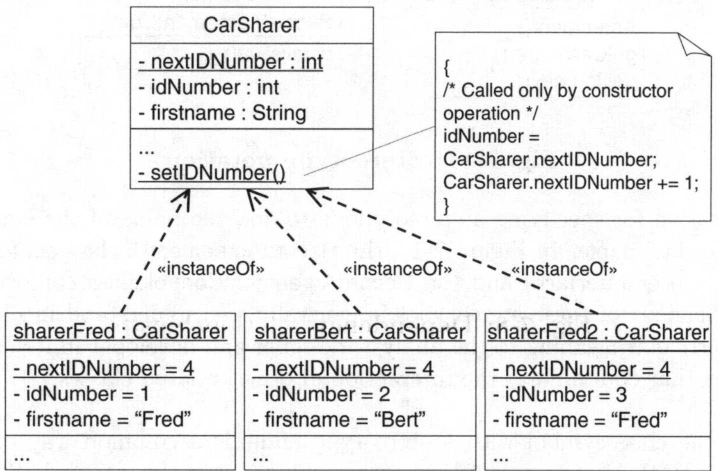

Fig. 7-10: Class-scope features

In this example, the CarSharer class also specifies a class-scope attribute, nextIDNumber, and a class-scope operation, setIDNumber. The class-scope attribute holds the same value over all instances of CarSharer. The nextIDNumber is used by setIDNumber to assign an incrementing IDNumber to each instance of a class on creation. As each instance is created and fires the setIDNumber operation, the value of nextIDNumber is incremented ready for access by the next instance of CarSharer to be created.

Figure 7-10 shows the instances after the creation of sharerFred2. At this point in time, nextIDNumber has a value of 4. When sharerFred was created, nextIDNumber had a value of 1, which was assigned to this instance. At the later point in time that is shown in Figure 7-10, nextIDNumber has been incremented through the creation of sharerBert then sharerFred2.

In UML, class-scope attributes and operations, whose scope encompasses all instances of a class rather than individual instances, are underlined. Other uses of class attributes might include: setting default sizes for graphical components such as shapes, windows, and panels or providing default values for text strings that can be changed in a running system, rather than being coded into an operation.

7.5 CLASS TYPES

Stereotyping is used in UML as a means of specifying that a modelling element conforms to the well understood pattern of behaviour or existence of the named stereotype. Stereotyping is used extensively in the UML Specification (Object Management Group, 1999*b*; Object Management Group, 1999*c*). In this section, the general notation for stereotypes is introduced first, followed by some specific examples of stereotypes provided by UML.

7.5.1 Stereotype

In the context of class diagrams, the stereotyping mechanism is normally applied to classes, associations and other dependencies between classes. Figure 7-11 shows the basic notation for specifying the stereotype of a class.

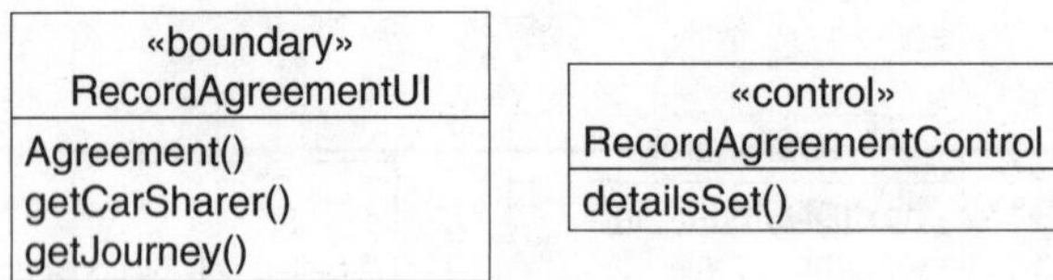

Fig. 7-11: Stereotype notation

The basic UML notation for specifying a stereotype is to add the name of the stereotype enclosed in guillemets above the class name. In Figure 7-11, the RecordAgreementUI class conforms to the «boundary» stereotype (as a user interface) and the RecordAgreementControl class conforms to the «control» stereotype. The behaviour of these stereotypes is generally well understood in object-oriented modelling and carries particular meaning to the analyst, designer and developer in its use. (For example, a «control» class is one that co-ordinates the interaction of other, related classes.)

The annotation of the class symbol with a stereotype name is a common way of specifying a class stereotype. However, UML also supports other notational means of stereotyping. Stereotyping came to UML through Jacobson's early work on object-oriented modelling (Jacobson et al., 1992). Jacobson et al. (1992) used iconic representation of three class stereotypes; boundary (which includes, for example, user interfaces), control and entity, as illustrated in Figure 7-12.

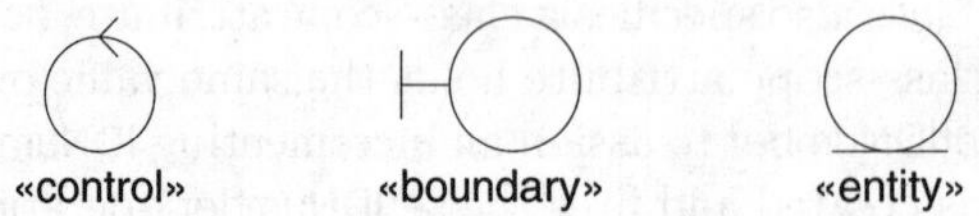

Fig. 7-12: Jacobson's three stereotype icons

UML permits the use of these iconic stereotypes (or, indeed, any other user-defined icon) to show the stereotype of a class. For example, Figure 7-13 shows the same stereotype specification as Figure 7-11. However, Figure 7-13 uses the iconic representation of the stereotypes.

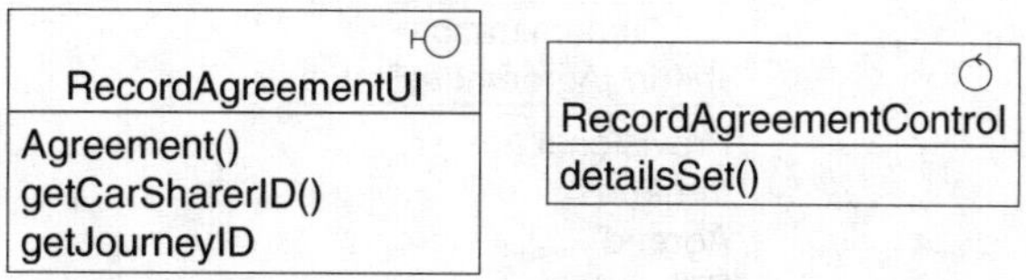

Fig. 7-13: Stereotype icon in class symbol

In line with Jacobson's original work, UML permits the class symbol to be collapsed to just the icon of the stereotype and the name of the class. Figure 7-14 illustrates this minimalist notation.

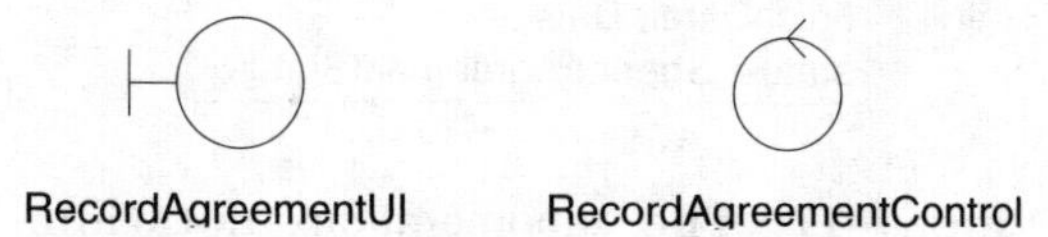

Fig. 7-14: Class symbol reduced to stereotype icon

If desired, UML permits the «stereotype» labelling notation shown in Figure 7-11 to be combined with the 'small icon' notation shown in Figure 7-13. Figure 7-15 illustrates the resultant notation.

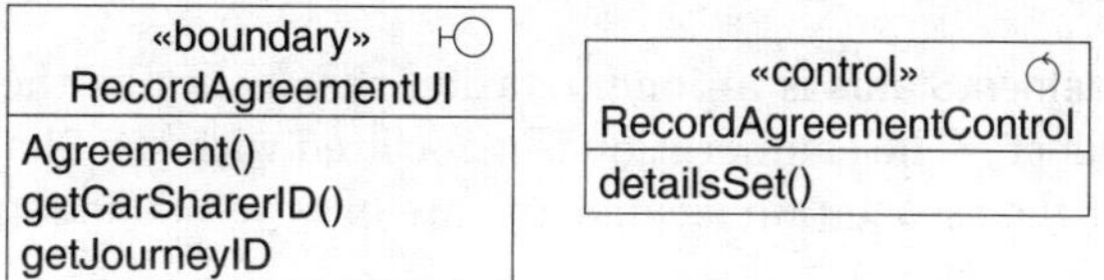

Fig. 7-15: Combined icon and label stereotype notation

The UML notation for an object, as introduced in Chapter 4, and elaborated earlier in this chapter, can also use the stereotype conventions discussed here. For example, an object could include the name of the stereotype using the stereotype label above the object name, or the 'small icon' notation. Figure 7-16 illustrates the notations for showing stereotyping of objects.

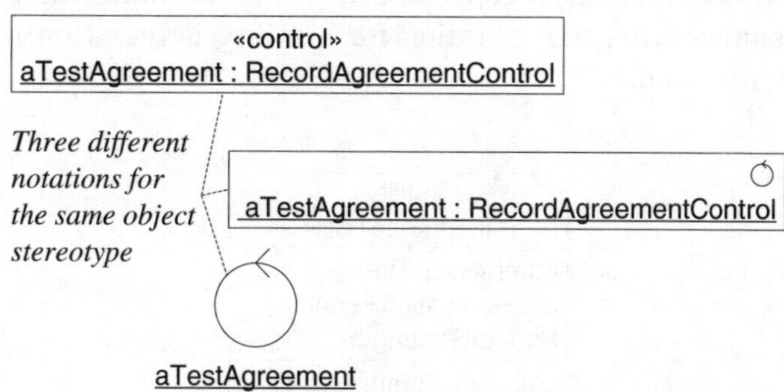

Fig. 7-16: Example object stereotype notations

7.5.2 Enumeration

It is sometimes useful to be able to specify a limited and predefined set of values from which the value of a particular attribute can be set. Figure 7-17 shows the notation for the enumeration stereotype in UML.

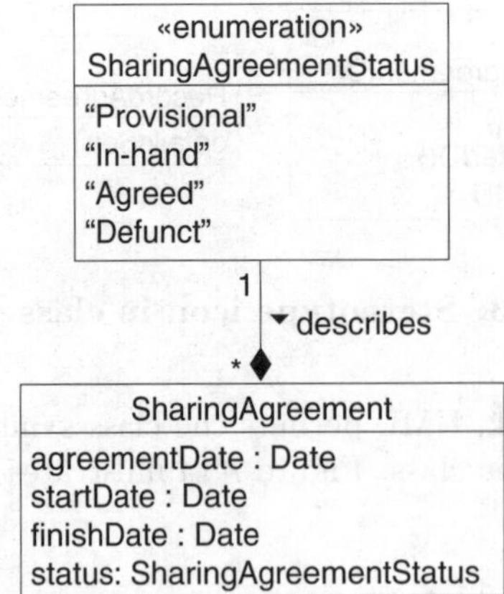

Fig. 7-17: The «enumeration» notation

The basic notation for an enumeration is a named class symbol. The inclusion of the «enumeration» stereotype above the class name indicates that this class represents an enumeration of values. The literal values for the enumeration are placed in the middle list compartment of the class symbol.

In Figure 7-17, SharingAgreementStatus is an enumeration that contains the literal values "Provisional", "In-hand", "Agreed", and "Defunct". The enumeration is associated with the SharingAgreement class and the probable implementation of the association as an attribute of type SharingAgreementStatus on SharingAgreement is shown.

An enumeration can have operations. The operations would be listed in the lower list compartment in the normal way as for classes.

7.5.3 Utility

UML provides a notation for modelling a collection of global attributes and operations as a «utility» stereotype. As with an enumeration, the notation for a utility is based on the class symbol. Figure 7-18 illustrates the utility notation.

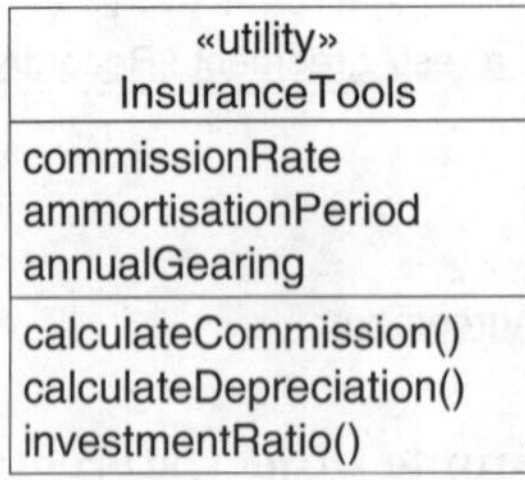

Fig. 7-18: The «utility» notation

In Figure 7-18, the InsuranceTools utility provides attributes and operations that can be used throughout the CarMatch system. It is not necessary to associate a utility with the classes that use the utility attributes or operations, as they are globally available.

7.5.4 Interfaces

Interfaces are classes that have no attributes and no direct instances (that is, they are abstract). The operations of an interface class have no method, that is, they are not implemented. Interface classes cannot participate in associations that are navigable from the interface class to the associated class as this may be considered to be a form of attribute feature of the class. Interfaces may participate in associations that are navigable only towards the interface class.

This means that the only features of an interface class are its operations. The set of non-private operations of an interface class specifies the functionality that must be supported by any class that realizes the interface class. Remember that the interface class itself does not provide its own implementation of the operations; the operations have no methods.

The concept of the realization of an interface is similar to that of generalization covered in Chapter 5. The key difference is that a class that realizes an interface is responsible for implementing the operations of the interface rather than inheriting and then specializing existing methods as in generalization.

Figure 7-19 illustrates the use of interfaces in UML using classes taken from the Java class library. The List class in Figure 7-19 illustrates the notation for specifying an interface stereotype in UML using the «interface» keyword.

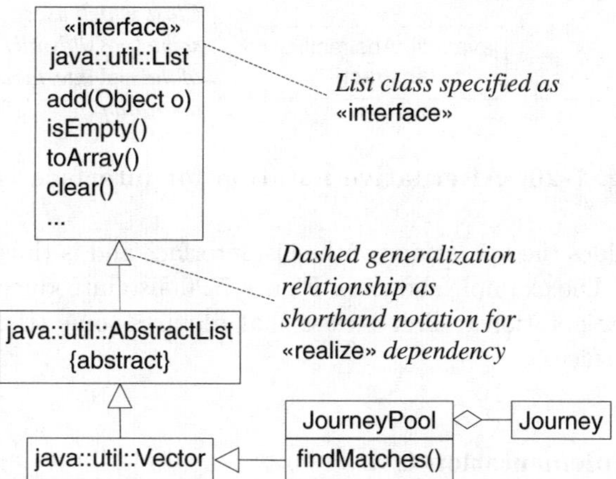

Fig. 7-19: Class based and association based interface notation

(Figure 7-19, shows an alternative UML notation for the «realize» dependency as a generalization relationship drawn with a dashed line rather than a solid line.)

The List interface class specifies an ordered collection of objects. The List interface class provides operations to support:

- insertion of objects into a list (for example, add(Object), which should allow an object to be added to the end of the list);
- interrogating a list regarding its contents (for example, isEmpty(), which should return a boolean true value if the list has elements in it);
- handling the list of objects (for example, toArray(), which should return an object of type Array containing all the elements of the list);
- removing objects from a list (for example, clear(), which should remove all the elements from the list).

To reiterate, the List class itself does not implement these operations, as it is an interface class. As shown in Figure 7-19, the AbstractList class realizes the List interface and thus provides methods to support the operations specified in the List interface class.

The example shown in Figure 7-19 shows the refinement in the Java class library down from List, through AbstractList to Vector. The example also illustrates how a class in the CarSharer package, JourneyPool might use the inherited behaviour of its ancestors. In the example, the JourneyPool class provides Vector-like operations plus the findMatches operation. The intention is that as instances of Journey are registered with CarMatch they are added to the JourneyPool collection, using Vector (and hence AbstractList and hence List) behaviour. The JourneyPool class then provides a specific operation findMatches to match up similar journeys that could be shared. The findMatches operation might well utilize Vector, AbstractList (and hence List) operations to provide the matching capability.

As a simpler notational form, UML allows an interface to be represented by a small circle labelled with the name of the interface. Figure 7-20 illustrates this notation, again using the List class first introduced in Figure 7-19.

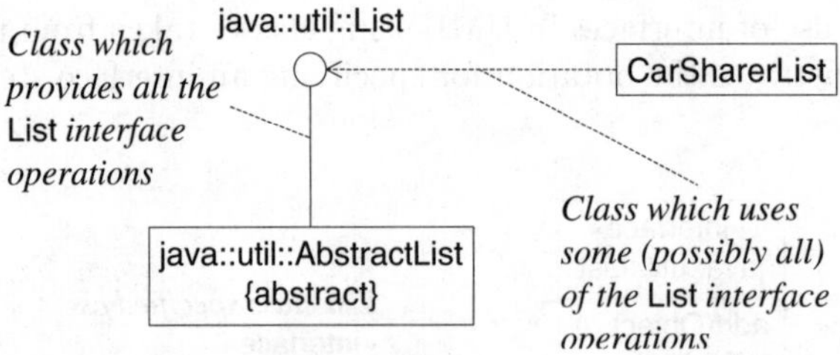

Fig. 7-20: Alternative notation for interface class

The AbstractList class provides the operations of the List interface and is thus attached by a solid line to the List interface element. The example shown in Figure 7-20 also introduces the CarSharerList class to illustrate the dashed arrow notation to link a class that requires some (though not necessarily all) of the operations on the interface.

7.5.5 Type versus Implementation Class

UML allows a distinction between «type» classes and «implementationClass» classes. A «type» class is similar in concept to an interface insomuch as it defines the operations to be provided for the class without implementing the methods for those operations. However, a type class differs from an interface class in that a type class may include attributes and may participate in associations that are navigable away from the type class. Any such attributes and associations are provided only to support the specification of operations.

It it important to be clear about the difference between type classes and abstract classes (classes with a tagged value property isAbstract=true). Neither type classes nor abstract classes have direct object instances. However, type classes are different from abstract classes because the operations of a type class are not implemented. An abstract class may provide methods for all of its operations, but still not permit direct object instances of that class.

In summary:

- **An «interface» class** has no attributes or outward navigable associations. The operations of an interface class have no methods; they are place holders that ensure that another class that realizes the interface provides all the required operations. From a specification and implementation perspective, as an interface class does not actually do anything, it cannot have direct object instances.

- **A «type» class** has operations and may have attributes and outward navigable associations. Those attributes and associations serve to support the specification of the operations of the class. The operations of a type class have no methods; they are place holders that ensure that another class that implements the type provides all the required operations. From a specification and implementation perspective, as a type class does not actually do anything it cannot have direct object instances.
- **An {abstract} class** may have attributes, operations and associations. The operations are implemented. An abstract class could support direct object instances in that it has attributes, operations with methods, and associations. However, abstract classes do not have direct object instances by the very nature of their being abstract.

The UML notation for a type class is based on the class symbol, augmented with a «type» stereotype. The class GatherCarSharerDetails shown in Figure 7-21 illustrates this notation.

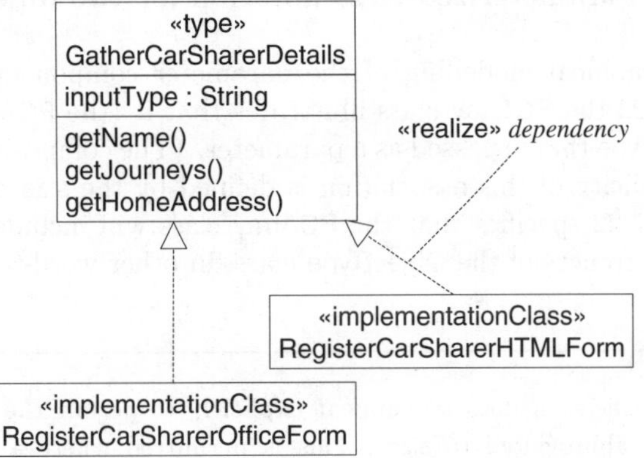

Fig. 7-21: Notation for «type» and «implementationClass» classes

From the preceding discussion it should not be too surprising to learn that an «implementationClass» is a class that realizes a type class by implementing the methods of the type class. Figure 7-21 shows two implementation classes, RegisterCarSharerOfficeForm and RegisterCarSharerHTMLForm. The office form would allow CarMatch staff to gather car sharer details for sharers who come into a CarMatch office. The HTML form would be served over the Internet to allow car sharers to register on-line. Figure 7-21 shows the two realization dependencies between the implementation classes and the type class.

The example shown in Figure 7-21, the GatherCarSharerDetails type class, illustrates the generic functionality that might be expected in any system interface that will be used to input car sharer details. As well as the operations, an attribute inputType is shown. The intention here is that whichever medium is used to input the car sharer details will be noted through the inputType attribute. With the class model shown, this would enable CarMatch to track on-line versus office based registrations.

The implementation of GatherCarSharerDetails will be tailored through the two implementation classes to suit the requirements of the particular environment in which the implementation class runs (via the Internet or as a desktop window). Each implementation class might introduce additional functional capability to meet the requirements of its environment or to provide added-value to the look and feel of the interface. For example, the desktop form implementation might make direct use of desktop functionality (and hence class libraries) such as drag and drop of icons on the form that are simply not available within an HTML based form.

7.6 PARAMETERIZED CLASSES AND BOUND ELEMENTS

The UML notation for a *parameterized class* (also called a *template*) is similar to the basic class symbol, with the parameters for the class being identified in a dashed box in the top right corner of the class symbol. Figure 7-22 illustrates the parameterized class notation for two different classes, PCSet and PCArray.

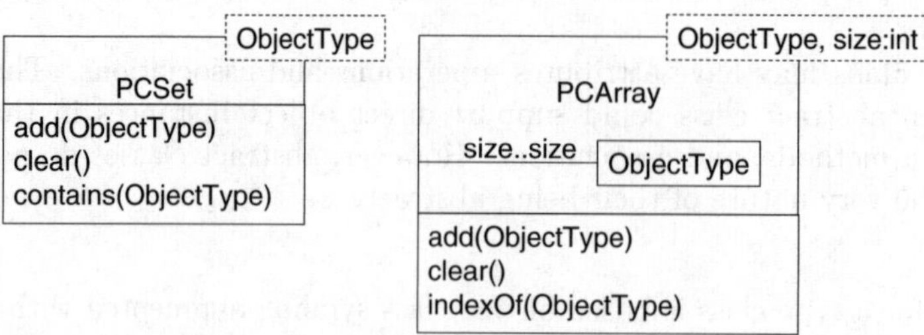

Fig. 7-22: Parameterized class notation for two different classes

UML also permits the graphical modelling of the parameter components of a parameterized class. For example, in Figure 7-22 the PCArray class illustrates that it (the PCArray class) has an composite association with the ClassType that is passed as a parameter. (The composition is shown using graphical containment). The multiplicity of this association is defined by the size parameter. In summary, the class definition in Figure 7-22 specifies that the PCArray class will include between size and size (the size..size multiplicity) occurrences of the ObjectType class, in other words, an array of size size.

> ***Aside***
>
> The UML Specification does not appear explicitly to permit the range definition size..size to be abbreviated to size. This is permitted where a specific value is known; for example, 1..1 may be truncated to 1 or a single integer value such as 7 may be used to specify a range of one value. This simplification has not explicitly been extended to a logical definition such as size..size.

What is a parameterized class though? Arguably, the most common use of parameterized classes is to support sets or collections of objects. Figure 7-23 illustrates this usage, showing two instantiations of the parameterized classes shown in Figure 7-22.

In Figure 7-23, the JourneyList class is bound to the PCSet parameterized class with the «bind» dependency. This binding also instantiates the ObjectType parameter to Journey. Thus, the operations of PCSet would actually be realized as, for example, add(Journey). So, the final effect of instantiating PCSet as JourneyList is that JourneyList will behave as a set with elements of type Journey.

EXAMPLE 7.1 What is the meaning of the binding between RequirementList and PCArray?

SOLUTION RequirementList binds to PCArray setting ObjectType to Requirement and size to 10. The effect of this is to instantiate RequirementList as an array that can hold up to 10 occurrences of type Requirement.

For the example shown in Figure 7-23, JourneyList and RequirementList are referred to in UML as *bound elements.* Bound elements can be shown using the notation in Figure 7-23. An alternative notation is shown in Figure 7-24.

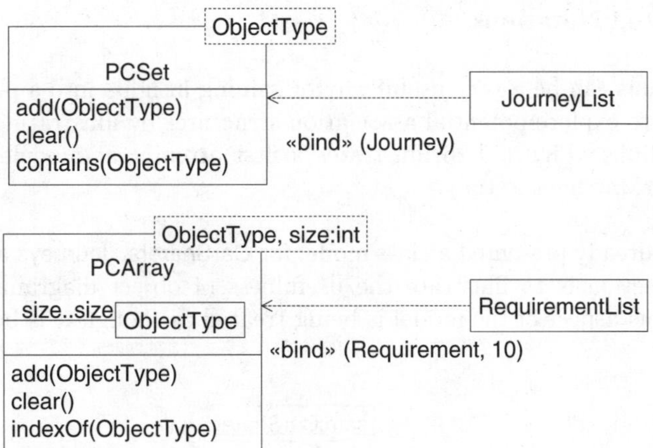

Fig. 7-23: Instantiation of parameterized classes

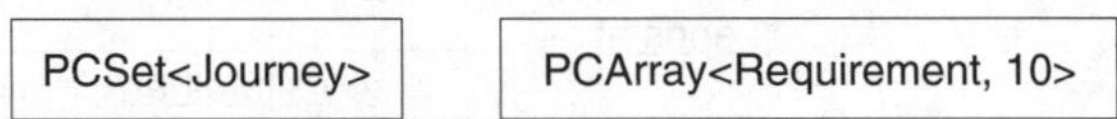

Fig. 7-24: Alternative notation for showing bound elements

This alternative notation is graphically more concise than the notation used in Figure 7-23. The name of the class is of the form `templateName <parameterList>`. However, the alternative notation does not allow the bound element to be named in the class diagram.

As a bound element is fully specified by the parameterized class of which it is an instantiation. The bound element cannot extend the functionality of the parameterized class by introducing further attributes or operations. Nor can the bound element change the functionality of the parameterized class beyond the instantiation to the particular bound element parameters. However, it is perfectly acceptable to specialize a bound element and then to extend or refine those specializations in line with the principles of generalization. Figure 7-25 illustrates this principle.

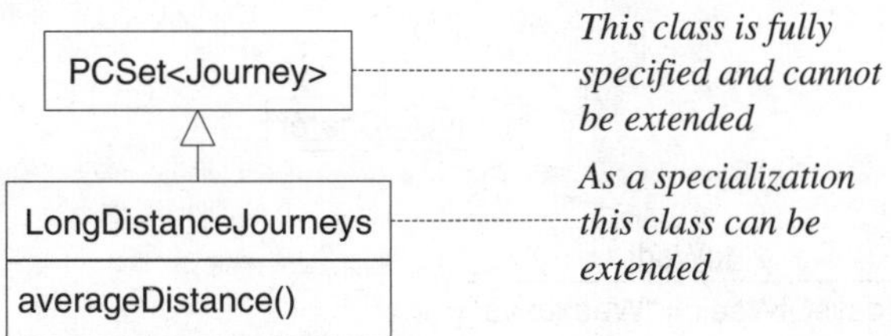

Fig. 7-25: Specialization of bound elements

7.7 MODELLING GUIDANCE

As with the previous chapter, this chapter covers relatively specialist annotations that can be used on class diagrams. Given this context, some of the modelling guidance given in this section focusses on the implications of using or not using the annotations.

7.7.1 Object Related Notations

Drawing object diagrams can be a very useful way of gaining insights into a problem domain. Objects and links can be used to explore potential association structures by illustrating possible configurations of those objects and links. Figure 7-26 illustrates a first attempt at modelling the core classes and associations in the CarMatch case study.

Earlier chapters have already presented a class model for CarSharers, Journeys and Addresses. However, the purpose of this section is to illustrate the usefulness of object diagrams in the early stages of modelling. As such, this aspect of the model is being treated as though it is being encountered for the first time.

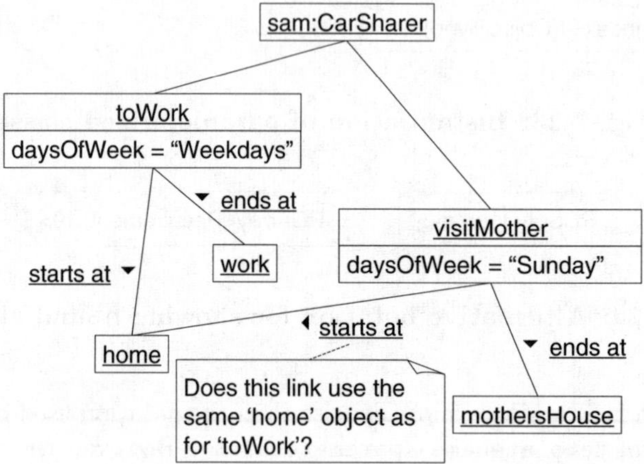

Fig. 7-26: First draft object diagram for core CarMatch model

This first draft object diagram has highlighted a problem in the interpretation of the object that a trip goes from or to. The analyst has used a note to indicate that they are unsure whether the same home object can be used for the from link for two different trips.

The analyst redraws the object model, using a slightly different structure. Figure 7-27 shows this second draft.

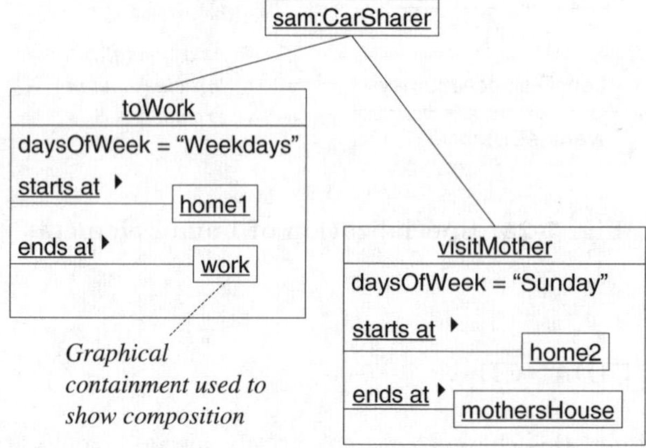

Fig. 7-27: Second draft object diagram for core CarMatch model

The second draft shows the from and to locations as components of each trip using the graphical containment representation of composition. Using this notation, it becomes necessary to use separate objects for the two occurrences of the home location for the two different trips. Redrawing the objects in this way causes the analyst to think about the nature of the existence of different locations, clarifying their role in the problem domain and their representation in the solution domain. In this case, based on this clarification, the analyst decides that this second draft more accurately describes the true nature of the relationship between trips and locations.

The next step is to think about suitable type (class) names for the instances represented in the model. The analyst already has the type name CarSharer and has thus far been using the informal terms trip and location. Having discussed the object diagram further with the client and using the language of the client (CarMatch) the analyst decides upon appropriate formal (class) type names for the objects. In this case study, trip becomes Journey and location becomes Address. Figure 7-28 shows the amended object diagram that now includes the class type of each object. In Figure 7-28 the analyst has also added notes about the multiplicity of the associations represented by the links on the object diagram.

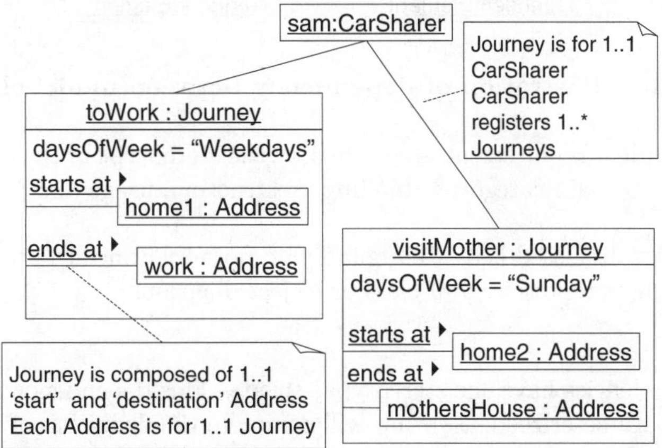

Fig. 7-28: Object diagram showing class types for core CarMatch model

Finally, the analyst switches from an instance based perspective to a type based perspective, that is, from an object diagram to a class diagram. The analyst draws a class diagram that reflects the general types illustrated on the object diagram. Figure 7-29 shows the class diagram drawn from the object diagram shown in Figure 7-28.

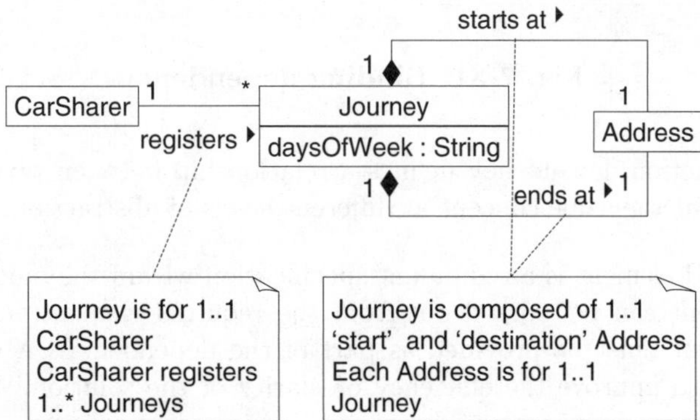

Fig. 7-29: Class diagram showing class types for core CarMatch model

So, objects and links, drawn as an object diagram, can be an extremely useful tool in the process of analysis to investigate particular aspects of the problem domain. Using an object diagram to give examples of possible structures in the problem domain can be an extremely useful tool to enable more effective communication with members of the user community.

7.7.2 Dependency

A dependency specifies that one model element requires the presence of another model element in order to function or be implemented. The implication of the dependency is that, if the model element upon which the dependency is specified is changed, then the dependent model element may also need to be changed (Figure 7-30).

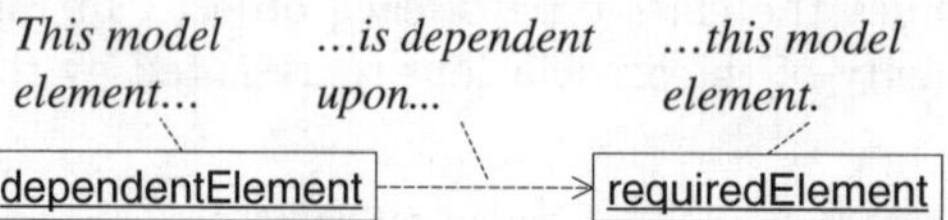

Fig. 7-30: Illustration of dependency between model elements

The nature of that dependent requirement is specified by the stereotype of the dependency relationship. Dependencies fall into four main categories, binding, abstraction, usage and permission.

Many of the dependencies discussed here are arguably of more relevance to process modelling concepts than to the static structures represented in class or object diagrams.

Binding Binding dependencies have one stereotype, «bind». This dependency relates a bound element to the template (parameterized class) that will complete the definition of the resultant class. The dependency should also include a list of values passed as parameters to the template. Figure 7-31 illustrates a «bind» dependency.

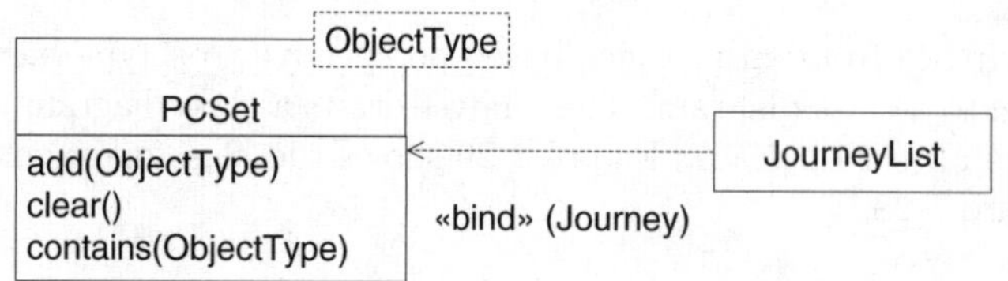

Fig. 7-31: Binding dependency

Abstraction An abstraction dependency defines a relationship between two elements or sets of elements that represent the same concept at different levels of abstraction.

«derive» A derived element is a redundant specification within the model as the value(s) of the derived element can be worked out from the required element(s). The specification of a derived element must be provided as part of the dependency. A derived element may be implemented to improve the efficiency or clarity of the solution. Figure 7-32 illustrates a derived specification.

«realize» A realization dependency specifies the relationship between an element in the implementation model and an element in the specification model.

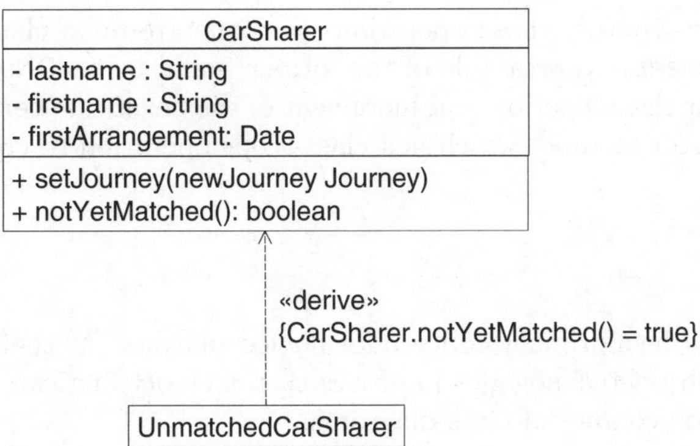

Fig. 7-32: Derivation dependency

- **«refine»** A refinement dependency specifies the relationship between model elements at different levels of abstraction, for example, analysis level and design level elements.
- **«trace»** A trace dependency specifies the relationship between two elements that represent the same concept in different models.

Usage Usage dependencies specify a requirement that one model element has for the presence of another model element.

- **«call»** A call dependency specifies a collaboration between two operations; one operation will call the other operation.
- **«create»** A create dependency implies that creation of an instance of the dependent class will result in the creation of an instance of the class that is the target of the dependency.
- **«instantiate»** An instantiate dependency implies that the operations on the dependent class will create instances of the class that is the target of the dependency.
- **«send»** A send dependency is specified between an operation and a signal. The dependency specifies that the operation sends the signal.

Permission Permission dependencies are used to specify the accessibility of model elements in one namespace to model elements in a different namespace.

- **«access»** An access dependency specifies that the dependent package can utilize the elements of the package that is the target of the dependency.
- **«import»** An import dependency specifies that the dependent package incorporates model elements from the package that is the target of the dependency.
- **«friend»** A friend dependency overrides normal visibility constraints, allowing the dependent element to access the target element regardless of the specified visibility.

7.7.3 Class-Scope Features

Class-scope features are useful in monitoring state across a group of classes. An example of this was used in Figure 7-10 on page 131. This example used a class-scope attribute nextIDNumber as an incremental count. As new object instances were created, they were assigned the current value of nextIDNumber. The value of nextIDNumber was then incremented, ready for assignment to the next instance. Class-scope attributes can also be useful to control state based behaviour, which is discussed in more detail in Chapter 11.

Class-scope operations are typically those operations that operate upon class-scope attributes or that manipulate instances of classes. An example of the former would be setIDNumber in Figure 7-10. This operation is responsible for the allocation and increment of the nextIDNumber count. An example of the latter would be a constructor method, which is a class-scope operation to create instances of a class.

7.7.4 Class Types

Use of stereotyping will not be a primary concern for novice analysts. As their understanding of object-modelling, patterns and object-technologies improves then stereotyping can be introduced as a means of enriching the information content of class diagrams.

Stereotyping provides a useful shorthand specification for the type conformance of a model element. The two principal uses of stereotyping that have been discussed here are for classes and dependency relationships. The usage of stereotyping to define dependencies has already been discussed in Section 7.7.2. By specifying a class as having a particular stereotype, the analyst is identifying the nature of the role played by a class in the overall model. For example, specifying a class as «control» clearly indicates the purpose of the class as controlling the interactions between other classes.

Parameterized classes (templates) and bound elements are again of primary relevance to the more experienced analyst. The notation has been covered in this book primarily for the sake of completeness. Fowler & Scott (1997) note that using templates has the advantage of re-use of the template code. However, the disadvantages of code bloat and increased complexity can outweigh the advantages.

The UML Specification (Object Management Group, 1999*a*) includes two stereotypes that directly support the extension of UML itself. These two stereotypes are «metaclass» and «powertype». A metaclass is a class whose instances are classes. Defining a new metaclass has the effect of extending the modelling elements available to the development team. A powertype is a meta-element whose instances are classes in a model. Both of these stereotypes are of little relevance to the vast majority of development work and are certainly only of interest to practitioners whose level of UML expertise puts them well beyond needing to read this book.

Review Questions

7.1 Discuss a situation where object diagrams can be useful during the analysis process.

7.2 Explain the difference between the «instanceOf» and link relationships.

7.3 On an object diagram, which association annotations are permitted and not permitted for links?

7.4 On an object diagram, what do each of the «become» and «copy» relationships show?

7.5 The 'shorthand' notation for «realize» dependencies is derived from two other UML notations. What are they?

7.6 On a class diagram, how are class-scope features distinguished from instance-scope features?

7.7 What is the semantic difference between class-scope features and instance-scope features?

7.8 What are the three general notations covered in this chapter for specifying stereotypes in UML?

7.9 What is the purpose of an «enumeration» class?

7.10 What is the purpose of a «utility» class?

7.11 UML supports two notations for specifying an «interface» class. What are they? What is the key semantic difference between the two notations?

7.12 In what way does an «implementationClass» differ from a «type» class?

7.13 What notation is used to relate «implementationClass» to its «type» class?

7.14 What is the basic notation for a parameterized class (template)?

7.15 What are the two notations for showing bound elements? What is the key semantic difference between the two notations?

7.16 Explain the differences between the following types of class: «type», {abstract} and «interface».

Solved Problems

7.1 Draw an object diagram to illustrate the 'evening talk' class diagram shown in Figure 6-36 in Problem 6.4 on page 124.

Three variant object diagrams are shown. Clearly there are many possible choices of object instances.

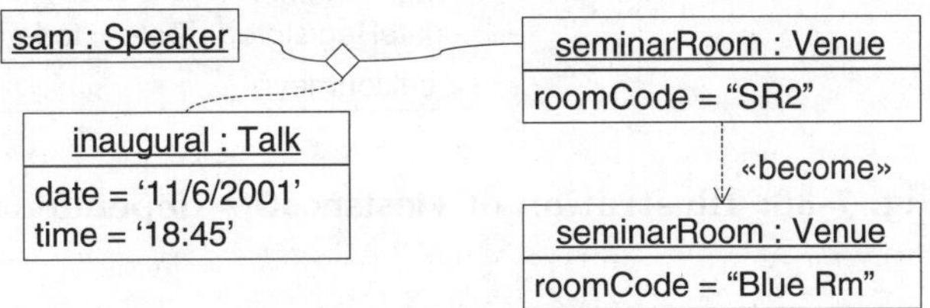

Fig. 7-33: A talk with no attendees registered yet

Figure 7-33 shows a talk that has been arranged for an identified date and time. The speaker has been identified as has the venue. The value of the roomCode of the venue is changed though and this is shown with the «become» dependency. As the object diagram suggests, the change of roomCode reflects a change in the state of the SeminarRoom : Venue object. It is still this same object instance that is involved in the association instance though.

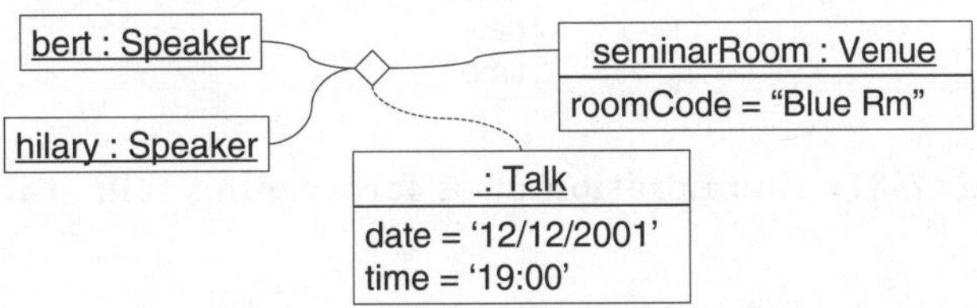

Fig. 7-34: A talk with two speakers

Figure 7-34 shows a talk with two speakers. Finally, Figure 7-35 shows a talk with two venues and several registered car sharers.

7.2 For any one of the objects drawn in Problem 7.1, draw a diagram showing the «instanceOf» dependency between the object and its class.

Figure 7-36 illustrates one possible «instanceOf» dependency.

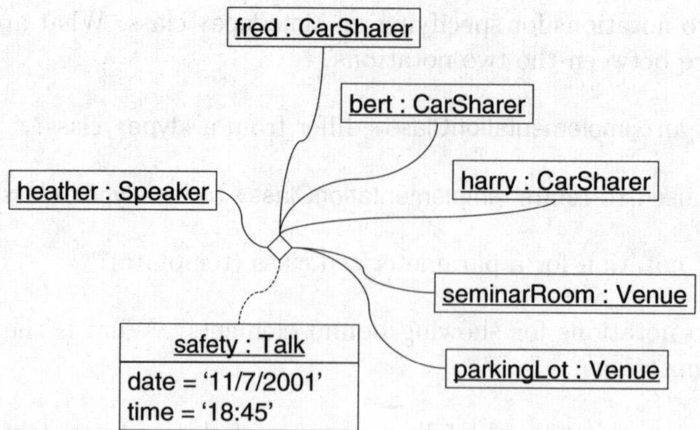

Fig. 7-35: A talk with three registered car sharers

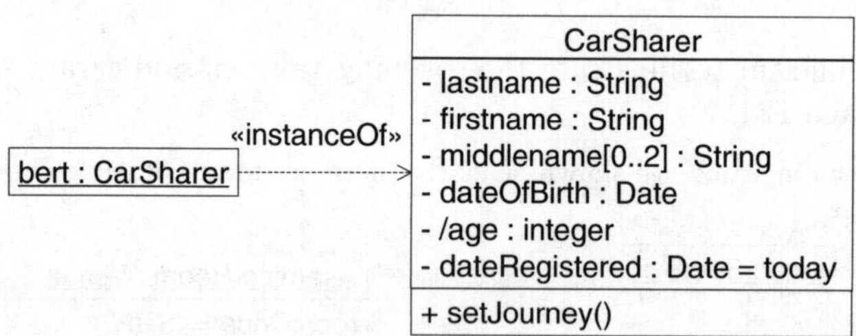

Fig. 7-36: Illustration of «instanceOf» dependency

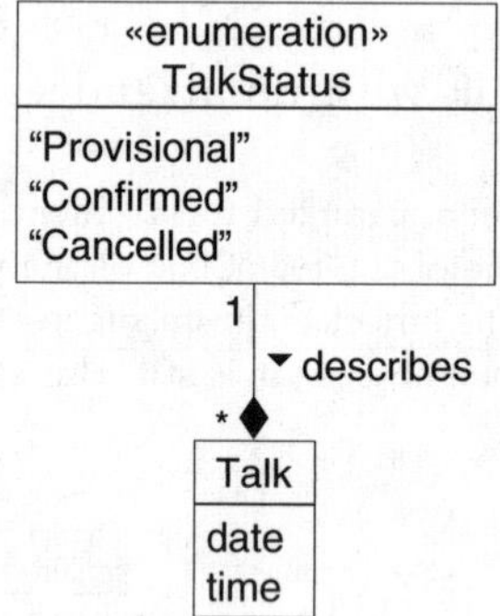

Fig. 7-37: Enumeration class for evening talk status.

7.3 Add an «enumeration» class to the 'evening talk' class model used in Problem 7.1. The enumeration class should be used to set the status of a Talk. A talk can be "Provisional", "Confirmed" or "Cancelled".

Figure 7-37 shows the relevant classes.

7.4 Draw a class diagram that shows the following requirements as a parameterized class with two bound elements. Use the more verbose notation with the parameterized class and «bind» relationships.

Janet Hoffner: We will need to keep a list of the requirements a CarSharer has. A car sharer could have no requirements, but we want to be able to list up to 10 requirements per car sharer. That '10' is a strict limit. We will also need to keep a list of the next of kin for a car sharer, we'll need to keep at least one and no more than three.

Figure 7-38 shows a possible solution. Other annotations have been suppressed.

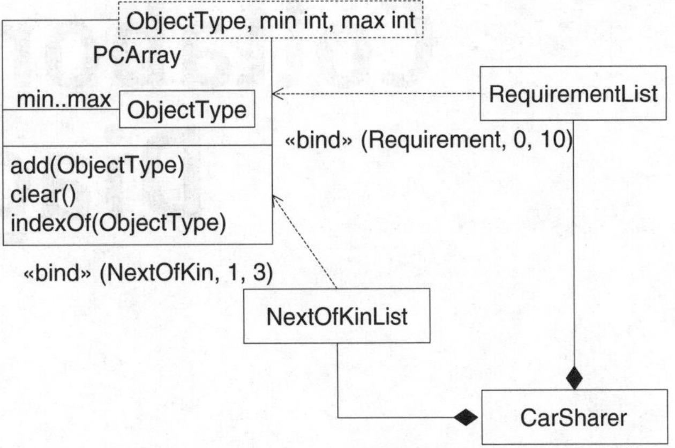

Fig. 7-38: Parameterized class and bound elements

Supplementary Problems

7.5 Draw an object diagram to illustrate the classes, n-ary association and association class in the class model you constructed for Problem 6.6.

7.6 Show the relationship between any one object and its corresponding class using the «instanceOf» dependency.

7.7 The VolBank system will make use of two operations getTimeInterval(fromTime:Time, toTime:Time) and getDateInterval(fromDate:Date, toDate:Date) in many different operations throughout the system. For example, to calculate time worked on an assignment, time available as banked time, length of time a volunteering opportunity has been registered, length of time a volunteer or organization has been registered. How could these two operations be modelled so as to specify that they should be globally available? Model a suitable class to show the notation in use.

7.8 Rather than holding a single contact for an organization, VolBank want to hold a list of contacts. Show how this could be modelled using both the 'terse' and 'verbose' UML notations for parameterized classes and bound elements.

Collaboration Diagrams

8.1 INTRODUCTION

In Chapter 3 on use cases, we said that use cases can be realized by collaborations. In this chapter we explain what is meant by a collaboration and how to draw collaboration diagrams.

8.2 WHAT IS A COLLABORATION?

In object-oriented systems, the functionality that users require of the system is produced by objects working together. Each individual object provides only a small element of the functionality—its particular responsibilities—but when they work together, objects are able to produce high-level functionality that people can use. In order to work together in this way, objects need to communicate with one another, and they do this by passing messages. This 'working together' to produce some useful result is what is meant by a *collaboration*.

In the UML Specification (Object Management Group, 1999*a*) a collaboration is described as something that 'defines a set of participants and relationships that are meaningful for a given set of purposes'. Let's look at an example and then work back to this definition.

We shall want to specify the participants in the use case Record sharing agreement. When an agreement is reached between two or more members of CarMatch to share a journey, a new SharingAgreement object is created. The SharingAgreement has an association with the Journeys rather than the CarSharers, as each CarSharer can have several Journeys that he or she wants to share, and each journey may be shared with a different car sharer. As a minimum, this use case will involve five objects, from the classes shown in Figure 8–1: two instances of CarSharer, two instances of Journey and one of SharingAgreement.

Strictly speaking, in UML terms, we are dealing here with roles rather than classes or objects (see Section 14.2.13 in Chapter 14). It is possible to use named roles in collaborations. If each car sharer was either a driver or a passenger, we could create two roles for the CarSharer objects involved in this collaboration, as in Figure 8-2. In the case of this system, however, the idea is to encourage people to take turns at driving if possible, so the roles /Driver:CarSharer and /Passenger:CarSharer do not apply.

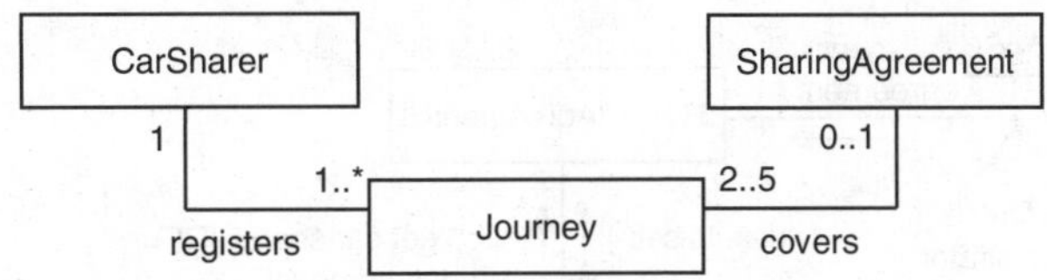

Fig. 8-1: Classes involved in the use case Record sharing agreement

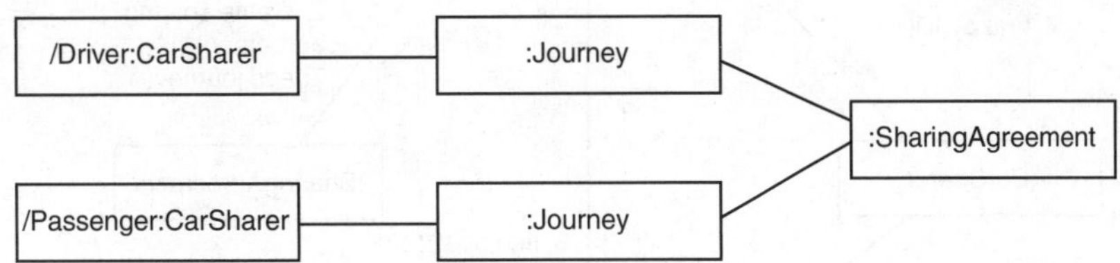

Fig. 8-2: Named roles for classes in the collaboration Record sharing agreement

The links between the roles in Figure 8-2 map onto the association between the classes CarSharer and SharingAgreement in the excerpt from the class diagram in Figure 8-1. This use case will also involve some additional classes, and these are shown in the collaboration in Figure 8-3. At this stage, we have tried to keep this collaboration simple: in a project that uses UML, we may want to get an idea of the domain classes that are involved in a collaboration, without worrying too much about the detail of how it will be implemented. For example, we have not included collection classes or classes to manage persistence. Because there is not a distinction between the roles played by different instances of CarSharer, we can show them as a single class role as in Figure 8-3.

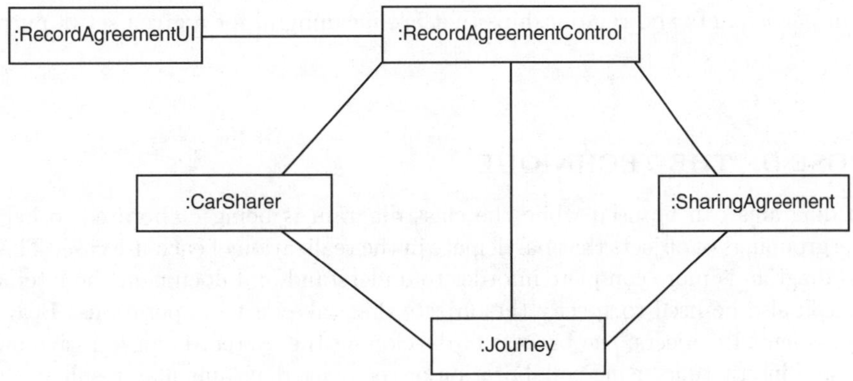

Fig. 8-3: Classes involved in the collaboration

The additional classes shown here are a user interface class RecordAgreementUI and a control class RecordAgreementControl. Association roles and multiplicities can be added to this diagram if required, although we have not shown them here. It is also possible to add the details of an interaction to the collaboration diagram. According to the UML definition, 'An interaction specifies the communication between instances performing a specific task...in the context of a collaboration.' In the early stages of a project, the messages that make up the communication of the interaction may be informally defined. Later they will be *signals* or *operations* sent between object instances. Figure 8-4 shows some informally defined messages on the collaboration diagram of Figure 8-3 and the inclusion of an actor to trigger the interaction.

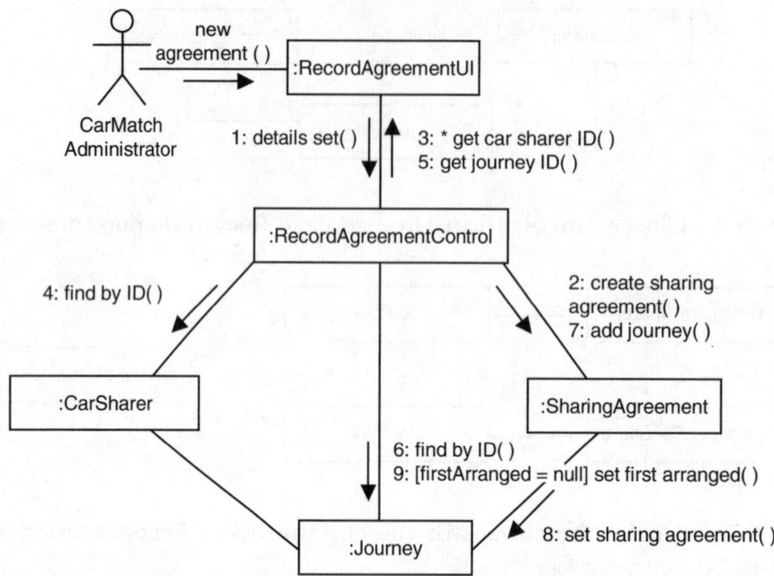

Fig. 8-4: Interaction added to the collaboration of Figure 8-3

This diagram shows which classes will participate in the realization of the use case Record sharing agreement and the relationships between them that are meaningful for the purpose of creating a new car sharing agreement. The relationships with the control class RecordAgreementControl, which will be used only in this use case, will not be meaningful in the context of another use case, such as Register car sharer, but equally the relationship between the classes CarSharer and SharingAgreement will not be relevant in many other use cases. It is in this sense that a collaboration is described as something that 'defines a set of participants and relationships that are meaningful for a given set of purposes'.

8.3 PURPOSE OF THE TECHNIQUE

Collaboration diagrams can be used while the class diagram is being elaborated to help the analyst understand the groupings of objects that participate in the realization of each use case. They can be used when the class diagram is more complete in order to understand and document the interactions among objects. They can also be used to specify the objects that take part in operations. Bear in mind that in many object-oriented projects, the process of developing the system is an iterative one. Modelling collaborations and interactions using collaboration or sequence diagrams may result in the recognition of the need for new classes, attributes or operations. These must be added to the class diagram. The addition of these new elements may result in the need for changes to existing collaboration or sequence diagrams or the addition of new ones to model the new operations. Ultimately, a line must be drawn somewhere on this process of iteration or no system would ever be finished. Where and how the line is drawn is an issue determined by project management and the development process. (Note that there are some people who claim that no system is ever finished. In his book on *Extreme Programming* (Beck, 2000), Kent Beck argues that systems should be put into production (that is into productive use) as soon as possible, even when partially developed.

The main purposes of producing collaboration diagrams are as follows.

- They are used to model collaborations between objects or roles that deliver the functionality of a use case.
- They are used to model collaborations between objects or roles that deliver the functionality of an operation.
- They are used to model mechanisms within the architectural design of the system.
- They are annotated with interactions. These interactions show the messages that are passed between objects or roles within the collaboration.
- They are used to model alternative scenarios within a use case or operation that involve the collaboration of different objects and different interactions.
- They are used in the early stages of a project to identify the objects (and hence classes) that participate in a use case. Each collaboration represents a partial view of the class diagram, and these partial models can be combined into a model of the whole system.
- They are used to show the participants in a design pattern (see Chapter 16).

8.4 NOTATION OF COLLABORATIONS

Before discussing the notation of collaboration diagrams, it is worth describing the notation of collaborations. This notation is, however, less commonly used.

Collaborations can be represented as a dashed oval with the name of the collaboration inside the oval or beneath it (see Figure 8-5).

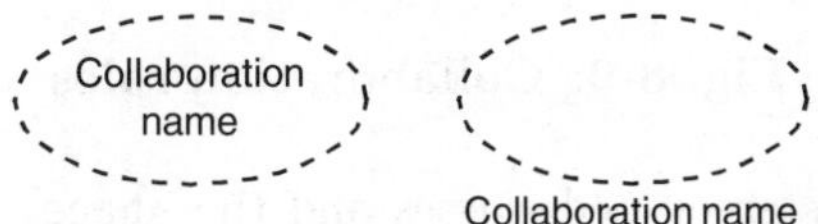

Fig. 8-5: Collaboration notation

Collaborations like this can be used to show the relationship between collaborations and the use cases that they realize, as in Figure 8-6.

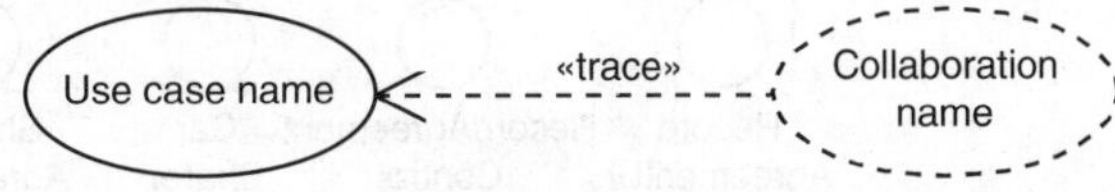

Fig. 8-6: Collaboration «trace» relationship

This approach can also be used to show the relationship between a collaboration and an operation, as shown in Figure 8-7.

However, these relationships are not usually represented explicitly in diagrams but by links between diagrams in a CASE tool. The UML Specification (Object Management Group, 1999*a*) refers to these as *invisible hyperlinks.* It is also possible to show a collaboration with the name of the operation that it realizes inside it (Figure 8-8.

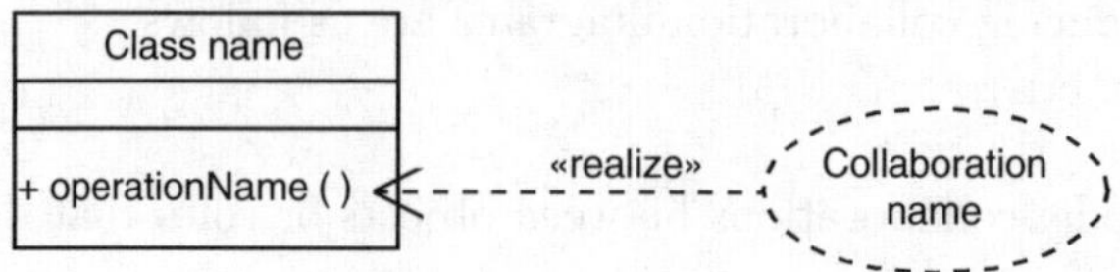

Fig. 8-7: Collaboration «realize» relationship

Fig. 8-8: Collaboration with represented operation

The dashed oval notation can also be used to show a collaboration in terms of the objects that participate in it. In this case, the collaboration is linked to the classes of those objects by dashed lines labelled with the names of the roles of the participants.

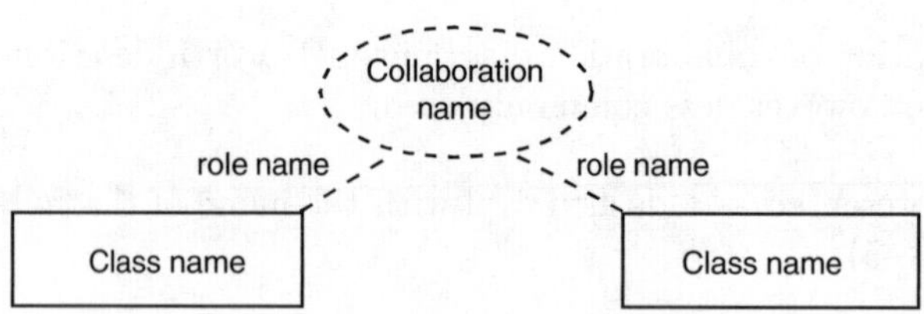

Fig. 8-9: Collaboration roles

This notation can be used with stereotyped classes and the «trace» dependency to show the classes involved in the realization of a use case, as in Figure 8-10.

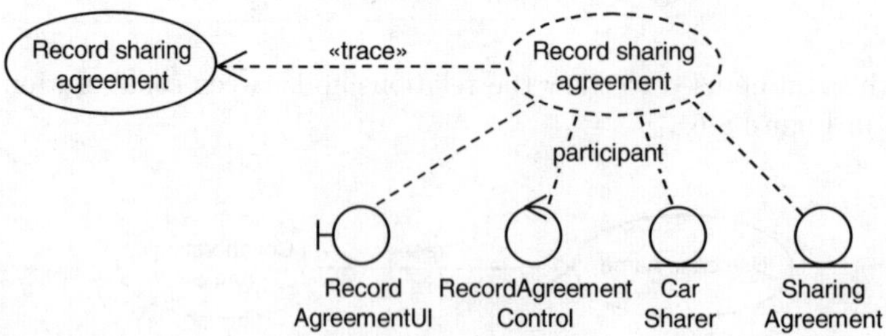

Fig. 8-10: Classes involved in the collaboration that realizes the use case Record Sharing Agreement

It is also possible to represent a design pattern in this way (see Chapter 16). In this case, the names of the roles can be shown using the template or parameterized notation (described in Chapter 7), as in Figure 8-11.

When the pattern is used, real classes must be bound to these roles. For example, the Façade pattern is widely used in systems where the developers want to hide the complexity of subsystems behind a single

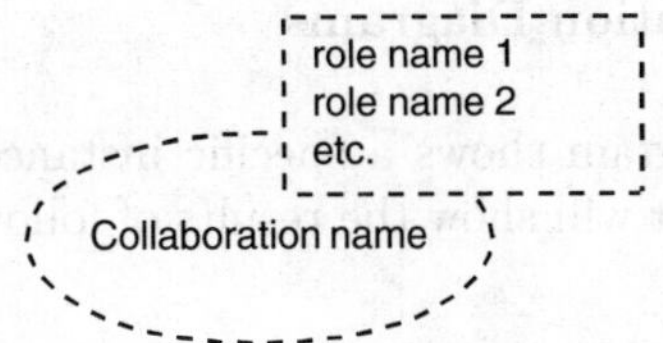

Fig. 8-11: Template (parameterized) collaboration

class which provides an interface to their functionality. Figure 8-12 shows this pattern with the façade role bound to the class InsuranceMatcher and the subsystem class role bound to the classes AgeMatcher, AreaMatcher and OccupationMatcher.

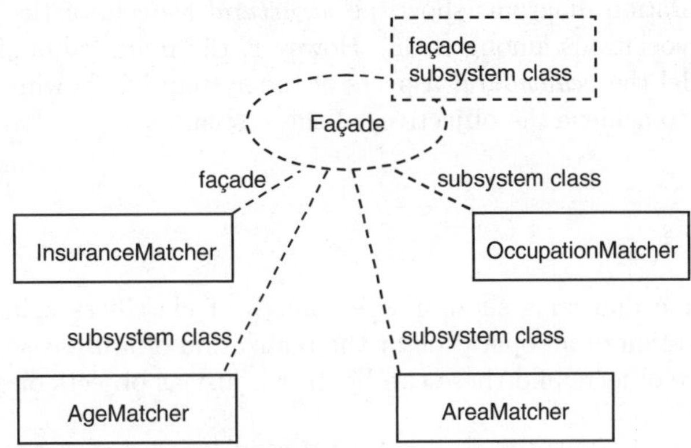

Fig. 8-12: Example of the use of a collaboration to document the use of the Façade pattern

8.5 NOTATION OF COLLABORATION DIAGRAMS

While collaborations are rarely used, collaboration diagrams are used extensively. They are most frequently used with an interaction superimposed on the collaboration to show the detail of the communication between the object instances that participate in the interaction.

Collaborations can be modelled at two levels: at *specification level* or at *instance level*. At specification level, the diagram shows classifier roles, association roles and messages; at instance level, the diagram shows objects, links and stimuli. (Chapter 14 explains what is meant by classifiers and roles.) Classes are the classifiers most often modelled in a collaboration diagram.

8.5.1 Specification Level Collaboration Diagrams

A specification level collaboration diagram shows the generic case of a collaboration. It includes possible alternative paths, loops that may execute an unspecified number of times and class roles rather than object instances.

8.5.2 Instance Level Collaboration Diagrams

An instance level collaboration diagram shows a specific instance of an interaction taking place and involving specific object instances. It will show the results of following a particular path where there is a choice.

The difference between specification level and instance level collaboration diagrams is similar to the difference between the general description of a use case and the scenarios that describe how particular instances of that use case will be worked through.

8.5.3 Collaboration Diagrams as the Context of an Interaction

Collaboration diagrams can also be drawn with no interaction in order to show the context of an interaction, effectively the subset of the class or object model that will be involved in the interaction.

Used in this way, collaboration diagrams show the *structural* aspects of the collaboration—the class roles involved and the associations among them. However, the main value of collaboration diagrams lies in using them to model the *behavioural* aspects of the system by showing the interaction between those class roles in order to achieve the objectives of the system.

8.5.4 Object Instances

Instance level collaboration diagrams show how instances of classifiers collaborate to achieve some objective—the implementation of an operation or the realization of a use case. The classifier instances that are most common are objects and these can be drawn just as objects or as instances of classes.

Objects that participate in a collaboration are drawn using the notation for instances that has been described in Chapter 4. They can be anonymous or named instances of a class, and they may or may not have a role name. The important thing to remember is that instance names are always underlined, whereas class names and role names never are (Figure 8-13).

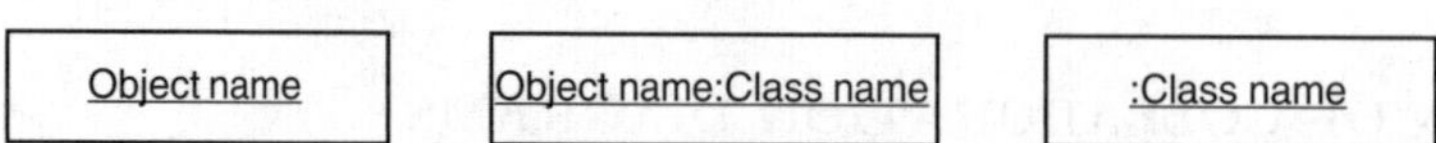

Fig. 8-13: Object instance names

Table 8-1 shows the various alternative forms that instance names can take.

8.5.5 Classes and Roles

Rather than using object instances, class roles can be drawn in a collaboration diagram. In a collaboration diagram, the classes that participate in a collaboration are drawn using the class notation, as rectangles with all the compartments apart from the class name suppressed. The name of the class is prefixed by a colon to show that it is a *class role* that is being modelled here. If the role has a name, the role name, prefixed by a forward slash '/', precedes the colon, as in Figure 8-14.

Table 8-2 shows the various alternative forms that role names can take.

Table 8-1: Syntax of instance names

Syntax	Explanation
o	An object named o.
o:C	An object named o of class C.
:C	An anonymous object of class C.
/R	An anonymous object playing the role R.
/R:C	An anonymous object of class C playing the role R.
o/R	An object named o playing the role R.
o/R:C	An object named o of class C playing the role R.

:Class name /Role name:Class name

Fig. 8-14: Role names

Table 8-2: Syntax of role names

Syntax	Explanation
/R	A role named R.
:C	An un-named role with the base class C.
/R:C	A role named R with the base class C.

8.5.6 Associations

Associations between the classes in the class diagram are added to the collaboration diagram if they are required to support the collaboration. These are called *association roles* in UML. If these are labelled, the names of the roles that the classes play in relation to the association can be added (see Figure 8-15), and the multiplicity of the associations can also be shown.

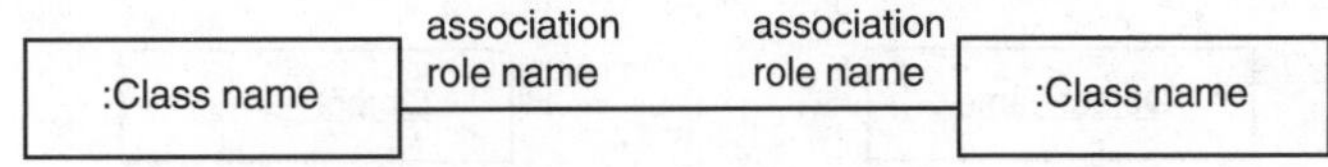

Fig. 8-15: Association role notation

Figure 8-16 shows an example of this for the CarSharer and their home address.

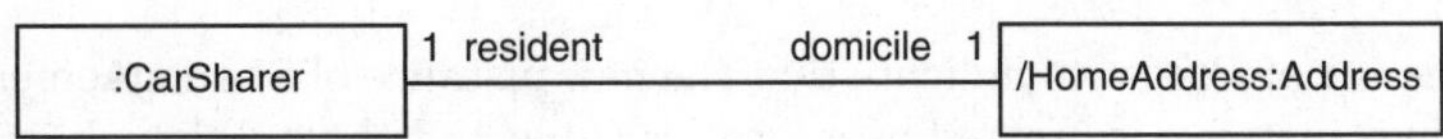

Fig. 8-16: Example of the use of association roles on a collaboration diagram

The collaboration diagram will become very cluttered if these role names are added throughout. They are best used when it is important to distinguish the roles that are played by different associations, although this can usually be done with class roles. It is only really necessary to distinguish the association roles when the same instance of a class will participate in the same collaboration in different roles, as in Figure 8-17.

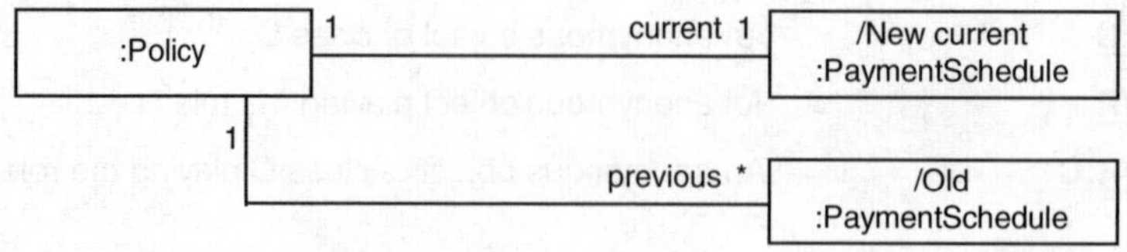

Fig. 8-17: Example of the essential use of association roles on a collaboration diagram

(In this example, a new payment schedule is added to an insurance policy. Each Policy has an association with one current PaymentSchedule and a set of zero or more previous instances of PaymentSchedule.)

Navigability of associations can also be shown, as in Figure 8-18, which indicates that the :Policy role needs to be able to send messages to the PaymentSchedule roles.

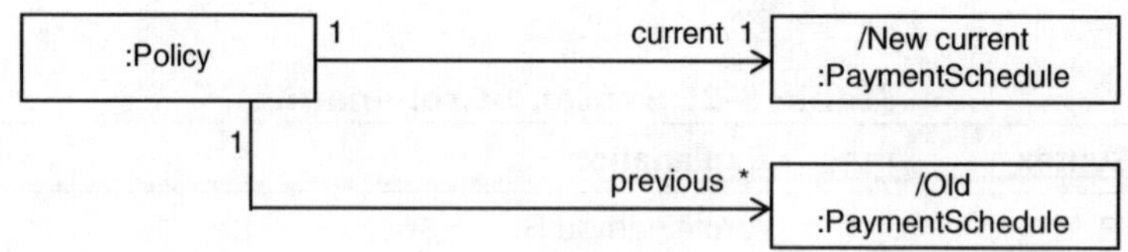

Fig. 8-18: Example of navigability of association roles on a collaboration diagram

8.5.7 Links

Links between object instances can be added to the collaboration diagram. Links may be instances of associations that are shown in the class diagram, or they may be temporary links between object instances that enable them to send messages to one another. For example, a control object may need to create an instance of a particular class as part of a collaboration, but the link between them is only temporary—it will not be shown on the class diagram—and it may represent the fact that the object instance is held in a local variable of the control object. Links can be stereotyped as «local» or «parameter» (see Figure 8-19).

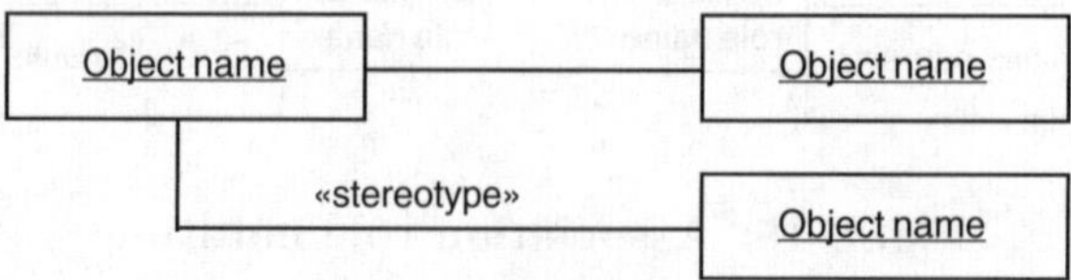

Fig. 8-19: Link with stereotype

Figure 8-20 shows the use of «local» to indicate that the new instance of SharingAgreement created by the RecordAgreementControl instance is created as a local variable and the link is only temporary—the link may be broken by the destruction of the RecordAgreementControl instance if the program terminates, or by the creation of another new instance of Sharing Agreement (called sa here).

Fig. 8-20: Stereotyped «local» link on a collaboration diagram

Compare this with the other links in Figure 8-21. The links between the new instance of SharingAgreement and the instances of Journey with which it has associations are permanent—these links must be maintained using some kind of persistence mechanism (files or a database) after the program terminates. These links are instances of the association covers, as shown on the class diagram in Figure 8-1. The link between the instance of RecordAgreementControl and the instance of the user interface, RecordAgreementUI, is stereotyped as «parameter». In this case, the control object will create an instance of the user interface class and pass the new instance some kind of reference to itself as a parameter (for example a pointer in C++, a reference in Java or a name in Smalltalk) so that the user interface can send events back to the control object.

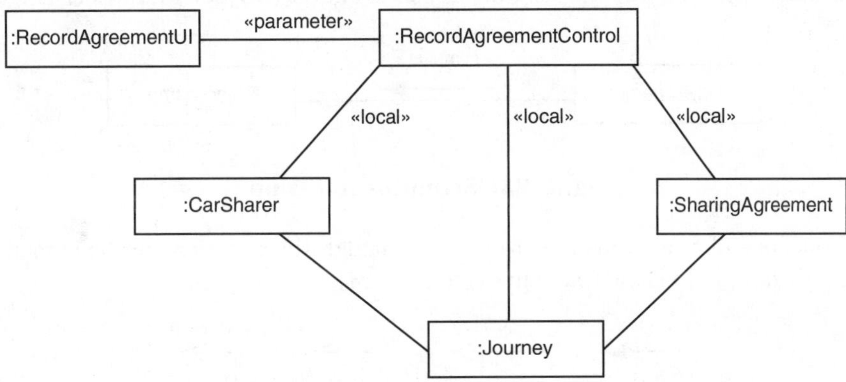

Fig. 8-21: Links on a collaboration diagram

8.5.8 Messages

The associations and links on a collaboration diagram are included to show the paths along which messages can be sent from one instance to another. The links can be labelled with the names of messages. In early versions of UML, messages was the only term used; however, in Version 1.3 a distinction was made between *messages* in specification level diagrams and *stimuli* in instance level diagrams. A message is the specification of a stimulus, and the stimulus represents a specific instance of sending the message, with particular arguments. The messages in a specification level collaboration diagram may be added to a diagram early in the development of a system, before the names of operations and events have been decided on and documented in the model.

A *stimulus* is defined as 'a communication between two objects that conveys information with the expectation that action will ensue' (Object Management Group, 1999*a*). A stimulus can be one of the following:

- an event sent from one object to another—for example a button press in a user interface object being sent to a control object;
- an operation being invoked on another object—for example a control object invoking the getName() operation of a CarSharer object in order to pass the name to the user interface to be displayed;

- the creation or destruction of an object instance—for example a control object creating a new instance of Sharing Agreement.

The term message is more widely understood and used than stimulus, and we shall refer to messages in the following description of how they work.

Messages are shown by an arrow pointing in the direction that the message is sent and a label which specifies the message (Figure 8-22).

Fig. 8-22: Message notation

Stimuli use the same notation, but the stimulus is sent from one **object** to another (Figure 8-23).

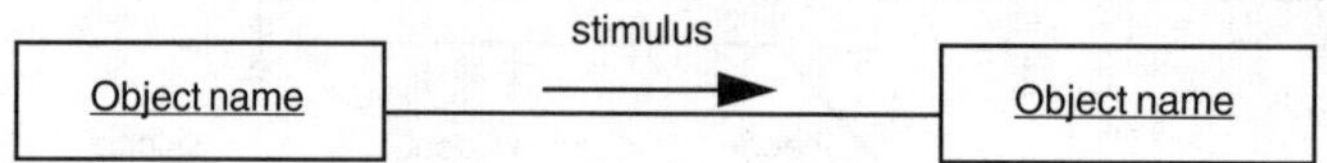

Fig. 8-23: Stimulus notation

The arrow can take one of four forms in core UML, although the notation can be extended by the use of stereotypes, for example to show time-outs (Figure 8-24).

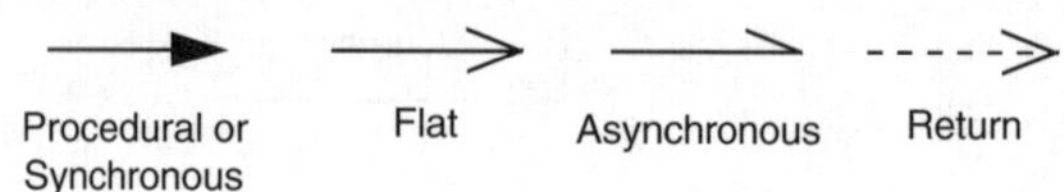

Fig. 8-24: Message flow notation

- **Procedural or Synchronous**—A message is sent by one object to another and the first object waits until the resulting action has completed. This may include waiting for the completion of actions invoked by the second object on other objects.
- **Flat**—Each arrow shows a progression from one step to the next in a sequence. Normally the message is asynchronous. A flat message can be used where it is not known whether the actual message will be synchronous or asynchronous.
- **Asynchronous**—A message is sent by one object to another but the first object does not wait until the resulting action has completed, it carries on with the next step in its own sequence of actions.
- **Return**—Represents the explicit return of control from the object to which the message was sent. Not normally shown on collaboration diagrams, but appears more often on sequence diagrams (see Chapter 9).

The arrow represents the flow of control. Where the flow of control is procedural or synchronous, there is only one thread of execution, and activity passes from one object to another. Where the flow of control is asynchronous, more than one object can be active at any one time.

The amount of detail about the message that is shown alongside the arrow can vary considerably. At its simplest, it is just the name of the message, but normally a sequence number is added, as in Figure 8-25.

Fig. 8-25: Message on a collaboration diagram

At its most complex, it can consist of all of the elements of the following syntax:

```
predecessor guard-condition sequence-expression return-value := message-name argument-list
```

All of these may be omitted, but the *message-name* is usually shown. The *return-value*, *message-name* and *argument-list* together are called the *signature* of the message.

Message-name—The message-name is the event that is sent to the target object. This may be the name of either an event or an operation in the class of the target object. If it is an operation, then it must be defined in the class of the target object. For example, setFirstArranged sent to an instance of the class Journey.

If an event is used, then the object that receives the event will almost certainly carry out some operation, but the name of the event and the name of the operation are not the same. The term *signal* is used to refer to events that are sent asynchronously from one object to another (to distinguish them from other kinds of events used in state transition diagrams). A signal can have attributes, for example a MouseDown signal may have the attributes button, xyCoordinate and timestamp. Signals can be organized in a generalization hierarchy like classes.

Argument-list—Operations are only uniquely defined if their full argument-list is also specified, as operation names may be overloaded—have different versions with the same name but different sets of parameters. Events may also have arguments. The argument-list is a comma-separated list of names of the arguments, for example setArranged(dateArranged) or MouseDown(button, xyCoordinate, timestamp). Arguments are normally references to objects or to variables containing primitive data types. They can also be expressions in pseudocode or a programming language, for example setArranged(Date.getCurrentDate()). The names of the arguments can be the names of attributes of the sending object, return values from previous operations or navigation paths that are reachable from the object concerned, for example journeyName := getJourneyName(i) followed by journey := find(journeyName).

Return-value—Events are asynchronous and do not have return-values. Synchronous operations may have a return-value that is sent back to the object that sent the message. We have already seen two examples above in journeyName := getJourneyName(i) and journey := find(journeyName). Return-values are a list of names that are returned at the end of the operation. As shown, these can be used as arguments to later messages. If an operation does not return a value, the return-value and the ':=' are omitted—there is no need to use the word void as in some programming languages.

Instead of using text for arguments and return-values, they may be shown using *data tokens*, which are small circles with an arrow attached and the name of the data value alongside, as in Figure 8-26.

Sequence-expression—The sequence expression defines the order in which the interactions take place. It is a dot-separated list of *sequence-terms* followed by a colon. Each term represents a level of nesting

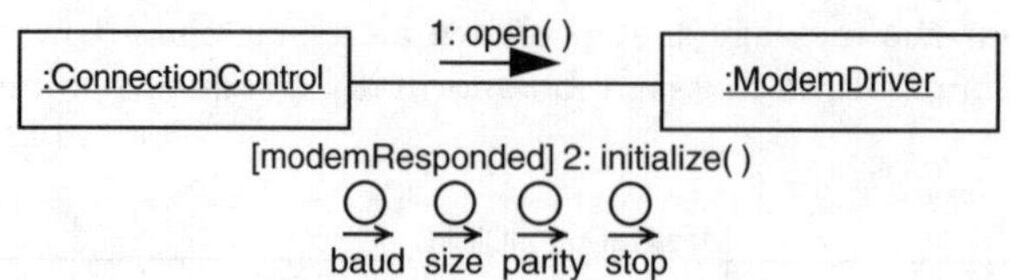

Fig. 8-26: Data tokens used as arguments

within the interaction. If an object receives an operation call numbered 1: and as a result sends an operation call to another two objects, then those operation calls will have sequence expressions 1.1: and 1.2:. If all the control is concurrent, then no nesting takes place and the messages can be numbered sequentially 1:, 2:, 3:, etc.

Each sequence-term can consist of an integer or a name with an optional *recurrence*. The UML Specification does not explain this clearly, as it states that each term is either an integer or a name, but it does not define a name in this context, and it is not clear whether it means a *name*, as discussed in Section 14.2.7. Examples given for message sequence-expressions incorporating names include 3.1a and A1. In (Booch et al., 1999), names of objects are used to prefix the sequence-numbers in messages originating from them.

Fig. 8-27: Prefixing a sequence-term with an object name

(Gomaa, 2000) suggests using initial names to represent the use case that is being realized by a collaboration, for example Use1.1.2, despite the fact that this is implicit in the meta-model. He also suggests the use of letters as suffixes to indicate both concurrent messages and alternative messages where there is a choice.

A name can be used in place of an integer to show concurrent nested operations; that is, the operations take place at the same time. So 3.1.1a and 3.1.1b are concurrent within the activation resulting from message 3.1. Names can also be used to distinguish alternative messages that result from a condition on the message, for example 3.1.2a[x <= 0] and 3.1.2b[x > 0].

The recurrence is used to denote messages that are sent iteratively or are sent depending on some condition. An iteration is denoted by an asterisk * and optionally an *iteration-clause* in square brackets, for example *[i:0..journeys.length] or *[while not end-of-file]. Where a name is used for an index in an iteration (like i in the first example), this can be used in subsequent sequence-terms, for example 2.1.i:, but the iteration-clause is not shown again at the nested level. If the operations within an iteration will be performed in parallel (in a device that provides parallel processing), then the asterisk is followed by two vertical lines, *||.

A condition uses the square brackets syntax without the asterisk, for example [dateArranged=null], and represents a point in the interaction where there is a choice.

Predecessor—The predecessor of a message is a list of comma-separated *sequence-numbers* followed by a slash. A sequence-number is a sequence-expression without the optional recurrence or the final colon, for example 2.1 rather than 2.1 *[while not end-of-file]:. The predecessor lists the sequence-numbers of messages that must have been completed before the current message can be sent, for example

2.1a,2.1b/2.2: drawLine(start, finish). If the list is empty, the slash is also omitted. According to the 'UML Semantics' section of the UML Specification, the sequence-numbers must have the same *activator* as the current message, although this does not seem to be the case in the examples in the 'UML Notation' section of the UML Specification. The effect of using the predecessor clause is to synchronize concurrent threads of execution before proceeding with the next message.

Guard-condition—A guard-condition is a condition that must evaluate to true before the message can be sent. The 'UML Notation' section on collaboration diagrams does not define a guard-condition, but it is defined in the context of *statechart diagrams* (see Chapter 11). A guard-condition is a Boolean expression, typically written in *Object Constraint Language*, that must be true for a transition in a statechart diagram to take place. The expression can be written in terms of parameters of the message, attributes of the current object, concurrent states of the current object or states of other objects that are reachable via links from the current object, for example [percentageComplete = 100]. In the context of a collaboration diagram, it would appear to indicate that a message will not be sent until the object instance meets some requirement, possibly as a result of another interaction in which it is also participating. The use of a guard-condition also has the effect of synchronizing threads of control. The circumstances in which you would use a guard-condition in a collaboration diagram are not clear, as it would have the effect of blocking the message being sent until the condition is true. This could cause the system to lock up if the condition is never met. It makes more sense to use the condition-clause version of the recurrence within a sequence-expression and to have an alternative branch. Figures 8-28 and 8-29 show the alternatives.

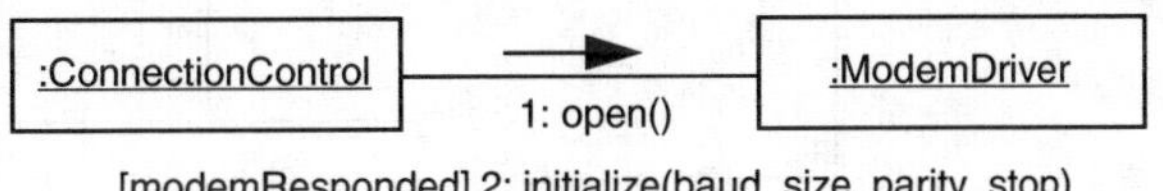

Fig. 8-28: Guarded message

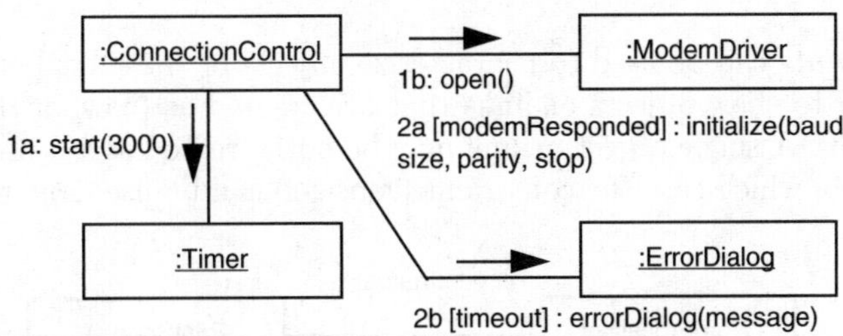

Fig. 8-29: Message with condition in sequence-expression

8.5.9 Further Notation

There are four additional aspects of collaboration diagram notation to be aware of:

- active objects
- multiobjects
- constraints
- flow relationships

Active objects—An *active object* is an object that owns a concurrent thread of control. This may be because it is an independent object running on its own processor, for example a database running on a server, or because it is running in a separate thread or process on a single processor, for example the print spooler in Windows. An active object is shown with a thick border or with the property keyword {active}, as in Figure 8-30.

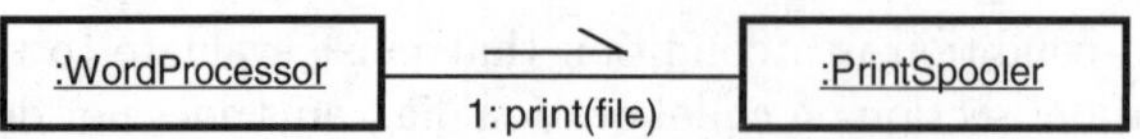

Fig. 8-30: Active object notation

Multiobjects—A *multiobject* is shown as two rectangles superimposed on one another and slightly offset. It is used to represent a set of objects at the 'many' end of an association, and to show that a message is sent to the set in order to obtain a link to each object in turn so that a further message can be sent to each. The individual object can be shown joined to the multiobject by a composition association, as in Figure 8-31.

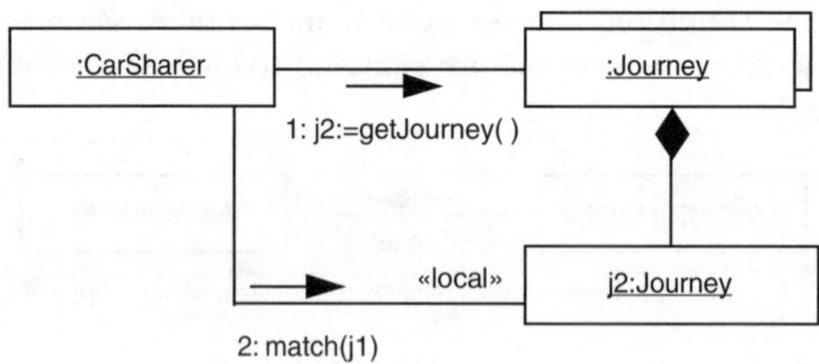

Fig. 8-31: Multiobject notation

Constraints—*Constraints* can be used to characterize objects or the links between them in a collaboration. They are used to show objects or links that are created as {new} or deleted as {destroyed} as part of the collaboration. A single object or link may be both created and destroyed within the course of a single interaction, in which case the constraint {transient} can be used, as in Figure 8-32.

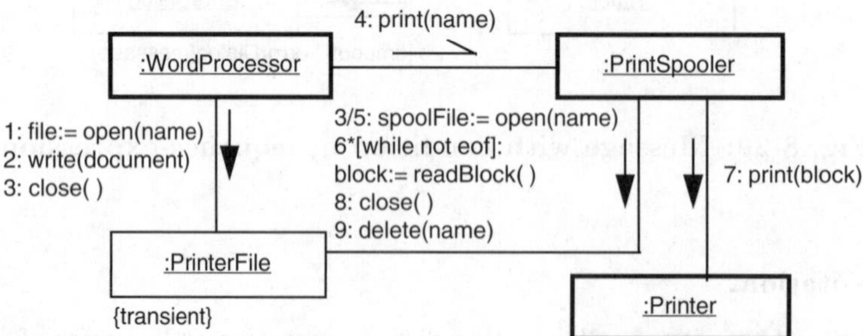

Fig. 8-32: Constraint notation

Flow relationships—*Flow relationships* can be used to show a dependency between two versions of an object at different points in time. The dependency can either be a «become» or a «copy» relationship, and indicates that an object has changed class or significantly changed state or has been copied. The stereotype label can be numbered to show where it belongs in the interaction sequence, as in Figure 8-33.

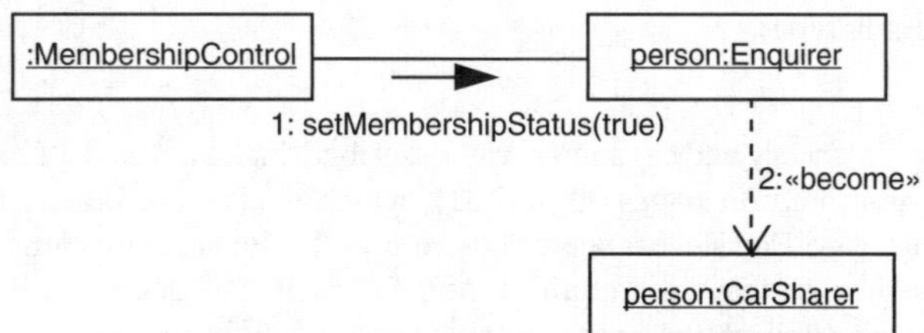

Fig. 8-33: Flow relationship notation

8.6 HOW TO PRODUCE COLLABORATION DIAGRAMS

Collaboration diagrams may be produced at a number of stages in the development of a system.

- Early in the development of a system, as part of the process of developing a class diagram. In this case, the objects participating in each use case can be modelled in a collaboration diagram, the objects can be assigned to possible classes and the classes in the collaboration diagrams merged to produce a first draft class diagram.
- Once the classes in a system are known, to specify the interaction that will take place between class roles in order to realize use cases.
- In order to specify the realization of operations that have complex behaviour.

Whatever the stage or purpose, the steps in developing a collaboration diagram are as follows.

- Decide on the context of the interaction: system, subsystem, use case or operation.
- Identify the structural elements (class roles, objects, subsystems) necessary to carry out the functionality of this collaboration.
- Model the structural relationships between those elements to produce a diagram showing the context of the interaction.
- Consider the alternative scenarios that may be required.
- Draw instance level collaboration diagrams, if required. (Alternatively, sequence diagrams can be drawn if the timing of messages is an important aspect of the interaction—see Chapter 9.)
- Optionally draw a specification level collaboration diagram to summarize the alternative scenarios in the instance level sequence diagrams.

8.6.1 Decide on Context

The collaboration diagram can model interaction at the system, subsystem, use case or operation level. The stage in the development of the project and the task being undertaken will determine which is to be modelled.

EXAMPLE 8.1 In this case, we are going to model a use case: the use case Register car sharer in the CarMatch system.

8.6.2 Identify Structural Elements

The first step is to identify the structural elements that will participate in the collaboration. These will include user interface elements, control elements and classes or objects that represent the business entities that the system deals with.

EXAMPLE 8.2 The use case Manually add car sharer was described in Chapter 3. This is a specialization of the use case Register car sharer (described on pages 30 and 31), which is also specialized by the use case Transfer car sharer from web server. The use case Register car sharer has to handle the common functionality of creating a new CarSharer, creating as many new Journeys as required, and for each new Journey validating the Addresses. For the purpose of this example, we shall assume that all this takes place in one go.

The classes involved here are CarSharer, Journey and Address. These can be drawn as a subset of the class diagram, as in Figure 8-34. There will also be an instance of some kind of control class that manages the collaboration, and either an interface class or a web transaction to provide the data, as in Figure 8-35.

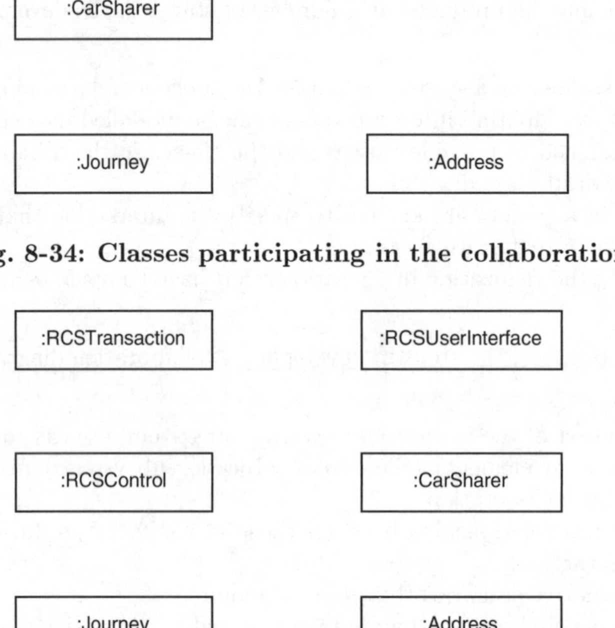

Fig. 8-34: Classes participating in the collaboration

Fig. 8-35: Interface and control classes added

Booch et al. (1999) suggests laying the objects out with the most important in the centre and the less important round the outside. Depending on the structure of the collaboration, this is not always appropriate. A top-down or left-right structure of message-passing may be easier to lay out.

8.6.3 Model Structural Relationships

The associations between classes are added to the collaboration diagram. In some cases, the same class will participate in different association roles. In such cases, it is best to distinguish between these by using different class roles. If the class role, state or attributes of a class or object change during the collaboration, place a copy in the diagram with the new values and connect the two with a message stereotyped as «become» or «copy».

EXAMPLE 8.3 There are associations between CarSharer and both Journey and Address, and two aggregation relationships between Journey and Address. These are shown in Figure 8-36. Control and user interface classes are also required. Without modelling the interaction in detail, it is not always obvious what the associations will be between such classes and the domain classes, so some possible associations have been added in Figure 8-37 and stereotyped as «local».

Drawing these structural relationships highlights the need for the class Address to appear in the diagram in different roles. These have been added in Figure 8-38.

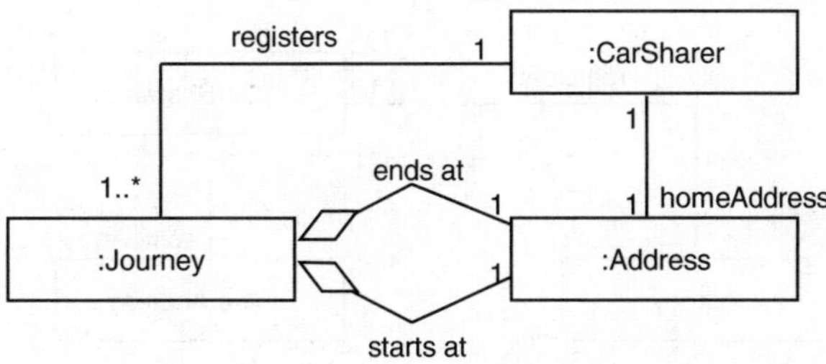

Fig. 8-36: Domain class associations

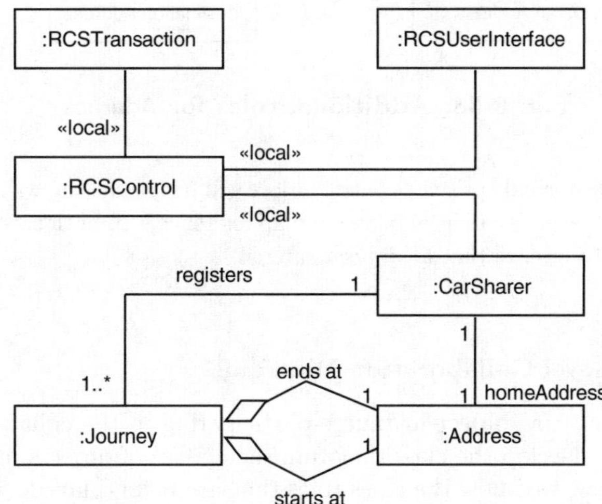

Fig. 8-37: Possible associations with interface and control classes

8.6.4 Consider Alternative Scenarios

There may be a number of different ways in which the interaction may develop, depending on inputs into the system or the state of existing objects in the system. These may already have been documented in behaviour specifications in the use case model, or the system developer may have to work through these alternatives as part of the process of producing collaboration diagrams. These alternatives may involve points in the interaction where one of two or more paths must be chosen, or they may involve iterations that execute a specific number of times. Collaboration diagrams with interactions can be drawn for the significant alternatives.

EXAMPLE 8.4 The two main alternatives for the realization of the use case Register car sharer depend on whether this use case's functionality is invoked from the use case Manually add car sharer or the use case Transfer car sharer from web server. In the first case, the control object will be interacting with a user interface object, and the address data will already have been validated against the geographical information system and a map

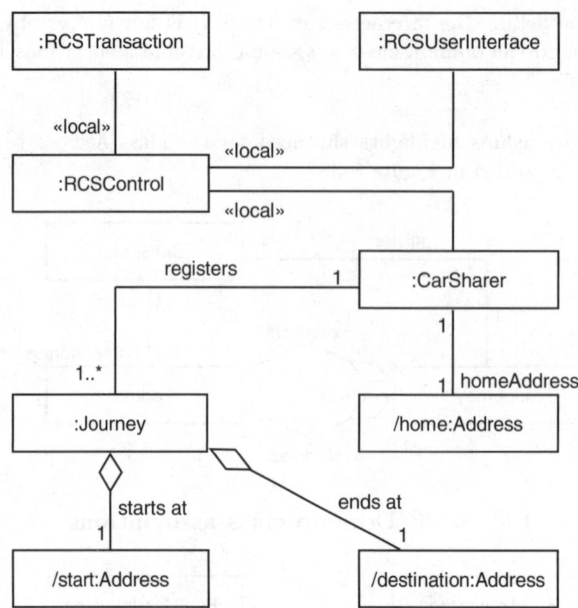

Fig. 8-38: Additional roles for Address

reference allocated to it. In the second case, the control object will be interacting with a web transaction object, and the addresses will have to be geolocated (allocated a map reference). In both cases, the number of iterations will depend on the number of journeys that have been entered.

8.6.5 Draw Instance Level Collaboration Diagrams

The instance level diagrams show object instances participating in the collaboration. If collaboration diagrams are being used to develop the class diagram, the classes of objects may not be known at this stage. In the example, below, we know the class roles that are being played.

Starting with the message that triggers the interaction, add each message to the appropriate link and add a sequence-term to each message. Add any necessary constraints to the objects or links.

EXAMPLE 8.5 Figure 8-39 shows the situation where the collaboration involves a user interface, and Figure 8-40 shows the situation where the collaboration involves a web transaction.

The constraint {new} has been added to the objects that are created in the interaction.

Some assumptions have been made here. Firstly, objects have been created using constructors that have the same name as the class. This is a convention in some languages, such as Java and C++. An alternative is to stereotype these messages as «create». Secondly, to keep the diagram simple, return-values and parameters have been left out in most cases. The exception to this is where a new instance of Journey is created by the control object and then added to the CarSharer. As an example, the parameters for the constructor operation CarSharer() would be firstname, lastname, dob, regDate, status and all those required for the home address. Thirdly, it is assumed that the CarSharer is responsible for creating its own Address object, but that Journeys are created by the control object. This is to avoid having to pass all the data associated with creating Journeys via the CarSharer. Fourthly, all the interaction associated with the user via the user interface or with the transfer of data via the web transaction is outside the scope of this use case realization. This collaboration provides the functionality that is inherited by the other two. In order for this to work, both the classes RCSTransaction and

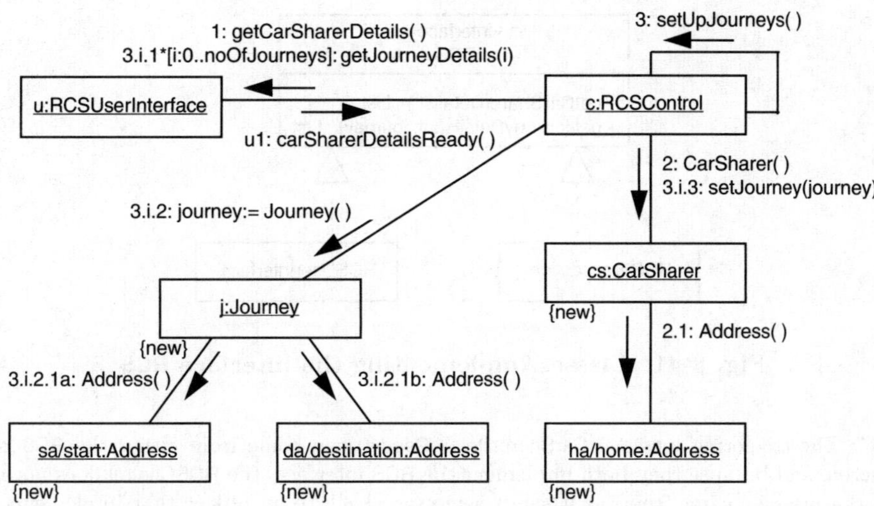

Fig. 8-39: Collaboration involving a user interface

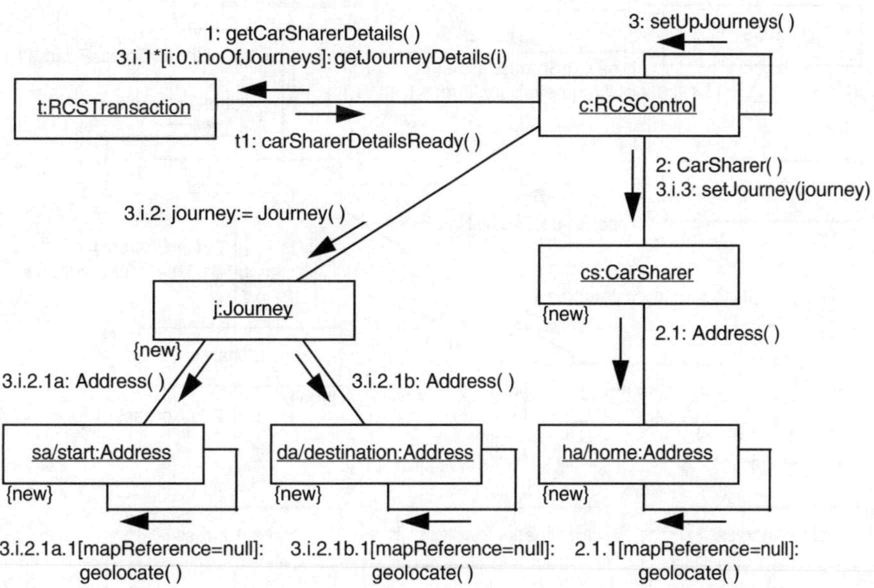

Fig. 8-40: Collaboration involving a web transaction

RCSUserInterface must support the operations getCarSharerDetails() and getJourneyDetails(). One way to do this is to define an interface which they both implement, as in Figure 8-41.

Note also that there are many alternative paths that could be taken as a result of incorrect input or invalid data, but it is not the role of the collaboration diagram to model all the possible error paths.

8.6.6 Draw Specification Level Collaboration Diagram

Optionally the instance level diagrams can be combined into a single specification level diagram. To do this, all alternative paths are shown on the diagram. Class roles are used rather than object instances.

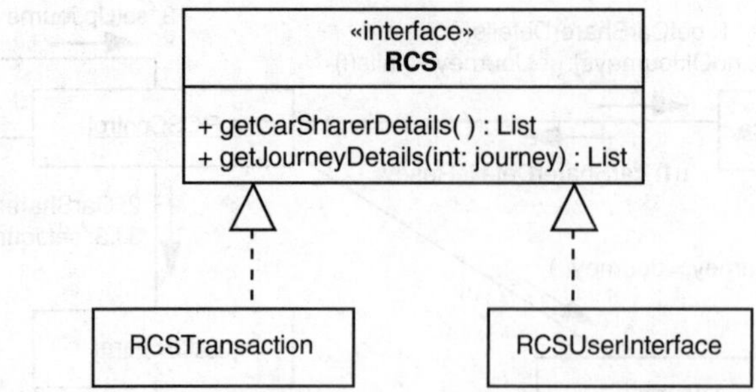

Fig. 8-41: Classes implementing the interface RCS

EXAMPLE 8.6 The triggering message CarSharerDetailsReady() can come from either the RCSUserInterface or the RCSTransaction, and because they both implement the RCS interface, the RCSControl does not need to know the class that the message came from, as it sends a message back to an object that implements the required interface.

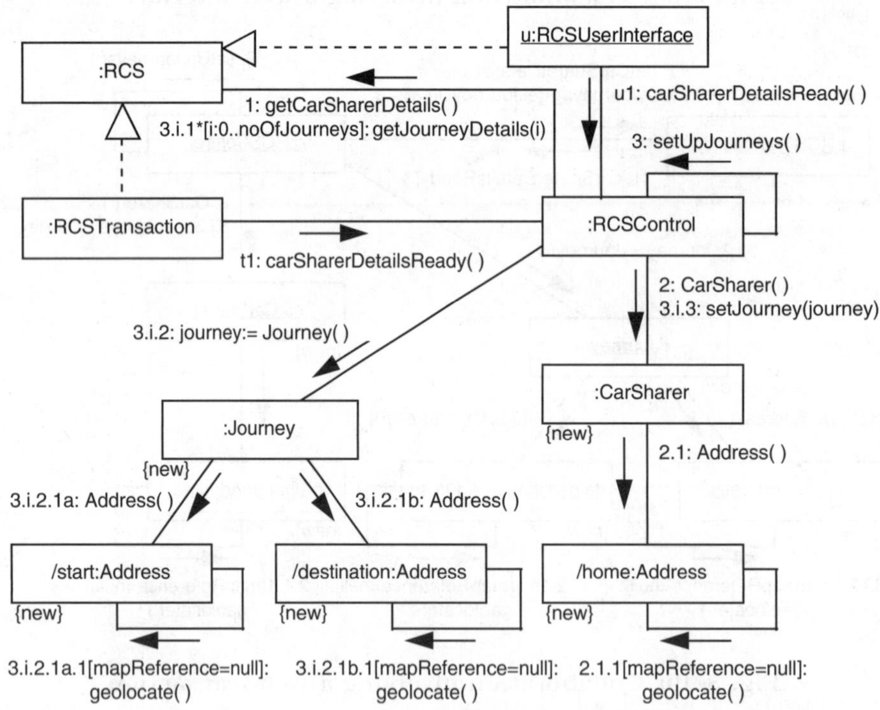

Fig. 8-42: Specification level collaboration

If there were any true alternative paths, then both paths would be shown in this diagram. Figure 8-42 shows a possible solution.

8.7 BUSINESS MODELLING WITH COLLABORATION DIAGRAMS

In the UML profile for business modelling, five class stereotypes are defined for business objects. These are: Actor, Worker, Case Worker, Internal Worker and Entity. Actors are defined in the UML. The meanings of the other stereotypes are as follows.

- **Worker**—an abstraction of a human who acts within a system to interact with other workers and manipulate entities in a use case realization.
- **Case worker**—a worker who interacts directly with actors outside the system.
- **Internal worker**—a worker who interacts with other workers and entities inside the system.
- **Entity**—a passive class that is manipulated by workers, participates in different interactions and usually outlives any single interaction. Entities are business classes, such as Address, Journey, Invoice and Product.

Entity classes have already been used, and are part of the UML software development process profile, together with user interface and control class stereotypes.

There are icons that can be used to represent these class stereotypes, and these are shown in Figure 8-43.

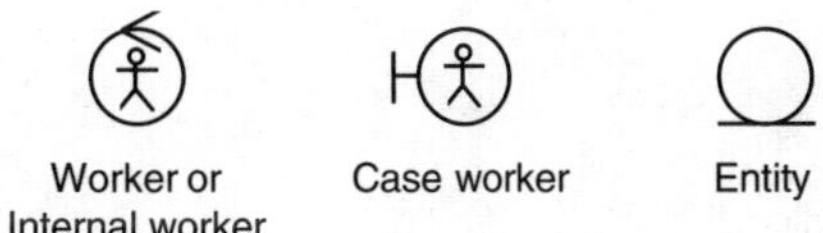

Fig. 8-43: Icons for business class stereotypes

These stereotyped icons can be used in collaboration diagrams to model the collaborations between workers and entities in use case realizations. Figure 8-44 shows their use in a collaboration diagram to model the use case Manually add car sharer.

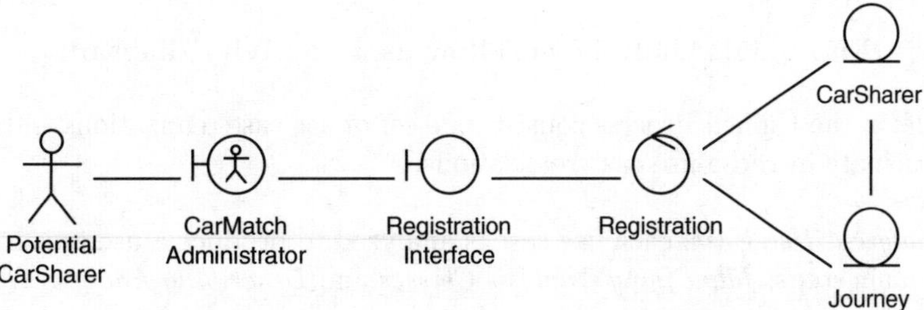

Fig. 8-44: Business collaboration diagram

This is the kind of diagram that would be produced at an early stage in the development of a system, as part of the business modelling and before detailed analysis is carried out.

8.8 RELATIONSHIP WITH OTHER DIAGRAMS

Collaboration diagrams can be used to model the realization of either use cases or operations of classes. In the latter case, each operation being modelled must exist in a class diagram. In an instance level diagram, the names of messages must be events or be operations of the class receiving the message. If states are referred to in guard conditions, they must be valid states of the relevant class and should appear in a statechart diagram (see Chapter 11).

Collaboration diagrams and sequence diagrams (see Chapter 9) model the same aspects of the system: the objects or class roles that collaborate together and the messages that are exchanged among them to achieve some objective. Collaboration diagrams and sequence diagrams can be converted into one another. Some CASE tools can do this automatically. They are almost but not quite interchangeable; some information is lost in the conversion: collaboration diagrams do not show information about timing constraints; sequence diagrams do not show the links between objects or the associations between class roles.

8.9 COLLABORATION DIAGRAMS IN THE UNIFIED PROCESS

Collaboration diagrams are used in the Unified Process first of all in the Analysis Workflow. This is shown in Figure 8-45.

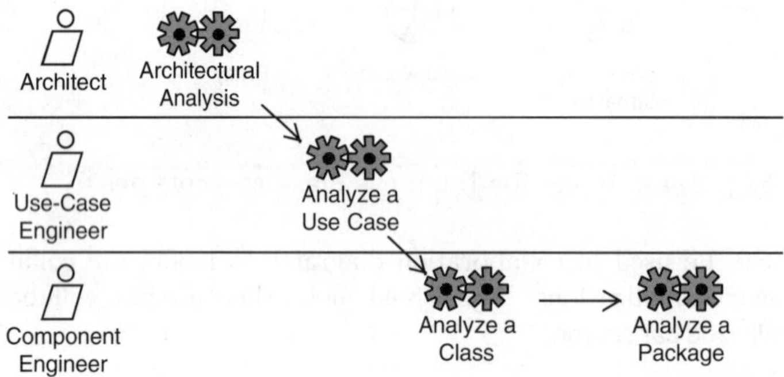

Fig. 8-45: Analysis workflow as an activity diagram

The Analysis Model in the Unified Process consists of a set of use case realizations and a set of classifiers (classes) that participate in those use case realizations.

In the activity *Analyze a Use Case*, each use case is analyzed to produce a use case realization. This is carried out in two main steps: *Identifying Analysis Classes* and *Describing Analysis Object Interactions*. First, the participating classes are identified and class diagrams produced to show just the classes involved in each use case, then the collaborations are analyzed to produce collaboration diagrams with interactions added to them. In the Analysis Model, these collaboration diagrams will use informal names for messages to show the intent of each message. These will be replaced later with event names or the names of specific operations of the design classes. Use cases are classifiers in UML terms, and can also be described by activity diagrams, statechart diagrams and sequence diagrams. Sequence diagrams can be used to represent the collaboration if there are important timing issues that are apparent during analysis. The collaborations can also be documented using *Flow of Events Analysis*. This uses text to describe the interaction taking place within a use case realization. These textual descriptions are different from those produced to specify the behaviour of use cases in the Requirements Workflow, as they describe the interaction between classes that are internal to the system, whereas use case descriptions describe the external behaviour of the use case (see Section 3.3.2). There is a third step, *Capturing Special Requirements*, in which all requirements relating to the use case are documented, including non-functional requirements, even if they are to be addressed in design rather than analysis.

The collaboration diagrams produced as part of the Analysis Model are refined in Design. Figure 8-46 shows the Unified Process Design Workflow.

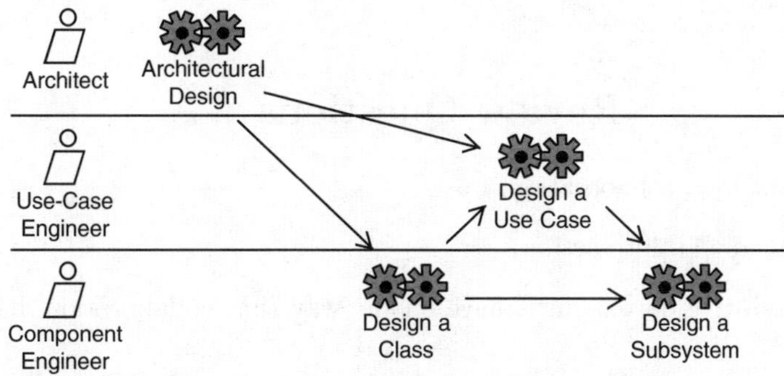

Fig. 8-46: Design workflow as an activity diagram

In the *Architectural Design* activity, the Architects look for and design generic collaborations that will be specialized by specific collaborations within the system. To do this, they look for common patterns of interaction in different collaborations. These involve similar actor roles and the same structure of participating class roles. In the CarMatch System, the use cases Process credit card payment and Notify insurer are both triggered by the completion of a financial transaction and involve the transfer of that transaction to an external system, and might therefore be candidates for this approach. (Note that they are different from the use case Transfer direct debit to ABTS which happens as a batch process: transactions take place and are stored for transfer as a batch at a later time or date.) A possible generic collaboration is shown in Figure 8-47.

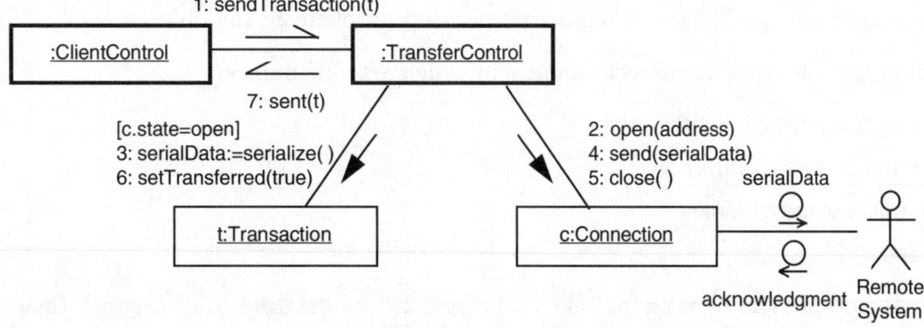

Fig. 8-47: Generic collaboration for transferring transactions to a remote system

The activity *Design a Use Case* is similar to the analysis activity of the same name, except for the fact that design classes are used and there are more steps, as more detail is required when a project gets closer to implementation. The main steps are: *Identifying the Participating Design Classes*, *Describing Design Object Interactions*, *Identifying the Participating Subsystems and Interfaces* and *Describing Subsystem Interactions*. Design classes may be different from analysis classes. For example, collection classes may be added in design to handle interactions that involve a set of objects. The interactions on the collaboration and sequence diagrams will have to be modified to include instances of these classes and their interactions. In the Unified Process, it is suggested that sequence diagrams rather than collaboration diagrams should be used to model the interactions in design. It is also possible to consider a use case in terms of interactions among design subsystems rather than design objects.

This provides a hierarchical decomposition of the interactions, as the detail of the interaction within a subsystem can be hidden in one diagram and shown in a separate lower-level diagram (see Chapter 9). In order to support this approach, the interfaces of subsystems must be identified, so that it is clear what operations or events each subsystem will handle. As in analysis, there is a fifth step, *Capturing Implementation Requirements*, in which requirements to be handled in implementation are documented.

Review Questions

8.1 Define what is meant by a collaboration.

8.2 Define what is meant by an interaction.

8.3 What effect does iterative development have on the way that collaboration diagrams are developed?

8.4 What are the main purposes of using collaboration diagrams?

8.5 What is the notation for a collaboration?

8.6 What dependencies can exist between collaborations and operations and use cases?

8.7 How can the template notation be used to represent a design pattern using a collaboration?

8.8 What is the difference between a specification level collaboration diagram and an instance level collaboration diagram?

8.9 What is the purpose of drawing a context collaboration diagram?

8.10 What distinguishes the names of object instances from the names of roles in collaboration diagrams?

8.11 What delimiter is used in a role name to separate the role from the object name?

8.12 Which of the following are object names and which are role names?

(a) /returnJourney:Journey

(b) /returnJourney:Journey

(c) j/returnJourney:Journey

(d) :Journey

8.13 What stereotypes can be used on links in a collaboration diagram to distinguish them from links that are instances of static associations in the class diagram?

8.14 Define what is meant by a stimulus in collaboration diagrams.

8.15 What is the distinction between a message and a stimulus?

8.16 What three kinds of stimulus can be used in a collaboration diagram?

8.17 What are the four types of messages that can be represented by different arrow styles in a collaboration diagram?

8.18 What distinguishes an event from an operation as a stimulus?

8.19 What is meant by a return-value?

8.20 What is a sequence-term in a message?

8.21 How can names be used in sequence-expressions?

8.22 What is meant by a guard-condition?

8.23 What is an active object?

8.24 What is the notation for an active object?

8.25 What is the notation for a multiobject?

8.26 What special constraints can be shown on links or objects in a collaboration diagram?

8.27 What dependencies can be shown by flow relationships?

8.28 What are the steps in producing a collaboration diagram?

8.29 What are the five class stereotypes defined in the UML Business Modelling profile?

8.30 Which two Unified Process workflows are collaboration diagrams used in?

8.31 What are the three steps in the Unified Process activity Analyze a Use Case?

8.32 How does a Flow of Events Analysis differ from a Use Case Description?

8.33 What is meant by a generic collaboration?

8.34 What are the five steps in the Unified Process activity Design a Use Case?

Solved Problems

8.1 One of the use cases in the CarMatch system is called Match car sharers. Here is a summary use case description.

> When a new member joins CarMatch as a car sharer, the member's journeys are matched against the unmatched journeys of other members to try to find suitable people with whom he or she could share travel. The automated part of the matching is carried out by passing the map references of the start and finish addresses of two journeys to a geographical information system (GIS). The GIS returns a percentage value which is a measure of how close together the two journeys are. If this percentage is greater than or equal to 80%, the journeys are looked at by a member of staff, who also looks at the members' requirements notes to decide whether they are compatible. If it looks like the journeys are similar and the people are compatible, a letter is sent out.

It is clear that the context of this collaboration is a use case. What are the domain classes that are involved in the use case Match car sharers? (You may want to look at the class diagrams in Chapter 5.)

There are three classes from the class diagram involved in this use case: CarSharer, Journey and Address.

8.2 What other subsystems are involved in this use case?

The geographical information system is a separate subsystem. We are not concerned here with how it works, only with the service it provides (matching journeys) and the interface that must be used to obtain that service. In this particular case, as with the geolocation of addresses in the earlier example, we shall not need to show it in the collaboration diagram. If we were drawing a collaboration diagram for the operation Address:geolocate() or Journey:matchJourney(journey), then we would need to show it.

8.3 What are the additional classes that will be required for this collaboration?

The collaboration will also require a control class and a user interface class: MCSControl and MCSUserInterface.

8.4 Draw a class diagram showing the associations between the classes, including stereotyped associations if required.

Figure 8-48 shows a possible solution. Note that the homeAddress association between CarSharer and Address is not required for this collaboration.

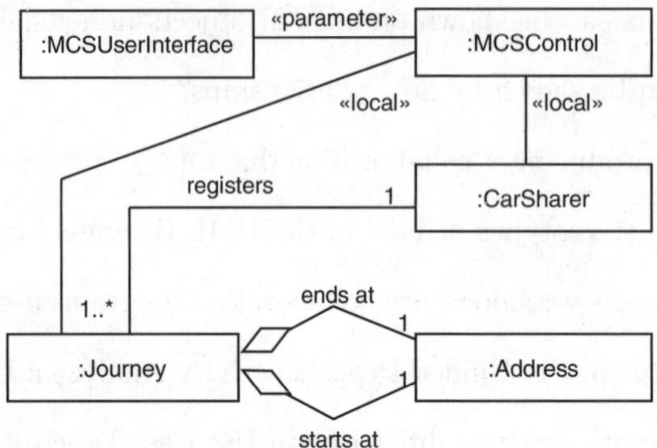

Fig. 8-48: Classes participating in the collaboration

8.5 What are the roles that the classes in Figure 8-48 take in this collaboration?

For each Journey there are two address roles: /start:Address and /destination:Address. This use case involves matching the Journeys from the set of existing unmatched Journeys against the Journeys for the new CarSharer, and this could involve the use of a multiobject as well as different roles for the different Journeys. Figure 8-49 shows the different roles involved.

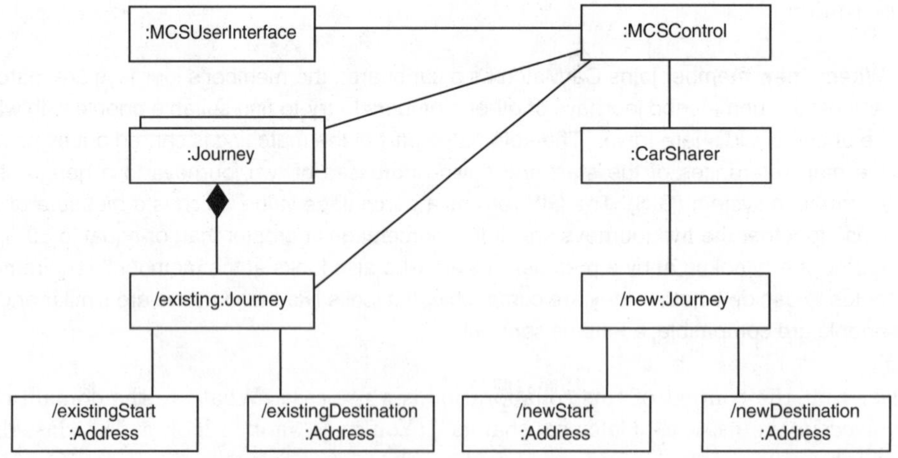

Fig. 8-49: Roles for classes participating in collaboration

8.6 What are the alternative scenarios that may occur?

There are two significant alternatives. In the first, a Journey is found that matches one of the new ones, and the details of the journeys and the car sharers' requirements are displayed to the Administrator. In the second, none of the Journeys has a match of 80% or more against the new ones, so no details are displayed for the Administrator. Thinking about the first scenario, we realize that in order to display the requirements of the existing car sharer whose journey matches one of the new ones we shall need another class role in the collaboration diagram. This has been added in Figure 8-50.

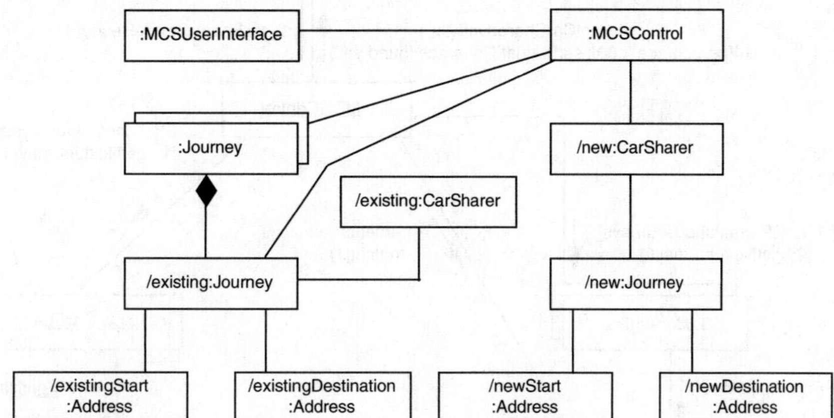

Fig. 8-50: Revised roles for classes participating in collaboration

8.7 Draw an instance level collaboration diagram for each of these scenarios.

The two different scenarios are shown in Figures 8-51 and 8-52. The messages have been numbered sequentially rather than using nesting, as the sequence expressions were getting very complex, for example 1.2.i.j.2.1.1a!

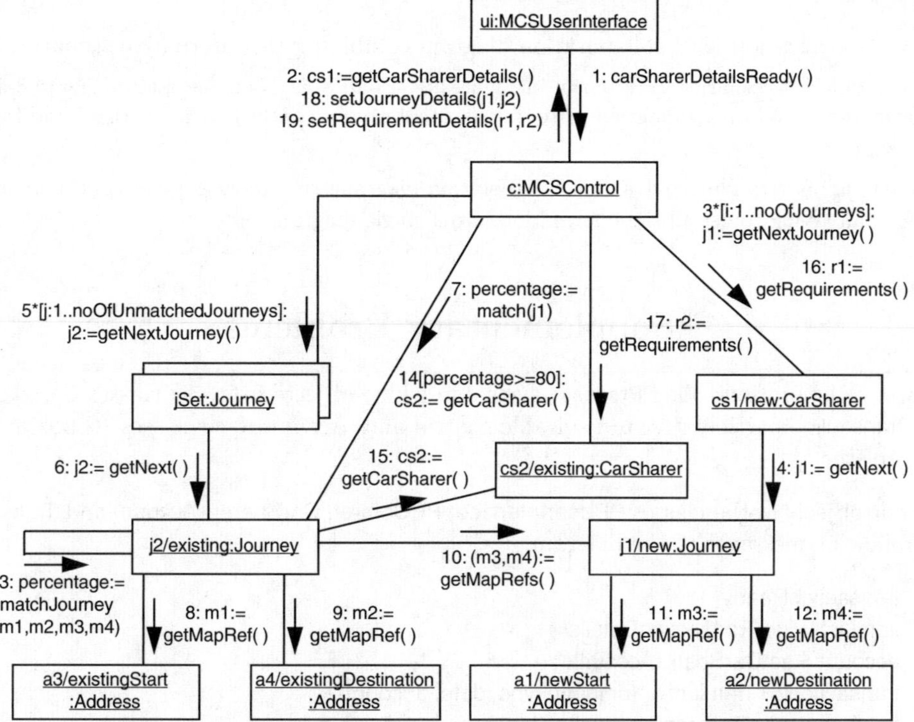

Fig. 8-51: Instance level collaboration diagram for the first scenario

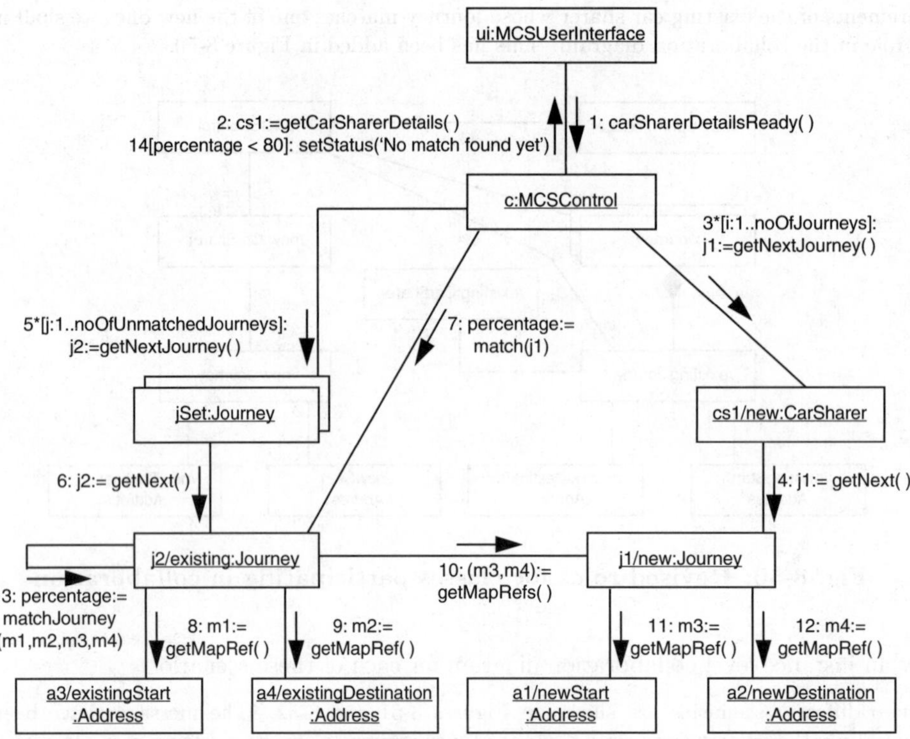

Fig. 8-52: Instance level collaboration diagram for the second scenario

8.8 Draw a specification level collaboration diagram combining the alternative scenarios.

The two different scenarios were shown in Figures 8-51 and 8-52. The diagram in Figure 8-53 shows the two combined into a single diagram, with one set of alternative paths labelled with 'a' and the other path with 'b'.

This diagram is very cluttered. Often collaboration diagrams are drawn for excerpts from an interaction rather than trying to get all the information into a single diagram.

Supplementary Problems

8.9 Draw a collaboration called Process payment in which objects from the classes CarSharer, Account and Transaction participate. Add suitable control and user interface classes. (Look at page 152 if you are stuck.)

8.10 Lay out objects of the classes PPUserInterface, PPControl, CarSharer, Account and Transaction. Add the following messages to the diagram.

1. transactionReady( )
2. itemList := getTransactionDetails( )
3. account:= getCarSharerAccount( )
4. transaction := Transaction(amount, type, date, account)
5. balance := postTransaction(transaction)
6. displayBalance(balance)

The variable itemList contains the following items: carSharerID, amount, type, date.

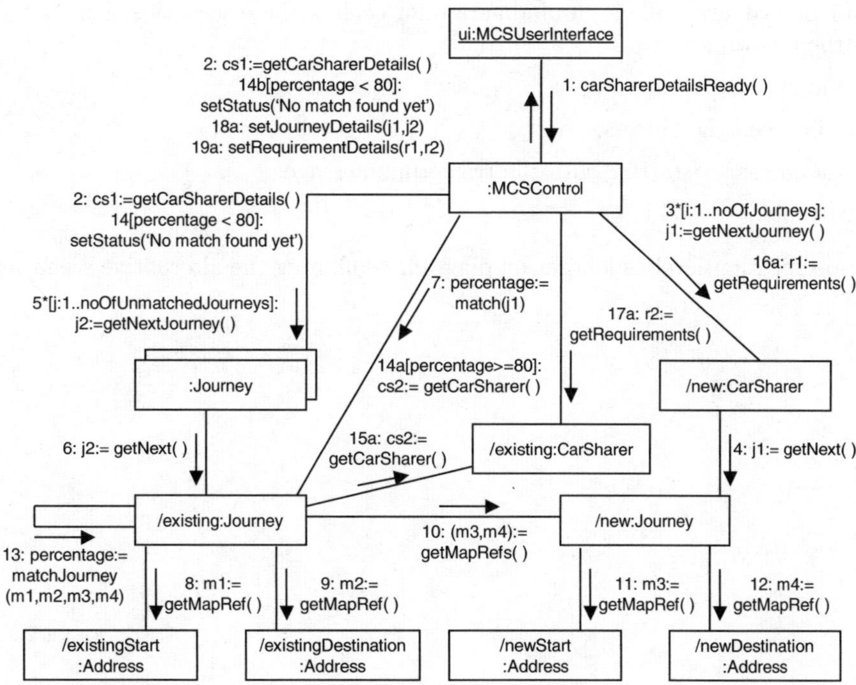

Fig. 8-53: Specification level collaboration diagram

8.11 One of the use cases that you found in Chapter 3 should have had a name such as Record an individual's request for help. In case you did not have a use case like this, here is a short summary description.

> Individuals can request help from VolBank. This includes volunteers requesting help themselves. The Volbank administrator first enters the details of the individual. If this is an existing volunteer, then the name is entered and the details are displayed. If there is more than one person with the same name, then a list is displayed with the first part of the address, and the administrator selects the right one. If this is not an existing volunteer, then the name, address and telephone number are entered. It is important that the zip or postal code is entered, as it is required to match this request with volunteers in the same area. Details of the help required are then entered: a text summary of the help and a code that describes the type of help wanted, for example DEC for decorating, GAR for garden work or PET for pet care. A start and finish date for when the help is required are also entered.

Again, the context of the collaboration is a use case. What are the domain classes that are involved in this use case?

8.12 What other subsystems (if any) are involved in this use case?

8.13 What are the additional classes that will be required for this collaboration?

8.14 Draw a class diagram showing the associations between the classes, including stereotyped associations if required.

8.15 What are the roles that these classes take in this collaboration?

8.16 What are the alternative scenarios that may occur?

8.17 Draw an instance level collaboration diagram for each of these scenarios. For each diagram work through the following steps.

Lay out the objects.

Add links between the objects.

Lay out the messages starting with the triggering message.

Add constraints.

8.18 Draw a specification level collaboration diagram combining the alternative scenarios.

Interaction Sequence Diagrams

9.1 INTRODUCTION

In object-oriented systems, tasks are performed by objects interacting with each other by passing messages. Interaction diagrams are used to model these object interactions. An interaction is a specification of the way in which messages are sent between objects or class roles in order to perform a task. In UML there are two kinds of diagram that are classed as *Interaction Diagrams*: *Sequence Diagrams* and *Collaboration Diagrams*. In this chapter we explain the notation and use of sequence diagrams; this builds on the explanation of the notation and use of collaboration diagrams in Chapter 8.

Class diagrams model the static structure of the system; interaction diagrams model the dynamic aspects of the system: they show how objects interact with one another to achieve some high-level functionality that individual objects cannot achieve on their own. Collaboration diagrams show this interaction in the context of the class roles that participate in the interaction and show the structural relationship of the classes to one another using association roles. Sequence diagrams are used to show the same interaction as in a collaboration diagram, but they emphasize the order of the messages over time.

9.2 WHAT IS A SEQUENCE DIAGRAM?

In Chapter 8 we showed how the interaction between objects or class roles can be added to a collaboration diagram as a series of stimuli or messages between those objects or roles. Figure 9-1 shows the collaboration diagram that we gave as an example at the start of that chapter with the interaction between the roles superimposed on it.

As a way of representing an interaction graphically, collaboration diagrams have two main characteristics: they show the structural relationships between the class roles or objects in terms of association roles or links—reflecting the structure of the class diagram—and they show the order of the interaction textually—using the sequence-numbers in the messages. Sequence diagrams represent some of the same information, but not all: they show object instances that play the roles defined in a collaboration; they do not show the structural relationships between objects and they show the order of the interaction visually by using the vertical axis of the diagram to represent time. Figure 9-2 shows the same interaction as Figure 9-1 as a sequence diagram.

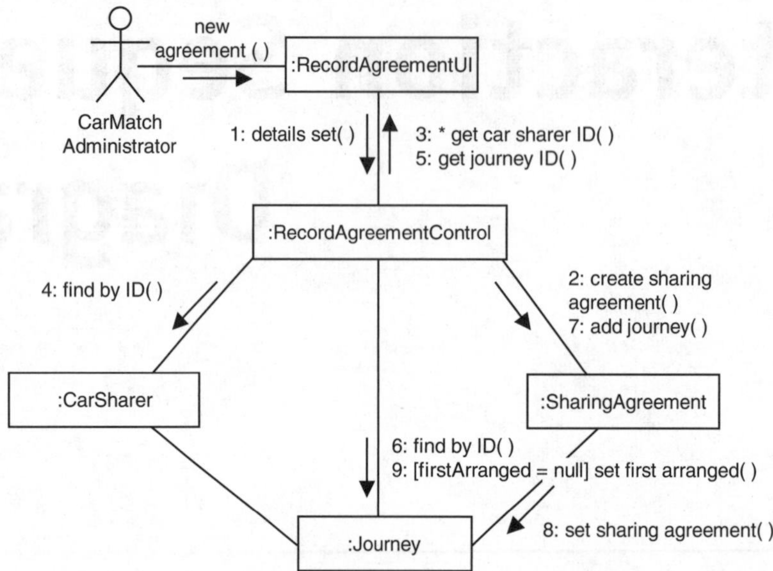

Fig. 9-1: Collaboration diagram with interaction

Figure 9-2 illustrates the way in which the order of the stimuli can be read from the diagram by looking at their sequence down the page, so there is no need for sequence numbers. Although this diagram illustrates the same collaboration as the collaboration diagram in Figure 9-1, the links between the objects are not shown. We cannot tell whether the ability of one object to send a message to another is based on a permanent association in the class diagram or a temporary link («local» or «parameter») created for the purpose of this interaction.

The sequence diagram does highlight some aspects that are not so obvious from the collaboration diagram. The creation of an object instance is shown explicitly by drawing the arrow to the rectangle containing its name (as in the case of the :SharingAgreement object, and its *lifeline* (the vertical dashed line) begins at the point when it is created. The *focus of control*, represented by the long, thin rectangles on the lifeline, shows when an object is active, either because it is performing some action or because it has sent a message to another object, which is carrying out an action on its behalf.

9.3 PURPOSE OF THE TECHNIQUE

Sequence diagrams are used to model the interaction between object instances in the context of a collaboration. The collaboration is implicit in a sequence diagram, rather than explicitly represented as in a collaboration diagram. Instances are used rather than roles, but it must be remembered that each instance is playing a role that has been defined in a collaboration.

Sequence diagrams can be used in the following ways.

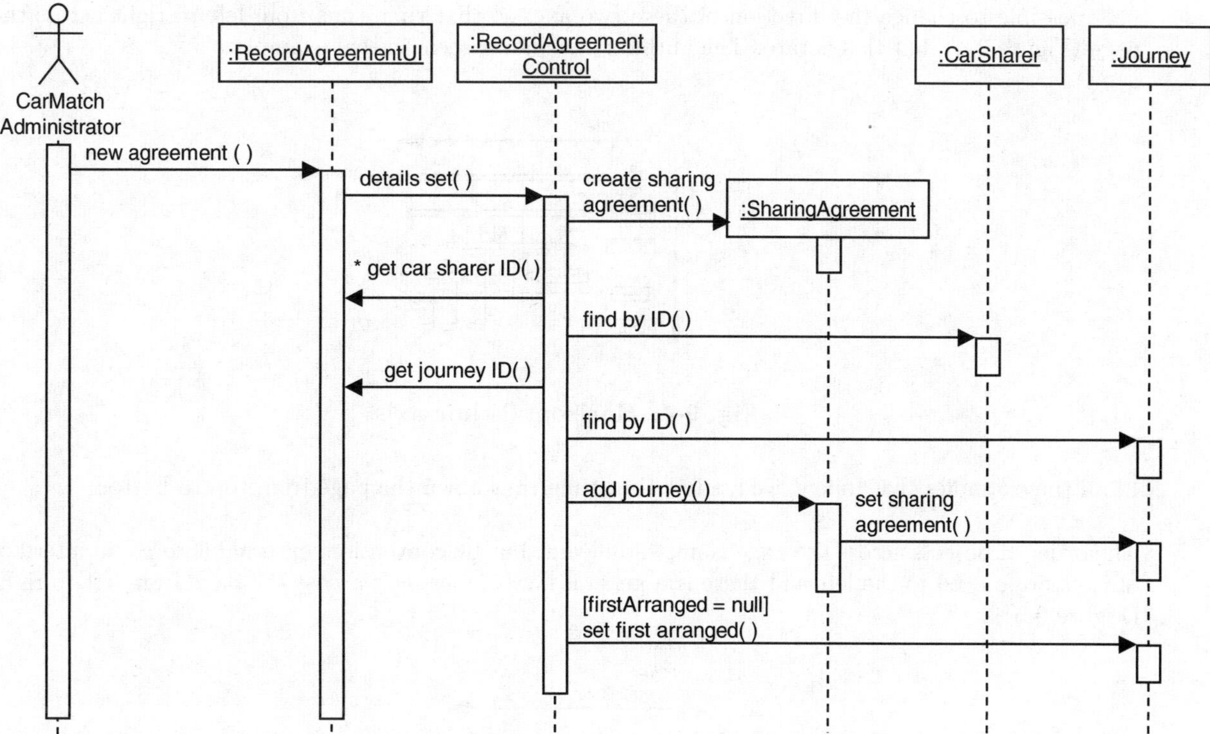

Fig. 9-2: Sequence diagram equivalent of Figure 9-1

- They are used to model the high-level interaction between active objects in a system.
- They are used to model the interaction between object instances within a collaboration that realizes a use case.
- They are used to model the interaction between objects within a collaboration that realizes an operation.
- They can be used either to model generic interactions (showing all possible paths through the interaction) or specific instances of an interaction (showing just one path through the interaction).

9.4 NOTATION OF SEQUENCE DIAGRAMS

In sequence diagrams, object instances are arranged horizontally across the page, and time runs vertically down the page (Figure 9-3).

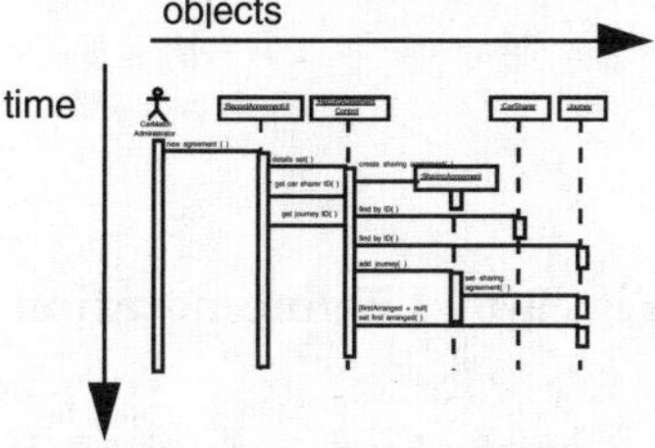

Fig. 9-3: Vertical time axis

It is possible to change the direction of these two axes so that time runs from left to right across the page (Figure 9-4), but this is rare. The authors have never seen an real example.

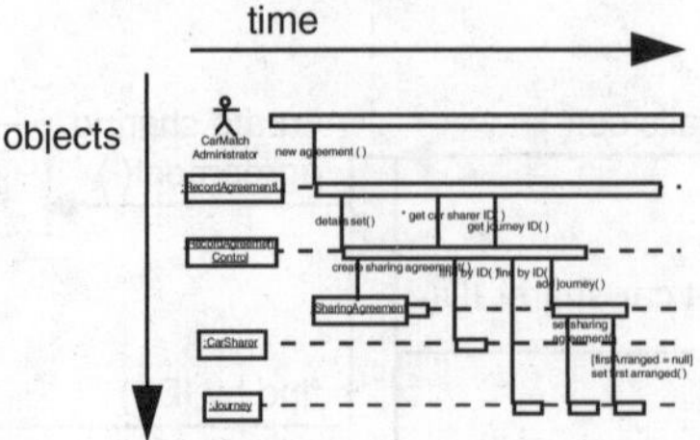

Fig. 9-4: Horizontal time axis

In all the examples that follow, we assume that time runs down the page from top to bottom.

The order of objects across the page is not significant, but by convention, external actors and interface objects are placed to the left and there is a general flow of messages across the page from left to right (Figure 9-5).

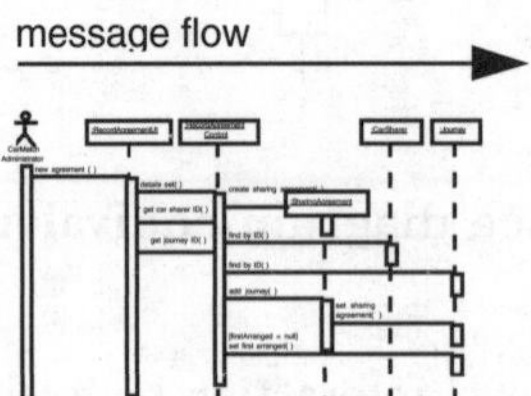

Fig. 9-5: Direction of message flow

9.4.1 Lifelines and Activations

Object instances are represented in sequence diagrams by a dashed vertical line with an object symbol at the top of the line. This dashed line is the *lifeline* of the object, as shown in Figure 9-6.

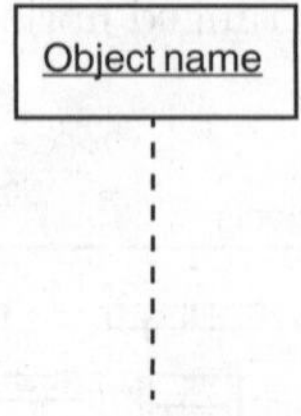

Fig. 9-6: Lifeline notation

The lifeline represents the time during which the object exists. If a particular object exists before an interaction starts and continues to exist after the interaction ends, then its lifeline runs from top to bottom of the diagram.

The same conventions apply to the names of object instances in sequence diagrams as in collaboration diagrams. Table 8-1 is repeated for convenience as Table 9-1 and shows the various forms that instance names can take.

Table 9-1: Syntax of instance names

Syntax	Explanation
o	An object named o.
o:C	An object named o of class C.
:C	An anonymous object of class C.
/R	An anonymous object playing the role R.
/R:C	An anonymous object of class C playing the role R.
o/R	An object named o playing the role R.
o/R:C	An object named o of class C playing the role R.

In a sequence diagram, a message or stimulus (see page 157) is shown using an arrow going from the sender to the receiver (see Figure 9-7).

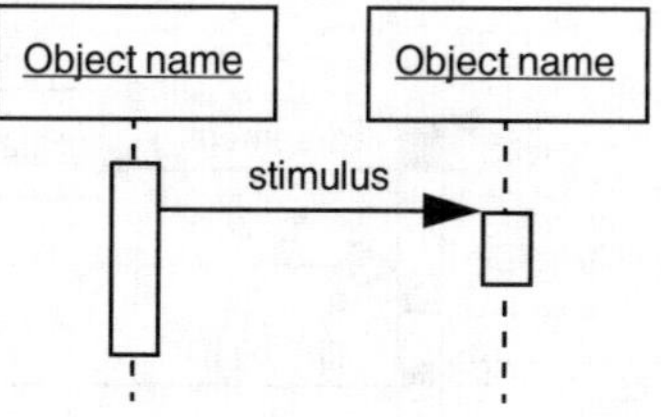

Fig. 9-7: Stimulus notation

The arrow is labelled with the message or stimulus that is being sent. From now on, we shall use the term message for the sake of simplicity.

The arrow is usually shown going from the *focus of control* region of the sending object to the focus of control region of the receiving object. The focus of control is shown as a narrow rectangle placed over the lifeline of the object. This is not always shown in sequence diagrams. The focus of control indicates which object is currently controlling the interaction because it is performing some task itself or because it has sent a message to another object requesting it to carry out a task. The idea of focus of control applies only when the messages that are sent are procedural calls from one object to another; these calls are synchronous. In an asynchronous interaction, one object can send a message to another object, and the first object then carries on with its next task without waiting for a reply; in a synchronous interaction each object waits for a response. The return of control in procedural interactions can be shown with a dashed arrow returning to the calling object, as in Figure 9-8.

The time when a particular object is active can be shown by shading the area of the focus of control, as in Figure 9-9. Figure 9-10 shows the sequence diagram of Figure 9-2 with explicit returns and shaded areas of activation in the flow of control. In a running program that uses procedural calls, the shaded areas represent times when program code is running in the particular object represented by the lifeline that owns that focus of control.

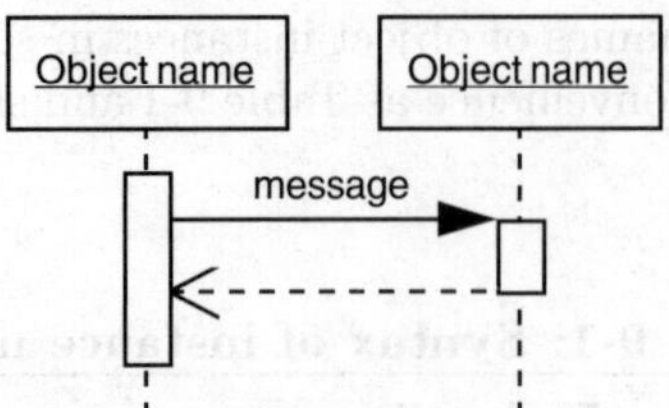

Fig. 9-8: Return notation

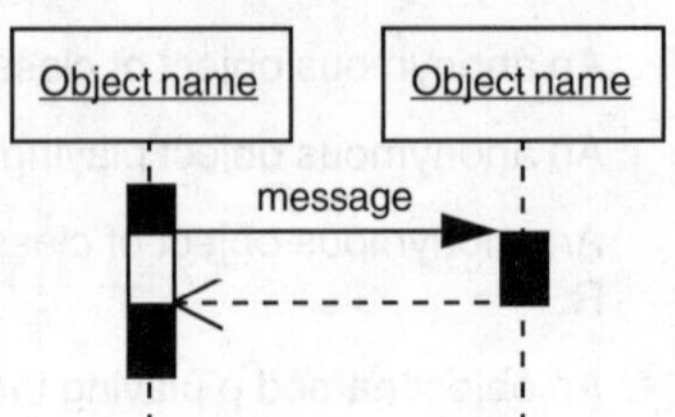

Fig. 9-9: Activation notation

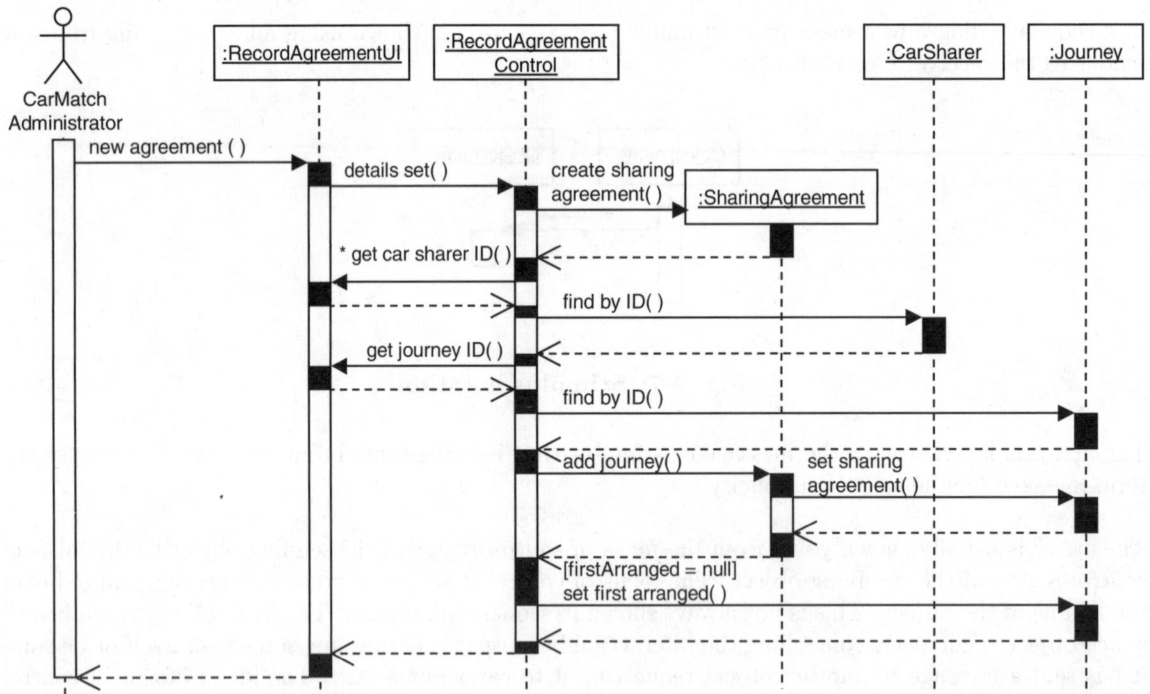

Fig. 9-10: Sequence diagram with explicit returns and shaded areas of activation

The focus of control rectangles in the objects to the right of the diagram are not continuous because they are active only for short periods of time; the user interface and control objects are active all the time and delegate responsibility for carrying out specific tasks to the other objects.

Sequence diagrams drawn like this give a much clearer picture than the equivalent collaboration diagram (Figure 9-1) of which objects are active when in an interaction. However, they can also become cluttered with lines and difficult to understand.

Not all messages are synchronous, and, as with collaboration diagrams, different style arrows can be used to represent different types of message (Figure 9-11).

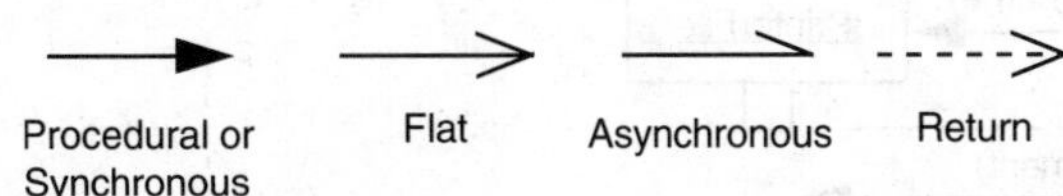

Fig. 9-11: Message flow notation

- **Procedural or Synchronous**—A message is sent by one object to another and the first object waits until the resulting action has completed. This may include waiting for the completion of actions invoked by the second object on other objects.
- **Flat**—Each arrow shows a progression from one step to the next in a sequence. Normally the message is asynchronous. A flat message can be used where it is not known whether the actual message will be synchronous or asynchronous.
- **Asynchronous**—A message is sent by one object to another but the first object does not wait until the resulting action has completed, it carries on with the next step in its own sequence of actions.
- **Return**—Represents the explicit return of control from the object to which the message was sent. Not normally shown on collaboration diagrams (see Chapter 8).

The arrow represents the flow of control. Where the flow of control is procedural or synchronous, there is only one thread of execution, and activity passes from one object to another. Where the flow of control is asynchronous, more than one object can be active at any one time. Figure 9-12 shows the collaboration diagram example from page 162 as a sequence diagram. Note that an asynchronous message is sent between the active objects, :WordProcessor and :PrintSpooler, which are drawn with a thick border (the notation for active objects—see page 161). The :Printer is also shown as an active object, but we have drawn it here with an explicit return to acknowledge that it has printed a block before it carries on with the next.

This diagram also illustrates the destruction of an object using a large 'X' at the end of the lifeline of an object where it has received a message that represents a *DestroyAction*. In this figure, the :PrinterFile object is both created and destroyed in the course of the interaction. This is the equivalent of the {transient} constraint in the collaboration diagram. In this example, the 'X' is shown at the end of a region of focus of control, as the :PrinterFile has to carry out some actions to delete itself and free up system resources, but it can be shown on the lifeline if the DestroyAction simply results in the destruction of the object. Also in this case, we have drawn the deletion as synchronous, as the :PrinterFile explicitly passes back control (and a result code) to the :PrintSpooler. Messages to create and destroy objects can be stereotyped as «create» and «destroy» (Figure 9-13).

Where a sequence of messages takes place within an iteration, the messages can be shown grouped together within a rectangle with the *recurrence condition* at the bottom of the rectangle (Figure 9-14). The Specification is not clear about whether the recurrence condition should have an asterisk or not, and gives no examples. We have added the asterisk to make it clear that an iteration is involved.

An example of this is shown in Figure 9-15, where the :PrintSpooler repeatedly reads a block from the :PrinterFile and writes it to the :Printer until it reaches the end of the file.

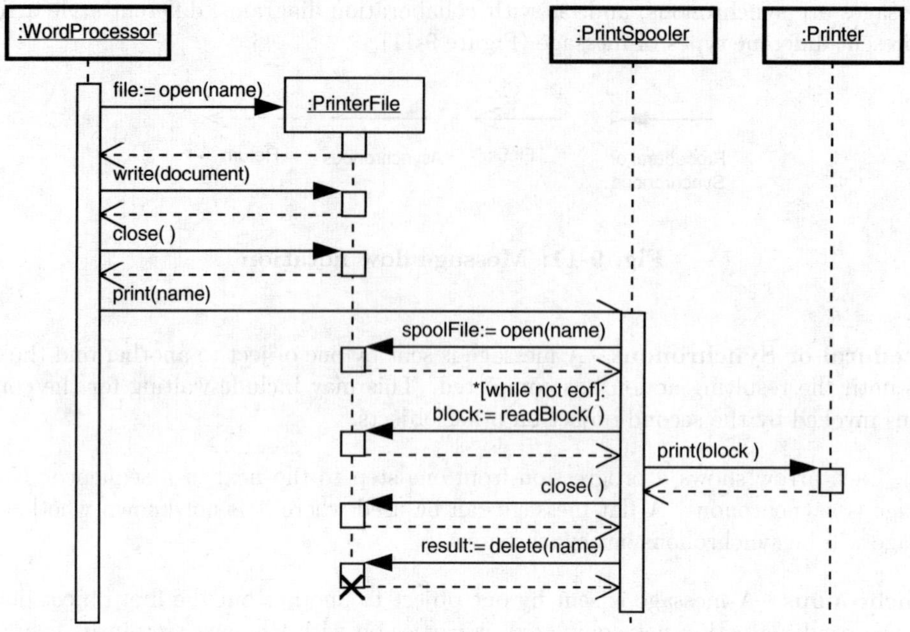

Fig. 9-12: Sequence diagram with asynchronous messages and active objects

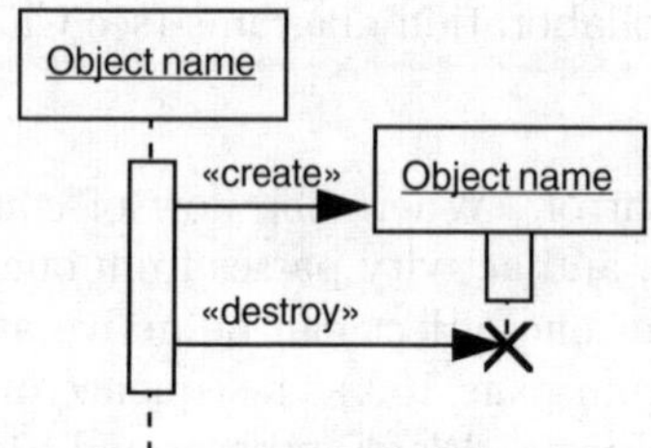

Fig. 9-13: Notation for creation and destruction of an object

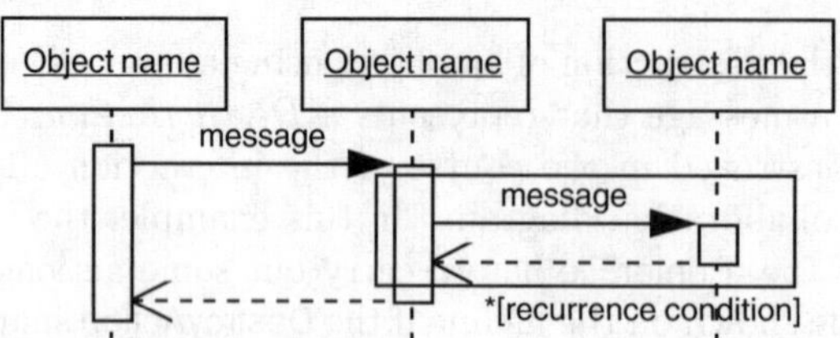

Fig. 9-14: Notation for iteration (recurrence)

An object can send a message to itself or call one of its own operations. This can be explicitly shown in the focus of control region by placing a separate rectangle over the existing one and offsetting it slightly to the right (Figure 9-16).

Branching can be shown in a sequence diagram by two arrows branching off from the same point. A condition-clause is added to the message to show the condition that is used to make the decision about which branch to take (Figure 9-17).

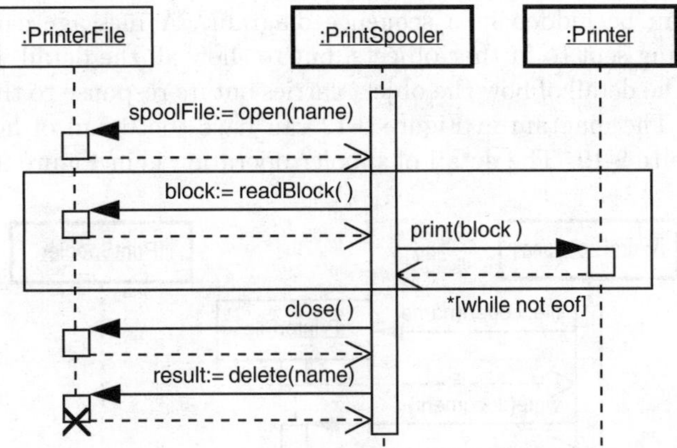

Fig. 9-15: Sequence diagram with iteration shown by grouping messages

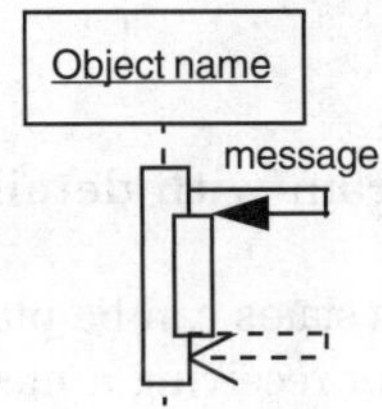

Fig. 9-16: Notation for recursion

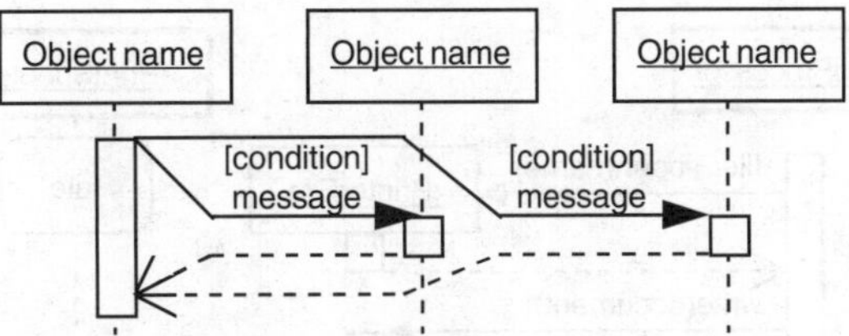

Fig. 9-17: Notation for branch

Where the branch results in a choice of two different messages (or operation calls) being sent to the same object, the lifeline of the object is shown forking with two different focus of control regions. The separate lifelines merge back together after the completion of different actions in response to the different messages (Figure 9-18).

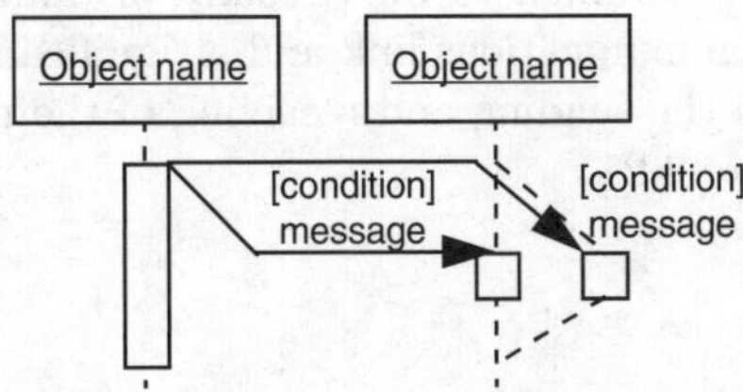

Fig. 9-18: Notation for branches to the same object's lifeline

Detail of interactions can be hidden in a sequence diagram. A message can be sent to an object, resulting in messages being sent to further objects, but to show all the detail would make the diagram unwieldy or cluttered. The detail of how the object carries out its response to the message can be shown in a separate diagram. The diagram in Figure 9-12 can have the detail of how the spooler operates removed to produce Figure 9-19. The detail of spooler operation is in Figure 9-15.

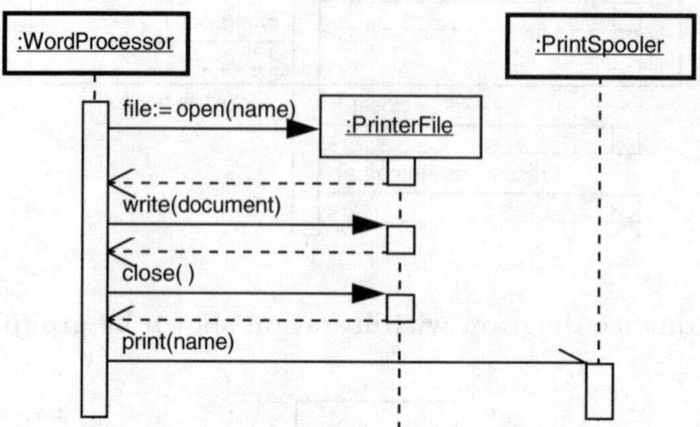

Fig. 9-19: Sequence diagram with detail removed to simplify it

According to Rumbaugh et al. (1999), object states can be placed on a lifeline to indicate the state that an object is in or transitions to as a result of receiving a message. States are explained in more detail in Chapter 11. Figure 9-20 shows an example of two states on a lifeline. The spooler is in the idle state until it receives the instruction to print, at which point it changes to the printing state. However, this notation is not covered in the section of the UML Specification on sequence diagrams.

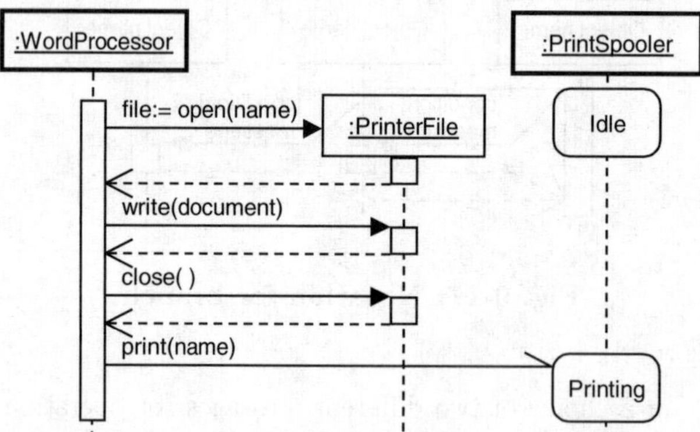

Fig. 9-20: Sequence diagram with states added

The sending of messages is usually assumed to be virtually instantaneous. However, in a situation where the message is sent over a communications link and a significant amount of time (in the context of the application) elapses between the sending and receiving of the message, the arrow can be shown slanting down the page, as in Figure 9-21.

9.4.2 Messages

The syntax for messages is essentially the same as for collaboration diagrams. This is summarized here. It is explained in more detail in Chapter 8 on page 159. Differences between the use of messages in

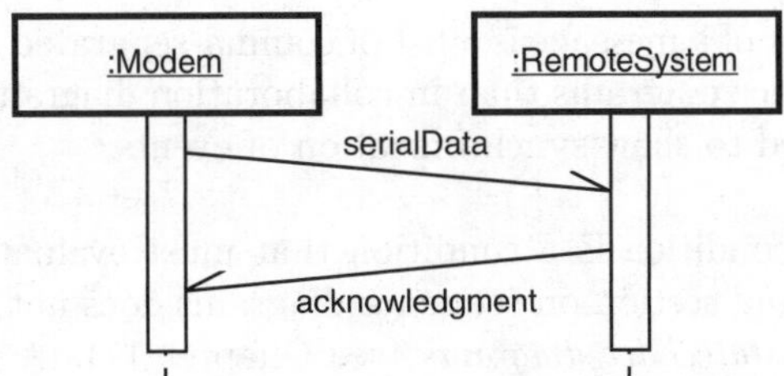

Fig. 9-21: Sequence diagram with message that takes time to reach its destination

sequence diagrams and in collaboration diagrams are mentioned below.

The amount of detail about the message that is shown alongside the arrow can vary considerably. At its simplest, it is just the name of the message. In sequence diagrams a sequence number is not normally added, as the placement of messages on the page shows their order.

At its most complex, it can consist of all of the elements of the following syntax:

```
predecessor guard-condition sequence-expression return-value := message-name argument-list
```

All of these may be omitted, but the *message-name* is usually shown. The *return-value*, *message-name* and *argument-list* together are called the *signature* of the message.

Message-name—The message-name is the event that is sent to the target object. This may either be the name of an event or of an operation in the class of the target object, for example, setFirstArranged.

The term *signal* is used to refer to events that are sent asynchronously from one object to another. A signal can have attributes, for example a MouseDown signal may have the attributes button, xyCoordinate and timestamp.

Argument-list—Operations and events are uniquely defined only if their full argument-list is also specified. The argument-list is a comma-separated list of names of the arguments, for example setArranged (dateArranged) or MouseDown(button, xyCoordinate, timestamp).

Return-value—Events are asynchronous and do not have return values. Synchronous operations may have a return-value that is sent back to the object that sent the message, for example journeyName := getJourneyName(i).

Sequence-expression—The sequence expression defines the order in which the interactions take place. It is a dot-separated list of *sequence-terms* followed by a colon.

Each sequence-term can consist of an integer or a name with an optional *recurrence*. The numbering part of sequence-terms is rarely used in sequence diagrams. (See page 159 in Chapter 8 for more detail.) Names are sometimes used in association with *constraints* (see Section 9.4.3).

The recurrence is used to denote messages that are sent depending on some condition or are sent iteratively, for example [dateArranged=null] or *[i:0..journeys.length].

Predecessor—The predecessor of a message is a list of comma-separated *sequence-numbers* followed by a slash. It is used less in sequence diagrams than in collaboration diagrams, because sequence-numbers are rarely used, but can be used to show synchronization of events.

Guard-condition—A guard-condition is a condition that must evaluate to true before the message can be sent. The 'UML Notation' section on sequence diagrams does not define a guard-condition, but it is defined in the context of *statechart diagrams* (see Chapter 11). A guard-condition is a Boolean expression, typically written in *Object Constraint Language*, that must be true for a transition in a statechart diagram to take place for example [percentageComplete = 100]. In the absence of sequence-numbers in a message in a sequence diagram, it is not possible to distinguish between a guard-condition and a condition-clause in a recurrence (unless both are present, in which case the guard-condition comes first).

9.4.3 Textual Annotation

Sequence diagrams can be annotated with textual information in three ways:

- comments
- constraints
- durations

Comments—Comments can be added to a sequence diagram. They are usually added on the left-hand side at the same vertical position on the page as the message or activation that they apply to. Figure 9-22 shows an example of this.

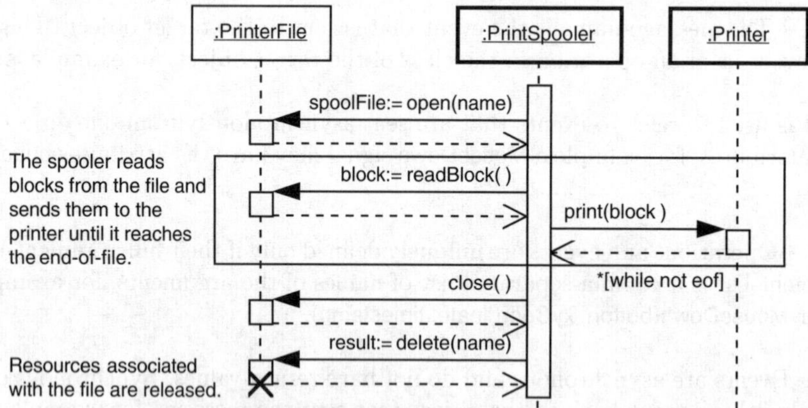

Fig. 9-22: Sequence diagram with comments

Constraints—Constraints are usually used to show timing constraints on messages. They can apply to the timing of one message or intervals between messages. A number of standard functions are assumed, for example *sendTime* and *receiveTime*, but users can define their own functions, for example *elapsedTime* or *executionStartTime*. Figure 9-23 shows examples using names for messages to distinguish them.

Durations—The duration of activations or the time between messages can be shown with construction marks (as used in engineering blueprints), although if the line representing the message is horizontal,

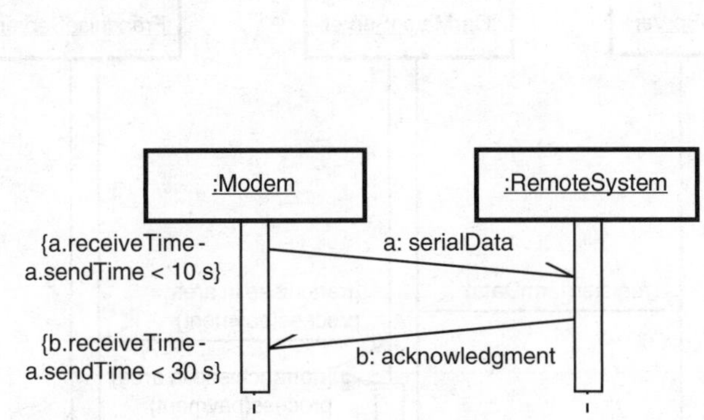

Fig. 9-23: Sequence diagram with timing constraints

it is not clear whether it applies to the time the message is sent or received. Figure 9-24 shows an example of this.

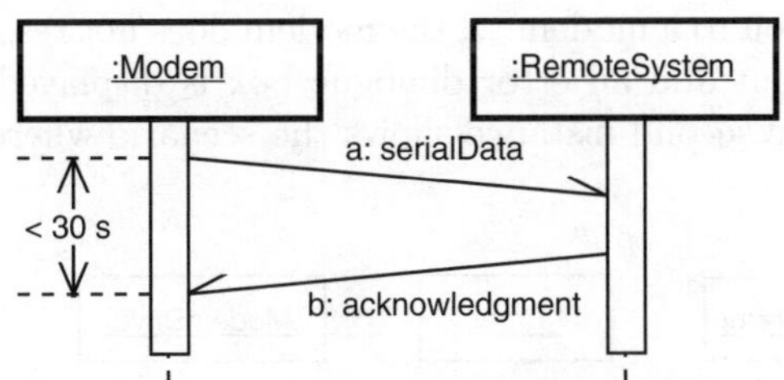

Fig. 9-24: Sequence diagram with duration

9.5 HOW TO PRODUCE SEQUENCE DIAGRAMS

Sequence diagrams can be drawn to model high-level interaction between users of the system and the system, between the system and other systems, or between subsystems (sometimes known as *system sequence diagrams*). In system sequence diagrams, the participants are drawn as active objects, as in Figure 9-25. Compare this with the activity diagram in Figure 10-1, which serves a similar purpose, but focuses on what activities are carried out rather than on the messages sent between the participants.

Sequence diagrams can also be used to model the interaction that takes place in a collaboration that realizes either a use case or an operation. The examples that we have used so far in this chapter fall into this category.

Sequence diagrams of this second type can be drawn either as *instance diagrams* or *generic diagrams.* An instance diagram shows one particular instance of an interaction, equivalent to a scenario in a use case.

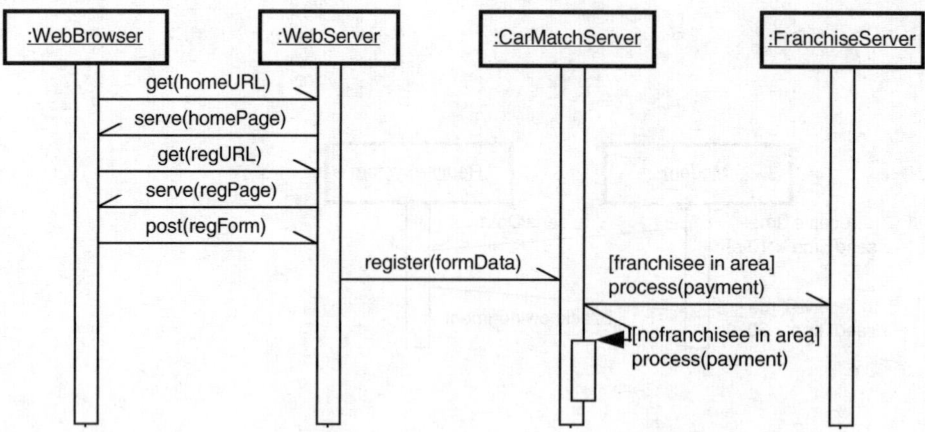

Fig. 9-25: High-level system sequence diagram

There may be several instance diagrams, with a slightly different path taken through the interaction in each. A generic diagram shows the combination of different possible paths through the interaction in a single diagram. This is similar to the distinction between instance-level and specification-level collaboration diagrams.

Figures 9-26 and 9-27 show two different instance diagrams for an application in which a ConnectionControl object has to open up a connection to a modem. If the modem does not respond within a certain amount of time, this operation times out and an error dialogue box is displayed. The first instance shows the successful connection and the second instance shows the scenario where the timeout occurs first.

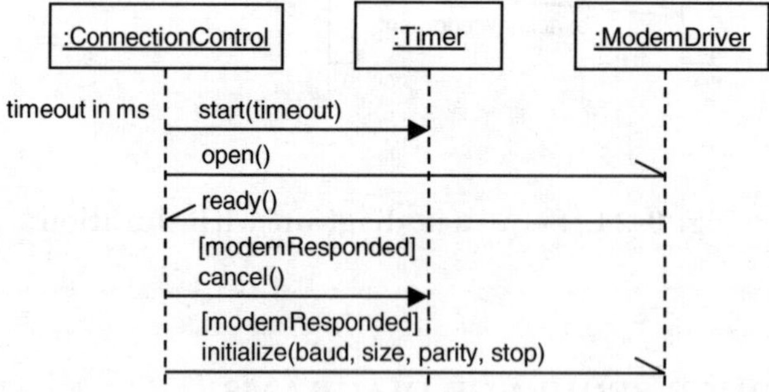

Fig. 9-26: Instance sequence diagram for first scenario

Figure 9-28 shows the two combined into a generic sequence diagram with alternative conditional actions.

The steps in drawing sequence diagrams are similar to those for drawing collaboration diagrams.

- Decide on the context of the interaction: system, subsystem, use case or operation.
- Identify the structural elements (classes or objects) necessary to carry out the functionality of the use case or operation. (There may already be a collaboration that defines these.)
- Consider the alternative scenarios that may be required.

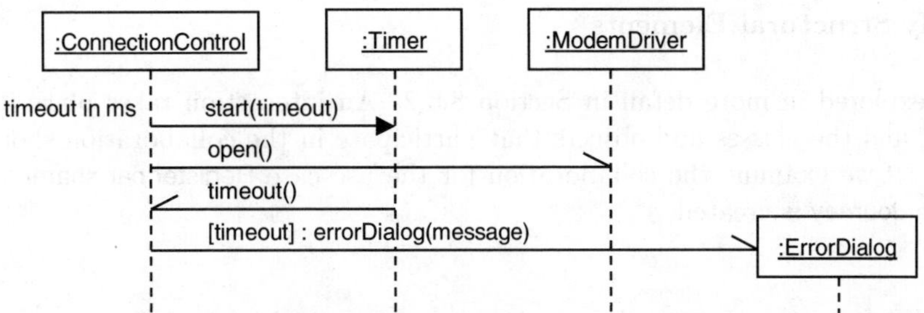

Fig. 9-27: Instance sequence diagram for second scenario

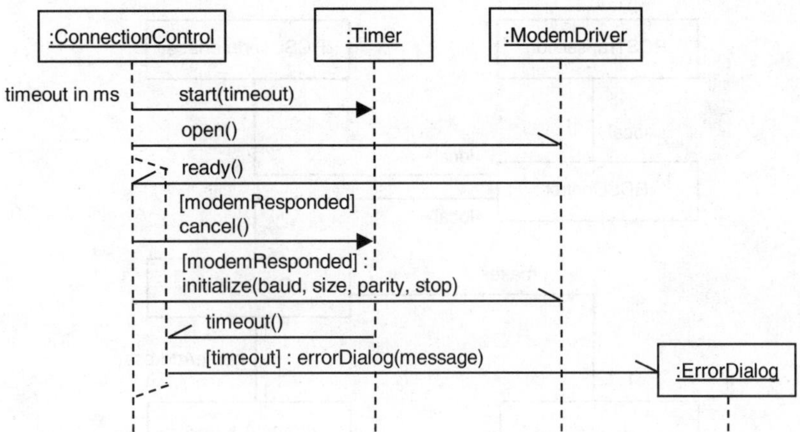

Fig. 9-28: Generic sequence diagram for both scenarios

- Draw instance sequence diagrams.
  - Lay out the objects from left to right.
  - Starting with the message that starts the interaction, lay out the messages down the page from top to bottom. Show the properties of the messages necessary to explain the semantics of the interaction.
  - Add the focus of control if it is necessary to visualize nesting or the point in time where an activation is taking place.
  - Add timing constraints if necessary.
  - Attach annotations to the diagram if required, for example pre- and post-conditions.
- If required, draw a generic sequence diagram to summarize the alternative scenarios in the instance sequence diagrams.

9.5.1 Decide on Context

The sequence diagram can model interaction at the system, subsystem, use case or operation level. The stage in the development of the project and the task being undertaken will determine which is to be modelled.

EXAMPLE 9.1 In this case, we are going to model an operation: the constructor operation that creates a new instance of the class Journey in the CarMatch system.

9.5.2 Identify Structural Elements

This has been explored in more detail in Section 8.6.2. An interaction takes place in the context of a collaboration, and the classes and objects that participate in the collaboration should already have been identified. If we examine the collaboration for the use case Register car sharer we can see what happens when a Journey is created.

EXAMPLE 9.2 When a Journey is created, it creates two instances of Address, one as the start address and one as the destination address. We are interested in part of the diagram in Figure 9-29.

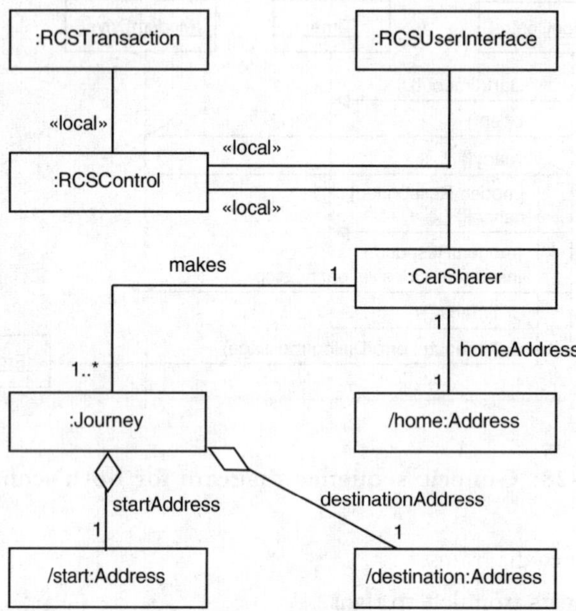

Fig. 9-29: Collaboration for Register car sharer

9.5.3 Consider Alternative Scenarios

We should check through the collaborations to see if there are any other use cases in which a Journey is created. In this case, there are not any. We also consider the different possible paths through the operation in response to different inputs.

EXAMPLE 9.3 For the use case Register car sharer, there are two different possible scenarios. In the first, the addresses have already been geolocated on the web server, and do not need to be geolocated again. In the second, they have not been geolocated, and this must be done when the new Address objects are created.

9.5.4 Draw Instance Diagrams

We now step through the process of drawing the instance diagrams for the two scenarios that have been developed. We shall explain the first in detail.

9.5.4.1 Lay out Objects

Lay the objects out from left to right, starting with the object that receives the message that triggers the interaction. If modelling a use case, there may be interface objects involved, and these should be shown at the left.

EXAMPLE 9.4 In this case, there are no interface objects. It is the new instance of Journey that receives the triggering message. It creates two instances of Address. These are shown in Figure 9-30.

Fig. 9-30: Objects involved in Journey constructor

9.5.4.2 Lay out Messages

The messages are laid out down the page. We have a lot of discretion about how much detail to show in the messages. We should show enough that someone looking at the diagram can understand the diagram and how it works.

EXAMPLE 9.5 The new instance of Journey that is created receives the triggering message. It in turn creates two instances of Address. Each of these is created by its constructor. We could just show all these messages as the stereotype «create», but that would not convey much information about how this works.

The Journey is passed a number of parameters when it is created. If we look at the class definition, we can see which values are set when a Journey is created. This is shown in Figure 9-31 with the required attributes in bold print.

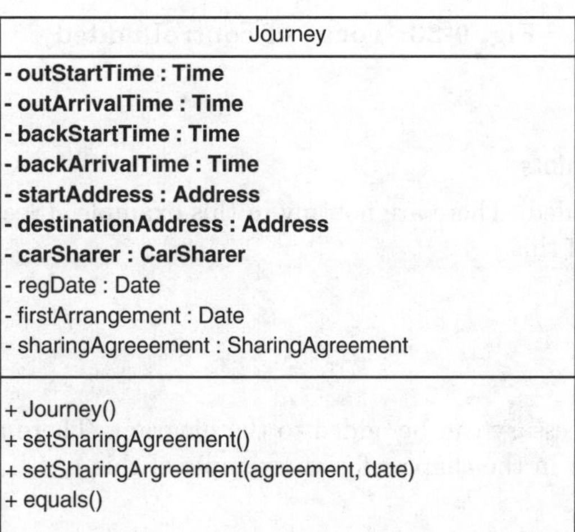

Fig. 9-31: Journey class (with constructor parameters in bold print)

The Address attributes will have to be created. The data that is passed in is unlikely to be an existing instance of Address; it is more likely to be a list of values, which will be passed on to construct the new instances of Address. Figure 9-32 shows the messages laid out with parameters. They are all synchronous operation calls.

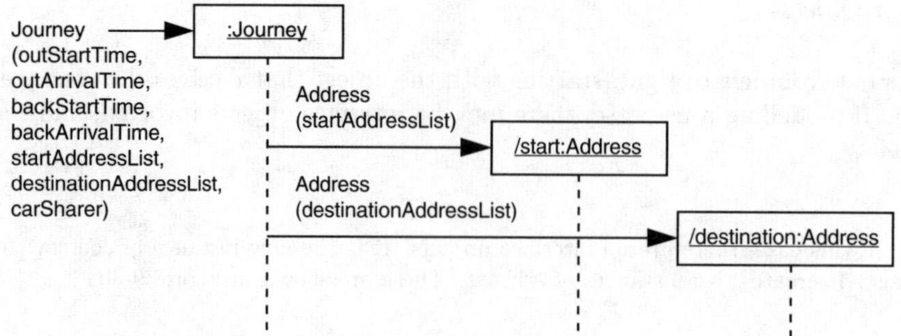

Fig. 9-32: Messages for the operations

9.5.4.3 Add Focus of Control

The focus of control region can be added if required.

EXAMPLE 9.6 The focus of control regions add nothing to the readability of the sequence diagram for this scenario, but will be useful for the alternative scenario, so we add them in here, as in Figure 9-33.

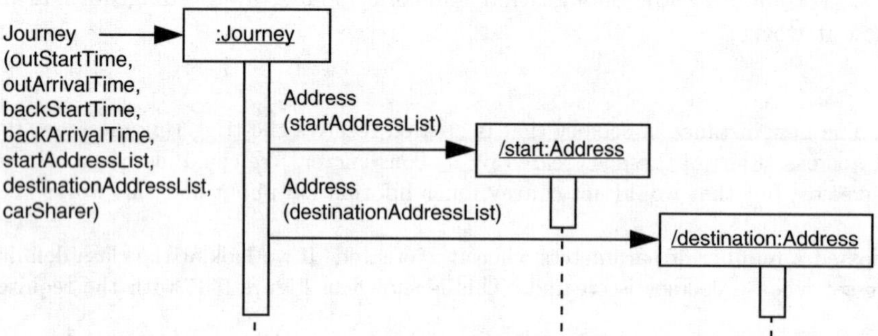

Fig. 9-33: Focus of control added

9.5.4.4 Add Timing Constraints

Timing constraints can be added. There are not any in this example. (See Solved Problem 9.9 later in the chapter for an example of this.)

9.5.4.5 Add Annotations

Any annotations that are necessary can be added to the diagram. There are not any in this example. (See Solved Problem 9.9 later in the chapter for an example of this.)

9.5.4.6 Repeat for each scenario

The same steps can be repeated for all the other scenarios.

EXAMPLE 9.7 In this case, we have one alternative scenario, in which the addresses have not yet been geolocated. This results in the diagram in Figure 9-34.

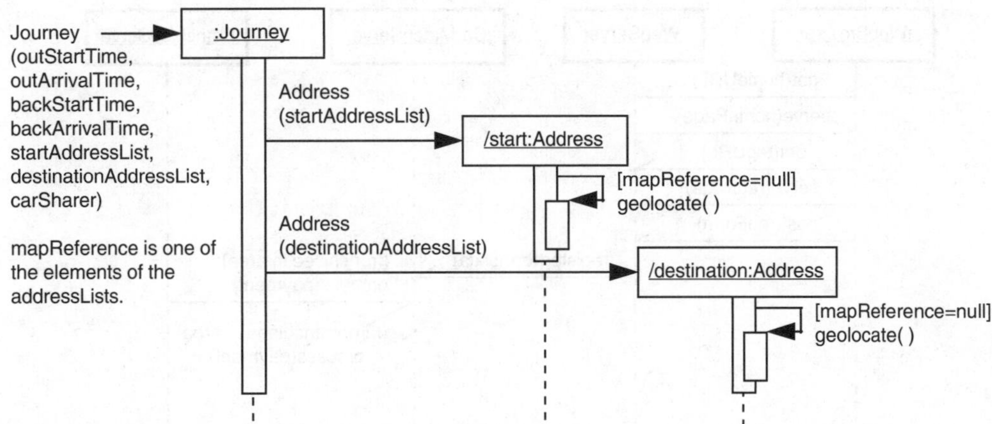

Fig. 9-34: Alternative scenario

We have added an annotation to explain where the mapReference comes from. This could also be shown as a UML note.

9.5.5 Draw Generic Sequence Diagram

We can now combine the alternative scenarios into a single diagram.

EXAMPLE 9.8 In this case, none of the alternatives adds additional messages or activations to the diagram. This means that the diagram in Figure 9-34 is the generic diagram and it is not necessary to draw a separate generic diagram.

9.6 BUSINESS MODELLING WITH SEQUENCE DIAGRAMS

In the UML profile for business modelling, five class stereotypes are defined for business objects. These are: Actor, Worker, Case Worker, Internal Worker and Entity. These have been explained in Section 8.7. These stereotyped icons could be used in sequence diagrams to model the collaborations between workers and entities in use case realizations.

High-level system sequence diagrams can be produced to model the interaction within business use cases. Figure 9-35 shows an example of this. Such diagrams are often drawn without the focus of control region on the lifeline.

This is the kind of diagram that would be produced at an early stage in the development of a system, as part of the business modelling and before detailed analysis is carried out.

9.7 RELATIONSHIP WITH OTHER DIAGRAMS

Sequence diagrams can be used to model the realization of either use cases or operations of classes. In the latter case, each operation being modelled must exist in a class diagram. The names of messages

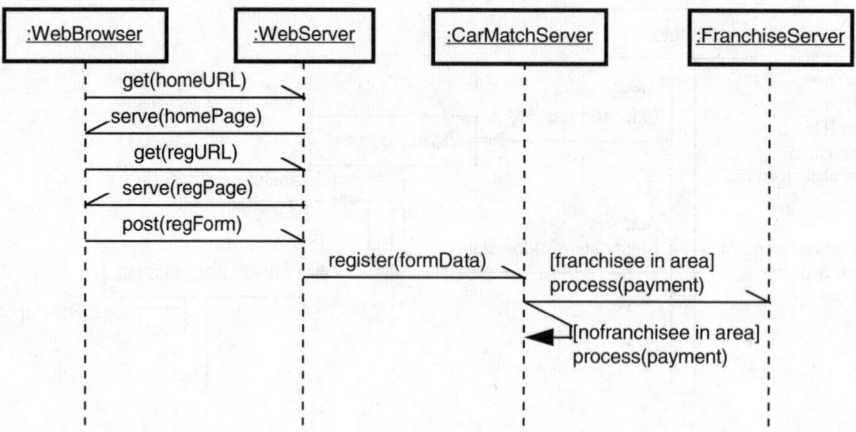

Fig. 9-35: High-level system sequence diagram

must be events or be operations of the class receiving the message. If states are referred to in guard conditions or shown on an object's lifeline, they must be valid states of the relevant class and should appear in a statechart diagram (see Chapter 11).

Sequence diagrams and collaboration diagrams (see Chapter 8) model the same aspects of the system: the objects that collaborate together and the messages that are exchanged among them to achieve some objective. Sequence diagrams and collaboration diagrams can be converted into one another. Some CASE tools can do this automatically. They are almost but not quite interchangeable; some information is lost in the conversion: sequence diagrams do not show the links between objects or the associations between class roles; collaboration diagrams do not show information about timing constraints.

9.8 SEQUENCE DIAGRAMS IN THE UNIFIED PROCESS

Sequence diagrams are used in the Unified Process first of all in the Design Workflow. This is shown in Figure 9-36.

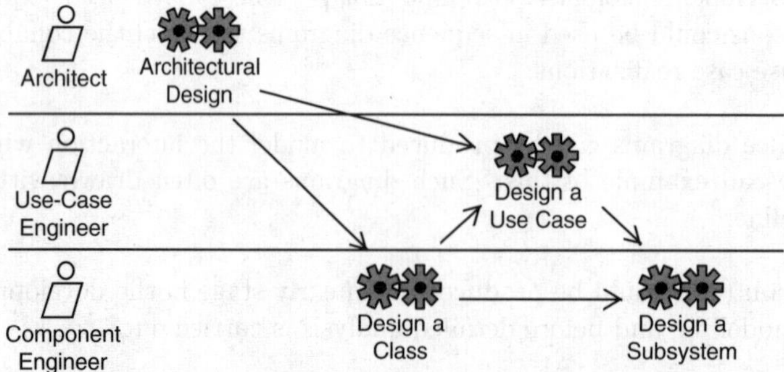

Fig. 9-36: Design workflow as an activity diagram

Collaboration diagrams are produced as part of the Analysis Model and are refined in Design. In the Unified Process, it is suggested that sequence diagrams rather than collaboration diagrams should be used to model interactions in the design phase.

The activity *Design a Use Case* is similar to the analysis activity of the same name, except for the fact that design classes are used and there are more steps, as more detail is required when a project gets closer to implementation. The main steps are: *Identifying the Participating Design Classes*, *Describing Design Object Interactions*, *Identifying the Participating Subsystems and Interfaces* and *Describing Subsystem Interactions*. Design classes may be different from analysis classes. For example, collection classes may be added in design to handle interactions that involve a set of objects. The interactions on the collaboration and sequence diagrams will have to be modified to include instances of these classes and their interactions. It is also possible to consider a use case in terms of interactions among design subsystems rather than design objects. This provides a hierarchical decomposition of the interactions, as the detail of the interaction within a subsystem can be hidden in one diagram and shown in a separate lower-level diagram. In order to support this approach, the interfaces of subsystems must be identified, so that it is clear what operations or events each subsystem will handle. There is a fifth step, *Capturing Implementation Requirements*, in which requirements to be handled in implementation are documented.

Sequence diagrams are also used in the Test Workflow. This is shown in Figure 9-37

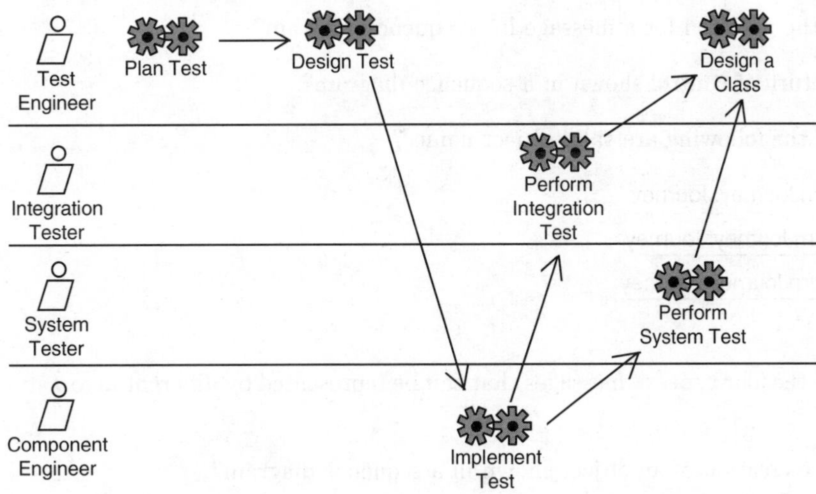

Fig. 9-37: Test workflow as an activity diagram

Sequence diagrams are used in the activity *Design Test.* This consists of the steps *Designing Integration Test Cases*, *Designing System Test Cases*, *Designing Regression Test Cases* and *Identifying and Structuring Test Procedures*. Sequence diagrams are used particularly in the first of these. Integration testing is concerned with ensuring that the different components of the system work correctly together. Most test cases can be derived from the use case realizations produced in design, as these describe how objects interact. The alternative paths through use cases documented by instance sequence diagrams provide the basis for test cases that handle (and test) the different possible routes that can be taken through the use case. Test designers will examine the sequence diagrams to find combinations of user input, output and system start state that will test the interaction between the participating objects. (System test cases are concerned with testing that the system functions correctly as a whole; regression test cases re-test test cases which have been passed to ensure that they have not been broken by changes made in subsequent iterations or to fix bugs.)

Some automated test tools can trace the interaction through a test case and produce output in the form of a sequence diagram that can be compared with the sequence diagrams produced in design.

Review Questions

9.1 Define what is meant by an interaction.

9.2 What are the differences between how sequence diagrams model an interaction and how collaboration diagrams model an interaction?

9.3 Explain how sequence diagrams represent time.

9.4 What are the main purposes of using sequence diagrams?

9.5 What is the difference between a generic sequence diagram and an instance sequence diagram?

9.6 What is the notation for the lifeline of an object?

9.7 What is the notation for the focus of control region?

9.8 How can it be shown that an object in a procedural sequence is currently carrying out some activity or computation?

9.9 What is the notation for a message in a sequence diagram?

9.10 How is return of control shown in a sequence diagram?

9.11 Which of the following are valid object names?

(a) returnJourney:Journey

(b) /returnJourney:Journey

(c) j/returnJourney:Journey

(d) j

9.12 What are the four types of messages that can be represented by different arrow styles in a sequence diagram?

9.13 How is the creation of an object shown in a sequence diagram?

9.14 How is the destruction of an object shown in a sequence diagram?

9.15 How can names be used in sequence-expressions?

9.16 What is meant by a recurrence?

9.17 What is an active object?

9.18 What is the notation for an active object?

9.19 In what two ways can iteration be represented in a sequence diagram?

9.20 What is the usual purpose of constraints in a sequence diagram?

9.21 What are the main steps in producing a sequence diagram?

9.22 Which two Unified Process workflows are sequence diagrams used in?

9.23 What are the five steps in the Unified Process activity Design a Use Case?

9.24 What are the four steps in the Unified Process activity Design Test?

Solved Problems

9.1 CarMatch refunds the membership fee to members if it is unable to match them up with another car sharer. The following is a description of the process.

> If it has not been possible to match a member's journeys with any other car sharer within three months, the member is entitled to a refund of the membership fee. The member's details are kept in the system. He or she is asked whether the records of the journeys requested can be kept for statistical purposes. If they are to be kept, they are flagged as defunct, otherwise the journeys are deleted. The accounting subsystem is requested to issue the refund (by cheque or by credit card, depending on how the member paid the fee in the first place.

The first task is to decide on the context of the sequence diagram.

This is a use case: Refund membership fee. The sequence diagram will be produced in the context of the collaboration that realizes this use case.

9.2 What are the structural elements of this collaboration?

This collaboration involves objects from the classes CarSharer and Journey. It also involves the Accounts subsystem. We shall treat this as a subsystem in this sequence diagram and not attempt to model the detail of what happens within the subsystem. When a Journey is deleted, the objects embedded within it (Addresses and the MapReferences embedded within them) must also be destroyed, but we can model this as a sequence diagram for the destructor operation for Journey as a separate sequence diagram, in the same way as we modelled the constructor in Section 9.5.4. The collaboration will also involve a user interface class and a control class.

9.3 What are the possible alternative scenarios for this sequence diagram?

There are two, which depend on input from the user.

In the first, the member allows their journey details to be kept, and the journeys are flagged as defunct.

In the second, the journey details are deleted.

There may be other alternative scenarios that depend on how the member originally paid the membership fee, but these are hidden inside the Accounts subsystem for the purpose of this example.

9.4 We now work through the steps of drawing instance diagrams for each of the scenarios. We shall first consider the scenario in which the journeys are kept. The first step is to lay out the objects involved.

Figure 9-38 shows the objects that are involved in this sequence diagram. Note that the user interface and control class have been drawn to the left of the diagram, then the CarSharer and Journey objects and finally the Accounts subsystem.

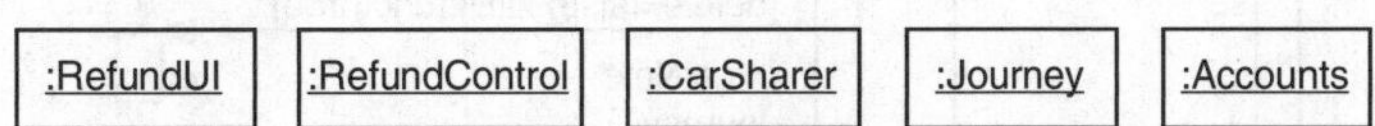

Fig. 9-38: Objects involved in the use case Refund membership fee

The second step is to lay out the messages down the page. The focus of control can be added at the same time.

Note that in some CASE tools, you may not have any choice about whether to add a focus of control region or not. If you are drawing the diagrams in a general purpose drawing package (not recommended), draw the focus of control regions from the start if you plan to include them.

The interaction is triggered by an event from the actor CarMatch Administrator. This could be a click on a Refund button on the screen. We shall assume that the CarSharer has been selected from a list and a

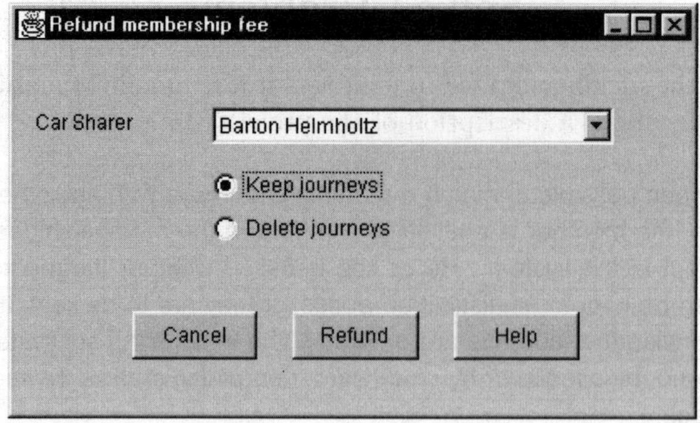

Fig. 9-39: User interface for the use case Refund membership fee

checkbox has been clicked to indicate whether the user wants his or her journey details kept or deleted. The interface could look something like the one in Figure 9-39.

When the user clicks on the Refund button, an event will be sent to the control object. This will get the data from the interface object: first the id of the CarSharer, which must then be found in the database or activated in some way; second the boolean value that tells the control object whether or not to delete the journeys. The CarSharer in this design contains a collection of Journey objects. There must be at least one, so we get the first one and set it to be defunct, then iterate through the collection, getting each Journey in turn, until we reach the end of the collection. Each CarSharer has a link to an Account object in the Accounts package, and a message is now sent to the Accounts subsystem, requesting it to pay the refund for the relevant Account. Figure 9-40 shows the resulting sequence diagram.

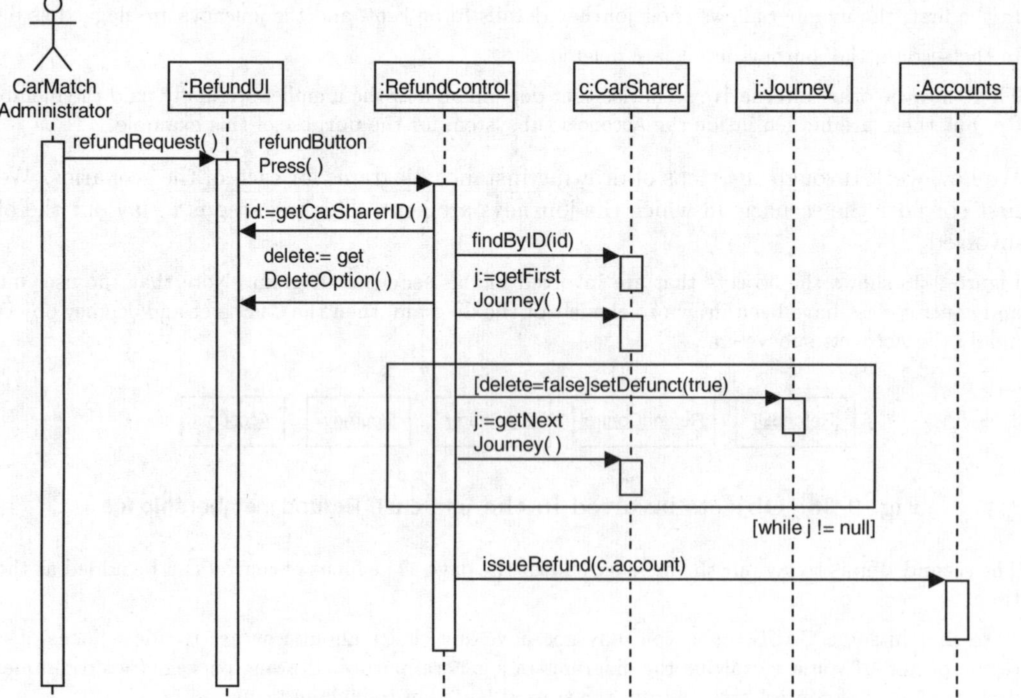

Fig. 9-40: Messages for the interaction in the first scenario

Finally, we add timing constraints and comments. In this case, there are not any to add.

We now repeat the exercise for the second scenario. This produces the sequence diagram in Figure 9-41.

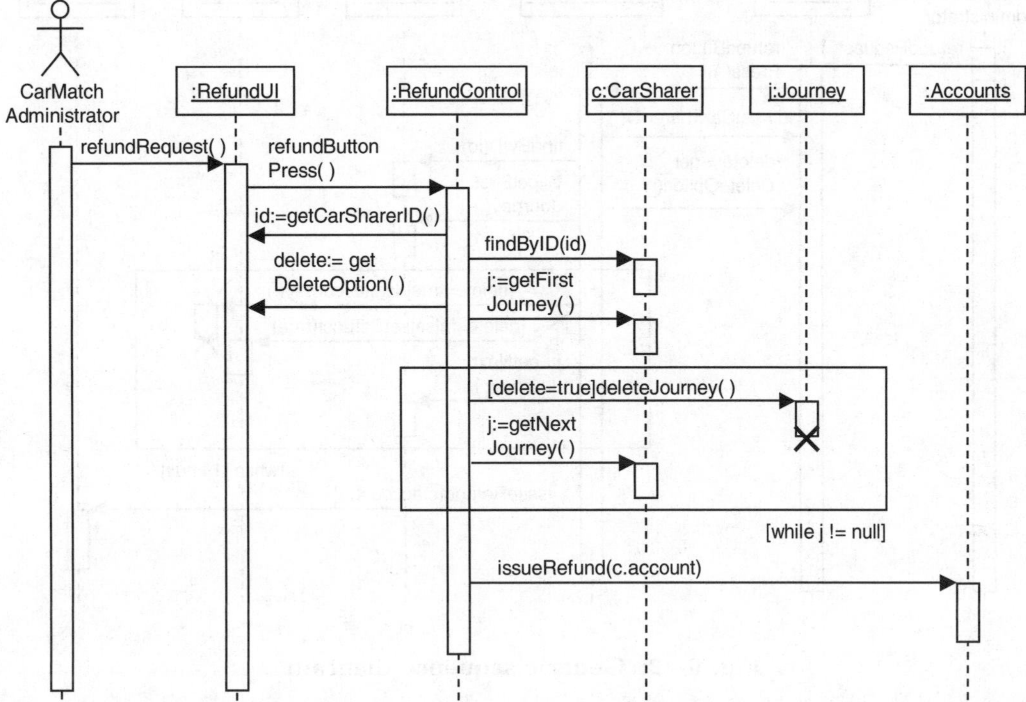

Fig. 9-41: Messages for the interaction in the second scenario

9.5 The final step is to combine the alternative scenarios into a generic sequence diagram.

Figure 9-42 shows this.

9.6 Draw a sequence diagram to model the interaction that takes place when a CarMatch member drives past a road charging beacon at the road-side, using a proposed in-vehicle radio transponder system to communicate with the beacon. The interaction is described as follows.

> The beacon at the road-side in constantly transmitting a signal to any transponder that passes. Whenever a transponder responds, the beacon and the transponder must exchange data within 0.25 s. The transponder transmits its identification to the beacon. The beacon transmits the charge information for that stretch of road to the transponder, which displays the information on an LCD screen for the driver. It also communicates with a central database to verify the identification. A response must come from the database within 1 s. If the identification is not valid, the beacon sends a request to a road-side camera to photograph the vehicle as it goes past.

The first task is to decide on the context of the sequence diagram.

This is a use case: Vehicle passes beacon. The sequence diagram we produce here will be a high-level diagram to model this use case rather than a detailed one with all the objects involved. It will be modelled in terms of subsystems.

9.7 What are the structural elements of this collaboration?

This collaboration involves four subsystems: Transponder, Beacon, Database and Camera. We could also include the LCDScreen associated with the transponder.

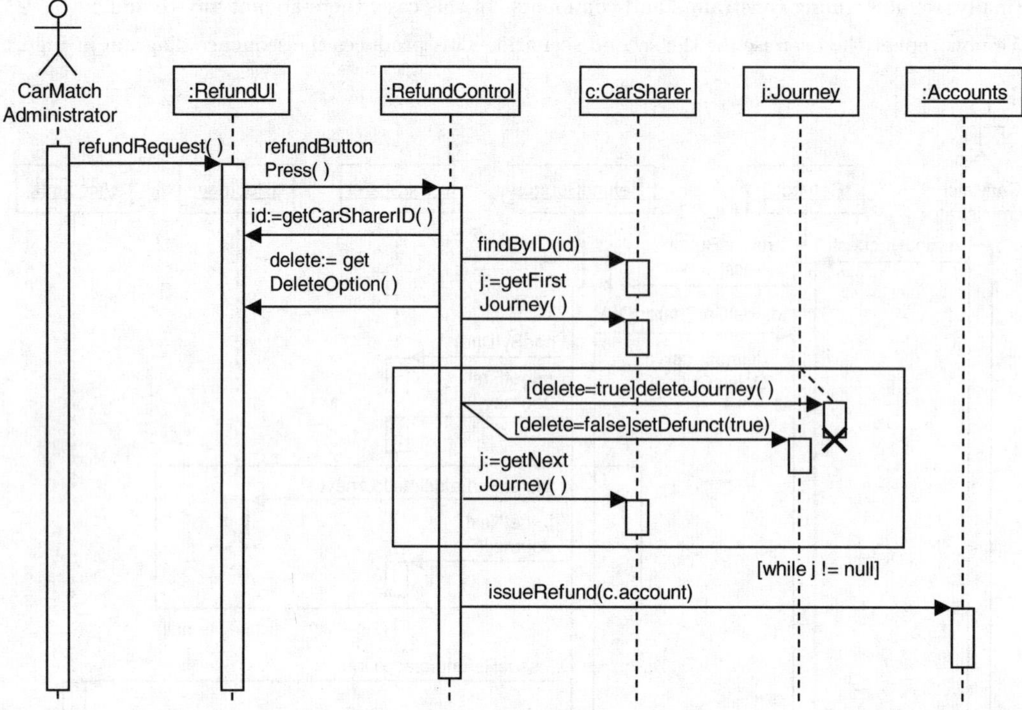

Fig. 9-42: Generic sequence diagram

9.8 What are the possible alternative scenarios for this sequence diagram?

There are two, which depend on the result that comes back from the central database.

In the first, the identification is valid; in the second, the identification is not valid and a message is sent to the camera.

9.9 We now work through the steps of drawing instance diagrams for each of the scenarios. We shall consider the scenario in which the identification is valid first. The first step is to lay out the objects involved. In this case, the objects are instances of the subsystems, and are active objects each operating independently on its own thread of control.

Figure 9-43 shows the objects that are involved in this sequence diagram.

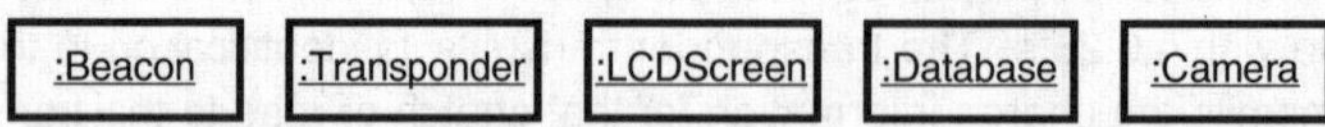

Fig. 9-43: Objects involved in the use case Vehicle passes beacon

The second step is to lay out the messages down the page. The communication here is asynchronous,and it is not necessary to draw the focus of control regions. Figure 9-44 shows the resulting sequence diagram.

We have assumed that the sending of signals locally is more or less instantaneous, whereas there is a significant delay in communicating with the remote database.

There are timing constraints on this interaction, and we may want to add a comment, as in Figure 9-45.

The procedure can be repeated for the second scenario, in which the identification is not valid, to produce the diagram of Figure 9-46.

This diagram is also the generic sequence diagram: by default it covers the case in which [result = valid] and no message is sent to the camera.

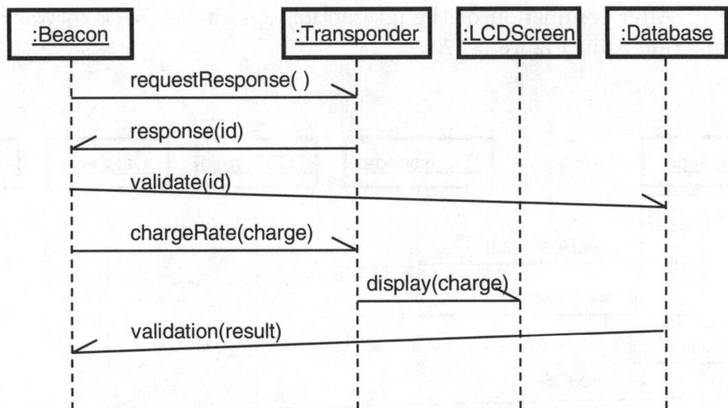

Fig. 9-44: Sequence diagram for Vehicle passes beacon, first scenario

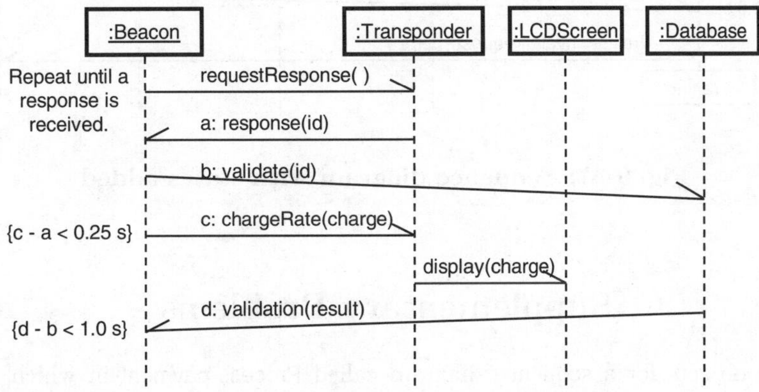

Fig. 9-45: Sequence diagram for Vehicle passes beacon, first scenario, with constraints

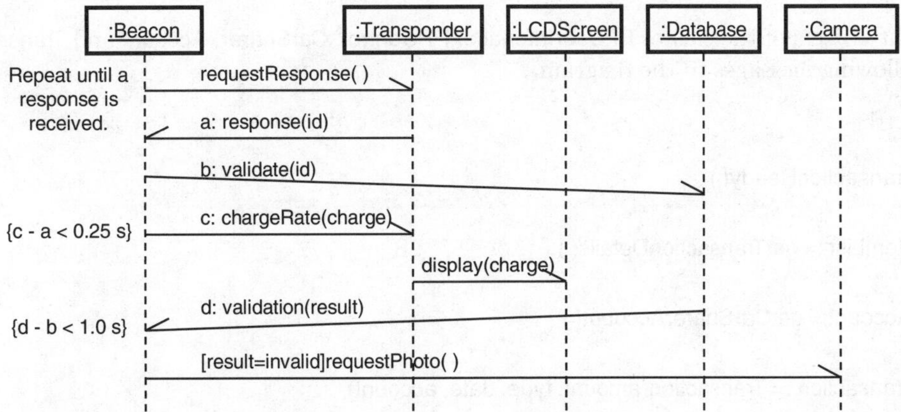

Fig. 9-46: Sequence diagram for Vehicle passes beacon, second scenario

9.10 The diagram in Figure 9-46 could be extended to show the states of the Beacon. At the simplest level, there could be two states: Waiting and Communicating. Add these to the sequence diagram.

The Beacon is Waiting until it receives a response from a passing Transponder. It then switches into the

Communicating state. After completion of the interaction it switches back to Waiting. This can be shown on the sequence diagram as in Figure 9-47.

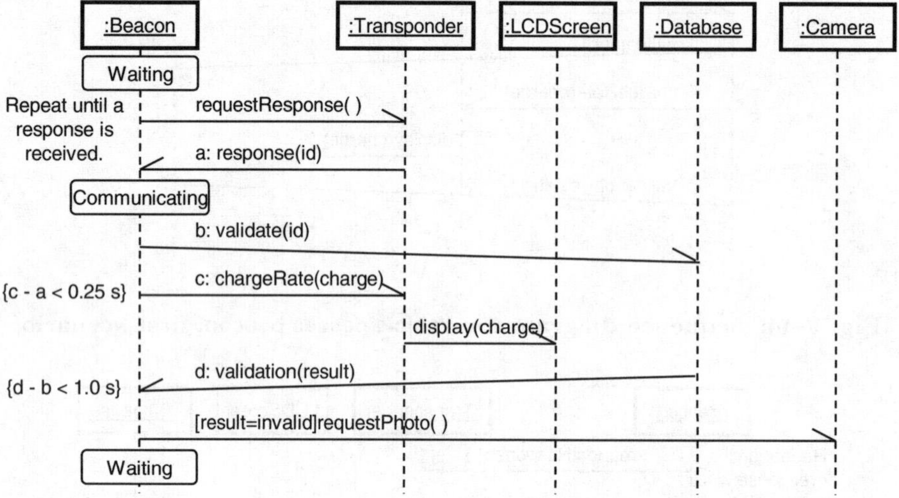

Fig. 9-47: Sequence diagram with states added

Supplementary Problems

9.11 Lay out the objects for a sequence diagram called Process payment in which objects from the classes CarSharer, Account and Transaction participate. Add suitable control and user interface classes. (Look at page 201 if you are stuck.)

9.12 Lay out objects of the classes PPUserInterface, PPControl, CarSharer, Account and Transaction. Add the following messages to the diagram.

1. transactionReady( )

2. itemList := getTransactionDetails( )

3. account:= getCarSharerAccount( )

4. transaction := Transaction(amount, type, date, account)

5. balance := postTransaction(transaction)

6. displayBalance(balance)

The variable itemList contains the following items: carSharerID, amount, type, date.

9.13 One of the use cases that you found in Chapter 3 should have had a name such as Record an individual's request for help. In case you did not have a use case like this, here is a short summary description.

> Individuals can request help from VolBank. This includes volunteers requesting help themselves. The Volbank administrator first enters the details of the individual. If this is an existing volunteer, then the name is entered and the details are displayed. If there is more than one person with the same name, then a list is displayed with the first part of the address, and the administrator selects the right one. If this is not an existing volunteer, then the name, address and telephone number are entered. It is important that the zip or postal code is entered, as it is required to match this request with volunteers in the same area. Details of the help required are then entered: a text summary of the help and a code that describes the type of help wanted, for example DEC for decorating, GAR for garden work or PET for pet care. A start and finish date for when the help is required are also entered.

If you produced a solution to the problems in Chapter 8 you will have the collaboration that is the context of this interaction. Otherwise you should work through the following steps.

What are the domain classes that are involved in this use case?

What other subsystems (if any) are involved in this use case?

What are the additional classes that will be required for this collaboration?

Draw a class diagram showing the associations among the classes, including stereotyped associations if required.

What are the roles that these classes take in this collaboration?

9.14 What are the alternative scenarios that may occur?

9.15 Draw an instance sequence diagram for each of these scenarios. For each diagram work through the following steps.

Lay out the objects.

Lay out the messages down the page.

Add constraints and comments.

9.16 Draw a generic sequence diagram combining the alternative scenarios.

9.17 When a volunteer registers with VolBank on the VolBank web server, he or she goes through the following interaction.

> Go to the VolBank home page. Request the VolBank registration page. Complete the form and submit it. The server validates the data. If there is any error, the form is redisplayed with the contents as entered by the volunteer and with the incorrect field highlighted. If there is no error, the data is submitted to a database.

Draw instance and generic sequence diagrams for this interaction.

CHAPTER 10

Activity Diagrams

10.1 INTRODUCTION

Activity diagrams are a means of describing *workflows* and can be used in a variety of ways. As an analysis tool they can describe business flows in varying levels of detail. They can also be used to describe complex flows within or between use cases. At the design level, they can be used to describe in detail the flow within an operation. In this sense, they are very flexible. They can be used before the identification of use cases in the determination of high level business requirements, as a means of describing complex use cases and as a means of describing complex behaviour within an object. Activity diagrams complement collaboration diagrams and sequence diagrams, which are alternative ways of describing workflows, and are closely related to statechart diagrams.

10.2 WHAT IS AN ACTIVITY DIAGRAM?

Activity diagrams consist of *activities*, *states* and *transitions* between activities and states. Let us look at a simple example. We have a business use case defined that allows a new member to register for CarMatch. This is drawn as in Figure 10-1.

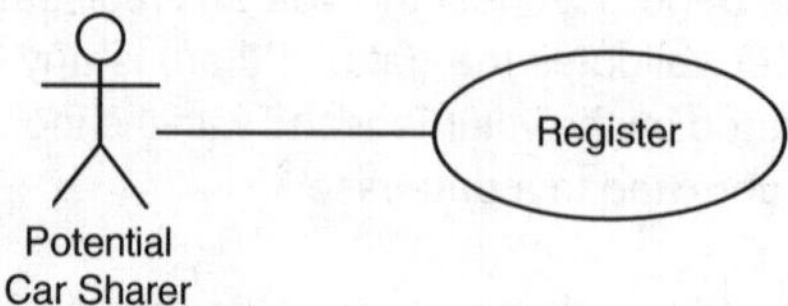

Fig. 10-1: Business use case for a potential car sharer registering with CarMatch

Before we define the system use cases, we may wish to understand the business process where the use cases fit. One way is to develop an activity diagram for a business process or business workflow as in Figure 10-2.

This activity diagram describes the main process (or primary path) for registering a new member of CarMatch. You can see that this is a simple flowchart describing business activities in the order that

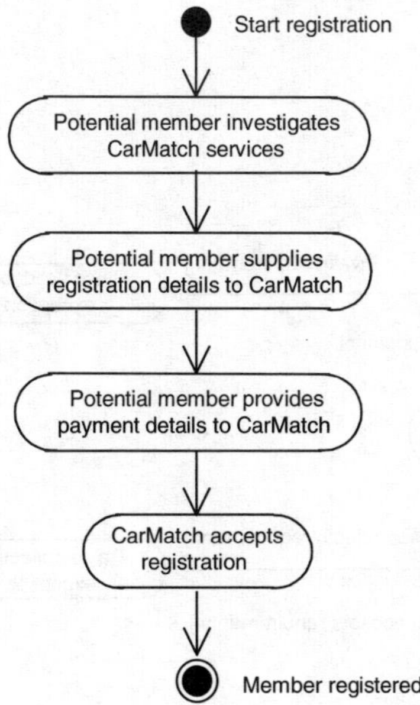

Fig. 10-2: Activity diagram to describe the business workflow of registration from the car sharer's perspective

they need to be followed. In this chapter we shall investigate how activity diagrams can be used to describe business workflows in detail. We shall explain how conditions can be added, how parallel workflows can be described, how conditions can be applied to workflows, and how the activities and states can be fully described.

At the other extreme, we may want to describe complicated flows within an operation. The CarSharer object has an operation addRequirement() as shown in Figure 10-3. We may realize during design that it is a complicated operation. We can then use an activity diagram to describe the flows through this operation. The first attempt might look at just the primary flow, as in Figure 10-4.

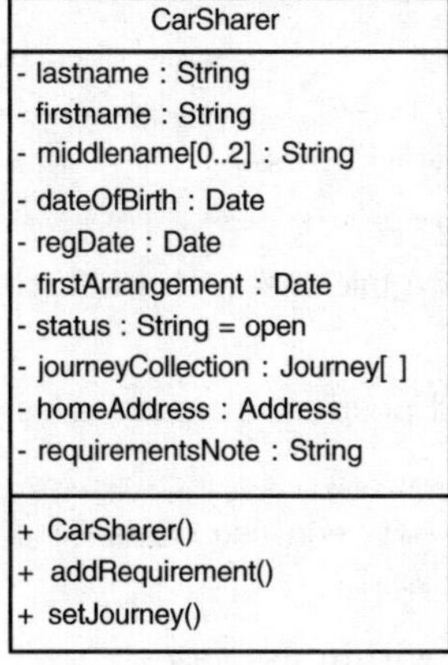

Fig. 10-3: Class definition for CarSharer object

In practice it would be unusual to describe any but the most complicated operations in this way, and the complexity would probably be well in excess of the above simple example. Each activity in such a

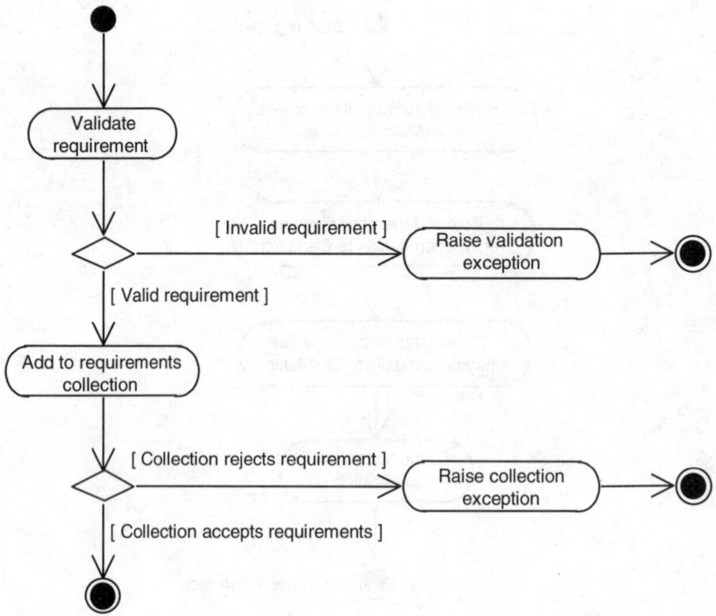

Fig. 10-4: Activity diagram to describe primary flow of addRequirement operation

workflow will map to one or a few simple instructions in a programming language, and it is acceptable to put program instructions in the text within the activity diagram, or as actions in the activity (see later).

10.3 PURPOSE OF THE TECHNIQUE

Activity diagrams can be used throughout a project, from business analysis through to program design. They can be attached to many types of object, such as business use cases, system use cases, use case diagrams, activities, and operations. They are generic flow diagrams with the uses listed below.

- They are used to model business workflows.
- They are used to identify candidate use cases, through the examination of business workflows.
- They are used to identify pre- and post-conditions for use cases.
- They are used to model workflow between use cases
- They are used to model workflow within use cases.
- They are used to model complicated workflows in operations on objects.
- They are used to model complex activities in a high level activity diagram in more detail.

10.4 NOTATION

The following notation is very rich. All aspects of the notation need not be used at any one time, and some aspects of the notation, such as control icons, are there to add visual impact rather than provide additional expressiveness. In the early stages of analysis, business workflows may not need the full notation for activity description and might better be described in simple text in a separate document. Swimlanes make sense only when there are significant organizational or technological boundaries that are crossed by a workflow.

10.4.1 Activities and Actions

An activity is a unit of work that needs to be carried out. In practice, this can be large or small, taking place over a long or short period of time. A business activity, such as debt recovery, might take many weeks. A computer activity, such as changing an attribute of a customer, can be almost instantaneous. We draw activities as rectangles with rounded ends, with a descriptive name for the activity inside, as in Figure 10-5. The name needs to be descriptive of the actions taking place in the activity. For design

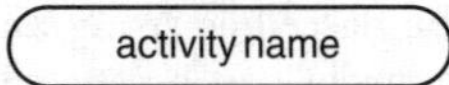

Fig. 10-5: The notation for an activity

level activities, it can even be a program instruction. Figure 10-6 shows an example of this.

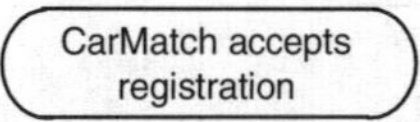

Fig. 10-6: An activity with a descriptive name

Activities carry out work. The work can be documented as actions in the activity, or separately in a text document. There are four ways in which an action can be triggered.

- On Entry: these actions are triggered as soon as the activity starts.
- Do: these actions take place during the lifetime of the activity.
- On Event: these actions take place in response to an event.
- On Exit: these actions take place just before the activity completes.

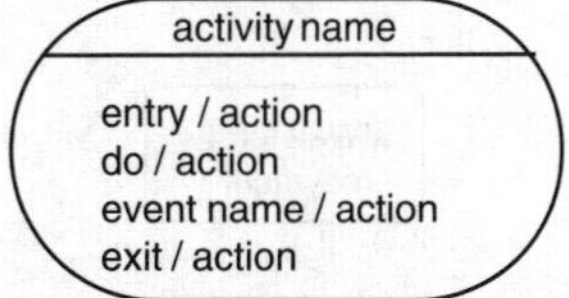

Fig. 10-7: The notation for actions

The action can be described in a simple English statement, or for more detailed design, using a programming language statement. An alternative form of action is the triggering of an event and this is written as:

```
^target.event(arguments)
```

where *target* is some object that needs to respond to the event, *event* is the name of the event, and *arguments* contain the information that is conveyed with the event.

An activity diagram can be used to document business decisions using actions.

EXAMPLE 10.1 Once CarMatch has accepted a registration, the member is notified immediately. The details of the applicant are added to the list of members and a registration fee is charged to his or her account. Payment is requested from the candidate member, with membership fee as one of the arguments, and fee request as the reason. Confirmation of payment is required before services can be enabled. There may be a problem with the payment, such as incorrect credit card details, and this is notified to the activity by an event paymentNotReceived, and that in turn triggers another event to request payment from the member, giving the reason from the paymentNotReceived event. When all the work of the activity is done, then the member services can be enabled for that member.

Thus we can elaborate the above activity as in Figure 10-8. Note that we are not fully specifying the order of the actions. An elaborate activity may best be described using an activity diagram, where the actions appear as activities in their own right, and where the order can be specified. This can be done by using subactivities on the same diagram (see Figure 10-25 later) or by producing a separate activity diagram. The activity could also be documented by a textual description stored in a file.

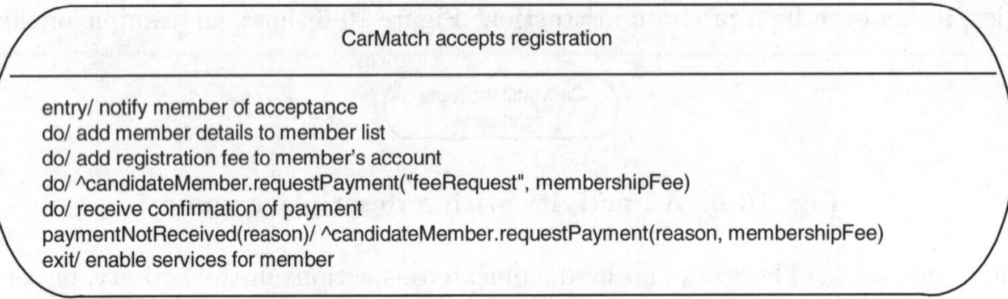

Fig. 10-8: An activity with actions specified

10.4.2 States

A state in an activity diagram is a point where some event needs to take place before activity can continue. Activities and states are roughly equivalent, and states can carry out actions just as activities can. However, activities need to complete all their actions before exiting normally. States are used to imply waiting, not doing. A state is drawn as a rectangle with rounded corners as in Figure 10-9.

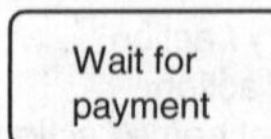

Fig. 10-9: A state

There are two special states. The start state is the entry point to a flow. Only one start state is allowed on a diagram. It is drawn as a black dot, and it can be labeled with a name as in Figure 10-10. Start states can have actions too, though mostly a start state is used as a marker to indicate that the flow has started. End states are drawn as black dots with a surrounding circle (a bulls-eye shape), as in Figure

10-11. End states can have actions too, as in Figure 10-12. You might use these to trigger events that start other processes, say in the registration process to signal that a new member has arrived so that some other process can do some matching.

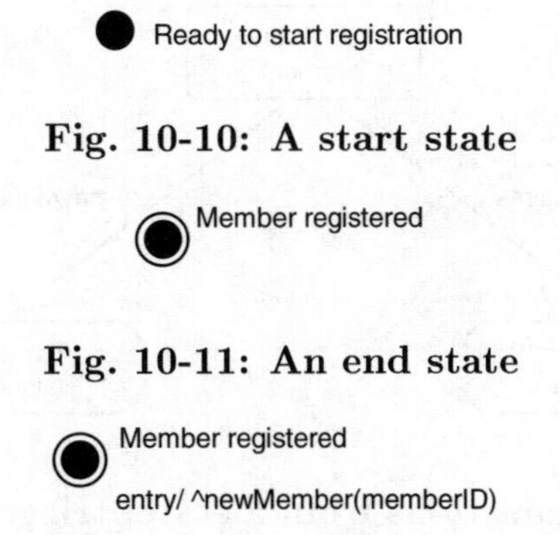

Fig. 10-10: A start state

Fig. 10-11: An end state

Fig. 10-12: An end state with an action

There can be several end states in a workflow. Multiple end states can be used to indicate different follow-on processes from a particular process. For example, bill processing may end with either successful payment of the bill, which will lead to the customer's being allowed to make further purchases, or unsuccessful payment, which will lead to the customer's being registered as a bad debtor.

10.4.3 Transitions

A *transition* is the movement from one activity to another, the change from one state to another, or the movement between a state and an activity in either direction. A transition normally occurs when all the actions of an activity have been completed, or when an event triggers the exit from a particular state or activity. Transitions are drawn as arrowed lines between two activities or states, as in Figure 10-13.

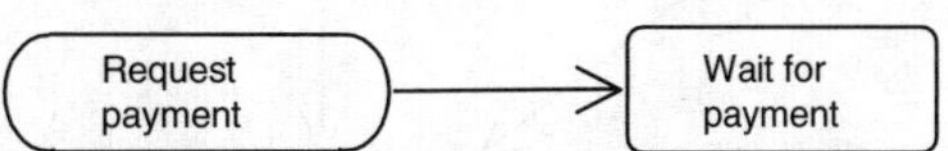

Fig. 10-13: A triggerless transition between an activity and a state

In this example, when a payment request has been made, waiting for payment begins. This is an example of a *triggerless transition* because no external event has caused it to take place and the transition starts when the activity has completed its work. Triggerless transactions are permissible when exiting activities, and the meaning is that the activity has completed all its actions and the next phase of the workflow can begin. When exiting a state, some event needs to trigger it. For example, when waiting for payment, exit from the state could be triggered by a paymentArrives event, with an argument describing the amount as in Figure 10-14.

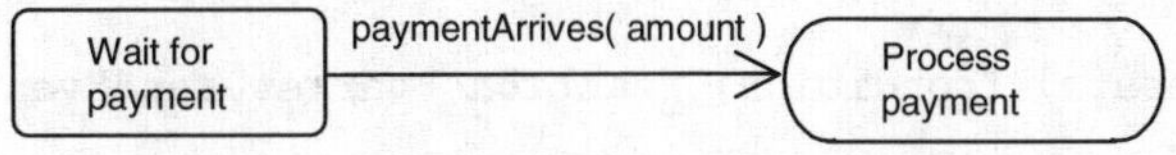

Fig. 10-14: A triggered transition from a state

There can be more than one transition out of a single activity or state. This is used when different events result in a state or activity terminating. An example would be if payment does not arrive in a specified period, which leads to a Chase payment activity instead of to a Process payment activity as indicated in Figure 10-15. Now we have the ability to model alternative paths through a workflow. (There is an additional notation to insert decision points that we will discuss later.)

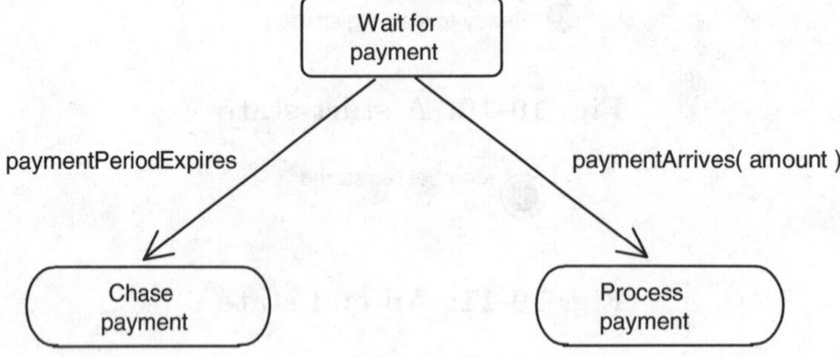

Fig. 10-15: Multiple transitions from a state, triggered by different events

Conditions can be set on transitions, and these are recorded in rectangular brackets and known as guards. The transition will then take place only if the condition is true. For example, suppose that in processing payments, there is an option to pay by cash, and that requires an extra step in modifying the cash balance before clearing the debt. The flow of work would then be as in Figure 10-16.

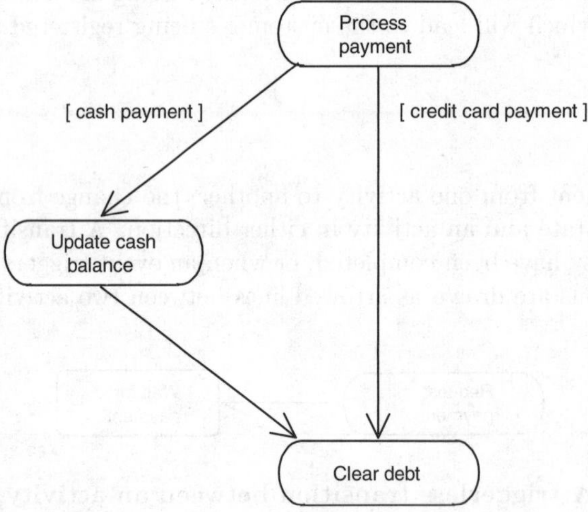

Fig. 10-16: Multiple triggerless transitions from an activity, using guards

A transition may also have one and no more than one associated action. An action is preceded by a forward slash. In an environment where cash is the only means of paying, then Figure 10-16 could be redrawn more simply, with an action on the transition updating the cash balance as in Figure 10-17.

An action on a transition may trigger an event. The full syntax for the transition label is as follows.

```
event (arguments) [condition] / action ^target.sendEvent (arguments)
```

The order of execution of actions is as follows. Once an activity or state completes, either because all the actions of the activity have finished or because some event triggers exit, then the exit actions of that activity or state are carried out, then the transition fires and any action on the transition fires, and finally the entry actions for the receiving activity or state are fired.

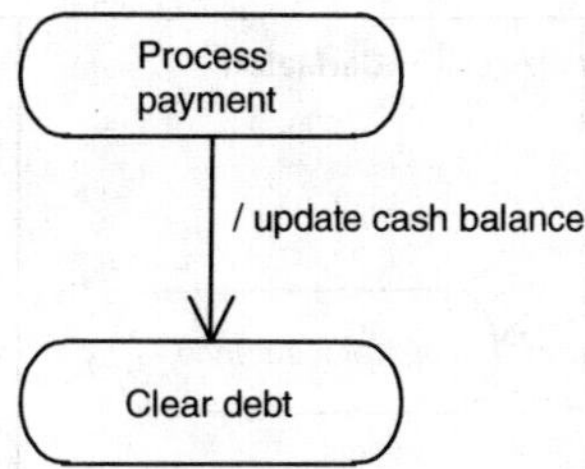

Fig. 10-17: Using an action on a transition

10.4.4 Decision Points

A *decision point* is a point in a workflow where the exit transition from a state or activity may branch in alternative directions depending on a condition. This is signified by a diamond shape. A decision can have one or more entry and two or more exit transitions. The exit transitions must be indicated by non-overlapping guards. In Figure 10-18 we see three options from a triggerless exit of a Process payment activity, that depend on whether the payment was by cheque, cash or credit card. Note that UML does not specify the syntax of the conditions. This might be structured text, or the logic syntax of a programming language, or the Object Constraint Language (OCL) described later.

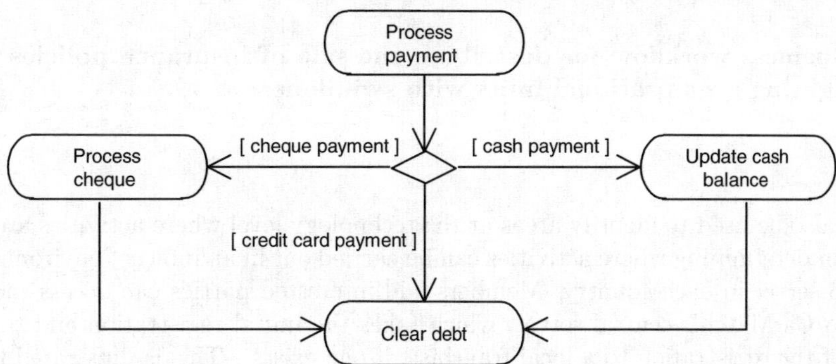

Fig. 10-18: Alternative paths described using a decision point

This is a more explicit way of describing alternative paths and indicating decision points, but it can clutter the diagrams. Sometimes it is easier to follow the flow if you use multiple exits from an activity or state, with guards or events to indicate the paths, as in Section 10.4.3.

10.4.5 Swimlanes

The *swimlane* is a very useful notation for indicating where an activity takes place. This may be where an activity takes place within a business, or where a system activity takes place in a complex system. Swimlanes are columns on an activity diagram, and the activities in the diagram are grouped in the swimlanes. For example, CarMatch offers insurance policies on behalf of insurance agents to its members. To take out a policy, activities are undertaken by the customer, by CarMatch, and by the insurer. The process can be mapped out in two dimensions as in Figure 10-19.

Note that a number of activities in the business workflow are carried out by the customer. In order to construct an information system to meet the requirements to support these activities, there would need to be use cases with actors from within the business to handle the results of customers' activities.

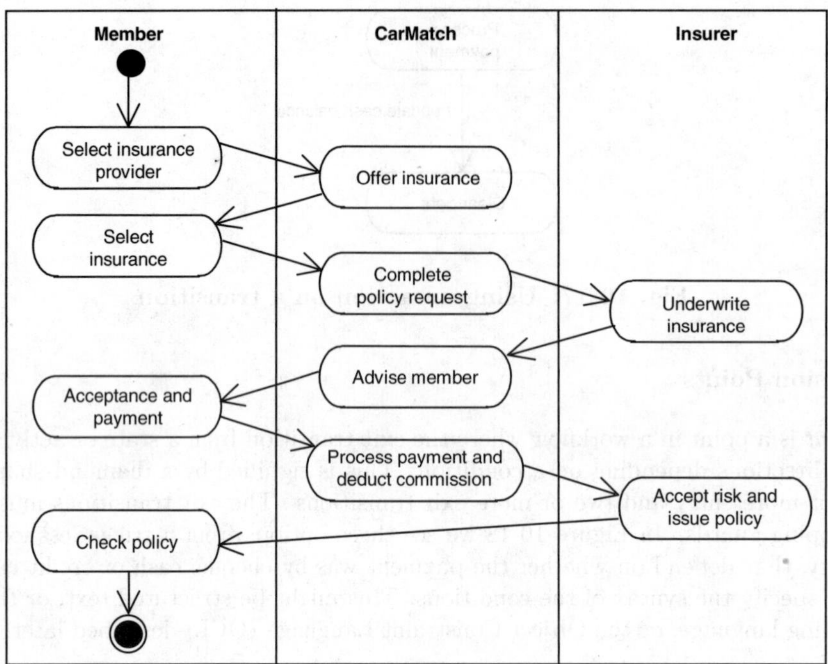

Fig. 10-19: Business workflow for describing the sale of insurance policies through CarMatch, highlighting organizational units with swimlanes

Swimlanes can also be used to identify areas at the technology level where activities are carried out. A common use is in determining where activities can be carried out in an internet environment. CarMatch has a main web-server in each country. Members and interested parties can access these web-servers. These link in to CarMatch's central server, which takes the initial registration and then delegate the final handling of the registration to a local franchise, if one exists . This is illustrated in Figure 10-20.

There are similarities with the use of sequence diagrams in the elaboration of business use cases. It is possible that the above flow could be modelled by a sequence diagram as in Figure 9-35. Although more complicated flows with more branching would be better described in an activity diagram.

10.4.6 Forks and Joins

Sometimes it makes sense to allow a number of activities to run in parallel. A transition can be split into multiple paths and multiple paths combined into a single transition by using a *synchronization bar*. Where the paths split is known as a *fork*, and where the paths meet is known as a *join*.

In the CarMatch case study, there is a use case Match car sharers. This can be modelled as a business process. Once the journeys have been matched, we realize that it is sensible to notify potential sharers in parallel. However, members will have to negotiate at the same time, and draw up an agreement together with the help of CarMatch. We would draw an activity diagram as in Figure 10-21.

A synchronization bar may have one entry transition and two or more exit transitions, or multiple entry transitions and one exit transition. It is important when workflow is split into parallel flows that these flows are re-combined on the same diagram.

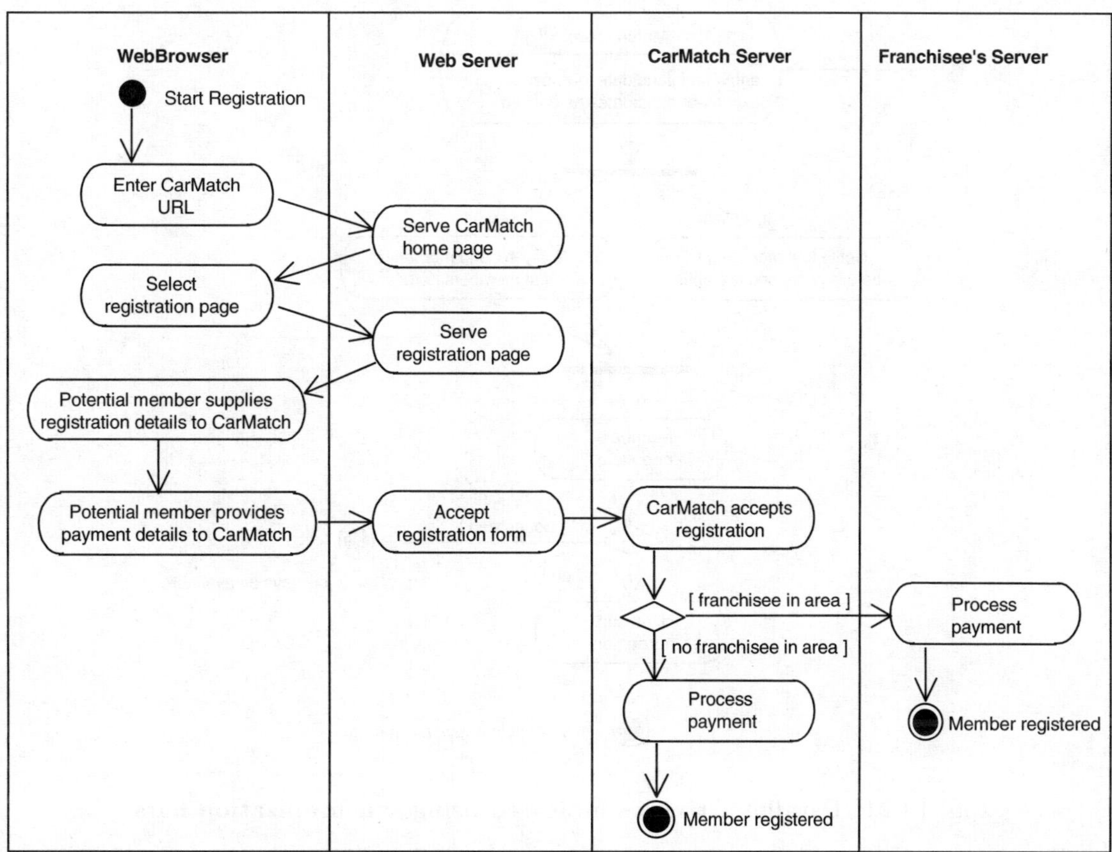

Fig. 10-20: Workflow describing registration of a CarMatch member through the web, highlighting technology areas with swimlanes

10.4.7 Objects on Activity Diagrams

So far, activity diagrams feel a little removed from objects. However, all activities need to be carried out by objects in an object-oriented implementation. Sometimes it is useful to indicate on an activity diagram where a flow affects an object. This is done by placing an object on the diagram and linking it to an activity by a dependency relationship. Such dependencies are known as *object flows* because they indicate how an object is used in a flow of control. The workflow will change the state of objects. Therefore, each object can have a state associated with it. We examine how to model the state of objects in Chapter 11 on statechart diagrams. In the Match car sharers use case we might want to see the impact the workflow has on the journeys in a matching process. We can place an instance of the class Journey, called j1, with a state Available on the diagram to indicate the state of the object, as in Figure 10-22.

We can then tie the objects to activities that transform them. Thus in the activity diagram we can show that there are two journeys that start in an Available state. The members offering those journeys are then notified of a possibility of each of them sharing and the journeys enter a Notified state so that the matching process does not try matching them again until this process is completed. Then finally the journeys either end up in either a Sharing state if the members agree to share, or an Available state if agreement is not reached. We show this in Figure 10-23.

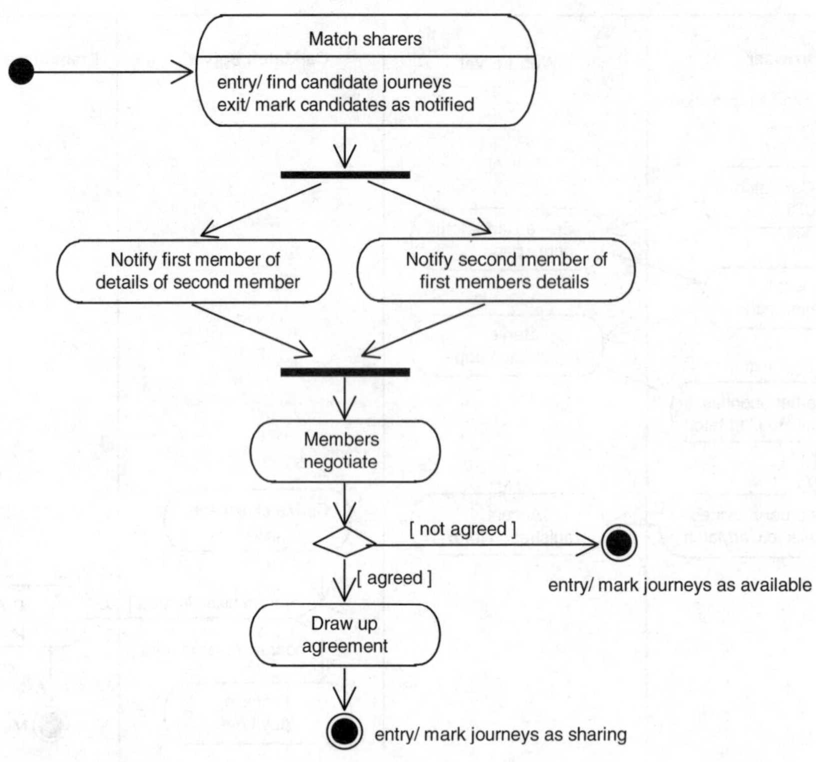

Fig. 10-21: Parallel activities indicated using synchronization bars

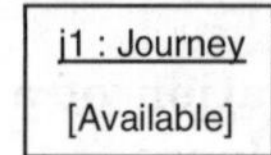

Fig. 10-22: An object on an activity diagram with an associated state

10.4.8 Nested Activity Diagrams

Activity diagrams can grow quite complicated. Activities within a diagram can be complicated too. To manage the complexity, an activity itself can be modelled by an activity diagram. Thus, the Match Sharers activity above may have an activity diagram to describe how the matching is done. In Figure 10-24 we see that to find a match, first an available journey is found, then a candidate journey for sharing is found. If no candidate journey to share is found, then the first journey would be skipped, and another sought, and so on until a pair is found.

Nesting of flows on a single diagram can also be shown as in Figure 10-25.

10.4.9 Control Icons

Transitions are triggered by events, either from an event external to the flow, or because the activity from which the transition issues has completed. Transitions can also trigger events themselves. We already have a sufficient notation to describe this fully, but there are two extra icons provided by UML to make the handling of events more explicit. These are *control icons*.

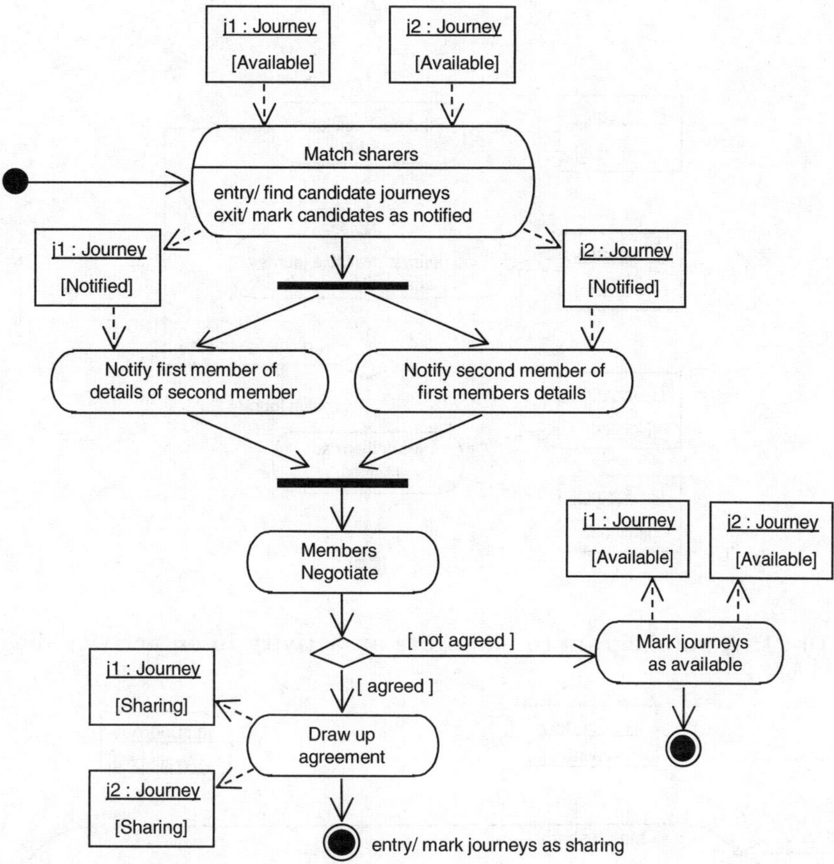

Fig. 10-23: Object flows on the journey matching use case

The first is an icon to indicate the sending of a signal (i.e. event). This is drawn as in Figure 10-26, with the point at either side of the icon, showing the issue of an event. In this case, it indicates that a car has passed a beacon on a road-pricing scheme. The second icon is to indicate the receipt of a signal. This is drawn as in Figure 10-26 with the triangular notch at either side of the rectangle, showing the receipt of an event. In this case, it indicates that a car has passed a beacon.

Events can pass between processes. We might have a process in a beacon to manage the capture of passing cars, and a process in a separate congestion monitoring system that takes the signal from the beacon and updates volumes of cars in a particular district, as in Figure 10-28. These processes would take place in separate computer systems, and be linked via some communication system along which the event would be carried. Note that, in this example, multiple beacons may be sending the same type of event to impact the same region.

Dependencies can also be added to the diagram between activities and the objects that need to process events. For example, in the beacon there may be an object to manage the car, that needs to respond to the signal that a car has passed the beacon, say to update the number of units that the owner needs to be charged. This would be indicated by putting a dependency link on the diagram, as in Figure 10-29.

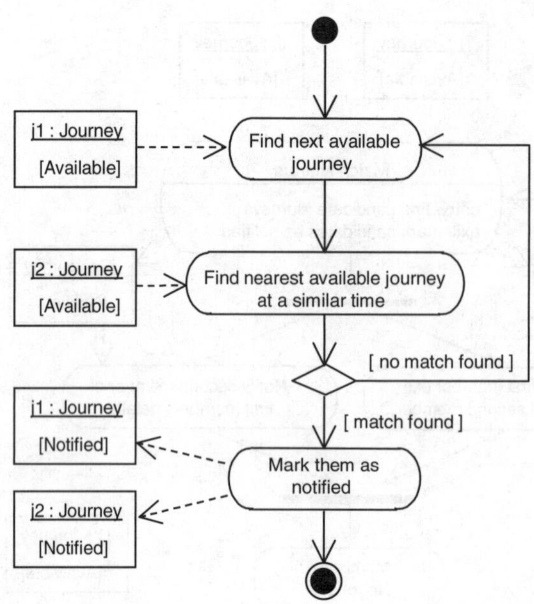

Fig. 10-24: A subdiagram to elaborate an activity in an activity diagram

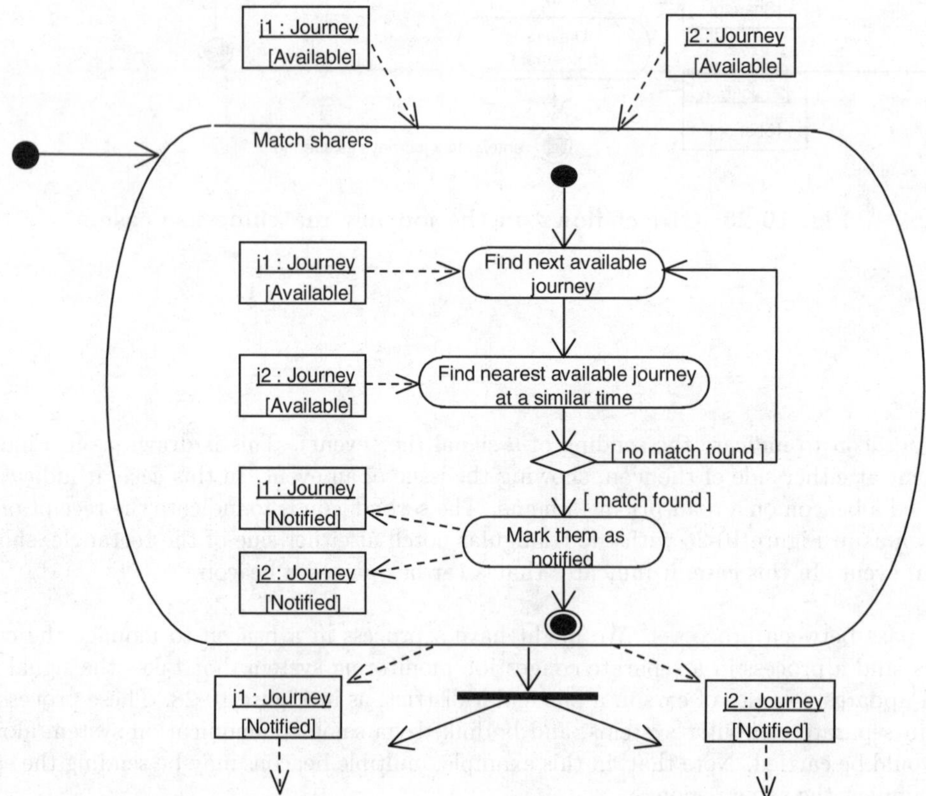

Fig. 10-25: A subdiagram workflow nested within an activity on an activity diagram

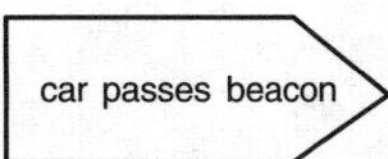

Fig. 10-26: The sending of a signal when a car has passed a beacon in a road-pricing scheme

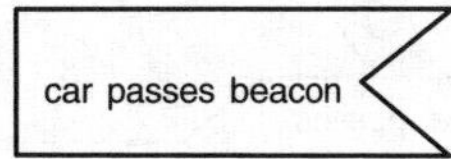

Fig. 10-27: The receipt of a signal when a car has passed a beacon in a road-pricing scheme

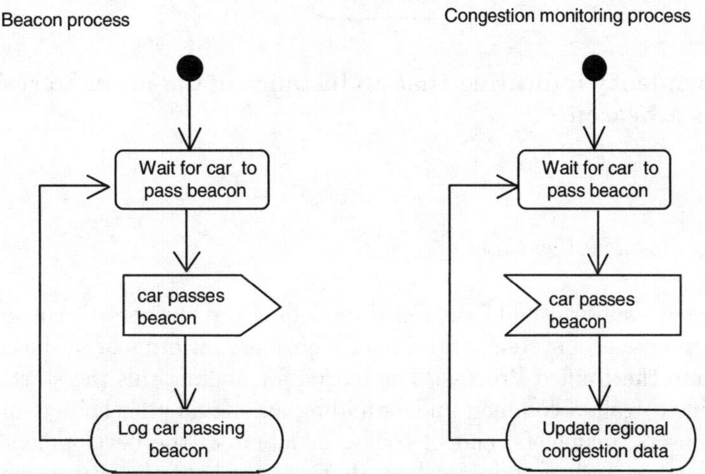

Fig. 10-28: Processes in the beacon and the congestion monitoring system to deal with cars passing beacons, linked by a signal

10.5 HOW TO PRODUCE ACTIVITY DIAGRAMS

10.5.1 Activity Diagrams for Business Modelling

Activity Diagrams are a means of describing workflows in the development of a business model. Business models consist largely of processes that can be described very comprehensively by activity diagrams. The development of business models consists of:

- finding business actors and business use cases;
- identifying key scenarios of business use cases, using primary and alternative paths;
- combining the scenarios to produce comprehensive workflows described using activity diagrams;
- where significant object behaviour is triggered by a workflow, adding object flows to the diagram;
- where appropriate, mapping activities to business areas and recording this using swimlanes;
- refining complicated high level activities in a similar fashion.

Once the business model has been described in this way, then the definition of system use cases can begin.

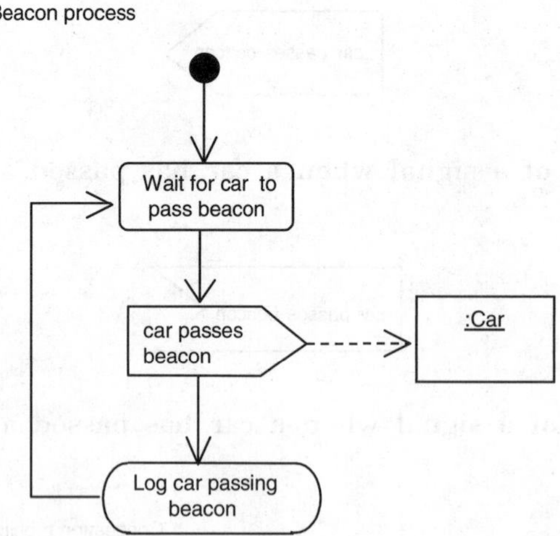

Fig. 10-29: A dependency indicating that an instance of Car needs to respond to the signal when a car passes a beacon

10.5.1.1 Identifying Business Use Cases

The first major stage of a substantial IT project is modelling the business. Jacobson, Ericsson & Jacobson (1995) view a business as a system, and model a business in terms of business use cases. This has been incorporated into the Unified Process. The reason for making this the starting point for analysis is that it is important to gain a common understanding among all stakeholders in a project, including funders, customers, users, managers, and of course members of the development team. Further, the context of a system very much determines how that system behaves. By viewing the business as a system, in which the computer systems are embedded subsystems, it is possible to model the behaviour of the environment in which a computer system operates. The first stage in this process is identifying the business actors that utilize the business, and this will include customers, investors, banks, suppliers, and maybe regulators. Each of these will invoke a set of business use cases. (These would be thought of as business processes in other approaches.)

10.5.1.2 Identifying Key Scenarios in Business Use Cases

A business use case typically consists of a complex workflow with many possible paths through it. When a business use case has been identified, the next stage is to analyze the key scenarios that are executed by the business use case. A scenario is best viewed as a simple sequence of business activities or actions. For the simplest business, the number of scenarios through a business use case can be very large.

The business analyst needs a structured method of acquiring a representative sample of scenarios from which a comprehensive description of the flows through the business use case can be determined. A recommended approach is to begin by looking for the *primary path*. This is the scenario that is most commonly used. The reasons for doing this are twofold. Firstly, the majority of instances of the use case will involve this primary path, at least in part, and the use case will be ineffective if it cannot at least cope with this. Based on the rule of thumb that 80% of activities use 20% of the capability of any system, implementing the primary path can provide a quick route to a usable system. Secondly, by identifying the primary path, a framework is established to identify representative alternative scenarios.

EXAMPLE 10.2 CarMatch wishes to sell consultancy. This is recorded at a high level as a business use case, as in Figure 10-30.

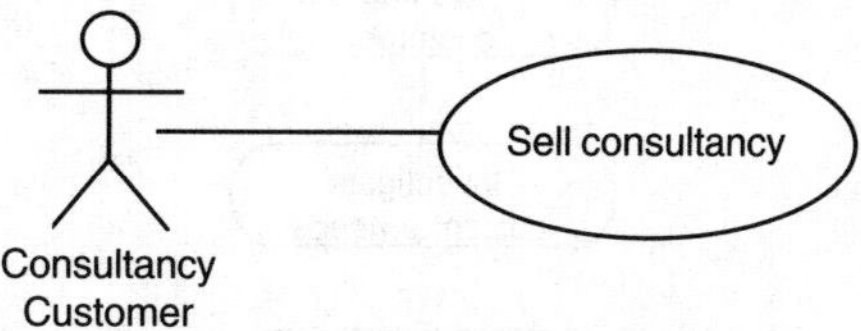

Fig. 10-30: Sell consultancy business use case

After discussions with the head of the new consultancy division, the following is the ideal process for the sale of consultancy.

1. Contact with potential consultancy customer. The contact can be direct from CarMatch, or by referral from an associate organization, or by direct contact from the customer.
2. Preliminary investigation of the customer's needs.
3. Construction of a project proposal.
4. Proposal accepted.
5. Contracts agreed.
6. Project executed.
7. Customer is billed, and project closed.

Now we have a primary path, we can look for alternatives by examining each stage of the primary path. In Stage 4, the ideal is that the customer has no objections and accepts the proposal, but in practice there may be minor or major changes required, or even withdrawal from the process altogether. After discussing this with the head of consultancy, three options have been identified in Stage 4.

4.1 The client wants changes to the proposal but is agreeable to the proposal as a concept, so revision of the proposal is required.

4.2 The client feels that this proposal does not meet his needs, but is prepared to consider alternative proposals.

4.3 The client no longer wishes to discuss a project with CarMatch, at least for the time being.

10.5.1.3 Merge Scenarios to Provide a Comprehensive Workflow

The workflow for each scenario can now be drawn, starting with the primary path and adding in the alternative paths one by one.

EXAMPLE 10.3 From the primary path of the Sell consultancy business use case, we can draw an initial straight line flow as in Figure 10-31. Then looking at the alternative paths we can start adding alternative flows. Figure 10-32 shows how we have used an event to take us out of the Accept proposal activity, and we make a decision as to whether to quit the proposal process, modify the current proposal, or seek another proposal idea; these decisions are recorded as guards. We can proceed with our analysis in this way, questioning each stage of the process as it is defined to look for alternative paths.

The outcome of this cycle will be a set of comprehensively defined business use cases with supporting business workflows. Clearly, it makes sense to elaborate in detail only those business use cases that are the focus of the project.

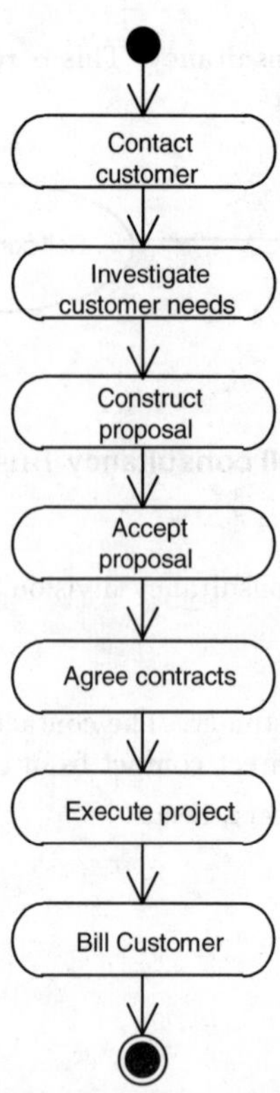

Fig. 10-31: The workflow for the primary path of the Sell consultancy business use case

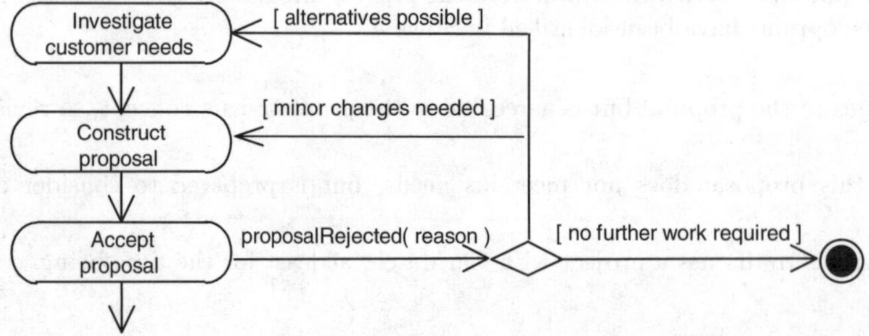

Fig. 10-32: An alternative path on the workflow of the Sell consultancy business use case

10.5.1.4 Assign Object Flows to Model Key Business Entity Behaviour

Objects are added to the workflow for key areas, where it is useful to model the changes of state that result from activities in the activity diagram.

EXAMPLE 10.4 In the CarMatch example of matching car sharers, we saw that the journeys that were matched went through significant state changes (see Figure 10-23). For example, it is not sensible to offer a journey to another potential sharer while it is being considered for sharing. Only for key areas like this is it appropriate to add objects to the workflow to indicate key state transitions. In this example (Sell consultancy) it is not appropriate to consider object flows, as the workflow is very high level.

10.5.1.5 Assign Activities to Business Areas using Swimlanes

Where a particular business organization is prescribed, and a workflow passes through a number of business areas, it is sometimes useful to draw workflows using swimlanes to indicate the business areas that carry out the activities (see Figure 10-19).

EXAMPLE 10.5 In this example, swimlanes would not be appropriate as the negotiation takes place in arbitrary and overlapping business areas.

10.5.1.6 Further Refine Activities

The top level activities identified in this way will often require further detail. The same process of refinement can be applied, looking for primary and alternative paths through the activity, then combining them to produce a comprehensive workflow. This can continue until sufficient detail has been gathered to describe the business model comprehensively for the purposes of the project. In practice, no more than three levels of activity decomposition are usually necessary and sometimes one is enough, though for complex processes this number can be much greater.

10.5.2 How to Produce Activity Diagrams for Use Case Modelling

The production of activity diagrams for system use case models is similar to that of preparing them for business workflows:

- identifying key scenarios of system use cases, using primary and alternative paths;
- combining the scenarios to produce comprehensive workflows described using activity diagrams;
- where significant object behaviour is triggered by a workflow, adding object flows to the diagram;
- where workflows cross technology boundaries, using swimlanes to map the activities;
- refining complicated high level activities in a similar fashion.

Remember that activity diagrams are just one way of recording workflow in a system. Sequence diagrams and collaboration diagrams give alternatives that link workflows more comprehensively to the underlying object models. Typically, you would use activity diagrams early in a project to describe those use cases where complex flows need a full description before an object model has been elaborated. The use case elaboration in Figure 3-11 illustrates a primary path for registering a car sharer. We can draw an activity diagram to illustrate the flow through the use case as in Figure 10-33.

Now, starting from this primary path, we could consider the alternatives, such as what might happen if the address is not found on the geographical database. For each of the points where the address is matched we might paste in a fragment as in Figure 10-34.

However, as it is repeated three times, then it would be sensible to represent this flow as a subflow of the activity that matches the address against the geographical database by attaching an activity diagram to the Match address against geographical database activity.

10.6 RELATIONSHIP WITH OTHER DIAGRAMS

Activity diagrams describe workflow, focusing on activities. They allow for sequential and parallel flows. Alongside collaboration diagrams and sequence diagrams, they provide a means of describing

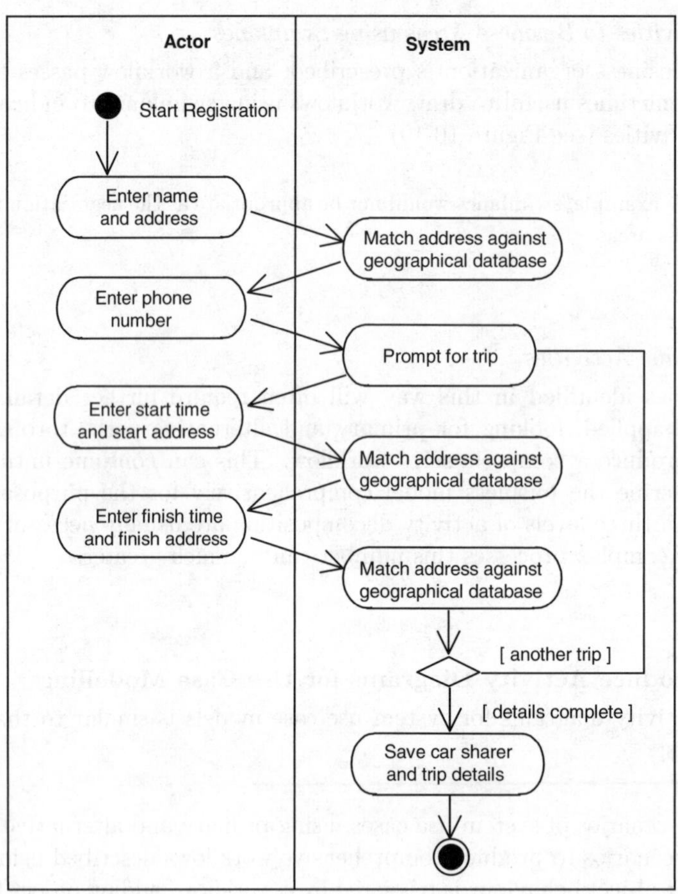

Fig. 10-33: Workflow for the primary path of the system use case Register car sharer

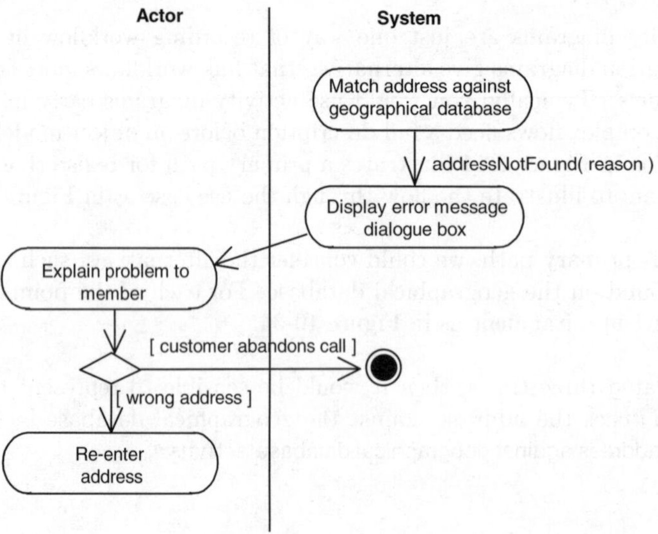

Fig. 10-34: An alternative path on the system use case Register car sharer

the dynamic behaviour of a system. Within a CASE tool, they would be linked as subdiagrams of business use cases, use cases, classes and operations.

10.7 ACTIVITY DIAGRAMS IN THE UNIFIED PROCESS

The Unified Process is itself a set of recommended workflows for the construction of software-intensive systems. These workflows are stereotyped activity diagrams. The Unified Process workflow for the development of requirements is given in Figure 10-35.

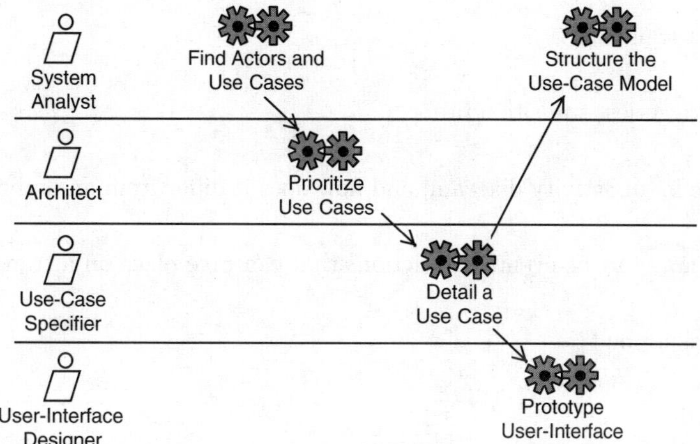

Fig. 10-35: Requirements workflow as an activity diagram

You can see that this is a very high level workflow, and quite simplistic. Most of the activities here are very long in execution, and within them there may be many parallel strands. The Unified Process defines five core workflows, spanning requirements, analysis, design, implementation, test. Unified process workflows provide an example of using workflow modelling to describe at a very high level a very complex business activity. The Unified Process is a use case driven approach, and use cases themselves are groupings of workflows. In business modelling, the definition of business use cases can be supported by activity diagrams to fully model the complex workflows that a business use case represents. Likewise, system use cases can be elaborated using activity diagrams fully to describe the complex workflows that need to be implemented in a computer system; in this case the analyst may also decide to use sequence diagrams and collaboration diagrams in order further to describe workflows and link them to the underlying object model.

In the Unified Process, activity diagrams are specifically used in the activity *Detail a Use Case.* In this activity, there is a step *Formalizing the Use-Case Descriptions*, and activity diagrams can be used to document the behaviour of the use case if a textual description is too informal.

Review Questions

10.1 What types of flow can be described by activity diagrams?

10.2 When would you first consider using an activity diagram?

10.3 Why do you draw activity diagrams?

10.4 What is an activity?

10.5 What are actions?

10.6 How long can it take for an activity to complete?

10.7 When do actions take place in an activity?

10.8 What is a transition?

10.9 What triggers a transition?

10.10 When does a triggerless transition fire?

10.11 What is a state in an activity diagram, and how does it differ from an activity?

10.12 What is the syntax for the events and actions that can take place on a transition?

10.13 What is a decision point?

10.14 What is a guard?

10.15 How many transitions can go into a decision point?

10.16 How many transitions can leave a decision point?

10.17 What is a swimlane?

10.18 Why would you use a swimlane?

10.19 What is a synchronization bar?

10.20 What is the rule about the number of transitions into and out of a synchronization bar?

10.21 What is an object flow?

10.22 What information can you keep about an object on an object flow?

10.23 Why would you nest an activity diagram within an activity?

10.24 With what UML elements can activity diagrams be attached?

10.25 What are control icons, and why would you use them?

Solved Problems

10.1 Here is a description of a business process in CarMatch.

> CarMatch intends that members could obtain a discount for road-pricing schemes. CarMatch negotiates with each authority independently. Each pricing scheme has its own computer system. CarMatch would prefer to take over the billing of its own members and attempts to negotiate this first, but sometimes that is not possible. They will then negotiate discounts for members. Finally, they will agree on the mechanism for exchanging information. It can take some time to agree standards, and the rest of the negotiations can be suspended temporarily. If negotiations are successful, then contracts will be drawn up and agreed. Sometimes the contract stage will cause some renegotiation. At any time, either party can suspend or cancel negotiations.

Draw a workflow for this process.

We identify the business use case as Obtain road-price discounts for members. This involves the CarMatch central office and the road pricing agency. We show this business use case in Figure 10-36.

Fig. 10-36: The business use case for Negotiate with road price agencies to obtain discounts for members

We then produce a primary path analysis, and alternative paths that result in the following steps.

1. Propose to road pricing agency that car match bill the members for road pricing.
2. Negotiate discounts with the agency.
3. Agree mechanism for data exchange.
4. Draw up contracts.

Further information from CarMatch leads to the recognition that there are some alternative paths.

3.1 There may be a suspension of the negotiation process while working on data exchange, that can lead to resumption at a later stage, or a cancellation.

4.1 There may be minor amendments to the contract, so return to Stage 4.

4.2 There may be issues with the data exchange when it comes to contract, so return to Stage 3.

4.3 There may be issues with the discounts, so return to Stage 2.

We are making the simplifying assumption here that after suspending negotiations, resumption would always start at the discount negotiation. Another simplifying assumption is that on contract changes, the process would backtrack to the point of negotiations where the area of dispute has arisen. In practice this is not a problem, because the other activities would run through with no action necessary, unless something changes earlier in the process. Too many decision points confuse the diagram. You should be able to identify more alternatives than this, but the above are representative. We then merge these scenarios to provide a combined workflow as in Figure 10-37.

This is a high level business process, so there is no point at this stage in identifying objects and placing them on the object flow. Later, there may be an appropriate linkage of a contract object to the flow. Following this analysis we may wish to break down any of the above activities into sub-activities, and provide activity diagrams to elaborate those workflows. Also, at this level, the activities are collaborative and it would not be appropriate to use swimlanes as the activities could not be assigned to particular business areas.

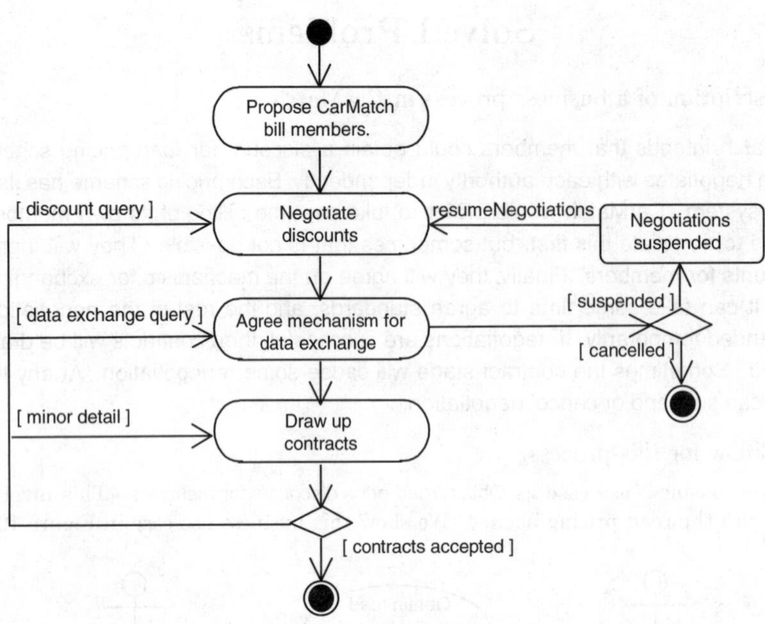

Fig. 10-37: The CarMatch process of negotiation with road pricing agencies

10.2 Assume that CarMatch has negotiated a deal with the pricing authority. Whenever a member passes a toll point, the toll beacon records the event then passes it on to the pricing authority. The pricing authority then calculates the fee and passes it on to the CarMatch system. To understand the linkages between the different computer systems involved, an activity diagram is needed.

After interviewing all parties, the following sequence of events is determined. This is the primary path scenario.

1. The member passes a road toll point. The member's car is detected by a beacon and its details are recorded on the beacon and transmitted to the charging authority's computer.
2. The charging authority determines that this is a CarMatch client, and calculates the discounted fee.
3. The charging authority adds the charge to the CarMatch account.
4. The charging authority computer notifies the CarMatch server that a charge is to be made.
5. CarMatch adds the charge to the member's account.
6. CarMatch adds the charge to the total outstanding for the Authority.

There are three technology areas: the pricing beacon itself, which can keep records, the pricing authority computer, to which it passes information, and the CarMatch server. We use swim lanes to indicate the three technology areas, and produce a workflow as described in Figure 10-38. Note that this is a process that could take place over a length of time. The transfer from the beacon to the pricing authority computer could be real time, or done on some regular batch basis. The transfer to CarMatch's server would almost certainly be done on a batch basis.

The next stage would be to identify system use cases from this business workflow, and these use cases may have activity diagrams or sequence diagrams to describe their internal flows.

Supplementary Problems

10.3 Look at the VolBank case study in Chapter 1, and draw up the process for matching a volunteer with voluntary organizations in his or her area and producing a volunteering agreement. Assume

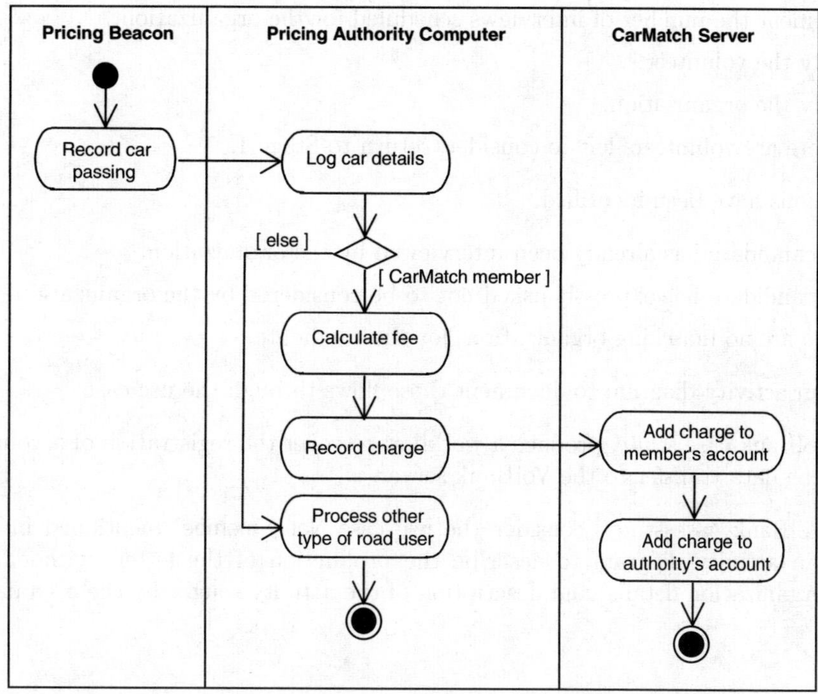

Fig. 10-38: The process of road-price charging via CarMatch

that a volunteer cannot be matched with more than one voluntary organization at a time, but that a voluntary organization will use many volunteers, up to a set limit.

10.4 After analyzing the business process in problem 10.3, it is decided that there will be a daily batch process to match volunteers with organizations. It is decided that an organization can have a maximum of three candidates in interview at any one time. The batch process is drawn up as a use case, Match candidates daily batch, that includes two other use cases, Notify volunteer and Notify organization, see Figure 10-39.

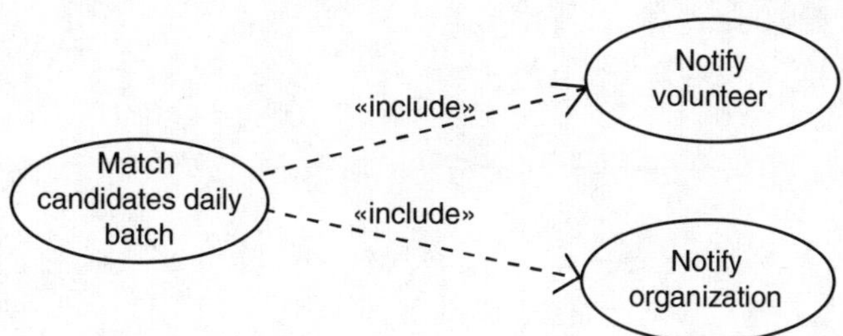

Fig. 10-39: The system use case for Match volunteers with organizations

The primary flow through the use case is as follows.

1. Get next volunteer who is available.
2. Get first matching organization seeking a volunteer who does not have three interviews active.
3. Mark the volunteer as notified.

4. Increment the number of interviews scheduled for the organization.
5. Notify the volunteer.
6. Notify the organization.
7. If there are volunteers left to consider, return to Stage 1.

Three options have been identified.

2.1 The candidate has already been interviewed by the organization.

2.2 The candidate has expressly asked not to be considered by the organization.

2.3 There are no matching organizations for the candidate.

Produce an activity diagram to document these flows through the use case.

10.5 For the VolBank case study, produce a workflow to cover the registration of a volunteer over the web and the data transfer to the VolBank server.

10.6 For the VolBank case study, consider the use case Notify member mentioned in Problem 10.4. Produce an activity diagram to describe the production of the letter, with date, volunteer's address, organization details, and description of the activity sought by the organization.

Statechart Diagrams

11.1 INTRODUCTION

Statechart diagrams are a means of describing the behaviour of dynamic model elements, and they are closely related to activity diagrams. Whereas activity diagrams describe flow between areas of work, statechart diagrams describe the changes between the *states* of instances. For example, a telephone is hung up, dialling, engaged in a call, or disconnected. These are states of the telephone, and we can use a statechart diagram to link the states together and determine the legal flows through the system. While an item is in a state, work may or may not be going on—when a phone is hung up, then there is no activity in the phone, but when it is making a call, there is lots of activity in the phone. States are useful logical views of an entity.

Statechart diagrams are used mostly to describe the behavior of classes, but they can be used to describe the behavior of other elements of a model, such as use cases, actors, subsystems, and operations. They can be used during analysis to describe complex behavior of elements in the system environment, such as the behavior of a customer. They can be used at the design level to describe the behavior of control classes, boundary classes (such as screens) or complex entity classes (such as accounts). The statechart diagram is one of a number of diagrams in UML that can be used to model workflow; namely, activity diagrams, collaboration diagrams, sequence diagrams. The difference is that a statechart diagram models behaviour from the perspective of a single entity, such as a class, whereas activity diagrams and collaboration diagrams can model the behaviour of many entities in a single diagram.

Figure 11-1 illustrates a simple statechart diagram for the Journey class in the CarMatch system. Once the journey is created, it enters the Available state. Once a car sharer has been found and agreement on sharing reached, then the journey becomes Active as far as the CarMatch system is concerned. Later the sharing agreement may terminate, say because one of the car sharers drops out of the agreement, and the journey goes back to being Available. At any time, the journey may be terminated.

In this chapter we shall introduce the notion of state, transition and event, and relate them to other UML elements. Some of these concepts are similar to those for activity diagrams. The term *state machine* is also used for the statechart that is shown in a statechart diagram.

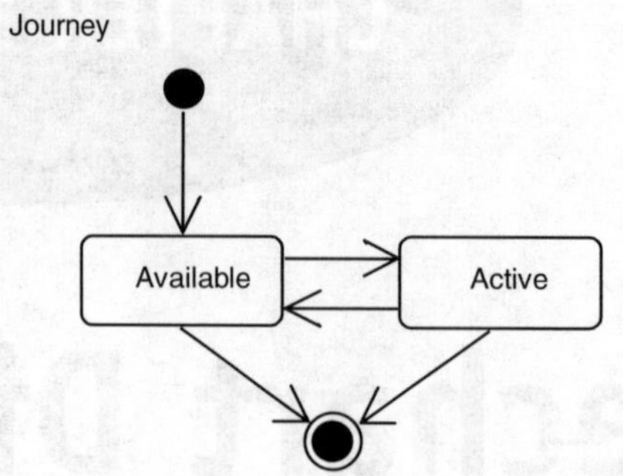

Fig. 11-1: A simple statechart diagram describing the Journey class in the CarMatch system

11.1.1 State

Systems and entities within a system, such as objects, can be viewed as moving from state to state. External events trigger some activity that changes the state of the system and some of its parts. In a banking system, money may be withdrawn from an account, and that account may move from a state of credit to an overdrawn state. An item can be in several states at once. For example, a customer may be waiting for a delivery, in debit, in dispute over a bill, all at the same time. States may also be nested. For example, the credit state of an interest-bearing bank account may move between high and low interest states dependent on the balance.

Viewing a system as a set of states and transitions between states is a very useful way of describing complex behavior. It is a way of describing the legal paths through a system. Understanding the legitimate transitions from one state to another is a key part of analysis and design. It is a common practice in the business world to think of entities as passing through a number of states.

11.1.2 Events

Systems are driven by *events*, both external and internal. Systems respond to events, and these events in turn trigger other events. An external event will usually cause a series of internal events to occur, and sometimes these may trigger external events too. For example, a customer depositing a cheque into her savings account will trigger an internal event to place an uncleared credit against her account, and trigger an external event to request transfer of the money by the banking system from the issuer of the cheque. Time is also a major source of events, such as the arrival of a billing date, which in turn may generate an event to print invoices.

Events pass information, expressed in UML as arguments. This information will flow around a system as events trigger other events. These arguments can be used as part of the decision-making, say to determine which state is the next appropriate state when an event occurs. (Note that a distinction is made between parameters and arguments. The signature of an operation or event includes parameters, which define the name and type of the values that can be passed in the operation or event; the arguments are the actual values associated with a particular instance of that operation or event.)

Ultimately events have to be realized by objects, in the form of operations (some programming languages include events, and operations can be implemented as event handlers), and the design process will involve examining all the events in a statechart diagram and considering how those events will be supported by the objects in the system.

11.2 PURPOSE OF THE TECHNIQUE

The key role of statechart diagrams is to describe complex entities that have significant states and complicated transitions between states. They are particularly useful for describing

- complex business entities, such as customers and accounts;
- behavior of subsystems;
- interactions in boundary classes during the definition of system interfaces such as screens;
- use case realizations; and
- complex objects, usually those that realize complex business or design entities.

11.3 NOTATION

The name of the entity being modelled (the class, use case or subsystem) can be displayed as a label on the diagram, as in Figure 11-1, normally at the top left of the diagram.

11.3.1 States

A state in a statechart diagram is a point in the lifecycle of a model element that satisfies some condition, where some particular action is being performed, or where some event is awaited. A state is drawn as a rectangle with rounded corners with the name of the state written inside, as in Figure 11-2, which describes a Debit state for an Account class. A state is considered to last for a period of time, though in practice this may be very brief for some states.

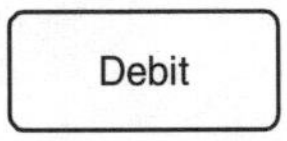

Debit

Fig. 11-2: The Debit state of an Account

States may be *simple* or *composite*. A simple state is not broken down further, and for an object it is likely to be represented by a simple set of values of attributes. A composite state is broken down further, usually by a nested state diagram or sometimes by embedding states within a state on a single diagram (see Section 11.3.4).

There are two special states. The start state is the entry point to a flow. Only one start state is allowed on a diagram, other than as part of a substate flow in a composite state. It is drawn as a black dot, and it can be labelled with a name as in Figure 11-3. End states are drawn as black dots with a surrounding circle (a bulls-eye shape), as in Figure 11-4. There can be several end states in a statechart diagram.

account opened

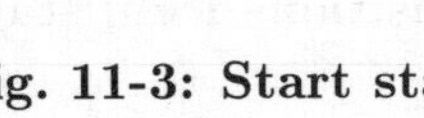

Fig. 11-3: Start state

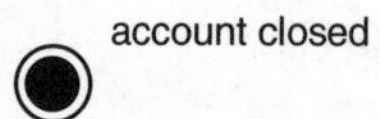

Fig. 11-4: End state

11.3.2 Transitions

A *transition* is the movement between states. Transitions are drawn as arrowed lines between pairs of states, as in Figure 11-5. This illustrates that an instance of Account can change between the Credit and Debit states. In a state diagram, transitions always occur in response to some event. (In activity diagrams, transitions out of activities can happen when the work of the activity is complete, and this is known as a triggerless transition.) The name of the event that triggers the transition is written next to the line.

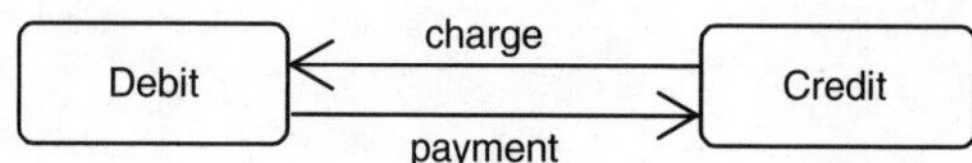

Fig. 11-5: Transitions between the Credit and Debit states of the Account class

More than one transition can leave a single state. This occurs either when different events result in a state terminating, or when there are *guard conditions* on the transitions. In Figure 11-6 we see an extra state introduced into the Account class to cover the possibility that an account has a zero balance. There are three events triggering exit from the Zero balance state, namely charge, payment and close. Conditions can be added to transitions, and these are recorded in square brackets and known as guards. The transition will then take place only if the condition is true. In Figure 11-6, the transition to Zero balance or Credit as a result of a payment depends on the value of the payment and the balance of the account.

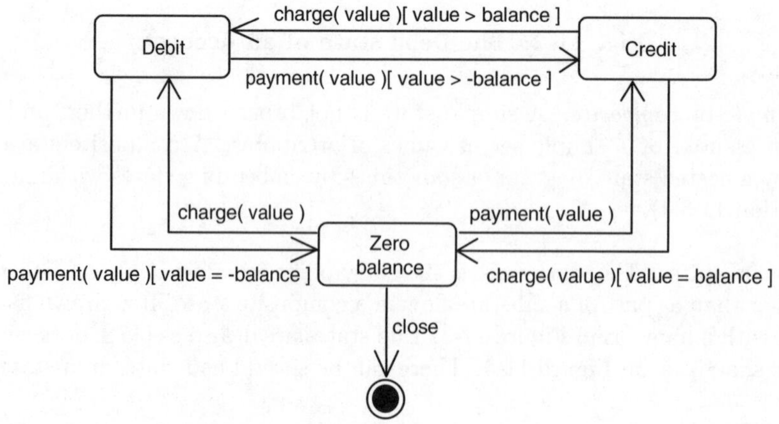

Fig. 11-6: Multiple transitions from states of the Account class

11.3.3 Actions

A state can trigger *actions*. There are five ways in which an action can be triggered:

- On Entry: these actions are triggered as soon as the state is entered;
- Do: these actions take place during the lifetime of the state;
- On Event: these actions take place in response to an event;
- On Exit: these actions take place just before the state exits;
- Include: invokes a *submachine*, represented by another statechart diagram.

Actions are shown in the diagram as in Figure 11-7. The name of the state is placed in the top compartment, separated from the list of actions below by a horizontal line. The syntax for actions is:

```
action-label / action
```

Where *action-label* is one of entry, do, exit, include, or the name of an event. In the special case of an event, the syntax for actions is:

```
event-name (parameters) [guard-condition] / action
```

where *parameters* is a comma-separated list of parameters supplied by the event, and *guard-condition* is a condition that must be true for the event to trigger the action.

Credit

payment(value)/ balance = balance + value
charge(value)[value < balance]/ balance = balance - value

Fig. 11-7: Actions within theCredit state of the Account class

The action can be described in a simple English statement, or for more detailed design, using a programming language statement. An alternative form of action is the triggering of an event in another object, and this is written as:

```
^target.event (parameters)
```

where *target* is some object that needs to respond to the event, *event* is the name of the event, and *parameters* are the information that is conveyed with the event, expressed as a comma-separated list.

Transitions can also trigger actions. The syntax is the same as for an event action inside a state, and written adjacent to the transition. If there is a single transition out of a state, the action is probably best expressed as an exit action on the state, but if there are multiple exits out of a state, that have different actions, then these actions need to be attached to the appropriate transitions.

In Figure 11-8 we see a full description of the states of the Account class. When an account is opened, the exit action of the start state sets the balance to zero and puts the instance in the Zero balance state. A payment will take the account to the Credit state, and a charge will take it to the Debit state. Credit balances remain in credit, until a charge is made that either zeroes the account (taking the instance back to the Zero balance state) or takes it to the Debit state. Likewise debit balances remain in debit until a payment takes them to the Zero balance state or the Credit state. The same event can be handled within a state or trigger a state change depending on the guards (for example, the payment event on the Debit state).

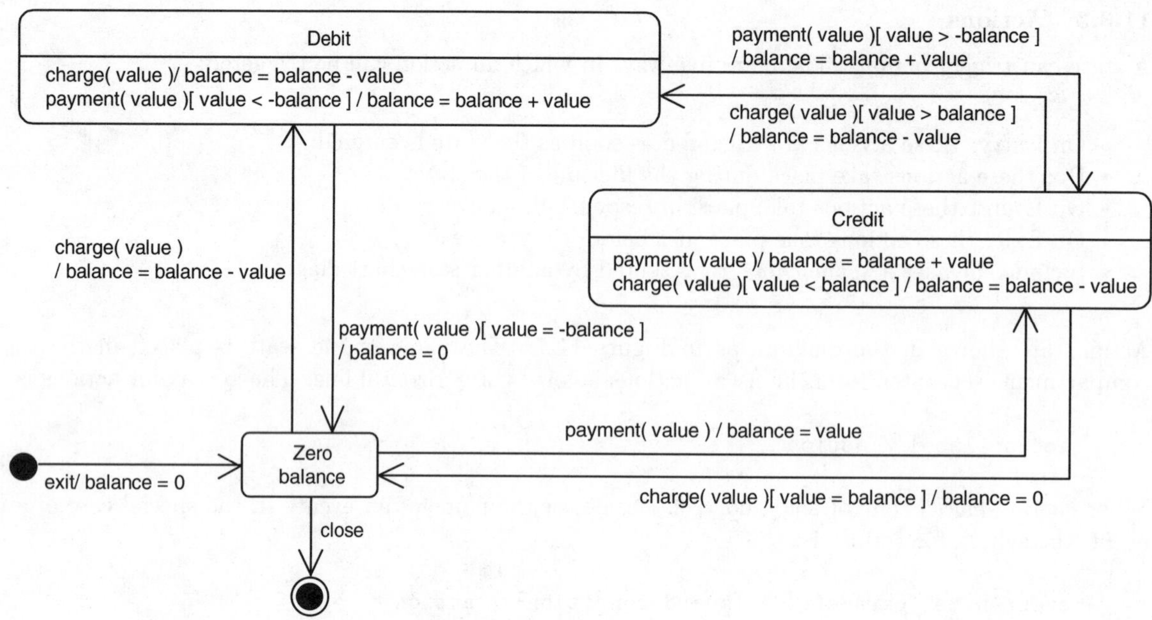

Fig. 11-8: The full description of the states of the Account class

11.3.4 Composite States

A *composite state* can be further broken down into *substates*. The substates can be drawn either within the state or in a separate diagram. Consider the statechart for the Journey class in Figure 11-9.

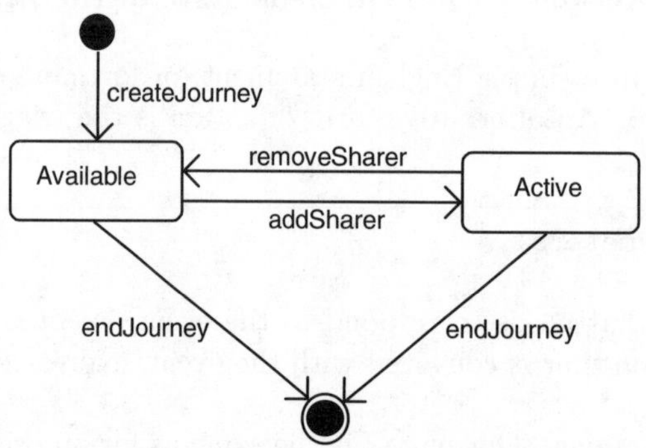

Fig. 11-9: Statechart diagram for the Journey class

Once a journey has been created, because someone wants to share that particular journey, it goes into the Available state. Eventually someone agrees to share on the journey, and the journey enters the Active state. One of the sharers may drop out, and the journey may return to the Available state because there is only one person registered on the journey. While the journey is active, additional drivers may join. The Active state can have two substates, Vacant representing that someone else could join the sharing, and Full indicating that the journey cannot take more sharers. We can therefore draw a statechart diagram to indicate this behavior as in Figure 11-10. We now have two choices to modify the top diagram, Figure 11-9, either by updating the Active state icon as in Figure 11-11, or by adding the substates to the diagram as in Figure 11-12.

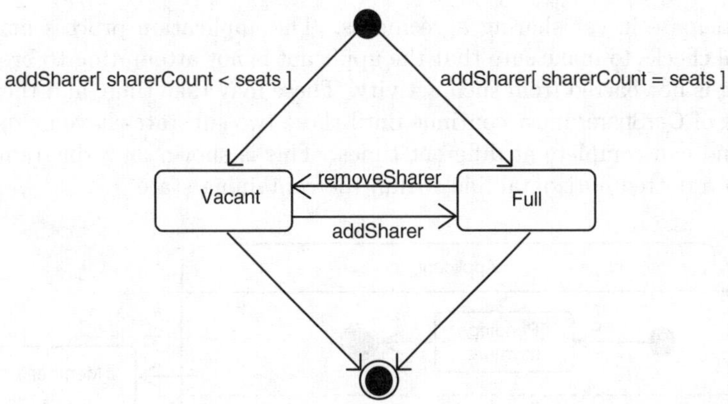

Fig. 11-10: Subflow of the Active state of the Journey class

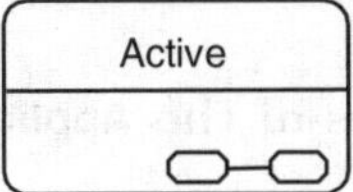

Fig. 11-11: Notation to show a subflow on a state

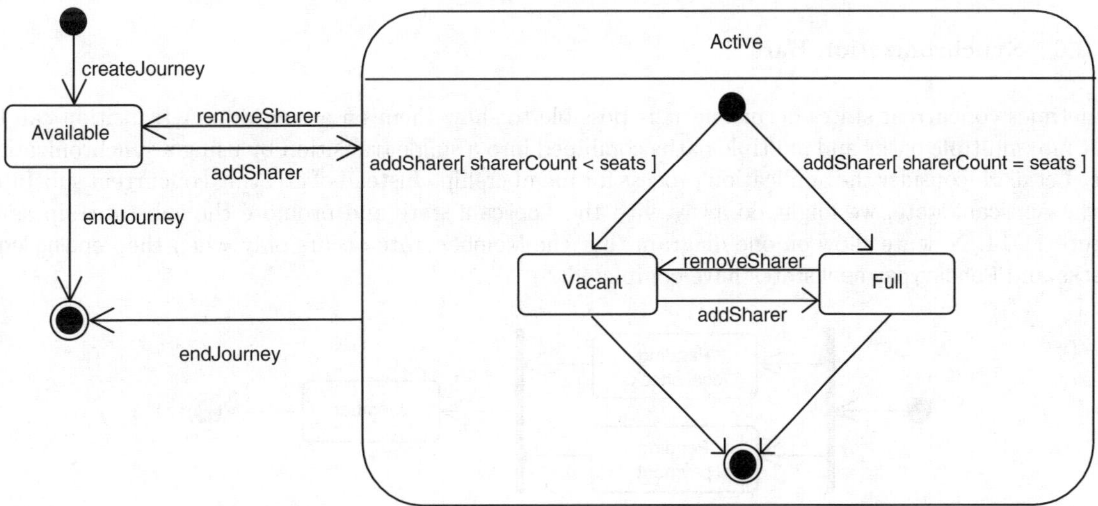

Fig. 11-12: Subflow drawn within a composite state in the statechart diagram for the Journey class

In this example, an instance of the Journey class that is in the Active state must also be in either the Vacant state **or** the Full state. Note the difference between this and the notation for concurrent substates in the next section.

11.3.5 Concurrent Substates

It is possible for a composite state to consist of multiple, *concurrent substates*. Consider Figure 11-13. When a car sharer applies for membership, he or she initially is considered to be an applicant, and unable to participate in car sharing agreements. The application process may involve payment processing and legal checks to make sure that the applicant is not attempting to break the law, or that the person applying is not barred from such activity. These may take time, and therefore the Applicant state of an instance of CarSharer must continue until these two substates have exited. These substates are independent, and can complete at different times. This is shown on a diagram by separating the concurrent flows by a dotted horizontal line within the containing state.

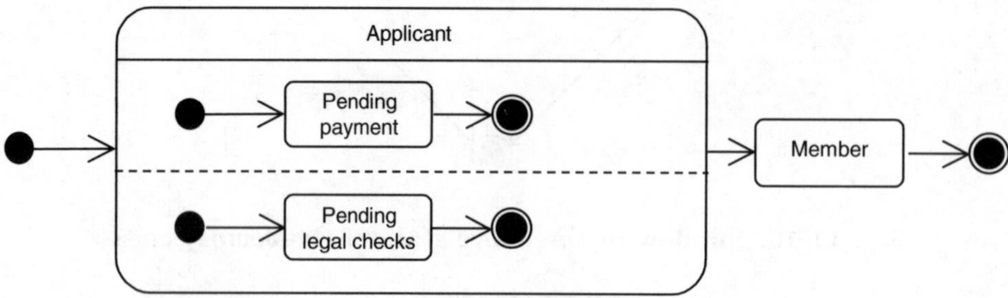

Fig. 11-13: Concurrent substates of the Applicant state for the CarSharer class

Note that in contrast to the previous example, an instance of the CarSharer class will be in both the Pending payment state **and** the Pending legal checks state.

11.3.6 Synchronization Bars

Sometimes concurrent states occur and it is possible to show them on a diagram. A transition can be split into multiple paths and multiple paths combined into a single transition by using a synchronization bar. Let us re-consider the application process for membership. Instead of creating concurrent substates of the Applicant state, we might do away with the Applicant state and promote the substates up as in Figure 11-14. Now we show on one diagram that the Member state occurs only when the Pending legal checks and Pending payment states have completed.

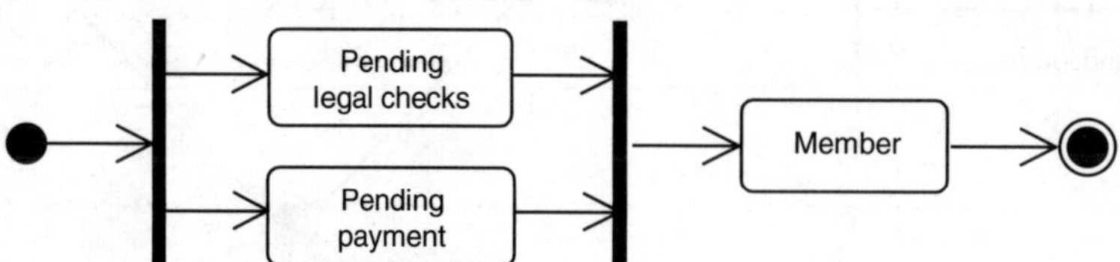

Fig. 11-14: Parallel states shown on a statechart diagram using synchronization bars

A synchronization bar may have one entry transition and two or more exit transitions, or multiple entry transitions and one exit transition. It is important when the overall state of a class is split into parallel states that these states are re-combined on the same diagram.

11.3.7 Transitions to and from Composite States

A transition drawn to the boundary of a composite state starts the subflow at the initial state of the composite state. If the composite state is concurrent, then the transition is to each of the initial states. The entry actions of the composite state are fired on entry, and then the actions of the start state (or states) are applied appropriately.

A transition drawn from the boundary of a composite state is immediate and effective on any of the substates; that is, the current substate (or substates if this is a concurrent composite state) exits and executes any exit actions.

Transitions may be drawn directly into substates of a composite state, or from a substate in a composite state out to other states. Consider Figure 11-15. We have re-introduced the idea of a state of membership prior to the full activation of membership, and called it Dormant. As in Figure 11-13, once a member joins for the first time, a legal check and payment clearance must be forced before the membership can be active. When the member's renewal is due, then the account can be switched to dormant, and this is indicated by taking a transition directly into the substate, Pending payment. Once payment has arrived, it is possible to reinstate membership without the legal check taking place, and this is indicated by a guarded transition that can fire only if this is a renewal.

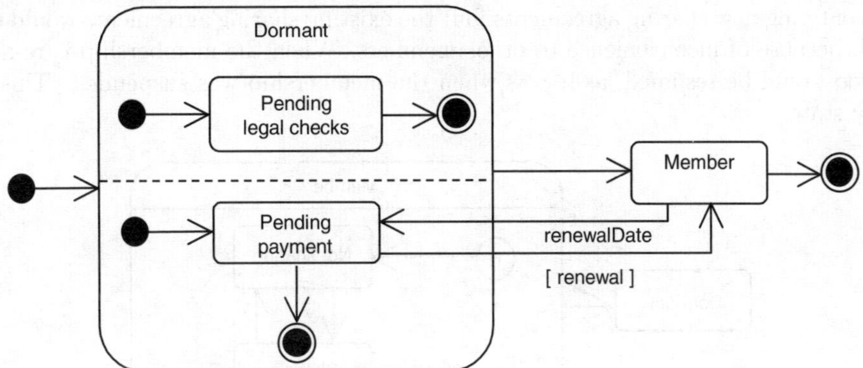

Fig. 11-15: Transitions into and out of substates in a composite state

11.3.8 Decision Points (Factored Transition Paths)

A decision point allows for a transition to be split along a number of transitions based on a condition, or for a number of transitions to converge at a single point, or both of these. Consider Figure 11-16. This models the behavior of a journey before it becomes active. This would be the elaboration of the composite state Available in Figure 11-9. The diamond shape represents the decision point at which the transition can take a number of alternative paths depending on some condition. (Confusingly, a black dot can be used in place of a diamond.) On start, there is a decision to be made whether there is a driver in the sharing agreement or not. If there is not, then the state No driver is entered. When another sharer is added, it makes sense to go back to the earlier decision point. If the new sharer is a driver, then the available state can complete, otherwise it goes back to No driver. If the first sharer is a driver, then it is necessary only to wait for another sharer, irrespective of his or her driving ability, to progress out of the Available state into the Active state.

11.3.9 History States

Ordinarily, when a composite state is entered, it begins at the initial state, (or the indicated substate if the transition is directly into that substate). Sometimes, however, it is useful to re-enter a composite state at the point at which it was last left. This is done by adding a *history state*, indicated by a circle with a letter H inside it. Consider the membership state in Figure 11-17. A member can be either Sharing or Not sharing. On entry for the first time, the member is Not sharing. If the member goes into the Dormant state, because the member is late paying a renewal fee, then it would be sensible to bar the

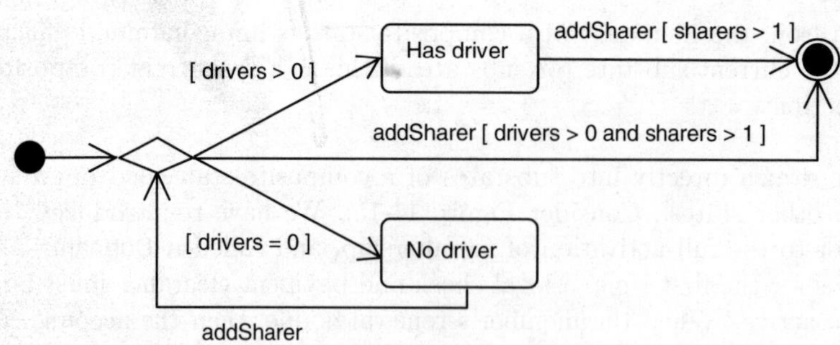

Fig. 11-16: A decision point on a statechart diagram

member from entering new sharing agreements, but the existing sharing agreements would not normally be suspended, because of inconvenience to other members. When the membership is re-activated, the state of Sharing would be resumed, as it was when the membership was suspended. This is indicated by the history state.

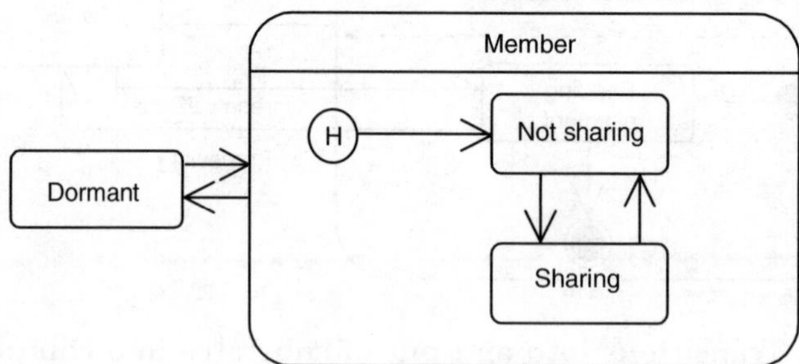

Fig. 11-17: A history state in a composite state

If the states within a composite state are themselves composite states, it may be necessary on some rare occasions to resume those nested states at the point at which they were suspended. If the history state indicator contains an *H, instead of an H, this is known as a deep history state, and the substates are re-started at the point where they left off; the re-start continues all the way down the nested states.

11.3.10 Synch States

Parallel flows in a composite state may sometimes need to synchronize. Consider Figure 11-18. An insurance policy has two separate concurrent flows, one for payments, and one for claims. However, the rule is normally that claims can be settled only when all outstanding fees are paid. To describe this, we can introduce two *synch states* indicated by a circle with an asterisk inside. Once a claim is made, the claims flow enters a state Settling outstanding fees, if the fees are not up to date, which runs in parallel with the state Fees due on the payment flow. The synch states can be considered as states in both of the concurrent flows, that can only be exited when both flows have reached them.

11.4 HOW TO PRODUCE STATECHART DIAGRAMS

Statechart diagrams model the behavior of entities (for example classes, use cases and subsystems), and are closely related to activity diagrams. While activity diagrams are good at describing processes,

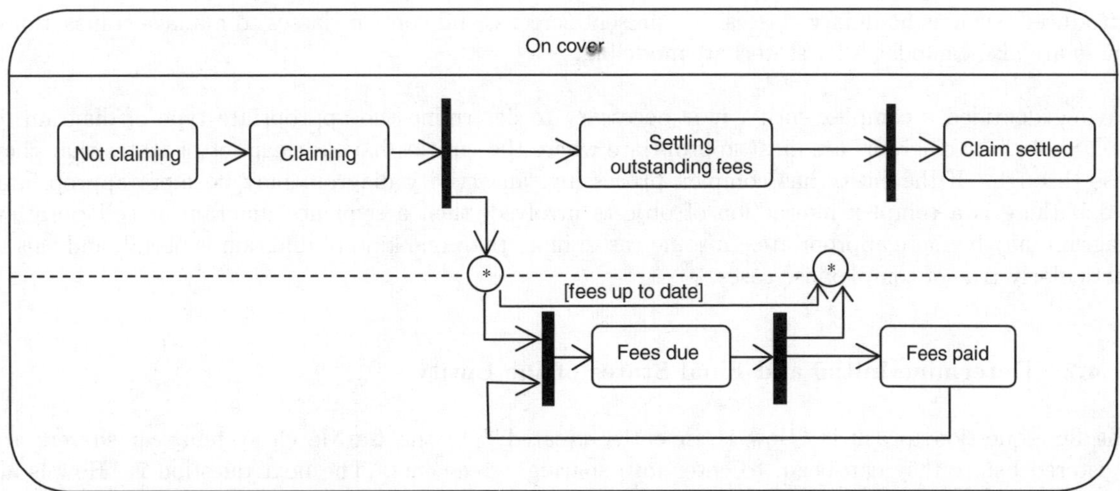

Fig. 11-18: Synchronization states in a composite state with concurrent subflows

statechart diagrams are better suited to describing the life history of classes in terms of the discrete stages that an object instance can pass through. The statechart diagram depicts the generic set of states and transitions between them for the class. Individual instances can take different paths through these states, depending on the sequence of events that affect each instance.

The classes that statechart diagrams model can be classes in the analysis domain, such as actors, or representations of parts of the system, or classes that need to be implemented. Statechart diagrams are not essential for all of the entities, just those that have reasonably complex behavior that can be represented as sets of states.

Statechart diagrams are developed as follows.

1. Identify entities that have complex behavior.
2. Determine the initial and final states of the entity.
3. Identify the events that affect the entity.
4. Working from the initial state, trace the impact of events and identify intermediate states.
5. Identify any entry and exit actions on the states.
6. Expand states using substates where necessary.
7. If the entity is a class, check that the actions in the state are supported by the operations and relationships of the class, and if not extend the class.

11.4.1 Identify Entities that have Complex Behaviour

At the analysis level, the entities to model are business actors that the system interacts with, and any real-world classes such as accounts, policies and agreements, that have changeable states and complicated relationships between states. At the design level, a number of complex classes are typically introduced, such as boundary classes to represent screens, and control classes to manage transactions. These are also candidates for statechart modeling.

Having identified a complex entity, it is necessary to determine the appropriate type of diagram to use. Statechart diagrams are most appropriate where the entities have a clear set of states that they pass through. If the entity has complex processing, an activity diagram may be more appropriate, and if there is a complex interaction of objects involved, then a sequence diagram or collaboration diagram may be more appropriate. In some cases, more than one kind of diagram is useful, and this is particularly true of complex use cases.

11.4.2 Determine Initial and Final States of the Entity

The first question to ask is "How is an entity created?" In the CarMatch system, car sharers are registered before they can begin to enter into sharing agreements. The next question is "How is an object destroyed?" (That is, how does it reach the point where it no longer needs to be processed by the system?) A car sharer may let his or her membership lapse, or may be disqualified from membership for reasons of misbehaviour, or may withdraw membership for reasons of moving away from the area, or may withdraw because of illness or disaffection with the service.

11.4.3 Identify the Events that Affect the Entity

The events that affect a car sharer would be registration, entering a journey, the matching of a journey with another car sharer, the entering of an agreement, the cancellation of an agreement, payment date arriving, and so on. The primary source of events for objects is the set of use cases. Use cases are groupings of events that provide meaningful functionality for a system, and a use case is realized by a group of collaborating objects.

11.4.4 Trace the Impact of Events and Identify Intermediate States

Start at the initial state, and ask what events may affect the initial state. A car sharer may have to pay membership and have a legal check carried out. As in Figure 11-15 we may decide to show this by creating a Dormant state that the CarSharer enters, and place two substates in it that operate in parallel, namely Pending legal checks and Pending payment. We continue in this way, examining what events took the CarSharer out of the Dormant state into the Member state, and then on out of the Member state either back into the Dormant state or to the end state.

11.4.5 Identify Entry and Exit Actions on States

When an instance of CarSharer enters the Pending payment state in Figure 11-15, entry actions would be to request payment from the car sharer, create an instance of the Account class, and debit that account with the membership fee. An exit action, responding to an event that signals payment has been received, would be to credit the account of the car sharer with the payment made.

11.4.6 Expand States Using Substates

A car sharer can be in the Dormant state for many reasons. Two of these would be payment being due, or legal checks being necessary. Alternatively, a car sharer may suspend membership while working away from home for an extended period. Each of these could be modelled as substates of the Dormant state that was shown in Figure 11-15.

11.4.7 Check that Operations Exist to Support the Actions

All actions have to be implemented as operations on classes. For the CarSharer class, there would need to be operations to support requesting payment, receiving payment, recording results of legal checks among others. These operations can either be directly on the class itself, or on related classes. The operation to handle payment, for example, would normally be implemented on the Account class, not on the CarSharer class itself.

11.5 RELATIONSHIP WITH OTHER DIAGRAMS

Statechart diagrams describe behaviour, focusing on states and transitions between states. They allow for sequential and parallel flows between states. Alongside activity diagrams, collaboration diagrams and sequence diagrams, they provide a means of describing the dynamic behavior of a system. They are closely related to activity diagrams, and the event flow notation in an activity diagram describes the states of objects in relation to workflow. Within a CASE tool, they would be linked as subdiagrams of business use cases, use cases, classes and (in some cases) operations.

11.6 STATECHART DIAGRAMS IN THE UNIFIED PROCESS

The Unified Process is a use case driven approach, and use cases themselves can have state dependent behaviour, which is best modelled using statechart diagrams. (In business modeling, the definition of business use cases can also be supported by activity diagrams to model fully the complex workflows that a business use case represents.) Statechart diagrams are used in the Requirements Workflow (see Figure 11-19) in the *Detail a Use Case* activity. They can be used to define formally the behaviour of a use case as a set of states and transitions between those states that are dependent on events initiated by the user or from within the system.

Statechart diagrams can be used to describe the behaviour of the classes that collaborate to realize a use case. These are typically classes with significant, complex behaviour. The work to create these statechart diagrams is carried out in the Design Workflow (see Figure 11-20) in the *Design a Class* activity. At the same time as the attributes, operations, associations and other features of each class are designed, statechart diagrams can be used to design and document state dependent behaviour.

Review Questions

11.1 What do statechart diagrams model?

11.2 What is a state?

11.3 How long can a state last?

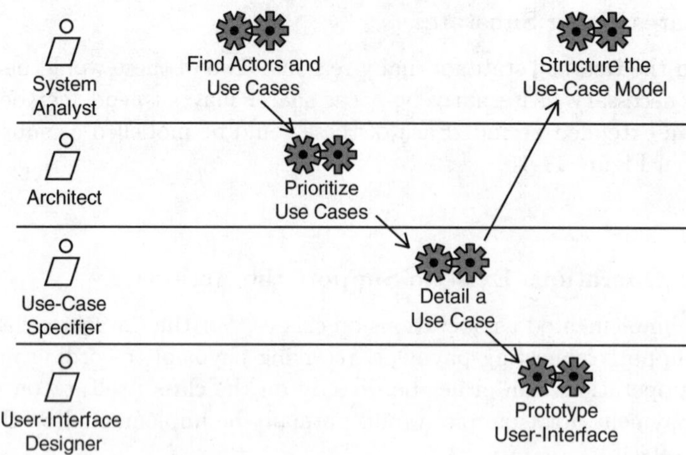

Fig. 11-19: Requirements Workflow

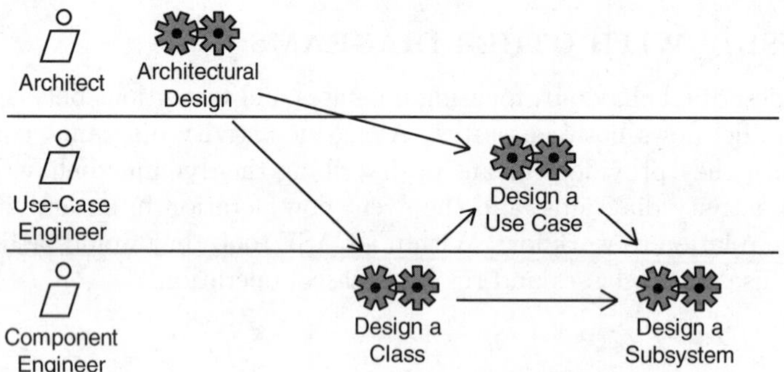

Fig. 11-20: Design Workflow

11.4 How do events affect states?

11.5 What types of entity can a statechart model?

11.6 Can you have a triggerless transition out of a state?

11.7 What are the five types of action on a state?

11.8 What is the syntax for an action?

11.9 What is the syntax for the action-label for an event?

11.10 How are actions shown on a state?

11.11 How many actions can be triggered by a transition?

11.12 What is a composite state?

11.13 How do you depict composite states?

11.14 What are concurrent substates?

11.15 What is a synchronization bar?

11.16 When a transition is direct to the boundary of a composite state, what happens?

11.17 When an event triggers a transition from the boundary of a composite state, what happens?

11.18 When a transition is to a substate of a composite state, what happens?

11.19 What is a factored transition point?

11.20 What is the difference between history states containing H and *H?

11.21 What is a synch state and what is its purpose?

Solved Problems

11.1 Consider Problem10.1 in which the CarMatch procedure for members to obtain a discount for road-pricing schemes is described. The Contract would be one candidate business entity that we might consider modelling. Draw a statechart diagram for the Contract class.

The first stage is to identify entities that need modeling with statechart diagrams. In the negotiations on road pricing, the key entity will be the Contract that will be drawn up, agreed and signed by all parties. We then consider the key events that affect the contract. These would be as follows.

1. Draw up the contract: this would be a detailed piece of work by lawyers, and once the contract is drawn up, it will be a draft for consideration by all parties.
2. Revise contract: this will be an event that will occur a number of times throughout the life of the contract until it is signed.
3. Agree contract: this will be when all parties accept the contract prior to signing.
4. Sign contract: this will be the point in time when all parties formally accept the contract.
5. Abort negotiations: prior to signing, all parties will be able to withdraw from negotiations, and the contract will terminate.
6. Dispute: during the lifetime of the contract, once in force, there may be disputes under the contract.
7. End contract: there are lots of ways a contract may end. It may expire, agreement may be reached between parties to terminate the contract, one of the parties may disappear and the contract would ultimately terminate.

The start state will be when the contract is drawn up. The end state will be either when negotiations are aborted, or when the contract terminates for whatever reason. We can now work from the start state, to the end state looking for the changes. The first attempt might be a diagram as in Figure 11-21.

If we consider the Draft state of the Contract, then we can see that this has to respond to the event to revise the contract. This does not involve a state change, and we enter this as an action in the state. It may also be allowed, though not commonly accepted, that even after agreement, before signing, there might be revisions requested that take the Contract back to the Draft state. Once the contract is signed, then during the lifetime of the contract there may be disputes that need to be handled. So the diagram is extended as in Figure 11-22.

In order to implement a system to maintain an electronic version of the contract, we would consider the events and actions identified above. Operations to create a contract, to create, update and delete clauses, to record that the contract is agreed and signed, and to record disputes would support the above. They would all have to be added to the Contract class.

11.2 In the CarMatch system, an agreement is drawn up to protect sharers against problems with insurance and taxation, and to formalize the relationship between sharers. This agreement can be drawn up when two or more sharers have been matched for a journey. Note that each sharer will have entered a journey on the system, and the matching takes place against journeys. Matching may take place against journeys where there is already an agreement, as there might be space in a car for an additional sharer. We have seen above how the journey registered for a sharer may

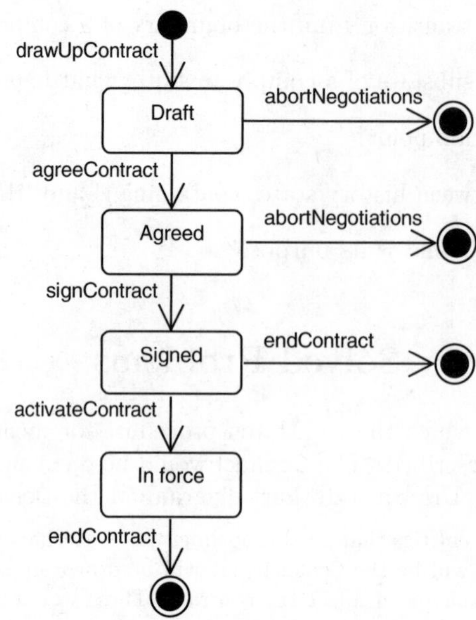

Fig. 11-21: First draft statechart diagram for Contract

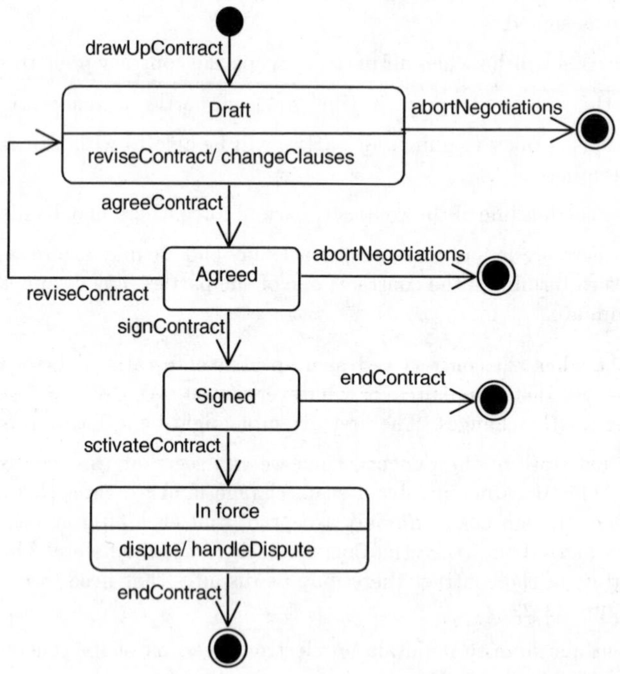

Fig. 11-22: Statechart diagram for Contract with actions

go from Available to Active when a sharing agreement has been reached, and that active journeys may be full or have vacancies. Draw the statechart diagram for the SharingAgreement class.

The start state for a sharing agreement is brought about when two or more sharers have been identified for a journey. The end state is when a sharer withdraws and there is only one sharer left. The agreement first enters a state of preparation, during which sharers are added to the agreement, and clauses of the agreement may be modified. Once the agreement has been accepted by all sharers, they sign copies and return them to CarMatch, which duly files them and records the state of the agreement on the system. During the life of an agreement, when it is in force, sharers may join the agreement or withdraw, and CarMatch keeps records of these changes on the system. The resulting statechart diagram is shown in Figure 11-23.

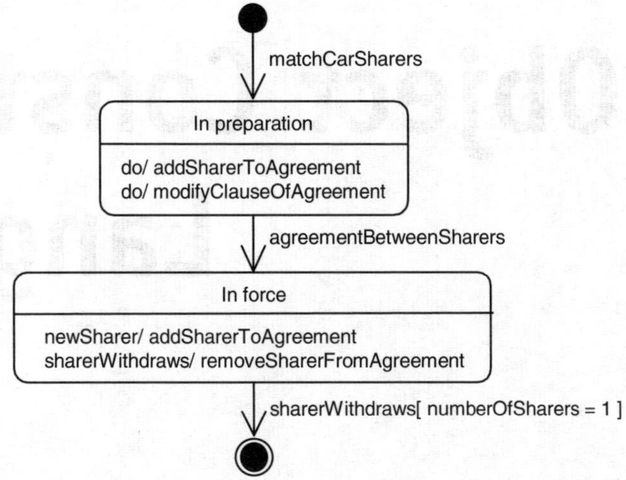

Fig. 11-23: Statechart diagram for SharingAgreement

Supplementary Problems

11.3 In the Volbank system, volunteering opportunities are registered, and matches are sought for people with time and skills that suit the opportunity. Opportunities can be open, partly filled or filled. Volunteers may have to withdraw from an opportunity, or the opportunity may require additional help from time to time. Whilst the opportunity is open, or partly filled, an interviewing process can go on. This involves identifying potential volunteers, inviting them for interview, considering candidates, and selecting them. For sensitive areas, there may also have to be some vetting of candidates, by checking police files or seeking references. Draw a statechart diagram with composite states to model the class Opportunity.

11.4 In VolBank, volunteers may register and enter into volunteering agreements. Before VolBank allows volunteering, it checks that the volunteer is not prevented for some reason (say by a previous disqualification from VolBank, or because of some queries on the application such as claimed qualifications that need to be validated). Certain voluntary activities involving care provision require additional checking before a volunteer can be matched against an opportunity. Volunteers may suspend membership for work reasons, or if they are moving temporarily out of VolBank's operational area. Volunteers may also withdraw or have their membership expire. Volunteers can also be expelled for reasons of misconduct. Draw a statechart diagram to model the class Volunteer.

Object Constraint Language

12.1 INTRODUCTION

A *constraint* is a rule that allows you to specify some limits on model elements. Warmer & Kleppe (1999) describe it as "a restriction on one or more values of (part of) an object-oriented model or system". Constraints exist in the real world, such as a car should not be driven beyond the speed limit, or voters in government elections need to be above a certain age. They are an important addition to a model, more precisely defining behaviour, notably in terms of limits of the system.

For example, it might be that in the CarMatch system an individual may not have more than 10 agreements for car sharing. In a car sharing agreement, there needs to be at least one sharer who can drive and owns a car. In the VolBank system, a member may not be able to offer more than five types of service.

As the analysis of a problem progresses, the details of constraints emerge. At first constraints can be imprecise, such as "a customer must not have a large outstanding debt". As the analysis progresses the constraints become more concrete, such as "before making an order, a standard customer should not have more than the standard limit of outstanding debt and have no invoice outstanding beyond the standard payment period".

Ultimately, the constraints need to be expressed in some language that can be translated into computer statements. UML itself does not specify either the particular language in which constraints can be expressed—English (for example) is perfectly acceptable—or the syntax or semantics of the implementation language. However, natural language statements are prone to ambiguity, and the implementation language may not be suitably expressive. UML therefore includes as an option the Object Constraint Language (OCL) for a more rigorous expression of constraints. (OCL is specified in an appendix to the UML Specification (Object Management Group, 1999*a*).) Various formal languages, such as Z, have been used for specification of constraints, but these can be onerous and difficult for non-mathematicians.

OCL has been designed as a formal language that is straightforward to read, and provides rigour in specification without great difficulty in either its construction or interpretation.

In a diagram, a constraint is shown as a text string enclosed in braces ({ }), and placed near the associated element or connected to that element by a dependency relationship. You may also put constraints in notes. Let us look at a simple example. In the CarMatch system, a journey has two addresses, for the start and end of the journey. It may be decided that CarMatch will register only journeys of greater than two miles. There is then a dependency between the startAddress and the destinationAddress, which is drawn as a dashed-line arrow, and a constraint on that dependency is written in braces, as in Figure 12-1.

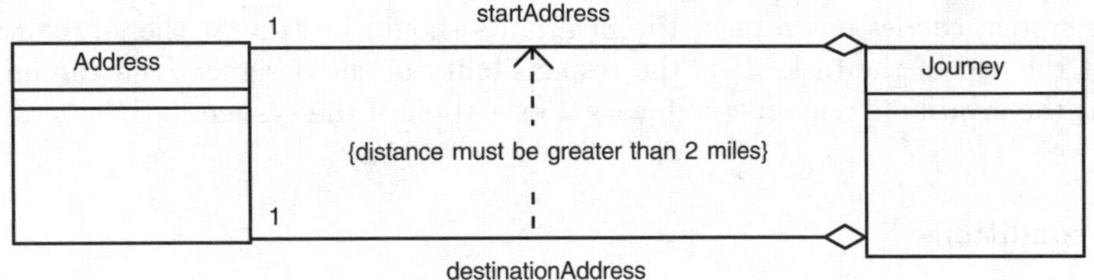

Fig. 12-1: A constraint attached to a dependency in a UML diagram

Another simple example would be if we wished to constrain the age of a car sharer to be 21 years or over for legislative or insurance reasons—this is known as an invariant as it is a property of the model that must not change. This could be shown by attaching a note to the CarSharer class and placing the constraint in the note, as in Figure 12-2. This constraint applies to all instances of this class.

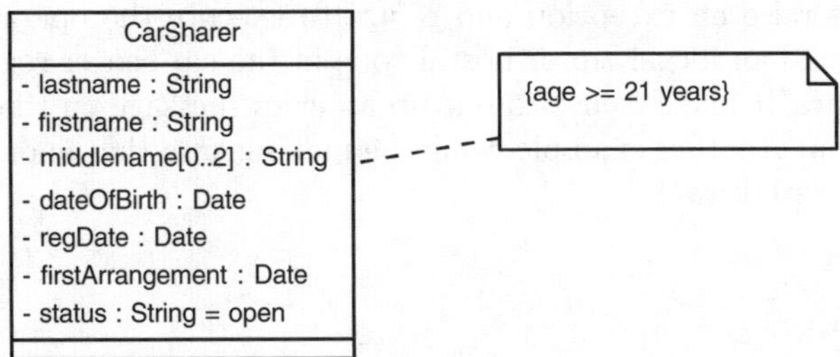

Fig. 12-2: A constraint on a class attached using a note in a UML diagram

An alternative approach is to keep the constraints in a separate text file. The constraint in Figure 12-2 could also be written as follows.

```
context CarSharer inv:
    age >= 21
```

The keyword context introduces a model element to which the invariant applies, and inv introduces the constraint as an invariant (this syntax will be explained fully later). This is much more concise, though it is often useful to indicate constraints on diagrams as illustrated in Figures 12-1 and 12-2.

This chapter will introduce the notions of invariant, post-condition and pre-condition, and explain how these can be expressed as constraints in the Object Constraint Language.

12.1.1 Invariants

An *invariant* is a property that must remain true throughout the life of a model element, such as an object. For example: a car sharer must be aged 21 years or older; a car sharer must have a valid driving licence to offer to drive in part of a sharing agreement; journeys must be two miles or over.

The reason for introducing invariants is to specify the constraints under which the system can operate. A system might be able to operate if the invariants are violated (ideally it should not), but the designer does not guarantee the results. Just as it is possible to use a hammer to force screws into wood, a computer system can be used for purposes for which it is not intended, but the results of such actions cannot be predicted.

Whenever the system carries out a task, the invariants should be true at the start of the task, and remain true at the end of the task. It is the responsibility of the designers and the implementers to make sure that the invariants remain true for legal execution of the system.

12.1.2 Pre-conditions

A *pre-condition* is something that must be true before a particular part of the system is executed. This can be applied to operations during design and implementation, and to use cases during analysis. (Use cases are implemented using operations, so that pre-conditions are translated through the design process from use cases to operations.) For example, to register as a car sharer, it must be true that the candidate is aged 21 or over. On registering a journey, the distance of the journey must be two miles or more. Pre-conditions can therefore be used to make sure that invariants are never violated.

The designer and implementer can use pre-conditions to perform checks before an operation is executed. This is a way of preventing the system from entering illegal states. If a pre-condition is violated, then the resulting action is to raise an exception and refuse to execute the operation. A simple example would be if someone entered an illegal zip or postal code in the car sharer registration screen. Instead of registering the candidate, it makes sense to put up an error message on the screen and ask the user to re-enter the information. Another example would be making sure that enough money is in a savings account before making a withdrawal.

12.1.3 Post-conditions

A *post-condition* is something that must be true after a particular part of the system is executed, if that execution was legal (that is, all pre-conditions were met), and the system has successfully carried out its action. For example, after registering a car sharer, the car sharer's details must be recorded, a request for payment must be sent to the car sharer or to his or her credit card or bank account, and the CarSharer instance must be enabled for submitting journeys. As with pre-conditions, post-conditions can be applied to operations or to use cases, and as use cases are translated into operations through the analysis and design process, so they ultimately become translated into post-conditions on operations.

Post-conditions are part of the definition of what an operation does. The designer and implementer must devise code to ensure that the post-conditions are met. In a formal development (for example for safety-critical systems) this might involve a rigorous proof that the code results in the post-conditions being true if the pre-conditions are true. It is possible to incorporate checks when operations have been completed to make sure that the post-conditions are true.

12.1.4 Design by Contract

Design of the operational elements of a system can proceed by a definition of pre-conditions and post-conditions. This is known as *design by contract.* This is not all that design is about—much of the design that is facilitated by UML is structural. Pre-conditions and post-conditions are used to define how parts of the model fit together and what their purpose is. The early phases of design focus on identifying the overall structure and the components. The later stages involve detailing the behavior of those components and how they interact.

The value of the Object Constraint Language is in providing a precise notation for the definition of the behavior of parts of the system. Ultimately any system must be implemented in a computer language that is unambiguous in its execution. OCL provides a stepping stone to that implementation that removes ambiguity.

12.2 PURPOSE OF THE TECHNIQUE

OCL is designed to provide a clear and unambiguous way of describing rules about the behavior of elements in a set of UML models. Constraints will be captured throughout the requirements and analysis phases, and translated in the design and implementation into checks on the system that is being constructed. The primary purposes of a constraint are as follows.

- They are used to specify pre-conditions and post-conditions on use cases and operations.
- They are used to describe invariants in operations.
- They are used to describe guards on transitions.
- They are used to describe invariants for classes and types in the class model.

The purposes of OCL are as follows.

- It is used to provide a clear and unambiguous language for the description of constraints.
- It is used to specify accurately the behavior of elements of the model.

12.3 NOTATION

The Object Constraint Language is an expression language that is guaranteed to be without side-effect. That means that the expressions do not change the value of any element of a model. Expressions simply return values. It is the developer's job to interpret OCL expressions and convert them into meaningful actions in a programming language. Consequently, OCL does not provide any notion of control. One can think of OCL, in programming language terms, as the expressions that are used in conditions to determine action, such as the condition on a while loop or an if statement, rather than as instructions that carry out an action.

OCL is a typed language. OCL statements must therefore conform to type rules, such as not comparing integers with strings. The results of OCL statements are of a particular type, determined by the rules of OCL for combining the elements of an expression.

12.3.1 Convention

All OCL statements must take place within a *context*. This might be a class, an association class or a use case. The statements themselves can be invariants, pre-conditions or post-conditions. The UML convention is that the keyword context is written in bold type, and the stereotype of the constraint is written in bold type as inv for «invariant», pre for «pre-condition», and post for «post-condition». Thus we could write the invariant that a sharing agreement must be for a number of days by the following statement.

```
context SharingAgreement inv:
    startDate < finishDate
```

12.3.2 Context

The context of an OCL expression must be a class (or type) for invariants, or an operation for pre-conditions and post-conditions. (Pre-conditions and post-conditions on use cases are not normally written in OCL, and are included in the use case description as natural language statements.) For invariants this can be simply the name of the class if that is unambiguous, or the package name can be used to define the context of the class. For pre-conditions and post-conditions, the name of the class is extended by the name of the operation and its full signature. (Because of overloading, the name of an operation is insufficient to fully determine the operation.) The syntax for an invariant context is as follows.

```
context Typename inv:
```

Where Typename is the name of the type or class for which the invariant constraint applies. Package names are introduced using the following syntax.

```
context Packagename::Typename inv:
```

Packages can be nested, so if package 2 is nested in package 1, the syntax would be as follows.

```
context Packagename1::Packagename2::Typename inv:
```

For pre-conditions and post-conditions on an operation the full syntax is as follows.

```
context Typename::operationName(param1 : Type1, ...): ReturnType
    pre: constraint
    post: constraint
```

For example, to specify the operation to subscribe on a CarSharer in the CarSharers package we might write the following.

```
context CarSharers::CarSharer::subscribe(d : Date, fee : Integer): Boolean
    pre: fee >= SubscriptionRate.fee
    post: active = true
```

Where SubscriptionRate is a class that is associated with CarSharers that contains the annual fee for membership for the car sharer, and active is a boolean value that is used to indicate whether the car sharer is active or suspended.

12.3.3 Navigation

Within a context, the navigation to an element of a model is by the left-to-right traversal of a path separated by full-stops. For example, to refer to a car sharer's account balance, with an association as in Figure 12-3, and placing an invariant on the class CarSharer that the balance should be no more than $100 overdrawn, we could write the following.

```
context CarSharer inv:
    Account.balance >= -100
```

Note that, strictly, the role name on the association is used to navigate to the class; where there is a missing role name, as is often the case, then the name of the type (i.e. Account in the above example) at the end of an association is the default role name, provided there is no ambiguity.

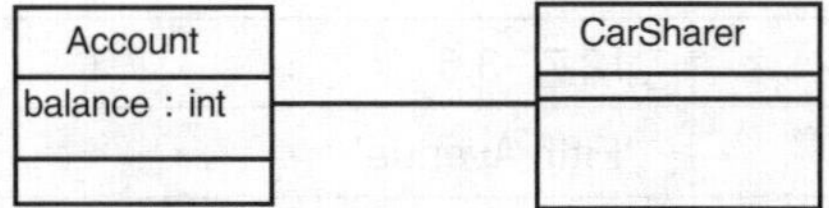

Fig. 12-3: Relationship between the classes Account and CarSharer

We could indicate the constraint on the model using a note as in Figure 12-4.

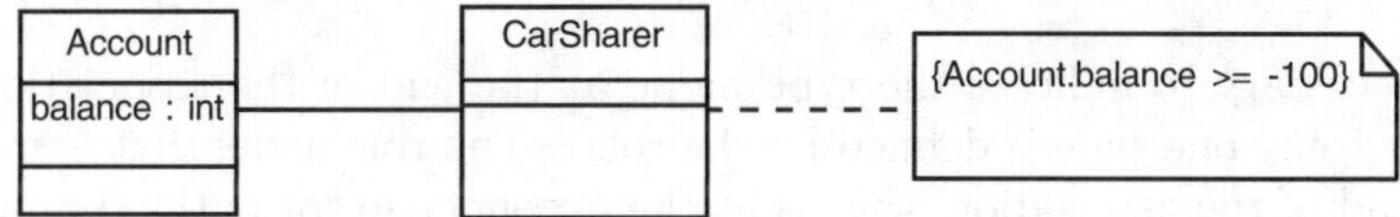

Fig. 12-4: Relationship between the classes Account and CarSharer with constraint attached as a note

There are three ways of referring to an item within a context. If the item is unambiguous, then the reference in the previous example is sufficient. If the expression is complex, however, then the word self can be used to refer to the instance of the class that is named as the context. So the following expression is equivalent to the previous one.

```
context CarSharer inv:
    self.Account.balance >= -100
```

This would be used in cases where another instance of the same class is involved in a different role, and it is necessary to distinguish between the two. Alternatively it is possible to refer to a named instance of the class and use the following syntax.

```
context c:CarSharer inv:
    c.Account.balance >= -100
```

Ordinarily we will not complicate expressions in this way, though the use of self is common to aid readability.

For associations, the role name can be part of the path. Suppose that CarMatch introduce separate accounts for members for their insurance. Then there may be two associations between CarSharer and Account, as in Figure 12-5, with a role name used to discriminate between the two types of association. To indicate that the insurance account must not be overdrawn by more than $500 we would write the following.

Fig. 12-5: Two relationships between Account and CarSharer delineated by roles

Table 12-1: Typical values of basic types in OCL

Type	Typical values
Boolean	true, false
Integer	0, 1, -1, 123, -256
Real	12.7, -3.6
String	'Fifth Avenue'

```
context CarSharer inv:
    insurance.balance >= -500
```

Note that it is unnecessary to indicate the type name at the end of the association (i.e. Account) as this is unambiguous (only one type is defined by the role). The role name that is used in navigation is the one at the far end of the association, that is at the Account end for paths running from CarSharer.

It is possible to navigate across a number of associations. So, for example, if it is made a condition that the driver in a journey has paid his or her insurance, using the associations in Figure 12-6 we can express this as follows.

```
context Journey inv:
    driver.insurance.balance >= 0
```

12.3.4 Types and Expressions

Elements of an OCL expression are made up of *types*. There are four basic types provided by OCL, namely Boolean, Integer, Real and String. Other types are obtained from the model. Typical values of basic types are provided in Table 12-1.

The basic types may be combined using operations, as indicated in Table 12-2. In addition, it is possible to use operations defined in the model, and where the values are model types then model operations are necessary.

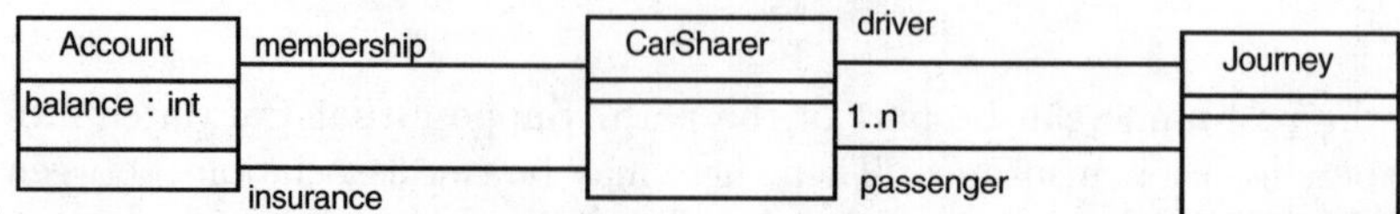

Fig. 12-6: Relationships between Journeys, CarSharers and Accounts

Table 12-2: Typical operations on basic types in OCL

Type	Typical operations
Boolean	and, or, xor, not, implies, if-then-else
Integer	multiply, add, subtract, divide, compare
Real	multiply, add, subtract, divide, compare
String	toUpper, concat

The result of an OCL expression using basic types is a basic type. The result of an expression involving model types may be a model type or a basic type.

Consider the model in Figure 12-7. We may want to express that the distance of any journey is two miles or more. To do this we construct an operation on an address that allows us to calculate the distance to any other address. We could express this using the following expression.

```
context Journey inv:
  startAddress.distanceTo(self.destinationAddress) >= 2
```

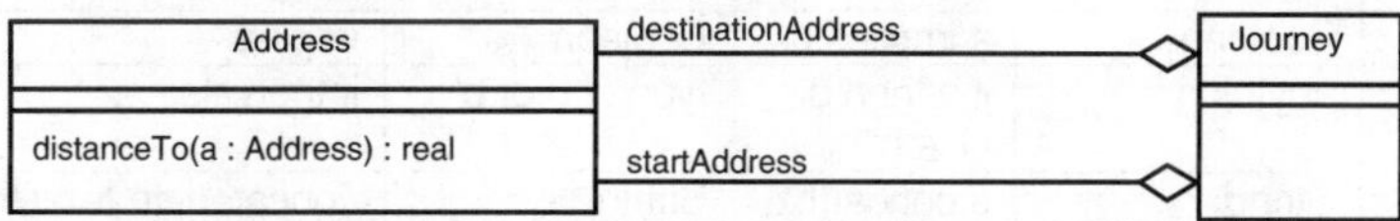

Fig. 12-7: Relationships between Journey and constituent instances of Address

This invokes a model operation distanceTo on the start address of the journey, indicated by the role name startAddress on the association with an Address. The argument is the destination address, indicated by self.destinationAddress, from the role name on the association with Address. The result is a real that is then compared with 2.

All types in an expression are considered to be subtypes of the type OclType whether they are basic types, collections or model types. OCL has a full set of operations on types, but these are not normally necessary to manipulate types for ordinary modelling purposes, and these are not all included in this chapter. The ability to check the type of an object, or whether it is a subtype is, however, often useful and is therefore included.

A comprehensive set of operations for basic types is given in Table 12-3. Some sample expressions and their results are given in Table 12-4.

12.3.5 Sets, Bags and Sequences

Because associations are rarely one-to-one, it is often necessary to deal with collections in object-oriented models. OCL provides three types of *collection*. A *set* consists of distinct instances; that is, there are no repetitions in the set. Sets have no ordering. A *bag* is an unordered collection that allows repetitions. A *sequence* is an ordered collection that allows repetition—the order is the order written or collected rather than the order of the values. Collections are written in braces, with the type of collection before it. Examples are as follows.

Table 12-3: Operations on basic types in OCL

a	b	Operation	Result type	Meaning
Integer or Real	Integer or Real	a=b	Boolean	equality
Integer or Real	Integer or Real	a<>b	Boolean	inequality
Integer or Real	Integer or Real	a<b	Boolean	less than
Integer or Real	Integer or Real	a>b	Boolean	greater than
Integer or Real	Integer or Real	a<=b	Boolean	less than or equal
Integer or Real	Integer or Real	a>=b	Boolean	greater than or equal
Integer or Real	Integer or Real	a+b	Integer or Real	addition
Integer or Real	Integer or Real	a-b	Integer or Real	subtraction
Integer or Real	Integer or Real	a*b	Integer or Real	multiplication
Integer or Real	Integer or Real	a/b	Real	division
Integer	Integer	a.mod(b)	Integer	modulus
Integer	Integer	a.div(b)	Integer	integer division
Integer or Real		a.abs	Integer or Real	absolute value
Integer or Real	Integer or Real	a.max(b)	Integer or Real	maximum
Integer or Real	Integer or Real	a.min(b)	Integer or Real	minimum
Integer or Real		a.round	Integer	round to nearest integer
Integer or Real		a.floor	Integer	round down (truncate)
Boolean	Boolean	a or b	Boolean	or
Boolean	Boolean	a and b	Boolean	and
Boolean	Boolean	a xor b	Boolean	exclusive or
Boolean	Boolean	not a	Boolean	negation
Boolean	Boolean	a <>b	Boolean	inequality
Boolean	Boolean	a implies b	Boolean	implies
Boolean	anything	if a then b else b'	type of b or b'	if then else
String	String	a.concat(b)	String	concatenate two strings
String		a.size	Integer	size of string
String		a.toLower	String	convert to lower case
String		a.toUpper	String	convert to upper case
String	String	a = b	Boolean	equality
String	String	a<>b	Boolean	inequality

set{4, 7, 2, 9}
sequence{2, 3, 8, 9, 3, 5, 7, 7, 9}
bag{3, 5, 4, 6, 8, 3, 5, 2, 5}
set{'orange', 'apple', 'banana'}

Because of the usefulness of sequences of consecutive integers, these can be shown by using n..m to denote the sequence in the range from n to m. For example sequence {2..6} is the same as sequence {2, 3, 4, 5, 6}.

Consider the association in Figure 12-8. A car sharer has the possibility of a number of agreements. An agreement can involve two to five car sharers. The expression self.agreement in the context CarSharer will return a set of agreements for that car sharer. The expression self.agreement.sharer will return a bag of all the people that a sharer shares with, including the CarSharer instance for him or herself repeated in the bag for each of the agreements. (Note that it is a bag and not a set because the same instance of CarSharer can occur more than once.)

Collections in OCL are flattened. That is, if you put a collection inside a collection, then the elements are promoted to the outer set. For example set { set {1, 2}, set {3, 4} } becomes set {1, 2, 3, 4}. The reasoning behind this is that in practice this situation occurs rarely, and it is very difficult to reason about collections of collections.

Table 12-4: Sample expressions on basic types in OCL

Expression	Result
1+2	3
3+4.5	7.5
(3+4)=7	true
3<4	true
(7.8).floor	7
(7.8).round	8
7.mod(3)	1
7.div(3)	2
true or true	true
true or false	true
false or false	false
(1>2) or (7>6)	true
if (7>6) then 2 else 3	2
if (7<6) then 2 else 3	3
'Washington'.concat(' State')	'Washington State'
'Washington'.toLower	'washington'
'New York' = 'new york'	false
'New York'.toLower = 'new york'	true
'Ohio'.size	4

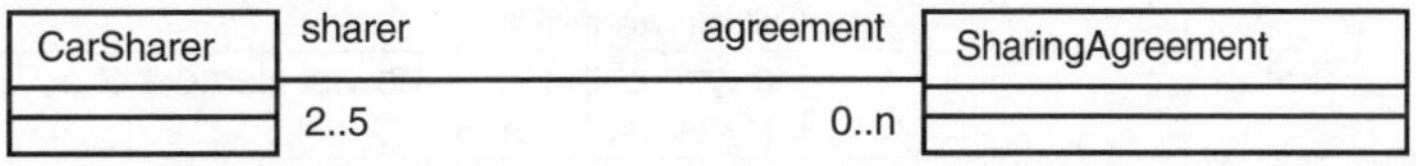

CarSharer sharer agreement SharingAgreement

2..5 0..n

Fig. 12-8: Relationship between the classes CarSharer and SharingAgreement

A list of some of the operations you can apply to collections is given in Table 12-5. A set of examples is given in Table 12-6. The majority of the operations are straightforward. However, some of the collection operations need explanation.

12.3.5.1 The Select Operation

The select operation picks out a subset of elements from a collection that meet a particular condition. The syntax for the select operation is:

```
collection->select(v | boolean-expression-with-v).
```

The action to implement the operation is to assign v to each of the values in the collection, evaluate the expression, and, if the result is true, add that to the resultant collection. The type of the resultant collection is the same as the source collection, with repetitions preserved for bags, and sequence preserved for sequences. For example, we may wish to select from a set the elements greater than a particular value. Thus

```
a->select(x | x>100)
```

would select all items in the collection a that are greater than 100 and provide a new collection.

Table 12-5: Some operations on collections in OCL

a	b	Operation	Result type	Meaning
set	set	a->union(b)	set	all elements in either a or b, without repetition
set	bag	a->union(b)	bag	all elements in a or b, repeated as often as in a and b together
set	set or bag	a->intersection(b)	set	all elements in both a and b, without repetition
set	any	a->including(b)	set	all elements of a with b added in if it was not in the set a
set	any	a->excluding(b)	set	all elements of a with b removed if it was in the set a
set	set	a-b	set	all elements of a not in b
set	set	a=b	boolean	true if a and be have identical elements, else false
set	set	a.symmetricDifference(b)	set	all elements in a not in b or in b not in a
set		a->asBag	bag	the elements of a in a bag
set		a->asSequence	sequence	the elements of a as a sequence of undefined order
bag	bag	a->union(b)	bag	all elements in either a or b, with repetition as many times as in both bags
bag	set or bag	a->intersection(b)	set	all elements in both a and b, without repetition
bag		a->asSet	set	the elements of a with repetitions removed
sequence		a->first	the type of the first element of a	the first element of a
sequence		a->last	the type of the last element of a	the last element of a
sequence	integer	a->at(b)	the type of the element at position b	the element of a at position b
sequence	any	a->append(b)	sequence	appends b to the end of the sequence a
sequence	any	a->prepend(b)	sequence	places b at the beginning of the sequence a
collection	expression	a->select(b)	collection	the subcollection of a for which the expression b is true
collection	expression	a->reject(b)	collection	the subcollection of a for which b is false
collection	expression	a->collect(b)	collection	the collection of results of the expression b applied to the elements of a
collection	expression	a->forall(b)	boolean	true if b evaluates as true for every element of a, otherwise false
collection	expression	a->exists(b)	boolean	true if b evaluates as true for at least one element of a, otherwise false
collection		a->size	integer	the number of elements in a
collection	any	a->count(b)	integer	the number of occurrences of b in a
collection	any	a->includes(b)	boolean	true if a includes b
collection	collection	a->includesAll(b)	boolean	true if a includes all the elements of b
collection		a->isEmpty	boolean	true if a is empty (i.e. has no elements)
collection		a->notEmpty	boolean	true if a is not empty
collection		a->sum	integer or real	the sum of the elements in a, all of which must be integer or real
any		a.oclType	OclType	the type of a
any	OclType	a.isTypeOf(b)	boolean	true if a is of type b
any	OclType	a.isKindOf(b)	boolean	true if a is of type b or any subtype of b

Table 12-6: Some examples of operations on collections in OCL

a	b	Operation	Result
set {1,2,3}	set{3,4,5}	a->union(b)	set {1,2,3,4,5}
set {1,2,3}	bag{2,3,3,4,5}	a->union(b)	bag {1,2,2,3,3,3,4,5}
set {1,2,3}	set{3,4,5}	a->intersection(b)	set {3}
set {1,2,3}	bag{3,3,4,5}	a->intersection(b)	set {3}
set {1,2,3}	5	a->including(b)	set {1,2,3,5}
set {1,2,3}	1	a->excluding(b)	set {2,3}
set {1,2,3}	set{3,4,5}	a-b	set {1,2}
set {1,2,3}	set{3,4,5}	a=b	false
set {1,2,3}	set{3,4,5}	a.symmetricDifference(b)	set {1,2,4,5}
bag {1,2,2,3}	bag{3,4,5,5}	a->union(b)	bag {1,2,2,3,3,4,5,5}
bag {1,2,2,3}	set{3,4,5}	a->union(b)	bag {1,2,2,3,3,4,5}
bag {1,2,2,3,3}	bag{3,3,4,4,5}	a->intersection(b)	set {3}
bag{3,3,4,5}	set {1,2,3}	a->intersection(b)	set {3}
bag {1,1,2,3}	5	a->including(b)	bag {1,1,2,3,5}
bag {1,1,2,2,3}	1	a->excluding(b)	bag {2,2,3}
bag {1,1,2,2,3}		a->asSet	set {1,2,3}
bag {1,2,3}	bag{3,2,1}	a=b	true
sequence {1,2,3,2,1}	sequence{3,4,5,4,3}	a->union(b)	sequence {1,2,3,2,1,3,4,5,4,3}
sequence {1,2,3,2,1}	3	a->including(b)	sequence {1,2,3,2,1,3}
sequence {1,2,3,2,1}	3	a->excluding(b)	sequence {1,2,2,1}
sequence {4,5,6}		a->first	4
sequence {4,5,6}		a->last	6
sequence {4,5,6}	integer	a->at(2)	5
sequence {7,2,3}	sequence {5,3,9}	a->append(b)	sequence {7,2,3,5,3,9}
sequence {7,2,3}	sequence {5,3,9}	a->prepend(b)	sequence {5,3,9,7,2,3}
set {2,4,5,7,9}	x | x>5	a->select(b)	set {7,9}
set {2,4,5,7,9}	x | x>5	a->reject(b)	set {2,4,5}
set {2,4,5,7,9}	x | x+1	a->collect(b)	set {3,5,6,8,10}
set {2,4,5,7,9}	x | x>1	a->forall(b)	true
set {2,4,5,7,9}	x | x>3	a->forall(b)	false
set {2,4,5,7,9}	x | x>1	a->exists(b)	true
set {2,4,5,7,9}	x | x>9	a->exists(b)	false
set {2,4,5,7,9}		a->size	5
set {2,4,5,7,9}		a->includes(7)	true
set {2,4,5,7,9}		a->includesAll(set {2,3})	false
set {2,4,5,7,9}		a->isEmpty	false
set {2,4,5,7,9}		a->notEmpty	true
set {2,4,5,7,9}		a->sum	27
bag {2,2,4,5,7,7,9}	x | x>5	a->select(b)	bag {7,7.9}
bag {2,2,4,5,7,7,9}	x | x>5	a->reject(b)	bag {2,2,4,5}
bag {2,2,4,5,7,7,9}	x | x+1	a->collect(b)	bag {3,3,5,6,8,8,10}
bag {2,2,4,5,7,7,9}	x | x>1	a->forall(b)	true
bag {2,2,4,5,7,7,9}	x | x>3	a->forall(b)	false
bag {2,2,4,5,7,7,9}	x | x>1	a->exists(b)	true
bag {2,2,4,5,7,7,9}	x | x>9	a->exists(b)	false
bag {2,2,4,5,7,7,9}		a->size	7
bag {2,2,4,5,7,7,9}		a->includes(7)	true
bag {2,2,4,5,7,7,9}		a->includesAll(bag {2,3})	false
bag {2,2,4,5,7,7,9}		a->isEmpty	false
bag {2,2,4,5,7,7,9}		a->notEmpty	true
bag {2,2,4,5,7,7,9}		a->sum	36
sequence {2,3,2,4,5,9,6}	x | x>5	a->select(b)	sequence {9}
sequence {2,3,2,4,5,9,6}	x | x>5	a->reject(b)	sequence {2,3,2,4,5}
sequence {2,3,2,4,5,9,6}	x | x+1	a->collect(b)	sequence {3,2,3,5,6,10,7}

Thus, if we apply this operation to the collection

```
bag {12,86,342,3,12,567,432},
```

the result will be

```
bag {342,567,432}.
```

The vertical bar can be read 'such that', for example 'x such that x is greater than 100'.

12.3.5.2 The Reject Operation

The reject operation picks out a subset of elements from a collection that fail a particular condition. The syntax for the reject operation is:

```
collection->reject(v | boolean-expression-with-v).
```

The action to implement the operation is to assign v to each of the values in the collection, evaluate the expression, and, if the result is false, add that to the resultant collection. The type of the resultant collection is the same as the source collection, with repetitions preserved for bags, and sequence preserved for sequences. For example, we may wish to select from a set the elements not greater than a particular value. Thus

```
a->reject(x | x>100).
```

would select all items in the collection a that are not greater than 100 and provide a new collection. Thus, if we apply this operation to the collection

```
bag {12,86,342,3,12,567,432},
```

the result would be

```
bag {12,86,3,12}.
```

12.3.5.3 The Collect Operation

The collect operation creates a new collection by applying an expression to each element of a collection. The syntax for the collect operation is:

```
collection->select(v | expression-with-v).
```

The action to implement the operation is to assign v to each of the values in the collection, evaluate the expression, and put the result in the returned collection. The type of the resultant collection is the same as the source collection, with repetitions preserved for bags, and sequence preserved for sequences. For example, to create a collection of squares of all numbers in a given collection we could use the expression:

```
a->collect(x | x*x).
```

12.4 HOW TO PRODUCE CONSTRAINTS

The acquisition of constraints will take place throughout the analysis and design process. To begin with these will inevitably have to be recorded as natural language statements. Continual refinement will be necessary until it is possible to express these more formally in an expression language such as OCL. Ultimately, the constraints will be used by developers to enable them to write clear and reliable code that conforms to the system specification. Constraints are identified by:

- determining pre-conditions and post-conditions on use cases;
- determining invariants on objects in the analysis model;
- translating use-case constraints to constraints on operations;
- translating pre-conditions, post-conditions and invariants to code in the implementation.

The refinement will be continuous and iterative throughout analysis and design. The ambiguity of natural language will mean that it is often necessary to ask further questions to clarify issues. Until the structural design is complete, it will not be possible to express all constraints fully in OCL because, for example, the complete set of objects and operations will not be available.

12.4.1 Determining Constraints on Use Cases

Use cases are legitimately invoked only under particular conditions. As part of the definition of use cases, it is important to capture these conditions. One way of doing this is to supply a document template for the description of use cases. This template will include the scenario descriptions as illustrated in Figure 3-11, and any additional requirements for the use case, including pre-conditions and post-conditions.

Consider the use case for registering car sharers, illustrated in Figure 12-9. The elaboration of the registration use case could be provided in a format as indicated in Figure 12-10. It would be infeasible at this stage to express these pre-conditions and post-conditions in OCL, as the underlying object structure is unlikely to be complete.

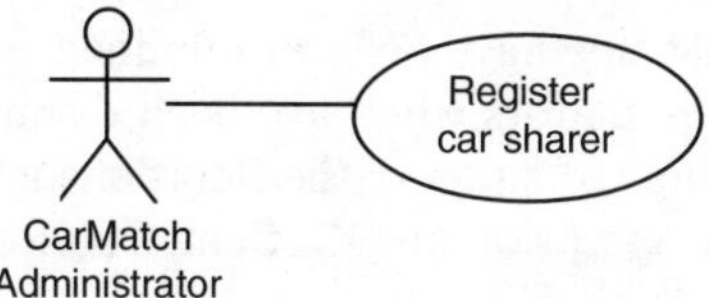

Fig. 12-9: The use case Register car sharer

12.4.2 Determining Constraints on Objects

The realization of use cases is through workflows that result in a network of communicating objects. These objects are configured to provide the use case functionality. Therefore, the pre-conditions and post-conditions for use cases must ultimately be translated into constraints on the objects. As part of realizing the Register car sharer use case, we have an class CarSharer with a date of birth attribute dateOfBirth. It does not make sense to store age as an attribute, so it is necessary to implement an operation on CarSharer to return the age. Translating the constraint from the use case for registration we arrive at an invariant for CarSharer expressed as follows:

Use Case: Register car sharer
Pre-conditions:
1. Car sharer must be older than 21 years.
2. If the car sharer offers to drive, he/she must have a current driving licence and valid insurance
3. Car sharer must not be already registered
4. Car sharer must not have been disqualified from membership in the past
Post-conditions:
1. Car sharer details registered
2. Car sharer has paid for membership
3. Welcome pack has been issued to car sharer
4. Registration of journeys for car sharer enabled
Description
etc.

Fig. 12-10: The use case description Register car sharer

```
context CarSharer inv:
    self.age() >= 21.
```

Note that the imprecise natural language expression 'older than 21 years' has been made more precise in OCL.

12.4.3 Translating Use Case Constraints to Operation Constraints

The CarSharer class is an entity class, instances of which are likely to have their operations called from a control object of the class RCSControl, which provides the implementation of the Register car sharer use case. To enforce the invariant on CarSharer, it makes sense to implement a pre-condition on the operation on RCSControl that creates the CarSharer

The constraint that car sharers must not have been disqualified from membership in the past implies that we need to keep a register of car sharers who have been disqualified. The class diagram in Figure 12-11 indicates the object relationships to support the Register car sharer use case. Now we can write a set of pre-conditions on the register operation on RCSControl as follows:

```
context RCSControl::register(name,address)
    self.CarSharer -> forall(self.name <> name and self.address <> address) and
    self.DisqualifiedCarSharer -> forall(self.name <> name
            and self.address <> address) .
```

12.4.4 Translating Constraints into Code

Pre-conditions and invariants are not, in themselves, executable. However, as they define the legal conditions under which a system operates, it makes good sense to provide checks in code to ensure that as far as possible they are not violated. If the constraints are violated, then it would be normal to raise some exception so that the system or the user of the system can take corrective action. Pre-conditions on operations can be translated into simple checks at the beginning of the code that implements the

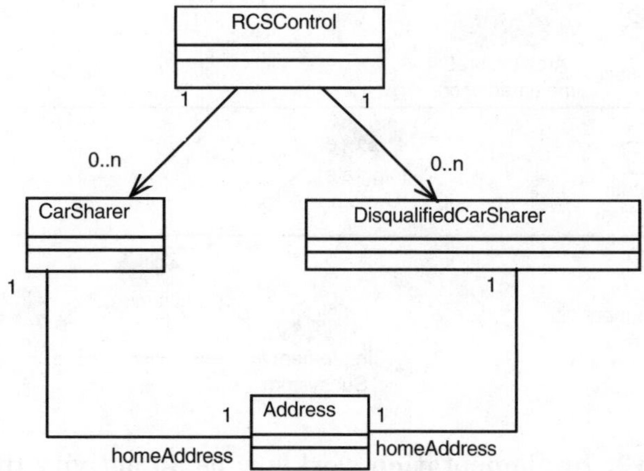

Fig. 12-11: Part of the class diagram to implement the use case Register car sharer

operations. Invariants can be checked by introducing code before a change to the attributes indicated by the invariant.

Post-conditions are part of the contractual requirement of an operation. The code should have left the post-conditions as true for legal execution of the operation. The post-conditions are used by the programmer as part of the specification. It is possible, though not routine, to check that the post-conditions are satisfied on exit from a procedure; this would be sensible if there is some complexity in the code or some safety-critical issue that means that the operation must be double-checked.

12.5 RELATIONSHIP WITH OTHER DIAGRAMS

OCL expressions can be held separately or tagged onto diagrams in some way. Invariants can be placed in a note and attached to the object to which they relate. Guards can be expressed in OCL, and are drawn on transitions in activity diagrams and statechart diagrams. There is no natural place to record pre-conditions and post-conditions on operations; placing them in notes is cumbersome, so that the only effective means is to record them separately. CASE tools support different means of associating text with elements in a UML model and these may be used to record OCL expressions.

12.6 OCL IN THE UNIFIED PROCESS

OCL is not specifically referenced in the Unified Process. Its primary role is to provide rigour to the recording of constraints. Because OCL expressions are constructed out of model elements, the model itself needs to be very well elaborated before constraints can be expressed in this way. OCL can be used to describe constraints in the business model once the business objects have been defined. Requirements are likely to be recorded in natural language, to be translated once object models have been defined through analysis and design. Unit testing can make use of pre-conditions and post-conditions to develop test plans. In the *Implementation Workflow* activities *Implement a Class* and *Perform Unit Test*, constraints would be used firstly to determine conditions in the program code for each class, and secondly to provide tests that can be applied to instances of each class. Figure 12-12 shows the workflow.

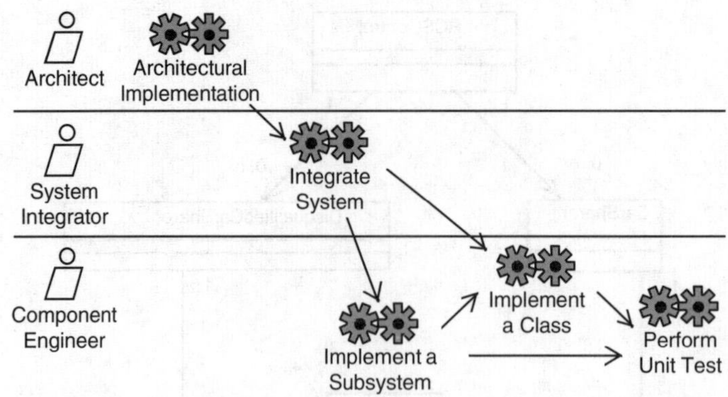

Fig. 12-12: Implementation workflow as an activity diagram

Review Questions

12.1 What is a constraint?

12.2 Why do you add constraints to a model?

12.3 What is OCL?

12.4 What is the problem with using natural language to define constraints?

12.5 What is a pre-condition?

12.6 What is a post-condition?

12.7 What is an invariant?

12.8 What is "design by contract"?

12.9 What is the context for a constraint?

12.10 What are the basic types in an OCL expression?

12.11 What types, other than basic ones, can be used in OCL expressions?

12.12 Evaluate the OCL expression: `if ((3+4)>=7) then 1 else 2`.

12.13 What are the different types of collection?

12.14 How do you find the first element of a sequence?

12.15 Flatten the collection: `set { set {2,4,7}, set {3,8,9} }`.

12.16 Evaluate the OCL expression: `bag { 2,5,2,3,8,3,4,6} -> select( x | x<5)`.

12.17 Evaluate the OCL expression: `bag {2,8,4,6,0,4,8,2} -> forall(x | x.mod(2) = 0)`.

12.18 Would you express pre-conditions and post-conditions on use cases in OCL?

Solved Problems

12.1 Consider the use case to sell insurance policies, indicated in Figure 12-13. As part of the discussions with the insurance companies, requirements are agreed as follows.

- Members must be fully paid up before taking out insurance.
- The first payment of the payment schedule must be made before cover is granted.
- Two policies must not be in force at the same time for a given car sharer.

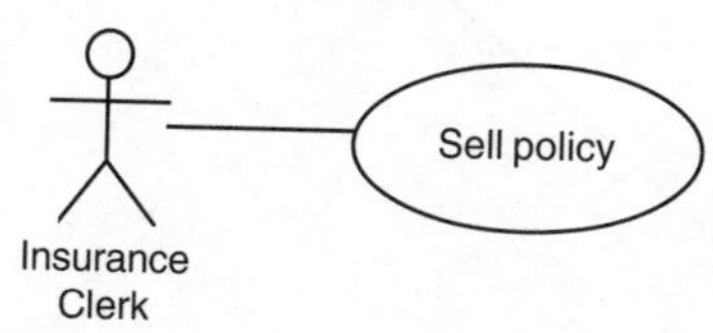

Fig. 12-13: The use case Sell policy

Write OCL constraints to handle these requirements.

These are added to the use case as pre-conditions and recorded as indicated in Figure 12-10 above. Then, as part of the design process a partial class diagram is devised as in Figure 12-14. Here a control object, SPControl, has been introduced to manage the use case transactions, and it has three operations (among others) to gather insurance details, to create a new policy and to create a new payment schedule. The first pre-condition should sensibly be checked before insurance details are gathered—it is not appropriate to gather information when there is something that is easily checked that could block the transaction. We would therefore put this as a pre-condition on the gatherInsuranceDetails operation, thus:

```
context SPControl::gatherInsuranceDetails( )
    pre: CarSharer.membership.balance >= 0.
```

Thus we have used the CarSharer that is linked to SPControl, and traced through the membership role to the account that holds the outstanding balance on membership fees, and checked that the balance is greater than zero.

The second requirement is sensibly mapped onto the createPaymentSchedule operation. Because dates are not basic types, an operation will have to be available on the date type to check that it is before another date, using the other date as the argument (this operation must return a boolean value). The constraint becomes:

```
context SPControl::createPaymentSchedule(startDate, regularDate, amount, frequency)
    pre: startDate.before(Policy.startDate).
```

The third requirement is an invariant on CarSharer, which can be expressed as 'the renewal date of a policy must fall before the start date of any later policy', and this becomes in OCL a set operation:

```
context CarSharer
    inv: Policy->forall( p1,p2 | p1<>p2 and p1.startDate.before(p2.startDate)
            implies p1.renewalDate.before(p2.startDate)).
```

In considering this, we need to place a constraint on Policy that makes sure that renewal dates fall after start dates, thus:

```
context Policy
    inv: startDate.before(renewalDate).
```

On further consideration of the design of the system, the invariant on CarSharer is ensured by placing a pre-condition on the createPolicy operation that can be expressed as:

```
context SPControl::createPolicy(startDate, renewalDate)
    pre: CarSharer.Policy -> forall( p | p.startDate.before(self.startDate)
            implies p.renewalDate.before(self.startDate)).
```

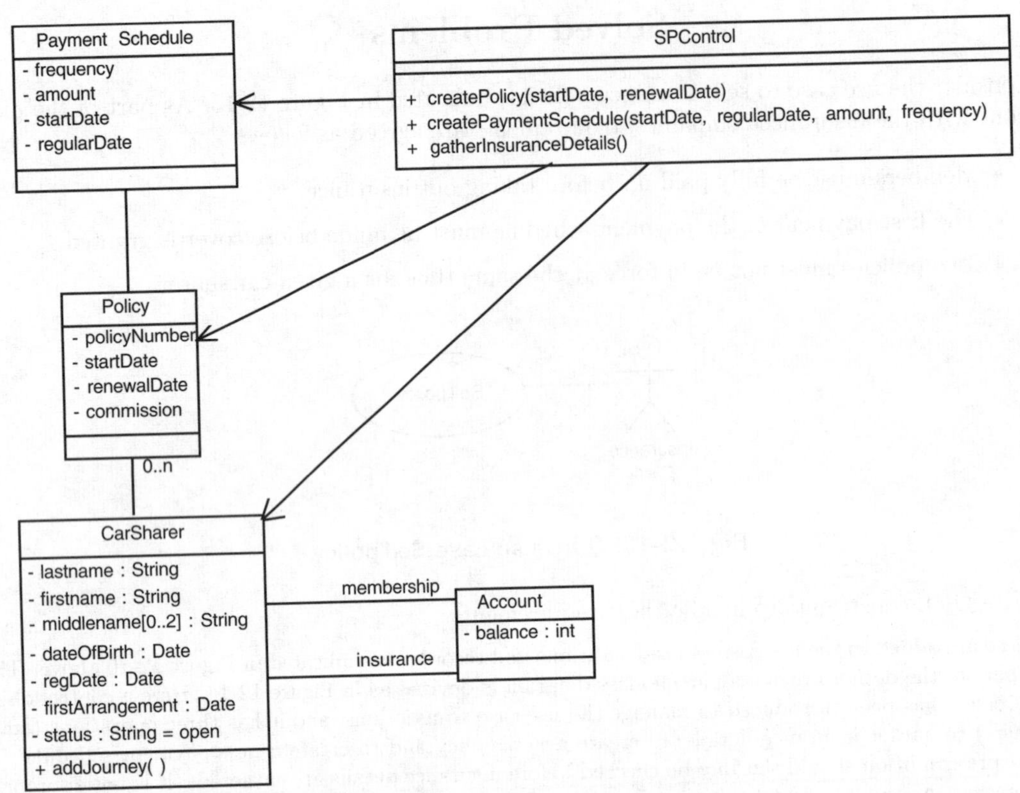

Fig. 12-14: Partial class diagram to implement the use case Sell policy

The translation of the pre-conditions into code would depend very much on the programming language chosen. However, in each case the operation would inevitably begin with some simple tests to check that the pre-conditions were true. If a pre-condition is false, then the operation would either exit with some return value set, or raise an exception.

12.2 Consider the use case Match car sharers. The requirements for sharing include the condition that to create a sharing agreement, there must be at least one driver, and at least two people in the agreement. Write OCL constraints to handle these requirements.

This would be a post-condition of the use case Match car sharers. We might then design a control class MCSControl with an operation to choose sharers for a particular journey and then create a sharing agreement. The object model is indicated in Figure 12-15. The requirement would mean that the chooseSharers operation must return a list of car sharers among whom is a driver. We clearly need a means of checking if a car sharer can drive, and we might elect to put a canDrive attribute in the object. The requirement can be expressed as a post-condition:

```
context MCSControl::chooseSharers(journey): list of CarSharer
    post: self->exists (x | x.canDrive) and (self->size) >=2.
```

This would then become a pre-condition on the createArrangement operation, expressed thus:

```
context MCSControl::createArrangement(agreementDate, startDate, finishDate, sharers)
    post:sharers -> exists (x | x.canDrive) and (sharers ->size) >=2.
```

Meeting these pre-conditions and post-conditions would be instrumental in implementing the invariant on a sharing agreement as follows:

```
context SharingAgreement
    inv: CarSharer->exists (x| x.canDrive) and (CarSharers->size) >=2.
```

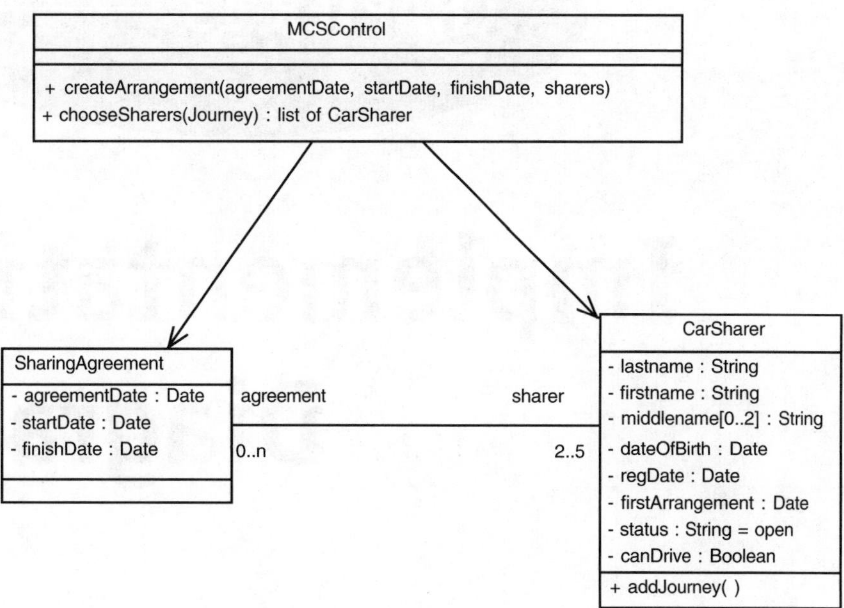

Fig. 12-15: Partial class diagram to implement the use case Match car sharers

Supplementary Problems

12.3 In VolBank, a requirement is made to prevent anyone depositing more than 200 hours, and no-one over-drawing more than 100 hours. Express this as a constraint in OCL.

12.4 In VolBank, a requirement is made to ensure that no volunteer works for more than three organizations at any one time. For the use case that matches a volunteer with an organization, express this as a pre-condition on the use case. Devise a set of objects to implement the use case, and express this constraint in OCL both as an invariant and as a pre-condition on an operation that implements the matching.

Implementation Diagrams

13.1 INTRODUCTION

There are two kinds of diagram in UML that are used to model aspects of the implementation of computer systems: *component diagrams* and *deployment diagrams*. Component diagrams are used to model the relationships between software components in the system. These relationships are usually between program source files, between run-time components or between source files and the executables that are compiled from them. However, they can be used to document any of the software components that make up a computerized system and the relationships among them. Deployment diagrams are used to model the hardware that will be used to implement the system and the links between different items of hardware. Components can be shown in a deployment diagram in order to model the deployment of run-time components on processors in the planned system. Figure 13-1 shows an example of a component diagram that models the relationships between a C++ source code file and two header files.

Figure 13-2 shows an example of a deployment diagram that models the hardware of a system and the way that the different processors will be linked together.

Components can be used in a deployment diagram to show where run-time components of a system will be deployed, as in Figure 13-3.

13.2 PURPOSE OF THE TECHNIQUES

Both component diagrams and deployment diagrams model aspects of the physical implementation of a system.

Component diagrams are used to model a static view of the components that make up a system. Components are things such as files, executable programs, documents, libraries and tables of data.

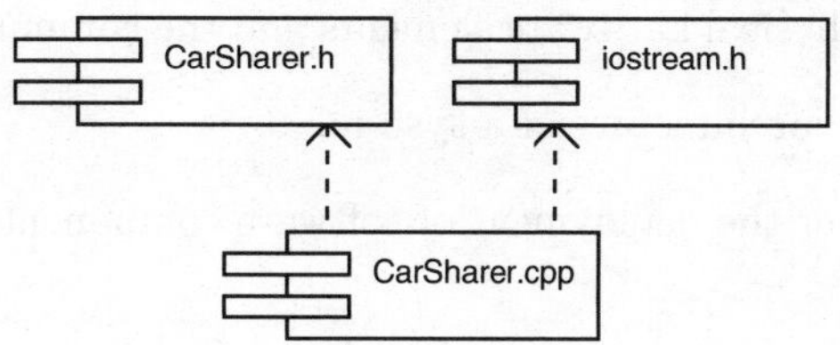

Fig. 13-1: A component diagram showing C++ source file dependencies

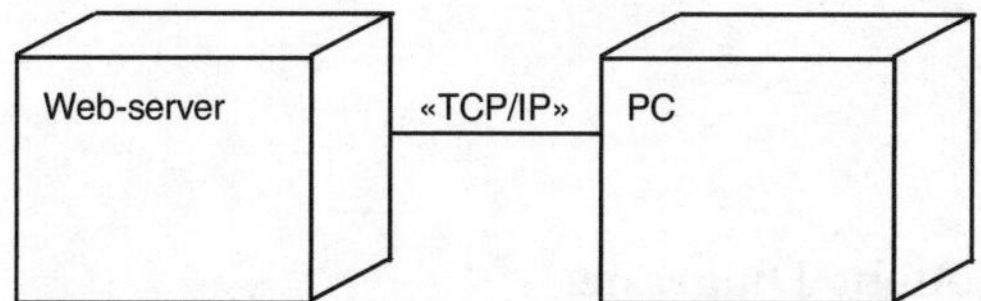

Fig. 13-2: A deployment diagram showing the communication association between a PC and a web-server

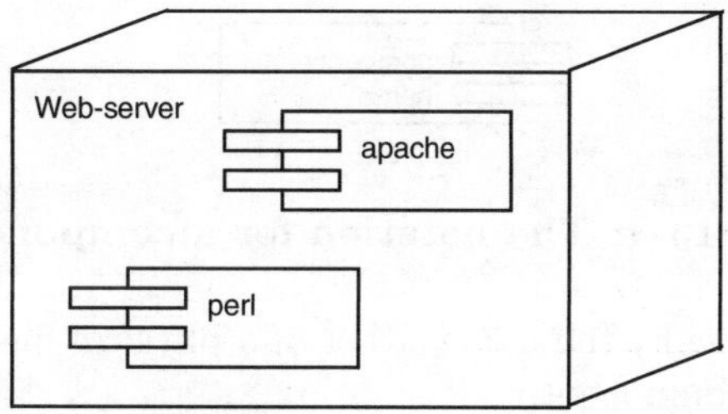

Fig. 13-3: A deployment diagram showing components

They are linked together in a component diagram by dependencies, generalizations, realizations and other associations. These relationships can be stereotyped using standard stereotypes such as «trace», or by stereotypes that apply to the domain that is being modelled. The main uses of component diagrams are as follows.

- They are used to model physical software components and the relationships between them.
- They are used to model source code and relationships between files.
- They are used to model the structure of releases of software.
- They are used to specify the files that are compiled into an executable.

However, they can be used to model any other software objects that make up a computerized system, for example the relationship between help files and the program files that invoke them or the structure of tables in a database.

Deployment diagrams are used to model the configuration of the hardware elements (or *nodes*) that make up the system. These include computers (clients and servers), embedded processors and devices such as sensors and peripherals. They are also used to show the nodes where software components reside in the run-time system. They are used for the following purposes.

- They are used to model physical hardware elements and the communication paths between them.
- They are used to plan the architecture of a system.
- They are used to document the deployment of software components on hardware nodes.

The components in component diagrams and the nodes in deployment diagrams can be stereotyped using icons to represent specific kinds of components or nodes.

13.3 NOTATION

13.3.1 Notation of Component Diagrams

A component diagram is a graph of *components* connected by dependency relationships. Components are shown using the notation of Figure 13-4.

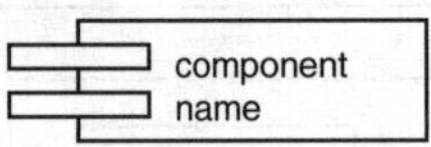

Fig. 13-4: The notation for a component

The name of a component is typically the name either of a physical file or of a subsystem of some sort that has been designed to be a component.

Dependencies between components are shown as dashed arrows drawn between components with the arrowhead pointing from the dependent component to the one on which it is dependent. Figure 13-5 shows a dependency between a compiled .class file and the .java source file.

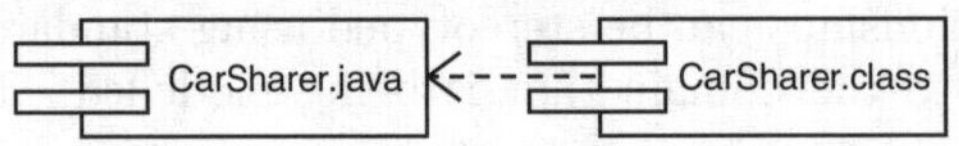

Fig. 13-5: Dependency between components

Dependency arrows can be labelled with a stereotype to indicate the nature of the dependency, as in Figure 13-6. There are a number of standard stereotypes in UML, such as «include», «derive», «friend» and «import». Additional stereotypes can be defined to meet the needs of a project or organization.

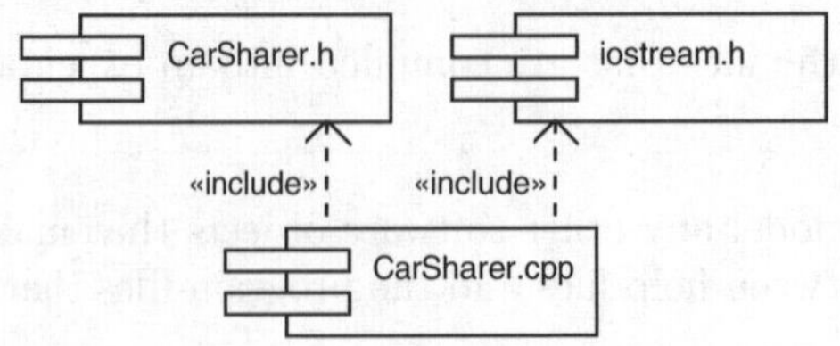

Fig. 13-6: Stereotyped dependency between components

A component may implement an interface, and the interface can be shown as a circle joined to the component by a line or as an interface class. Components that use the interface are shown with a dependency arrow going to the interface rather than to the component itself. Figure 13-7 shows a GIS (geographical information system) as a component that implements the Geolocation interface that is used by the Address Matching component.

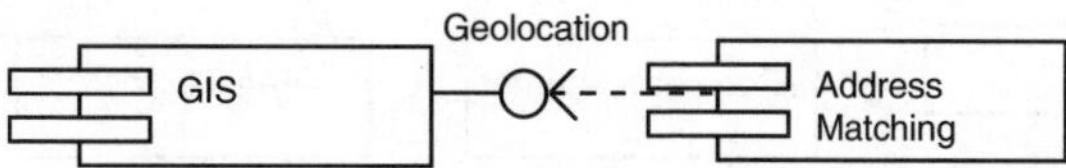

Fig. 13-7: A component diagram showing a dependency on an interface

The containment of one or more components within another component can be shown by enclosing the contained components within the container component, as in Figure 13-8. This represents a composition relationship between the container component and the components that it contains.

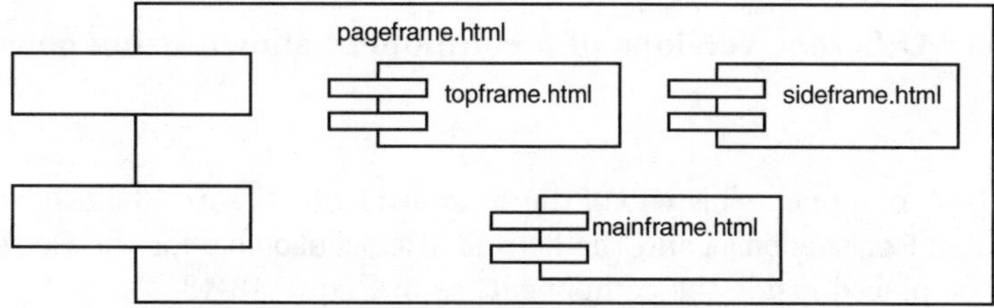

Fig. 13-8: A component diagram showing contained components

According to the UML Specification, because it is a kind of classifier (see Chapter 14), a component may have operations (and presumably also attributes). Other information about the component, such as the classes that it realizes can be shown in compartments in the component icon, as in Figure 13-9.

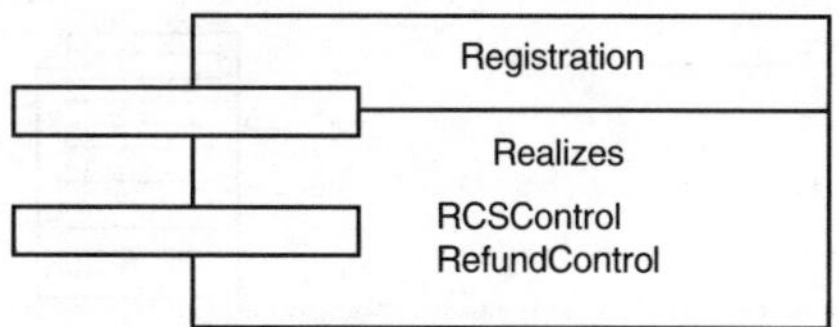

Fig. 13-9: A component with a compartment to show realized classes

The classes that are implemented by a component can also be shown contained within it. The class names can be labelled with a plus or minus sign to show their visibility to other classes or components outside the component that implements them. Figure 13-10 shows an example of this for the façade pattern example of Figure 8-12. The InsuranceMatching component implements the four classes shown, but only one of them, which plays the role of the façade class in the pattern, is visible to other components. The other three classes, which play the role of subsystem classes in the pattern, provide specific services but these services are only accessible through the façade class.

Constraints can also be added to components, and can be used to show information such as version numbers, as in Figure 13-11. A constraint can either be shown inside the component or alongside it on the diagram.

The component icon made up of a large rectangle with two small rectangles on the left-hand side, which we have used so far, is the standard notation for a component. It has its origins in a notation for an program component. If you wish to emphasize the fact that a component is not a program, then you can

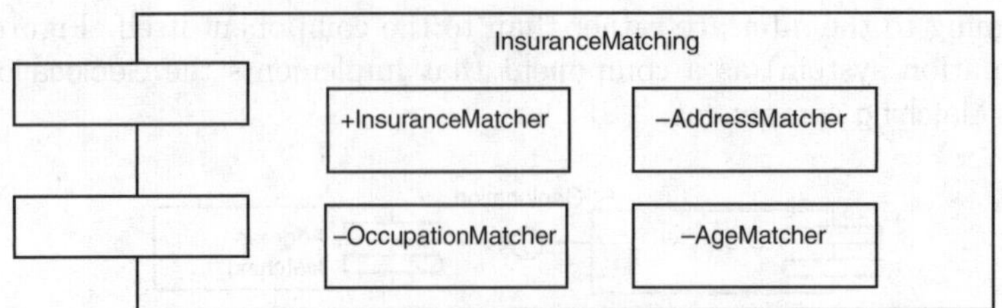

Fig. 13-10: A component showing contained classes

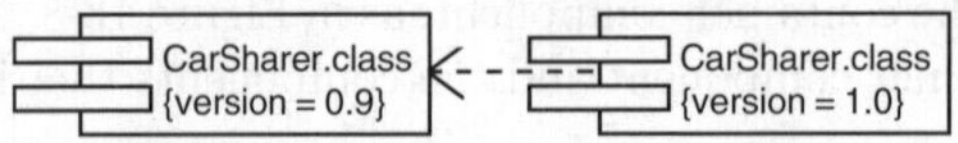

Fig. 13-11: Different versions of a component shown using constraints

use stereotyped icons for components instead of the standard icon. Figure 13-12 shows stereotyped icons for the configuration file Registration.ini and the help file Registration.hlp for the Registration component. Stereotypes can also be placed inside the component, as in Figure 13-13.

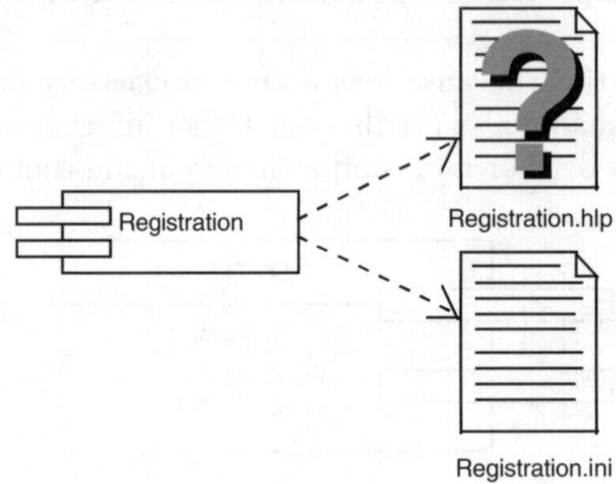

Fig. 13-12: Stereotyped component icons

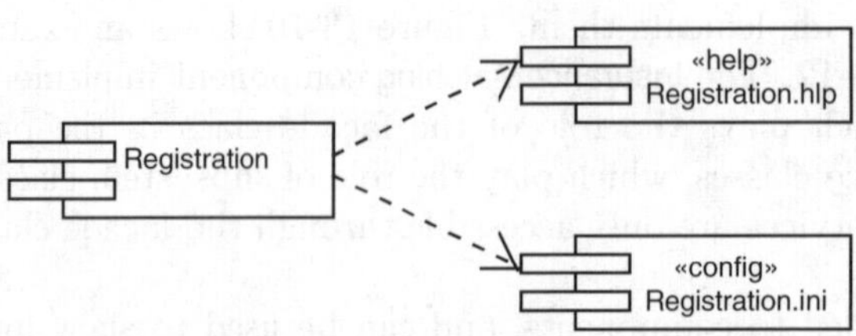

Fig. 13-13: Stereotyped components

Components in a component diagram are always types rather than instances. Instances of components can be shown in deployment diagrams.

13.3.2 Notation of Deployment Diagrams

Deployment diagrams show *nodes* connected by *communication associations*. The notation for a node is a cuboid, as in Figure 13-14.

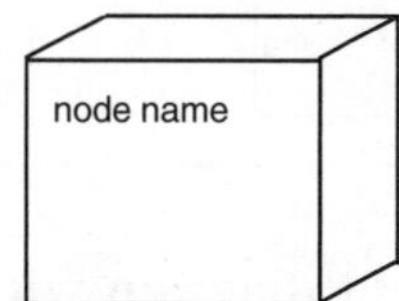

Fig. 13-14: The notation for a node

Nodes represent the processing resources in a system, typically computers with processing power and memory, but can also be used to represent sensors, peripherals or embedded systems. Nodes are connected by communication associations, which can be stereotyped to show the nature of the communication between the connected pair of nodes. Figure 13-15 shows a client and a server connected using the TCP/IP network protocol.

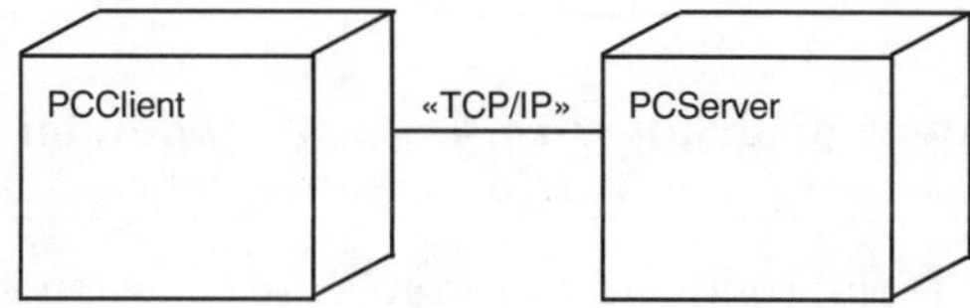

Fig. 13-15: The stereotyped communication association between a client and a server

Deployment diagrams can be used to show node types, as in Figure 13-15, or instances of nodes, as in Figure 13-16, which depicts the specific clients and servers that will be in an implemented system.

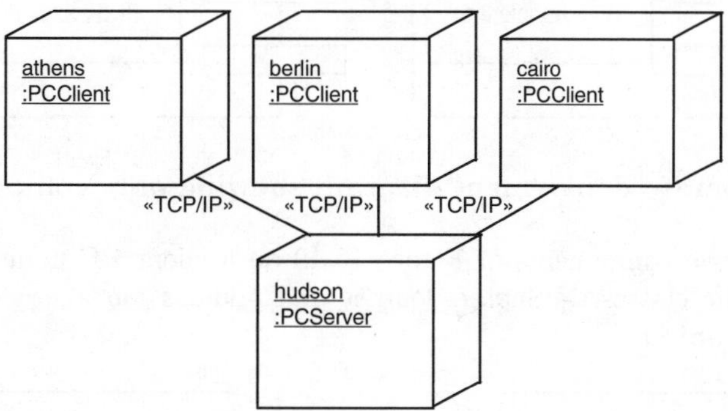

Fig. 13-16: Instances in a deployment diagram

Instances of components can be shown residing on nodes in deployment diagrams. Only run-time components are shown: source files that will be compiled into program executables do not appear in deployment diagrams, but the executables do. Components can be shown either by nesting them within the node or by joining them to the node with a dependency stereotyped «support», as in Figures 13-17 and 13-18.

Objects can also be shown as contained within node instances, and these are often active objects (see Chapter 8). Objects can also be shown contained within instances of components. A component

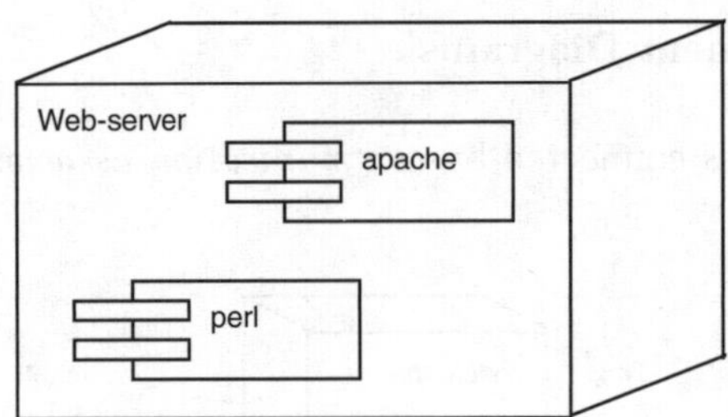

Fig. 13-17: A deployment diagram with nested components

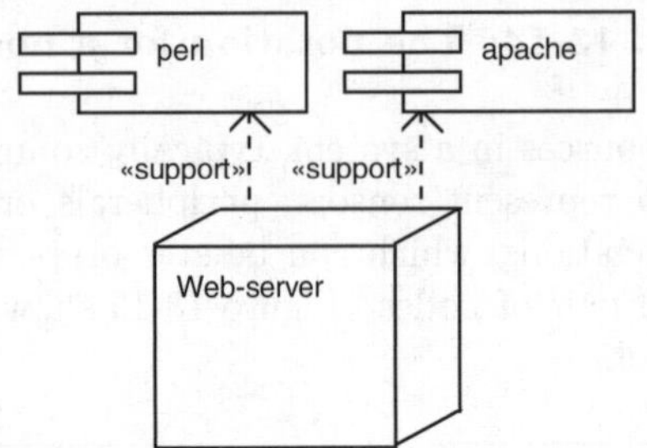

Fig. 13-18: A deployment diagram with «support» dependencies on components

diagram shows only component types; component instances are shown in a deployment diagram, and it is possible to produce a deployment diagram with no nodes, only component instances, which is known as a degenerate deployment diagram. Figure 13-19 shows a degenerate deployment diagram consisting of only components and objects related to the use case Register car sharer.

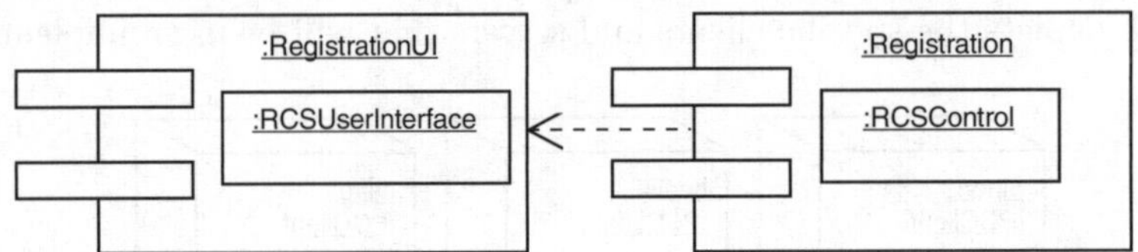

Fig. 13-19: A degenerate deployment diagram showing only components and objects

Figure 13-20 shows the two components of Figure 13-19 on a client PC node and a CarSharing component, which realizes the classes CarSharer, Journey and Address, on a server node together with a CarMatchDatabase active object.

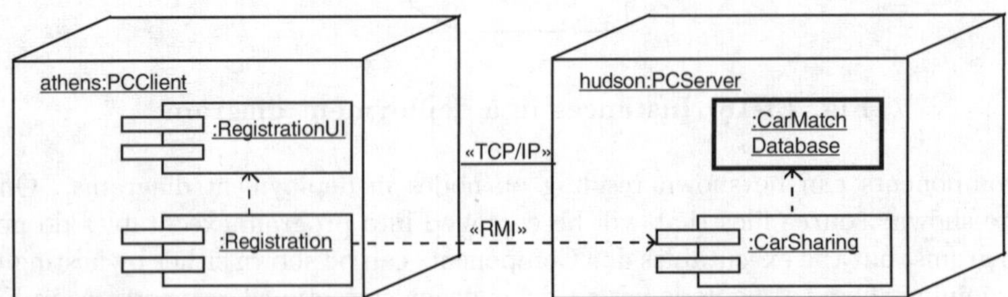

Fig. 13-20: A deployment diagram showing components and an active object

Note that the communication association between the nodes is stereotyped as «TCP/IP» while the dependency between the Registration component and the CarSharing component is stereotyped «RMI» because it uses Java's Remote Method Invocation (RMI) to call operations on the instances of CarSharer, Journey and Address.

The nodes in a deployment diagram can be shown using stereotypes or stereotyped icons if required. This is most useful when many different kinds of node are to be shown in a single diagram, and it helps to distinguish among them. Figure 13-21 shows an example.

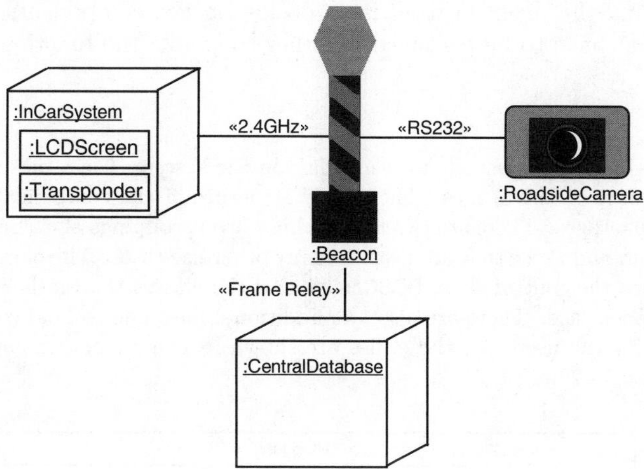

Fig. 13-21: A deployment diagram with stereotyped nodes

13.4 HOW TO PRODUCE IMPLEMENTATION DIAGRAMS

13.4.1 How to Produce Component Diagrams

Component diagrams can be used for a number of purposes, and what constitutes a component will depend on the development environment that is used to implement the system. For example, in the implemented system, components might be *packages* in Java or *projects* in Visual Basic. During the implementation process, component diagrams may be produced that show lower level components such as Java .java or .class files or Visual Basic forms or modules. However the general approach can be set out as follows.

1. Decide on the purpose of the diagram.
2. Add components to the diagram, grouping them within other components if appropriate.
3. Add other elements to the diagram, such as classes, objects or interfaces.
4. Add the dependencies between the elements of the diagram.

13.4.1.1 Decide on Purpose

The first step is to decide on the purpose of the diagram. Is it being used to model relationships between classes and components, between source code components, between source code and executables or between executables and supporting components? (In the Solved Problems for this chapter, we model all four.)

EXAMPLE 13.1 In this example, we are going to model the components involved in the registration of new car sharers. The purpose of the diagram is to show the relationships among executable components and other supporting components. The system is to be implemented in Java, so these components will be .class files and other files such as help and configuration settings.

13.4.1.2 Add Components

The first step in producing the diagram itself is to decide on the components that will be included. These will be the files that have to be packaged together to enable the functionality of registering car sharers to be carried out.

EXAMPLE 13.2 Java produces one .class file for each class in the system. Class files can be grouped together into packages held in .jar (Java Archive) files. The nested structure of the components can reflect the nested structure of classes within packages. There are two natural high-level groupings of classes: those that are specific to the process of registration, and those that are used in many other use cases. The ones that are concerned with registration can be split into the control class, RCSControl, and the classes that gather the data for processing, RCSTransaction and RCSUserInterface. There are also two additional files, one to hold configuration settings and the other to provide help for the user. All these files are shown as components, some of them nested within other components, in Figure 13-22.

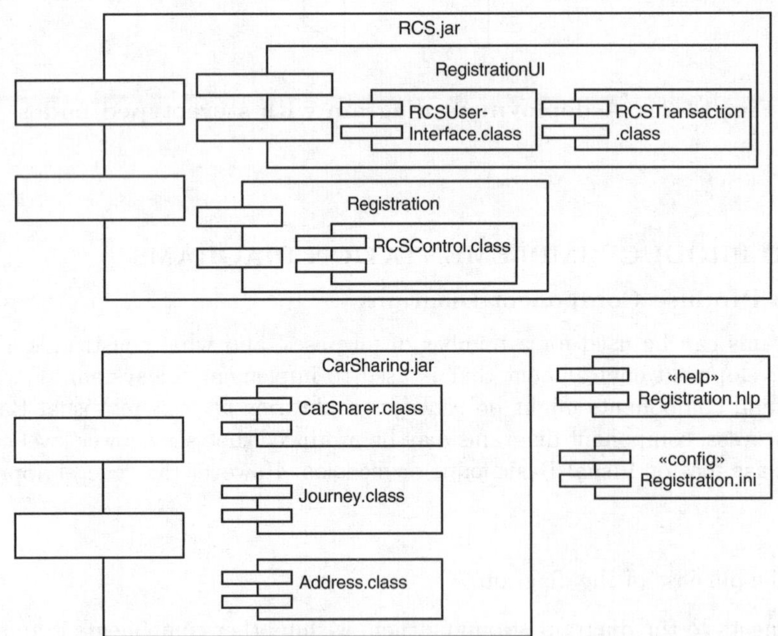

Fig. 13-22: Components for car sharer registration

13.4.1.3 Add Other Elements

The next step is to add other elements that are required. These include interfaces, classes and objects.

EXAMPLE 13.3 There are no classes or objects involved in this example, but both RCSUserInterface and RCSTransaction implement the RCS interface. This interface is used by the class RCSControl. (The dependency will be added in the next step.) The interface is added in Figure 13-23, which shows part of the component diagram.

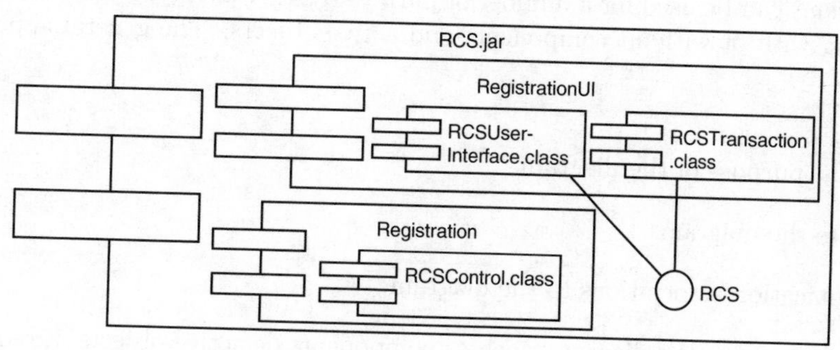

Fig. 13-23: Interface RCS added to partial diagram

13.4.1.4 *Add Dependencies*

The final step is to add in dependencies between components or between components and other elements in the diagram. The dependencies can be stereotyped to clarify the diagram, if required.

EXAMPLE 13.4 In this case, there are dependencies between the RCSControl component and the RCS interface (to use the services of the user interface and transaction components), the CarSharing component (to use services from the components within it) and the help and configuration files. Figure 13-24 shows these dependencies added to the diagram. In this case, we have stereotyped only the Java «RMI» dependency between RCSControl.class and the CarSharing component classes.

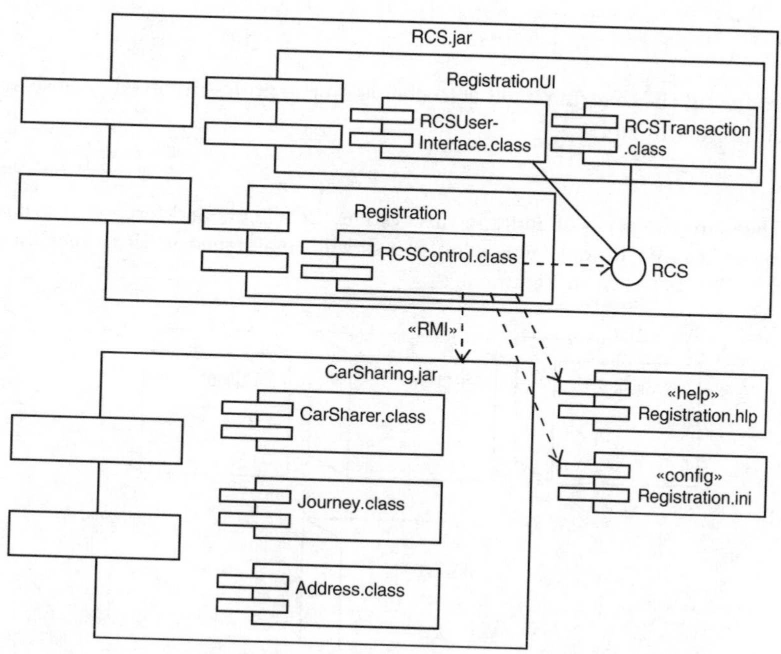

Fig. 13-24: Dependencies added to component diagram

13.4.2 How to Produce Deployment Diagrams

Deployment diagrams can be used for a number of purposes, either as a type diagram or as an instance diagram and either with or without components and active objects. The general approach can be set out as follows.

1. Decide on the purpose of the diagram.
2. Add nodes to the diagram.
3. Add communication associations to the diagram.
4. Add other elements to the diagram, such as components or active objects, if required.
5. Add dependencies between components and objects, if required.

13.4.2.1 Decide on Purpose

The first step is to decide on the purpose of the diagram. Is it being used to model only nodes or the deployment of components and other objects on nodes? (In the Solved Problems for this chapter, we model both types.)

EXAMPLE 13.5 In this example, we are going to model the deployment of components involved in the registration of new car sharers. The purpose of the diagram is to show where the components will reside. This will be an instance diagram.

13.4.2.2 Add Nodes

The first step in producing the diagram itself is to decide on the nodes involved. These are the processors on which the executables will run.

EXAMPLE 13.6 There are two types of nodes in this system: PC clients and servers. A typical office will have three clients and one server. We do not know what names will be assigned to these machines, so they will be anonymous instances. This is shown in Figure 13-25.

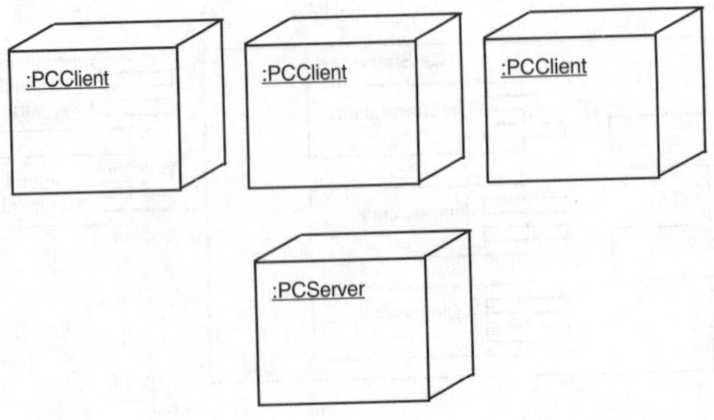

Fig. 13-25: Nodes in the deployment diagram

13.4.2.3 Add Communication Associations

The channels for communication between pairs of nodes must be added. Stereotypes are used to show the protocol for the communication.

EXAMPLE 13.7 The clients communicate with the servers using TCP/IP. We could show a network as a node in the diagram, to illustrate the fact that each client can also communicate with the other clients. However, for this diagram, we are interested only in the communication between clients and the server. The result is shown in Figure 13-26.

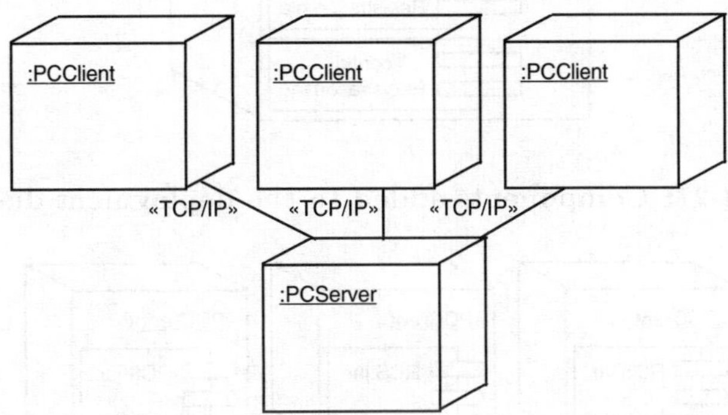

Fig. 13-26: Communication associations in the deployment diagram

13.4.2.4 Add Other Elements

Components and active objects can be added to the diagram if the purpose of the diagram is to show where they reside in the system.

EXAMPLE 13.8 In this system, the RCS.jar component will reside on each of the clients, but the components that implement the entity classes will reside only on the server. The help file is held on the server. Depending on its purpose (to set up a global configuration or a configuration for individual machines), the configuration file could reside on the clients or the server. In this case, we have decided that it sets up the configuration globally, so it is on the server. The result is shown in Figure 13-27.

13.4.2.5 Add Dependencies

It may help to show dependencies between components or between components and objects in the deployment diagram. However, the diagram can become very cluttered with lines. It may be better to produce a set of deployment diagrams, each of which illustrates a different facet of the implementation architecture.

EXAMPLE 13.9 In this case, we have chosen to show the «RMI» dependencies between each of the RCS.jar components and the CarSharing.jar component, as Java Remote Method Invocation is used to call operations of the CarSharing classes. This is shown in Figure 13-28.

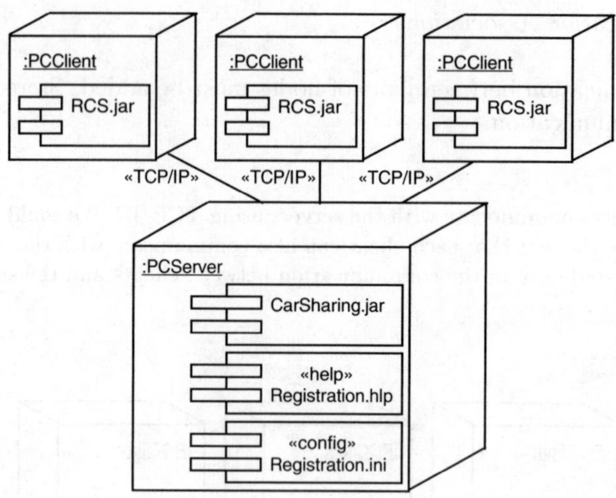

Fig. 13-27: Components added to the deployment diagram

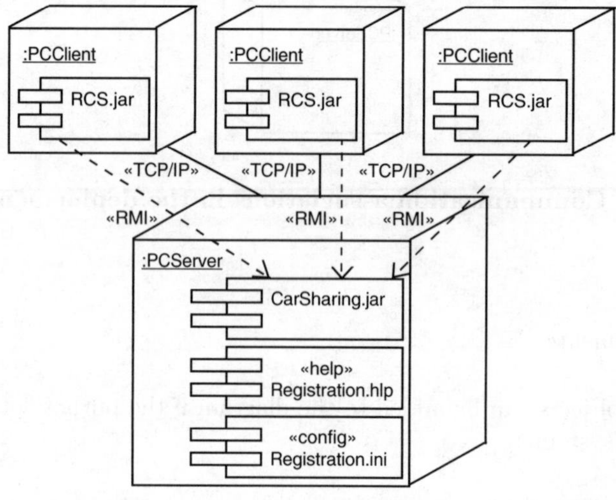

Fig. 13-28: Dependencies added to the deployment diagram

13.5 IMPLEMENTATION DIAGRAMS FOR BUSINESS MODELLING

Both types of implementation diagram can be used for modelling business operations in general rather than software systems.

Components in component diagrams can be used to model business procedures and documents. Many businesses that sell vehicle parts deal with ordinary retail customers and trade customers (other businesses). At the trade counter in the parts department, there may be a paper copy of a set of rules about what discounts to give and a list of trade customers and the discount rates that they are given. Although these are paper documents they could be modelled as components, as in Figure 13-29. This would be a suitable model in which to use stereotyped icons.

Deployment diagrams can be used to model the non-computerized 'run-time structure' of the business. The nodes in this can be organization units and other resources, including people. In the vehicle parts example, nodes could be used to represent the Trade Counter, the Retail Counter and the Parts Store.

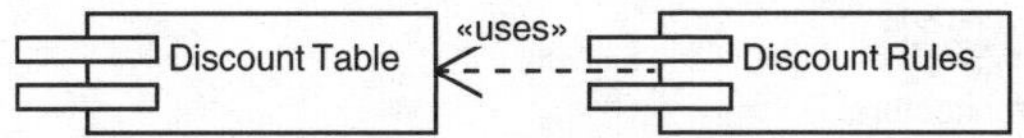

Fig. 13-29: Business components that are not software components

Figure 13-30 shows this, with the components from Figure 13-29 residing in the Trade Counter node.

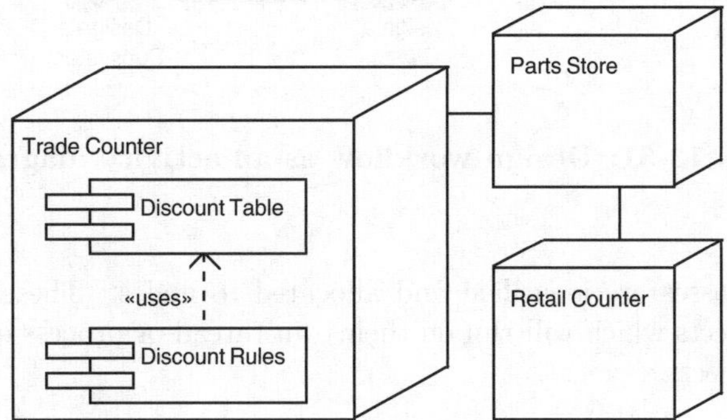

Fig. 13-30: Use of deployment diagram for business modelling

13.6 RELATIONSHIP WITH OTHER DIAGRAMS

There is a strong link between component diagrams and deployment diagrams, as instances of components can be depicted on deployment diagrams.

Components provide the mechanism for implementing classes, and are often used to show «trace» dependencies between components and classes. Component instances may include active objects, which can be shown contained within the component icon.

In designing the components for a system, use cases and collaborations can be used to determine which classes belong together in components. Classes that are always used together in a small number of related use cases can often be packaged together into one or a few components; classes that are used in many different use cases should be packaged into components that can be reused across the system without being coupled to any particular use case or group of use cases.

13.7 IMPLEMENTATION DIAGRAMS IN THE UNIFIED PROCESS

Deployment diagrams are used in the Design Workflow (see Figure 13-31) in the *Architectural Design* activity. One of the products of this activity is an Outline Deployment Model. The first step in the activity is *Identifying Nodes and Network Configurations*, during which the Architect produces a high-level architectural model of the nodes in the system and the channels of communication that they will use. Factors such as performance requirements, capacity, network protocols and data security are considered and any decisions are recorded in supporting text documents.

Deployment diagrams are also used in the step *Identifying Subsystems and their Interfaces*, in which an initial allocation of subsystems to nodes is made. In the step *Identifying Architecturally Significant*

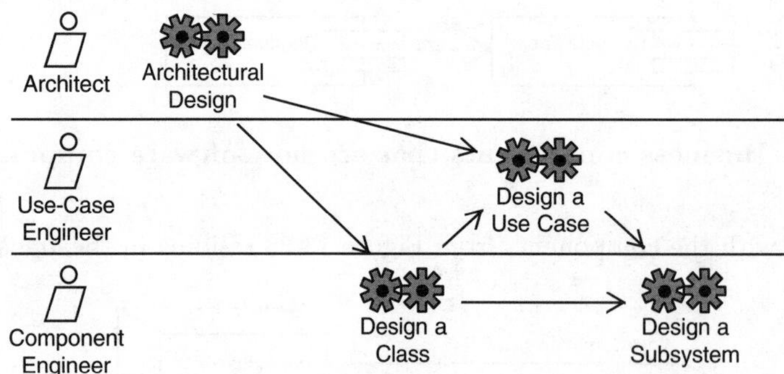

Fig. 13-31: Design workflow as an activity diagram

Design Classes, active classes are identified and allocated to nodes. These are classes that will be instantiated as active objects which will run on their own thread or process on a node and coordinate the operation of other objects.

Both component diagrams and deployment diagrams are used in the Implementation Workflow, which is shown in Figure 13-32.

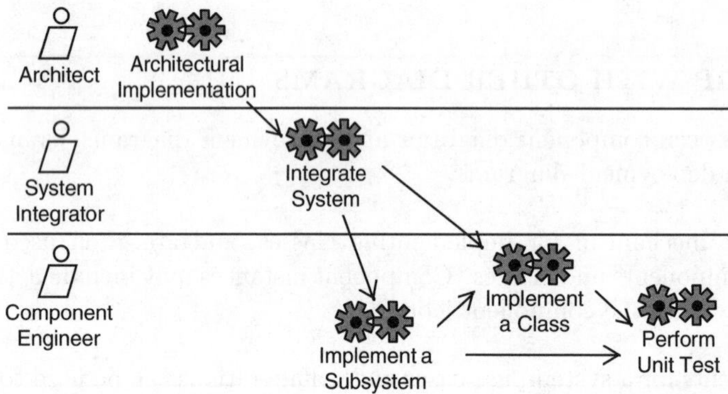

Fig. 13-32: Implementation workflow as an activity diagram

Component diagrams are used in most of the activities in this workflow. In the activity *Architectural Implementation* they are used in the step *Identifying Architecturally Significant Components*, when important components are identified and a decision is made about the nodes on which they will reside. Deployment diagrams are also used to show the allocation of components to nodes.

In the activity *Integrate System*, components are used in planning a build of the system. The activity *Implement a Subsystem* uses component diagrams to model how components will be used to implement the design classes that have been allocated to each subsystem. Component diagrams are also used in the activity *Implement a Class* to model the file components that make up the implementation of each class (source code and header files, for example). Finally, components are the 'units' in the activity *Perform Unit Test*. Components are subjected to black-box testing to ensure that each component produces the correct outputs in response to different sets of input values, and to white-box testing to verify that the component works internally as it is designed to do. This can include coverage tests to ensure that all code is executed at least once under some circumstance.

Review Questions

13.1 Define what is meant by an component.

13.2 Define what is meant by a node.

13.3 Define what is meant by a communication association.

13.4 What is the notation for a component?

13.5 What is the notation for a node?

13.6 What are the main purposes of using component diagrams?

13.7 What are the main purposes of using deployment diagrams?

13.8 What is the difference between components in a component diagram and components in a deployment diagram?

13.9 How are dependencies shown in a component diagram?

13.10 Give two examples of how stereotypes can be used in component diagrams.

13.11 Give two examples of how stereotypes can be used in deployment diagrams.

13.12 Give an example of how constraints can be used in component diagrams.

13.13 What are the main steps in producing a component diagram?

13.14 What are the main steps in producing a deployment diagram?

13.15 In which Unified Process workflow are component diagrams used?

13.16 In which two Unified Process workflows are deployment diagrams used?

Solved Problems

13.1 In this set of solved problems, we are going to draw four separate component diagrams; we shall model relationships between classes and components, between source code components, between source code and executables and between executables and supporting components. We shall work through the first of these in detail and then simply provide a solution for the other three.

We developed the realization of the use case Match car sharers in Chapter 8. This is to be implemented in Java.

What is the purpose of the first component diagram?

This first diagram is to model the components that will be implemented and their dependencies on design classes.

13.2 Draw the required components.

There are three entity classes that are used in the collaboration: CarSharer, Journey and Address. Each of these classes will be implemented by a .java source file. We have already seen that these classes are used in a number of use cases and are packaged together into a CarSharing component as Java .class files. Here we are just dealing with the source files. There are also two other classes MCSUserInterface and MCSControl. Each of these will also be implemented by a .java file. Figure 13-33 shows the components.

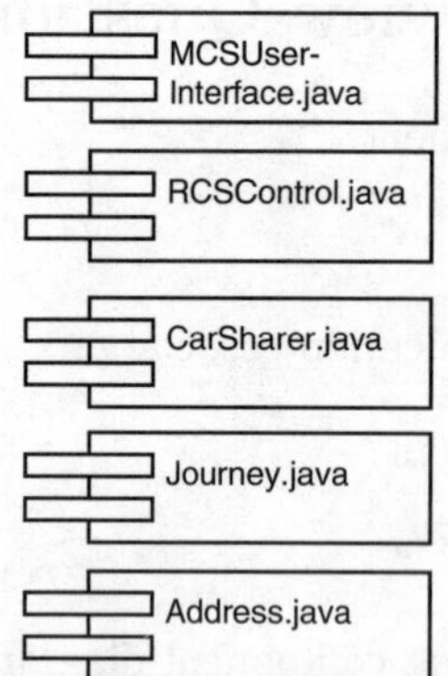

Fig. 13-33: Source code components for the use case Match car sharers

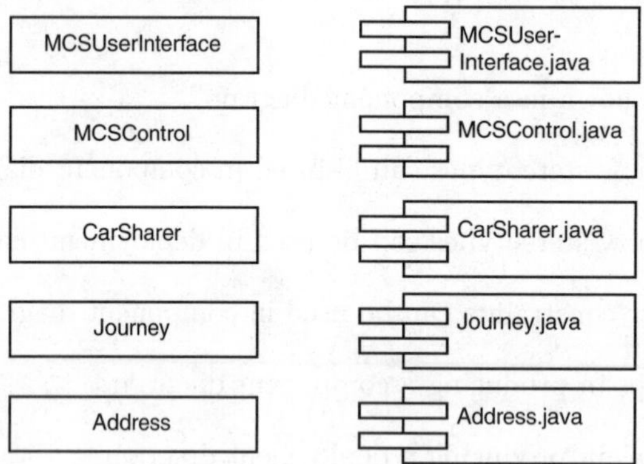

Fig. 13-34: Source code components and classes

13.3 What other elements are required in this diagram?

The classes that are implemented by the components need to be shown. These are: CarSharer, Journey, Address, MCSUserInterface and MCSControl. They are shown in Figure 13-34.

13.4 What dependencies need to be added to the diagram?

There is a «trace» dependency between each of the classes and the component that implements it. These are shown in Figure 13-35. Note that there are only simple dependencies here, as there is a one-to-one correspondence between classes and source files. This is not always the case.

13.5 The second diagram is used to model dependencies between source code components. Draw the component diagram. (We shall produce this and each of the following diagrams in one step rather than working through the four steps above.)

The purpose here is to model dependencies between source files. The components are the source files that we have already identified. The source files that will be compiled into the CarSharing component can be shown grouped together here in a single component. The MCSControl component has a dependency on the CarSharing component and on the MCSUserInterface component (Figure 13-36).

13.6 The third diagram is used to model the source code and executables as components and the dependencies between them. Draw the component diagram.

The purpose here is to model the dependencies of Java executables on source code components. Each of the .java components will be compiled into a single .class file (Figure 13-37).

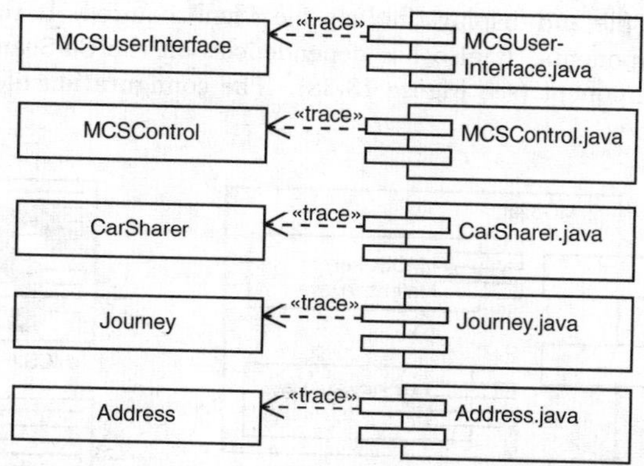

Fig. 13-35: Source code components and «trace» dependencies on classes

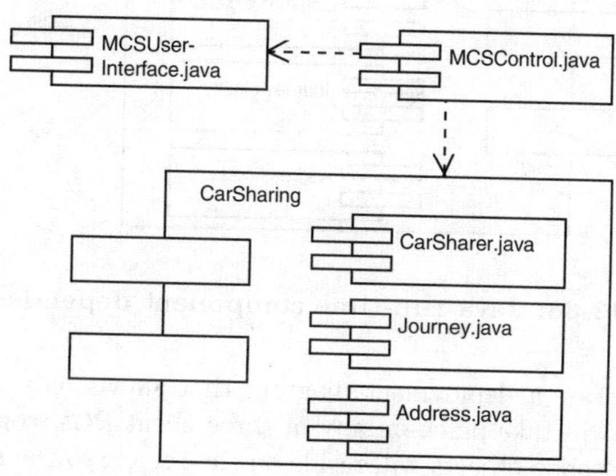

Fig. 13-36: Source code dependencies

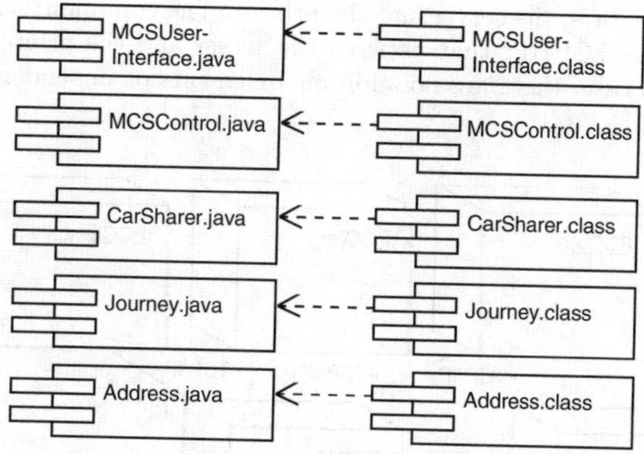

Fig. 13-37: Java .class file dependencies on source code

13.7 The final component diagram is used to model other supporting components and the dependencies between the executables and these components. A help file and a configuration file are required. Draw the component diagram to include them.

The purpose here is to show the dependencies between components in the run-time system. The .class files will be packaged together into two Java archive (.jar) files. The MCSControl.class component will need to read the configuration file and display the help file when required. It therefore has a dependency on these two additional components. It also has dependencies on the CarSharing.jar component and on the MCSUserInterface.class component (see Figure 13-38). The configuration file and the help file have been stereotyped.

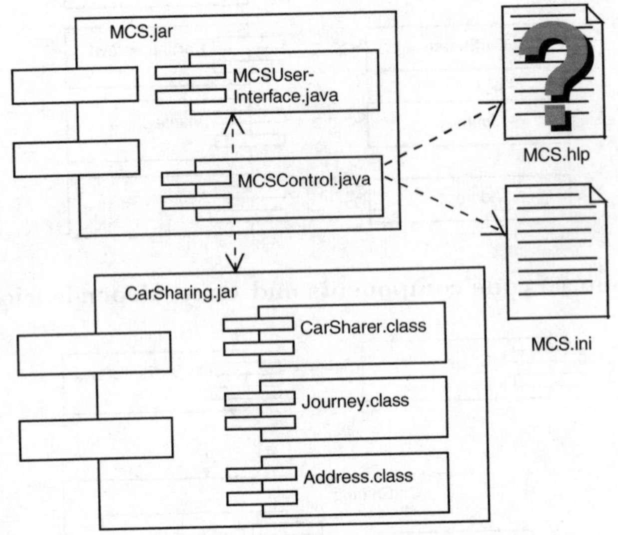

Fig. 13-38: Java run-time component dependencies

13.8 The next task is to draw a deployment diagram that shows only the nodes for this system. Matching car sharers will take place on any of three client PCs, connected to the server using TCP/IP, but the CarSharing objects will reside on the server, so the server needs to be included in the deployment diagram. A parallel printer is attached to the server to print out details of car sharers who have been matched up. Draw the deployment diagram.

The purpose of this deployment diagram is to show the nodes that will be required in this system. The nodes are the three client PCs, the server and the printer. The communication associations between the clients and the server use TCP/IP; that between the server and the printer uses the standard parallel printer protocol. In this case, there are no additional elements or dependencies between nodes to show (Figure 13-39).

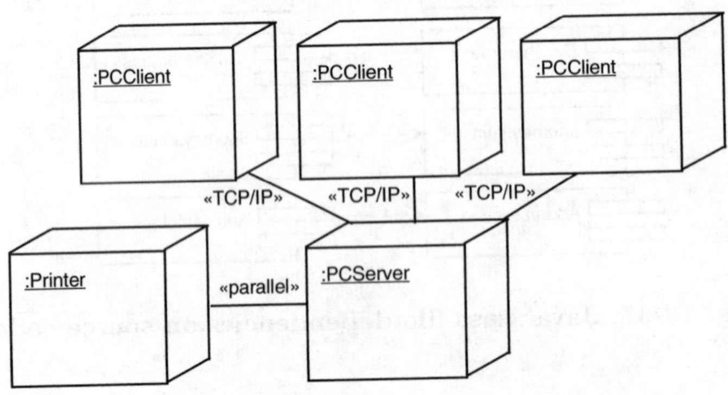

Fig. 13-39: Deployment diagram showing nodes only

13.9 Finally, we need to model the deployment of components on the nodes in the system. Draw a diagram deploying the components from Problem 13.7 on the nodes of Problem 13.8.

The purpose of this diagram is to show the deployment of specific components. (Note that there are many other run-time components that have to be deployed for this system to work: the Java run-time environment, printer drivers, maybe a database, even the operating system for the PCs. However, we limit this diagram to the things that we are interested in for this particular purpose.)

The user interface and control objects will run on the clients, so the MCS.jar component needs to be on each client. The other components need to be on the server (Figure 13-40).

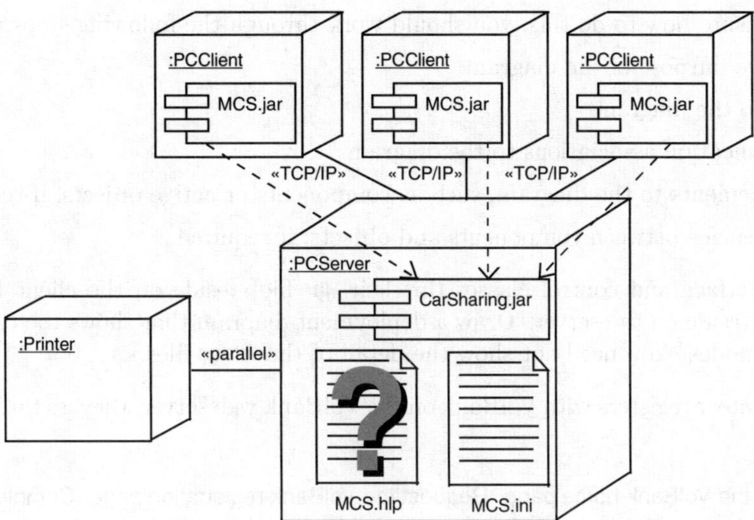

Fig. 13-40: Deployment diagram with components

Supplementary Problems

13.10 In Supplementary Problems 8.9 onwards you produced a collaboration diagram for the use case Process payment. Using the classes from those problems (PPUserInterface, PPControl, CarSharer, Account and Transaction), draw a component diagram to show the .java files to implement each of those classes.

If you are unsure how to do this, you should work through the following steps.

Decide on the purpose of the diagram.

Add components to the diagram, grouping them within other components if appropriate.

Add other elements to the diagram, such as classes, objects or interfaces.

Add the dependencies between the elements of the diagram.

13.11 Draw a component diagram to show the dependencies between .java files for the components in your answer to 13.10.

13.12 Draw a component diagram to show the dependencies between the Java .class files and the .java source code files from your solution to 13.11.

13.13 The CarSharer.class file already belongs in the CarSharing.jar Java package. This use case requires two classes that belong in a different Java package. Choose a suitable name for it and show these classes in a separate component to represent this Java package.

13.14 In the run-time environment for the Process payments use case, there will be a configuration file, a file of tax rates and a help file. There are dependencies between the PPControl.class file and the configuration and help files, and between the Transaction.class file and the tax rates file. Draw a component diagram to include all the .class files in their appropriate .jar files and the dependencies on these three additional files.

13.15 The Process payments use case runs only on a single PC Client. It is connected to a server via TCP/IP. A modem is connected to an RS232 port on the server for transferring data to the banking system. Draw a deployment diagram.

If you are unsure how to do this, you should work through the following steps.

Decide on the purpose of the diagram.

Add nodes to the diagram.

Add communication associations to the diagram.

Add other elements to the diagram, such as components or active objects, if required.

Add dependencies between components and objects, if required.

13.16 The user interface and control classes (in their .jar file) reside on the client PC; all the other components reside on the server. Draw a deployment diagram that shows the components on the appropriate nodes. You need not show the detail of the .class files.

13.17 When a volunteer registers with VolBank on the VolBank web server, they go through the following interaction.

> Go to the VolBank home page. Request the VolBank registration page. Complete the form and submit it. The server validates the data. If there is any error, the form is redisplayed with the contents as entered by the volunteer and with the incorrect field highlighted. If there is no error, the data is submitted to a database and a confirmation is displayed.

Draw a component diagram to show the components that are displayed in the web-browser on the client machine with any dependencies that you think apply.

13.18 For the scenario of Problem 13.17 draw a component diagram to show the components on the server. These are a web-server program, a database management system (DBMS) and a Java servlet (a Java application that runs on a server) to handle the registration.

13.19 For the scenario of Problem 13.17 draw a deployment diagram to show the components deployed on either the client or the server. Include a communication association that uses the hypertext transfer protocol (HTTP).

UML Common Notational Conventions

14.1 INTRODUCTION

Many UML diagrams have features in common. Within the notation there are a number of standard ways of representing the things that are of interest to the system developer, and these standard elements are set out early in the UML Specification (Object Management Group, 1999*a*). We have included this chapter towards the end of the book to pull together common features that you may come have across as you worked through the other chapters.

In this chapter we first cover the common diagram elements that are used extensively throughout UML. Secondly we explain the extension mechanisms that exist within UML that make it possible to extend it or to specialize it for particular kinds of systems. We have included an example of how these extension mechanisms can be applied from the work of Jim Conallen on the use of UML to model web applications (Conallen, 1999). There is no 'How To' section in this chapter, as the application of the diagram elements that we discuss here is covered in other chapters.

14.2 COMMON DIAGRAM ELEMENTS

14.2.1 Graphs

Most diagrams in UML are *graphs.* A graph in this sense is not something like a histogram or an x-y graph used to represent statistical information graphically. A graph is a collection of nodes joined together by paths. Graphs are used to represent information about many kinds of problems. Often the term vertex is used instead of node, and edge or arc is used instead of path. Figure 14-1 shows an example of a graph used to represent the travelling salesperson problem (in which a salesperson wishes to visit each of a number of locations by the shortest route, visiting each location once and only once). The locations at the nodes are represented by letters. The numbers labelling the paths represent the distances between nodes.

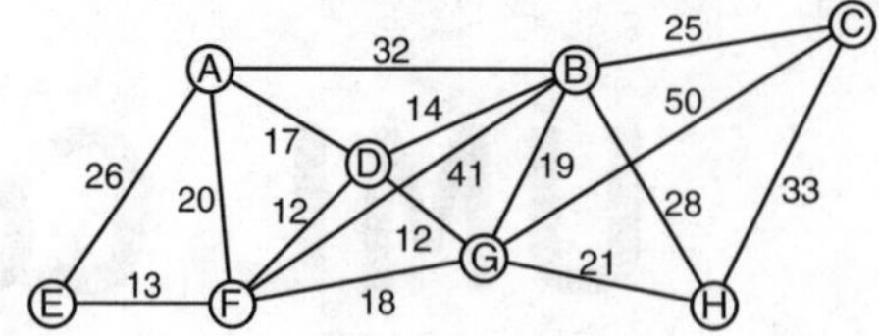

Fig. 14-1: Example graph representing a travelling salesperson problem

Graphs are used extensively in UML. Figure 14-2 shows a use case diagram in which there are two different kinds of nodes—actors and use cases—and paths connecting them.

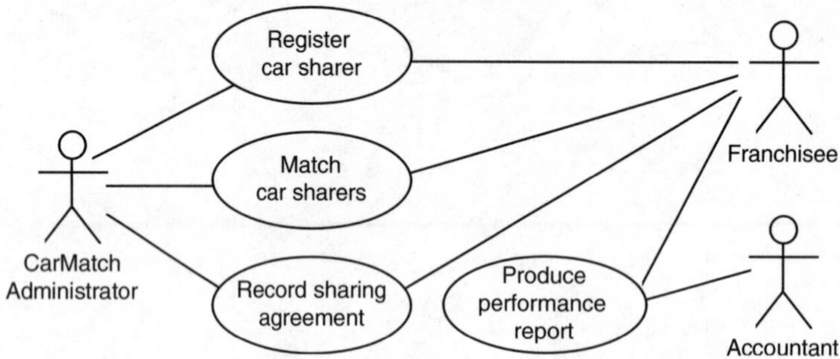

Fig. 14-2: Example of a graph—a use case diagram

14.2.2 Visual Relationships in Graphs

In most graphs in UML, it is the relationships among symbols that are important rather than their size: the fact than one class is drawn larger than another in a class diagram is not intended to convey information. The one exception to this is in some sequence diagrams where the time axis is drawn to scale—for example, to show one second as one centimeter.

There are three kinds of visual relationships in UML diagrams that are important:

- connection (usually symbols and two-dimensional shapes connected by lines);
- containment (usually of symbols by two-dimensional shapes);
- visual attachment (text or a symbol being close to a symbol on a diagram).

These relationships can be represented by graphs. In Chapter 2 we said that UML is a visual language. If you parse the visual representation into an internal representation using the rules of the UML grammar, then the result is a graph. Figure 14-3 shows examples of these three kinds of visual relationships in a package diagram.

Figure 14-4 shows the relationships among the elements of the diagram in Figure 14-3 as a graph. (The

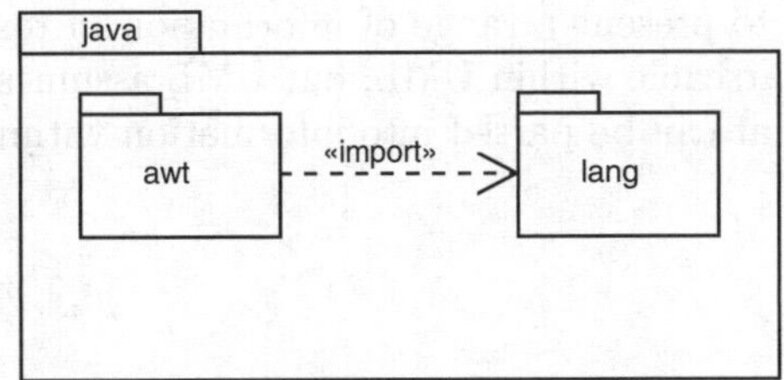

Fig. 14-3: Example of a package diagram showing visual relationships

notation used here is an adaptation of UML notation, but it has no formal meaning and is simply used to show the relationships as a graph.)

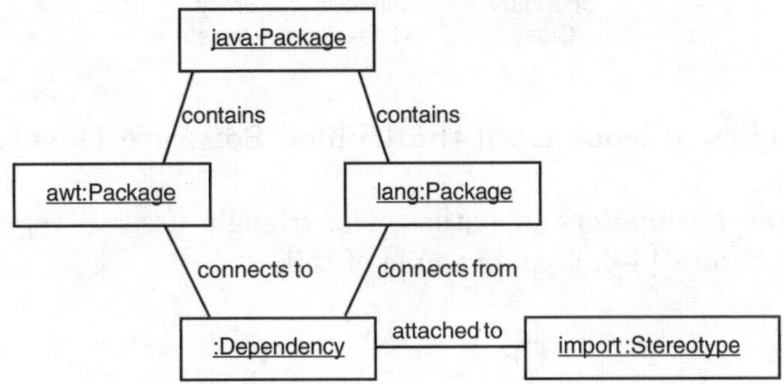

Fig. 14-4: Graph of visual relationships between elements of Figure 14-3

Note in particular that something being contained within something else and something being visually attached to something else (in this case as a label) can be converted into paths in the graph. CASE tools use some kind of internal representation such as this to hold the details of the relationships between pairs of model elements. For most CASE tools, it will be the UML metamodel that is used for this purpose (see Chapter 2).

There are four kinds of element used in UML notation: icons, two-dimensional symbols, paths and strings. These are explained below.

- *Icons.* An icon is a graphical element of a fixed size and shape. It does not change shape to hold other elements. In UML, icons are often used as stereotypes for classes (see Section 14.3.1). Icons can be used as standalone elements in diagrams, within other elements or as terminators of paths (see below).

- *two-dimensional symbols.* Two-d symbols can be used to contain other symbols and will change their size accordingly. They can be divided into separate compartments. Paths connect two-d symbols to each other and to icons. In a CASE tool, if you move a two-d symbol, all its contents and all the paths connected to it move with it.

- *Paths.* Paths are used to connect together two-d symbols and icons. A path is made up of a sequence of lines whose endpoints are attached. Paths may not have dangling ends—they must always be attached at both ends to some other element. Paths may have *terminators* at their ends (where they attach to other symbols), and these terminators convey meaning about the path symbol.

- *Strings.* Strings are used to present a range of information in textual form. It is not necessary for them to be formally parseable within UML, but UML assumes that they are written in some language with a syntax that can be parsed into information within the model.

14.2.3 Icons

Icons are used to represent stereotyped graphical elements in UML. The stick-person symbol used to represent actors is an example of an icon. The Unified Software Development Process uses icons to represent three different kinds of classes: boundary classes, control classes and entity classes. These are shown in Figure 14-5.

Fig. 14-5: Examples of icons from the Unified Software Development Process

Icons are also used on the *terminators* of paths. The triangle used to represent the generalization relationship, as shown in Figure 14-6, is an example of this.

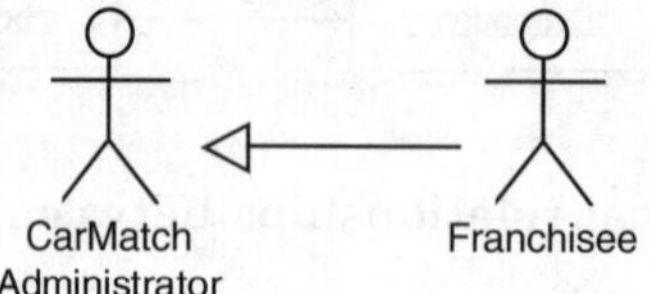

Fig. 14-6: Example of an icon as a terminator on a path

14.2.4 Two-dimensional Symbols

Two-dimensional symbols are used to represent many elements within UML. The obvious example is the class in class diagrams. Figure 14-7 shows an example of a class divided into compartments for the class name, attributes and operations.

MapReference
- externalForm : String - internalForm : Coordinate
«abstract» # convertToInternal(String) : Coordinate «abstract» # convertToExternal(Coordinate) : String

Fig. 14-7: Examples of a class as a two-dimensional symbol with compartments

As well as containing strings, two-dimensional symbols can also contain other symbols, including icons. Figure 14-8 shows a deployment diagram with icons to represent executables deployed on the Web-server node.

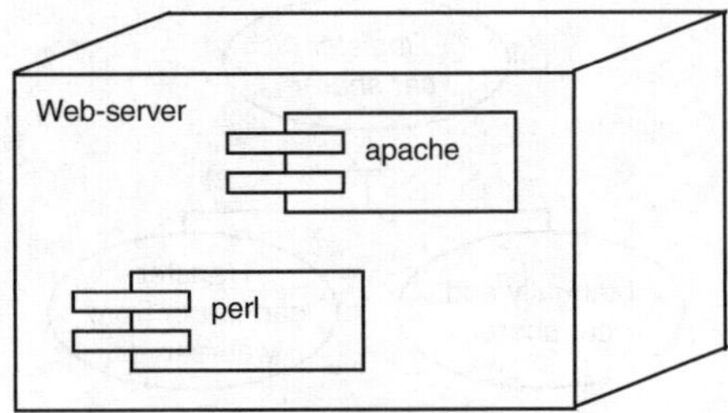

Fig. 14-8: Examples of a deployment diagram as a two-dimensional symbol containing icons

Of course, the symbol that represents the node designated Web Server is a two-dimensional projection of a three-dimensional symbol. Currently UML expects diagrams to be presented in only two dimensions. Until three-dimensional CASE tools become widespread, it is likely that such symbols will stay two-dimensional!

14.2.5 Paths

Paths are used to represent all the many links among other symbols on UML diagrams. A path is made up of line segments for graphical display. It may be possible in a CASE tool to manipulate an individual segment, for example to drag it around on the diagram, but an individual line segment cannot exist without the rest of the path. As mentioned above, paths must always be attached to some symbol at both ends. It is not possible to have a path that is left with a dangling end in a diagram. (They are attached logically, but do not always touch.) Paths may have icons as terminators at the point where they join onto another symbol.

Figure 14-9 shows two paths each of which is made up of three line segments and terminated with an icon that signifies generalization.

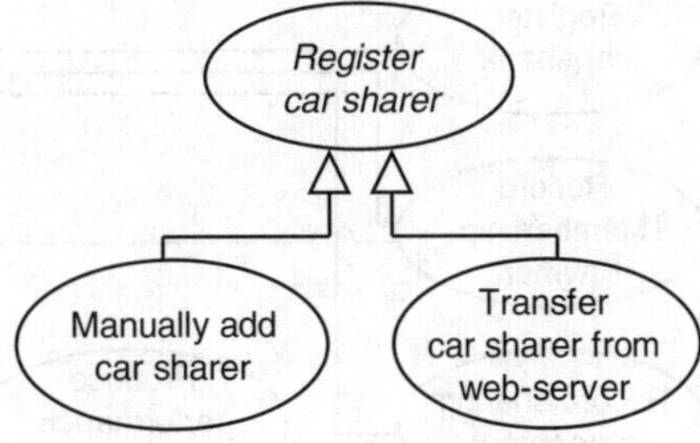

Fig. 14-9: Example of paths made of line segments terminated with icons

Some paths may be combined into branching tree structures as in Figure 14-10. However, the physical appearance of the paths in the diagram hides the fact that these are conceptually still two separate paths.

The choice of how paths are laid out on diagrams is a presentation issue, and may be configurable within a CASE tool. Figure 14-11 shows some possible options. Normally only a single style will be used in a model.

Paths should be drawn to avoid crossing wherever possible, but where crossing line segments cannot be

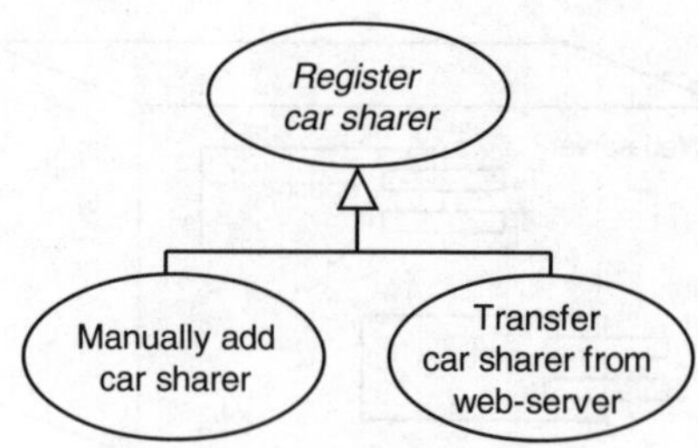

Fig. 14-10: Example of branching paths

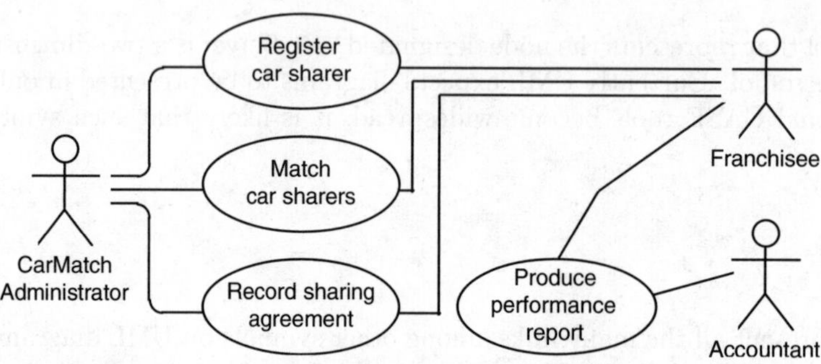

Fig. 14-11: Different path styles

avoided, a small 'jog' can be included, to make it clear that the lines cross but do not join. An example of a jog is shown in Figure 14-12 (although this diagram could be redrawn to eliminate the need for a jog).

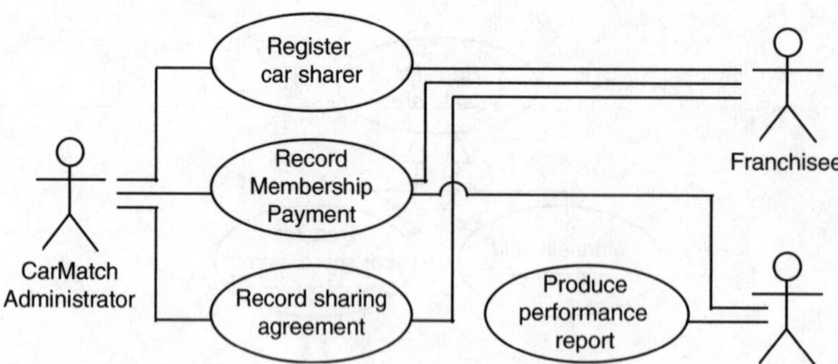

Fig. 14-12: Jog introduced to show where paths cross

14.2.6 Strings

Strings are sequences of characters in a particular character set that are used to display information about the model. The character set that is used need not be limited to Roman characters. UML assumes that the character set is capable of handling multi-byte characters. Eight-bit character sets such as ASCII (American Standard Code for Information Interchange) cannot handle more than 256 distinct character codes, and so cannot represent the full range of characters used by human languages.

Unicode would provide this capability, although it is not singled out as a likely candidate in the UML Specification.

Strings are displayed in UML as text string graphics. Printable characters should be printed directly. Non-printable characters (control codes) are platform-dependent. Strings may be printed out as single lines or as paragraphs with line breaks. The choice of font or typeface can be used to indicate properties of the model. For example, in UML, italic typeface is used to indicate an abstract class name. Figure 14-13 shows the use of different types of string.

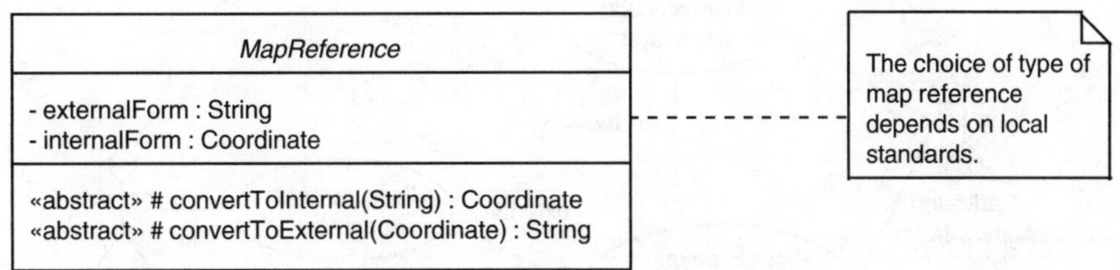

Fig. 14-13: Examples of strings in UML

14.2.7 Names

Strings are used as *names* to identify model elements. Model elements are uniquely identified within a particular scope. The scope may be a system, it may be a package, or it may be a class. For example, different classes may contain attributes or operations with the same name, but they can be distinguished from one another by the name of the class to which they belong. The term *namespace* is used to identify the scope of a name.

Pathnames can be used explicitly to show the scope of a name. In UML, packages are the normal mechanism for defining namespaces (see Chapter 2), and package names can be linked together using pairs of colons as delimiters, for example java::awt::Applet or CarMatch::Insurance::Policy.

14.2.8 Labels

Strings are also used as *labels* on diagram elements. Labels are attached graphically to another symbol on a diagram, either by being contained within or displayed adjacent to them. In a CASE tool, if a symbol is moved, then any label attached to it will move with it. Figure 14-14 shows examples of labels that are contained in and adjacent to other symbols, including the names of two classes qualified by paths.

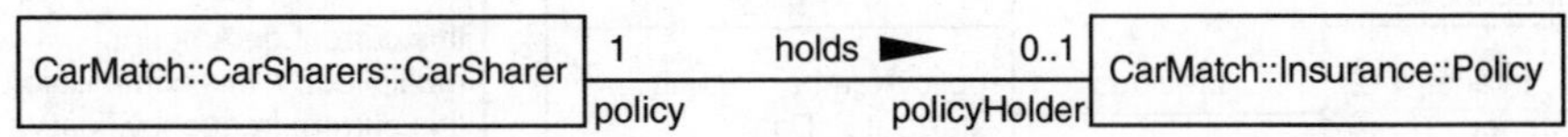

Fig. 14-14: Examples of labels and names in UML

14.2.9 Keywords

Keywords are used in places within UML to distinguish model elements that do not have a distinct visual representation. For example, there are a number of types of dependency in models, all of which are represented by a dashed arrow with an open arrowhead. The use of keywords in guillemets distinguishes these different types of dependency. Figure 14-15 shows two different kinds of relationship in a use case diagram distinguished by the use of keywords.

Appendix A of the UML Specification lists a number of keywords as *standard elements.* These are reserved words within UML and should not be used except for their defined purpose. Other words can be used by modellers as stereotypes to extend the use of UML (see Section 14.3.1).

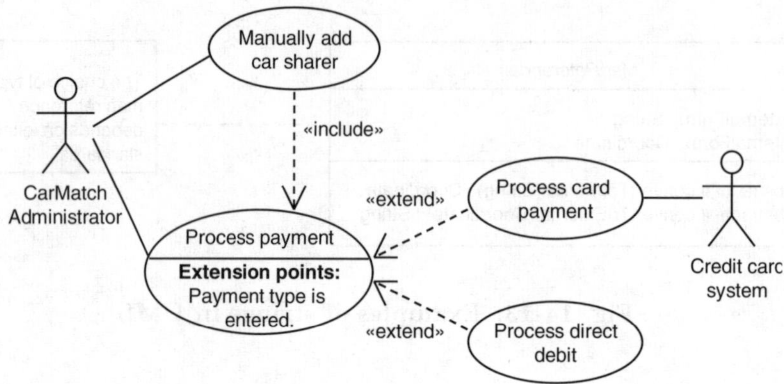

Fig. 14-15: Examples of keywords in UML

14.2.10 Expressions

An *expression* is a string that is displayed in a particular language. It is assumed that the expression can be evaluated appropriately or analyzed to produce a meaningful result. It may be that the expression is in a language that will be used by a case tool to generate code, and will be placed directly into the generated code, it may be in some specification language that will be translated into an expression in the target language, or it may be used by the tool at run-time to simulate some element of the running system.

The choice of language is dependent on the user and the options available in the CASE tool being used. Expressions can be used in the specification of operations, as default values for attributes, as constraints (see Section 14.3.3) or as code fragments in notes (see Section 14.2.11). Figure 14-16 shows examples of some expressions. The note contains a short piece of Java code to calculate the commission for an insurance policy.

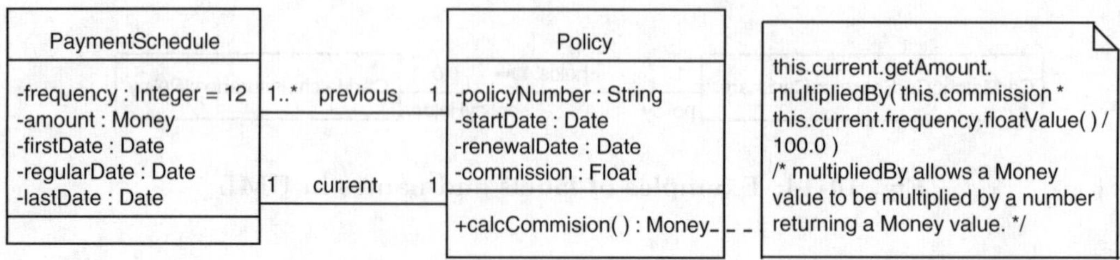

Fig. 14-16: Examples of expressions in UML

Expressions can be defined in Object Constraint Language (OCL), which is explained in detail in

Chapter 12. The specification for OCL is part of the UML Specification. OCL is used particularly for expressing constraints such as pre-conditions and post-conditions for operations.

14.2.11 Notes

Already in this chapter you have seen the use of *notes* in diagrams. A note is a two-dimensional symbol containing a string. The string can be a constraint, a code fragment in some language or a note about the model in natural language. Figures 14-13 and 14-16 show examples of the use of notes in class diagrams. Notes are drawn using a rectangle with a 'turned down' top right-hand corner. They are joined to the thing they are documenting by a dashed line. Note the distinction between the end point of the line in Figure 14-13, where the note describes the class, and Figure 14-16, where the note describes the operation. Strictly speaking, the line should be a dependency arrow (with an open arrow head), but because the dependency is always from the note to the model element, the arrow head can be omitted without loss of information. A note placed on a diagram with no dashed line usually describes the diagram in some way, for example to provide details of the author, the date on which it was produced or the source of information for the model.

14.2.12 Classifiers

Classifiers is a term that we have tried to avoid using in this book, although it is used extensively in the UML Specification, because it is central to the semantics of UML. However, it is so abstract as to make explanations of how UML works more difficult to understand. A classifier is a model element that describes behavioural and structural features of a model. Classifiers include classes, actors, use cases, data types, components, interfaces, signals, nodes and subsystems. In the UML metamodel, classifiers are specializations of both GeneralizableElement and NameSpace which are both specializations of ModelElement. As namespaces, classifiers may have features, such as attributes and operations that are uniquely identified by belonging to their particular classifier. As generalizable elements, classifiers may be further specialized in an inheritance hierarchy; stereotypes (see Section 14.3.1) provide a mechanism for this. The Boundary, Control and Entity Classes of the Unified Software Development Process are stereotyped specializations of Class. Some things that apply in general to classifiers can be applied to all the specializations of classifier. For example, classifiers can participate in associations or own state machines. Classifiers can match to interfaces, so, for example, an actor could be drawn with an interface, although the UML specification is not explicit about the notation, and we cannot decide whether we prefer the 'two-headed actor' or the 'tennis playing actor' in Figure 14-17!

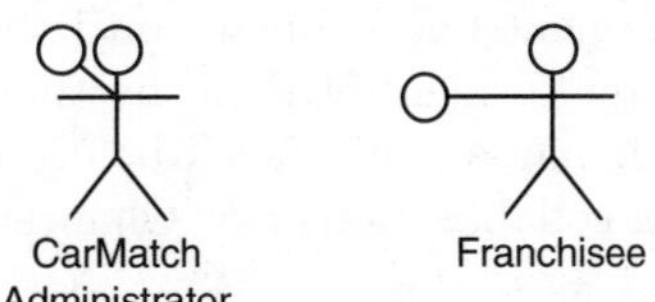

Fig. 14-17: Possible notations for an actor with an interface

Some things are not classifiers. These include collaborations, interactions, relationships and states.

14.2.13 Types, Instances and Roles

Many UML models define general cases that will be instantiated in the working system: classes and objects, attributes and links, and parameters and values. This distinction between types and instances has been explained in most detail in the chapters on objects and classes (see Chapters 4 to 7). In UML diagrams, the distinction is made between types and instances in the following way. Both the type and the instance are drawn using the same geometrical symbol. The name of the instance is underlined. The name of an instance may be just the string that identifies the instance, or that string followed by a colon and the name of the type (if known), or a colon followed by the name of the type (an anonymous instance). These are shown in Figure 14-18. (Note that in Rumbaugh (Rumbaugh et al., 1999) the term ***descriptor*** is used rather than type, which has a more specific meaning as the data type to which instances of a descriptor belong.)

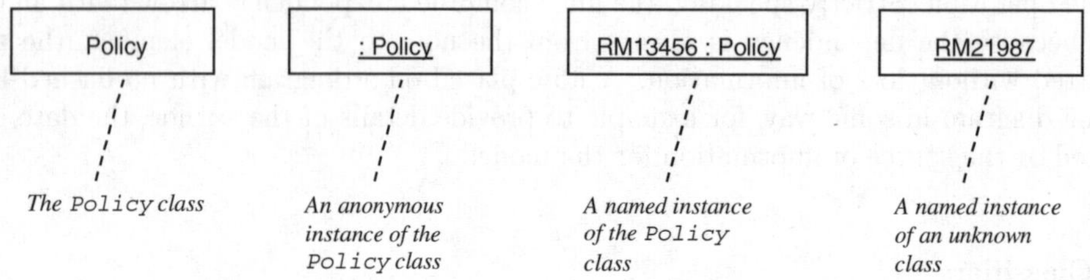

Fig. 14-18: A class and some instances

It is not clear in UML whether the name of the instance is some unique identifier of the instance or equivalent to some kind of attribute or variable name. In the section of the UML Specification on the language architecture, object instances are given names such as <Acme_Software_Share_98789> (for an instance of StockShare), while elsewhere names such as p1 (for a Point) are used and Jill (for a Person). The first of these cases is probably a unique identifier of an object instance. The second case is the name of an attribute within an instance of the class Rectangle, and while it may uniquely identify the point within the namespace of the Rectangle class, there will presumably be a p1 (and a p2) for every instance of Rectangle—r1.p1, r2.p1, r3.p1, etc.—this only defers the question of what is meant by these names. The last case above is clearly not a good name to give to an object instance: it is neither a unique identifier nor necessarily unique within a namespace.

Often anonymous instances are used to avoid having to name the instances. However, there are often situations in which multiple instances of a Class appear, for example in a collaboration diagram. For example, to draw a path in a drawing package an array of anonymous instances of the Point class may be used. To draw the path, a line segment must be drawn from the first point to the second, then from the second to the third, and so on until the last point in the array. In each case, one point plays the role of the start of the line segment and the other the end of the line segment. Then the point in the end role becomes the start of the next line segment until the last point is reached. Rather than naming the instances, it may be better to identify them by these *roles*: start and end. Figure 14-19 shows the notation for roles. The role name is displayed before the classname, separated by a colon, but not underlined. Roles are used in collaborations (see Chapter 8).

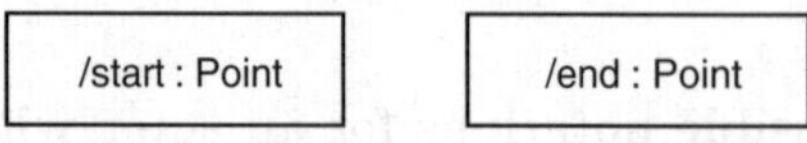

Fig. 14-19: Examples of roles

Role names can be included in instances, indicating that a particular instance takes on a particular role in a collaboration. In this case, the name of the instance is displayed first, separated from the role name by a forward slash, and then the role name is separated from the class name by a colon. Figure 14-20 shows an example of this. An instance may take on more than one role, in which case a list of role names, separated by commas, is included. Because we are dealing here with an instance, the complete name is underlined.

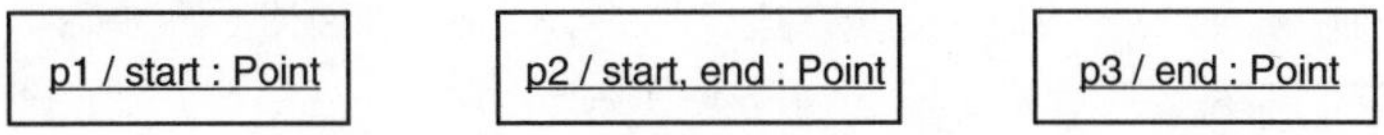

p1 / start : Point   p2 / start, end : Point   p3 / end : Point

Fig. 14-20: Examples of instances in roles

14.3 EXTENSION MECHANISMS IN UML

UML has been designed to be extensible. The aim is to enable developers to create specialized versions of UML for specific kinds of development task. It should be possible to do this without having to invent new or conflicting elements of notation. Three mechanisms exist within UML to support the process of extending it: ***stereotypes***, ***tagged values*** and ***constraints***. Some of the examples that are used here come from the work of Jim Conallen on the use of UML to model web applications (Conallen, 2000).

14.3.1 Stereotypes

A stereotype is a new metamodel class that is introduced in order to model a special kind of class in a system. Stereotypes are used in UML itself, for example the «abstract» stereotype that is used to identify abstract classes in a generalization hierarchy, and the «include» and «extend» stereotypes that are used to distinguish dependencies in use case diagrams.

Stereotypes are most often used as adornments to classes and associations. The name of the stereotype can be displayed above the name of the class or adjacent to the association in guillemets. Alternatively, the stereotype can be represented as an icon. Either this icon can be placed in the top compartment of the class symbol, at the top right, or the class symbol can be 'collapsed' and represented by the icon alone. Figure 14-21 shows these three options for classes using one of the stereotypes from Jim Conallen's web application modelling.

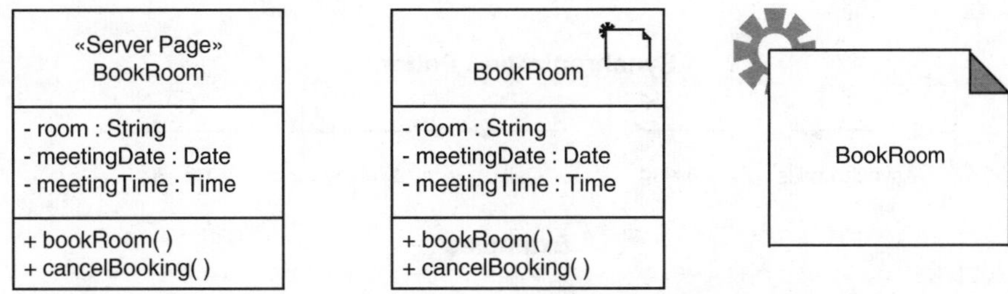

Fig. 14-21: Example of different notations for stereotypes

Conallen's extensions to UML provide the following class stereotypes: «Server Page», «Client Page», «Form», «Frameset» and «Target». These stereotyped classes represent the building blocks of web applications. For example, «Form» is an HTML (HyperText Markup Language) form, and «Server Page» is an HTML page that contains scripts that are executed on the web-server. The icons for «Form» and «Client Page» contain elements that look like HTML forms and web pages respectively, other icons are more abstract in their design. Conallen also stereotypes associations that represent the typical relationships between the elements of a web application, such as «link», «submit», «targeted link» and «build». Figure 14-22 shows some of these.

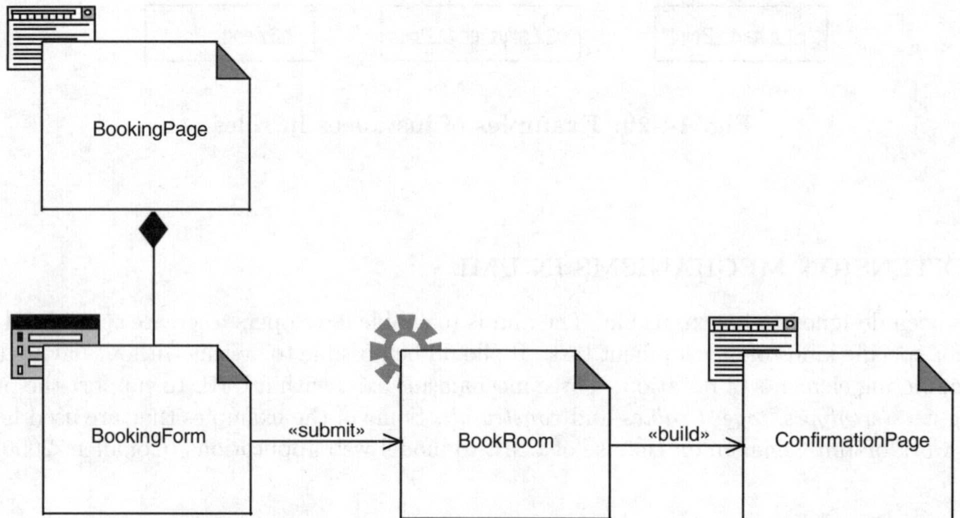

Fig. 14-22: Example of stereotyped associations

Stereotypes can be applied to other model elements. Bruce Powel Douglass' real-time extensions to the UML notation includes stereotypes for messages (Douglass, 1998). There are two kinds of stereotypes: those that relate to the arrival of the messages and those that relate to their synchronization. The two can be combined into single icons, as shown in Figure 14-23.

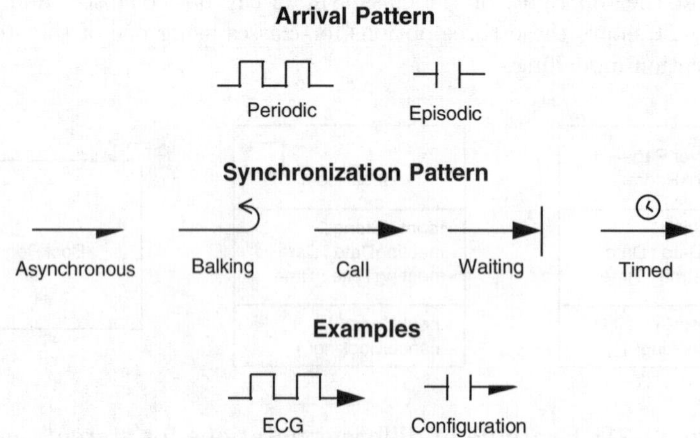

Fig. 14-23: Example of stereotyped messages

The ECG (Electro-Cardiogram) example indicates that a value is obtained at regular intervals by calling an operation of the target object.

14.3.2 Tagged values

Many model elements have properties that cannot be represented visually. These may be predefined values from the metamodel or they may be user-defined values. Tagged values consist of a *tag* or name and the associated value. Tagged values can be represented by strings in braces.

Figure 14-24 shows the use of a tagged value to show the name and value of one of the parameters passed in from the web forms to the server program in a web application, using Conallen's extensions to UML.

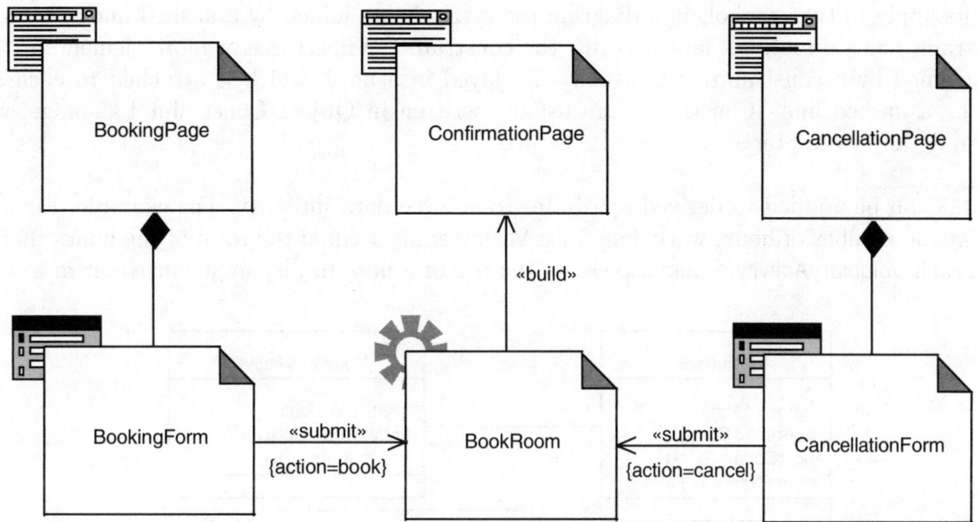

Fig. 14-24: Example of tagged values

If a tagged value has a Boolean value (true or false), then if the default value is true the word 'true' can be omitted: {abstract}. Boolean properties often have the form *{isPropertyName}* where *PropertyName* is the name of the value that may be true or false. The property {abstract} is equivalent to {isAbstract=true}. Tagged values can also be used to provide information about the status of a model, for example {author="Simon Bennett", date=16-July-2000, status=draft}. Multiple values are separated by commas.

14.3.3 Constraints

A constraint defines a relationship between model elements that must be true, otherwise the system described by the model ceases to be valid. Constraints are displayed in curly braces: {subset}. Some constraints are predefined in UML as keywords or standard elements (see Section 14.2.9). For example, the {xor} constraint can be used in class diagrams to show that instances of a class participate in one of two optional associations but not both. (Simply making the multiplicity of the relationships 0..1 does not provide this piece of information.) This is a constraint on the associations and this is shown by joining them together with a dashed line that is labelled with the constraint. Figure 14-25 shows an example of this.

Constraints on classes are usually shown beneath the class symbol. Constraints on attributes or operations are shown as text strings in the appropriate compartment of the class to which they belong. Constraints that apply to a group of attributes or operations can be shown as an entry in the compartment and apply to all succeeding items until another constraint is included or the end of the list. This implies that unconstrained attributes or operations should appear at the start of the list. When

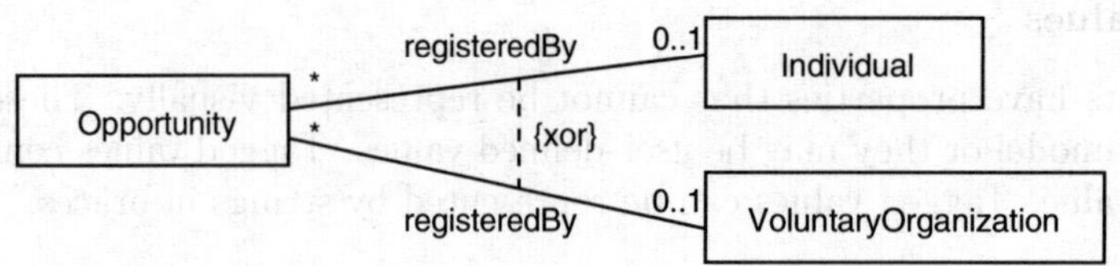

Fig. 14-25: Example of {xor} constraint on associations

constraints apply to two symbols in a diagram the symbols are joined by a dashed line or an arrow (if the constraint has a direction), labelled with the constraint. When three or more elements in a model are constrained by a constraint, it is usually displayed in a note, which is attached to each affected element by a dashed line. Constraints are usually written in Object Constraint Language, which is covered in detail in Chapter 12.

Constraints can be applied to derived attributes to enforce data integrity. For example, Figure 14-26 shows that the number of hours work done by a Volunteer must equal the total of the hours that person spent on each VoluntaryActivity. This also shows the use of a note to display a constraint in a diagram.

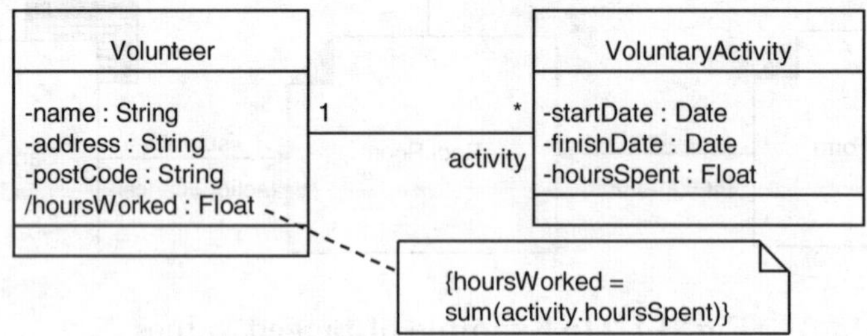

Fig. 14-26: Example of a constraint on a derived attribute

Constraints are the last of the mechanisms that can be used to extend the UML notation. Many constraints are implicit in stereotyped classes. For example, the stereotyped classes of the Unified Software Development Process shown in Figure 14-5 have implicit constraints: boundary classes are constrained to handle the interface between the system and the user, while entity classes are constrained not to participate in the user interface.

Constraints can be applied to models other than class diagrams. For example, constraints are used in sequence diagrams to show timing constraints between events (see Chapter 9).

Review Questions

14.1 What are the two elements of graphs?

14.2 Give three examples of diagrams in UML that are graphs.

14.3 What are the three kinds of visual relationships between elements in graphs in UML?

14.4 (a) What are the elements of graphs in UML?
(b) Explain what is meant be each of these elements.
(c) Give an example of each.

14.5 What is the difference between a name and a label in UML?

14.6 How are keywords shown on UML diagrams?

14.7 Give two examples of keywords from different UML models.

14.8 How are notes shown on UML diagrams?

14.9 Define what is meant by a classifier in UML.

14.10 Give three examples of model elements that are classifiers in UML.

14.11 Give three examples of model elements that are not classifiers in UML.

14.12 What is the notation for each of the following?

(a) the name of a class
(b) the name of an anonymous instance of a class
(c) the name of a named instance of a class
(d) the name of a named instance of an unknown class
(e) the name of a role
(f) the name of an named instance in a role

14.13 Define what is meant by a stereotype.

14.14 How are stereotypes used to extend the UML notation?

14.15 Describe the three ways in which stereotyped classes can be represented in a diagram.

14.16 Give an example of a stereotyped class.

14.17 Give an example of a stereotype of another kind of model element.

14.18 Define what is meant by a tagged value.

14.19 How are tagged values displayed in a diagram?

14.20 Define what is meant by a constraint.

14.21 How are constraints displayed in a diagram?

14.22 Give an example of a constraint.

14.23 What is the name of the language often used to represent constraints?

Solved Problems

14.1 We want to extend UML to cover applications developed to use Wireless Access Protocol (WAP) and Wireless Markup Language (WML). These two standards are used to deliver Internet content to wireless devices such as mobile telephones and personal digital assistants (PDAs). Here is a summary of how WML works.

WML uses the metaphor of decks of cards. An application is typically made up of a single deck. Each deck consists of a number of cards; each card displays a screen-full of information on the screen of the mobile device. The whole deck is transferred onto the mobile device, and the user then moves between cards. This saves the delay associated with loading pages. The content of decks is transferred to the mobile device using a binary format to minimize the bandwidth required (GSM telephones transfer data at 9,600 baud).

What stereotyped classes and associations might be created to extend UML to cover these elements of WAP?

The Application is probably the first class. This seems to involve server-side and client-side pages, but we know only about the client-side. An Application «delivers» a Deck to the mobile device and the Deck consists of Cards. The user can move to the «next» Card or to the «previous» Card.

Using stereotype strings displayed with the class name, we might develop something like Figure 14-27 for a hypothetical deck of cards containing static content about CarMatch. (You might like to try to devise suitable icons.)

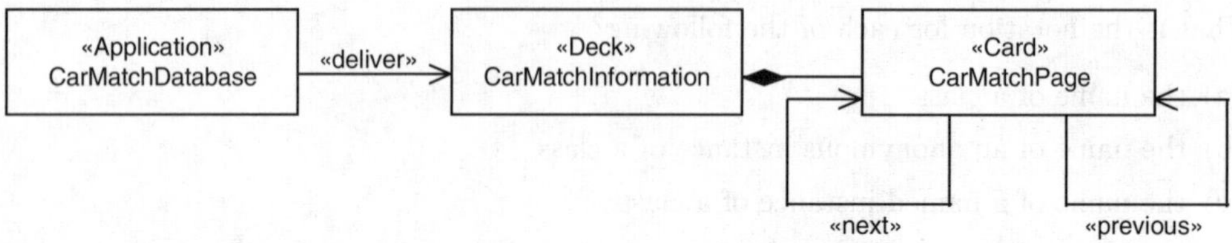

Fig. 14-27: Possible solution for WAP/WML extensions to UML

14.2 Different mobile devices, telephones and PDAs, have different sized screens and navigational techniques. The browser on a mobile device is known as the user-agent and transfers information about the device it is running on to the server, so that appropriately formatted cards are sent to the mobile device.

We have not included the user-agent or device as classes in Figure 14-27, but what tagged values might be sent from the client to the server to ensure that correctly formatted WML pages are delivered?

We might want two tagged values, one for the user-agent and one for the device. This assumes that the server keeps some database of devices and their characteristics. Alternatively, it might be necessary to transmit those characteristics. Here are examples of two possibilities.

{device="MyPDA Z99", useragent="Mobile Browser 1.21"}

{width=640, height=240, colour=false, greyscale=true, shades=16, navigation="touchscreen"}

14.3 The user moves through a set of cards in a deck from start to finish. It is possible to move forwards through the deck unless the card displayed is the last in the deck. Similarly, it is possible to move backwards through the deck until the first card is reached.

What constraints might be applied to the «next» and «previous» associations defined above?

The obvious constraint is that the user can only move forwards to the end or move back to the beginning of the deck. Moving to the end does not result in looping back to the beginning. This could be represented by two constraints, one each on the next and previous associations. These are shown in Figure 14-28.

Supplementary Problems

14.4 Draw a class PDA that is stereotyped as «device» and a class WAP Explorer that is stereotyped as «user-agent».

14.5 Design your own icons to represent the stereotyped classes «device» and «user-agent».

14.6 Draw a class diagram to show a stereotyped association, «runs», between the classes PDA and WAP Explorer.

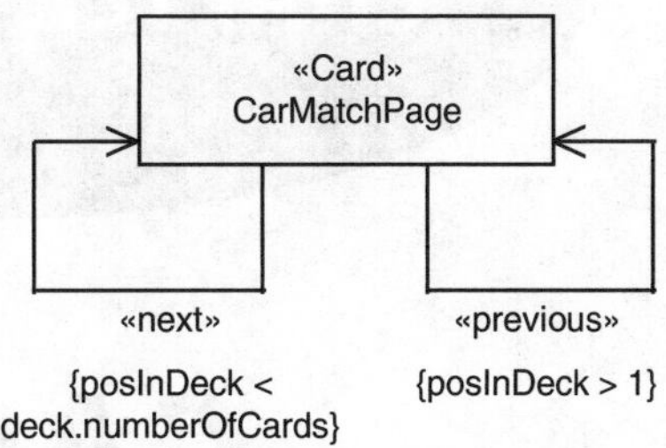

Fig. 14-28: Possible constraints on associations

14.7 The application WAP Explorer runs only on the PDAOS operating system. Add a constraint to the «runs» association in your solution to the previous problem to show this.

14.8 Enterprise Information Portals (EIPs) are becoming widespread as a way of delivering a range of different types of information to employees of an organization.

Typically a portal application runs on a server. It delivers web pages to the client. The user must log in to the portal, sending their username and password to the application. Having logged in they are presented with a number of pages. They can move to any page by clicking on its number in a list of pages. Each page is made up of panes. Panes are small windows within the page presenting different kinds of information (for example, a calendar, a notice board, a search engine, a table of stock prices). If the user does not interact with the portal for a specified period of time, they are logged out, and the next time they attempt to change anything on the portal it will take them to the login page.

Suggest some stereotyped classes and associations that you could use to extend UML to model portals.

14.9 What tagged values might be needed in this particular extension of UML?

14.10 What constraints might apply to a «moveTo» association between pages?

CHAPTER 15

CASE Tools

15.1 INTRODUCTION

The production of software models for any substantial system is a time-consuming task, and almost universally requires the use of computer-based tools, known as CASE tools. CASE stands for Computer Assisted Software Engineering (or sometimes Computer Aided Software Engineering or Computer Aided Systems Engineering). CASE tools aim to automate as far as possible the software engineering process. Pressman (2000) characterizes a good workshop for the production of any artifact, be it a car, a piece of furniture or a computer program, as having three parts: there is a set of tools to aid the building of the product; there is an organized layout to enable the tools to be applied effectively; and finally there is a skilled team of craftspeople who know how to apply the tools. CASE supplies the tools for the various craftspeople in a software engineering process. The term CASE is very generic and covers the broad range of software engineering activities, of which modelling and the use of UML (or other modelling notations) are only a part. This chapter will look at some of the key characteristics of UML-based software modelling CASE tools, and how these relate to other tools used in the development of substantial software systems.

The modelling of a system is part of the much broader aspect of the construction of a system. Computer system development is a people-intensive activity. All but the smallest projects require co-operation among a wide number of stakeholders, including the sponsors and customers of the proposed system, the potential users, project managers, analysts, developers, testers, technical deployment teams, and finally the actual users themselves. An essential factor in effective development is good communication. Comprehensive and consistent use of an integrated suite of CASE tools to support the various work products of a software engineering process is an important facilitator of good communication.

UML is a key enabler of the communication within a project, providing integration between CASE tools through technical interchange of software models, and supplying a standard presentation of models to the many people involved in a project. In the process of development, there may be a number of CASE tools involved, from project inception through to project delivery, covering business analysis, requirements analysis, project management, through software modelling to implementation, testing and deployment. Software modelling CASE tools can integrate with each other and with a variety of other tools, such as planning and testing tools. For the purposes of this chapter we shall concentrate on CASE tools that specifically incorporate UML, and that are focussed on the generation and management of software models.

An appropriate CASE tool can assist you in drawing the various UML diagrams, and usually much more. Different tools have different foci and different ways of achieving results, and often incorporate additional, non-UML notations; increasingly though, because of the development of the UML standard, there is growing commonality in the presentation and content of the software modelling aspects of many tools. Switching between modelling tools is more straightforward if they each comply with the UML standard. One of the key goals of UML has been to reduce the amount of wasted time and effort necessary to switch between notations when developers move between projects, or when projects need to change tools.

CASE tools contribute to model development in a variety of ways. Firstly they aid in the construction of accurate UML diagrams, and provide checks to make sure that the diagrams are complete and consistent with each other. A good CASE tool will organize UML elements in a repository that keeps objects, activities, states, relationships, diagrams and so on grouped together. The various diagrams represent different views of the underlying repository that supplies the storage of the model elements and their linkages. The development process often produces many documents other than UML diagrams, such as use case descriptions, and a CASE tool should be able to integrate these into the repository. As all but the most trivial projects involve a number of people co-operating, the repository needs to be able to cope with people sharing different elements, and either allow shared access to the repository with some means of protecting against conflict, or some means of merging and reconciling repositories. The end result of any development project is a system, and CASE tools offer a variety of means of generating program code, or importing program code, and even the generation of test plans.

It would be very foolish today to embark on a substantial IT development without incorporating a comprehensive set of computer-based tools, including a software modelling CASE tool, to facilitate the project. Of course, use of IT tools does not ensure an effective development. Management and maturity of the organization are critical too. Jacobson et al. (1992) discuss organizations at different levels of maturity. At the initial level, no documented method is in place, and developers are working in their own, often quite diverse, ways. At the second level, an informal method is widely adopted. At the third level a formal method is in place. At the fourth level, there is close management tracking of the application of the method and the productivity of the development process. At the highest level, systematic changes are made to the method to optimize it for the organization. A modelling CASE tool may be used at any of these levels of organization, but is likely to be most effective at the third level and above. As with any craft, good tools do not ensure success, but they are very important in helping the craftspersons achieve a good product efficiently and effectively.

15.2 UML AND CASE TOOLS

UML has a number of primary goals that relate to the use of CASE tools. It is a notation that allows for the specification of systems independently of the chosen programming language. It is designed to be extensible, so that other modelling features can be integrated into UML models. It is intended to encourage the growth of the object tools market, and to support higher-level development concepts such as frameworks and patterns.

Programming-language independence is essential, partly because languages are textual and there is a great need for a visual representation of a system, partly because systems are commonly built from a number of components implemented in different languages. However, there is a strong correspondence between object-oriented languages and UML. A language-independent description of the system is important for many stakeholders in a project, while linkage between UML and the programming language is extremely valuable in the construction phase. CASE tools can support this linkage through automatic generation of program code and reverse engineering of programs to construct UML models.

Extensibility is a core aspect of UML, through tagged values and stereotypes (see Section 14.3). This is important because UML cannot possibly cover all possible aspects of software modelling and remain concise enough to be manageable. CASE tools need to support extensibility and also depend on this for implementing many aspects of the software development process such as the embedding of documentation, integrating programming code into the models, and linkage to other tools.

UML has enhanced the object tools market by shifting the area of competition away from notation. CASE tools add value to the software development process over and above providing a modelling notation, by enforcing methods and by integrating with other tools and with programming languages; it is in these areas that UML-based CASE tools compete rather than in the notation itself. The use of UML makes it easier for developers to move between projects using different tools, and between different tools in the same project.

15.3 FEATURES OF CASE TOOLS

15.3.1 UML Diagrams

A good CASE tool will provide a means of drawing the majority of the UML diagrams, and certainly the core diagrams such as use case, sequence, statechart and class diagrams. A CASE tool will generally only allow legal diagrams, and can do some elementary checking of consistency, say by preventing cycles of inheritance, or highlighting potential name conflicts. This is particularly important when a number of people are working on a system and consistency between parallel development of the models is essential.

The construction of diagrams is usually a drawing activity, supplemented by entry of detailed information on UML elements through forms. For example, a typical tool will allow the drawing of a class by clicking on a class icon and placing the icon on a background. Completion of details such as attributes will involve typing into a form the name of the attribute and choosing the type from a list. Pre-built elements can be incorporated on diagrams by dragging and dropping from the repository or choosing from pick-lists. Diagrams and the repository are complementary views of UML elements such as classes and use cases, and CASE tools can provide different ways of managing these elements.

UML has emerged from a number of earlier notations, and many CASE tools have evolved from these notations. At the time of writing, many tools still incorporate elements of an earlier notation (such as Booch or OMT), either as an alternative or alongside the UML notation. This is partly to support projects that started before UML was defined or became widely adopted, and partly because the construction of CASE tools is a large-scale undertaking itself and the vendors of these packages may still be in the process of catching up. There are also other notations, such as business process modelling, that UML does not fully cover, and these may be incorporated alongside UML in a CASE tool.

15.3.2 Compliance to UML Standards

UML is a standard, and CASE tools should state the extent to which they comply with the standard. The UML specification provides a number of compliance points, including the diagrams (use case, class, statechart, activity, sequence, collaboration, component, and deployment), UML profiles (software development process, and business modelling), and OCL. Each of these can be rated as 'no/incomplete' or 'complete'. There are other elements of compliance from the UML metamodel that we shall not consider here—these ensure that the semantics of the model elements used to compose the diagrams are standard. Compliance with a diagram implies being able to support all the associated adornments (such as stereotypes, tagged values and constraints).

To declare accurately that a CASE tool is compliant to the UML specification, the vendor should refer to the language elements and the compliance points, rather than simply state that they are "UML compliant". CASE tools need not comply with the whole of the UML specification, but partial compliance will significantly reduce the interchangeability of models. Care is advised in the selection of CASE tools, and due consideration is needed to make sure where possible that vendor-independence is maintained in the application of tools to prevent projects from becoming subject to the whims or problems of suppliers.

15.3.3 The Repository

The repository in a CASE tool holds all the UML elements, such as objects, attributes, operations, activities, states and relationships, as well as the diagrams themselves. UML diagrams are in fact only views of the repository. It is common to produce many different views of the repository with an element or set of elements repeated in different diagrams. For example, it is often useful to construct a class diagram for a use case to describe object collaborations in the use case; as a class usually supports more than one use case, the class may appear in multiple diagrams.

The repository is usually organized in a hierarchical way, much as the file store in an operating system is organized, and browsers are supplied to view the hierarchy. Figure 15-1 illustrates a possible organization of a repository. The repository is split into requirements, analysis, design and implementation models. Each high level model is then broken down into packages, and under the packages are the UML elements and diagrams that constitute that model. The repository will be substantial, typically holding hundreds or thousands of elements even for a small project, and the view of the repository will allow opening and closing of parts of the hierarchy to zoom in and out of aspects of the project. The package concept of UML is particularly important for structuring the view of the repository.

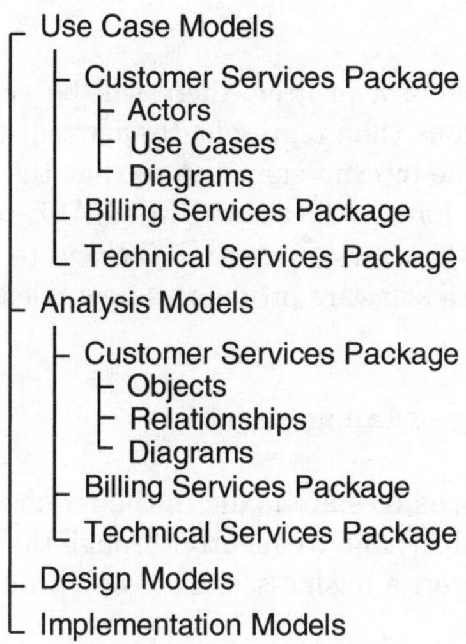

Fig. 15-1: A typical repository structure in a CASE tool

The repository in some CASE tools can also incorporate non-UML elements. Commonly, other documents, such as word processing documents, can be linked into the repository and accessed through the repository. Linkage may be made out to other CASE tools, such as those supporting requirements analysis. Some CASE tools also incorporate links from the repository to programming language source code.

15.3.4 Shared Access to the Repository

For any but the most trivial project, the development of UML models will require a number of people to develop models simultaneously. There are two basic approaches to this. The first is to allow people to have separate copies of the repository, and to merge those repositories periodically, checking for mutual consistency. The second and much better approach is to provide a single shared repository, with analysts and developers checking out parts of the repository they are working on. Variants of these are commonly used.

If a single repository is used, then team members are allowed, subject to privileges, to check out elements of the repository. While these are checked out, other team members may not update them, but they are usually allowed to read a write-locked version that has been checked out. Once a person has checked out a set of elements, he or she is allowed to merge them back into the repository, overwriting the versions that were checked out, and release them for others to view and update. A middle-ground option that can be used is to break a large repository into subrepositories. These subrepositories are then checked out, modified, merged back and checked in.

15.3.5 Integrity of the Repository

A key role of the repository is to validate entries and maintain integrity. Changes to a model element may have an impact across a number of other model elements. For example, removing an operation from a class may affect the collaborations represented by (for example) a sequence diagram. A CASE tool will adopt a variety of tactics to ensure that consistency and integrity are maintained, from preventing illegal changes, through warnings, to consistency checks initiated by the user.

15.3.6 Version Control

At critical milestones in the lifetime of a project, there will be versions of the software models that need to be stored as baseline versions that represent the current state of the project. This may be for a release of the products, or some interim snapshot so that the project can be rolled back if there are problems with the development for some reason. UML CASE tools need either to support version control directly, or to integrate with a version control package to manage this. Version control will continue throughout the lifetime of a software product as new releases are issued.

15.3.7 Traceability and Change Management

During the lifecycle of any project, changes are made to the requirements. This may take place before the initial delivery of a software product, and frequently through the life of the product as improvements or adjustments are necessary to support a business. Changes to product specifications have implications for models.

As changes are requested, it is necessary to trace through all aspects of the system that are affected by the change, and protect those that are not affected. A large part of the requirements might be held outside a UML compliant CASE tool, for example in text documents. The notion of use case is the key linkage between the analysis models and user requirements. The grouping of classes through collaborations to support a use case makes it possible to trace through from a requirement to the use case that supports the requirement. From the use case it is possible to trace the classes that support the design to realize the use case, and ultimately the classes used to implement the design.

CASE tools assist in this by integrating with requirements capture and programming tools, and by structuring the repository in ways that support traceability (say by grouping collaboration diagrams with the use cases they support). The issue of traceability is project-wide, not just related to models, and requires careful application of a method, such as the Unified Process. CASE tools and UML are facilitators in this process.

15.3.8 Tagged Values

UML supports tagged values that may be attached to any model element (see Section 14.3.2). This is a simple mechanism for attaching information that goes beyond the basic semantics of UML. It is a pair, usually represented as {tag=value}, where tag is a name that indicates the property and value is some value expressible as a string. CASE tools use tagged values for a variety of purposes. Commonly there is a tag for documentation of the model element, allowing the storage of a textual description of (for example) classes and use cases. Some CASE tools support tags for recording the primary and alternative paths in use cases, thereby embedding the use case descriptions in the repository. Tagged values are sometimes used to structure model elements such as use cases and operations, by allowing pre-conditions and post-conditions to be attached. Linkages to code can be embedded to provide tighter integration between the modelling CASE tool and the programming environment.

15.3.9 Icons

We have seen the standard icons defined by UML, such as for an actor. UML allows the attachment of an icon to a stereotype. All objects with that stereotype may then, optionally, be displayed with the icon. Figure 15-2 shows a worker stereotype from the UML profile for business modelling displayed both as an icon and in the standard class notation with the stereotype name in guillemets. CASE tools are free to add extensions of this type to provide improved visual descriptions of models.

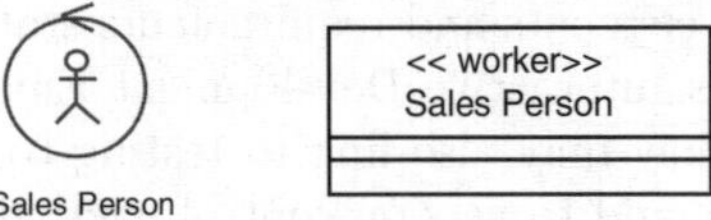

Fig. 15-2: A worker stereotype from the UML business modelling profile in iconic and standard notation

15.3.10 Code Generation

To improve the speed and accuracy of programming, many CASE tools offer code generation of programs and database schemas. At the simplest level, this involves the generation of classes in the programming language syntax, for the programmer to complete, and database table definitions. Some CASE tools also provide generation of the logic code from models such as sequence diagrams. Currently the degree of integration between CASE tools and programming environments varies considerably. At one end, the CASE tool can be treated as a programming environment itself. At the other, the CASE tool is only a way of bootstrapping the development of the code.

CASE tools can also import programs and database schemas and construct a UML repository from them. The amount of information that can be imported is again very variable, being dependent on the CASE tool and the programming language. At the very least, a set of classes can usually be generated, with operations and attributes defined.

Most CASE tools offer some notion of *round trip engineering*. This means that some of the program code can be generated from the CASE tool and modified in the programming environment. Then the modified program can be imported and any changes made in the programming environment are reflected in the CASE tool repository. This is a very valuable facility, as it provides a means of keeping the implementation, the analysis and the design models in step, and thereby maintaining traceability.

15.3.11 Model Interchangeability between CASE Tools and Other Tools

UML models can be described in a standard textual language, known as XMI, which is an acronym for XML Metadata Interchange. XML stands for Extensible Markup Language, which is an international standard for the description of documents. CASE tools commonly have the facility to produce an XMI version of the models they contain, and to import XMI models.

This means that CASE tools supporting XMI can exchange models. There are many good reasons for this. Some CASE tools are tightly integrated with a particular development environment, and XMI allows for the import of UML models developed elsewhere. Increasingly, large systems are built by integrating subsystems that may be developed in different languages by different suppliers, and access to the various models used to develop the subsystems is essential. XMI permits the choice of the best tool for a particular task, with minimal cost in translation.

15.3.12 Relationship between Modelling CASE Tools and Other Tools

CASE tools support only certain parts of a project, and UML is designed to cover specifically the modelling aspects of the system development. CASE tools usually link to other tools. At the simplest level, word processor documents can be linked into the models to support requirements capture and documentation of aspects of modelling not necessarily supported by UML CASE tools, such as textual descriptions of use cases. Requirements analysis tools exist that can be linked into CASE tools to provide traceability between model elements and requirements statements. CASE tools are commonly linked to development tools such as Interactive Development Environments (IDEs) that support the development of executable code. They may also link to testing tools for the generation, tracking and (sometimes) execution of test plans, and to version control packages to support versioning of systems. UML and the XMI interchange format are a key element in facilitating these linkages.

15.3.13 Method Support and Enforcement

UML is a notation, not a method. Most tools aim to support a particular software development method. This may be based on the Unified Process, perhaps with a proprietary slant, or some other method. Method support is provided in a number of ways. At the elementary level, the tool will incorporate guidance in the form of help text and supporting documentation. Repositories can be structured according to the rules of the method—some tools permit you to re-arrange the structure of the repository to adapt it to different methods. In some cases the CASE tool may enforce the rules of a particular method.

15.3.14 Frameworks

A framework is a reusable design that can be adapted to support and enhance the development of systems and to supply a generic structure to systems developed by an organization. Alongside design patterns, they aid in the standardization and optimization of approaches to software development. A variety of types of framework exist. There are technical frameworks, such as the classes in the Java Development Kit, that provide predefined classes and components for a variety of programming tasks. There are application frameworks such as that developed by the IBM San Francisco project, that focus on the development of generic classes and components for business systems (accounting systems, etc). There are development-oriented frameworks that structure the repository according to some development method such as the Unified Process. Some CASE tools permit the incorporation and definition of frameworks, represented as a set of predefined models available at the start of a project.

15.3.15 OCL

At the time of writing, OCL is often partially integrated into CASE tools for the definition of constraints. Full integration with generation of code to check pre-conditions is not yet achieved. CASE tools usually allow constraints to be expressed in any textual form, as intended by the UML specification.

15.3.16 Document Generation

UML models are of value to a wide number of stakeholders in a project. For example, end-users may wish to see use case models in the requirements capture phase. CASE tools support the production of paper-based documentation, merging UML diagrams with text and tabular descriptions of model elements. Some tools permit the generation of web-based views of their repositories, so that access to the models can be made widely available over an intranet to people without access to the CASE tool.

Review Questions

15.1 What does CASE stand for?

15.2 Is CASE just for UML?

15.3 In what way does UML support CASE tools?

15.4 What is XMI?

15.5 What is a repository in a CASE tool?

15.6 What is a tagged value?

15.7 Why are tagged values important?

15.8 What is *round trip engineering*?

Solved Problems

15.1 The project manager for the CarMatch system development wishes to choose a suite of CASE tools, including a modelling tool that supports UML. He has two months in which to select the suite of tools. Knowing that the market is unlikely to provide the perfect tool he commissions a consultant to run a tendering process for the supply of CASE tools. What might be the key questions that the consultant incorporates in the tender document regarding the software modelling tools?

The consultant provides a general section requesting information on prices, technical platforms and requirements, the supplier's track record, market penetration, turnover and profitability, plus a request for reference sites. She then adds the following specific questions relating to the software modelling CASE tools.

1. How closely does the tool comply to the UML standard? Specifically rate the compliance of the tool to the diagrams: use case, class, statechart, activity, sequence, collaboration, component, and deployment.
2. How is shared access to the repository managed?
3. How are repositories merged?
4. How is integrity of the repository managed?
5. How is version control of the repository contents managed?
6. What other CASE tools does this tool integrate with?
7. How is traceability from requirements through to implementation supported?
8. What notations other than UML are supported by the tool?
9. For which programming languages does the tool support code generation, reverse engineering or both?
10. Is XMI supported?
11. What methods are supported by the tool?
12. What support is there for document generation, including web-based documentation?

Supplementary Problems

15.2 The VolBank project manager has not supplied an adequate budget for CASE tools to support the development of the system. Supply a one-page memo that argues for the use of a CASE tool for software modelling. Highlight the benefits of using a software modelling CASE tool that supports UML, and the risks involved in not using a CASE tool.

Design Patterns

16.1 INTRODUCTION

Patterns are not a part of core UML, but are widely used in object-oriented system design, and UML provides mechanisms that can be used to represent patterns in graphical form. For these two reasons, we have included this short chapter about design patterns.

A *design pattern* is a solution to a common problem in the design of computer systems. It is a solution that has been recognized as worth documenting so that other developers can apply it to solve the same problem when they come up against it. In the same way as object-oriented analysis and design claims to promote reuse of class libraries and components, the use of patterns is claimed to promote the reuse of standard solutions to frequently-occurring design problems.

Patterns are discovered not invented: they are techniques that people have used for some time to solve particular problems, and which have been recognized as good solutions; they are not clever tricks that someone has just invented to solve a problem and then decided to promote to other developers.

An example of a pattern was given in Chapter 8 (see Figure 8-12). The Façade pattern is widely used in systems where the developers want to hide the complexity of a subsystem behind a single class, which provides an interface to its functionality. This is a common problem in system design. If a subsystem contains a lot of classes that collaborate together to provide the services of that subsystem, there is a risk of creating a complex interface to that subsystem. Every class might have several operations, and other subsystems will need to be capable of sending messages to instances of each class. This creates a high degree of *coupling* between the subsystems: changes to the classes in the subsystem providing the services will result in a lot of work tracking down all the places in other subsystems where the operations of all these classes are called.

One way of simplifying this situation is to create a façade class, which provides a single interface into the subsystem and co-ordinates the actions of the instances in the subsystem. In this way, changes to the implementation of classes in the subsystem will have a limited impact on other subsystems: it may be possible to limit the changes to the subsystem itself, as the messages to changed classes (within the subsystem) will come from the façade class; otherwise, tracking down the effect of changes is made easier, as it is necessary only to find the points in other subsystems where messages are sent to instances of the façade class—one class instead of many.

The Façade pattern is just one of many patterns that have been documented by experienced developers. Before giving further examples and explaining how they can be represented in UML, we shall first explain their origin.

16.2 ORIGIN OF DESIGN PATTERNS

The idea of using patterns comes from architecture. Alexander, Ishikawa, Silverstein, Jacobson, Fiksdahl-King & Angel (1977) first proposed the idea of using standard patterns in the design of buildings and communities. They identified and documented related patterns that could be used to solve recurring problems in the design of buildings. These patterns are ways of designing buildings that have evolved over hundreds of years as solutions to the problems faced by people constructing buildings of all sorts. The best solutions have come through to the present day by a process of natural selection. These patterns have authority—as good solutions—without being the work of any one individual. Although software development does not have the same history as architecture, patterns have been found that represent good solutions to the problems of constructing software systems.

Evitts (2000) provides a summary history of the way that patterns infiltrated the world of software development. (His book is about patterns that can be used in UML rather than UML representations of more general patterns.) He credits Kent Beck and Ward Cunningham with the development of the first patterns in their work with Smalltalk reported at the OOPSLA'87 conference. These were five patterns found by Beck and Cunningham in conjunction with the users of a system that they were designing. These five patterns applied to the design of user interfaces in a windowing environment.

During the early 1990s patterns were discussed at conference workshops, and many attempts were made to draw up lists of patterns and to document them. The participants were driven by the need to provide some kind of structure at a higher conceptual level than objects and classes that could be used to organize classes. This was the result of a recognition that the use of object-oriented techniques alone was not delivering the claimed improvements in quality and effectiveness of software development. Patterns were seen as a way of organizing object-oriented development and encapsulating experience and good practice.

In 1994 the first Pattern Languages of Program Design (PLoP) conference was held. Also that year, *Design Patterns: Elements of Reusable Object-Oriented Software* (Gamma, Johnson, Helm & Vlissides, 1995) (sic) was published in time for OOPSLA'94. This was the seminal text in the emergence of patterns for software development; its contribution was to structure patterns into a *catalogue* with a standard format that was used to document each pattern. It is known as the *Gang of Four* book, and its patterns are often referred to as the Gang of Four patterns. Other books on patterns appeared in the following couple of years, and other 'standard' formats were proposed.

The first patterns were exclusively design patterns, intended to solve problems facing designers. Since then other kinds of pattern have emerged, notably analysis patterns, which represent concepts that are used in domain modelling, and organization patterns, which propose solutions to the common problems of managing business processes, including software development.

Frameworks and *idioms* are related to patterns, but should be distinguished from them. A framework is more comprehensive than a pattern and is essentially a partially completed application that can be applied to a specific domain. For example, a financial framework would contain a set of financial classes in relationships determined by patterns, and could be developed to produce a financial application. (In

UML, *framework* has a specific meaning and is defined as either a stereotyped package that contains mainly patterns or an architectural pattern that provides an extensible template for applications in a specific domain.) An idiom is a set of guidelines for how to implement aspects of a software system in a particular language. Coplien (1992) first published a set of idioms for use in C++. These idioms captured the experience of expert C++ programmers in a way that could be used by inexpert programmers facing common problems in writing C++ programs.

16.3 DOCUMENTING PATTERNS

Patterns are grouped together in *pattern catalogues* and *pattern languages.* A pattern catalogue is a group of related patterns that can be used either together or separately. A pattern language documents patterns that work together and can be applied to solving problems in a particular domain.

Patterns are documented using templates, which provide headings under which to enter details of the pattern and how it works that will enable users to decide whether it is an appropriate solution to their problem and, if it is, to apply it to that problem. There are different templates available; two of the most widely used are Coplien's and Gamma's (Gamma et al., 1995). The headings listed below are from Coplien's template.

- *Name*—The name of the pattern, ideally describing the solution in some way.
- *Problem*—The question that the pattern helps to resolve.
- *Context*—The context of the application of the pattern: architectural or business context and the critical success factors for the pattern that will make it work in a particular situation.
- *Forces*—The constraints or issues that must be resolved by the pattern. The forces create an imbalance, which the pattern helps to balance.
- *Solution*—The solution that balances the conflicting forces and fits the context.
- *Sketch*—Symbolic sketch of the forces and how they are resolved.
- *Resulting context*—The context as it is after being changed by the solution.
- *Rationale*—The reason and motivation for the pattern.

Documentation of patterns can include sample code and diagrams. UML diagrams can be used to illustrate the way that each pattern works. The choice of diagram type depends on the nature of the pattern. Design patterns have been classified as *creational*, *structural* and *behavioural.*

- *Creational*—Concerned with the creation of object instances, separating the way in which this is done from the application.
- *Structural*—Concerned with the structural relationships between instances, particularly using generalization, aggregation and composition.
- *Behavioural*—Concerned with the assignment of the responsibility for providing functionality among the objects in the system.

For structural patterns, class diagrams are more likely to provide the necessary information about the pattern; for behavioural patterns, interaction diagrams or statechart diagrams will illustrate the way that the functionality will be delivered; for creational patterns, the choice of diagram will depend on the nature of the pattern (whether it is more about behaviour or structure).

However, the UML Specification (Object Management Group, 1999*a*) specifically proposes template collaborations as the way to model patterns, and these are explained in the next section.

16.4 HOW PATTERNS ARE REPRESENTED IN UML

One of the goals of UML is 'to support higher-level development concepts such as components, collaborations, frameworks and patterns' (Object Management Group, 1999*a*, p.1-5). The intention is to support these concepts by providing a mechanism for clearly defining their semantics, so that it is easier to use them to gain the benefits of reuse that are claimed for object-oriented methods. The structural aspects of patterns are presented in UML using template collaborations (see Section 8.4).

A template collaboration is represented by a dashed ellipse with a dashed rectangle overlaying its top right-hand quadrant, as in Figure 16-1.

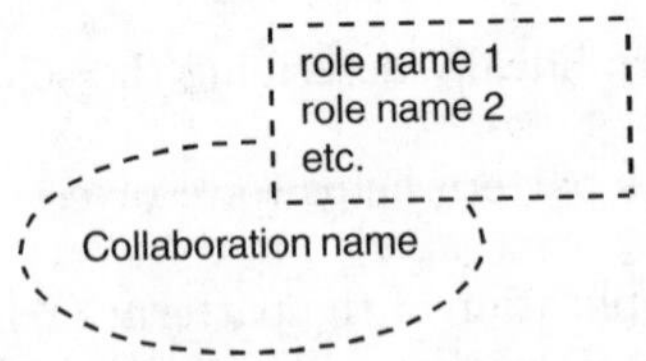

Fig. 16-1: Template collaboration notation

The names of the roles played by participating classes are written in the dashed rectangle as in Figure 16-2.

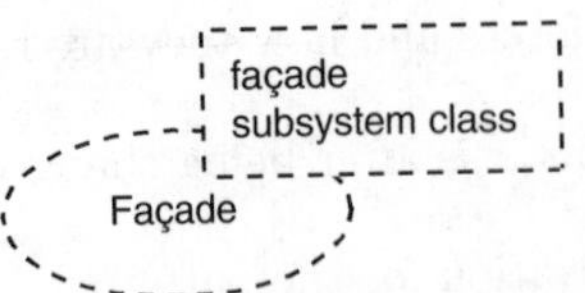

Fig. 16-2: The class roles involved in the Façade pattern

This notation can also be used to show the actual classes that are bound to the roles, as in Figure 16-3.

The template collaboration shows only the participating roles and classes that fill those roles. In order to show the structure of the collaboration, we need to draw a class diagram for the participating classes. This can be done in terms of the class roles, as in Figure 16-4, which is a rather simple diagram, because there are only two roles in this pattern. Note the navigability of the association.

When a pattern is applied to a particular problem in the design of a system, the structural relationships among the classes that participate in the collaboration can be shown in a class diagram. In the CarMatch system, there is a requirement to match insurance policies to members based on three sets of characteristics of the members: age, home address and occupation. One way of hiding the complexity

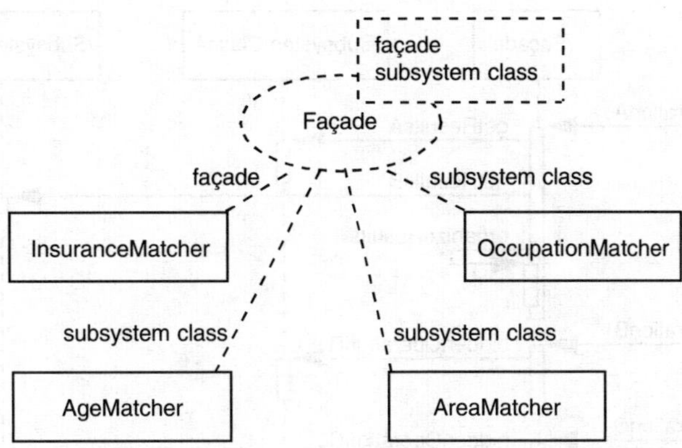

Fig. 16-3: Example of a collaboration to document the use of the Façade pattern

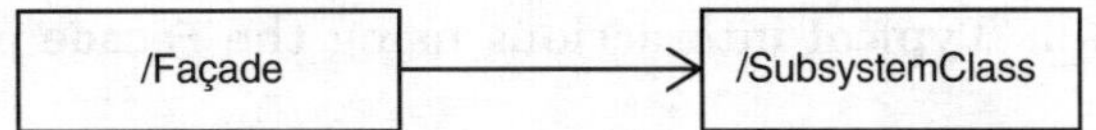

Fig. 16-4: The roles played by classes in the Façade pattern

of the different classes that implement these three kinds of matching process is to create a façade class, in this case InsuranceMatcher, to provide a single interface to client objects, as in Figure 16-5.

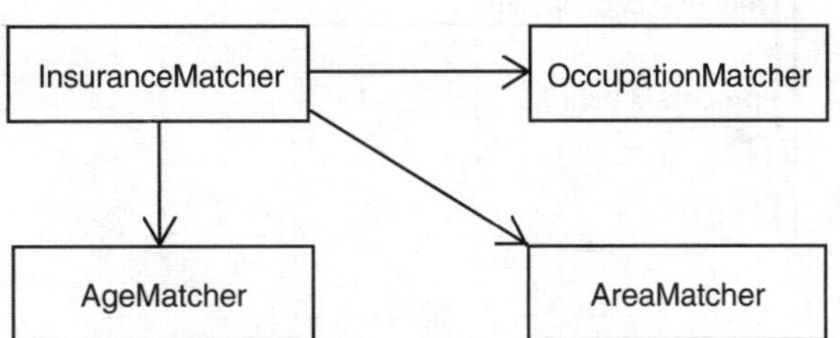

Fig. 16-5: The InsuranceMatcher example of the Façade pattern

The interaction involved in a pattern can be modelled with an interaction diagram. Figure 16-6 shows three typical patterns of interaction that can be provided by the use of the Façade design pattern. In the first case (operationA), the façade class invokes operations of the subsystem classes to obtain some results and then organizes the results before passing them back to the client. In the second case (operationB), the façade class simply hides the operation that is invoked from the client. In the third case (operationC), the façade class again hides the operation that is invoked, but the operation involves interaction between roles in the subsystem.

In the case of the InsuranceMatcher example, the interaction is likely to be of the first type: the InsuranceMatcher receives a request from another object, despatches requests to each of the subsystem classes in turn, processes the results and returns a single result to the client, as in Figure 16-7.

Other non-structural aspects of patterns are recorded in text or in tables using a template like the Coplien template described in Section 16.3.

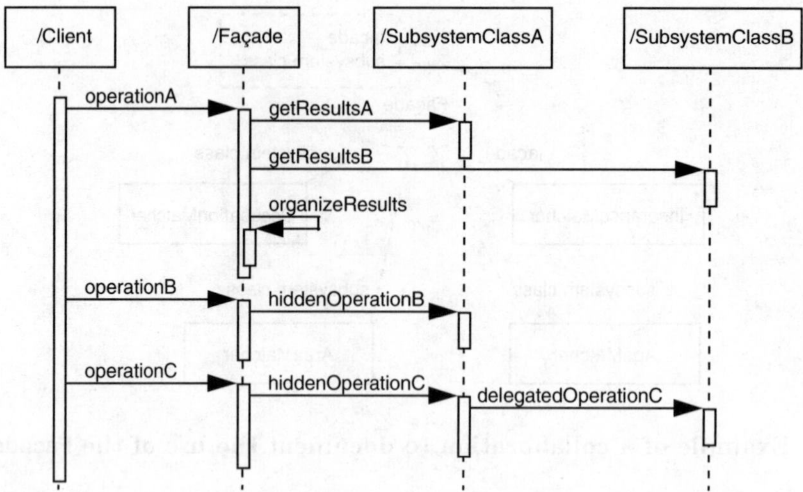

Fig. 16-6: Typical interactions using the Façade pattern

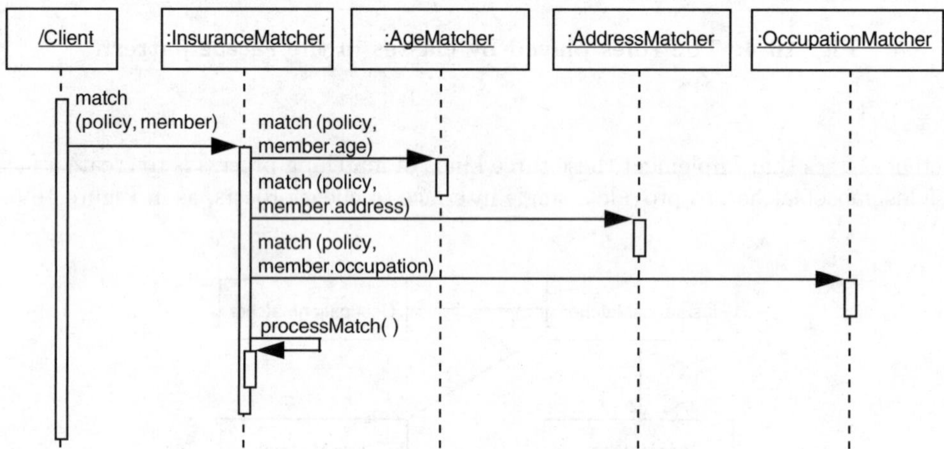

Fig. 16-7: Sequence diagram for the Façade pattern

16.5 APPLICATION OF PATTERNS

Patterns are applied at different stages in the development of systems. Organizational patterns can be used in planning a project; analysis patterns can be used in structuring the domain model; architectural patterns can be applied in determining the overall architecture of the system; design patterns can be used to design the relationships and interactions among design classes. Our focus here is on design patterns.

Patterns are intended to allow novice developers to make use of the accumulated experience of experts who have developed systems in the past and from whose work examples of good practice and effective solutions have been collected as patterns. However, in order to use these patterns, the novice developer needs to have at least some knowledge of what they are and the kinds of problems that they solve. Faced with a problem in the development of a system, it is not easy to find a pattern from scratch. In this section, we shall examine one design problem in the CarMatch system and propose a solution to this problem based on patterns.

EXAMPLE 16.1 In each CarMatch franchise office there will be a computer system that is used to run the business of that franchise. There is a need to hold local information about the franchise, such as the address and perhaps a company registration number. So the class diagram should include a CarMatchOffice class as in Figure 16-8. Unless the intention is to build a distributed system connecting all the franchise offices (which it is not), there should only ever be one instance of this class in any one system. How can we ensure that only one instance is ever created?

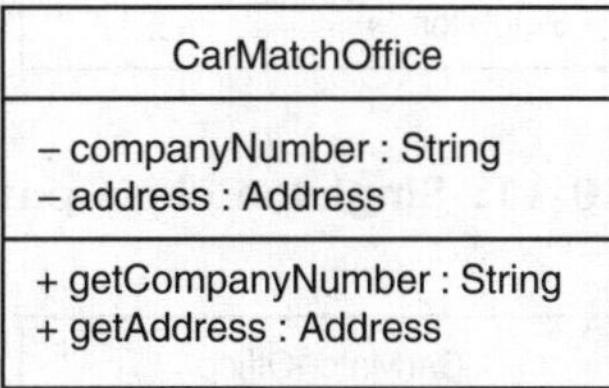

Fig. 16-8: CarMatchOffice class

One approach to this problem is not to create any instances but to use the class itself and to make all the attributes and operations into class-scope attributes and operations as in Figure 16-9. This approach was illustrated in Section 7.4.

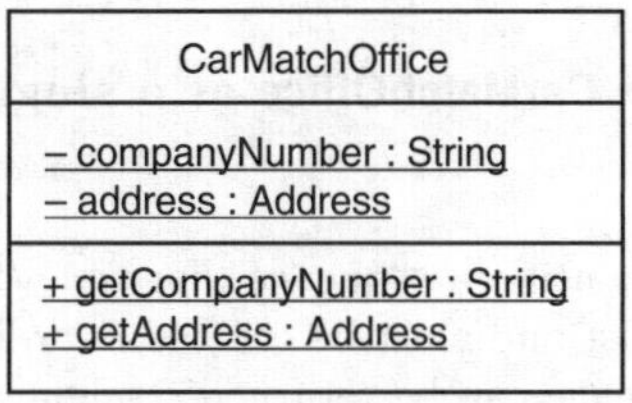

CarMatchOffice
– companyNumber : String
– address : Address
+ getCompanyNumber : String
+ getAddress : Address

Fig. 16-9: CarMatchOffice class with class-scope attributes and operations

This approach has shortcomings, as we may later want to subclass the class, and class operations cannot be redefined by subclasses in some languages. So, we may decide to create an object instance, but ensure that only one is ever created. The Singleton pattern is a way of doing this. The Singleton can be applied as a solution to the problem *How can a class be constructed that should have only one instance and that can be accessed globally within the application?* This is a creational pattern.

In the Singleton pattern, a class-scope operation getInstance() is added to the class definition. This operation returns a reference to a single instance of the class or creates that single instance if it does not already exist. The reference to the instance is held as a class-scope attribute within the class. To prevent other objects calling the constructor of the singleton class directly, the constructor is made private.

The Singleton pattern is very simple, involving only one class, so it is hardly worth drawing the template collaboration of Figure 16-10.

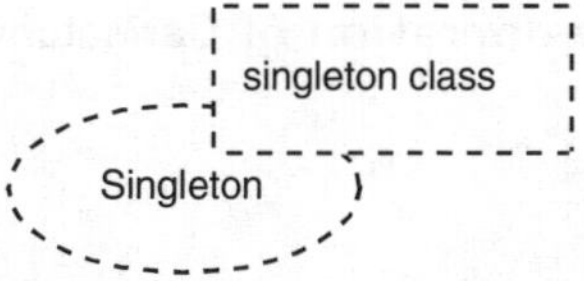

Fig. 16-10: Template collaboration for the Singleton pattern

A singleton class will look something like the example in Figure 16-11.

This pattern can be applied to the CarMatchOffice class, and the result is shown in Figure 16-12.

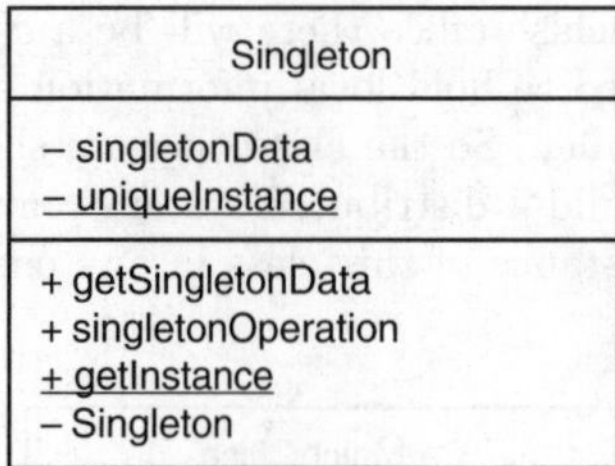

Fig. 16-11: Singleton class pattern

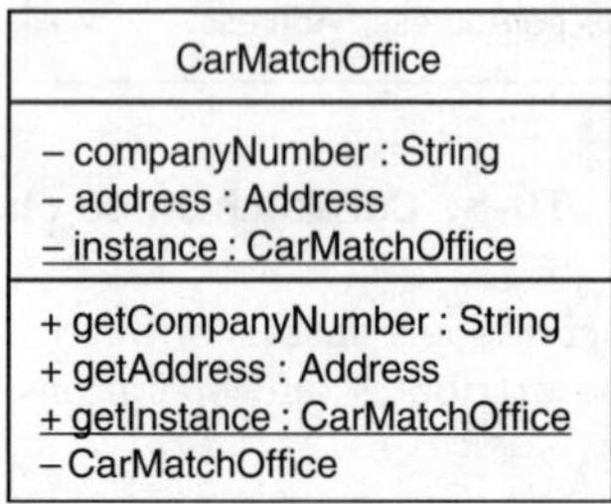

Fig. 16-12: CarMatchOffice as a singleton class

We can model the getInstance() operation using a sequence diagram. There are two possible scenarios: in the first, the unique instance does not yet exist and must be created in order for a reference to it to be returned; in the second, it already exists, and a reference can be returned straight away. The client object can then invoke an operation on the instance. This is shown in Figures 16-13 and 16-14. Note the distinction between the class CarMatchOffice and the instance :CarMatchOffice.

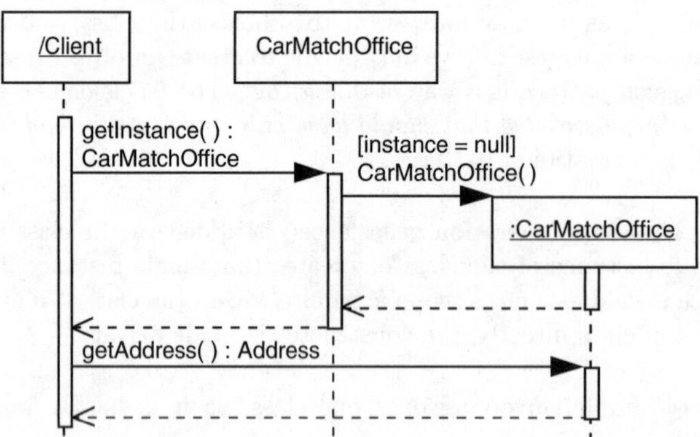

Fig. 16-13: The getInstance operation of CarMatchOffice creating an instance

16.6 HOW TO USE PATTERNS

Patterns are not always the answer to every problem in the design of a system. However, they can provide significant benefits by shortcutting the process of finding solutions to design problems in complex systems. If you plan to use patterns in a project, it is important that members of the team receive appropriate training before you even begin to consider individual patterns as design solutions.

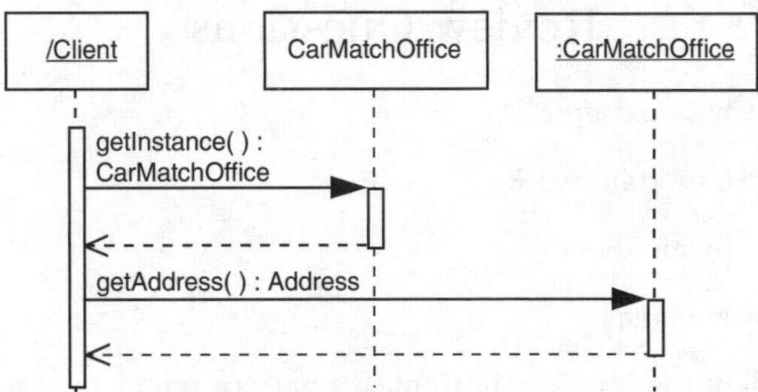

Fig. 16-14: The getInstance operation of CarMatchOffice returning an existing instance

When you face a problem in the design of a system, the following points should be considered.

- Does a pattern exist that addresses this or a similar problem?
- Does the documentation for this pattern suggest any other solutions that may be more acceptable?
- Is there a simpler solution? (Do not use patterns just for the sake of it.)
- Is the context of the pattern consistent with the context of the problem?
- Are the results of using the pattern acceptable?
- Are there constraints imposed by the software being used that would conflict with the use of the pattern?

Gamma et al. (1995) suggest seven steps in the application of a pattern in order to ensure that it is used successfully.

1. Read the pattern to get a complete overview.
2. Study the structure, participants and collaborations of the pattern in detail.
3. Examine the sample code to see an example of the pattern in use.
4. Choose names for the pattern's participants (i.e. classes) that are meaningful to the application.
5. Define the classes.
6. Choose application-specific names for the operations.
7. Implement operations that perform the responsibilities and collaborations in the pattern.

Patterns can be very helpful, but should not be applied without careful thought. They bring the benefit of reusing the experience of other developers and examples of good practice that have shown themselves to be widely applicable. They also provide a language for discussing architectural and design issues at an abstract level.

However, the use of patterns can result in over-design of simple systems, making them more complex than they need to be. Some patterns may have performance implications for the system, and should not be used without weighing up their advantages and disadvantages in the same way as is done with any other design decision.

Review Questions

16.1 Define what is meant by a pattern.

16.2 Define what is meant by a framework.

16.3 Define what is meant by an idiom.

16.4 How are patterns documented?

16.5 List and explain each of the headings in Coplien's pattern template.

16.6 What three different types of design pattern are there?

16.7 Explain what is meant by each of the types of pattern that you have listed in answer to the previous question.

16.8 What is the notation for a template collaboration?

16.9 What four UML diagram types could you use to model a pattern?

16.10 List the steps that Gamma et al. (1995) suggest should be carried out to check that a pattern is appropriate.

Supplementary Problems

16.1 Find out about other design patterns (by reading a book or researching on the Internet). Consider which patterns could be applied to the CarMatch and VolBank case studies.

16.2 Choose a design pattern from those about which you have read. Draw UML diagrams to model the structure and behaviour of this pattern.

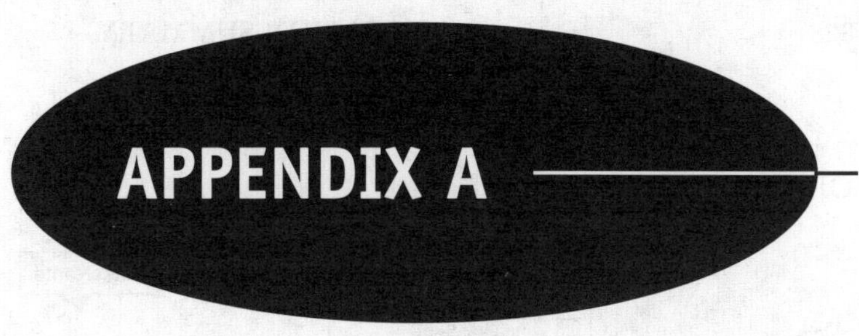

APPENDIX A

Notation Summary

USE CASE DIAGRAM

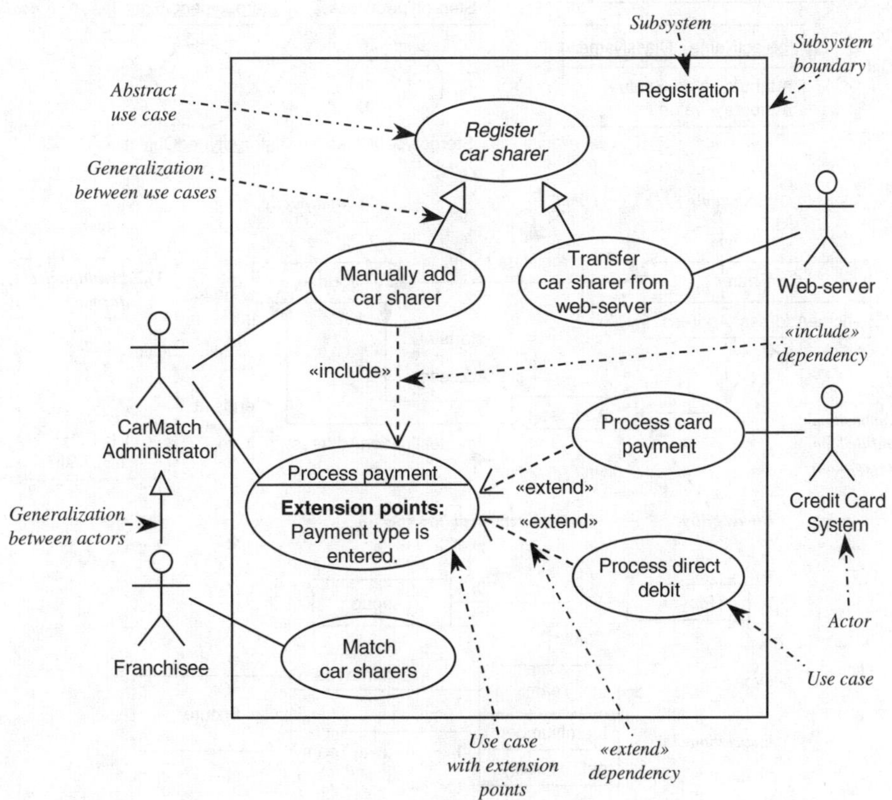

CLASS DIAGRAM

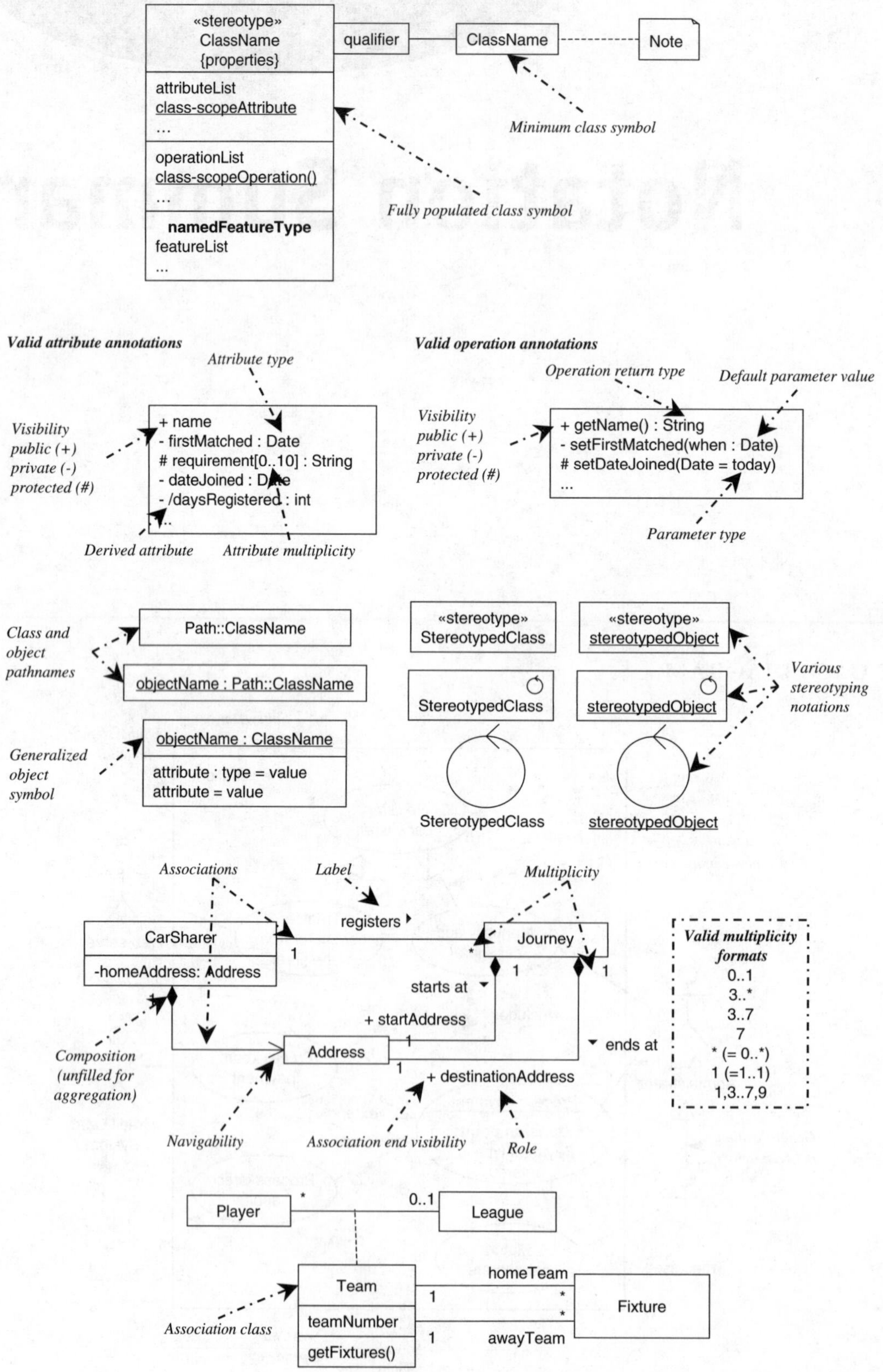

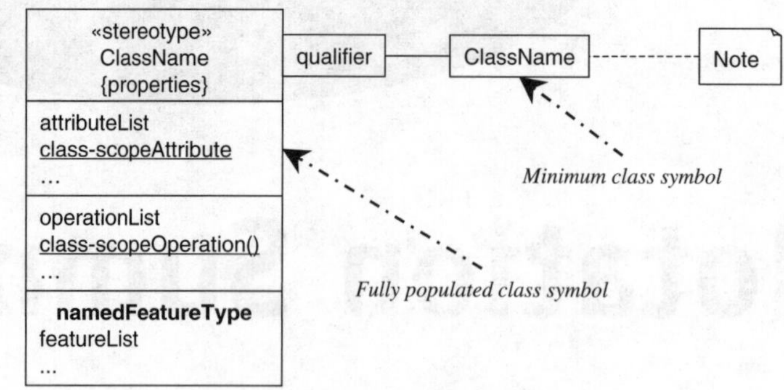

Valid attribute annotations

Attribute type

Visibility
public (+)
private (-)
protected (#)

+ name
- firstMatched : Date
requirement[0..10] : String
- dateJoined : Date
- /daysRegistered : int
...

Derived attribute
Attribute multiplicity

Valid operation annotations

Operation return type
Default parameter value

Visibility
public (+)
private (-)
protected (#)

+ getName() : String
- setFirstMatched(when : Date)
setDateJoined(Date = today)
...

Parameter type

Class and object pathnames

Path::ClassName
objectName : Path::ClassName

Generalized object symbol

objectName : ClassName
attribute : type = value
attribute = value

«stereotype»
StereotypedClass
«stereotype»
stereotypedObject
StereotypedClass
stereotypedObject
StereotypedClass
stereotypedObject

Various stereotyping notations

Associations
Label
Multiplicity

registers ▸
CarSharer
-homeAddress: Address
Journey
1
*
1
1
starts at ▾
+ startAddress
1
Address
1
▾ ends at
+ destinationAddress

Composition (unfilled for aggregation)
Navigability
Association end visibility
Role

Valid multiplicity formats
0..1
3..*
3..7
7
* (= 0..*)
1 (=1..1)
1,3..7,9

Player
*
0..1
League
Team
teamNumber
getFixtures()
homeTeam
1
*
*
1
awayTeam
Fixture

Association class

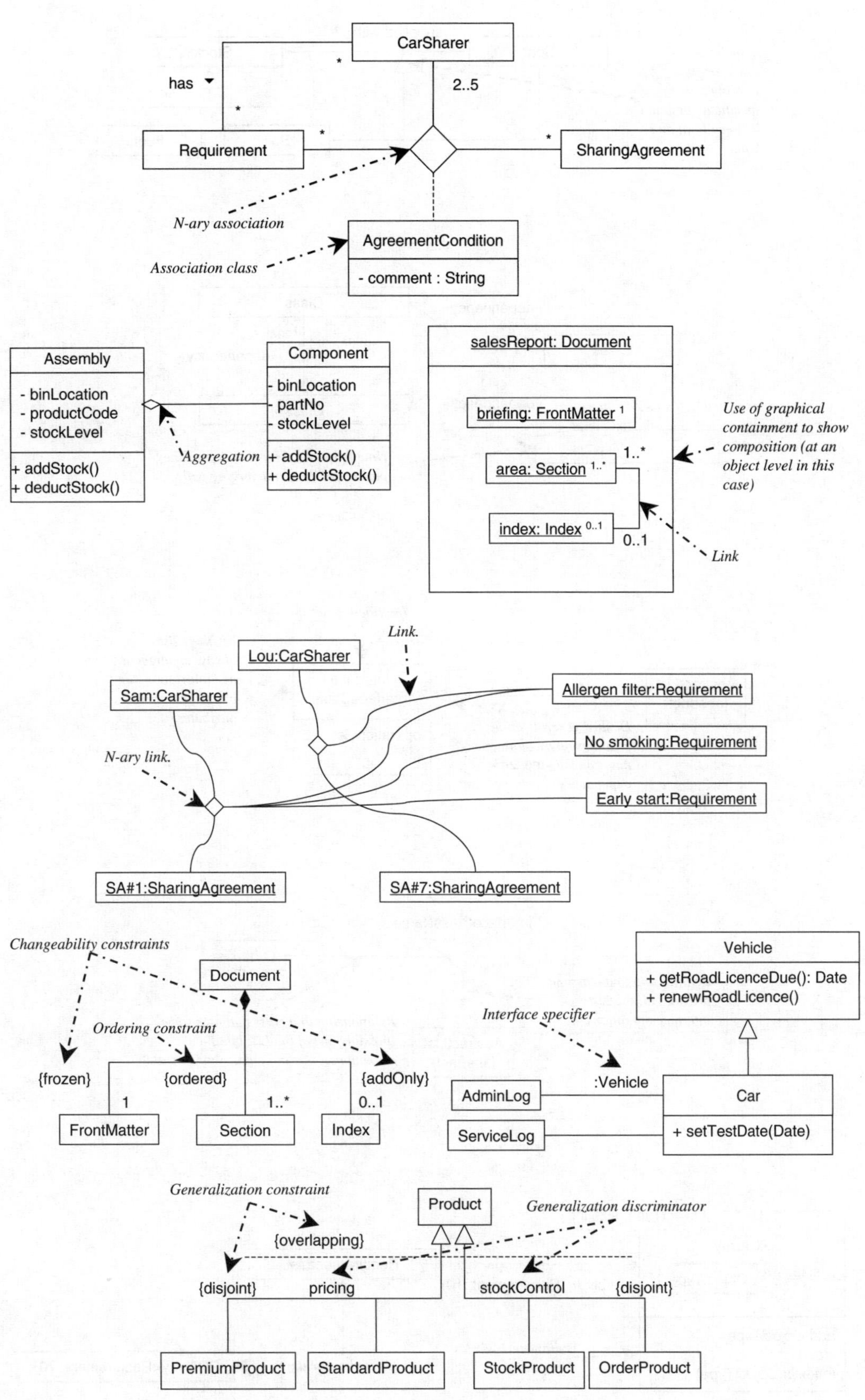
CarSharer
has
2..5
Requirement
SharingAgreement
N-ary association
AgreementCondition
Association class
- comment : String
Assembly
- binLocation
- productCode
- stockLevel
+ addStock()
+ deductStock()
Component
- binLocation
- partNo
- stockLevel
+ addStock()
+ deductStock()
Aggregation
salesReport: Document
briefing: FrontMatter 1
area: Section 1..*
index: Index 0..1
1..*
0..1
Use of graphical containment to show composition (at an object level in this case)
Link
Link.
Lou:CarSharer
Sam:CarSharer
Allergen filter:Requirement
No smoking:Requirement
Early start:Requirement
N-ary link.
SA#1:SharingAgreement
SA#7:SharingAgreement
Changeability constraints
Document
Ordering constraint
{frozen}
{ordered}
{addOnly}
1
1..*
0..1
FrontMatter
Section
Index
Vehicle
+ getRoadLicenceDue(): Date
+ renewRoadLicence()
Interface specifier
:Vehicle
AdminLog
ServiceLog
Car
+ setTestDate(Date)
Generalization constraint
Product
Generalization discriminator
{overlapping}
{disjoint}
pricing
stockControl
{disjoint}
PremiumProduct
StandardProduct
StockProduct
OrderProduct

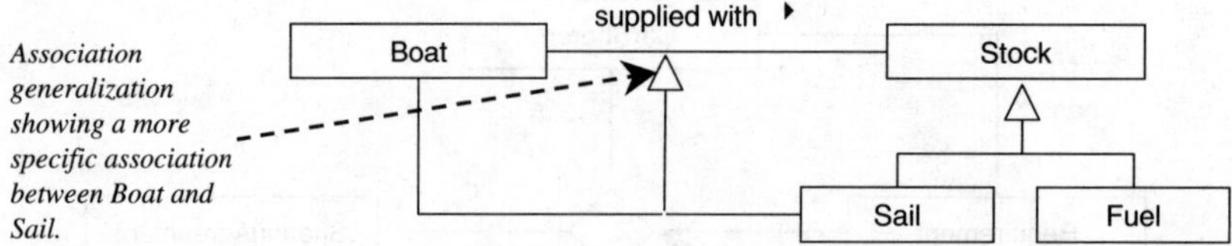
supplied with
Boat
Stock
Association generalization showing a more specific association between Boat and Sail.
Sail
Fuel

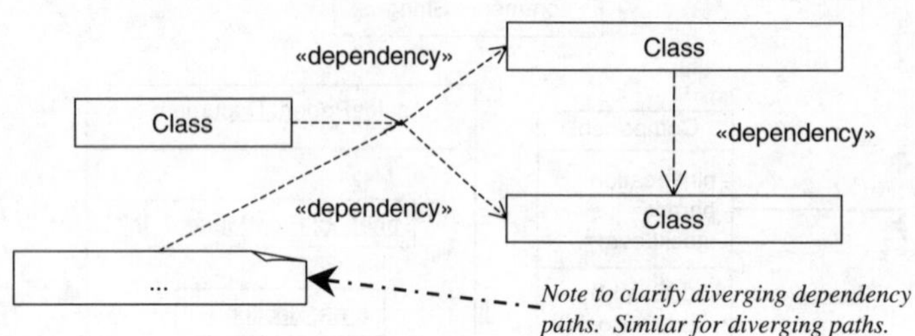
«dependency»
Class
Class
«dependency»
«dependency»
Class
...
Note to clarify diverging dependency paths. Similar for diverging paths.

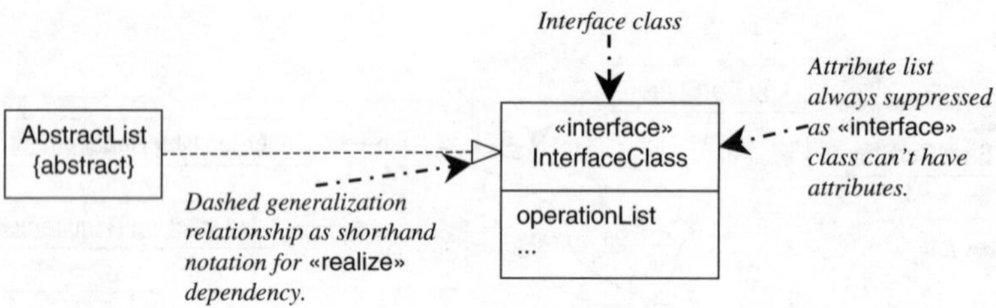
Interface class
Attribute list always suppressed as «interface» class can't have attributes.
AbstractList {abstract}
«interface» InterfaceClass
operationList
...
Dashed generalization relationship as shorthand notation for «realize» dependency.

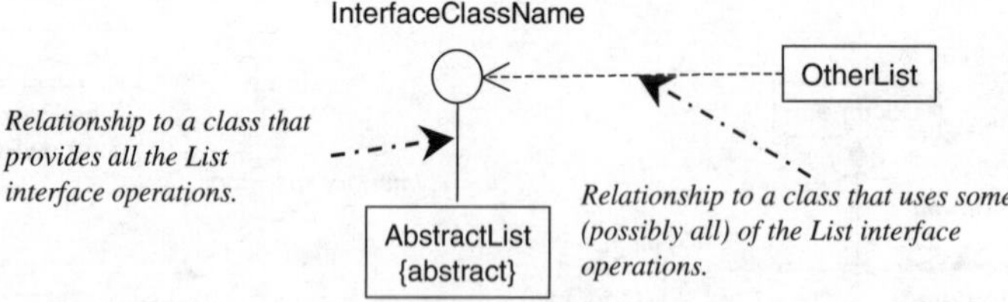
InterfaceClassName
OtherList
Relationship to a class that provides all the List interface operations.
Relationship to a class that uses some (possibly all) of the List interface operations.
AbstractList {abstract}

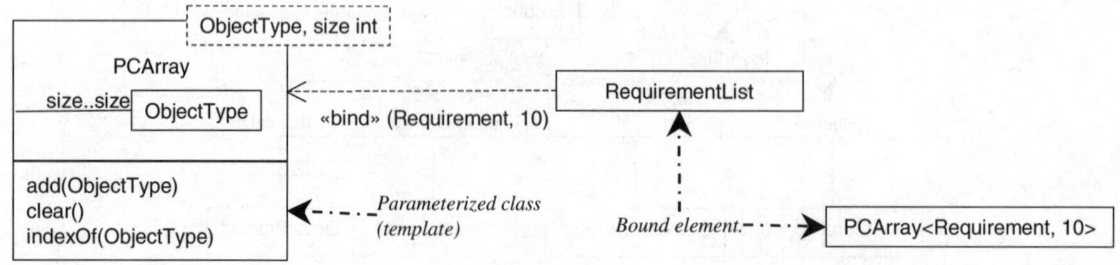
ObjectType, size int
PCArray
size..size
ObjectType
RequirementList
«bind» (Requirement, 10)
add(ObjectType)
clear()
indexOf(ObjectType)
Parameterized class (template)
Bound element.
PCArray<Requirement, 10>

COLLABORATION DIAGRAM

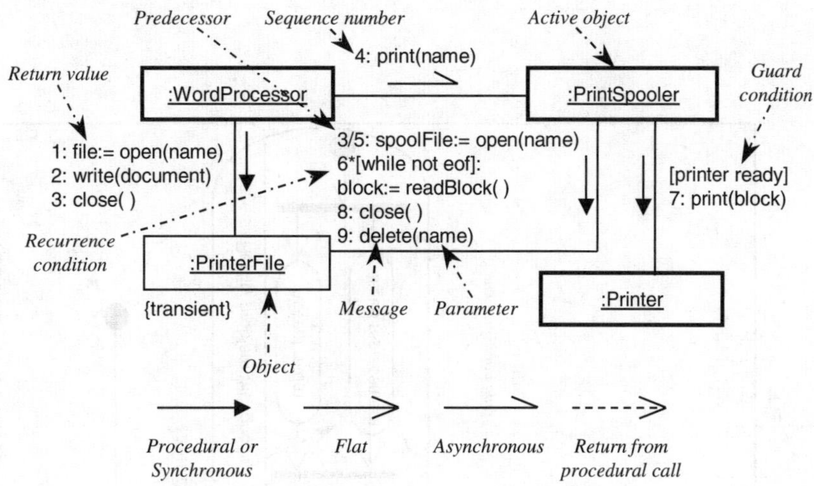

SEQUENCE DIAGRAM

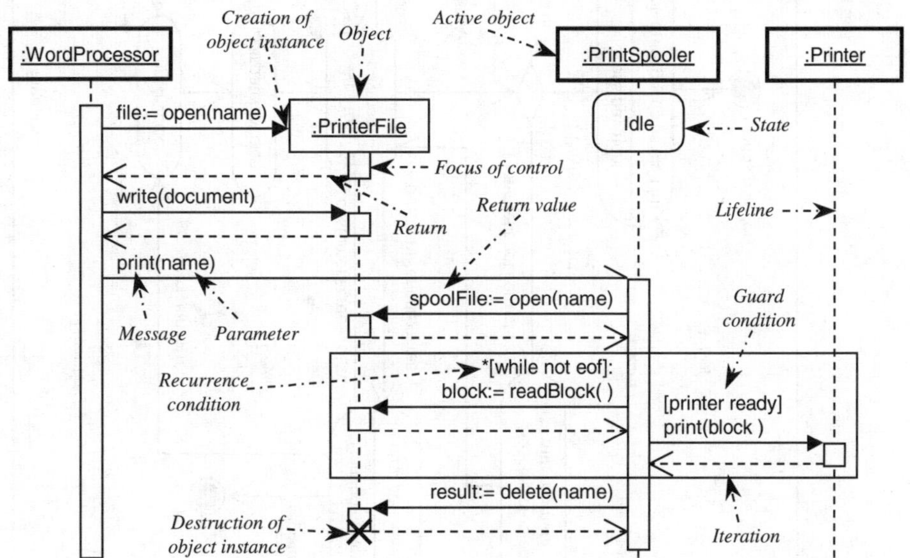

ACTIVITY DIAGRAM

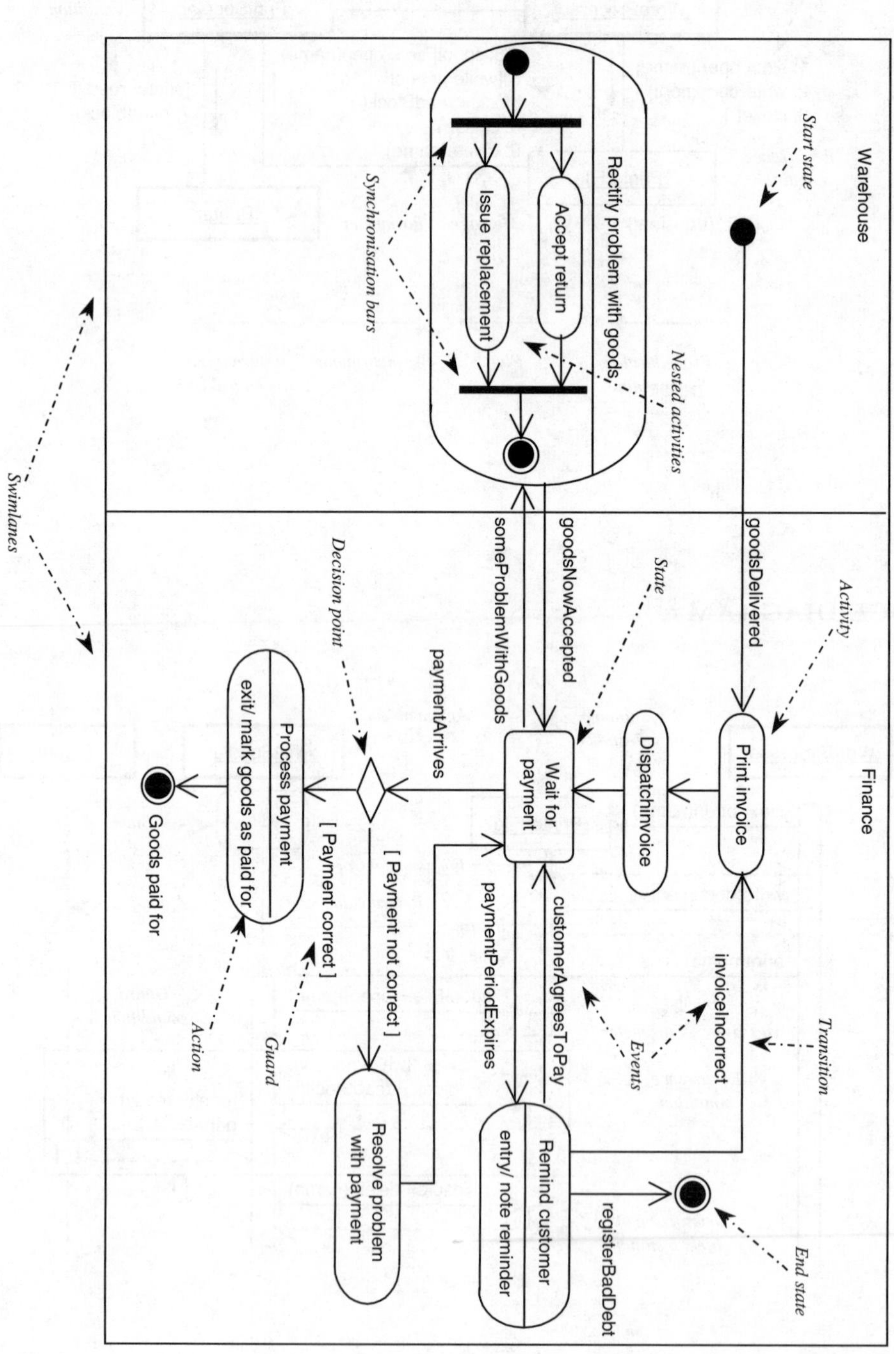

STATECHART DIAGRAM

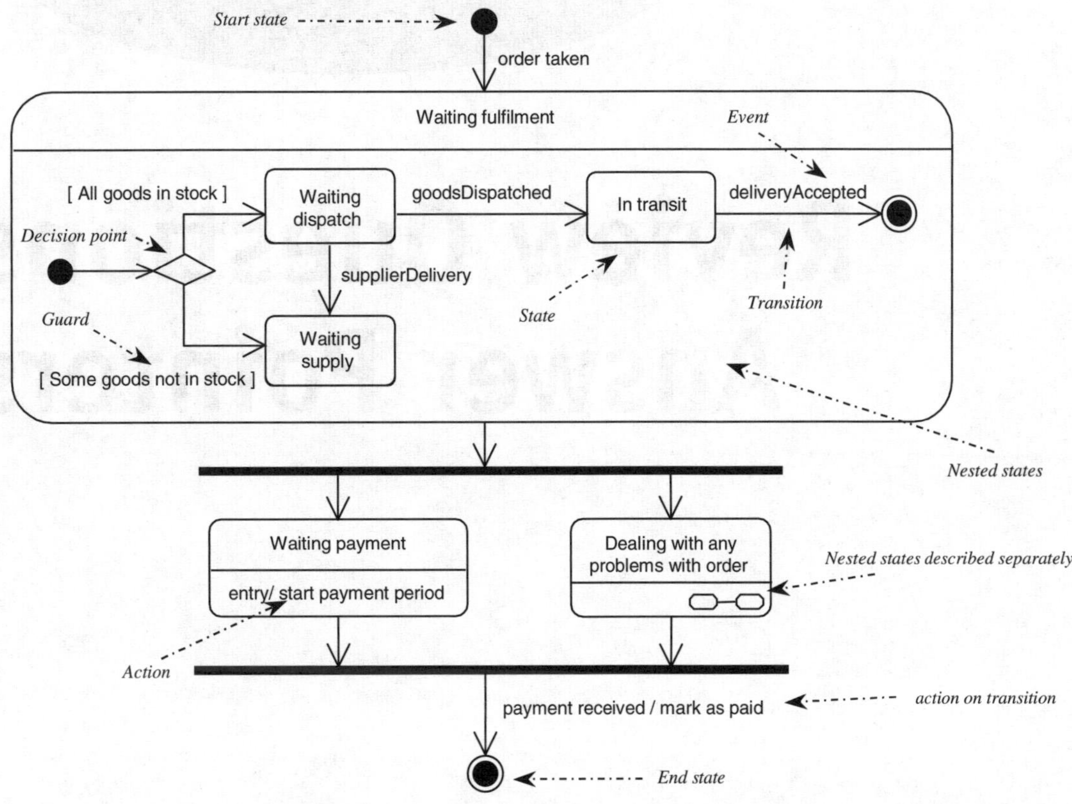

IMPLEMENTATION DIAGRAMS

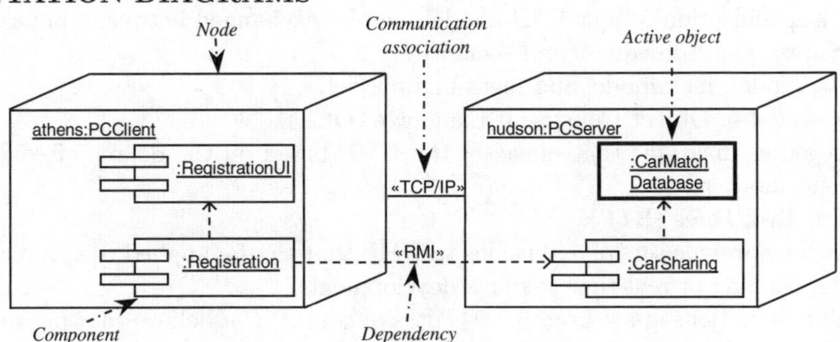

MODEL MANAGEMENT

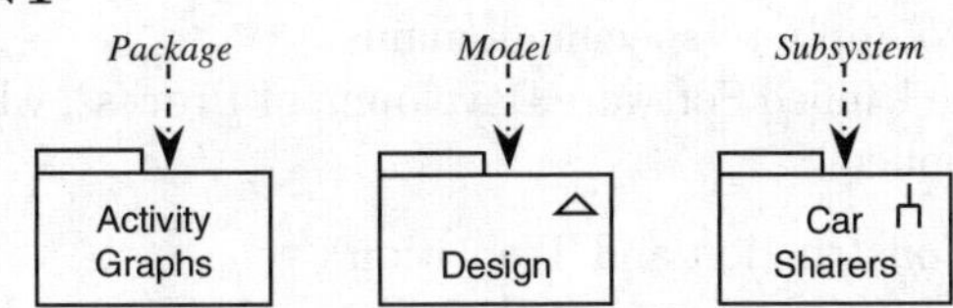

Review Questions Answer Pointers

CHAPTER 2 BACKGROUND TO UML

2.1 James Rumbaugh, Grady Booch and Ivar Jacobson.
2.2 The Object Management Group (OMG).
2.3 It provides a specification of how UML models can be exchanged between applications.
2.4 Abstract syntax, well-formedness and semantics.
2.5 User objects, model, metamodel and meta-metamodel.
2.6 They are specified in Object Constraint Language (OCL).
2.7 To group together diagrams that make up the UML based on the degree of cohesion that they have with one another.
2.8 The Revision Task Force (RTF).
2.9 They are used to provide sets of extensions to UML that can be applied to specific domains, such as business modelling or real-time systems development.
2.10 They are all abstractions apart from (c). (Unless of course, you believe that because it is just the name 'London, England' printed on a piece of paper, it must be an abstraction!)
2.11 They are all models apart from (d).
2.12 Choose three reasons from the following.

- It has become the *de facto* industry standard.
- It unifies the approaches of different authors in a single notation.
- It can be extended to apply to specific domains.
- It is supported by the Unified Software Development Process, which provides a process model for how it can be applied.

2.13 Inception, Elaboration, Construction and Transition.
2.14 Workflows specify the activities in a project that are carried out and the roles of the workers who

will carry out the activities. Workflows group activities together into major project tasks, such as requirements elicitation. Activities specify the work that must be done, and are defined in terms of a sequence of steps that describe the detail of the work to be done.

CHAPTER 3 USE CASES

3.1 A sequence of activities carried out by the system that produce a meaningful outcome for an external user or system.

3.2 An oval with the name of the use case written in or below it.

3.3 An external user or another system that communicates with the system or subsystem that is being modelled.

3.4 A stick figure with the name of the actor written beneath it.

3.5 One of a number of possible different paths that can be taken through a use case, depending on different circumstances, the state of the system or the responses of actors.

3.6 Business modelling or requirements elicitation (as part of early analysis work).

3.7
- They are used to model sequences of actions that are carried out by the system and that provide an observable result to someone or something outside the system, known as an actor.
- They provide a high level view of what the system does and who uses it.
- They provide the basis for determining the human–computer interfaces to the system.
- They can be used to model alternative scenarios for specific use cases that may result in different sequences of actions.
- They use a simple diagrammatic notation that is comprehensible to end users and can be used to communicate with them about the high level view of the system.
- They can be used as the basis for drawing up test specifications.

3.8 Generalization.

3.9 Generalization associations and «include» and «extend» relationships.

3.10 The include relationship means that the included use case will always occur as part of the use case that includes it. In the extend relationship, the extending use case may or may not occur.

3.11 A line joining the two model elements with a triangle icon at one end of the line, pointing at the supertype.

3.12 An open arrow head and a dashed line, with the arrow pointing at the included use case, with the stereotype «include» alongside the line.

3.13 An open arrow head and a dashed line, with the arrow pointing at the extended use case, with the stereotype «extend» alongside the line.

3.14 The point in the execution of a use case when another use case, which extends the functionality of the first, may or may not occur, depending on some condition.

3.15 The Requirements Workflow.

3.16 Find Actors and Use Cases, Prioritize Use Cases, Detail a Use Case, Structure the Use-Case Model and Prototype User Interface.

CHAPTER 4 CLASS DIAGRAM—CLASSES AND ASSOCIATIONS

4.1 Class diagrams consist mainly of classes and associations. Other symbols that you might see on a class diagram are notes and objects. A diagram that consists solely of objects would more correctly be referred to as an object diagram though. See Chapter 7.

4.2
- They are used to document the classes that constitute a system or subsystem.
- They are used to describe the associations, generalization and aggregation relationships between those classes.

- They are used to show the features of classes, principally the attributes and operations of each class.
- They can be used throughout the development lifecycle, ranging from the specification of the classes in the problem domain to the implementation model for a proposed system, to show the class structure of that system.
- They can document how the classes of a particular system interact with existing class libraries.
- They can be used to show individual object instances within the class structure.
- They can show the interfaces supported by a given class.

4.3 A class represents the generic features and properties of a set of instances (objects) that exist in either the problem domain, or the solution that is implemented to support the problem domain. Classes have properties (shown in curly braces { and }), and features (attributes and operations).

4.4 The class name in a rectangle.

4.5 The class pathname reflects the model management structures within which the class exists. This is also known as the namespace of the class.

4.6 A class in the Accounts package within the Finance package would have the class pathname Finance::Accounts::Class.

4.7 An attribute is a data item that a class is responsible for maintaining.

4.8 The most basic notation for an attribute is to show its name alone. Attribute names start with a lower case letter and have no spaces within them. Each component word in an attribute name starts with an uppercase letter.

4.9 Other properties could include the data type, attribute properties, visibility, derivation, initial value and multiplicity.

4.10 In outline:

- Data type is shown with attributeName **: type**.
- Attribute properties are shown in curly braces ({ and }).
- Visibility is shown with –, + or # (or a user-defined symbol).
- Derivation is shown by preceding the attribute name with '/'.
- Initial value is shown with attributeName [: type] **= initialValue**.
- Multiplicity is shown in the form attributeName[lower..upper].

4.11 An operation is a functional responsibility that a class has. 'Fine-grain' operations on classes collaborate to provide some externally visible functionality (see chapters on interaction diagrams).

4.12 A parameter is a data item that is passed to an operation. The type of the data item could be either a standard library type (e.g. String, int, Date) or a class type from the problem domain (e.g. CarSharer).

4.13 Passing by reference passes the underlying memory location of a parameter. Any change to the parameter made by an operation is a direct change to the attribute that was passed as the parameter. Passing by value means that a copy value of the underlying attribute is taken. Changes to the parameter do not affect the underlying attribute.

4.14 The most basic notation for an operation is operationName : type. The operation could be annotated with its visibility.

4.15 A list of parameters is shown in brackets after the operation name. Each parameter in the list can be of the form parameterName : type = defaultValue. Type and initial value can be omitted either independently or together. The parameter type alone can be shown.

4.16 At a conceptual level, classes will reflect the problem domain. Such classes might arguably be more reflective of the data handling requirements of the system. Moving into the specification and implementation level, the emphasis shifts to functional responsibilities of the classes. Classes relating to the implementation of the system will be introduced and component operations of larger collaborations will be added to the (simplistic) get and set operations.

4.17 Initial value can be shown with attributeName [: type] **= initialValue**.

4.18 Default value can be shown in the form parameterName : type = defaultValue or parameterName =

defaultValue.

4.19 An association specifies that two classes will pass messages to each other.

4.20 The most basic notation is a solid line between two classes. The label (name) of the association is suffixed or prefixed with a solid arrow-head to indicate the direction in which the label is intended to be read.

4.21 The role played by a class can be shown by adding a role name to the end of the association nearest the concerned class. The format of the role name is the same as the format of an attribute name.

4.22 In the context of attributes, multiplicity specifies the number of distinct values that the attribute can hold. In the context of associations, the multiplicity specifies the number of instances that may be involved in the appropriate end of an association.

4.23 Multiplicity is shown in the form lowerBound..upperBound. For an attribute the multiplicity is enclosed in square brackets. The lower bound can be any non-negative integer, including zero. The upper bound can be any non-negative integer that is equal to, or greater than the lower bound, or '*'. Several different multiplicity ranges can be specified as a comma-separated list.

4.24 Attributes and associations.

4.25 Conceptual, specification and implementation.

4.26 By taking either a data-oriented or a functionality-oriented approach. A data-oriented approach suits initial investigation and identification of data responsibilities. A functionality-oriented approach builds a class diagram from the collaborations which should take place to fulfil some externally visible function.

CHAPTER 5 CLASS DIAGRAM—GENERALIZATION, AGGREGATION AND COMPOSITION

5.1 Aggregation implies that a 'whole' end of the association groups together instances of the 'part' end of the association. Furthermore, the 'whole' end is considered to be composed of instances of the 'part' end.

5.2 Semantically, aggregation associations imply a stronger coupling between whole and part than a normal association might.

5.3 Composition is a more strict form of aggregation where the 'part' instances have a lifecycle that is co-incident with the 'whole'. Parts cannot be created before the whole and are deleted when the whole is deleted.

5.4 In aggregation the part instances do not have a lifecycle co-incident with the whole. They are capable of independent existence alongside of, or instead of, their participation in the aggregation association.

5.5 Aggregation associations have an unfilled diamond annotation at the 'whole' end.

5.6 Either with a filled diamond annotation at the whole end of the association or by graphical containment,

5.7 'Normal' associations indicate that the operation of two classes is inter-related. Aggregation and composition clarify the nature of this inter-relationship as being one of 'whole-part'.

5.8 Generalization implies that objects of one class are 'a kind of' object of another class. The generic concept of generalization is well-understood, for example, a banana is a kind of fruit. In a class diagram for a banking application it might be specified that a Debit and a Credit are both kinds of Transaction.

5.9 Generalization is shown with a solid line from the subclass to a triangular arrow-head at the parent class end.

5.10 The path of a generalization relationship can be shown as a solid line with either separate or converging paths.

5.11 Generalization constraints can specify two things. First the inter-relationship between different generalization hierarchies that share the same parent class (i.e. overlapping or disjoint). Second, the extent to which a generalization hierarchy in the problem domain is reflected in the class model (i.e. incomplete or complete). The four generalization constraints are: overlapping, disjoint, incomplete and complete. A hierarchy showing a subset of different employee or customer types might be constrained as being incomplete. A parent type of Vehicle might have disjoint sub-class hierarchies for fuel type and cabin type.

5.12 One example could be mapReferenceType to discriminate between OS, Tiger and Latitude-Longitude map references in the GeoLocation package.

5.13 By using Object Constraint Language (OCL).

5.14 If inappropriately used, aggregation and composition could be implemented too rigidly for the problem domain. Care should be exercised in their use.

5.15 In a top-down approach, likely parent classes in generalization structures may be identified by the analyst. The implications of introducing generalization can be explored and considered. This particular approach is usually based primarily on the experience of the analyst.

5.16 In bottom-up generalization the approach is to look for shared class responsibilities. Similar operations and attributes might well suggest the presence of an undetected generalization structure.

CHAPTER 6 CLASS DIAGRAM—MORE ON ASSOCIATIONS

6.1 The visibility indicator (–, +, # or user-defined) is prefixed onto a role name.

6.2 Changeability can be either {changeable}, {addOnly} or {frozen}.

6.3 At a conceptual level the notation is {ordered}, and at a specification or implementation level {sorted}.

6.4 Navigability is shown with an arrow-head indicating the direction of navigability. Where it is standard practice to implement relationships of a given multiplicity combination in a particular way, then it may be necessary explicitly to specify that an association must be implemented so as to make it navigable in both directions.

6.5 An association interface specifier is shown in the form : Class at the end of the association that the specifier relates to. The interface specifier indicates that the source of the association requires only the publicly available operations of the specified interface rather than the public interface of the associated class itself.

6.6 Qualifiers allow the specification of the attribute(s) that can be used to identify occurrences of instances related by an association to be specified.

6.7 The names of both derived attributes and derived associations are prefixed with '/'.

6.8 UML provides the n-ary association, a diamond symbol linked by a solid line to the classes involved in the association.

6.9 The association class symbol can be used to show those attributes and operations. The notation for an association class is identical the normal class symbol. An association class is connected to the association (either binary or n-ary) that it represents with a dashed line.

CHAPTER 7 CLASS DIAGRAM—OTHER NOTATIONS

7.1 Object diagrams can provide a useful way of illustrating points of discussion and to illustrate the effects of modelling classes in one way or another.

7.2 The «instanceOf» relationship shows the dependency between an object and the class of which it is an instance. A link shows an occurrence of an association between two objects.

7.3 Permitted: association label, role names, interface specifier, visibility, navigability, aggregation, composition, qualifier. Not permitted: multiplicity. Multiplicity has no sense. The link is an instance of an association and relates the objects that it is seen to join.

7.4 These stereotypes are used to show the effect of dynamic behaviour on the static object model. The «become» relationship is used to show a change in state of an object. The «copy» relationship shows the cloning of an object instance. One possible use of «copy» would be to illustrate the effect of passing an object parameter by value.

7.5 The «realize» dependency is derived from the generalization relationship and the 'normal' dependency relationship. The generalization relationship provides the triangular arrow-head of the «realize» relationship. The dependency notation provides the dashed line. The notation of realization is one that combines generalization with dependency—one class realizes other class(es).

7.6 Class-scope features are underlined. This is arguably confusing since the UML notation for an object instance is to underline the class name. This could be seen as using the same annotation to indicate diametrically opposed concepts.

7.7 Instance-scope features are those that relate to individual objects. For example, an operation to add 10% to an attribute value of an object is operating upon the value of that attribute for that object. Class-scope attributes hold the same value across all instances of that class. Class-scope operations either operate upon class-scope attributes or operate upon instances of the class (for example constructor operations).

7.8 Stereotypes can be shown using the stereotype name in guillemets («»), using a small icon of the stereotype in the upper right corner of the object/class name compartment or using the stereotype icon with the object/class name underneath it and no other object/class features or properties shown.

7.9 Enumeration classes provide a specified list of values that the enumeration class can hold.

7.10 Utility classes provide a notationally convenient way of collecting up system-wide attributes (global variables) and operations (utility functions) into one clearly identified place.

7.11 Interface classes can be shown using either the «interface» stereotype or as a small circle with the name of the class either just above or below the circle. When using the small circle notation, no features or properties of the interface are listed.

7.12 A «type» class has operations and may have attributes and outward navigable associations. Those attributes and associations serve to support the specification of the operations of the class. The operations of a type class have no methods, they are place holders that ensure that another class that implements the type provides all the required operations. An «implementationClass» is a class that realizes a type class by implementing the methods of the type class.

7.13 By a «realize» dependency from the «implementationClass» to «type».

7.14 A parameterized class is similar to the 'normal' class symbol with the addition of a dashed box overlaid on the top-right corner of the class symbol. In the dashed box, the parameters of the class are shown as a comma-separated list. The multiplicity and type of attributes in the parameterized class and the return type of operations of the parameterized class may be defined in terms of the parameters identified in the dashed box.

7.15 Bound elements can be shown using either a «bind» dependency or a class named TemplateName <arguments>. If the bind dependency is used, the «bind» stereotype is suffixed with <arguments> to instantiate the parameters of the parameterized class.

7.16
- **A «type» class** has operations and may have attributes and outward navigable associations. Those attributes and associations serve to support the specification of the operations of the class. The operations of a type class have no methods; they are place holders that ensure that another class that implements the type provides all the required operations. From a specification and implementation perspective, as a type class does not actually do anything, it cannot have direct object instances.

- **An {abstract} class** may have attributes, operations and associations. The operations are implemented. An abstract class could support direct object instances in that it has attributes, operations with methods, and associations. However, abstract classes do not have direct object instances by the very nature of their being abstract.

- **An «interface» class** has no attributes or outward navigable associations. The operations of an interface class have no methods; they are place holders that ensure that another class that realizes the interface provides all the required operations. From a specification and implementation perspective, as an interface class does not actually do anything, it cannot have direct object instances.

CHAPTER 8 COLLABORATION DIAGRAMS

8.1 A set of participants, objects or roles, that work together to achieve some meaningful outcome in the context of the system.

8.2 A sequence of messages sent between objects or roles in the context of a collaboration to achieve the functionality of that collaboration.

8.3 It may result in the recognition of the need for new classes, attributes or, particularly, operations.

8.4
- They are used to model collaborations that deliver the functionality of a use case.
- They are used to model collaborations that deliver the functionality of an operation.
- They are used to model mechanisms within the architectural design of the system.
- They are annotated with interactions. These interactions show the messages that are passed between objects or roles within the collaboration.
- They are used to model alternative scenarios within a use case or operation.
- They are used in the early stages of a project to identify the objects (and hence classes) that participate in a use case.
- They are used to show the participants in a design pattern

8.5 A dashed oval with the name of the name of the collaboration written in it or beneath it.

8.6 «trace» and «realize» dependencies.

8.7 By showing the roles of the participants in the collaboration as the parameterized roles that will be filled by actual participants.

8.8 The specification level diagram shows the generic roles that are filled and all the possible options in the collaboration as it develops. The instance level diagram shows a particular instance of the collaboration, in which the roles are filled by instances of objects, and a single path is taken through the collaboration.

8.9 To show the structural aspects of the context of a collaboration in terms of the class roles and the association roles between them.

8.10 The names of object instances are underlined.

8.11 A forward slash, '/'.

8.12 (a) Role. (b) Object. (c) Object. (d) Role.

8.13 «local» and «parameter».

8.14 A communication between two objects that conveys information with the expectation that action will ensue.

8.15 A message is the specification of a stimulus, and the stimulus represents a specific instance of sending the message, with particular arguments.

8.16 An event, an operation call and the creation or destruction of an object instance.

8.17 Procedural (or synchronous), flat, asynchronous and return from a procedure call.

8.18 An event is asynchronous.

8.19 The value returned from a procedural call that invokes an operation synchronously on another object.

8.20 An integer or name followed by an optional recurrence.

8.21 To represent the use case in which a message is sent, to represent the name of the object sending the message and to label alternative paths after a branch.

8.22 A conditional statement that must evaluate to true before the message is sent.

8.23 An object running on its own thread of control.

8.24 A rectangle with a thick border or the keyword {active}.

8.25 Two rectangles superimposed on one another and slightly offset.
8.26 {new}, {destroyed} and {transient}.
8.27 «become» and «copy».
8.28
- Decide on the context of the interaction: system, subsystem, use case or operation.
- Identify the structural elements (class roles, objects, subsystems) necessary to carry out the functionality of this collaboration.
- Model the structural relationships between those elements to produce a diagram showing the context of the interaction.
- Consider the alternative scenarios that may be required.
- Draw instance level collaboration diagrams, if required.
- Optionally draw a specification level collaboration diagram to summarize the alternative scenarios in the instance level sequence diagrams.

8.29 Actor, Worker, Case Worker, Internal Worker and Entity.
8.30 Analysis Workflow and Design Workflow.
8.31 Identifying Analysis Classes, Describing Analysis Object Interactions and Capturing Special Requirements.
8.32 Flow of events analysis describes the interaction between classes internal to the system rather than between the system and external actors.
8.33 A collaboration that defines a common pattern of interaction between roles that can be applied or specialized in different collaborations.
8.34 Identifying the Participating Design Classes, Describing Design Object Interactions, Identifying the Participating Subsystems and Interfaces, Describing Subsystem Interactions and Capturing Implementation Requirements.

CHAPTER 9 INTERACTION SEQUENCE DIAGRAMS

9.1 A sequence of messages sent between objects or roles in the context of a collaboration to achieve the functionality of that collaboration.
9.2 Sequence diagrams model an interaction in terms of the time-ordered sequence of messages that are sent, whereas collaboration diagrams show the messages in the context of the structural relationship among the class roles and object instances involved.
9.3 Time is represented as running vertically down the page, so a message that is lower on the page is sent after one that appears above it. (Optionally, time can be represented as running from left to right across the page.)
9.4
- They are used to model the high-level interaction between active objects in a system.
- They are used to model the interaction between object instances within a collaboration that realizes a use case.
- They are used to model the interaction between objects within a collaboration that realizes an operation.
- They can be used either to model generic interactions (showing all possible paths through the interaction) or specific instances of an interaction (showing just one path through the interaction).

9.5 An instance diagram shows one particular instance of an interaction, equivalent to a scenario in a use case. There may be several instance diagrams, each with a different path taken through the interaction. A generic diagram shows the combination of different possible paths through the interaction in a single diagram.
9.6 A dashed line hanging from the rectangle that represents the object.
9.7 A white rectangle drawn on the lifeline of an object.
9.8 By shading the area of the focus of control region in black when the object is carrying out the activity.

9.9 An arrow going from the lifeline or focus of control region of one object to another (or possibly to itself), with the message signature written (normally) above the arrow.

9.10 Using a dashed line with an open arrow head going from the object whose operation was called back to the object that invoked the operation.

9.11 (b) and (c), because they are underlined.

9.12 Procedural (or synchronous), flat, asynchronous and return from a procedure call.

9.13 By a message arrow going to the rectangle representing the object, and the object's lifeline starting immediately below the rectangle.

9.14 By a bold x-shaped cross at the lower end of the object's lifeline, at the point where it is destroyed.

9.15 To represent the use case in which a message is sent, to represent the name of the object sending the message and to label alternative paths after a branch.

9.16 Either an asterisk or an asterisk followed by a condition in square brackets to indicate that a message is sent repeatedly while the condition is true.

9.17 An object running on its own thread of control.

9.18 A rectangle with a thick border or the keyword {active}.

9.19 Either by the use of a recurrence (asterisk and condition) on the message arrow, or by placing a rectangle around the messages that are iterated with the condition at the bottom of the rectangle.

9.20 To indicate that there are constraints on the time that is allowed to elapse either between the sending and receipt of a message, or between the sending of one message and the sending of another, usually a response.

9.21
- Decide on the context of the interaction: system, subsystem, use case or operation.
- Identify the structural elements (classes or objects) necessary to carry out the functionality of the use case or operation. (There may already be a collaboration that defines these.)
- Consider the alternative scenarios that may be required.
- Draw instance sequence diagrams.
  - Lay out the objects from left to right.
  - Starting with the message that starts the interaction, lay out the messages down the page from top to bottom. Show the properties of the messages necessary to explain the semantics of the interaction.
  - Add the focus of control if it is necessary to visualize nesting or the point in time where an activation is taking place.
  - Add timing constraints if necessary.
  - Attach annotations to the diagram if required, for example pre- and post-conditions.
- If required, draw a generic sequence diagram to summarize the alternative scenarios in the instance sequence diagrams.

9.22 The Design Workflow and the Test Workflow.

9.23 Identifying the Participating Design Classes, Describing Design Object Interactions, Identifying the Participating Subsystems and Interfaces, Describing Subsystem Interactions and Capturing Implementation Requirements.

9.24 Designing Integration Test Cases, Designing System Test Cases, Designing Regression Test Cases and Identifying and Structuring Test Procedures.

CHAPTER 10 ACTIVITY DIAGRAMS

10.1 Activity diagrams are used to describe business workflows (business processes), workflows within use cases, worflows between use cases, and, for complex operations, the workflow within the operation.

10.2 Activity diagrams can be first used in business analysis, as a way of elaborating business use cases, or to support some other business workflow method.

10.3 Activity diagrams are a graphical two-dimensional illustration of the complicated flows that take place within a system, be it a business or a computer system. They are useful for describing systems to a range of stakeholders.
10.4 An activity is a unit of work.
10.5 Actions are the elements of work that activities carry out. An activity can consist of one or many actions. A transition can fire one action.
10.6 An activity can be instantaneous, or it can take place over an extended period.
10.7 Actions can take place on entry, during the execution of the activity, in response to an event, or on exit from the activity.
10.8 A transition is the movement between activities and/or states.
10.9 A transition normally occurs when an activity completes. Transitions can also be triggered when an event occurs.
10.10 When the activity completes.
10.11 A state is similar to an activity, but is used to indicate that the workflow is waiting for an event to occur before progressing. It can have actions associated with it. It differs in that an activity can exit when all its work is complete, and a state exits only when an event occurs.
10.12 `event (arguments) [condition] / action ^ target.sendEvent (arguments)`
10.13 A decision point is a point in a workflow where the transition on exit from a state or activity may go in a number of alternative directions depending on a condition.
10.14 A guard is a condition on a transition. The transition can take place only when the condition in the guard is satisfied.
10.15 A decision point can have one or more transitions entering it.
10.16 A decision point can have two or more transitions leaving it. Each exit transition must have a guard, and the guards from all transitions leaving a decision point must not overlap.
10.17 A swimlane is a column on an activity diagram, used to indicate some organizational or technology unit that takes care of the activity.
10.18 Swimlanes are useful for allocating activities to business units or technology areas.
10.19 A synchronization bar is used to split a transition and open up parallel workflows, or to merge multiple transitions into a single transition to synchronize the end of parallel workflows.
10.20 There can be one transition into a synchronization bar and many out, or many in and one out.
10.21 Objects can be placed on activity diagrams, and dependencies used to indicate how activities affect the states of the objects. This is known as an object flow.
10.22 You can keep state information about an object on an object flow.
10.23 Some activities are complex workflows themselves. Therefore it is often necessary to elaborate those activities with workflow elements.
10.24 Activity diagrams can be attached to business use cases, system use cases, activities, objects and operations.
10.25 Control icons are visual icons to indicate the point on a diagram where events are triggered or responded to. They are an additional notation, not strictly necessary, that makes the event handling more explicit.

CHAPTER 11 STATECHART DIAGRAMS

11.1 The states that entities in the system can take and their changing state, defined by the transitions from one state to another.
11.2 A state is a condition that an object can enter, and remain in for a period of time.
11.3 A state lasts for an indefinite period of time, but it can be very brief.
11.4 Events can either trigger an action in a state, or trigger the exit from a state.
11.5 A statechart is usually used to model objects, but it can be used to model actors, use cases and occasionally operations.

11.6 No.

11.7
- On Entry: these actions are triggered as soon as the state is entered;
- Do: these actions take place during the lifetime of the state;
- On Event: these actions take place in response to an event;
- On Exit: these actions take place just before the activity completes;
- Include: invokes a submachine, represented by another statechart diagram.

11.8 action-label / action
where action-label is one of entry, do, exit, include, or the name of an event.

11.9 event-name(arguments) [guard-condition] / action
where arguments is a comma-separated list of arguments supplied by the event, and guard-condition is a condition that must be true for the event to trigger the action.

11.10 By dividing the state into two compartments and listing the actions in the second compartment.

11.11 One or none.

11.12 A composite state is a state that can be viewed as having substates, and for which those substates are defined.

11.13 Composite states can be depicted either by using a separate statechart diagram, or by drawing the subflows on the same diagram nested inside the state.

11.14 A composite state may have parallel workflows. Thus a composite state may be in multiple substates at any one time.

11.15 A synchronization bar allows the splitting of a diagram to represent parallel flows between states, and the subsequent re-joining of those parallel flows.

11.16 The entry actions for the composite state are fired. The subflow starts at its start state, or if there are concurrent subflows then each of the subflows start at their start states. The exception to this is when there is a history state, and the subflows resume at the point they exited.

11.17 Any substate in the composite state terminates, applying exit actions. The composite state terminates, applying its exit actions.

11.18 The subflow starts at the substate indicated by the transition. The entry actions for the composite state and the substate are fired.

11.19 A transition triggered by an event may take a number of routes depending on a condition. A decision-point can be introduced to indicate the alternative routes.

11.20 History states containing "H" mean that a composite state resumes at the point in the top-level flow where it last exited. "*H" indicates that the composite state resumes at the point in any nested composite state where it last exited; the point of resumption will be at whatever level of nesting is defined.

11.21 A synch state is a shared state between parallel flows in a composite state. It allows the parallel flows to synchronize.

CHAPTER 12 OBJECT CONSTRAINT LANGUAGE

12.1 A constraint is a rule about the values in a model, expressed as a restriction on the values.

12.2 They are used to define the behaviour of the model, and to define the legal use of the model.

12.3 OCL is the object constraint language, which is a language for the rigorous definition of constraints.

12.4 Natural language can be ambiguous. Models ultimately need unambiguous descriptions of their behaviour.

12.5 A pre-condition is a statement that defines the legal conditions under which an operation or use case can function. If the pre-condition is met, then the system is obliged to perform according to specification.

12.6 A post-condition is a statement about the model that defines the state of the model after an operation or use case has completed, given that it was invoked with the pre-conditions met.

12.7 An invariant is the property of an object or operation that must remain true at all times.
12.8 Design by contract involves specifying the behaviour of systems in terms of pre-conditions and post-conditions. The constraints form a contract.
12.9 The context of a constraint is a class or operation.
12.10 Boolean, integer, real and string.
12.11 Sets, and types defined in the model.
12.12 1
12.13 Sets, sequences and bags.
12.14 a->first
12.15 set {2,4,7,3,8,9}
12.16 bag {2,2,3,3,4}
12.17 true
12.18 Not usually. At the time of defining the use cases, the objects will not be adequately defined.

CHAPTER 13 IMPLEMENTATION DIAGRAMS

13.1 A physical element of a system, usually a file of some sort. Can be a source file, used in producing the software for the system, or an element of the runtime system.
13.2 Processor in the implementation of a system, shown in a deployment diagram.
13.3 Association between nodes in a deployment diagram, normally stereotyped with the communication mechanism or protocol.
13.4 A rectangle with two narrow rectangles overlapping the left-hand end, with the name of the component in the larger rectangle.
13.5 A cuboid with the name of the node in the top left-hand corner.
13.6
- They are used to model physical software components and the relationships between them.
- They are used to model source code and relationships between files.
- They are used to model the structure of releases of software.
- They are used to specify the files that are compiled into an executable.

13.7
- They are used to model physical hardware elements and the communication paths between them.
- They are used to plan the architecture of a system.
- They are used to document the deployment of software components on hardware nodes.

13.8 Components shown in a deployment diagram model the deployment of run-time components on processors in the planned system. They are normally instances of components. Components in a component diagram are usually source files or other elements of the system software under development.
13.9 As dashed arrows with an open arrow head.
13.10 Stereotyped icons can be used to replace the standard icon. The name of the stereotype in guillemets can be placed above the name of the component.
13.11 Stereotyped icons can be used to replace the standard icon for a node. Communication associations can be stereotyped with the protocol for the communication in guillemets.
13.12 To show model information, such as version numbers of components.
13.13
- Decide on the purpose of the diagram.
- Add components to the diagram, grouping them within other components if appropriate.
- Add other elements to the diagram, such as classes, objects or interfaces.
- Add the dependencies between the elements of the diagram.

13.14
- Decide on the purpose of the diagram.
- Add nodes to the diagram.
- Add communication associations to the diagram.
- Add other elements to the diagram, such as components or active objects, if required.

- Add dependencies between components and objects, if required.

13.15 Implementation Workflow.
13.16 Design Workflow and Implementation Workflow.

CHAPTER 14 COMMON NOTATIONAL CONVENTIONS

14.1 A graph is a collection of nodes joined together by paths.
14.2 For example, use case diagrams, class diagrams, collaboration diagrams, component diagrams, deployment diagrams.
14.3 Connection, containment and visual attachment.
14.4 (a) Icons, two-dimensional symbols, paths and strings.
(b)
- An icon is a graphical element of a fixed size and shape. It does not change shape to hold other elements.
- Two-dimensional symbols can be used to contain other symbols and will change their size accordingly. They can be divided into separate compartments.
- Paths are used to connect together two-d symbols and icons.
- Strings are used to present a range of information in textual form.

(c) The icon for an actor; the two-dimensional symbol for a class; the association between classes; the name of an association.
14.5 Names identify model elements; labels are attached to model elements to provide information about them.
14.6 As stereotypes in guillemets («...»).
14.7 «include» and «realize». There are many others.
14.8 In a rectangle with a 'turned down' corner attached to the model element to which the note applies by a dashed line.
14.9 An umbrella term used for a model element that describes behavioural and structural features in a model.
14.10 Classifiers include classes, actors, use cases, data types, components, interfaces, signals, nodes and subsystems.
14.11 States, attributes, operations.
14.12 (a) Classname.
(b) <u>:Classname</u>.
(c) <u>objectname:Classname</u>.
(d) <u>objectname</u>.
(e) /Rolename:Classname.
(f) <u>objectname/Rolename:Classname</u>.
14.13 It is a means of specifying that a model element conforms to the well understood pattern of behaviour or existence of the specified stereotype. Stereotypes are specified in guillemets («...») or as graphical icons.
14.14 A stereotype is a new metamodel class that is introduced in order to model a special kind of class in a system.
14.15 As an icon; by placing the name of the stereotype in guillemets in the class above the class name; by placing an icon in the class above the class name.
14.16 Classes from Bruce Conallen's web extensions, such as the «ServerPage» class.
14.17 A stereotyped message arrow for use in sequence diagrams.
14.18 It is a pair, usually represented as {tag=value}, associated with a model element such as a class, where tag is a name that indicates the property and value is an arbitrary value expressible as a string.
14.19 As {tag=value} alongside the model element to which the tagged value applies.
14.20 A constraint defines a relationship between model elements or on a model element that must be

true, otherwise the system described by the model ceases to be valid.

14.21 As {constraint} alongside the model element to which the constraint applies, where the actual constraint is placed in the braces, usually as an OCL expression. Where a constraint applies to the relationship between two objects, they can be joined by a dependency and the constrain written alongside the dependency. They can also be shown in a note.

14.22 $\{age <= 21years\}$.

14.23 Object Constraint Language (OCL).

CHAPTER 15 CASE TOOLS

15.1 Computer Assisted Software Engineering or Computer Aided System Engineering.

15.2 No. CASE tools may support all aspects of the software engineering process, not just those involving UML. CASE tools may also incorporate other modeling notations.

15.3 UML provides a common notation and common semantics for models developed in different CASE tools, and provides an interchange standard so that models can be exchanged between tools.

15.4 XMI stands for XML metadata interchange. XML stands for Extensible Markup Language. XMI is the standard definition for a textual language to describe UML models, defined to enable interchange of models between different CASE tools.

15.5 The repository is where all the model elements are stored. Additional elements over and above UML may be stored in the repository.

15.6 It is a pair, usually represented as {tag=value}, associated with a model element such as a class, where tag is a name that indicates the property and value is an arbitrary value expressible as a string.

15.7 Tagged values are important because they permit UML to be extended.

15.8 Round trip engineering is where the CASE tool can both generate program code, and reverse engineer code, managing updates to software models and program code.

CHAPTER 16 DESIGN PATTERNS

16.1 A design pattern is a solution to a common problem in the design of computer systems. It is a solution that has been recognized as worth documenting so that other developers can apply it to solve the same problem when they come up against it.

16.2 A framework is more comprehensive than a pattern and is a partially completed application that can be applied to a specific domain.

16.3 An idiom is a set of guidelines for how to implement aspects of a software system in a particular language.

16.4 Using a template in a pattern catalogue.

16.5
- *Name*—The name of the pattern, ideally describing the solution in some way.
- *Problem*—The question that the pattern helps to resolve.
- *Context*—The context of the application of the pattern: architectural or business context and the critical success factors for the pattern that will make it work in a particular situation.
- *Forces*—The constraints or issues that must be resolved by the pattern.
- *Solution*—The solution that balances the conflicting forces and fits the context.
- *Sketch*—Symbolic sketch of the forces and how they are resolved.
- *Resulting context*—The context as it is after being changed by the solution.
- *Rationale*—The reason and motivation for the pattern.

16.6 Creational, structural and behavioural.

16.7
- *Creational*—Concerned with the creation of object instances, separating the way in which

this is done from the application.

- *Structural*—Concerned with the structural relationships between instances, particularly using generalization, aggregation and composition.
- *Behavioural*—Concerned with the assignment of the responsibility for providing functionality among the objects in the system.

16.8 A dashed oval with a dashed rectangle superimposed on the top right-hand quadrant of the oval. The name of the template collaboration is written in the oval, and the names of parameterized roles are written in the rectangle.

16.9 Template collaboration, collaboration diagram, class diagram, sequence diagram.

16.10
- Read the pattern to get a complete overview.
- Study the structure, participants and collaborations of the pattern in detail.
- Examine the sample code to see an example of the pattern in use.
- Choose names for the pattern's participants (i.e. classes) that are meaningful to the application.
- Define the classes.
- Choose application-specific names for the operations.
- Implement operations that perform the responsibilities and collaborations in the pattern.

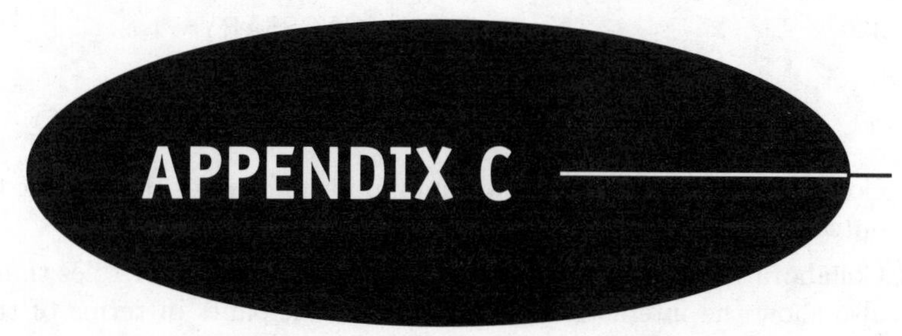

APPENDIX C

Glossary

Action: An executable statement, commonly associated with an activity, state or transition.

Activation: Rectangular area shown on the lifeline of an object or role in a sequence diagram to indicate when that object or role is executing an operation.

Activity: A step in a workflow used to represent where work is taking place, either in the business or within the system being modelled. The activity continues until all its work is complete, or an event triggers an exit.

Activity Diagram: A means of describing workflows, linking activities and states. Used to describe business and system workflows.

Actor: External user of a system or an external system, shown in a use case diagram, which communicates with a system or subsystem being modelled.

Aggregation: Specifies that the nature of an association is one of 'whole-part'. One class is part of the other class.

Ancestor: Any superclass of a class regardless of the number of generalizations between the class and the superclass.

Association: A relationship between two or more classes. Specifies that the classes concerned collaborate with each other.

Association Class: The representation of an association as a class. Allows the association to have data and functional responsibilities (attributes and operations).

Attribute: A data item for which a class is responsible.

Behaviour Specification: Description of the behaviour provided by a use case.

Bound Element: A class that is specified in terms of an instantiation of a parameterized class. (See Parameterized Class).

Class: A generalized type representing a collection of objects which share the same data items and functional responsibilities.

Class Diagram: Shows the static structure of a set of classes. This static structure can include, but is not limited to, classes, attributes, operations, associations and generalization.

Class-scope [Feature]: An attribute or operation that exists on the class itself, rather than the instances of the class. A class attribute would hold the same value across all instances of that class.

Classifier: An umbrella term in term used for a model element that describes behavioural and structural features in a model. Classifiers include classes, actors, use cases, data types, components, interfaces, signals, nodes and subsystems.

Collaboration: A set of participants, objects or roles, that work together to achieve some meaningful outcome in the context of the system.

Collaboration Diagram: Diagram showing the objects or roles that participate in a collaboration. May also show the interaction between the participants in terms of the messages or stimuli sent between them.

Communication Association: Association between nodes in a deployment diagram, normally stereotyped with the communication mechanism or protocol.

Component: A physical element of a system, usually a file of some sort. Can be a source file, used in producing the software for the system, or an element of the runtime system.

Component Diagram: Diagram to show components and the relationships between them.

Composition: A more strict form of aggregation where the 'part' class has a lifecycle co-incident with the 'whole' class. (See *Aggregation*).

Constraint: A restriction on the model, expressed as a condition, used to specify pre-conditions, post-conditions and invariants.

Control Icon: A diagrammatic means of making the sending of an event on a transition more explicit.

Data Token: Icon representing data sent in a message in an interaction diagram.

Decision Point: A point in a workflow where a transition may branch according to certain conditions.

Dependency: A stereotyped relationship between two modelling elements. The stereotype indicates the nature of the relationship. Typically dependencies reflect process oriented concepts. For example, «realize» or «refine».

Deployment Diagram: Diagram to show the implementation of the runtime system in terms of nodes (processors), communication associations among nodes, and the components that are deployed on the nodes.

Design by Contract: Design using pre-conditions and post-conditions to specify the behaviour of parts of a system.

Enumeration Class: A class that groups a set of defined members.

Event: A notable occurrence at a particular point in time. In activity and statechart diagrams events are used to trigger transitions.

Expression: A string in a particular language that can be evaluated to produce a result.

[Class] Feature: An attribute, operation or other user-specified concept (e.g. event) for which a class is responsible.

Generalization: The abstraction of the shared common features of model elements (often classes) into an appropriate supertype.

Guard: A condition that must be satisfied for a transition to fire.

Icon: Graphical representation of a stereotyped model element.

Instance: An occurrence of a class.

Instance-scope [Feature]: The normal scope of an attribute or operation. An attribute whose value relates to only one instance of a class or an operation whose method acts upon the attributes of that same instance as opposed to the attributes of the class as a whole.

Interaction Diagram: Generic term for collaboration diagrams and sequence diagrams, which can be used to show the interaction between collaborating objects or roles.

Interface: A way of organizing a set of operation signatures that can be implemented by a model element such as a class.

Invariant: A condition on a class or use case that must always be true.

Lifeline: Line in a sequence diagram that indicates the existence of an object or role that is participating in the interaction.

Link: An occurrence of an association.

Message: The specification of the communication sent between objects or roles in a collaboration. Defined in terms of its name, the types of its parameters and the type of its return value.

Method: The implementation of an operation.

Model: Abstraction of a physical system for a specific purpose. Used of the various views of a system that are developed at different stages of a project.

Multiplicity: The range of occurrences that may be found in the model element. One typical example is the multiplicity of an association end, that is how many instances of a class could be associated with an instance of the source class.

N-ary Association: An association that links three or more classes.

Node: Processor in the implementation of a system, shown in a deployment diagram.

Note: A text string attached to a model element to provide additional infomation about it.

Object: An occurrence of a class.

OCL: Object Constraint Language—a formal language for the expression of constraints.

Operation: A functional or behavioural responsibility of a class.

Operation Signature: A collective reference to the name, parameter list and return type of an operation.

Package: Mechanism for organizing the different views of a project or system.

Parameter: An attribute or object passed as an argument to an operation.

Parameterized Class: A class definition consisting of attributes and operations specified in terms of parameters that are passed to the parameterized class in order to instantiate it. Also known as a template. See also *Bound Element.*

Parent Class: The class immediately above another class in a generalization is known as its parent class.

Pattern: A documented solution to a common problem in computer system design.

Post-condition: A condition that must be true if an operation or a use case has been legally executed.

Pre-condition: A condition that must be true for an operation to be legally executed, or for a use case to be legally applied.

Relationship: In UML, a generic name for some kind of semantic and notational join between two model elements. Associations, generalizations and dependencies are all specific types of relationship.

Repository: A facility for storing UML elements and diagrams, and associated documents.

Role: A named behaviour of a model element in a particular context, typically the part played by an object in an association or a collaboration.

Sequence Diagram: Interaction diagram that shows the interactions among the participants in a collaboration or an operation. Shows the passage of time, usually on the vertical axis of the diagram.

Signal: An asynchronous message sent between instances in a collaboration.

Specialization: The inverse of generalization. A specialized class is one which differs from the superclass and any other sibling specializations of the same superclass in terms of its attributes, operations or methods.

State: A collective term for the attribute values of an object and the relationships it has with other objects at an instant in time. Objects may be in multiple states at any one time. States are terminated by events.

Statechart Diagram: A means of depicting how elements of a model move from state to state. Changes of state are the result of transitions.

Stereotype: In UML, a means of specifying that a model element conforms to the well understood pattern of behaviour or existence of the specified stereotype. Stereotypes are specified in guillemets

(«...») or as graphical icons.

Stimulus: An instance of a message.

Subclass: A specialized class in a generalization hierarchy.

Subflow: Activities or states may be broken down into subflows.

Subsystem: A meaningful division of a system into parts.

Subtype: See *Subclass.*

Superclass: A generalized class in a generalization hierarchy.

Supertype: See *Superclass.*

Swimlane: A column in an activity diagram used to indicate an area of responsibility for the activities.

Synchronization Bar: A point in an activity diagram or in a statechart where either a transition may split into multiple parallel flows, or multiple parallel flows can be synchronized to meet and fire a single transition.

Tagged Value: Mechanism for attaching (name, value) pairs to model elements. One of the ways of extending UML.

Template: See *Parameterized Class.*

Transition: A relationship between states and/or activities. When one state or activity ends, the transition indicates the next state or activity to commence. When a transition is applied, it is said to fire.

Use Case: Sequence of actions carried out by the system to achieve some purpose that is meaningful for an external user or system. Graphically represented in a use case diagram and defined by behaviour specifications.

Use Case Diagram: Diagram showing use cases and actors and the associations between them. provides a high-level model of the functionality of a system.

Utility Class: A collection of globally available attributes and operations. Specified using the «utility» stereotype.

Workflow: In UML, a generic term for modelling tasks in terms of a sequence of activities. In the Unified Process, a grouping of activities to carry out a particular system development task.

Visibility: Typically applies to attributes and operations, but may also apply to an association end. Specifies the accessibility of the model element to other associated model elements. UML specifies three options for visibility, public (+), private (-) or protected (#).

BIBLIOGRAPHY

Alexander, C., Ishikawa, S., Silverstein, M., Jacobson, M., Fiksdahl-King, I. & Angel, S. (1977), *A Pattern Language: Towns, Buildings, Construction*, Oxford University Press.

Beck, K. (2000), *Extreme Programming Explained*, Addison-Wesley.

Beck, K. & Cunningham, W. (1989), 'A laboratory for teaching object-oriented thinking', *Proceedings of OOPSLA 89. SIGPLAN Notices* **24**(10), 1–6.

Bellin, D. & Simone, S. (1997), *The CRC Card Book*, Addison-Wesley, Reading, MA.

Bennett, S., McRobb, S. & Farmer, R. (1999), *Object-Oriented Systems Analysis and Design using UML*, McGraw-Hill.

Booch, G. (1991), *Object-Oriented Analysis and Design with Applications*, Benjamin/Cummings.

Booch, G., Rumbaugh, J. & Jacobson, I. (1999), *The Unified Modeling Language User Guide*, Addison-Wesley.

Brown, D. (1997), *An Introduction to Object-Oriented Analysis: Objects in Plain English*, John Wiley.

Coad, P. & Yourdon, E. (1990), *Object-Oriented Analysis*, Yourdon Press; Prentice-Hall.

Coad, P. & Yourdon, E. (1991), *Object-Oriented Design*, Yourdon Press; Prentice-Hall.

Conallen, J. (1999), 'Modeling web application architectures with UML', *Communications of the ACM* **42**(10), 63–70.

Conallen, J. (2000), *Building Web Applications with UML*, Addison-Wesley.

Constantine, L. (1997), 'The case for essential use cases', *Object Magazine, May, 1997*.

Cook, S. & Daniels, J. (1994), *Designing Object-Oriented Systems: Object-Oriented Modeling with Syntropy*, Prentice-Hall.

Coplien, J. O. (1992), *Advanced C++: Programming Styles and Idioms*, Addison-Wesley.

Douglass, B. P. (1998), *Real-Time UML: Developing Efficient Objects for Embedded Systems*, Addison-Wesley.

Eriksson, H.-E. & Penker, M. (1998), *UML Toolkit*, John Wiley.

Evitts, P. (2000), *A UML Pattern Language*, MTP.

Fowler, M. (1999), `http://ourworld.compuserve.com/homepages/Martin_Fowler/`.

Fowler, M. & Scott, K. (1997), *UML Distilled: Applying the Standard Object Modeling Language*, Addison-Wesley.

Gamma, E., Johnson, R., Helm, R. & Vlissides, J. (1995), *Design Patterns: Elements of Reusable Object-Oriented Software*, Addison-Wesley.

Gomaa, H. (2000), *Designing Concurrent, Distributed and Real-Time Applications with UML*, Addison-Wesley.

Jackson, D. (n.d.), 'A comparison of object modelling notations: Alloy, UML and Z', `http://sdg.lcs.mit.edu/~dnj/abstracts.html#alloy`.

Jacobson, I., Booch, G. & Rumbaugh, J. (1999), *The Unified Software Development Process*, Addison-Wesley; ACM Press.

Jacobson, I., Christerson, M., Jonsson, P. & Övergaard, G. (1992), *Object-Oriented Software Engineering: A Use Case Driven Approach*, Addison-Wesley.

Jacobson, I., Ericsson, M. & Jacobson, A. (1995), *The Object Advantage: Business Process Reengineering with Object Technology*, Addison-Wesley.

Kobryn, C. (1999), 'UML 2001: A standardization odyssey', *Communications of the ACM* **42**(10), 29–37.

Larman, C. (1998), *Applying UML and Patterns*, Prentice Hall.

Lee, R. C. & Tepfenhart, W. M. (1997), *UML and C++: A practical Guide to Object-Oriented Development*, Prentice Hall.

Martin, J. & Odell, J. (1998), *Object-Oriented Methods: A Foundation (UML Edition)*, Prentice-Hall.

Muller, P.-A. (1997), *Instant UML*, Wrox Press.

Object Management Group (1999*a*), OMG Unified Modeling Language Specification 1.3, Technical report, Object Management Group.

Object Management Group (1999*b*), OMG Unified Modeling Language Specification: UML Notation, Technical report, Object Management Group. Part 3.

Object Management Group (1999*c*), OMG Unified Modeling Language Specification: UML Semantics, Technical report, Object Management Group. Part 2.

Page, W. (n.d.), 'Alloy and its Alcoa analysis tool', `http://sdg.lcs.mit.edu/alcoa/`.

Pressman, R. S. (2000), *Software Engineering: A Practitioner's Approach*, 5th edn, McGraw-Hill.

Priestley, M. (2000), *Practical Object-oriented design with UML*, McGraw-Hill.

Rumbaugh, J., Blaha, M., Premerlani, W., Eddy, F. & Lorensen, W. (1991), *Object-Oriented Modeling and Design*, Prentice Hall.

Rumbaugh, J., Jacobson, I. & Booch, G. (1999), *The Unified Modeling Language Reference Manual*, Addison-Wesley.

Selic, B., Gullekson, G. & Ward, P. (1994), *Real-Time Object-Oriented Modeling*, John Wiley.

Shlaer, S. & Mellor, S. (1988), *Object-Oriented Systems Analysis: Modeling the World in Data*, Prentice-Hall.

Sun Microsystems (1999), 'Java platform 1.2 API specification: JDK 1.2 distribution documentation', `...\docs\api\index.html`.

Warmer, J. & Kleppe, A. (1999), *The Object Constraint Language: Precise Modeling with UML*, Addison Wesley Longman Inc.

Wirfs-Brock, R., Wilkerson, B. & Wiener, L. (1990), *Designing Object-Oriented Software*, Prentice-Hall.

INDEX